I0888626

Fundamentals of Transfer Pricing

Fundamentals of Transfer Pricing

Industries, Regions, New Technologies, and Other Topics

Edited by

Raffaele Petruzzi
Giammarco Cottani
Michael Lang

TAX
Institute for Austrian and
International Tax Law Vienna
WU Transfer Pricing Center

Wolters Kluwer

Published by:
Kluwer Law International B.V.
PO Box 316
2400 AH Alphen aan den Rijn
The Netherlands
E-mail: lrs-sales@wolterskluwer.com
Website: www.wolterskluwer.com/en/solutions/kluwerlawinternational

Sold and distributed by:
Wolters Kluwer Legal & Regulatory U.S.
7201 McKinney Circle
Frederick, MD 21704
United States of America
E-mail: customer.service@wolterskluwer.com

ISBN 978-94-035-3515-9

e-Book: ISBN 978-94-035-3520-3
web-PDF: ISBN 978-94-035-3521-0

© 2022 Raffaele Petruzzi, Giammarco Cottani & Michael Lang

All rights reserved. No part of this publication may be reproduced, stored in a retrieval system, or transmitted in any form or by any means, electronic, mechanical, photocopying, recording, or otherwise, without written permission from the publisher.

Permission to use this content must be obtained from the copyright owner. More information can be found at: www.wolterskluwer.com/en/solutions/legal-regulatory/permissions-reprints-and-licensing

Editors

Dr Raffaele Petruzzi, LL.M. is the Managing Director of the WU Transfer Pricing Center at the Institute for Austrian and International Tax Law at WU (Vienna University of Economics and Business) and an international tax advisor specializing in international tax and transfer pricing at Baker McKenzie, where he is part of the EMEA Transfer Pricing Group and is the Head of the Austria Transfer Pricing Group.

Raffaele has gained extensive experience in dealing with topics related to international tax and transfer pricing for many years, from both a professional and an academic side. He is a frequent speaker in international conferences and lecturer of numerous courses all over the world, as well as author of many publications. Finally, among others, he is a member of the United Nations Subcommittee on Transfer Pricing, of the International Fiscal Association (IFA), and of Transfer Pricing Economists for Development (TPED).

Raffaele holds a Ph.D. in International Business Taxation and an LL.M. in International Tax Law from WU, as well as an MSc in Business Administration and Law from Bocconi University, Italy.

Dr Giammarco Cottani joined Netflix in 2019 as director of global tax policy where he oversees all direct and indirect tax public policy-related issues that the group faces in the countries in which Netflix operates.

Previously, Dr Cottani was a partner of the international tax law firm Ludovici Piccone & Partners where he coordinated the international and transfer pricing practice with regard to dispute prevention and resolution and complex audit assistance for large multinational enterprises.

Prior to that, he was an adviser to the Italian tax authorities on international tax and transfer pricing issues and was one of the delegates for Italy involved in the OECD BEPS Project. He also worked as a transfer pricing adviser in the transfer pricing unit of the OECD where he was involved in the introduction of the new Chapter IX of the OECD Transfer Pricing Guidelines concerning business restructurings. He has (co-)led over twenty events in the area of transfer pricing for a number of non-OECD countries and has also been involved in a number of technical assistance projects for the tax administrations on behalf of international and regional organizations in various parts of the world.

He served as a member of the UN Subcommittee in charge of the draft of the Practical Manual on Transfer Pricing for Developing Countries.

Dr Cottani was recently involved in a number of ongoing technical assistance projects for the tax administrations of three EU Member States mainly in the areas of transfer pricing, attribution of profit by using permanent establishments, and aggressive tax planning. Furthermore, he regularly lectures at postgraduate courses in international taxation in Europe.

He received his degree in Law from LUISS Rome University, Italy, in 2003, an LL.M. in European and International Taxation from the European Tax College, Tilburg and Leuven in 2005, and a Ph.D. in Corporate Taxation from LUISS Rome University, Italy, in 2009.

Prof. Dr DDr H.c. Michael Lang is the head of the Institute for Austrian and International Tax Law of WU (Vienna University of Economics and Business) and academic director of both the LL.M. Program in International Tax Law and the Doctoral Program in International Business Taxation (DIBT) of this university. He is the president of the Austrian branch of the IFA and has been a visiting professor at Georgetown University, US; New York University, Sorbonne University, Paris; Bocconi University, Milan; Peking University (PKU), China; University of New South Wales, Sydney, Australia, and others.

Assistant Editor

Abhishek Padwalkar, LL.M. is a Research and Teaching Associate at the WU Transfer Pricing Center at the Institute for Austrian and International Tax Law at WU (Vienna University of Economics and Business). He has worked as a tax counsel in Mumbai, India where he advised clients on matters related to international tax, transfer pricing, arbitration, and company and constitutional law. He has also litigated before various fora including the Bombay High Court and the Income Tax Appellate Tribunal. Abhishek holds an advanced LL.M. in International Tax Law from the University of Amsterdam (IBFD), the Netherlands and another LL.M. in Constitutional and Administrative Law from the University of Mumbai, India. Abhishek is also a Doctoral Candidate in Business Law at the WU (Vienna University of Economics and Business).

Contributors

Tatiana Amba is a senior transfer pricing economist and international tax practitioner at DLA Piper London. Her expertise spans across the entire transfer pricing cycle with a particular focus on the preemptive defence strategies, value chain transformations, and M&A transactions. Tatiana supported multinational clients across the three continents having worked in New York, London and Singapore. Tatiana is a Fulbright Scholar specializing in international economics, public policy and multinational enterprises. She is a lecturer in the Executive Program in Transfer Pricing, University of Lausanne, Switzerland and a contributor to the 'Practical Guide to U.S. Transfer Pricing' – a legal treatise for tax counsel, tax authorities, and policymakers – published by Lexis Nexis. Tatiana has contributed to Chapter 19 of this book.

Pietro Bricchetto is a junior partner at the Italian law firm Gatti Pavesi Bianchi Ludovici. His main areas of expertise include international and EU tax law as well as the VAT, customs, and excise. He has been a member of L&P - Ludovici Piccone & Partners - since its foundation. Before that, he worked with Maisto e Associati for three years and, previously, with the indirect tax team at PwC in Italy for two years. Pietro is the author of several contributions on VAT matters. Pietro has contributed to Chapter 31 of this book.

Barend Broen is an international tax and transfer pricing professional with almost two decades of experience. He spent most of his career as an in-house tax and transfer pricing specialist with multiple multinational companies (Shell, Unilever, ABN AMRO) and currently works as the head of tax for Mambu. Barend is a lecturer in transfer pricing at the Erasmus University, Rotterdam, the Netherlands, and deputy director of the EFS Top-Level Transfer Pricing Seminar. He holds a Master of Science in Fiscal Economics and a Master of Law in Financial Law. Barend has contributed to Chapter 20 of this book.

Gabriela Capristano Cardoso, LL.M. is an analyst at the Transfer Pricing Unit of the Centre for Tax Policy and Administration at the OECD. She has previously worked as a researcher and teaching associate at the WU (Vienna University of Economics and Business) as Consultant for the UNDESA, an International Tax and Transfer Pricing Senior Consultant at EY, the Netherlands and the United Arab Emirates, a lawyer for the Public Agency of Economic Development of Pernambuco, Brazil, as well as in the public notary and law firms in Brazil. Gabriela received her degree in Law from the Catholic University of Pernambuco, Brazil, an advanced LL.M. in International Tax Law from the International Tax Center, Leiden University, the Netherlands, and is currently a Ph.D. candidate at WU with a focus on transfer pricing. Moreover, she has lectured at WU and at Xiamen University, China, and has been a speaker at international conferences and workshops as well as published numerous articles on international tax and transfer pricing topics in international journals. Gabriela has contributed to Chapters 22 and 28 of this book.

These chapters were finalized before the author joined the OECD and the opinions expressed in it are the author's and do not reflect those of the Organization, or its member countries.

Andrea Costa Chaves is the head of the International Affairs Division at the Inspection Undersecretariat of the Brazilian Tax Administration, Ministry of Economy. She was the delegate to the OECD Working Party No. 6 and its bureau during the BEPS Project until August 2021. She was directly engaged in the implementation in Brazil of the minimum standards agreed on the BEPS Project. Andrea has held different positions at the Brazilian Tax Administration since 2001. Her areas of work have included drafting legislation on international taxation and issuing rulings on the application of tax legislation related to transfer pricing, taxation of income and capital gains from foreign sources, withholding tax, and double taxation agreements. She managed and developed systems for risk assessment in international taxation and customs. Andrea holds a Master's in Economics from the University of Brasília, Brazil (2010) and a mathematics degree from the Fluminense Federal University, Brazil (1997). Andrea has contributed to Chapter 22 of this book.

Marco D'Ostuni is a partner in the Rome office of Cleary Gottlieb Steen & Hamilton LLP. He is a graduate of Columbia Law School, the College of Europe, and the University of Naples, Italy and holds a Ph.D. from the University of Perugia, Italy. Marco's practice focuses on competition law and regulation in the energy, telecommunications, and media sectors. He has represented clients in some of the leading EU and Italian competition law cases, often in heavily regulated sectors. He has widely published on antitrust matters and lectures at conferences and universities. Marco has contributed to Chapter 29 of this book.

Jacopo Figuz Diaz is a counsel in the Rome office of Legance – Avvocati Associati. He is a graduate of Columbia Law School, the College of Europe, and the Universities of Poitiers and Rome. Jacopo advises companies on a wide range of issues under European and Italian competition law, in particular complex cartel and merger control matters, where he has extensive experience in various sectors including pharmaceuticals, automotive, financial services, and industrials, as well as horizontal and vertical cooperation arrangements. He is widely published on antitrust and European law matters. Jacopo has contributed to Chapter 29 of this book.

Dr Karol Dziwiński is a senior associate in transfer pricing at PwC Austria in Vienna, as well as lecturer in transfer pricing at WU (Vienna University of Economics and Business). Previously, he was a research and teaching associate at the WU Transfer Pricing Center at the Institute for Austrian and International Tax Law at WU Vienna and worked with TPA in Austria, Henkel AG & Co. KGaA in Germany and KPMG in Poland. He received a Master's Degree in Law from the University of Warsaw, Poland; a first-level Master's Degree in Italian Law from the University of Catania, Italy, and a doctoral degree from WU (Vienna University of Economics and Business), specializing in transfer pricing with a dissertation on the DEMPE concept and intangibles. Karol has contributed to Chapters 30 and 31 of this book.

Axel Eigelshoven is a transfer pricing partner in PwC's Düsseldorf office and serves as head of the PwC's German transfer pricing practice. He has more than twenty years of experience in international taxation and transfer pricing.

Axel lectures at the Mannheim Business School and the WU (Vienna University of Economics and Business) and is a frequent speaker on transfer pricing at national and international seminars. He is the co-author of Vogel/Lehner, *Doppelbesteuerungsabkommen*, a leading commentary on tax treaties; co-author of Kroppen/Rasch, *Handbuch der Verrechnungspreise*, a leading publication on transfer pricing; and is contributing the German country chapter in IBFD's *Global Transfer Pricing Explorer*. Moreover, he has published numerous articles in national and international tax journals.

Axel holds a degree in Business Economics (Diplom-Kaufmann) from the University of Cologne, Germany. He is a certified tax advisor (Steuerberater) and is a member of the Tax Advisors Association and the IFA. Axel has contributed to Chapter 14 of this book.

Eva Frehner has been a head of group tax at Sulzer (a large industrial multinational company headquartered in Switzerland) since 2019. Prior to joining Sulzer, she worked for eight years as a corporate tax director at Vontobel (a medium-sized, globally acting bank and asset manager headquartered in Switzerland). She started her career at KPMG. Eva Frehner is a regular speaker at seminars and conferences and publishes articles on corporate tax and transfer pricing topics. She lectures on transfer pricing and corporate tax planning at the University of Zurich, Switzerland and EXPERT Suisse (Swiss expert association for audit, tax, and fiduciary). She was the Swiss IFA country reporter for 2020 on Exchange of Information: issues, use and collaboration. Eva obtained an LL.M. in International Tax Law from the WU (Vienna University of Economics and Business) in 2011. She is a Swiss Certified Tax Expert and wrote her dissertation on Tax Accounting/Tax Reporting at the IFF-Institute of St. Gallen, Switzerland. Eva Frehner is the co-head of the working group Swiss Taxation at Swiss Holdings and a member of other technical groups (e.g., transfer pricing, European and international tax, the VAT, and customs). When working at Vontobel, she represented the Swiss Bankers Association at the OECD BIAC and

European Banking Federation in transfer pricing/BEPS topics. Eva has contributed to Chapter 15 of this book.

Dr Gregor Gehauf is a senior tax manager at the central tax department of a premium automobile company. He has almost twenty years of experience in transfer pricing and has led the transfer pricing team of the company for the last five years. The focus of his work is the planning and documentation of international supply chain projects as well as its defence in audits. Gregor has managed numerous bilateral and unilateral controversy cases in recent years and is a frequent speaker on international tax and transfer pricing matters at international conferences.

Gregor is a certified tax advisor (Steuerberater) and holds a Ph.D. in Economics from the University of Munich, Germany. Gregor has contributed to Chapter 14 of this book.

Erik Jan van Sten is the global transfer pricing lead at Shell. Erik Jan van Sten has been a transfer pricing professional since 1999. As a senior member of Shell's transfer pricing team, he is currently responsible for Shell's long-term transfer pricing strategy, audits and tax controversy, operational transfer pricing, corporate reorganizations, and M&A projects. His prior roles include transfer pricing support for Shell's upstream, integrated gas, projects and technology, and treasury businesses. Particular experience includes the management of major projects in the areas of business integration and audit defence. Erik Jan has contributed to Chapter 20 of this book.

Philipp Kaiser is Bayer's global head of transfer pricing and business models and is responsible for all divisions (Pharmaceuticals, CropScience and Consumer Health). He has more than fifteen years of experience in the area of transfer pricing. Before joining Bayer in 2011, Philipp spent six years with EY's transfer pricing expert group in Düsseldorf, Germany and New York. During his career in consulting and industry, Philipp worked on various transfer pricing projects, including the preparation of transfer pricing documentation (global and EU master file, US, etc.), transfer pricing audits on a global scale, several competent authority procedures (mutual agreement procedures and advance pricing arrangements). He furthermore focused on strategic transfer pricing planning, including business model effectiveness and intellectual property planning. During his time in consulting, and especially since joining Bayer, Philipp has a strong focus on and in-depth knowledge of the pharmaceutical, agricultural, and chemical industries. Between 2015 and 2019, he was a non-government member of the EU Joint Transfer Pricing Forum. Philipp has contributed to Chapter 21 of this book.

Neal M. Kochman is a senior counsel at Caplin & Drysdale, Chartered, a law firm in Washington, DC. Neal's practice focuses on international tax planning, taxation of settlements, and bankruptcy tax matters. His experience covers a broad range of international, domestic, and state tax issues associated with transfer pricing, foreign tax credit planning, corporate restructurings, qualified settlement funds, and withholding and reporting. Prior to joining Caplin & Drysdale, Neal spent over twenty years performing quantitative and policy analyses for federal government agencies. Neal has contributed to Chapter 26 of this book.

Dorottya Kovács is a senior transfer pricing associate at PwC, Austria. Before joining PwC, she was a research and teaching associate in the WU Transfer Pricing Center at the Institute for Austrian and International Tax Law at WU (Vienna University of Economics and Business). Dorottya has also gained practical experience in international tax and transfer pricing while working at the tax department of Sberbank Europe, Vienna and at Bella Beratung, Mönchof. Her main responsibilities included *inter alia* global transfer pricing documentation, consolidation of country-by-country reports, calculation of head office charges, group tax risks monitoring and reporting, development of tax methodologies and procedures, tax communications on projects, and transfer pricing audit defence. Dorottya is a doctoral candidate in Economics and Social Sciences at the WU (Vienna University of Economics and Business). Dorottya has contributed to Chapter 27 of this book.

Dr Martin Lagarden, MBA, has been with Henkel Group in Germany and the US for more than twenty-five years, holding various managerial positions in R&D and finance. Since 2008, he has been the head of global transfer pricing in Henkel's tax and trade unit. His responsibilities span system development; international audit management and dispute resolution; documentation and related topics; and digitalization in operational transfer pricing. He was awarded his academic degrees from the Universities of Aachen, Bochum, Düsseldorf and Reading/Henley Business School, United Kingdom. To date, Martin has (co-)authored several publications on different aspects of transfer pricing, including but not limited to intangibles, their valuation, and related documentation issues. Moreover, he is a member of the editorial board of IBFD's *International Transfer Pricing Journal* and a regular presenter on various transfer pricing topics in different university contexts and professional conferences in Germany and abroad. Martin has contributed to Chapter 17 of this book.

Srini Lalapet is a transfer pricing executive with leadership experience and expertise in the area of transfer pricing economics and international tax planning acquired within multiple industries (information technology, financial services, energy, industrial products, chemicals, consumer products, manufacturing, etc.) and jurisdictions (United Kingdom, US, Canada, Switzerland). Srini has had stints managing the transfer pricing function for companies as diverse as Dell Technologies, UiPath, AIG, and Siemens. He has also worked for big four consulting firms such as EY and PwC at a senior level and got his start in transfer pricing at BDO in Canada.

Srini holds dual MBA degrees from Cornell University, US, and Queen's University, Canada; a Master's in Global Affairs from Yale University, US where he specialized in the political economy of international markets, and a Bachelor's in International Relations from Bennington College, US. He has written and contributed to numerous articles in international tax/transfer pricing publications and has spoken at numerous transfer pricing conferences as well. Srini has contributed to Chapter 19 of this book.

Shimeng Lan is a tax consultant at KPMG in Switzerland and is pursuing a Ph.D. in International Tax Law at the Institute for Austrian and International Tax Law, WU (Vienna University of Economics and Business). She studied at the University of International Business and Economics, China, where she graduated in Law in 2016.

She also holds an Advanced Master's in International Taxation from Leiden University, the Netherlands, and had practical experience with an international advisory firm and the secretariat of the OECD-hosted Global Forum on Transparency and Exchange of Information for Tax Purposes. Shimeng has contributed to Chapter 23 of this book.

Kalale Mambwe is an economist and international tax and transfer pricing specialist working for the Zambia Revenue Authority's international taxation unit. After her graduating with an honours degree in Economics from the University of Namibia, Kalale went on to pursue her Master's in Business Administration (MBA) from the University of Zambia. Kalale has over six years' experience in transfer pricing. She has worked as a transfer pricing specialist since the inception of the specialized unit handling transfer pricing and other international taxation issues. Kalale is currently a technical committee member with the ATAF and IGF on 'The Future of Resource Taxation' in the extractive industry. Kalale also works with ATAF in providing technical assistance to tax administrations in Africa with the aim of building capacity in transfer pricing and other international taxation matters. Kalale is currently a member of the OECD Inclusive Framework on Pillar 1 and Pillar 2 and the OECD Task Force on Digital Economy. Kalale has contributed to Chapter 16 of this book.

Rahul Mitra has over twenty-seven years of experience in handling transfer pricing, supply chain management projects, international taxation, BEPS, profit attribution to permanent establishments, etc. Rahul was a tax partner with PwC and KPMG in India for an aggregate period of almost twenty years, including having served both organizations as the leader of their national transfer pricing practices. Rahul was a country reporter on the topic 'Non-Discrimination in International Tax Matters' for the IFA Congress held in Brussels in 2008. Rahul was invited by the OECD to speak at the 2012 Paris roundtable conference on APAs. Rahul was invited by the tax tribunal in 2012 and the Indian Revenue Board in 2015 and 2019 to impart training on the topic of transfer pricing to members of the tax tribunal and senior officials of the Indian Revenue, respectively. Rahul has been rated as a leading transfer pricing professional and tax litigator in India by *Euromoney* and *International Tax Review* since 2010. Rahul received the 'International Tax Contributing Author of the Year' award in the subject of transfer pricing in 2019 from Bloomberg Tax. Rahul is a member of global editorial board of the international web-based tax magazine, *Bloomberg Tax Transfer Pricing Forum*. Rahul has authored a book on transfer pricing, styled as *Decoding Transfer Pricing for Selling Functions*. Rahul independently handles litigation for top companies before tax tribunals and has won several landmark rulings creating precedents in India in matters relating to the berry ratio, marketing intangibles; selection of tested party; corporate guarantee; profit split method; etc. Rahul has handled several APAs and MAPs in India covering complex transactions, e.g., industrial franchise fees under non-integrated principal structures; contract R&D service provider model; distribution models with related marketing intangible issues; financial transactions; profit split model for royalties; etc. Rahul has contributed to Chapter 25 of this book.

Jérôme Monsenego is full-time professor of International Tax Law at Stockholm University, Sweden and Chairman of IFA Sweden. He obtained his Ph.D. summa cum laude and was awarded an honourable mention by the jury of the IFA Mitchell B. Carroll Prize for his doctoral thesis 'Taxation of Foreign Business Income Within the European Internal Market – An Analysis of the Conflict Between the Objective of Achievement of the European Internal Market and the Principles of Territoriality and Worldwide Taxation' (IBFD Doctoral Series, 2012). He has published articles in English, French, and Swedish on various topics of international taxation, a book on transfer pricing (*Introduction to Transfer Pricing*, Kluwer Law International, 2015), and a book on fiscal state aid (*Selectivity in State Aid Law and the Methods for the Allocation of the Corporate Tax Base*, Kluwer Law International, 2018) that was shortlisted for the 2019 IBFD Frans Vanistendael Award. Before joining academia on a full-time basis, he worked for twelve years as an international tax advisor at PwC in Paris and Stockholm. Jérôme has contributed to Chapter 24 of this book.

Velio Alessandro Moretti, MBA, is the group head of transfer pricing at the Generali Group with the responsibility to coordinate and steer the Transfer Pricing affairs at Group level. He joined Generali in 2012 after having worked in big four consultancy firms such as EY and Deloitte for almost five years focusing on Transfer Pricing and International Taxation. Velio specializes in transfer pricing issues related to insurance, asset management and banking transactions. He is an Italian chartered accountant and certified auditor and is a speaker at seminars and conferences on transfer pricing topics.. He also holds an executive master's in Transfer Pricing at the University of Lausanne, Switzerland, an executive MBA from MIB School of Management and a Master of Laws in International Tax Law from the Italian Ministry of Finance. He graduated cum laude with a Master of Science in Business Administration (Dissertation Title: Related Party Transactions in MNEs: Economic and Law Perspective). Velio has contributed to Chapter 18 of this book.

Nitin Narang possesses rich professional experience of more than eighteen years in handling international tax and transfer pricing matters of domestic and multinational enterprises. Since 2005, he has been involved in various transfer pricing assignments, including local transfer pricing documentation and compliance, master file and country-by-country reports, global transfer pricing documentation, APAs, MAPs, representation at the tax office at various levels, business restructuring, implementation of tax-effective supply chain structures, profit attribution analyses, FIN 48 analysis, implementation of global cross-charge mechanisms, transfer pricing planning analyses, etc. Nitin has also handled litigation for many companies and has successfully represented his clients at the level of the Income Tax Appellate Tribunal, commissioner of income tax (appeals), and dispute resolution panel. He has also assisted various legal counsels in high court and other legal matters. Nitin has worked across a wide spectrum of various industries like oil and gas, IT/ITeS, automotive, pharma, FMCG, chemicals/ink, EPC, sogo shosha, sourcing support, industrial products, consumer durables, etc.

Prior to joining Nangia Andersen India, he worked at Ernst & Young and PwC in tax and regulatory services in international taxation and transfer pricing teams. His experience also includes a one and half year secondment to Ernst & Young US, Atlanta,

Georgia. Nitin has been a speaker at various tax conferences and forums on transfer pricing. He has also contributed to various articles on transfer pricing and international tax matters, in leading financial dailies like *ETCFO*, etc., and various tax journals like *Taxsutra, Taxmann*, etc. Nitin has contributed to Chapter 25 of this book.

Tarini Nijhara possesses rich professional experience of more than thirteen years in handling transfer pricing matters of domestic and multinational enterprises. She has extensive experience in assisting multinationals to resolve complex transfer pricing disputes at almost all appellate forums and has also assisted various multinationals in resolving disputes through the mutual agreement procedure and APA proceedings. Since 2005, she has been assisting her clients across a wide spectrum of industries like IT/ITeS, automotive, FMCG, chemicals, services, industrial products, EPC, sogo shosha, travel, consumer products, etc. She has been handling various transfer pricing projects, including global transfer pricing documentation spanning a number of countries, APAs, representation at the tax office at various levels, FIN 48 analysis, advisory on cost allocation mechanism/process, transfer pricing diagnostic of existing models, determination of target arm's length margins for various business models, etc. She has also handled litigation for many companies across numerous industry sectors along with the legal counsels at the level of the Income Tax Appellate Tribunal and above. She has also contributed inputs and articles on transfer pricing matters in leading financial dailies like *ETCFO*, etc., and various tax journals like *Taxsutra, Taxmann*, etc. Prior to joining Nangia Andersen Consulting Pvt. Ltd, she worked with the KPMG and PwC in tax and regulatory services in transfer pricing practice. Tarini has contributed to Chapter 25 of this book.

Katarina Petovska has more than fifteen years of transfer pricing experience and is currently leading the global transfer pricing economics and operations team at Dell Technologies. She is responsible for the design and implementation of a worldwide operational transfer pricing policy, supply chain planning; implementation and management of the global transfer pricing models reflecting current BEPS developments; pricing strategy in respect of intercompany financing transactions; supports global transfer pricing lead in transfer pricing planning and strategy, M&A transactional support, acquisitions integration, and APA negotiations. Previously Katarina worked in the PwC Prague Office and was specialized in international tax advisory. Katarina has a Master's in International Trade, is a registered tax advisor, and is ADIT qualified. Katarina has contributed to Chapter 19 of this book.

Prof. Dr Robert Risse is the Director of WU Tax Law Technology Centre at the Institute for Austrian and International Tax Law at WU (Vienna University of Economics and Business). Previously, he was the global head of the tax and trade department at Henkel AG & Co. KGaA and has also held leading positions at Deutsche Post AG, Mannesmann AG, and Kaufhof Holding AG during his career. He is also an Honorary Professor of Tax Compliance and Applied Tax Planning for Business Taxation at the University of Leipzig, Germany. His teaching activities focus mainly on international taxation, tax compliance and tax planning, and tax technology in practice. Robert has contributed to Chapter 17 of this book.

H. David Rosenbloom is an attorney specializing in international tax matters. He is a member of Caplin & Drysdale, Chartered, a law firm in Washington, DC; the James S. Eustice Visiting Professor of Taxation; and director of the international tax program at New York University School of Law. Born in New York, NY in 1941, Mr Rosenbloom attended Princeton University, US; the University of Florence, Italy; and Harvard Law School, US. He served as president of the *Harvard Law Review*, assistant to Ambassador Arthur Goldberg at the US Mission to the UN, and clerk to Justice Abe Fortas in the US Supreme Court.

Mr Rosenbloom was international tax counsel and director of the office of international tax affairs in the US Treasury Department from January 1978 through January 1981. A frequent speaker and author on tax subjects, he has taught International Taxation and related subjects at Stanford, Columbia, the University of Pennsylvania, Harvard, and New York University Law Schools, and at educational institutions in Taipei, Mexico City, Milan, Bergamo, Sydney, Mainz, Heidelberg, Rio de Janeiro, and Pretoria. He has also served as a tax policy advisor for the US Treasury, the OECD, AID, the World Bank in Eastern Europe, the former Soviet Union, Senegal, Malawi, and South Africa. Mr Rosenbloom has contributed to Chapter 26 of this book.

Dr Niraja Srinivasan is a director in the global transfer pricing practice at NERA based out of Washington DC. In that role, she assists multinational companies and law firms with expert economic analyses and dispute resolution in transfer pricing for intellectual property and global supply chains as well as in tax valuation audits. She has over twenty years of consulting and corporate experience leading strategy and risk mitigation for Fortune 50 companies and, prior to joining NERA, she held the position of vice president in Dell Technologies' Global Tax Group. Niraja received her Ph.D. in Economics and MA in Public Policy and Management from the Wharton School of the University of Pennsylvania. Niraja has contributed to Chapter 19 of this book.

Sing Yuan Yong is currently the tax director at the Inland Revenue Authority of Singapore dealing with transfer pricing and dispute resolution matters. She has experience in tax policy work and international taxation matters. Sing Yuan holds a Bachelor of Accountancy with honours from the Nanyang Technological University, Singapore and a Master of Advanced Studies in International Tax Law cum laude from Leiden University, the Netherlands. She is also an accredited tax advisor with the Singapore Institute of Accredited Tax Practitioners. Sing Yuan is the course advisor and ad hoc trainer for programmes run by the tax academy. She has also contributed to external journals such as the *Bulletin for International Taxation* by IBFD. Sing Yuan has contributed to Chapter 28 of this book.

Florian Zirnstein is co-leading the transfer pricing and business models for the CropScience division at Bayer. He has more than ten years of experience in the area of transfer pricing. Before joining Bayer in 2013, Florian spent five years with EY's transfer pricing expert group in Düsseldorf, Germany. During his career in consulting and industry, Florian worked on various transfer pricing projects, including strategic transfer pricing planning (i.e., business model effectiveness and intellectual property planning), the preparation of transfer pricing documentations (global and EU master file), transfer pricing audits, and business integration. Furthermore, he focused on various types of intercompany financing concepts within the Bayer group, including cash pools and loan transactions. Florian has contributed to Chapter 21 of this book.

Summary of Contents

List of Figures

List of Tables

List of Abbreviations

AAC	Average Avoidable Cost
AERR	Actually Experimented Return Ratio
AI	Artificial Intelligence
ALM	Asset/Liability Management
ALP	Arm's Length Principle
AMP	Advertisement, Marketing and Promotion
AO	Assessing Officer
AOA	Authorized OECD Approach
APA	Advance Pricing Agreement/Arrangement
API	Application Programming Interface
APMA	Advance Pricing and Mutual Agreement Program
ARERA	Authority for Energy Networks and Environment
ART	Alternative Risk Transfer
ATAD	Anti-tax Avoidance Directive
ATAF	African Tax Administration Forum
ATC	Average Total Cost
ATO	Australian Tax Office
AVC	Average Variable Cost
B2B	Business-to-Business
B2C	Business-to-Customer
BCB	Brazil's Central Bank
BCB	Central Bank of Brazil
BEPS	Base Erosion and Profit Shifting
BMDA	Baseline Distributor and Marketing Activities

BOI	Binding Origin Information
BPMN	Business Process Model and Notation
BTI	Binding Tariff Information
CAP	Custo de Aquisição ou de Produção mais Tributos e Lucro
CARF	Administrative Council for Tax Appeals, Brazil
CbCR	Country-by-Country Report
CBDT	Central Board of Direct Taxes (India)
CCA	Cost Contribution Arrangement
CE	Constituent Entity
CFR	Cost and Freight
CIAT	Inter-American Center of Tax Administrators
CIF	Cost, Insurance and Freight
CIT(A)	Commissioner of Income Tax (Appeals)
CJEU	Court of Justice of the European Union
CKD	Completely Knocked-Down
CMS	Compliance Management Systems
CNY	Chinese Yuan
COGS	Cost of Goods Sold
COR	Combined Ratio
CPG	Consumer Packaged Goods
CPL	Custo de Produção mais Lucro
CPM	Cost-Plus Method
CRISPR	Clustered Regulatory Interspaced Short Palindromic Repeats
CRM	Customer Relationship Management
[year] OECD Commentary, if a reference to the latest version, just OECD Commentary	Commentary to the OECD Model Tax Convention on Income and Capital
[year] UN Commentary, if a reference to the latest version, just UN Commentary	Commentary to the United Nations Model Double Taxation Convention Between Developed and Developing Countries
CSP	Captive Services Provider
CST	Cost Sharing Transaction
CTAIS	China Taxation Administration Information System
CU	Currency Unit
CUP	Comparable Uncontrolled Price

CUT	Comparable Uncontrolled Transaction
CWI	Commensurate with Income
DAC	Directive on Administrative Cooperation
DAEMPE	Development, Acquisition, Enhancement, Maintenance, Protection, Exploitation
DCF	Discounted Cash Flow
DEMPE	Development, Enhancement, Maintenance, Protection, Exploitation
DEMPEP	Development, Enhancement, Maintenance, Protection, Exploitation, Promotion
DLT	Distributed Ledger Technology
DNA	Deoxyribonucleic Acid
DPA	Data Processing Agreement
DRP	Dispute Resolution Panel
DST	Digital Service Tax
DTC	Double Tax Treaty/Double Tax Convention
EBIT	Earnings Before Interest and Tax
EBITDA	Earnings Before Interest, Tax, Depreciation and Amortization
EC	European Council
ECJ	European Court of Justice
EITL	Enterprise Income Tax Law
EMEA	Europe, the Middle East and Africa
ERP	Enterprise Resource Planning
ESG	Environment, Social and Governance
EU	European Union
EU JTPF	European Union Joint Transfer Pricing Forum
EU TPD	European Union Transfer Pricing Documentation
FAR	Functions, Assets and Risks
FCA	French Competent Authority
FCM	Flexible Consumption Model
FCMU	Full Cost Mark-Up
FDI	Foreign Direct Investment
FMCG	Fast-Moving Consumer Goods
FOB	Free on Board
FTA	Forum on Tax Administration
FTE	Full-Time Equivalent
FY	Financial Year
GAAPs	Generally Accepted Accounting Principles

GDP	Gross Domestic Product
GDPR	General Data Protection Regulation
GMP	Good Manufacturing Practice
GST	Goods and Services Tax
GVC	Global Value Chain
GVCA	Global Value Chain Analysis
HC	High Court
HNTE	High and New Technology Enterprise
HNWI	High Net-Worth Individual
HQ	Headquarters
HR	Human Resources
HTVI	Hard-to-Value Intangibles
ICAP	International Compliance Assurance Programme
ICT	Information and Computer Technology
IF	Inclusive Framework
IFA	International Fiscal Association
IFRS	International Fiscal Reporting Standard
IGF	Intergovernmental Forum
INPI	National Institute of Industrial Property
INR	Indian Rupee
IOC	Integrated Oil and Gas Company
IoT	Internet of Things
IP	Intangible Property
IQR	Interquartile Range
IRC	Internal Revenue Code
IRS	Internal Revenue Service
IT	Information Technology
ITAT	Income Tax Appellate Tribunal
ITeS	Information Technology Enabled Services
JA	Joint Audit
JCC	Japanese Crude Cocktail
JOA	Joint Operating Agreement
JTPF	Joint Transfer Pricing Forum
JV	Joint Venture
KERT	Key Entrepreneurial Risk Taking
KPI	Key Performance Indicator
LB&I	Large Business and International

LBMA	London Bullion Market Association
LIBOR	London Inter-Bank Offered Rate
LMB	London Metal Bulleting
LME	London Metal Exchange
LNG	Liquefied Natural Gas
LRAIC	Long Run Average Incremental Cost
LRD	Limited-Risk Distributor
LSA	Location-Specific Advantage
LSCCs	Local Operative Supply Chain Companies
LSMC	Local Sales and Marketing Company
LVAS	Low Value-Adding Services
M&A	Merger and Acquisition
MAP	Mutual Agreement Procedure
MAT	Marine, Aviation, and Transport
MiFID2	Markets in Financial Instruments Directive II
MLI	Multilateral Instrument
MNE	Multinational Enterprise
MTC	Model Tax Convention
NPV	Net Present Value
NSR	Net Smelter Return
O&G	Oil and Gas
OCI	Other Comprehensive Income
OECD	Organisation for Economic Co-operation and Development
[year] OECD MTC, if a reference to the latest version, just OECD MTC	OECD Model Tax Convention on Income and Capital
[year] OECD TPG if a reference to the latest version, just OECD TPG	OECD Transfer Pricing Guidelines for Multinational Enterprises and Tax Administrations
OPEX	Operating Expenses
ORA	Options Realistically Available
P&L	Profit and Loss
PCI	Preço sob Cotação na Importação
PCT	Platform for Collaboration on Tax
PE	Permanent Establishment
PECEX	Preço sob Cotação na Exportação
PEVEX	Preço de Venda nas Exportações

PIC	Preços Independentes Comparados
PLI	Profit Level Indicator
PPM	Parts per Million
PRRR	Period Return Ratio Range
PSC	Production Sharing Contracts
PSM	Profit Split Method
PVA	Preço de Venda por Atacado no País de Destino, Diminuído do Lucro
PVV	Preço de Venda a Varejo no País de Destino, Diminuído do Lucro
R&D	Research and Development
RAB	Reasonably Anticipated Benefits
RC	Refining Cost
RFB	Receita Federal do Brasil
ROA	Return on Asset
ROC	Return on Cost
ROCE	Return on Capital Employed
ROE	Return on Equity
ROI	Return on Investment
ROS	Return on Sales
RPA	Robotic Process Automation
RPM	Resale Price Method
SC	Supreme Court of India
SCM	Services Cost Method
SCPP	Supply Chain and Procurement Entrepreneur/Principal
SDT	Specified Domestic Transaction
SHR	Safe Harbour Rule
SKD	Semi Knocked Down
SME	Small and Medium Enterprise
SPE	Special Purpose Entity
SPFs	Significant People Functions
SSA	Shared Services Agreement
SSA	Shared Services Agreement
STA	State Tax Administration, China
STPI	Software Technology Parks in India
SWOT	Strengths, Weaknesses, Opportunities and Threats
TC	Treatment Cost
TCCV	Technical Committee on Customs Valuation
TCJA	Tax Cuts and Jobs Act, 2017

TFEU	Treaty on the Functioning of the European Union
TIEA	Tax Information Exchange Agreement
TNMM	Transactional Net Margin Method
TP	Transfer Pricing
TPD	Transfer Pricing Documentation
TPO	Transfer Pricing Officer
TPSM	Transactional Profit Split Method
TREAT	Tax Risk Evaluation and Assessment Tool
UCC	Union Customs Code
UK	United Kingdom
UN	United Nations
[year] UN MTC if a reference to the latest version, just UN MTC	United Nations Model Double Taxation Convention Between Developed and Developing Countries
[year] UN TPM if a reference to the latest version, just UN TPM	United Nations Practical Manual on Transfer Pricing for Developing Countries
UPE	Ultimate Parent Entity
US	United States
UStAE	Umsatzsteuer-Anwendungs-Erlass
UStG	German Value Added Tax Act
UTP	Uncertain Tax Positions
UZK	Union Customs Code
VAT	Value-Added Tax
VAT Directive	Council Directive 2006/112/EC of 28 November 2006 on the Common System of Value-Added Tax
VCLT	Vienna Convention on the Law of Treaties
VIES	VAT Information Exchange System
WACC	Weighted Average Cost of Capital
WARA	Weighted Average Return on Assets
WCO	World Customs Organization
WCO Guide	World Customs Organization Guide to Customs Valuation and Transfer Pricing
WHO	World Health Organization
WTI	West Texas Intermediate
WTO	World Trade Organization
WTO Valuation Agreement	Agreement on Implementation of Article VII of the General Agreement on Tariffs and Trade

XaaS	Anything-as-a-Service
ZRA	Zambia Revenue Authority

Note to Readers

This book forms the second volume of the series 'Fundamentals of Transfer Pricing'. The first volume (second edition) consists of thirteen chapters of detailed guidance on general transfer pricing topics and specific transactions. Since this book is the next volume in the series, the chapters are numbered from 14 until 31. Both the volumes together form a comprehensive set thereby giving the reader understanding of the principles of transfer pricing, their application to specific kind of transactions, regional guidance, technological developments and their interaction with other tax and legal fields.

Preface

Transfer pricing continues to be one of the most significant and debated issues in international taxation. The increasing number of disputes between taxpayers and tax administrations concerning the interpretation of the arm's length principle and the constant review of the guidance provided by international organizations as well as all relevant stakeholders are among the evidence of its relevance. Rapid transformations in the economic, political, and social climate bring about inevitable changes in the functioning of MNEs that consequently influence transfer pricing. Such a dynamic field of tax law requires invariably updating and revisiting the core principles on which it was built.

It gives us immense pleasure to introduce the second volume of the book *Fundamentals of Transfer Pricing*. The first volume of the book, introduced in 2019, focused on the basic principles of transfer pricing and their application to specific transactions. The second edition of the first volume, published in 2021, added numerous updates, examples, and cases to the previous edition. The current second volume consists of four parts. It starts with the application of transfer pricing topics to particular sectors. As industry knowledge forms the basis of any transfer pricing analysis, this part provides ample information on the functioning of leading sectors, their value creation, and ways to determine the related arm's length outcomes. The following part fleshes out some country- and regional-specific profiles where the reader can gain an overview of the transfer pricing rules in various jurisdictions. Later, the authors provide a peek into the use of new technologies to facilitate transfer pricing analyses. The final section presents the interaction of different areas of law with transfer pricing. Specific changes in the tax world like the 2021 update of the UN Transfer Pricing Manual, the Two-Pillar solution proposed by the OECD, the 2022 OECD Transfer Pricing Guidelines, the ongoing cooperative compliance work under the ICAP, EU State Aid issues and, among others, discussions on digitalization and taxation also influence the content of this book and warrant changes in intervals throughout the writing and editing process.

This book not only provides a comprehensive understanding but also delves deeper into the practical aspects of the topic. It represents a collaboration of leading transfer pricing experts from all around the globe. Their expertise and knowledge are reflected in the detailed and lucid explanation through the chapters. We are grateful to the authors and contributors for taking time from their busy professional lives and committing to this project. We would also like to thank Abhishek Padwalkar and the entire WU Transfer Pricing Center staff for their hard work and constant support. Finally, thanks to Jenny Hill for the excellent language editing and to Wolter Kluwers for the continuous trust in publishing this book.

Vienna, 6 June 2022
Dr Raffaele Petruzzi
Dr Giammarco Cottani
Prof. Dr Michael Lang

Industries

CHAPTER 14

Transfer Pricing in the Automotive Sector

Gregor Gehauf & Axel Eigelshoven

1 INTRODUCTION

The automotive industry includes companies involved in the design, development, and manufacture of automobiles and is one of the most important industries worldwide in terms of value creation. This includes car manufacturers (so-called OEMs) and suppliers. In 2019, OEMs produced 67.15 million passenger vehicles and 24.64 million commercial vehicles. Pre-COVID-19 sales exceeded 91 million vehicles in 2019.[1] Within the EU, the automotive industry accounts for approximately 7% of its total GDP and features 14.6 million direct and indirect jobs which equal a share of 6.7% of all EU jobs or 11.5% of EU manufacturing jobs.[2] Automotive suppliers and OEMs are the main drivers of innovation with average R&D spending of EUR 60.9 billion p.a. which is 29% of the total R&D spending in the EU.[3] Hence, even taking into account that all numbers reflect a pre-COVID-19 world economy, the importance of the automotive industry for job creation and economic growth around the globe cannot be emphasized enough. In a globalized economy, the automotive value chain is highly diversified and encompasses supply and service transactions spanning all continents.

Its importance also means that the automotive industry pays a substantial share of taxes into government pockets as MNEs – whether they are OEMs or suppliers – have a significant taxable presence in all major markets. Consequently, tax authorities generally place intensive scrutiny on TP in the automotive industry. Many countries use specialized auditors who are trained in the specific TP issues of the industry to ensure that tax audits are conducted with the appropriate focus. As a result, attention is generally paid to traditional goods and service transactions in TP audits in the automotive industry. As in all industries, transactions on IP become increasingly important in value creation and therefore become a major component of audits. This chapter shall provide an overview of the most important TP issues of OEMs and suppliers. Although they are closely interlinked in their supply chains, each party features somewhat different TP issues. The structure of this chapter reflects this in two distinctive parts, i.e., one for OEMs and one for suppliers.

2 TP OF OEMs

The business of an automotive OEM is a classic product business. Regardless of the numerous services offered and the recent trend of digitalization (*see* the end of this chapter), the OEM supply chain is still centred overwhelmingly around the vehicle itself.[4] From a TP perspective, this means that the focus in the analysis is primarily on tangible goods transactions and their respective price calculations. These calculations are often straightforward, and there is not much discussion on which TP methodology is used (as further detailed below). However, as finished products in the automotive industry feature a higher value compared to, e.g., fast consumer goods, minimal TP adjustments (such as, a 0.1% return on net sales of a typical wholesale distribution company that might often have a sales volume of several billion euro) may have a significant impact on the profit allocation along the value chain of the MNE.

1. Cf. *OICA*, www.oica.net/category/production-statistics (last accessed 30 January 2022).
2. Cf. *ACEA*, www.acea.be/automobile-industry/facts-about-the-industry (last accessed 30 January 2022).
3. *Ibid.*
4. The term 'car' or 'vehicle' is used in the following; this includes all trucks and other commercial vehicles as well.

The value chain of an automotive OEM is simple: It consists of the development/design, the production, and the sale of a car. As the product (including the technology and brand embedded within the product) forms the core of the OEM business, MNEs organize all value-creating functions along this rather simple supply chain. Any risk-taking functions are also set up to be able to efficiently manage the value chain for which three types of typical tangible transactions exist within an automotive OEM:

(1) R&D services on behalf of the core IP owner/development entity;
(2) manufacturing activities/transactions; and
(3) the sale of products to a wholesale/retail entity.

These transactions (along with some corresponding services) will be illustrated in detail from a TP point of view in the following sub-chapters.

Before beginning, a quick aside is necessary. Any TP topic regarding the tangible goods transactions within an automotive OEM is also subject to the laws and regulations of customs authorities worldwide. While the arm's length principle is adopted by both international tax and customs regulations, this does not mean that disputes with customs and tax authorities adhere to the same interpretation of these principles. In particular, customs authorities focus on individual transactions, whereas the tax authorities, in general, take an aggregated view. Moreover, while a jurisdiction importing vehicles might want to see a high transfer price from a customs perspective (creating a base for higher duty revenues), the same jurisdiction calls for a lower transfer price in order to increase the tax base of the importing legal entity. This chapter focuses on the issues of TP for tax purposes. Nevertheless, the implications of any TP policy on customs and respective import levies always need to be carefully considered in the industry.

2.1 Central Entrepreneur Model

As mentioned above, the typical value chain of an OEM is organized around the development, production, and sale of a vehicle. In its internal organization, the centre of the value chain is formed by the classic *central entrepreneur* model; i.e., in most cases, a central legal entity (generally the ultimate parent) is responsible for the overall strategy and set-up of the business model and assumes the role of a residual risk-taker. This central entrepreneur entity is generally the owner of all significant IP relevant for the business model of the OEM. The two major types of IP that are pertinent for the success of an automotive OEM are technology and brand.

In contrast to a central entrepreneurial entity, other legal entities of an MNE will often have a routine functional profile and bear routine risks from their operations. Transactions between such entities and the central entrepreneur will generally be designed in such a way that remuneration for the functions performed is somewhat limited but stable given the routine risk profile. In turn, the central entrepreneur is entitled to the residual profit (or loss) from the business of the MNE.

Figure 14.1 Central Entrepreneur Model

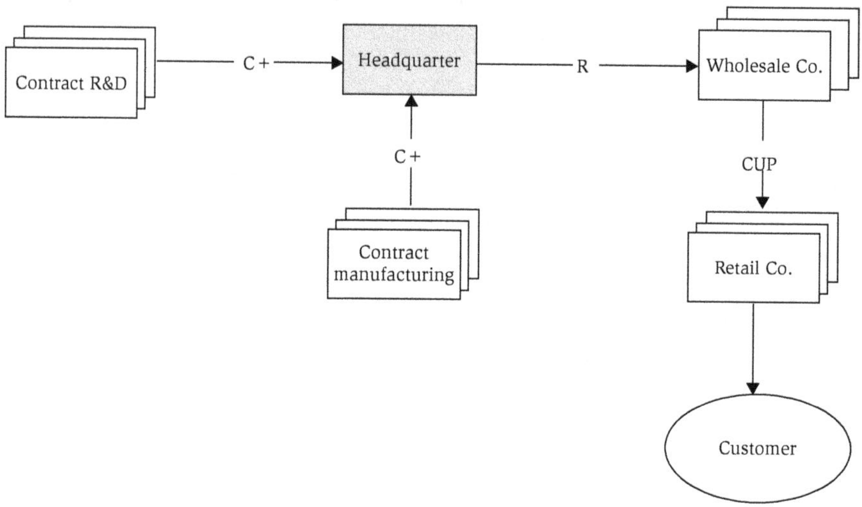

However, there may be some variations of the central entrepreneur model (Figure 14.1):

- Some OEMs own *several brands* within the group. These brand owners often have their own historic technology IP, and new IP is charged either by way of a cost-sharing arrangement or through a licence agreement. Central entrepreneurial entities may consequently exist for every brand within an MNE.
- Some OEMs operate manufacturing through *licence manufacturers*; e.g., in China, OEMs were forced into joint venture structures for regulatory reasons. Such joint ventures are typically set up as a licence manufacturer. A significant number of OEMs also operate in South Africa through local production entities as this government has created large economic incentives on localizing production. Such production entities are also often set up as licence manufacturers and many times feature an extended functional and risk profile.
- For certain markets, OEMs set up manufacturing plants for CKD or SKD assembly as they are able to access favourable customs regimes. This structure is often seen in Southeast Asia, e.g., Indonesia, the Philippines, Thailand, and Vietnam. The IP is either included in the product price of the components or a separate licence agreement is established.

If an OEM adheres to the simple central entrepreneur model, typical transaction partners of the central entrepreneur are R&D service providers (development), contract manufacturers (production), wholesale as well as sales companies (sale). The following chapters describe in detail the transactions between such entities and the entrepreneur as well as the TP implications.

2.2 Development/Design of a Car

R&D activities in the automotive industry typically concentrate around the following main topics: vehicle platform, engine and drivetrain, vehicle integration, and – more recently – software development and connectivity of the car. The phases of the process are generally divided into two parts: a general conception of a new vehicle (or a new generation of vehicles) and the so-called industrialization of the product (i.e., developing the technical solution, integration of all planned product features into a finished car, and a definition of necessary production processes). Once all of these features have been developed, the focus of R&D is on testing pre-series vehicles as well as making processes suitable for series production. At the very end of the R&D cycle is the so-called homologation of the vehicle in various countries (i.e., adapting the vehicle to the respective regulations of any specific country for public road allowance). The 'handover' from R&D responsibility to production usually occurs at the initiation of series production.

Traditionally, OEMs have a large development centre at their main site that is responsible and controls the complete R&D process. It retains the process ownership from the original conceptualization of the car to its industrialization for production processes. Hence, the process is generally quite centralized within an MNE, and respective organizational aspects of the R&D process reflect that. Smaller engineering centres around the globe support central processes. However, the scope of services and activities of smaller engineering centres is mostly limited and focuses on a specific part of the development process. Primary examples of such limited activities are technology scouting, testing, and homologation. Technology scouting refers to research on features that might be crucial for the next generation of cars (e.g., connectivity with personal mobile devices). Such activities are typically conducted in close collaboration with universities and start-up companies. Testing, on the other hand, features specialized teams to test certain characteristics of a car in development (e.g., hot/cold weather conditions, driving performance). Finally, during the homologation process, special country teams ensure that the newly designed vehicle is properly adapted to local traffic regulations.

From a TP point of view, the R&D process is structured in a rather straightforward manner. The functions of smaller or specialized R&D centres – being responsible only for certain elements of the R&D process even if that means that it features many qualified people – are characterized and legally structured as a service.[5] The activities of the engineering centre – integrating all R&D activities into the respective vehicle project – are considered entrepreneurial functions that eventually result in the respective technological IP (know-how, patents, software). As smaller centres perform support services for the central engineering department, their remuneration is based on the cost-plus method (contract R&D services) with their services typically including a

5. Cf. para. 7.41 OECD TPG.

markup of 5%-8%. The engineering centre is then entitled to the respective entrepreneurial return or a royalty if the technology is licensed to another manufacturing entity within the OEM (e.g., to another entity owning its own brand).

Assume a case of a European OEM that has a central engineering centre located in Germany that features all of the primary functions of the R&D process involved in a new car. Support in the early concept phase is provided by a technology scouting site in the US that features a large start-up scene that provides for future trends in individual mobility concepts (e.g., Silicon Valley). This R&D site is then tasked with adapting certain new technologies for the industrialization of a new vehicle as a service. Moreover, an R&D office in China needs to adapt the car's new features to the respective local regulations and register certain items with local authorities in order to obtain a sign-off for use on public roads. Both service sites are remunerated on a cost-plus basis.

From an organizational perspective, this involves some outsourcing of less important activities to a service partner within the MNE, while the overall responsibility for the R&D process remains with the main development centre (e.g., in Germany as the country of the headquarter). In particular, although legal entities performing R&D services may operate with a certain level of discretion, the central R&D departments develop the framework and guidelines of the service function to be performed by the service provider and define the goals and requirements of the services and retain all major decision rights. In the past, this general composition and the respective characterization of transactions as a service have not been questioned by tax authorities.

From a TP viewpoint, three areas are of concern. The first is the question of an arm's length markup for the services being rendered. Second, there is controversy about the cost base. The third issue is regarding the question of who actually controls the R&D function and should receive the intangible-related return.

The markup may be subject to discussions with tax authorities as tax officers often hold the opinion that the applied markup is not sufficient to remunerate the important functions performed by the R&D service providers within their country. In particular, tax authorities in emerging markets may question the quantum of the markups as a bottom-line remuneration of an R&D entity may be quite low if the cost base of the markup is limited (e.g., operations in low-cost markets). As there are no safe harbour rules[6] for engineering or R&D services in general, tax authorities in emerging markets may object to the standard markups between 5% and 8% that are often applied by MNEs. In fact, there are a number of large international contract R&D service providers, such as Bertrandt, EDAG, IAV, and Ferchau, that provide R&D services to the automotive industry and should be an adequate indication of third-party markups. The cost-plus margins of 5%-8% are generally in accordance with such independent companies. However, if independent service providers, for instance, in India are analysed, much higher markups of 15%-20% can often be observed, and MNEs are well advised to differentiate markups by countries, especially if labour costs are low.

6. Chapter VII. D OECD TPG does not apply to contract R&D transactions.

Another problem is the cost base as actual profitability might deviate due to:

- differences between budget and actual costs;
- differences between the accounting periods and accounting treatment; or
- exclusion of costs from the cost base, e.g., costs relating to third-party service providers.

As these problems become even more pronounced in a cost-plus manufacturing set-up, section 2.3 below will cover these in more detail.

In recent years, R&D processes have become increasingly specialized, and, as a result, authorities have begun to question if the central engineering centre actually exercises the control of the development process that is necessary to be entitled to the respective intangible-related return. Sometimes, specialized R&D sites have become more self-reliant. Thus, a pure funding of the service activities without being able to exercise control of the service provider leads to the question of the arm's length profit allocation regarding the R&D process. The end of this debate is well known: The original BEPS Project resulted in a recharacterization of IP-generating value chain processes with the newly introduced DEMPE concept in the chapters on hard-to-value intangibles (BEPS work packages 8-10). This is now reflected in Chapter VI of the OECD TPG.

The most significant change for the R&D process of an OEM is that IP ownership for economic/tax purposes must align with the important value-creating functions actually performed and controlled by associated legal entities involved in a transaction related to the DEMPE IP functions. Legal ownership of IP serves only as a beginning for analysing controlled transactions relating to IP and for determining an appropriate remuneration.[7] Hence, the actual controlling of the DEMPE functions in terms of relevant personnel (so-called people function) is the deciding factor for allocating the intangible-related return. In particular, IP does not automatically accrue to the legal entity (e.g., by contract) that has funded R&D activities if it does not exercise sufficient control over it.

As a result of these new developments, it has become more important to provide detailed documentation about IP-generating processes in an MNE. From a TP perspective, an MNE can no longer rely on TP policy and respective agreements to document the service character of a transaction. Instead, it must reflect exactly who is doing what along the value-generating process and describe the corresponding decision-making processes. This includes describing the organizational composition of the R&D process and the designated MNE bodies making final decisions.

Hence, future discussions with tax authorities will likely focus more on determining the DEMPE functions and the attribution of intangible-related return instead of the appropriate amount of a profit markup. Obviously, claiming a part of the entrepreneurial return will have a greater impact on fiscal revenues.

While the value chain of automotive OEMs is still quite simple (being organized around a central engineering centre, as explained above), the development of software solutions in the car may pose a new dimension of complexity in this discussion. Work

7. Cf. para. 6.43 OECD TPG.

on software is often performed around the clock with developers beginning work in Asia, passing it on to Europe, and then on to US developers. Due to its cyclical nature, it is very difficult to determine in the end who added what to the final software solution and when the breakthrough was achieved. Disputes will certainly arise regarding which entity should receive part of the intangible-related returns. Ultimately, taxpayers may need to resolve such questions with bilateral tax procedures such as APAs or joint audits to obtain legal certainty concerning their business models.

A simple conflict may arise if Country A takes a more legal view on IP-generating processes by investigating the respective intra-group contractual arrangements (e.g., most notably the US) while Country B fully applies the DEMPE regulations and analyses the individual value-adding processes between the two transaction partners.

However, the allocation of intangible-related returns is not the only TP topic from a practitioner's point of view. There is a risk that the DEMPE concept makes the use of traditional transactional TP methods (in the case of R&D, the cost-plus method) less applicable. Once IP-related transactions become more relevant, local tax auditors might require the use of a profit split method.[8] This raises the question on the value of R&D within the value chain of an OEM and its quantification. While the DEMPE concept is only qualitative in nature, the question on an appropriate quantification of contributions along the value chain remains a difficult one.[9] The discussion is not about HTVI for nothing![10] At least from a tax risk perspective, OEMs are well advised to ensure central control of their R&D processes which allows centralizing their IP.

As a brief aside, note that IP is separately defined for TP purposes by the OECD TPG (not adhering to accounting or legal principles).[11] Therefore, it was rather 'easy' during the BEPS Project to assign economic/tax ownership to the company actually performing the value-generating function as a theoretical concept. However, these divergent definitions will very likely lead to more disputes with tax authorities around IP ownership in the future.

2.3 Production

Similar to the R&D process, an OEM will generally have a significant number of manufacturing operations in its home country. However, over the last decades, OEMs have followed a global footprint strategy and have set up significant manufacturing operations in all larger markets.

Production entities in foreign countries customarily manufacture products based on technological IP owned by the entrepreneurial entity of the OEM group. They also follow instructions and guidelines in their manufacturing processes, including necessary process know-how. As a result, such entities perform, in most cases, routine

8. Cf. Chapter II, Part III OECD TPG.
9. In fact, Chinese regulations require such a quantitative analysis in theory from the very beginning.
10. As stated in para. 2.126 OECD TPG, 'it can be difficult to determine the relative value of the contributions that each of the associated enterprises makes to the controlled transactions'.
11. Cf. para. 6.5 OECD TPG.

functions (sometimes a mere assembly of preprocessed components in the case of SKD or CKD production) and bear routine risks. Usually, such entities are often qualified as contract manufacturers while, at other times, licence manufacturers are set up. The size of such operations can be significant, and plants generate revenues of several billion euros; thus, the choice of the TP method and exact steering is key to gaining legal certainty.

Typically, TP discussions on contract manufacturing circle around the right profit level indicator when testing for arm's length purposes. Contract manufacturing activities usually do not feature non-routine IP-related functions; therefore, the TNMM should be applicable for intra-group transactions. If such manufacturing entities do not have a significant sales function, the TP policy is usually on a cost-plus basis (in accordance with the business concept of a cost centre). IP-related manufacturing processes that are more complex in the automotive industry predominantly apply to the OEM suppliers and are therefore handled in more detail below.

One core question regards the choice of the appropriate profit level indicator. In essence, tax authorities apply full cost-plus methods, but some tax authorities are in favour of a Berry ratio analysis and exclude material costs from the cost base. For example, German tax authorities often take the view that material costs for supplies that are provided to the group internally are based on contracts negotiated by the principal company should be excluded from the profit markup.[12] In this case, a contract manufacturing company realizes a profit only on its own value-adding costs, but excluding material cost.

Applying the same markup to the full cost base or on value-adding costs makes a tremendous difference in the bottom-line profitability of the contract manufacturer. Profits may become quite high when applying a profit markup on a full cost base. However, as 80%-90% of a complete car assembly consists of material costs, profits could become ridiculously low if such a slim cost base is taken for markup only (as envisaged, e.g., by the approach of German tax authorities). As an alternative, the arm's length profit could be tested through the use of an ROA approach. This may be more robust for arm's length testing in the mid to long term as the asset base of a plant does not change significantly during normal operations. Audit discussions can thus be alleviated. However, a proper arm's length definition of the asset base is required in such cases. In most cases, tax authorities have agreed on full cost-plus methods with a markup on the lower end of the benchmark range of independent contract manufacturers.

In addition, typical discussions with tax authorities concern *ex ante* price setting versus the *ex post* outcome testing and bottom-line profitability. Taking into consideration factors such as deviations between budgets and actuals, timing differences in TP calculation versus accounting, impact of FX fluctuation, plant expansions, and other factors, it can easily be seen that there is a risk of complex discussions with tax authorities around the effects that drive the deviation from the target profitability. Given that many OEMs operate contract manufacturing plants that have a sales volume

12. Cf. *Kolb*, in Seer/Lüdicke/Rasch, Festschrift Kroppen, p. 319.

of billions of euros, the risk level must be checked carefully even if operations qualify as limited-risk operations. In particular, it is crucial to implement appropriate control and true-up mechanisms in price-setting policies (i.e., a mechanism that corrects transfer prices used during the year) which bring planned and actual profitability inline within a limited period of time (three-five years). If such a mechanism is not in place, it may prove very difficult to be in accord with the arm's length testing in the TPD.

The recent COVID-19 crisis emphasized another risk of a contract manufacturer: capacity risk. Plants were required to close down due to safety regulations, and idle capacity costs were incurred by contract manufacturers. While many OEMs incorporate a take-or-pay clause in their contracts, it may prove difficult in reality to fulfil such a commitment in times of a liquidity crunch. Moreover, such idle costs cannot always become part of the transfer price of the manufactured products as prices might increase manifold if a lockdown continues over a long period of time. In such cases, proper documentation of the adopted policies is the only chance to avoid difficult audit discussions later on with authorities.[13]

Problems may also arise in the start-up phase of a contract manufacturer as start-up costs may add up to three-digit million figures. The TP policy must ensure that any start-up losses may be recovered over an appropriate period of time. Alternatively, the principal may reimburse start-up losses, and the contract manufacturer would charge for a service transaction to the principal. However, as such costs are significant, the issue can easily become part of controversy. Therefore, a diligent analysis is recommended.

2.4 Sales & Distribution

The most visible part of the OEM value chain is the sales function that includes operations at wholesale and retail levels that are usually separate. While the wholesale operation is normally part of the OEM group, retail is operated by third parties in most cases. The distribution of vehicles is generally steered and managed by the OEMs' respective related wholesale company of the market. The central entrepreneurial entity not only sells vehicles to its respective wholesale company in a specific country but also provides the central framework for marketing.

The TP policy for the sales component of the value chain almost exclusively uses the resale minus method/TNMM at the wholesale level.[14] For group retailers, CUP methods are often employed as the pricing logic, and the steering is very much aligned with third-party dealers. As stipulated by the OECD TPG, the transfer prices to the MNE's wholesalers are set to enable the distributor to realize an arm's length gross

13. Note that audits will generally begin after a crisis is over. Hence, hindsight may prove some of the planning as being plainly erroneous. However, documentation laid out at the point of the decision should help overcome such a discussion.
14. The exception being the cost-plus method in the case of agency distribution in smaller markets. However, such a set-up is normally used with independent third-party agents only.

margin in order to cover distribution costs, including an appropriate profit margin.[15] The discussion on the arm's length operating margin is one of the most prominent in the business model of the OEM. Profitability is dependent on the regulatory framework, market specifics, and the competitive environment in a given market. While markets can be clustered to a certain degree regarding competition and regulations (e.g., EU markets), it is still a common discussion on how to take into account specific market characteristics for arm's length pricing.

Quite often, arm's length margins are validated by benchmarking with independent retailer companies using the TNMM; i.e., typical arm's length testing is performed on the operating margin level. Benchmarking an OEM's TP policy is a difficult exercise as very few independent wholesale distributors of vehicles exist in major markets. Hence, finding the right mix of comparable companies from the automotive industry (in general, retailers) and companies with a similar function and risk profile (wholesalers of a different industry) is the focus of any TPD of a distributor. Naturally, benchmarking and the corresponding 'right' level of arm's length profitability is at the centre of any automotive distributor's TP audit. As always in the automotive industry, even small adjustments to transfer prices can have an enormous impact on profitability as transaction volumes are usually substantial: sales values of billions of euros to industrialized countries are common features of the industry.

To ensure an arm's length outcome for their wholesale companies, many OEMs use year-end adjustments in their TP policies in order to adjust profitability for any adverse impacts during a financial year not foreseen during the price setting in their budgets. Such a policy is taken to avoid exposing a related wholesale distributor to a tax risk as tax authorities take the viewpoint that independent distributors do not have the financial capability to absorb the complete market risk. Market risks[16] can quickly impact the operating profitability of a wholesale company when sales to retailers decline and wholesale stocks overly accumulate. As this is not in line with the routine characteristics in the TP set-up of a wholesale company (at least not over a longer period of time),[17] OEM entrepreneurial companies need to develop a way to adjust for such developments at year end. Typically, such adjustments are done as a lump sum correction of transfer prices used during the respective financial year. Given that such lump sum adjustments may entail significant amounts of money, OEMs may have to comply with a rather stringent set of rules to be in accordance with the arm's length principle: a clear TP policy, a written agreement in advance of the adjustment, and

15. Notably, the same reasoning is applied when determining the import value of a vehicle for custom's purposes. As mentioned, international customs regulations also use the arm's length principle in determining appropriate transfer prices as a base for import levies. However, the respective focus of authorities is, of course, very different: While tax authorities would want to see (*ceteris paribus*) a lower transfer price (which results in a higher taxable profit), customs authorities favour a (*ceteris paribus*) higher transfer price (which results in a higher price as a base for import duties).
16. Market risks include '... risks caused by the economic environment, political and regulatory events, competition, technological advance, or social and environmental changes' (cf. para. 1.72 a OECD TPG).
17. Cf. para. 1.129 OECD TPG where reference is made that unrelated companies would not accept loss-making over a longer period of time.

proper documentation.[18] In recent years, the practice of year-end adjustments has become less controversial in transactions between industrialized countries as many APAs foresee such adjustments. Thus, acceptance among tax authorities has increased.

Over the years, audit discussions have also started including the marketing function of the distributors. As the automotive industry is a consumer-facing business, marketing activities of OEMs and their distributors are usually quite intensive. This not only includes classic television, press, and online advertising but also sponsoring, trade fairs, showroom events, etc. As a consequence, marketing costs of an automotive distributor are generally higher than those of independent wholesale companies, especially in the case of premium brands. This results in a discussion on whether such high marketing efforts are part of a routine distribution function or should entitle a distributor to earn more than a routine remuneration. In the latter case, tax auditors in some markets claim that a high level of marketing adds to the brand value of the OEM and thus entitles the distributor to a higher return.[19]

The discussion focuses on the second major type of IP in the automotive industry: the brand. The OEM brand is central to the success of the respective MNE as the brand and its respective image are often important sales arguments for consumers around the globe, especially if the car manufacturer is a premium brand. Hence, brand development is central to the sales function of any OEM. As with R&D, a central brand development department at the OEM headquarters company is usually in charge of all relevant functions and decisions concerning the brand. In the past, there was not much discussion around brand IP (and the corresponding entrepreneurial returns), and tax authorities respect that the intangible related return is accrued in the central entrepreneurial company. However, the DEMPE regulations added significant complexity to this reasoning. In particular, compared to technological IP, it is much more difficult to analyse which activities add to the value of a brand.

Often, the brand must be adapted to specific market requirements. In some markets, the OEM brand may be promoted a bit differently by the distributor (e.g., by focusing on a specific brand element that other markets do not focus on). The crucial question is ultimately whether such an activity of a related distributor actually provides the brand with a unique, long-lasting facet that adds significantly to the market success (and is not based on concepts of the central brand/marketing department). Tax authorities have recently focused on exactly such features of wholesale companies (including the automotive industry) in that respect.

For example, an OEM may decide to target a 'sportier' image for its brand and urges its wholesale companies to do additional sports sponsoring. Typically, the decision on what to sponsor is left to the respective wholesaler as its local marketing department knows best which type of sports may have the highest positive impact on sales (e.g., high marketing impact of soccer in European markets whereas lower impact in China or the US).

The approach to marketing activities appears differently in many markets. Some tax authorities may contend that IP is directly created by the marketing function of a

18. Cf. paras 1.77-1.81 OECD TPG on the contractual assumption of risks.
19. This is at the heart of current regulatory discussions of the Inclusive Framework at the OECD.

wholesaler, although this is rather difficult to substantiate as brand image only moves slowly. Instead, emerging markets in particular use different regulatory concepts around brand IP. China, for example, adds another feature to the DEMPE concept in its national TP regulations by using the DEMPE-P concept.[20] The additional 'P' is for promotion which is a typical feature of the individual market. In India, tax authorities often claim that local marketing adds to brand development of an OEM. However, they do not claim an entrepreneurial return for such activities but deem a service of the distributor to the OEM central marketing department. As a result, for certain marketing costs in excess of what independent distributors feature as costs, a deemed charge is added to income using a rather high arm's length markup. As a result, court cases around brand development and respective royalties have increased significantly over the years. One of the most prominent cases is that of Maruti Suzuki.[21]

Maruti Suzuki India Ltd. (MSIL) began its business operations in 1982 as a 100% subsidiary of the Government of India. Suzuki Motor Corporation, Japan (SMC), was selected as a business partner in 1982 and held 54.21% of the shares in MSIL. MSIL entered into a licence agreement with SMC for the manufacture of specified models of cars using the licensed information and licensed trademark. Under the agreement, MSIL made composite royalty payments for the rights and licences granted by SMC. The TPO held in an audit that the royalty paid by MSIL was towards the use of technology and the trademark/brand name and consequently divided the total royalty payments into royalty for use of technology and for use of trademark. For the purpose of splitting the royalty, the TPO took into consideration the advertisement and marketing expenses incurred by SMC. The TPO determined the arm's length price of royalty that was allegedly paid for use of the brand name as nil on the pretext that Suzuki was a weak brand and therefore attributed the economic brand ownership to India.

However, the court ruling in favour of the taxpayer held that the entire business of MSIL was based on the licence agreement (including the brand) without which the business of MSIL would cease to exist. Moreover, the court held that the decision to use the Suzuki brand name was taken by the taxpayer in order to advance its own commercial interest and therefore legitimates the payment of a royalty.

2.5 Financing

One important element of the wholesale activities of any OEM is the financial services function of a respective related leasing/captive company in a specific market. Wholesale distributors and leasing companies team up to ensure maximum sales of the OEM products by offering not only the car but also financial options for the customer's purchase. Taking this activity into account for TP purposes means analysing complementary functions and risks of a joint business effort which normally does not even involve a cross-border transaction. Depending on the competitive situation of the

20. Cf. SAT Bulletin Gonggao (2017) No. 6 issued 1 April 2017.
21. Delhi High Court, 15 December 2015, *Maruti Suzuki India Ltd. v. CIT*, ITA 110/2014.

market, the wholesale unit would provide support payments to the financing division so that the financing company can earn an arm's length financial return. The arm's length nature of the return (normally measured on a return on asset or return on equity basis) depends on risks such as market and volume risks, credit default risks, residual value risks, and risk of interest rate fluctuations. Thus, the transfer price between the entrepreneurial company and the wholesale distributor takes into account such subsidies, and tax authorities might analyse the financing companies' return although it is not directly engaged in a cross-border transaction. Depending on the importance of the leasing/financing business of a market (e.g., high in Germany, the United Kingdom, and the US), the impact of the financial services part of the OEM's sales efforts may be substantial.

3 AUTOMOTIVE SUPPLIER INDUSTRY

3.1 Typical Value Chain in the Automotive Supplier Industry

The hundred largest automotive supplier industries have a combined global sales volume of EUR 900 billion p.a.[22] Over the last decades, suppliers have followed the global footprint of OEMs and are present in most of the markets where the OEMs' headquarters are located. Moreover, many OEMs establish production facilities in their target markets to balance FX risk, to realize customs benefits, and/or to receive government incentives for localization. Suppliers have also relocated part of their production to low labour cost locations, such as Eastern Europe, Mexico, North Africa, and Southeast Asia. This has led to significant cross-border intercompany transfers of products, licences, and service transactions which have given rise to significant tax challenges. Although the volumes at stake are not as high as in the OEM business, transaction volumes are often greater than in other industries. Thus, TP is one of the most pressing tax issues in the supplier industry.

The value chain of a supplier is somewhat similar across multinationals (Figure 14.2).

22. Cf. *PwC Automotive*, https://www.strategyand.pwc.com/de/de/studien/2020/die-zuliefererindustrie-von-morgen/thesen-zur-zuliefererindustrie-von-morgen.pdf (last accessed 10 March 2021).

Figure 14.2 Graphical Representation of Value Chain in Automotive Supplier Industry

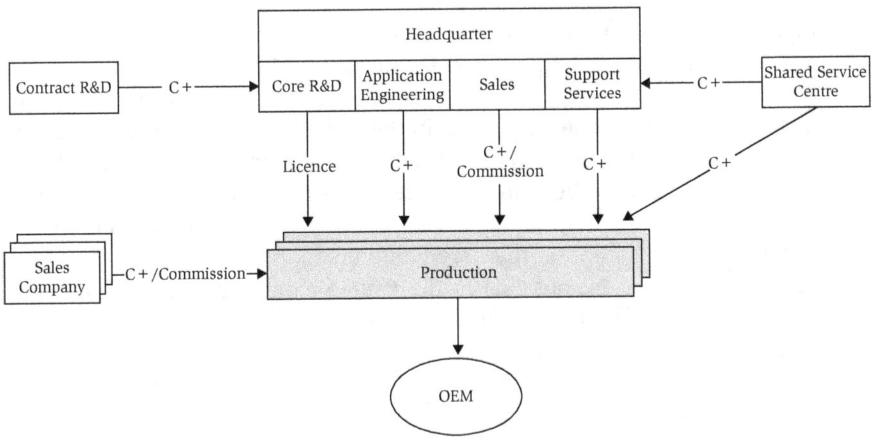

- *R&D:* The supplier industry typically invests approximately 2%-6% of their sales in R&D.[23] The R&D investment is a core value driver of the industry.[24] Typically, the R&D in product and production-related intangibles must be differentiated. In the case of product-related R&D, there are two types of R&D activities: ground and/or platform R&D and application engineering. Ground and/or platform R&D is independent of a customer-specific application. Suppliers drive innovation so that new technologies are used across OEMs. In the case of application engineering, the supplier invests in a customer-specific project. Thus, the core intangible of the supplier is applied to a customer-specific project, e.g., the headlamps of a 3 series of BMW. The supplier is therefore embedded in the development of the OEM and follows the same product life cycle, which is usually seven to eight years. In the event that products are part of the so-called facelift (at the midterm of the life cycle), life cycles can be shorter which tends to be more often the case in car electronics. The OEM compensates the R&D investment of the suppliers through upfront payments, or costs are recovered through the product price in series production. In most cases, the development is pre-financed by the supplier.
- *Sales:* The sales function of a supplier for the OEM business is closely linked to application engineering. Sales teams are typically organized by OEMs and are globally coordinated. The sales teams are predominantly located close to the

23. Cf. *Roland Berger*, 2017, Global Automotive Supplier Study 2018, p. 84, https://www.rolandberger.com/en/Insights/Publications/Global-Automotive-Supplier-Study-2018.html (last accessed 30 January 2022), https://www.vda.de/en/services/Publications/vda-anual-report-2020.html (last accessed 30 January 2022).
24. Cf. *PwC Automotive*, https://www.strategyand.pwc.com/de/de/studien/2020/die-zuliefererindustrie-von-morgen/thesen-zur-zuliefererindustrie-von-morgen.pdf (last accessed 10 March 2021).

headquarters of the OEMs. Thus, the main sales locations are typically found in Brazil, China, France, Germany, India, Italy, Japan, Russia, South Korea, Spain, Sweden, the United Kingdom, the US and in the country where the supplier's headquarters/main engineering capabilities are located. In the case that the product range includes replacement parts such as tires, brakes, filters, and batteries, many suppliers operate an aftermarket business and have sales entities in the target markets of end consumers. Aftermarket parts are subsequently sold through several levels in the distribution chain and ultimately to a garage which in turn sells the product to the end customer within their service offering. Suppliers are typically active only on an importer or wholesale level. Only the large global tire suppliers are active in the retail market.

- *Production:* Production is the core value creation of a supplier. As stock is reduced to the extent possible in the value chain, suppliers' operations are highly integrated with the production of the OEM. Any disturbance in the value chain can lead to significant risks on the supplier side. In most cases, just-in-time and just-in-sequence production is required by the OEMs. Moreover, efficiencies must be constantly increased as they require yearly price reductions in the course of a series production. In some cases, lead plants ensure that production processes are optimized, and efficiencies are gained globally. The market differentiates between Tier 1, 2, and 3 suppliers. Tier 1 suppliers are system integrators that produce an entire system and receive products from Tier 2 suppliers. These are, in most cases, determined and controlled by OEMs. In recent years, increasing focus has been placed by OEMs on the integrated supply chain and respective Tier-n suppliers of important products. Tier 3 suppliers often specialize in single products. A Tier 1 supplier can also operate as Tier 2 or Tier 3 supplier in certain markets or for specific customer projects.
- *Support services:* An MNE group has a major flow of intercompany services that need to be carefully managed from a TP perspective. Since production sites invoice the OEM and thus generate the ultimate sales of the group, service costs need to be recharged to the production entities. Thus, suppliers need to ensure that such costs are allocated from the headquarters countries' perspective. On the side of the recipients, the benefit of such services must be carefully documented.

Typically, suppliers are exposed to significant risks as OEMs require suppliers to bear their part of the volume and market risk of the specific vehicle. In the case of a weak performance of a vehicle type, the volume of the supplier project might not allow the supplier to recover its fixed costs. In some cases, quality issues can result in significant risks. Suppliers are bound by a contract to very high-quality standards that are measured by the defect PPM rate. In the event of failure, the supplier is exposed to significant additional costs of rework, increased logistic costs, contractual penalties, and product liability issues. If raw materials play an important role (such as in the case of a catalyst), the risk of raw material price fluctuations is often shared between the supplier and the OEM or is completely borne by the OEM. From a TP perspective, the risk allocation and the profit opportunities within the supplier group should be clearly documented and be in accordance with a diligent TP analysis.

3.2 Role of DEMPE Functions

As mentioned above in section 2.2, the OECD has changed its view on the role of legal contracts. Under the pre-2017 OECD TPGs, a reclassification of risk allocation was only possible in well-defined exceptions.[25] For the automotive supplier industry, this meant that the factories executing the customer contracts legally often bore the majority of the risks. The sales and application engineering functions received a cost-plus compensation. Core R&D was compensated through a licence fee that was expressed as a fixed percentage of net sales. This structure led to the result that volume, price, and market risk were typically borne by the production entities abroad. The headquarter company received licence and service fees that allowed it to recover its costs and to realize a profit in line with the service and IP contribution.

In its 2017 guidelines, the OECD changed its interpretation of the arm's length principle. The OECD was concerned about low substance locations where, through a legal allocation of development risks and the financing of an IP, the intangible-related return was borne by an offshore entity. As a countermeasure, the OECD introduced the DEMPE concept. Under it, the assumption of risks must be supported by the ability to control risks; contracts are explicitly only a 'starting point' of the analysis.[26] Under the revised guidelines, it is required to control the risk of DEMPE of an intangible.[27] In such cases, the intangible-related return would be attributable to the entity performing the functions which is, in principle, impossible for an offshore entity. From a political perspective, the concept seems logical for offshore IP structures. However, the concept is applicable to the supplier industry in which tax-driven IP structures are only seen in exceptional cases as the margins and profits attributable to IP are often limited.

The new concept is applied not only to risk associated with IP but to any type of risk that is allocated within an MNE group. The new concept of the OECD is described in paragraph 1.48 of the OECD TPG with the example describing a very typical set-up in the supplier industry where a production entity allegedly has limited control over major risks:[28]

> Company S is a wholly-owned subsidiary of Company P. The parties have entered into a written contract pursuant to which Company P licenses intellectual property to Company S for use in Company S's business; Company S agrees to compensate Company P for the licence with a royalty. Evidence provided by other economically relevant characteristics, and in particular the functions performed, establishes that Company P performs negotiations with third-party customers to achieve sales for Company S, provides regular technical services support to Company S so that Company S can deliver contracted sales to its customers, and regularly provides staff to enable Company S to fulfil customer contracts. A majority of

25. Cf. paras 1.52, 1.64-1.69, 2010 OECD TPG.
26. Cf. para. 1.42 OECD TPG.
27. Cf. paras 6.12, 6.32 OECD TPG.
28. Paragraph 1.48 OECD TPG.

> customers insist on including Company P as joint contracting party along with Company S, although fee income under the contract is payable to Company S. The analysis of the commercial or financial relations indicates that Company S is not capable of providing the contracted services to customers without significant support from Company P, and is not developing its own capability. Under the contract, Company P has given a licence to Company S, but in fact controls the business risk and output of Company S such that it has not transferred risk and function consistent with a licensing arrangement, and acts not as the licensor but the principal. The identification of the actual transaction between Company P and Company S should not be defined solely by the terms of the written contract. Instead, the actual transaction should be determined from the conduct of the parties, leading to the conclusion that the actual functions performed, assets used, and risks assumed by the parties are not consistent with the written licence agreement.

For the industry, it is somewhat unsatisfactory that risk allocation and the underlying contracts shall not be respected. It also disregards the fact that a contract manufacturing set-up as implied by the example of the OECD can often not be applied for various reasons; e.g., if sales were routed through the sales entity, IT processes would need to be changed, VAT and customs implications might not be manageable. From a TP viewpoint, it is also questionable if an entity that controlled the sales process before the start of production shall be part of the invoicing flow as it is typically no longer involved in the ongoing project that is executed years after the project was acquired. A potential solution would be to use a royalty rate that commensurates with the ability of the production entity to control the risk (*see* section 3.3, a, bb below). Under such a concept, the risk would be allocated to the entities that have the central control over the IP and/or negotiated the conditions with the customer contracts and had major control over volume and price risks.

The issue of risk allocation for an automotive supplier was also dealt with by a Swedish Court. In the set-up under review, the sales branch assumed the volume risk but ended up incurring ongoing losses. The court held that the branch did not execute the significant people function and should thus not bear such risks.[29]

3.3 TP Implications of Major Transaction Flows

a) Licence Manufacturer

Suppliers have a global network of factories and follow the global footprint of OEMs. Production is the core value creation of the suppliers and drives cost-efficiencies as suppliers are often required to gain cost savings over the lifecycle of a project. In most cases, foreign manufacturing plants are operated as licence manufacturers. Thus, the licence manufacturer must compensate the IP owner through a licence, and the sales function (*see* section 3.4) and service providers must be compensated for various services such as application engineering. Four types of compensation schemes can be differentiated to remunerate the core IP:

29. Kammarrätten (Swedish Administrative Court of Appeal), 10 October 2019 Case Nos 2552-2555-17, 2557-2558-17, 3422-18.

aa) Fixed licence fee.

Historically, the most common method in the industry is compensation through a royalty, which might vary by product. The arm's length royalty rate could be tested through a TNMM or profit split analysis. However, the most appropriate method for a fixed licence fee is the use of the comparable uncontrolled price method. Under such a method, external databases such as RoyaltySource, RoyaltyRange, KT Mine, and RoyaltyStat are used to identify third-party royalty rates. The royalty rates are often identified through public filings in the US. In the automotive industry, the interquartile range of a royalty rate for automotive parts is often between 2% and 6%.[30] However, in the case of high tech and/or software-driven products, the royalty rates can be significantly higher. Tax authorities sometimes use R&D costs as a sanity check for royalty rates; i.e., the royalty income should at least cover the R&D cost plus a certain markup. The OECD is sceptical about the use of cost-plus methods as the value of the IP is not driven by its costs but through its value.[31]

In the case of high profits of licensees, the royalties are often challenged by the tax authorities of the IP owner. It is argued that the value of the IP is driven by its profit potential; therefore, in the case of high profits, the royalty rates should have been higher. Vice versa, if the licensee is incurring a loss, the royalty rates are challenged by the tax authorities in the licensee's country. In such cases, they propose the arguments of the OECD (*see* section 3.2) and suggest that the licensee does not control the risks that often led to the losses, e.g., because of missing volumes, too low prices, and product failures caused by a wrong design.

bb) Profit-oriented licence fee.

A concept that is more often introduced by European and US suppliers is what is referred to as a profit-oriented licence fee.[32] Under such a concept, the production entity would receive a return that is in accordance with an arm's length return of a third-party manufacturer not owning significant IP. The return would be determined using a TNMM benchmark. The arm's length royalty should then ensure that the licensee earns an arm's length return. If, for instance, a production entity had a return of sales of 8% and an arm's length return of sales were 5%, the arm's length royalty would be 3% of net sales. If, in another country, the production entity had a return of sales of 18%, the royalty rate would then be 13%. The royalty could be determined within a certain time period (e.g., every three years) or could be adjusted at year end to ensure an arm's length return for the production entity.

30. Cf. *Royalty Range*, Benchmarking Report – Automotive, 2017 reports rates of 2%-6%, www.royaltyrange.com/wp-content/uploads/2017/12/benchmarking-study-report-example.pdf (last accessed 30 January 2022).
31. Cf. para. 6.143 OECD TPG.
32. Cf. *Kolb*, in IWB 2009, p. 587; *Renz*, Absauglizenzen in der Automobilindustrie, PwC Transfer Pricing Perspective Deutschland Volume 34, May 2017, p. 13.

If companies decide to implement such concepts, a variety of issues need to be considered such as VAT, withholding taxes, currency control, and customs requirements. In some countries, the concept will not be accepted by tax authorities. Brazil, China, and Russia, for instance, do not allow profit-oriented licence fee schemes.

cc) Mixed concept

Some suppliers use mixed concepts when companies attempt to balance the two views. Thus, royalty rates are fixed and might be changed after a certain time period if the long-term or midterm profit expectation of the production entity strongly deviates from the margins of unrelated manufacturers. Moreover, the production entities shall bear a greater share of the risk but correspondingly receive a higher return if the materialized risks are less than expected.

dd) Cost-sharing concepts

Some suppliers have also used cost contribution arrangements to share core R&D costs. Thus, all factories bear core R&D costs and correspondingly become an owner of the intangibles. However, such structures are currently rarely used for the following reasons:

- Buy-in payments are required for new entities which would lead to significant payments, one-time taxation effects, and significant legal uncertainty as the IP value might be a hard-to-value intangible.
- From a cash flow perspective, participating entities need to pre-finance R&D costs, whereas new entities or entities with an increasing production volume over the years might not have sufficient capital to pre-finance them.
- For the fulfilment of substance requirements, the OECD requires that a member of the cost contribution arrangements controls the R&D risk, which might be disputed in the case of pure production entities.[33]
- Finally, the cost contribution arrangement potentially leads to withholding tax issues if licences are granted to non-pool members. Technically, it must be analysed whether the tax treaty rate of each beneficiary is applicable if the licence income is shared among the pool members.

3.4 Brand Value

In some cases, tax authorities take the position that the brand of a supplier creates value and that, as a consequence, compensation for the brand value is payable. The German tax authorities use a Federal Court case in 2000 as a reference point. In the underlying case, a foreign automotive supplier of brakes introduced a brand royalty of 1.5% for its OEM business.[34] The tax authorities argued that the company name could be used free of charge; however, the Federal Tax Court agreed with the taxpayer that

33. Cf. para. 8.15 OECD TPG.
34. Cf. Germany's Federal Tax Court ruling dated 9 August 2000 – I R 12/99 BStBl. 2001 II p. 140.

the company name and the brand name must be considered separately. Thus, the royalty charge was allowed as it was made for the brand and not the company name. The German tax authorities now use this case and subsequently require that German-headquartered suppliers charge for the value of its brand.[35] The value of the brand is well accepted for the aftermarket, but it is very unclear if the brand in fact creates an additional value in the OEM business for which technology, reliability, quality and price are the success factors. Hence, the B2C component of the brand (i.e., its visibility to end customers) is rather limited. That a brand may have a limited value is also evidenced by suppliers sometimes changing their names, e.g., in the course of a divestment, as can be seen by global players such as Adient (former JCI), Aptiv (former Delphi), Autoneum (former Rieter), and Vitesco (former Continental); thus, it is implied that a brand can easily be replaced by the supplier without forfeiting business. Another argument is that the OEM often requires the supplier not to use the brand on the product itself. On the other hand, it can be argued that certain costs for establishing the brand are incurred and thus value is created.

3.5 Contract Manufacturer/Delivery of Semi-finished Products

In some cases, products are supplied within the group or a contract manufacturing business model is set up. In most cases, suppliers use a cost-plus mechanism to determine product prices. *See* section 2.3 for further details.

3.6 Contract R&D

Most suppliers have contract R&D structures in place and use cost-plus compensation schemes. *See* section 2.2 for further details.

3.7 Sales Function for OEM Business

As mentioned above, sales teams can often be seen in countries where the OEMs are headquartered. There are three areas of concern from a tax/TP perspective. The value contribution of the sales function needs to be determined; however, this is difficult as there are no independent companies providing sales services for the OEM business. Moreover, the sales activities can lead to PE risks that need to be carefully managed. Another challenge is that OEMs require quick savings and such costs need to be carefully analysed.

a) Arm's length sales compensation

The first question would be to determine an arm's length compensation for sales teams. As the entity employing it would typically not invoice the products, the most common approach in the industry is to compensate sales through a cost-plus mechanism. Many

35. Cf. Germany's Ministry of Finance Ordinance dated 7 April 2017 – BStBl. 2017 I p. 701.

suppliers use a cost-plus remuneration of 5%-8%. An alternative approach – which would be more in line with other industries – would be to provide a commission that is expressed as a percentage of sales as a compensation for the sales function. The commission would allow the sales function to recover the costs and to earn a net margin (expressed as a percentage of solicited sales). Some tax auditors have required operating margins of 1%-3% of net sales. However, considering that the industry earns overall operating margins of 4%-7%, sales functions would be allocated a significant part of the group's profit, which seems unrealistic given that sales costs are a relatively minor part of the overall value chain of the supplier. Another argument could be that the customer base is well known in the industry and that the impact of the sales function is limited compared to other functions within the group. Moreover, it seems reasonable to compensate the sales functions at cost plus as this compensation scheme implies that selling costs are recovered at the time of the sales activities and not at the time when sales are made. This seems to be the only practical way as customer projects are typically won three-four years prior to the initiation of production; in the case of a typical product life cycle, the sales entity would receive the compensation up to ten years after the sales were actually made, which seems to be impractical.

b) PE risk

The sales function also leads to a significant agency PE risk. Under Article 5, paragraph 5 of the OECD MTC, an agency PE is established if the agent concludes contracts on behalf of the principal. Under its revised version of 2017, it is even sufficient if the agent plays the principal role in the conclusion of contracts. Under a typical set-up of a supplier, a legal entity is established in the country of the OEM that takes the responsibility to negotiate new contracts. Legally, however, the entity does not conclude contracts on its own behalf but on behalf of the production entity that later executes the project. Thus, if the production entity located in the Czech Republic, for instance, executes contracts that were negotiated by a related party in Italy (for a customer such as FIAT), Germany (for BMW, Mercedes, or Volkswagen) and France (for PSA or Renault), the Czech Republic would establish PEs in Italy, Germany, and France. The result would be that, with a large supplier group for which each production entity most probably executes contracts that were negotiated in many locations, the group would need to declare hundreds of agency PEs.

Such multiple PE issues would be extremely complex, and it would lead to a significant compliance burden. Therefore, a more detailed analysis is recommended to identify ways to mitigate the risk. One possible solution would be to analyse whether the agent actually has the authority to conclude contracts. The updated version of the model tax treaty allows a PE only in the event of 'material modifications by the enterprise'.[36] In many cases, one would identify that approval processes exist which shows that the selling entity cannot make such decisions. It is, in fact, observed that the

36. Cf. note 28 OECD, BEPS Action 7: Additional Guidance on the Attribution of Profits to Permanent Establishments, 3/2018.

authority of the sales entities is limited. However, the sales process is normally not controlled by the executing manufacturer but by the parent company.

Another solution would be to review whether the agent is acting independently as Article 5, paragraph 6 of the model tax treaty suggests that a PE shall not be assumed in cases of independent agents. The 2017 version of the OECD MTC clarifies that, in the case of a sales entity that acts exclusively or almost exclusively on behalf of one or more enterprises to which it is closely related, the selling entity shall not be considered to be independent.[37]

The most convincing argument from a TP perspective would be to contend that there is no profit attributable to the PE. As set forth above, the activity is executed through a legal entity that receives an arm's length compensation. The OECD has put forth significant effort in expanding the agency PE definition but has admitted that it might be practical and agreeable between Member States to not assume a PE.[38]

c) Quick Savings

Under quick savings, an OEM would grant new projects if a one-time payment is made by the supplier to the OEM or if a further discount is granted on an ongoing basis.[39] The grant of quick savings is among the most complex forms of payments from a tax perspective, and the concept must be closely monitored from a legal perspective to identify its limits. From a pure TP perspective, concerns arise if an entity with ongoing supplies to an OEM grants a discount on its products for the potential benefit of a new customer project with the OEM of another legal entity of the supplier's group in another country but with the result that its own profit decreases. The tax authority in the country where the existing project is executed would require that the entity that grants the discount receive compensation from the entity in the other country.[40] However, as there are legal limitations to agreeing on quick savings measures, a supplier and the OEM might only agree informally on a discount with any legal documentation being insufficient from a tax perspective.

3.8 Sales in the Aftermarket

Depending on the type of product, suppliers may be active in the aftermarket business. The products are then sold not only to the OEM but also through the group's sales subsidiaries in the target markets. Moreover, the supplier might also develop and manufacture aftermarket products where other suppliers have produced the original product. Finally, the supplier might purchase certain products from other suppliers to complete the offered product range. Products are usually sold under the name of the supplier. Typically, it can be seen that original OEM parts receive the highest prices in a market. Meanwhile, some supplier brands are then still referred to as OEM brands

37. Cf. Article 5 para. 6, OECD MTC.
38. Cf. notes 43, 44 OECD, BEPS Action 7: Additional Guidance on the Attribution of Profits to Permanent Establishments, 3/2018.
39. Cf. *Kolb*, in Seer/Lüdicke/Rasch, Festschrift Kroppen, p. 317.
40. *Ibid.*

and receive price premiums. Finally, there are a number of trade organizations that have established their own names.

From a TP perspective, the foreign sales subsidiaries are generally tested using the TNMM method. As a profit level indicator, 'return on sales' is used. Typically, there are a number of independent retailers or wholesalers of spare parts that could be used as comparables.

3.9 Shared Services

Another major transaction stream within a supplier company is the provision of intra-group services. As external net sales are made by foreign production companies, the supplier should have an elaborate system to charge intercompany services. The main challenge is to determine the beneficiary and to document the benefit. Some services should qualify as low value-adding services in the sense of section 7.61 of the OECD TPG. Thus, a cost-plus markup is often applied by the suppliers for their intercompany services. For other core services, markups of 5%-8% are commonly applied.

4 OUTLOOK: DATA-DRIVEN BUSINESS MODELS AND DIGITALIZATION

During the last couple of years, the digitalization of the economy as a whole has significantly increased. Back in 2015, the BEPS Project still considered it feasible to attempt to effectively address the questions from digitalization for the international tax system within the existing framework.[41] However, the rise of Amazon, Google, Facebook, etc., has renewed the question on how to capture the profits from the digitalized economy for tax purposes. The Inclusive Framework of the OECD is focusing on answers to this question.

During the renewed discussion around an update of the regulative framework, it quickly became clear that any revised international tax system cannot be based on a ring-faced digital economy. Instead, all industries need to be investigated regarding the respective digitalization. For an automotive OEM, this basically has two characteristics: the digitalization of the car in its driving characteristics (e.g., over-the-air updates, autonomous driving, connected services) and the vehicle as a digital platform.

From a TP perspective, these two issues have very different consequences. Enhancing digital features of a car or enabling it to offer connected services are a part of the traditional product business of an OEM. A significant number of data analyses and digital developments result in a feature/option that any customer can purchase either when he originally buys the car or at a later stage by buying a digital product online. In the end, even a very complex development like autonomous driving will be part of the OEM's product offer and will mostly adhere to traditional TP rules for the sale of goods.

41. Cf. OECD (2015) BEPS Report on Action 1: Addressing the Tax Challenges of the Digital Economy.

On the other hand, when using the car as a data platform where OEMs sell (or facilitate sales) based on customer and/or car data, this will certainly have very different implications. In such cases, the OEM will be offering a digital platform where a broader range of digital business models is conceivable.

The collaboration of OEMs and suppliers is quite common when developing digital products and creating a connected car. In particular, sharing of data is crucial to ensure a successful transition of the industry. Such an exchange (among OEMs as well as between OEMs and suppliers) will develop a next-generation business model that needs to be integrated into an appropriate regulatory framework. TP implications from such businesses will be strongly impacted by the upcoming OECD regulations, and new TP challenges will arise in the industry in the future.

CHAPTER 15

Transfer Pricing in the Banking and Asset Management Sector

Eva Frehner

1 INTRODUCTION

1.1 Typical Activities

The banking sector usually includes retail banking, wealth management, and investment banking.

Retail banking – also known as consumer, commercial, or traditional banking[1] – is the typical mass-market banking in which individual customers use local branches of larger commercial banks. The services that are offered include savings and checking accounts, mortgages, personal loans, debit and credit cards, and certificates of deposit. In retail banking, the focus is on the individual consumer.[2] Notably, there is no minimum threshold (e.g., minimum deposit) to qualify as a client in retail banking that is intended to be the one-stop shop for as many financial services as possible on behalf of individual retail clients. Most consumers utilize local branch banking services that provide onsite customer service for all of a retail customer's banking needs. Through local branch locations, financial representatives provide customer service and financial advice. Customer relationship managers are also the lead contact for underwriting applications related to credit-approved products. In the last two decades, a movement towards digitalized operations has also broadly expanded the offerings to retail banking customers. Several online banks even provide banking services to customers purely through the internet and mobile applications.[3] While there is an obvious trend

1. OECD, *Report on the Attribution of Profits to Permanent Establishments* (Paris: OECD Publishing, 2010), Part II, para. 3.
2. Investopedia, https://www.investopedia.com/articles/professionals/092515/career-advice-investment-banking-vswealth-management.asp (last accessed 30 January 2022).
3. *Ibid.*

towards more digital engagement, human interactions are still relevant. For banks and customers alike, this means that local branches remain an important channel in some geographic areas. However, the share of retail banking customers using internet banking at least sometimes has increased from 2015 to 2019 by 23% according to a Boston Consulting Group study.[4] The author believes that the recent outbreak of the global pandemic of the coronavirus disease in 2019 (COVID-19) will lead to an acceleration of the digitalization trend in all banking sector areas.[5]

Wealth management – also known as private banking – consists of personalized financial services and products offered to the HNWI clients. Services include investing and portfolio management,[6] tax services, insurance, and trust and estate planning. In contrast to retail banking, wealth management provides services to only exclusive clientele. While an individual may be able to conduct some private banking with USD 50,000 or less in investable assets, most financial institutions establish a benchmark of six figures worth of assets, and some exclusive entities only accept clients with at least USD 1 million to invest. If they are managing a client's investments, wealth managers often provide the client with extensive resources and opportunities not afforded to the average retail banking client. For example, an HNWI may be allowed access to an exclusive hedge fund or a private equity partnership or some other alternative investments.[7] In addition to tailored products or services, face-to-face meetings with a dedicated investment advisor are typically offered. Although digitalization remains highly relevant on the agenda of wealth management institutions globally, the degree of digital strategy implementation among private banks varies significantly depending on the digital affinity of their clients.[8] According to the LGT Private Banking Report 2018,[9] the following trends could be observed in the wealth management markets Austria, Germany, and Switzerland:[10]

- generation gap further narrows: The age-related differences observed in the past in terms of the utilization of online channels are visibly diminishing. This

4. Boston Consulting Group, Global Retail Banking 2019: The Race for Relevance and Scale, https://www.bcg.com/publications/2019/global-retail-banking-race-for-relevance-scale.aspx (last accessed 30 January 2022).
5. The following institutions offer (among others) retail banking: Citibank, Maybank and Sberbank.
6. OECD, *Report on the Attribution of Profits to Permanent Establishments* (Paris: OECD Publishing, 2010), Part II, paras 2 et seq.
7. Investopedia, https://www.investopedia.com/terms/p/privatebanking.asp (last accessed 30 January 2022).
8. KPMG, Assessing the impact of digitalisation on wealth management, https://home.kpmg/cn/en/home/insights/2019/04/assessing-the-impact-digitalisation-wealth-management.html (last accessed 30 January 2022).
9. LGT, Private Banking Report 2018, https://www.lgt.com/shared/.content/publikationen/bankdienstleistungen/180604_LGT_Private_Banking_Report_2018_de.pdf (last accessed 30 January 2022).
10. *The following institutions offer (among others) Wealth Management Services: Bank of America Merrill Lynch, BNP Paribas Wealth Management, China Merchants Bank, Citi Private Bank, Credit Suisse, J. P. Morgan Private Bank, Morgan Stanley, UBP and UBS.* Business Insider, https://www.businessinsider.com/the-15-biggest-wealth-managers-in-the-world-2018-6?r=US&IR=T (last accessed 30 January 2022).

is because the older generations of clients frequently use online banking at present;

- the gender gap is closing: Compared to the 2016 responses, there has been a significant rise in the relevance of online order placement from home among the women surveyed which results in an alignment with the figures as they apply to men;
- need for private banking 24/7: The possibility of having a ubiquitous overview of an individual's own investments at all times is important to approximately half of respondents. In contrast, the possibility of conducting transactions from anywhere and at any time is only important to around one-third of respondents. The latter is more significant particularly for the younger client generations more so than for the older ones;
- preference for humans over machines: For a clear majority, the opinion of a relationship manager is personally of more value than a recommendation from a robo-advisor. The statement that an individual would never let their own assets be managed by a robo-advisor also met with a high level of agreement. Those who are convinced that a robo-advisor is better able to process information than a relationship manager are in the minority.

Investment banking mainly offers financial services and advice to corporate entities rather than to individuals. It is the area of the financial sector that handles M&A, business restructurings, spin-offs, stock splits, share buy-backs, capital raising transactions (e.g., initial public offerings), and secondary stock or bond issues (e.g., structured products or derivatives).[11] In addition, investment bankers may handle the short-term investments of their corporate clients. Occasionally, investment banking also includes commodity trade financing. In this part of investment banking, banks lend to traders of energy as well as to agricultural and metal commodities through facilities encompassing borrowing bases, revolving credit lines, guarantees, and simple letters of credit.[12] Digitalization has also found its way to investment banking. On the one hand, artificial intelligence helps in creating M&A prediction models or dealing with origination ideas for corporate actions. On the other hand, a wide range of investment banks and fintechs offer online platforms for structured products. They enable investors to design tailored financial products by combining selected underlying securities. Finally, online platforms link demand with the matching offer for private placements and credits. Institutional investors gain access to attractive financing projects of public sector bodies such as cities and municipalities that were previously absent from the capital markets. One of the major benefits of such a platform is to obtain financing that is tailored to their individual needs – in terms of the volume, term and form of financing, and pricing due to increased transparency.[13]

11. OECD, *Report on the Attribution of Profits to Permanent Establishments* (Paris: OECD Publishing, 2010), Part III, paras 2 et seq.
12. Financial Times, European banks lose appetite for commodity trade financing, https://www.ft.com/content/a61cb821-edaf-41b5-b7dd-f667f3eab81b (last accessed 30 January 2022).
13. Vontobel, Media releases and news, https://www.vontobel.com/en-ch/about-vontobel/media/communications/vontobel-launches-cosmofunding-the-digital-platform-for-private-placements

Some integrated universal banks also still operate asset management businesses; however, in the last decade, there was a clear separation trend observed in financial services. Either the asset management business was spun-off from the entity with the banking licence to a new legally distinct entity,[14] or it was sold.[15] This is a result of low synergetic effects within an integrated business model with both asset management and the remaining three 'traditional' banking areas.

In *asset management* business, the clients comprise institutions such as public or private pension funds and intermediaries, including (e.g., smaller privately owned) banks, insurance companies, and financial intermediaries (e.g., external asset managers). Their investments are structured either as investment funds or as mandates and investment advisory solutions (e.g., portfolio design or asset allocation).[16] Typically, asset managers offer a broad variety of asset classes such as fixed income, money markets (liquidity solutions), public and private equity, commodities, hedge funds, and real estate. The blending of individual classes is referred to as multi-assets. They can be combined with geographic focus, e.g., emerging markets equities or European real estate. In addition, individual clients of asset management businesses usually pursue different strategies. First, with increasing interest and activity in ESG and impact investing, clients are seeking ways to enhance the ESG alignment of their investments and have a positive impact while generating financial return.[17] Second, as the market environment grows increasingly complex, and organizational resources evolve, institutional investors (e.g., smaller private banks or insurances) are seeking outsourced solutions to help balance strategic priorities and day-to-day decision-making based on their distinct investment objectives. For this purpose, fiduciary services are offered. Finally, pension solution strategy helps pension plans achieve improved total investment outcomes by providing innovative and bespoke solutions.[18] In comparison to other financial services areas, asset management tends to be the least digitalized sector. Despite revenue pressures driven by increased competition, the shift to lower-fee passive investments, and the need to comply with new regulations, only a minimal number of firms are creating value through greater investments in digitizing their operations and technology functions.[19]

-and-loans/ (last accessed 30 January 2022). *The following institutions offer (among others) corporate actions and capital raising advisory services: Credit Suisse, Deutsche Bank, Goldman Sachs, JP Morgan Chase, Morgan Stanley and UBS.* Investopedia, *The following institutions offer (among others) secondary stock and bond products and related services: Deutsche Bank, Goldman Sachs, Leonteq, Morgan Stanley, UBS and Vontobel*, https://www.investopedia.com/articles/investing/111114/worlds-top-10-investment-banks.asp (last accessed 30 January 2022).

14. Julius Bär, History, History (juliusbaer.com) (last accessed 26 March 2022).
15. CNN Money Switzerland, Does UBS really need an asset management division?, https://www.cnnmoney.ch/shows/living-markets/videos/adriano-lucatelli-descartes-finance-ubs-asset-mgmt-division (last accessed 30 January 2022).
16. *The following universal banks offer asset management services: Credit Suisse, Deutsche Bank, Goldman Sachs, Pictet, UBS and Vontobel.*
17. Thomas Berndt, Andreas Weyer, *Wesentliche und (scheinbar) unwesentliche Themen in der GRI-Nachhaltigkeitsberichterstattung*, ZCG 1/22, pp. 38-46.
18. Goldman Sachs Asset Management, https://www.gsam.com/content/gsam/nc/en/institutions/homepage.html (last accessed 30 January 2022).
19. McKinsey & Company, Financial Services Insights, https://www.mckinsey.com/industries/financial-services/our-insights/achieving-digital-alpha-in-asset-management (last accessed 30 January 2022).

1.2 Regulation

When a bank fails, it can cause problems for financial markets and the real economy.[20] People and businesses can lose the money they have placed with the bank. This can mean they also lose confidence in banks and are thus unwilling to again deposit their money with them. It can also disrupt the services that banks provide to customers. For example, if payment systems collapse – because of a bank insolvency – clients might not be able to use their account for a while. Therefore, governments regulate the banking sector. Stated differently, they subject banks to certain requirements, restrictions, and guidelines that are designed to create market transparency between banking institutions and the individuals and corporations with whom they conduct business.[21]

Regulation helps to ensure that banks have effective management so they do not make bad investments or are too risky. Regulation also makes banks hold shock absorbers referred to as capital to help deal with bad investments. There are frequently minimum capital requirements for operating a banking business in individual countries.[22] Finally, a financial institution that wants to operate a banking business usually needs a banking licence that presents a legal prerequisite. Under the laws of most jurisdictions,[23] a business must not include words such as 'bank' in their name unless it holds a corresponding licence.[24] Depending on their banking regulations, jurisdictions may offer different types of banking licences, such as:

(a) full banking licence for general banking activities such as taking deposits from the general public;
(b) international banking licences (offshore banking licences) that prohibit any onshore banking activities besides representation;
(c) non-banking financial institution licence for institutions that provide financial services but have to comply with fewer regulations than those with a full banking licence.

Typically, asset managers are either divisions of universal banks or independent international asset management boutiques. Generally, they are subject to lower regulatory requirements than banks. However, the phenomenon of increasing compliance costs could be observed even in this area of financial services.[25]

20. Swiss Financial Market Supervisory Authority FINMA, Factsheet, New 'too big to fail' capital requirements for global systemically important banks in Switzerland, https://www.finma.ch/en/documentation/finma-publications/fact-sheets/ (last accessed 30 January 2022).
21. Bank of England, How does regulation help?, https://www.bankofengland.co.uk/KnowledgeBank/why-do-we-regulate-banks (last accessed 30 January 2022).
22. Swiss Financial Market Supervisory Authority FINMA, Factsheet, New 'too big to fail' capital requirements for global systemically important banks in Switzerland, https://www.finma.ch/en/documentation/finma-publications/fact-sheets/ (last accessed 30 January 2022).
23. For example: Hong Kong Banking Ordinance, Swiss Banking Act, Banking Act of Singapore.
24. For example, Article 1(3) Swiss Banking Act.
25. FINMA, Authorisation, Asset Management, https://www.finma.ch/en/authorisation/asset-management/ (last accessed 30 January 2022).

1.3 Recent Challenges

The banking sector has been in transition for many years, especially since the onset of the financial crisis. As a result, many international banks are facing numerous challenges. They operate in a difficult macroeconomic environment with record low (negative) interest rates and a demanding investment environment. Moreover, the implementation of national and increasingly international regulatory requirements is reflected in banks' margins and cost structures. Proven business models are, to a certain degree, being put into question, and some banks are primarily concerned with the past - due to compliance issues - and not with forward-looking innovations and growth strategies.

The environment is characterized by volatility, uncertainty, complexity, and ambiguity. In the last few years, banks were particularly concerned with the implementation of new regulatory requirements that governing bodies have adopted in the wake of the financial crisis. This tendency has been strengthened by regulatory standards created by international organizations and governments focusing mainly on capital and liquidity, consumer protection, and tax transparency. The ever-increasing occurrence of international banking regulations is a reaction to the globalization of financial markets that has been taking place since the late twentieth century.[26]

Regardless of their size and diversification, all businesses have to negotiate their way through this labyrinth of regulatory changes. Failure to comply means risking sanctions and fines. At the moment, aside from understanding the changes, banks focus on the efficient, holistic and pragmatic implementation of these regulations.

2 VALUE CREATION IN THE BANKING AND ASSET MANAGEMENT SECTOR

2.1 Preliminary Remarks

Back in 2015, the OECD/G20 BEPS Project brought a new concept of value creation into TP language.[27] This new term and approach helps to understand key enterprise functions while different industry sectors manifest these concepts in various ways.[28] In addition, BEPS 13 requires that the master file contains a brief written functional analysis describing the main contributions to value creation by individual entities within an MNE, i.e., key functions performed, major risks assumed, and valuable assets used.[29]

In the banking and asset management sector, it is very common to label individual functions as 'front-office', 'middle-office', and 'back-office' depending on whether the

26. OECD, *Report on the Attribution of Profits to Permanent Establishments* (Paris: OECD Publishing, 2010), Part II, para. 2.
27. OECD, *BEPS Actions 8-10 Final Reports*, para. 1.51.
28. Raffaele Petruzzi et al., Editor's Preface, Transfer Pricing and Value Creation, p. 4 (Linde 2019); see also Isabel Verlinden, Bram Markey, From Compliance to the C-Suite: Value Creation Analysed Through the Transfer Pricing Lens, Intertax, p. 774, Volume 44, Issue 10 (2016).
29. OECD, *BEPS Action 13*, Final Report, Annex I to Chapter V.

activity is linked with client contact.[30] Although such a categorization is not decisive for the determination of which function is key from a TP perspective, it helps to better understand the entire value chain. The business models with specific key functions as well as those that are routine vary depending on the area of banking and asset management. Several OECD documents use a variety of terms for the categorization of functions, e.g., SPF, KERT, non-routine functions,[31] high-value adding functions, (non)-auxiliary functions, and key functions. However, for banks, all of these categories refer to activities that usually contain a higher level of complexity, belong to the core business, are not of auxiliary nature, and their contribution to the value chain is significant. To simplify this chapter, the following terms are consequently used: key functions or high-value adding functions as opposed to routine functions. The section 'Transfer Pricing Issues in the Banking and Asset Management Sector' thoroughly discusses the challenges arising with the variety of the above terms.

2.2 Retail Banking

2.2.1 Functions

Interestingly, it is the OECD Report on Attribution of Profits to Permanent Establishments of July 2010, Part II (2010 OECD PE Report, Chapter II) that is used in the practice as a major reference for classifying functions in the retail banking sector. As neither the OECD TPG nor the BEPS reports describe value creation in the banking sector in sufficient detail, the approach used in the 2010 OECD PE Report, Part II is applied to intra-group functions between legally distinct and separate enterprises in retail banking. However, it is worth mentioning that some of the functions presented in the 2010 OECD PE Report, Part II as KERT became less important in the banking value creation due to increasing automation and digitalization. As such, their position is nearly that of a routine qualification. Figure 15.1 depicts a value chain with individual functions contributing to the value creation in retail banking.

30. OECD, *Report on the Attribution of Profits to Permanent Establishments* (Paris: OECD Publishing, 2010), Part II, para. 12 and Part III, para. 67.
31. *Ibid.*, Part II, para. 171, as well as OECD, para. 6.133 OECD TPG.

Figure 15.1 Value Chain in Retail Banking

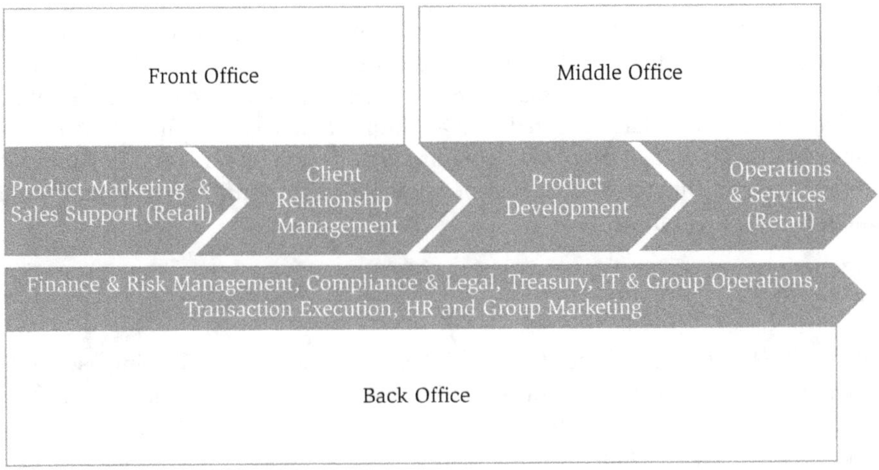

A typical business model in retail banking consists of the following functions: product marketing and sales support for retail; client relationship management; product development; operations and services for retail as well as finance and risk management; compliance and legal; treasury; IT and group operations; transaction execution; HR; and group marketing. As employees performing product marketing, sales support, and client relationship management regularly face client contact, the indicated functions belong to the category 'front-office'. Next, 'middle-office' functions in retail banking are mentioned under letters (c) and (d). Finally, 'back-office' functions include finance and risk management; compliance and legal; treasury; IT and group operations; transaction execution; HR; and group marketing complete the value chain.

In this respect, it is important to understand the difference between 'front-office' and 'back-office' marketing. Whereas product marketing promotes specific products offered by the retail bank to its clients (e.g., mortgages or credit cards), group marketing focuses on public awareness of the enterprise brand. In addition, Figure 15.1 shows two categories of operations. While 'middle-office' operations provide the necessary infrastructure for client relationship management and product marketing (e.g., maintenance of platforms for digital retail banking), 'back-office' operations focus on processes and infrastructure in supporting functions (e.g., software solutions for accounting).

Client relationship management includes acquisition of new clients and retention of those already existing. It requires direct exposure to the client in, e.g., meetings and educational seminars. Client relationship management is a key function in both the acquisition and retention phases.[32] The other high-value adding functions are product

32. OECD, *Report on the Attribution of Profits to Permanent Establishments* (Paris: OECD Publishing, 2010), Part II, paras 8 and 9.

development and related risk management. The remaining functions can be considered - despite their undisputable contribution to value creation - as routine or low-value adding functions.

It is also worth mentioning that retail banks conduct fewer cross-border transactions than, e.g., private or investment banks or asset managers. This results from the retail banking regulations and the necessary capital requirements for each country in which deposits from the public are accepted.[33] In addition, clients usually choose the bank in the neighbourhood that offers all of the required retail banking services from one place for retail banking. Due to the omission of internationalization, the TP issues in retail banking are usually limited.

2.2.2 Risks

Similar to the key functions, the 2010 OECD PE Report, Part II is still being used today as a major reference for the identification of risks inherent to retail banking. Although the said report focuses on attributing risks and assets between the head office and its PE, it mentions all relevant risks that are taken by legally distinct and separate enterprises. Commonly, the following risks are assumed in retail banking when performing functions along the value chain (*see* Figure 15.1).

Credit risk is the risk that the customer to whom a credit was granted will be unable to pay the interest or to repay the principal of the loan in accordance with its terms and conditions.[34] Credit risk is very important in retail banking regarding borrowing and lending money. The development of credit derivatives has permitted banks to manage this risk by passing the credit risk arising from their loans to independent global trading enterprises. However, the credit risk outsourced to these enterprises must be managed just as with other risks assumed from other customer transactions. It is also worth mentioning that banks may also be assuming risk through credit derivatives which should be taken into account in the determination of the overall risk exposure and capital adequacy.[35]

Market interest rate risk is the risk that market interest rates will increase above the rates used when entering into the loan agreement. Consequently, the retail bank will receive interest rate revenues from the client that are lower than the interest expense that it has to pay its lender, e.g., other banks.[36]

Foreign exchange risk appears when the retail bank grants a loan in a currency other than its functional currency, i.e., the main currency used by a business. Such a situation can negatively influence the revenues from this transaction.[37]

---

33. For example, EU, *Regulation (EU) No. 575/2013 of the European Parliament and of the Council of 26 June 2013 on prudential requirements for credit institutions and investment firms and amending Regulation*.
34. *Ibid.*, para. 17.
35. OECD, *Report on the Attribution of Profits to Permanent Establishments* (Paris: OECD Publishing, 2010), Part II, para. 93.
36. *Ibid.*
37. OECD, *Report on the Attribution of Profits to Permanent Establishments* (Paris: OECD Publishing, 2010), Part II, para. 93.

Operational risk refers to the risk of human error or lapses in procedures or control leading to errors in, e.g., a transaction execution that could lead to a client's financial loss.[38]

Market risk arises when a company is subject to adverse sales conditions due to increased competition in the marketplace, adverse demand conditions within the market, or the inability to develop markets or position products to service targeted customers.

Reputational risk refers to the risk of losing existing and potential clients and investors through a negative impact on reputation. Reputational risks can occur due to a number of reasons, e.g., regulatory compliance failure or corporate governance failure.

2.2.3 Assets

The OECD TPG requires that compensation should not reflect just functions performed but also the assets used and risks assumed in performing those functions.[39] Again, the 2010 OECD PE Report, Part II is still being used today as a major reference for the identification of economic ownership of key assets inherent to retail banking. However, even here, the key assets have evolved since 2010. Due to automation and digitalization, the relevance has decreased of, e.g., physical assets such as retail bank office equipment.[40] Conversely, the author believes that highly qualified people are currently not only a link for allocation of functions[41] but also the most important asset. The assets discussed below are used in retail banking when performing functions along the value chain (*see* Figure 15.1).

The retail banking business needs *highly qualified personnel* that understand the financial market products offered to their clients (e.g., investment funds solutions or mortgages), used instruments (e.g., retail banking portal), and the interaction between individual banking functions (e.g., client relationship management and treasury).

In the banking area, marketing *intangibles* represented by the name, reputation, and trademark of the bank are commonly used.[42] In contrast, other intangibles - also known as trade intangibles - such as proprietary systems, ingenuity, and patents are less spread in banking than, e.g., in the engineering industry. However, in some instances, there are complex algorithms developed for risk calculation or portfolio management that could be considered as other intangibles.[43]

38. *Ibid.*, para. 18.
39. Paragraph 1.34, OECD TPG.
40. *Ibid.*, para. 14.
41. *Ibid.*, Part I, para. 15.
42. OECD TPG Glossary (Ch. I).
43. *Ibid.* As well as OECD, *Report on the Attribution of Profits to Permanent Establishments* (Paris: OECD Publishing, 2010), Part II, para. 15.

Currently, retail banks work with various *IT applications and platforms*. Some of them are used by clients (e.g., e-banking portals and apps); others are for the internal use only and include, e.g., compliance tools and fee calculators.[44]

The international regulatory framework[45] requires banks to reserve enough *capital* to cover unexpected losses and keep themselves solvent in a crisis. As a main principle, the amount of capital required depends on the risk attached to the assets of a particular bank. Consequently, a sufficient amount of capital is a precondition of operating the banking business.

2.3 Wealth Management

2.3.1 Functions

2.3.1.1 General Remarks

Figure 15.2 depicts a value chain with individual functions contributing to value creation in wealth management and private banking.

Figure 15.2 Value Chain in Wealth Management

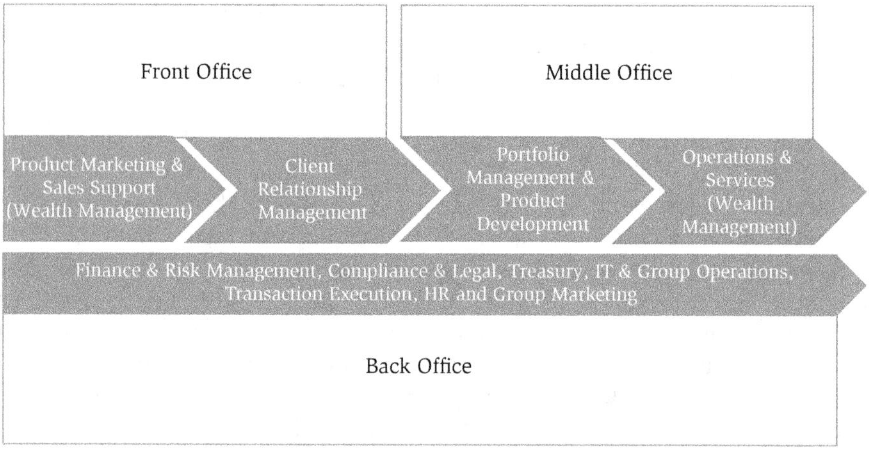

In contrast to retail banking, private banking uses Part III (Global Trading of Financial Instruments) of 2010 OECD PE Report as a major reference for classifying functions.[46]

44. OECD, *Report on the Attribution of Profits to Permanent Establishments* (Paris: OECD Publishing, 2010), Part III, para. 68.
45. Bank for International Settlements, *Basel III: international regulatory framework for banks*, https://www.bis.org/bcbs/basel3.htm (last accessed 30 January 2022).
46. OECD, *Report on the Attribution of Profits to Permanent Establishments* (Paris: OECD Publishing, 2010), Part III, paras 12 et seq.

Although the value chain for wealth management shows some similarities with retail banking,[47] there are a few significant differences in the value creation. First, the role of client relationship management is intrinsically much more important. This is because private banking clients usually have higher expectations in terms of service quality and performance.[48] At the same time, for most of the private banking clients, personal interaction with the client relationship manager still remains an important part of the service. In contrast to retail banking clients, they tend to also be more mobile and flexible. On the client's side, a generational shift is under way, and clients are now demanding easier and more convenient ways to manage their assets. To meet the constantly increasing expectations of private banking clients, successful relationship managers must possess special skills, e.g., in-depth knowledge of investments in derivative instruments such as options.

Second, portfolio management, product development and the related risk management cover a much broader universe of products than in retail banking in which, typically, the use of Lombard credits are rather rare. Conversely, wealthy clients in a private banking commonly expand their portfolios by obtaining a loan secured by their financial products (e.g., bonds or shares). On top of that, the financial crisis has increased the investor's sensitivity to risk, and the current low yield environment has made it more challenging to meet the client's expectations of returns while limiting risk.[49]

Consequently, client relationship management is a key function in both the acquisition and retention phases.[50] The other high-value adding functions are portfolio management as well as product development and related risk management. The remaining functions can be treated - despite their undisputable contribution to value creation - as routine or low-value adding functions.

It is worth mentioning that the digitalization of the industry, the broad availability of investment information on the internet, and the generational shift among wealthy clients to digital natives gave rise to a new private banking segment that does not seek any human interaction with relationship managers. They rather advise themselves in terms of portfolio management and limit the interaction with the private bank to mere use of the infrastructure, i.e., transaction execution. However, the traditional wealth management business model with relationship management still prevails.

The following paragraphs describe individual functions from the value chain depicted in Figure 15.2.

47. *See* Figure 15.1 Value Chain in Retail Banking.
48. OECD, *Report on the Attribution of Profits to Permanent Establishments* (Paris: OECD Publishing, 2010), Part III, para. 43.
49. Deloitte, *Wealth Management and Private Banking: Connecting with Clients and Reinventing the Value Proposition*, https://www2.deloitte.com/content/dam/Deloitte/ch/Documents/financial-services/ch-en-financial-services-efma-wealth-management-private-banking-032015.pdf (entered on 23 March 2020).
50. OECD, *Report on the Attribution of Profits to Permanent Establishments* (Paris: OECD Publishing, 2010), Part II, paras 8 and 9.

2.3.1.2 *Product Marketing & Sales Support*

Product marketing is the process of introduction and promotion of a product to the market that encourages sales to wealth management clients. Otherwise stated, it raises the awareness of the wealth management core competencies among the target client groups. It focuses on maintenance and enhancement of a consistent market image of individual products in terms of style and messages. Furthermore, the Product Marketing & Sales Support function supports the wealth management teams in their targeted distribution activities by creating marketing instruments, e.g., drafting brochures and leaflets. Conversely, group marketing rather raises the awareness of the private bank's brand and strengthens its positioning.

The main tasks and competencies include comprehensive planning and budgeting for the marketing activities for all target client markets. They usually take the form of premium meet-and-greet events or educational seminars for client retention and acquisition. Further, the product marketing and sales support team elaborates promotional content (messages) and assumes responsibility for media planning. It also develops and defines the content of brochures and presentations. Finally, yet importantly, the team is also responsible for market research and performance monitoring of the marketing activities as well as the initiation and tracking of follow-up activities.

2.3.1.3 *Client Relationship Management*

This key function focuses on the acquisition and retention of client relationships.[51] Client relationship managers provide comprehensive advice and a broad range of investment products and services tailored to the complex needs of HNWIs. Although client advisors work for specific individuals, market segments, and revenue targets, the competitive industry of wealth management constantly forces banks to enter into new markets and entice new customers. However, even more important is the need for increased loyalty of the current customers. The client relationship managers help to create cohesion between the client and wealth management business. They are responsible for acquiring and retaining clients by creating and maintaining strong relationships that increase client satisfaction and the sale of products and services. Depending on the level of client involvement, different services are provided in private banking as further discussed.

Execution only – as the name indicates – means that the private bank carries out the investment decisions of the client. In other words, the client directly instructs the wealth manager to buy and sell assets on their behalf. Such a mandate could be provided with market insights and news but without the advice of a professional investment manager. It tends to be only suitable for highly experienced investors and financial professionals because the investment strategy in this mandate is fully determined by the client.

51. *Ibid.*, paras 40 et seq.

With an *advisory investment management* mandate, the client relationship manager advises the client on investment strategy; however, the client himself makes the final decision. This type of service requires a substantial amount of investment expertise and affords the wealth management firm a far less stable income stream from the private banking business than discretionary mandates.

Discretionary mandates are a popular option for those who have little experience in financial markets or lack the time or appetite to be involved in investment decisions. Should the client opt for a discretionary service, he and his client relationship manager work out his investment objectives and risk appetite. In the next step, the private bank develops an investment strategy that precisely aligns with the client's profile and requirements. How much investment risk he is willing to take on, the level of returns the client aims to receive for taking on that risk, and the asset classes and markets he wishes to be invested in are questions that will all be addressed.[52]

The client relationship manager will then take responsibility for all investment decisions and will not require consent for individual transactions. Should the bank operate within the agreed-upon conditions for discretionary mandates, the client cannot require compensation for a negative performance. Discretionary investment services are offered by most private banks. Moreover, it is the most common choice for private clients. This option frees the client from involvement in day-to-day investment management decisions and makes it easier to benefit the most out of long-term investments (e.g., investment funds and pensions.) As the client's needs evolve and form a core part of the service, the agreed client's investment strategy is regularly reviewed.

The technical complexity of the function of the client relationship management is relatively low compared to other functions in the value chain. However, it represents the key function in terms of generating revenues. As such, from the TP perspective, it represents a high-value adding function.

2.3.1.4 Portfolio Management and Product Development

The primary goal of portfolio management and product development is to actively manage client assets. This function consists of accurately monitoring financial markets, anticipation of trends and opportunities, and developments of individual solutions. There is usually close interaction between client relationship management and portfolio management in order to develop investment decision guidelines that meet the current client's needs. In addition, portfolio managers organize seminars for both client relationship managers and clients to inform about the present investment trends and support sales activities.

Portfolio management and product development are other high-value adding functions or key functions.

52. OECD, *Report on the Attribution of Profits to Permanent Establishments* (Paris: OECD Publishing, 2010), Part III, paras 44 et seq.

2.3.1.5 *Operations & Services*

Although these functions are indispensable in the wealth management business, they do not belong to key functions from the TP perspective. Operations and services are middle-office functions consisting of three areas. The first area is *operations* that comprise a centralized middle-office services provision such as payment processing, account administration, as well as a tool and system support. The second one is *process management* that consists of design and implementation of efficient banking processes. Finally, yet importantly, the third area is *services* in the private banking middle office that presents a competence centre for various wealth services relating to financial, tax, succession, and pension planning. Typically, there are wealth and tax planning services offered to high net-wealth individuals that take the form of succession or inheritance planning for family businesses.

2.3.1.6 *Back-Office Services*

In order to provide the entire wealth management group with the same quality standard of back-office services, private banks typically establish a group-servicing centre that provides management and administrative services to all entities. There is a wide range of these services that are typically provided, among which are accounting, finance and controlling, group tax, treasury, corporate business development, HR, internal audit, investor relations, IT, legal, marketing and communication, risk control, etc.[53]

The back-office *accounting function* commonly books clients' and corporate transactions. In addition, it collects and assesses data to create periodic reports, such as monthly, quarterly, and yearly balance sheets as well as profit and loss statements.

The *finance and controlling function* prepares budgets, compares them with the actual figures, and explains deviations. In addition, it analyses costs and provides support with financial projects.

Tax compliance of the group in all locations, tax accounting, managing the effective tax rate, minimizing tax risks related to new products, and set-ups and regulatory tax topics are the main goals of the *group tax function*. The back-office function of group tax rather takes care of the tax topics related to the multinational group, e.g., TP, VAT/GST, and tax accounting. On the contrary, there is usually another middle-office function providing services directly to wealthy individuals relating to inheritance tax topics or succession planning. In addition, certain tax topics (e.g., collection of stamp duties and financial transactions tax) are fully digitalized and outsourced to the transaction execution part of operations.

The back-office *function treasury* optimizes liquidity within the organization. It develops and implements a detailed quarterly cash flow forecasting model to ensure the availability of required funding and adherence to target cash metrics. In addition, it manages the full accounting cycle including accounts payable, accounts receivable,

53. Paragraph 7.14 OECD TPG.

and expense claims. Finally, it manages the daily operations of the fund, and coordinates the attribution of the repayments and the calculation of the repayments in the portfolio with investment analysts.

The corporate business development function develops and retains the strategy of the private banking group. It participates in due diligence (e.g., strategic M&A, new products, and set-ups and business process optimization.)

The *HR function* takes care of the development and education of employees. In addition, it is in charge of the hiring process, payroll and compensation policy, global mobility, secondments, and social security topics.

The *internal audit* plans and executes financial, operational, and compliance audits worldwide. It identifies and analyses business risks as well as advises in the field of internal auditing. Their findings are communicated and discussed with local and senior management.

The *investor relations function* drafts press releases and compiles interim financial reports and analyst presentations. In addition, it provides perspective on all investor communications, helping to advance the private bank story to address investor perceptions and needs. Finally, it proactively – in rapid time – analyses, prepares, and communicates on market moving events to investor communities for specific regions. Often, there is a close interaction between investor relations and communication.

The *IT function* is in charge of application management that is related to a bank's webpage and other system support. It manages the IT set-up and processes including ongoing IT security operations and monitoring. Moreover, it manages all external providers contributing to the development and maintenance of business support infrastructure.[54]

The *legal function* supports all stakeholders, including analysing and monitoring legal and regulatory developments and advising the front, middle, and back offices in a wide variety of legal matters in close cooperation with department heads. The legal function provides legal advice with respect to local or regional and global regulatory projects (e.g., MiFID2 and GDPR/DPA). It supports the HR department in a variety of employment law-related questions and manages (in cooperation with external counsels) litigation cases (including client complaints, HR cases, internal investigations, etc.)

The *marketing and communication* function develops and executes the globally planned marketing and media concepts in private banking. Furthermore, it has to deliver a consistent global marketing framework across digital marketing, client marketing, and brand communication.

The *risk control function* analyses the product portfolio and assesses specific topics for special transactions. In addition, it constantly reviews and further develops risk methods, models, processes, and systems. Moreover, it ensures daily monitoring of the Lombard credit portfolios. Finally, it identifies and cleans up potential loss positions in the bank's balance sheet.

54. OECD, *Report on the Attribution of Profits to Permanent Establishments* (Paris: OECD Publishing, 2010), Part III, para. 68.

From a TP perspective, all management and administrative services are considered as routine, low-value added, and low inherent risk containing supporting services.

2.3.2 Risks

There are the same risks assumed in the value chain for wealth management as those in retail banking.[55]

2.3.3 Assets

There are the same assets used in the value chain for wealth management as those in retail banking.[56,57]

2.4 Investment Banking: Financial Products

2.4.1 Functions

Figure 15.3 Value Chain in Investment Banking: Financial Products

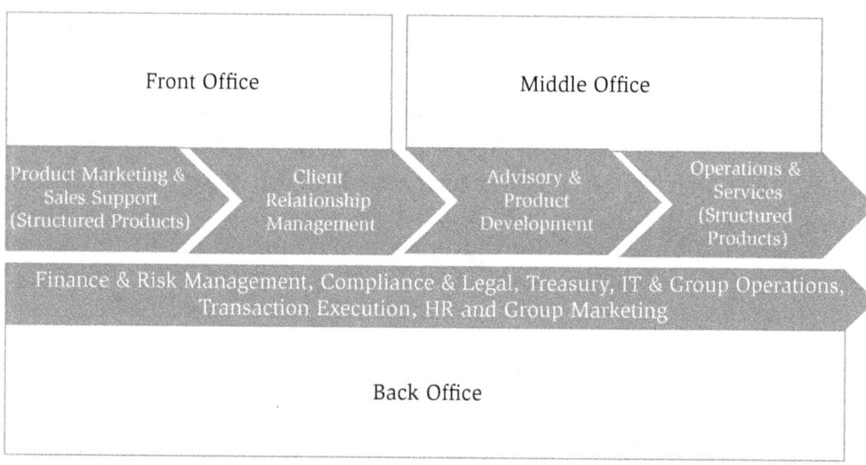

Similar to private banking, investment banking-structured products uses Part III (Global Trading of Financial Instruments) of the 2010 OECD PE Report as a major reference for classifying functions.[58]

55. *See* 15/2.2.2 above.
56. *See* 15/2.2.3 above.
57. OECD, *Report on the Attribution of Profits to Permanent Establishments* (Paris: OECD Publishing, 2010), Part III, paras 106 and 107.
58. *Ibid.*, paras 12 et seq.

Although the value chain for investment banking-financial products resembles that of retail banking[59] and wealth management,[60] there are a few significant differences in the value creation (Figure 15.3). First, the client relationship management has more facets. There are more distribution channels than in private banking. Besides the sales to the high wealth individuals (usually via the distribution channel wealth management), structured products are also offered to professional investors (e.g., hedge funds, pension funds, state funds, or traders and portfolio managers). Even if personal relationships still play some role, it is rather the ability to swiftly react to market trends and develop new products with an attractive performance that is the key function.[61] The role of client relationship managers in the wholesale market is rather limited. Stated differently, the key function is the ability to create tailor-made structured products consisting of individual components depending on the underlying and the requested payoff structure. Based on these input parameters, the pricing of the products will be calculated and negotiated with the client.[62] In the case of a consensus, the product will finally be issued. During the lifetime of a structured product, the issuer is expected to ensure proper market-making support for the product in order to offer the client the opportunity to sell the product back to the issuer.[63]

Second, risk management together with risk assumption also plays a key role as some of the structured products require that the bank holds the underlying products (e.g., corporate bonds) in its balance sheet.

2.4.2 Risks

There are the same risks assumed in the value chain for investment banking-financial products as those in wealth management and retail banking.[64] In addition, the most significant risk is the market risk connected with the structured products. The issuer takes the risk on their balance sheet that has to be properly managed according to the risk policy reflecting the issuer's risk appetite and the corresponding maximum risk limits. The issuer risk positions always have to be in accordance with these limits. Therefore, hedging transactions are undertaken, and the risk positions are actively managed during the trading day. For some structured products - usually those containing options - it may be difficult to segregate the risk assumption from the risk management function.[65]

59. *See* Figure 15.1 Value Chain in Retail Banking.
60. *See* Figure 15.2 Value Chain in Wealth Management.
61. OECD, *Report on the Attribution of Profits to Permanent Establishments* (Paris: OECD Publishing, 2010), Part III, paras 44 et seq.
62. *Ibid.*, para. 47.
63. *Ibid.*, para. 48.
64. *See* 15.2.2.2 above.
65. OECD, *Report on the Attribution of Profits to Permanent Establishments* (Paris: OECD Publishing, 2010), Part III, para. 50.

2.4.3 Assets

There are the same assets used in the value chain for investment banking-financial products as those in wealth management and retail banking.[66]

2.5 Asset Management

Figure 15.4 Value Chain in Asset Management

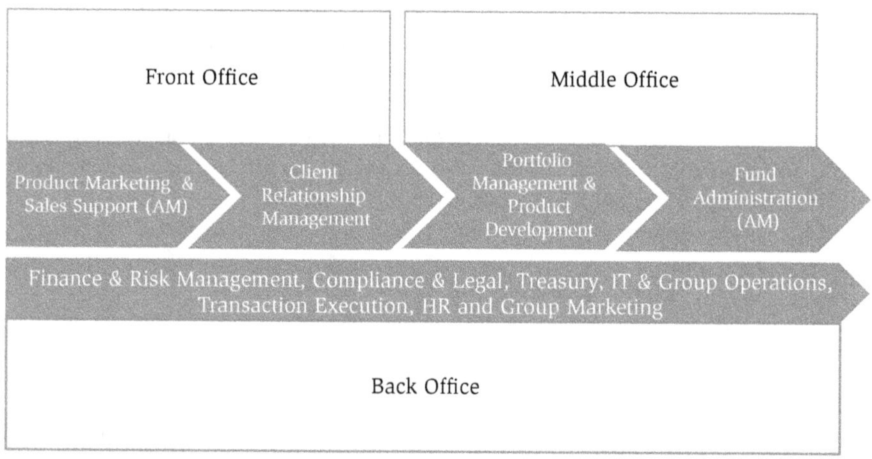

2.5.1 Functions

Like private banking and investment banking-structure products, asset management uses Part III (Global Trading of Financial Instruments) of the 2010 OECD PE Report as a major reference for classifying functions.[67]

Despite similar value chains as those of retail, private and investment banking-financial products, there are a few significant divergences in the value creation of the asset management sector (Figure 15.4). First, although client relationship management is still a high-value adding function, it is less important than portfolio management. This is because institutional clients (i.e., state and private pension funds) tend to focus on performance and fee structure to achieve long-term pension scheme goals. Even if personal relationships still play some role, it is rather the strong investment performance that is decisive for an institutional client. Frequently, pension fund representatives regularly compare investment performance of key players in the asset management market. Asset managers performing below the benchmark for individual asset classes tend to have fewer numbers of assets under management. Continuous weak

66. *See* 15.2.2.3 above.
67. *Ibid.*, paras 7 et seq.

performance tends to result in the loss of clients. Conversely, successful asset managers with investment performance above the benchmark tend to also generate performance fees on top of management fees. In addition, their positive performance attracts new assets under management.

Second, there is a specific routine function referred to as fund administration that deals with requirements from regulators for investment funds, e.g., consistent reporting to the regulator and drafting of terms sheets. Typically, this function also takes care of the refund of withholding taxes.

2.5.2 Risks

There are the same risks assumed as those in the value chain for asset management as in retail, private and investment banking-financial products.[68]

2.5.3 Assets

There are the same assets used in the value chain for asset management as those in retail, private and investment banking-financial products. However, until recently, asset managers generally benefited from a number of exemptions and national discretions regarding capital requirements.[69]

3 IMPACT OF DIGITALIZATION ON THE VALUE CREATION IN THE BANKING AND ASSET MANAGEMENT SECTOR

As with many other industries, the banking sector has been facing a tremendous change due to digitalization. In contrast to other businesses, it is combined in the banking field with ever-increasing compliance and regulatory requirements as well as globalization of financial markets.[70] Although all the three phenomena significantly changed proven business models that maximized shareholder values for decades, digitalization is transforming the financial services industry most significantly. The primary drivers behind this process are the enormous developments in IT and the convergence of related technologies such as smartphones and tablets with new electronic services, i.e., electronic banking marketplaces and investment platforms. These developments not only enable new business processes but also lead to completely new business models and even indicate an entire change of the banking value chain. Notably, in the same way, value chains in other industries – such as the media

68. *See* 15.2.2.2 above.
69. KPMG, New capital requirements ... and much more – The main elements of the Investment Firm Directive and Regulation have broadly been welcomed, April 2019, https://home.kpmg/xx/en/home/insights/2019/04/new-capital-requirements-and-much-more-fs.html (last accessed 30 January 2022).
70. *See also* section 15.1.3 *supra*.

or travel industry – were radically transformed a few years ago.[71] According to the study, *Digital Banking 2025*,[72] the banking industry is currently undergoing transformations in six areas.

First, decreasing physical client advisory and intensified use of electronic channels forces many banks to adapt to new client processes in order to keep retain contact. Future client contact with the bank will be in the form of a hybrid client interaction. It will take place among different banking channels and even across different companies bridging the digital and the physical world. An example of this is a client journey that begins with a personal financial planning process on a tablet app guided by a digital bot. It includes exchanges with other clients on social networks, contact with a client support person via video chat, and finally a visit with the client relationship manager.

Second, operating models of banks still rely on a strong vertical integration of management, core, and support processes. A recent development termed 'hyperspecialization' indicates that sourced services will tend to be more granular in the future and new sourcing models, such as crowdsourcing, will thus emerge. Due to developments in IT (e.g., blockchain) and standardization, banks are now able to outsource services on the level of single tasks. This atomization of the value chain may lead to organization structures that are more decentralized, as we know them today.

Third, decreasing market share through intensified competition with other banks and new non-banks (i.e., fintechs), a low interest rate environment, and increasing costs because of regulatory requirements have led to lower profitability for banks. The development of new digital ecosystems enables banks to reposition themselves in the banking value chain and in other value chains as well as develop new revenue models. Among such examples are collaborations with other providers of innovative services such as investing platforms or the development of new services such as social community platforms for banking clients.

Fourth, new hybrid client journeys of Generation Y clients are characterized by an increasing degree of electronic client services and cross-company processes that will integrate clients, banks, and third-party service providers over new digital platforms across various parts of banking. These open digital banking platforms seamlessly integrate innovative services such as social banking services, self-profiling services, or automated advisory services into new client journeys and allow all involved parties to access the same end-user applications and data.

Next, data analytics is an enabler of new client-related services and internal services with the purpose of gaining operational efficiency. The increasing amount of unstructured internal and external data allows banks to obtain a more comprehensive view of their clients and to offer new services for them such as targeted product marketing. Consequently, the internal use of big data enables optimizing product offerings based on the transactions thus far executed by the client.

71. Gasser U. et al., *Digital Banking 2025*, April 2018, https://www.fintech.uzh.ch/dam/jcr:2ef31105-1a60-43da-a657-8b140e47b3b4/Digital%20Banking%202025%20FINAL.pdf (last accessed 30 January 2022).
72. *Ibid.*

Finally, in recent years, many non-banks entered the banking value chain. For example, there are technology companies that disintermediate banks' client relationships by providing their services directly to clients and only use banks as transaction execution providers. Another example of this is providers that offer investment services without banks, or peer-to-peer lending in financing. These new developments indicate a shift towards new banking value chains and force banks to radically rethink their existing business models.

The digitalization of the banking sector – taking the form of apps and internet portals – will reduce the importance of the function of client relationship management in the upcoming years. It could be reasonably expected that the element of human interaction will gradually lose its importance in the sales function. On the contrary, the user-friendliness of digital solutions and unique digital experience will become a part of the distribution function.

Although financial institutions have globally begun the shift to competing in the digital economy, asset managers have generally remained digital laggards. Despite constant profitability pressures driven by increased competition, the shift to lower-fee passive investments and the need to comply with new regulations, only a small number of asset managers are creating value through greater investments in digitizing their operations and technology functions.[73] Consequently, there are no changes in the value chain expected in the upcoming years.

4 TP ISSUES IN THE BANKING AND ASSET MANAGEMENT SECTOR

4.1 Categorization of Functions

In contrast to other businesses, banks and asset managers provide only services. There is no manufacturing, no product fabrication, extract, and assembly and no product design and engineering. In addition, banks and asset managers do not perform technological research and development or transportation and warehousing.[74] However, they provide a broad variety of services, most of which have only a digital (and rather abstract) form, e.g., conducting buy/sell transactions of shares for a client or providing a Lombard credit. Therefore, the accurate delineation of the actual transaction[75] is limited to only a provision of services. Such an analysis requires an in-depth business understanding rather than one that is broad based.[76]

One of the major difficulties in the TP of the banking sector is the lack of up-to-date detailed guidance on the categorization of services functions regarding value creation.[77] Both the OECD TPG and the UN TPM require that the selection of a TP method

73. McKinsey & Company, *Achieving digital alpha in asset management*, https://www.mckinsey.com/industries/financial-services/our-insights/achieving-digital-alpha-in-asset-management (last accessed 30 January 2022).
74. US IRS Reg. 1.482.
75. Paragraph 1.33 OECD TPG and 2017 UN TPM, B.2.3.1.4.
76. Paragraph 1.34 OECD TPG.
77. *See* 15.2.1, 15.2.2.1, 15.2.3.1 and 15.2.4.1 *supra*.

should consider the nature of the controlled transaction.[78] The nature of the tested transaction should be determined particularly through a functional analysis that will conclude whether that function is routine (and low-value adding) or non-routine (and high economic value adding and risk containing).[79] Once the functional analysis is complete, it is then necessary to determine an arm's length remuneration using the TP methods listed in the OECD TPG and UN TPM for those transactions.

As mentioned in the section on value creation, the 2010 OECD PE Report, Parts II and III are still used as a reference for classifying a specific service function as routine or non-routine.[80] However, due to the constant evolution of business models and offered products in the banking and asset management sector, some parts of the report have become obsolete.[81] Second, Parts II and III do not cover all of the activities performed in the banking and asset management sector. More specifically, Part II describes (some) service functions typical for the borrowing and lending of money, which is one small component of retail banking.[82] Part III mentions some functions of 'global trading' of financial instruments that is a 'catch-all' phrase including underwriting and distribution of products on a worldwide basis, market-making in physical securities, and derivative instruments.[83] 'Global trading' covers the part of investment banking dealing with financial products,[84] brokerage, and an element of wealth or asset management that underwrites its own products, e.g., investment funds.[85] However, the traditional private banking business in which a bank advises clients on how to invest their wealth by buying shares, bonds, or other third products is not covered. The same applies to any other banking activity for which assumption and ongoing management of market risk for the bank's own books does not take place, e.g., corporate actions advisory services or trade financing.

Third, Part III of the 2010 OECD PE Report discusses KERT functions in 'global trading'. The author of this chapter believes that the terms 'marketing and sales' and 'trading and day-to-day risk management' – identified in paragraphs 40 et seq. as KERT functions – are overly generic. They both encompass several routine and non-routine functions.[86] For example, marketing is a typical low-value adding and low-risk containing intra-group function.[87] Conversely, sales as in global trading are a high-value adding and non-routine function. They are one of the most important functions in any area of banking or asset management[88] as it is ultimately the only one generating revenues.

78. Paragraph 2.2 OECD TPG and 2017 UN TPM, B.2.1.2.
79. OECD, *Report on the Attribution of Profits to Permanent Establishments* (Paris: OECD Publishing, 2010), Part III, para. 114.
80. *See* 15.2.1, 15.2.2.1, 15.2.3.1 and 15.2.4.1 *supra*.
81. OECD, *Report on the Attribution of Profits to Permanent Establishments* (Paris: OECD Publishing, 2010), Part III, paras 40, 41, 45, 62, 63 and 66 and 2021 UN TPM, A.1.3.3.
82. *See* 15.2.2.1 *supra*.
83. OECD, *Report on the Attribution of Profits to Permanent Establishments* (Paris: OECD Publishing, 2010), Part III, para. 7.
84. *See* 15.2.4.1 *supra*.
85. *See* 15/.3.1 and 15.2.5.1 *supra*.
86. *See* 15.2 *supra*.
87. Paragraph 7.44 OECD TPG.
88. *See* 15.4.1 *supra*.

Fourth, there are instances in which risk assumption – supported with sufficient capital equipment – is entirely separated from any function. Consequently, the company performing, e.g., a risk management or product structuring function does not necessarily have to be the one assuming the market or credit risk.[89]

4.2 Outsourcing

There is an increasing trend in the banking and asset management sector to outsource functions to either intra-group or to third parties (e.g., to independent specialist companies).[90] One reason for outsourcing certain functions is the centralization in one location, e.g., European equity research services in Frankfurt, London, or Zurich as they are locations with a high concentration of highly qualified equity research analysts. The other (and, most likely, even more common) motivation for outsourcing is cost reduction achieved due to location savings. Back-office low-value adding functions such as routine IT, HR, or credit receivables accounting are often outsourced to countries with lower labour costs (e.g., CEE countries,[91] China, or India). In this respect, several TP questions arise.

First, when significant location savings are derived following a business restructuring, the question arises of whether and how the location savings should be shared among the affected group entities.[92] Generally, developing countries tend to argue that the economic benefit arising from moving operations to a low-cost jurisdiction should be taxed by them.[93] The OECD TPG emphasizes that the allocation of the savings between affected countries depends on what would have been agreed upon by independent parties in similar circumstances.[94] However, the UN TPM admits that developing countries could have a different view on the allocation of location savings.[95] More specifically, the part of the UN TPM presenting the country practice in China explains that location savings should be split by applying, e.g., an increased markup on costs.[96] Similarly, India takes the position that location savings should be allocated between affected countries by using the PSM in cases when comparable unrelated party transactions are not available.[97] It is also worth mentioning that CEE countries – as OECD Member States – follow the approach described in Chapter IX of the OECD TPG.[98] Finally, it is assumed that the COVID-19 outbreak will force several MNEs in the banking sector to insource (i.e., bring back) certain functions from China and India to Europe. It will be interesting to observe whether such TP restructuring steps will have any impact on the location savings country practices.

89. OECD, *Report on the Attribution of Profits to Permanent Establishments* (Paris: OECD Publishing, 2010), Part III, paras 49 et seq.
90. *Ibid.*, para. 87.
91. For example, the Czech Republic, Hungary, Poland and the Slovak Republic.
92. Paragraph 9.127 OECD TPG.
93. 2017 UN TPM, B.1.10.14. et seq.
94. Paragraph 9.128 OECD TPG.
95. UN TPM, 3.4.5.6-3.4.5.13.
96. UN TPM, Part D, 2.20.1-2.20.4.
97. UN TPM, Part D, 3.8.3.
98. Paragraph 9.128 OECD TPG.

Second, the decision to outsource certain functions to low-cost locations could also bring challenges in terms of comparability. This is usually the case if the arm's length remuneration is determined based on the CUP method.[99] Typically, banks and asset managers outsource their routine IT services (e.g., help desk services) to low-cost locations at certain levels of internationalization. Should the remuneration for such intra-group services reflect market prices in the original western European country, the new low-cost location might challenge them as not being comparable.[100] In such instances, a change to the CPM might be a reasonable solution. This is because the cost basis changes with the lower cost, whereas the profit markup remains the same.[101]

Third, the outsourcing in banking and asset management leads to the question of which functions, risks, and assets remain at the outsourcing entity that very often appears vis-à-vis third-party clients as the fully fledged entity (so-called subdelegation of functions). In other words, the outsourcing entity is still responsible for the timely delivery of service quality to clients. The subdelegating entity supervises the services quality, selects the preferred service provider, and assumes the market risk. The combination of these functions and risks – sometimes also referred to as 'contractual management' – tend to be remunerated based on a CUP method. The subdelegation of function is common in the asset management sector in which the management company concludes agreements with institutional investors and outsources certain functions, e.g., portfolio management and fund administration, to other group entities.

4.3 Overview of the TP Methods

4.3.1 General Remarks

Both traditional transaction methods and transactional profit methods are common in the banking and asset management sector. However, there are a few interesting features regarding the TP methods. First – and in contrast to other industries – there are many external and internal CUPs available for certain functions (e.g., for portfolio management or for client advisory and relationship management). Many external CUPs are available in the commercial database that is used for financial services (i.e., Thomson Reuters Lipper) presenting data from primarily US collective investment vehicles (i.e., funds).[102] This database is used for the identification of CUPs in both the banking sector and asset management. Second, as these are areas in which no goods are sold, there is no use of the RPM.[103] Third, for determining the arm's length compensation for routine services, the CPM is commonly used. For example, marketing and sales supports as well as other supportive administrative services are typically remunerated with the CPM with a profit markup of 5%-9%. Interestingly, the

99. Paragraph 1.144 OECD TPG.
100. 2017 UN TPM, B.1.6.23.
101. Paragraph 1.144 OECD TPG.
102. *See*: Refinitiv Lipper Funds Data, https://www.refinitiv.com/en/products/lipper-fund-research (last accessed 30 January 2022).
103. 2017 UN TPM, Subchapter 4.3.

benchmarking studies conducted in commercial databases (e.g., Orbis or Amadeus) usually present as comparables entities acting out of the financial services businesses. Finally, yet importantly, the TPSM – in particular the residual analysis – is frequently applied in situations with a high level of integration and cooperation between functions and locations.[104]

The UN TPM admits that the choice of a TP method, availability of different types of them, and the priority to be given to various different TP methods are matters often covered by domestic legislative frameworks.[105] They tend to take the form of administrative guidance or other subsidiary materials rather than taxation laws following the hierarchy developed by the OECD.[106] However, there are also several court cases in which the tax authorities required the application of the TPSM (residual analysis) instead of traditional transaction methods.

Court Case

In the *A AG* case, the tax authorities of the Canton of Zurich adjusted the taxable profits of the A Group operating in asset and wealth management by applying TPSM – residual analysis – instead of CUP. However, the hierarchy of the TP methods as presented by the OECD in paragraphs 2.5, 2.49, and 3.49 was not questioned. The tax authorities of the Canton of Zurich admitted that traditional transaction methods should be preferred over transactional profit methods. In addition, among the former category of the TP methods, the CUP should be given priority. However, the precondition for the application of the CUP method is the existence of comparable data that could be reasonably applied. The tax authorities of the Canton of Zurich challenged the comparability of the presented external CUPs by arguing that the database results show enterprises with different types of clients (i.e., mainly institutional professional investors) than A Group dealt with (i.e., primarily individuals). In addition, the benchmarking study mainly showed multinational asset and wealth managers and the prices they applied in transactions with related parties. Therefore, they cannot be used as a reference for a comparable uncontrolled price.

Besides the hierarchy of the TP methods, the *A AG* case describes another relevant TP issue in the banking and asset management sector. It presents the most common reason for the denial of the CUP application. In addition, there are rare instances in which tax authorities accept adjustments to CUPs that should eliminate the effect of differences.[107] Such adjustments tend to be treated by tax authorities as discretionary.[108]

104. OECD, *Report on the Attribution of Profits to Permanent Establishments* (Paris: OECD Publishing, 2010), Part III, para. 119.
105. UN TPM, para. 10.1.6.3.
106. *Ibid.*
107. *See* Jens Wittendorff, *Transfer Pricing and the Arm's Length Principle in International Tax Law*, pp. 715 et seq. (Kluwer Law International 2010).
108. US Tax Court, 13 November 1985, *Paccar Inc. v. Commissioner*, 85 TC 754 (1985).

4.3.2 *Transactional Profit Split Method*

In the banking and asset management sector, highly interrelated contributions or those that are interdependent upon each other often occur. Typically, financial institutions involved in private banking, asset management, and investment banking at the same time use an integrated business model. In such a scenario, the application of the TPSM (residual analysis) as the most suitable TP method should be considered.[109] The TPSM might be applied to any type of activities in the banking sector. What is decisive for the application of the TPSM is that two or more associated enterprises make non-routine contributions to an intra-group transaction.[110] However, it is sometimes difficult to prove that the level of integration is so high that one-sided TP methods (e.g., CUPs and CPM) cannot be equally effectively used in the same situation. If both a traditional transaction method and a transactional profit method can be applied in an equally reliable manner, the traditional transaction method is preferable to the transactional profit method.[111] In addition, the application of the CUP method has priority over any other traditional TP method. Such a clear hierarchy of TP methods tends to give tax authorities strong arguments against any application of the TPSM, especially when one-sided TP methods allocate more profit to the location where the tax audit takes place. Frequently, the application of the two options (PSM versus CUPs with CPM) results in different profit allocation between involved entities. The selection of the most suitable TP method is a common field of disputes in tax audits not only in the banking sector.[112] Even if several authors and TP practitioners believe that the PSM is a TP method that will be increasingly used in the future,[113] it tends to be difficult to defend it in a tax audit as the most suitable TP method against traditional methods.[114] The OECD addressed the issue in paragraph 2.116 of the OECD TPG18. According to OECD TPG, the following aspects indicate that the TPSM is the most applicable method to apply:

- unique and valuable contributions (e.g., unique and valuable intangibles) by several parties of the transaction;[115]
- highly integrated operations or business model;[116]
- lack of comparable data for functions that build the integrated business model; i.e., it is not possible to apply one-sided methods for all transactions;[117] and
- industry practice.[118]

109. Paragraph 2.138 OECD TPG.
110. *See* Jens Wittendorff, *Transfer Pricing and the Arm's Length Principle in International Tax Law*, p. 755 (Kluwer Law International 2010).
111. Paragraph 2.3 OECD TPG.
112. Paragraph 2.2 OECD TPG and UN TPM, 4.1.1.
113. *See* Raffaele Petruzzi, Claire (Xue) Peng, *The Profit Split Method: Historical Evolution and BEPS Insights*, Transfer Pricing International, pp. 44-54, Volume 1/February (2017).
114. *See* Magdalena Bonna, Iris Burgstaller, Birgit Fassbender, Eva Frehner, Ulrike Wolff-Seeger, *Profit Split in der Praxis*, Transfer Pricing International, pp. 255-258, Volume 6/December (2021).
115. OECD TPG Chapter 2 Parts III.C-III.D.
116. *Ibid.*, para. 2.120.
117. *Ibid.*
118. *Ibid.*

Example

Company A, located in Country X and Company B, located in Country Y, are part of the ABC Group. ABC Group is in the business of banking and uses an integrated business model in the area of structured products. Company A structures the composition of products and bears the entire hedging risk from the emission of structured products. Company B (head office) and its branches are the major distribution entities. In addition, Company B develops a digital platform for the distribution of structured products. As both Company A and Company B and its branches make unique and valuable contributions to a highly integrated business model in the area of structured products, several criteria for the application of the TPSM are fulfilled. A residual analysis would be applicable.

Overall, the application of the TPSM residual analysis is connected with significant discretionary elements.[119] In the implementation phase of this analysis, it must be decided which revenues and costs relate to the integrated business model. Otherwise stated, a link between generated revenues, incurred costs, and functions has to be established. Already in this step, certain pragmatic simplifications have to be made, e.g., in terms of allocating overhead costs for the use of the infrastructure. Since the method is applied to entities located in several countries with different local accounting standards, it is necessary to bring their financials to the same accounting standard, e.g., the IFRS.[120] The deviation between financials prepared according to local GAAPs and the IFRS figures lead to difficult discussions in tax audits. The tax authorities usually cannot establish an exact link between the figures used in the residual analysis (TPSM) and the local GAAPs that are used as the starting point for the determination of taxable profits.

In addition, there is still lack of guidance for the allocation of the residual profits (i.e., the part that remains after routine functions are remunerated) in the residual analysis approach. The OECD partly addressed the topic in paragraphs 2.152 and 2.166 of the OECD TPG. Usually, the allocation of the residual profit among the parties is based on the relative value of their non-routine contributions. Should there be more of them (e.g., performance of several valuable functions and major risk assumption), the profit attributable to any contributions should be determined based on a CUP reference whenever possible.[121] Fortunately, the banking and asset management sectors benefit from a broad availability of internal and external CUPs so that, at least for some valuable contributions, a CUP reference could be used. This is usually the case for product structuring or portfolio management-related activities and distribution.

119. *See* Jens Wittendorff, *Transfer Pricing and the Arm's Length Principle in International Tax Law*, p. 755 (Kluwer Law International 2010) as well as *Eli Lilly & Co. v. Commissioner*, 31 August 1988, 856 F 2d 855 (7th Cir. 1988).

120. *Ibid.*, para. 2.123.

121. *Ibid.*, para. 2.167.

Example (continues from previous example)

To determine CUP references for Company A and Company B and its branches, either of the agreements with third parties for product structuring could be used as internal CUPs. Alternatively, a search for independent providers of product structuring services could be performed in commercial databases, e.g., Thomson Reuters Lipper.

Should there remain a high-value adding function and risk assumption that contribute to the creation of residual profit, the OECD suggests in paragraph 2.171 of the OECD PSM Report that profit-splitting factors be based on:

- assets or capital (e.g., intangibles or fixed assets); or
- costs (e.g., relative spending and/or investment in key areas such as marketing and distribution);[122] or
- others (e.g., sales or salaries).[123]

Example (continues from previous example)

After remunerating product structuring based on a CUP reference, the question arises of how to remunerate the remaining high-value adding functions, i.e., distribution. Should there be no internal or external CUP reference available, the residual profit could be split according to sales revenues generated by Company B and all of its individual branches.

Moreover, it is also worth mentioning that obtaining a corresponding adjustment (i.e., reduction of taxable income)[124] in the remaining locations – after one country made a TP primary adjustment – participating in the TPSM (residual analysis) might be burdensome or even partly impossible. This is particularly the case if there is a disagreement about the appropriateness of the primary adjustment in principle and regarding the amount[125] or substantially different statutes of limitations in individual countries. The more countries that participate in the TPSM (residual analysis), the more difficult it is to obtain the corresponding adjustments. Should there be a dispute between participating countries concerning the amount and character of the adjustment, the MAP according to Article 25 OECD MC might be invoked among treaty partners.[126]

122. *Ibid.*, para. 2.171.
123. *Ibid.*, para. 2.172.
124. *See* Jens Wittendorff, *Transfer Pricing and the Arm's Length Principle in International Tax Law*, p. 241 (Kluwer Law International 2010).
125. Paragraph 6 of OECD Commentary on para. 9 of OECD MTC and para. 4.35 OECD TPG.
126. Paragraph 11 of the OECD Commentary on para. 9 OECD MC.

Example (continues from previous example)

In 2022, the tax authorities in Country Y make an upward TP adjustment of Company B's profits for FY 2015 attributable to the distribution function in the residual analysis (TPSM). In Country Z where the first branch of Company B is located, a corresponding adjustment is not granted as the tax authorities do not agree that the adjusted remuneration for the head office in Country Y is at arm's length. Recourse could be taken to a MAP if there is a need to reach a consensus between tax authorities in Countries Y and Z. In Countries U and V where the second and third branches are located, the statutes of limitations for corresponding adjustments have already elapsed. Thus, no adjustment is possible either. Only Country X where Company A has its seat is willing to make a corresponding adjustment.

4.4 Interaction of VAT and TP

One of the political goals pursued when introducing a modern VAT system is to achieve a non-cumulative cascade turnover tax aspect of the system. It should be always the final consumer who – irrespective of the business model – bears the VAT burden. An enterprise should have the possibility to either claim an input VAT refund suffered on his purchases or offset the input VAT against the output VAT in respect of his sales. The process of nullifying the VAT impact on enterprises is known as VAT neutrality. Any modern VAT system worldwide would generally ensure that the concept of neutrality is adhered to in order to avoid double taxation.[127]

However, the concept of neutrality usually fails in the banking and asset management sector. This is because some of the functions performed (e.g., provision of loans, trading in securities, or distribution and management of investment funds)[128] are VAT exempt. Therefore, the VAT-registered enterprise performing such functions does not impose VAT on such revenues. At the same time, the enterprise is allowed to claim an input VAT refund only in the proportion of the VATable revenues to total revenues (i.e., VATable/(VATable plus exempt revenues)). The rest of input VAT that cannot be refunded is treated as an additional cost of conducting banking and asset management business. Such a constellation often influences the choice of a service recipient in the banking and asset management sector. In other words, financial services enterprises tend to provide VATable functions to related entities with a high-input VAT refund quote to minimize the input VAT loss.

127. *See* Michael Lang, Ine Leujene, *Improving VAT/GST, Designing a Simple and Fraud Proof Tax System*, pp. 1, 23, 111 and 138 (IBFD 2014).
128. Article 21/2/19/a, c and f Swiss VAT Act.

Example

Company A, Company B and Company C are part of the ABC Group. ABC Group is in the business of banking. Company A is a broker and investment advisor. Consequently, it provides both chargeable and VAT-exempt services. Company B carries out wealth management advisory services that are taxable. Company C is a product developing company that is considering whether Company A or Company B should provide distribution support (i.e., advisory and marketing) services for Company C products. As Company B's input VAT refund quote is higher than that of Company A, ABC Group will choose to channel the distribution function via Company B.

4.5 Guarantees and Cash Pools

In the banking sector, structured products and corporate bonds are often issued from offshore locations with beneficial withholding tax regime for interests. For this purpose, an SPE is established that is disclosed in the investment prospects as the issuer. As investors (i.e., individuals and institutions) in structured products bear not only market risk but also the issuer default risk, they usually require that guarantees are provided to an SPE to reduce the latter to the minimum. The increased sensitivity to issuer default risk is a rather new phenomenon in the structured product market that appeared in the wake of the insolvency of the investment bank Lehman Brothers Inc. in 2008. The decrease of the issuer default risk via guarantees from other group entities positively influences the creditworthiness of the SPE. The guarantee is granted either by the top holding company of the banking group (i.e., a downstream guarantee) or by the entity with the full banking licence depending on their ratings (i.e., a side-stream guarantee). The improved creditworthiness of the SPE does not a have direct impact on the interest yield paid to investors – in contrast to borrowing of funds[129] – of such products; it is rather the precondition for finding investors at all. Nevertheless, the same rules apply for the determination of arm's length remuneration, as for intra-group financial guarantees that increase the debt capacity of the borrower and enable him to obtain a more favourable interest rate.[130] The issuer guarantees belong to explicit guarantees and usually take the form of downstream or side-stream guarantees. There are several approaches of how to determine the arm's length guarantee fee. Most often, the internal, external or hypothetic CUP method is applied. Frequently, banks acting in the area of international trade financing provide third-party clients guarantees.[131]

129. Paragraph 10.155 OECD TPG.
130. *Ibid.*, para. 10.157.
131. R. Petruzzi, *Transfer Pricing and Intra-group Financial Transactions*, in: Lang, Cottani, Petruzzi, Storck (eds), *Fundamentals of Transfer Pricing: A Practical Guide* (Vienna: Wolters Kluwer, 2018), p. 409.

Example

Company A, located in Country X, is in the business of engineering solutions. Company A intends to be voluntarily registered for the VAT Country Y to operate its new logistics centre. For this purpose, Company A has to appoint a provider of accounting services as its tax representative in Country Y. The tax representation role in Country Y is connected with private liability and severe penalties for any VAT compliance mistakes. In practice, the VAT representative will require from Company A a guarantee from a bank offering international trading services. If sufficiently comparable, the guarantee fee charged to Company A could be used as an internal CUP reference for other guarantees given within the banking group.

In addition, in the banking sector, the use of keep-well agreements is quite common. This is, for example, the case if a financial institution (A SPA) with its seat in Country A intends to sell products that should be listed on the stock exchange in the same country. Usually, the stock exchange in Country A requires a keep-well agreement between A SPA and A AG (i.e., another group entity with a full banking licence). A keep-well agreement belongs to the category of implicit guarantees that does not require any guarantee fee.[132]

Next, banks provide larger industrial MNEs with the necessary infrastructure and function as enablers of notional and physical cash pooling. In contrast to industrial MNEs, though, the use of cash pools for its own intra-group needs is less prevalent in the banking and asset management sector. This could be ascribed to several factors. First, the primary purpose of a cash pool is the optimization of liquidity and working capital needs.[133] Whereas working capital[134] belongs to the KPI of industrial MNEs, it is less relevant for banks and asset managers. In fact, the most important KPIs for banks and asset managers are: Assets under Management, Cost/Income Ratio, Net New Money; Tier 1 Capital and Return on Assets. Second, within a banking group, only entities with a full banking licence – so-called booking platforms – are allowed to keep deposits and current accounts of other group companies. Therefore, there are only a small number of booking platforms within one banking group with regional relevance. The liquidity optimization takes place only among them. Third, banks can optimize their interest expense via borrowings from national banks.

4.6 Intangibles and CCAs

In contrast to industrial MNEs, banks and asset managers usually do not have patents or industrial aptitude, nor do they perform research and development activities to

132. Paragraph 10.164 OECD TPG.
133. *See*: Santander, Standard cash-management tools that support a customer's liquidity and working capital requirements, https://www.santandercb.co.uk/financing/corporate-lending/specialised-finance/sweeping-and-pooling (last accessed 30 January 2022).
134. Working Capital = Current assets – Current liabilities.

invent, e.g., proprietary ingenuity. However, banks and asset management institutions sometimes develop digital platforms and mobile phones applications. Should the development of such a software solution require that participants share the costs, risks, and the rights to results in the project, the rules for the CCA apply.[135] The participating entities may exploit the results individually to generate revenue from the sale of services incorporating the software solution.[136] In such concepts, it is essential to define contractual terms from the beginning of the project (i.e., legal and economic ownership of the software solution and cost coverage). A solid record of all investments made by involved parties is – together with an intra-group agreement – the necessary minimum to defend such a CCA concept in a future tax audit. The exact evidence of costs shared between participating entities is decisive for the determination of the ratio in which revenues from the use of the developed platform will be shared.[137] Typically, the revenue takes the form of a platform fee that is paid by third-party users. It is also worth mentioning that not only the development costs but also the maintenance costs for ongoing updates and upgrades should be considered.

Example

Company A, located in Country X, and Company B, located in Country Y, are part of the ABC Group. ABC Group is involved in the business of banking. Company A and Company B agreed on the common development of a software platform that will enable Company B's wealth management clients to create tailor-made structured products by combining a wide variety of underlying financial instruments (e.g., corporate bonds with options). Both Company A and Company B employed software developers and portfolio managers that commonly program the new software tool. In the initial phase of development, both parties concluded in a written contract that they will split the future benefits from the platform between each other in the same ratio in which they bear the development costs. The development took four years and the related development cost amounted to CU 50 Million. The project manager maintained records of the development and maintenance costs incurred. Company A invested 60% (CU 30 Million) and Company B 40% (CU 20 Million). Starting from the fifth year, a platform fee from third-party banks – that will enable their clients to create their own products – will be received. The total revenue received from third banks amounts to CU 1 Million in Year 5. Company A receives CU 600,000 and Company B CU 400,000. In a tax audit, Company A and Company B substantiate the arm's length character of the revenue split be presenting the CCA agreement and the overview of related incurred costs.

135. OECD TPG, paras 8.1 et seq. and UN TPM, section 8.1 *See* Jens Wittendorff, *Transfer Pricing and the Arm's Length Principle in International Tax Law*, pp. 537 et seq. (Kluwer Law International 2010).
136. *Ibid.*
137. OECD TPG, para. 8.5.

Finally, banks and asset managers often have a brand structure in which the group name plays a central role. The economic owner of the brand is usually the entity that bears the brand-related costs[138] and employs the brand management team. The same team performs the development, enhancement, maintenance and exploitation activities of the DEMPE[139] or D(A)EMPE[140] concepts. Conversely, the brand protection activity is carried out by the group legal team and partly even outsourced to specialized IP law firms when it regards the breach of IP rights and litigation cases. Sometimes, the protection component is performed and managed by another group company.[141] In such a case, the protection function is remunerated with a CPM (e.g., cost + 5%) as it is a low-value adding administrative function for which the OECD allows applying the markup safe harbour.[142] The entity employing the brand management team and bearing, e.g., the branding campaigns costs is entitled to receive the royalties paid by other group companies.[143] The economic ownership of an intangible for TP purposes will usually be ascribed to a single entity in an MNE.[144] Sometimes, in tax audits, the question arises of which marketing costs are brand-building costs as not all marketing costs result in a creation or enhancement of an intangible.[145] In banking and asset management TP, product-related marketing costs are considered only partially as brand-building costs. As such, they should be only partially borne by the economic owner of the brand. On the contrary, brand campaign costs create or enhance the brand fully.

5 CONCLUSIONS

The term 'banking sector' usually includes retail banking, wealth management, and investment banking. Retail banking offers services such as savings and checking accounts, mortgages, debit/credit cards, and certificates of deposit. In this banking area, the focus is on the individual consumer. Notably, there is no minimum threshold (i.e., minimum deposit value) to qualify as a client in retail banking. Several online banks even provide retail banking services to customers purely through the internet and mobile applications.

Wealth management offers services such as investing and portfolio management, tax and pension scheme advisory services, insurance, and trust and estate planning. In contrast to retail banking, wealth management provides services only to exclusive clientele, and some exclusive wealth managers only accept clients with at least USD 1

138. *Ibid.*, para. 6.48 (Ch. VI).
139. Paragraph 6.45.
140. 2017 UN TPM, paras B.1.6.12. et seq.
141. Paragraph 6.42. *See* Raoul Stocker, Patrick Schmid, *Markenrechte: Entschädigung des rechtlichen Eigentümers vs. Ausübung von DEMPE Funktionen*, Transfer Pricing International, pp. 216-220, Volume 4/October (2018).
142. Paragraph 7.16; UN TPM, 5.5.2.
143. *See* Jens Wittendorff, *Transfer Pricing and the Arm's Length Principle in International Tax Law*, p. 624 (Kluwer Law International 2010).
144. *Ibid.*
145. OECD TPG, para. 6.11.

million to invest. The degree of digital strategy implementation among private banks varies and depends on the digital affinity of their clients.

Investment banking provides financial services to corporate entities rather than to individuals. It is the area of banking focusing on M&A, business restructurings, spin-offs, stock splits, share buy-backs, capital raising transactions, and secondary stock or bond issues (e.g., structured products and derivatives). Occasionally, investment banking also covers commodity trade financing. Investment banking has also found its way to digitalization. On the one hand, AI helps to create M&A prediction models or origination ideas for corporate actions. On the other hand, a wide range of investment banks and fintechs offer digital platforms for structured products. They enable investors to create tailored financial products by combining selected underlying instruments (e.g., bonds, options and shares). In addition, other digital platforms link demand with the matching offer for private placements and credits.

Some integrated universal banks still also operate asset management businesses. However, in the last decade, there was a clear separation trend observed in financial services. In an asset management business, the clients comprise institutions such as public or private pension funds, insurance companies, and financial intermediaries. Their investments are structured either as investment funds or as mandates and investment advisory solutions (e.g., portfolio design or asset allocation).

When a bank is insolvent, it can create difficulties for financial markets and the real economy. Therefore, governments regulate the banking sector. Such regulations also make banks hold shock absorbers referred to as capital to help deal with bad investments. There frequently are minimum capital requirements for operating banking businesses in individual countries. Finally, a financial institution that wants to operate a banking business usually needs a banking licence that presents a legal prerequisite. The banking sector has been in transition for many years, especially since the onset of the financial crises. Many banks operate in a difficult macroeconomic environment with negative interest rates and a demanding investment situation. Moreover, the implementation of national and increasingly international regulatory requirements are reflected in banks' margins and cost structures. Regardless of their size and diversification, all banks have to find their way through this labyrinth of regulatory developments, as failure to comply means risking sanctions and fines.

The term 'value creation' assists in understanding key enterprise functions performed, major risks assumed, and valuable assets used in the banking and asset management sectors. It is common to label individual functions as 'front-office', 'middle-office', and 'back-office' in both business areas depending on whether the activity is linked with client contact. Although such a categorization is not decisive for the determination of which function is a key function from a TP perspective, it helps to better understand the entire value chain. The business models with specific key functions and routine functions vary depending on the financial services area.

The approach used in the 2010 OECD PE Report, Part II (Banks) is also applied to intra-group functions between legally distinct and separate enterprises in retail banking. However, it is worth mentioning that some of the functions presented in the 2010 OECD PE Report, Part II as KERT became – due to increasing automation and digitalization – less important in the retail banking value creation. As such, their position closely resembles that of a routine qualification. A related point to consider is that retail banks conduct fewer cross-border transactions than, e.g., private banks, asset managers, or investment banks. This is a result of the retail banking regulations and the necessary capital requirements for each country in which deposits from the public are accepted.

In contrast to retail banking, wealth management uses Part III (Global Trading of Financial Instruments) of 2010 OECD PE Report as a major reference for classifying functions. Although the value chain for wealth management shows some similarities with retail banking, there are a few differences in the value creation. First, the role of client relationship management as such is much more important. This is because wealth management clients usually have higher expectations in terms of service quality and performance. Client relationship management is a key entrepreneurial function in both the client acquisition and retention phases. Second, portfolio management, product development, and the related risk management encompass a much broader universe of products than in retail banking. The remaining functions can be treated as routine or low-value adding functions. Another important aspect to consider is that digitalization of the industry, the broad availability of investment information on the internet, and the generational shift among wealthy clients to digital natives gave rise to a new private banking segment that does not seek any human interaction with relationship managers.

Similar to private banking, investment banking-structured products uses Part III (Global Trading of Financial Instruments) of 2010 OECD PE Report as a major reference for categorizing functions. Although the value chain for investment banking-financial products resembles those for retail banking and wealth management, there are few significant differences in the value creation. First, client relationship management has more facets, and there are more distribution channels than in private banking. Besides the sales to the high wealth individuals, structured products are also offered to professional investors (e.g., hedge funds, pension funds, state funds or traders, and portfolio managers). Even if personal relationships still play some role, it is rather the ability to swiftly react to market trends and develop new products with attractive performance that are the key functions; therefore, the actual role of client relationship managers is rather limited. In other words, the key function is the ability to create a tailor-made structured product consisting of individual components depending on the underlying instruments and the requested payoff structure. Second, risk management together with risk assumption also plays a key role as some of the products require that the bank includes the underlying instruments (e.g., corporate bonds or shares) in its balance sheet.

Like wealth management and investment banking-structured products, asset management uses Part III (Global Trading of Financial Instruments) of 2010 OECD PE Report as a major reference for classifying functions. Despite the similar value chains of wealth management and investment banking-financial products, there are a few significant divergences in the value creation of asset management. First, although the client relationship management is still a high-value adding function, it is less important than portfolio management. This is because institutional clients (i.e., state and private pension funds) tend to focus on performance and fee structure to achieve long-term pension scheme goals. Even if personal relationships still play some role, it is rather the strong investment performance that is decisive for an institutional client.

One of the major difficulties in the TP of the banking and asset management sectors is the lack of up-to-date detailed guidance on the categorization of services functions regarding value creation. The 2010 OECD PE Report, Parts II and III are still used as a reference for classifying some banking and asset management functions as routine or non-routine. However, due to the constant evolution of business models and offered products, some parts of the report became outdated. In addition, many banking functions are missing in Parts II and III. Second, there is an increasing trend in the banking and asset management sector to outsource functions either intra-group or to third parties. When significant location savings are derived further to a business restructuring, the question arises of whether and how the location savings should be shared among the affected group entities. Third, there are many external and internal CUPs available in a banking and asset management business. The TPSM residual analysis is a frequently applied TP method. However, it is sometimes difficult to prove that the level of integration is so high that one-sided TP methods cannot be equally effectively used. In addition, the application of a TPSM residual analysis is connected with significant discretionary elements. It applies especially to the determination of cost and revenues that relate to the integrated business model and the allocation of the residual profits. Another aspect to consider is the interaction between the VAT and TP. Next, banks and asset managers use the CCA to develop platforms and software solutions. Finally, banks and asset managers often apply the DEMPE or DAEMPE concept to their brand structures.

CHAPTER 16

Transfer Pricing in the Commodities Trade Sector

Kalale Mambwe

1 INTRODUCTION

The increasing integration of cross-border transactions in the commodity trade sector and commodity trading has, in the past decade, effectuated the way that these transactions are analysed at every stage of the value chain. The commodity trade sector encompasses transactions involving mining and extraction of natural resources such as oil, gas, and minerals as well as agricultural commodities such as wheat, coffee, cocoa, fruit, sugar, and meat. TP issues relating to intra-group transactions in the commodity trade sector are often present at every stage of the value chain from the conception, that is, the production process and to the marketing and sale of the commodity. This chapter will focus on the general approach to identifying TP issues throughout the value chain of commodity sectors with a specific focus on the mining sector with relevant examples to this effect. It will also discuss the approach that the tax authorities and policymakers may take in their risk analysis of the identified TP issues.

2 VALUE CREATION IN THE COMMODITIES TRADE SECTOR

2.1 The Commodity Value Chain Lifecycle

A value chain has been defined as the range of activities or processes that are required to transform a product or service from conception through the different phases of production, delivery to the final consumer, and final disposal after use.[1] The value chain, therefore, brings a commodity from the initial input supply stage to the final market destination, i.e., the target market. The UN TPM emphasizes the role that a value chain plays in a business by stating the aim of MNE as that of maximizing profit that it achieves through its production and sales. The starting point being the understanding of the company's value chain which links the set of activities the business performs to create value. The following guidance was provided in the UN TPM:[2]

> An MNE's value chain is fundamentally used to convert its economic resources of lower value into economic resources of higher value, which may involve the following steps:
> (1) Mapping out a generic value chain for the industry;
> (2) Mapping out an MNE's specific value chain;
> (3) Comparing the generic value chain to the group's value chain and analysing the differences which may explain why an MNE has a competitive advantage over its competitors;
> (4) Distinguishing between an MNE's main functions and its support functions;
> (5) Identifying and understanding which of the MNE's main functions are critical to the success of the organization (i.e., a critical success factor);

1. Raphael Kaplinsky & Mike Morris, A Handbook For Value Chain Research 2002, Brighton Institute of Development Studies.
2. *See* para. 1.3.3.3 of the UN TPM.

(6) Identifying and understanding which activities performed by an MNE add value to the goods and services it produces, and which activities distinguish the MNE from its competitors, i.e., value-adding activities; and
(7) Understanding and confirming how the various functions across the value chain are split by the MNE between its various constituent legal entities.

TP in the commodity industry has undeniably claimed more limelight in the past decade. This limelight is attributed to the risks associated with each process at every point in the value chain of the commodity industry. Evidently, in order to accurately identify the commercial or financial association between related parties in this business, it is critical to understand the operations of the industry sector in which the entity and the MNE under evaluation belong to. This requires having a reasonable understanding of the factors affecting the performance of the business and other businesses operating in that sector associated to it, the conditions under which they operate, and the economically relevant factors and circumstances of the business.

The process of the trade of commodities including silver, gold, copper, etc., often involves performing different support functions by other related parties such as providing financing, technical support, and marketing. The process may also involve the transfer of assets (mining rights) or intermediate mineral products (such as ore, crushed ore, the concentrates, or the refined mineral) to other related parties along the value chain. This chapter, as mentioned, mainly focuses on the value chain of mining and hence analyses the mining chain life cycle in detail.

2.2 The Mining Value Chain Lifecycle

The mining value chain life cycle of a fully integrated mining entity has seven main components starting from acquisition and exploration to the sale of the product. The extent of the integration depends on several factors in mining such as the type of mineral commodity. Another factor considered is whether the size of the mineral resource or deposit warrants investment in processing facilities such as a concentrator, smelter, or refinery. Each stage of the mining life cycle contains distinct processes with different potential TP issues. Figure 16.1 illustrates a typical mining value chain.

Figure 16.1 Mining Value Chain: Phase 1-Phase 7

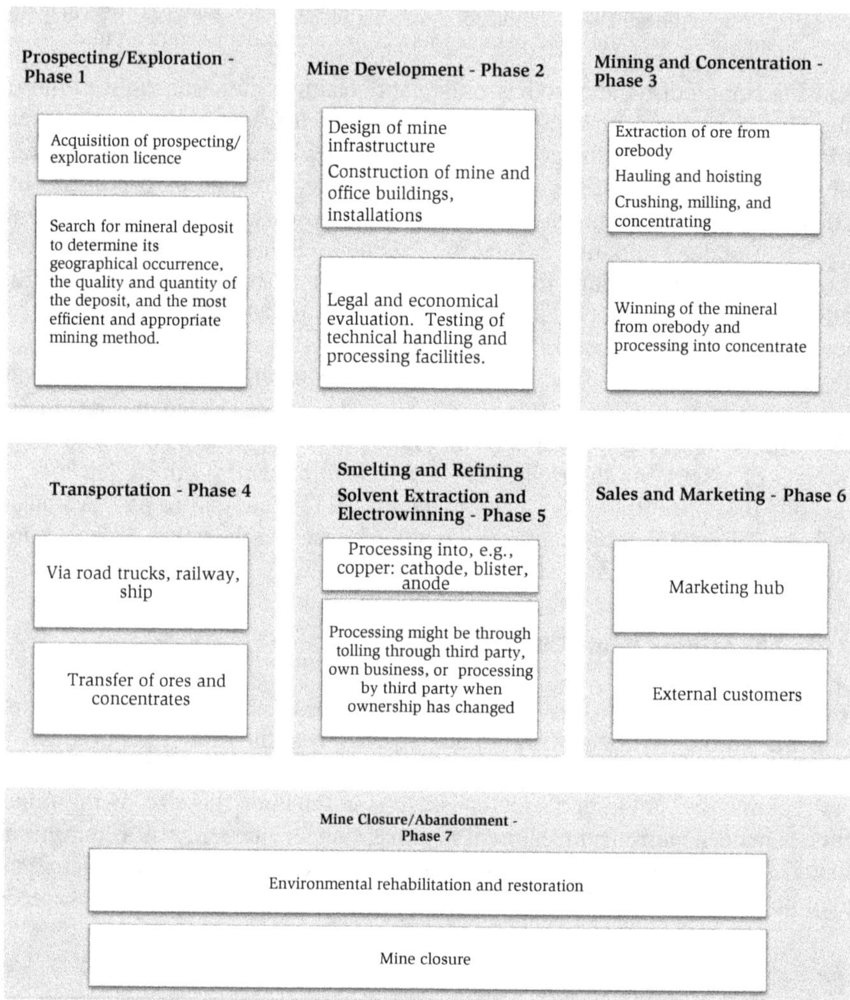

Source: Modified Adaptation from – Transfer Pricing in Mining with a Focus on Africa: A Reference Guide for Practitioners (Guj, Martin, Maybee, & Cawood, 2017).

2.3 The Phases in the Mining Value Chain

2.3.1 The Paragraphs Below Discuss in Further Detail the Phases in the Mining Value Chain Outlined in Figure 16.1

Acquisition and Exploration

The first step to this stage is the acquisition of the right from the host country's government to explore the land for mineral deposits and exploit them if found. The exploration and prospecting stage is typically carried out by an exploration company under an exploration right or licence. These rights or licences are either granted directly from the government department in charge of mining or acquired from another company at a consideration. The acquisition of prospecting and exploration licences normally forms the first stage of any mining operation. In broad terms, prospecting operations are primarily for the purpose of searching for mineral deposits (the orebody). Exploration operations are, however, mainly for the purpose of defining the quantity. This involves the geographic mapping and determination of the quality of the mineral deposit and, subsequently, the value of a mineral deposit.

The two processes involve the mathematical resource estimation of the size and grade of the mineral deposit. This estimation is used to conduct a prefeasibility study to determine the theoretical economics of the ore deposit. This identifies at an early stage whether further investment in estimation and engineering studies is warranted and identifies key risks and areas for further work. This stage is very critical as it allows for the evaluation of the economic viability of the mineral deposits discovered to support the project.

This stage of the lifecycle has the greatest uncertainty and therefore poses significant risk to investments. The assets explored during this stage in mining can only generate profits for the entity in instances when they are leased out or traded in. The time span for prospecting/exploration activities to the eventual commercial production can last up to ten years, and, thus, when the exploration is unsuccessful, the investors bear significant sunk costs of the invested capital funds. Figure 16.2 summarizes the exploration activities discussed above.

Figure 16.2 Exploration Activities

Licensing

- Acquiring the legal right (licence) to explore and exploit for mineral deposit in a host country
- The licences may specify the type of minerals under exploration
- The licence may have a time limit after which it may expire

Exploration and Resource Delineation

- Geographical mapping, determining the economic value of the mineral deposit, and the characteristics of the orebody

Feasibility Study

- Determining the economic viability of any eventual mining based on the level, geographical location of the mineral reserve, and market variables
- Business case is formulated on whether to proceed with mine development
- This leads to commissioning of the mine

Figure 16.2 summarizes the activities in the first phase of any mining operation which is the exploration activities.

2.3.2 Mine Development

Depending on whether the results from the feasibility study taken during the exploration activities indicate that the mining project is commercially and financially viable, the subsequent next stage in the mining value chain is undertaken which is the mine construction and development. The primary purpose of mine development is to create access to the orebody. This stage typically involves additional in-depth geological and geothermal studies that are necessary to target and plot the mine orebody. The stage further reconfirms the economic viability of the mine by analysing the quantity and quality of the mineral ore. It also provides for a more detailed mine design and plan.

This mine development stage is typically very highly capital intensive in terms of the required cash outflows depending on the size and type of mineral resource. The cash flows are required to build a solid asset base in preparation for the mining operations to follow. Mine investment costs can vary considerably between mining operations. This is due to the differences in ore grade, mine sizes, mining method, topography, and ground condition.

At this stage, the mining method of either underground or open-pit mining would have been determined. Generally, underground mine development is considerably more expensive than open-pit mine development per annual tonne of mine ore. This and the high cost of operating underground mines explains why the underground ore bodies must contain a higher percentage of a mineral, such as most copper ore deposits, than open-pit ore bodies to be economically viable.

It is during this stage that environmental impact assessments of the planned mine development on the environment and society are performed, particularly on the surrounding local communities. These assessments are generally included in the mine plan and design.

The required mine infrastructure, mining equipment such as conveyers, crushers, processing plants, and related assets are constructed or procured during this phase of the life cycle in accordance with the architectural, mining, and engineering designs developed under the mine plan. The final phase of mine development is the commissioning of the mine that involves exposure of the mine orebody and trial production. The completion of the construction and development phase up to actual production may take up to four or more years depending on the scale of the operation and mineral product (Figure 16.3).

Figure 16.3 Typical Activities under Mine Development Stage

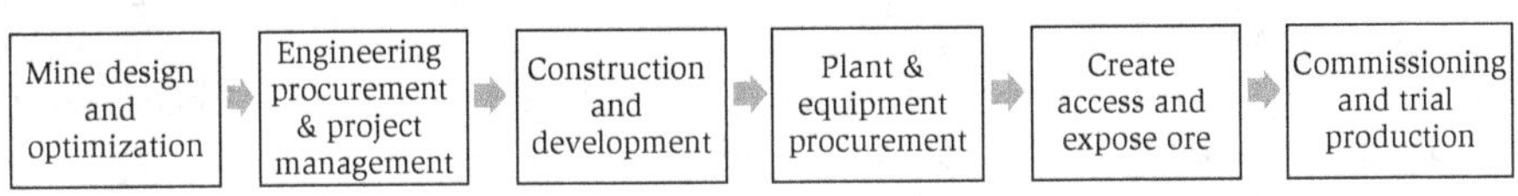

Source: Transfer Pricing in Mining with a Focus on Africa: A Reference Guide for Practitioners.[3]

2.3.3 *Mining and Concentration*

The mining and concentration phase is when the actual production begins from the physical extraction of the ore to hauling, crushing, grading, grinding, and milling to the eventual processing into a concentrate. During this process, the valuable minerals are separated from the ore and transformed into a concentrate as is the case for base metals such as copper, cobalt, and nickel as well as precious metals including gold, palladium, selenium, silver, and platinum. The mining and concentration life, i.e., the mine life, is determined by the quantity and grade of the available mineral resource in a mine that is economically viable for extracting.

Depending on the scale of operation in terms of vertical integration and type of mineral product, a mining company may engage in the following activities in the value chain:

- sale of the bulk ore to a concentrate producer;[4]
- sale of bulk ore to final consumer who may be a related party or third party;[5]

3. Pietro Guj, Stephanie Martin, Bryan Maybee, Frederick Cawood, Boubacar Bocoum, Nishana Gosai, Steef Huibregtse. Transfer Pricing in Mining with a Focus on Africa. A Reference Guide for Practitioners, World Bank, Washington, D. C., 2017.
4. This is typically the case for small mining companies for which the mineral resource cannot economically warrant investment in a mill and concentrator.
5. (i) this would be in cases when the ore already contains the valuable mineral in high proportion and, hence, there is no need for any concentrating but just further crushing and screening. This is the case for most industrial minerals and other bulk commodities like iron ore, limestone,

- sale of concentrates locally or export to a smelting/refinery company;
- toll treatment, i.e., having the concentrate processed by a smelting company (without actually selling the concentrate to it) while maintaining ownership of the concentrate or having a third party, in this case, a smelting company, process it;
- the mining company processes the concentrate in its own smelting/refinery facility.

2.3.4 Transportation

This phase involves the transportation of mineral products to the market for further processing. Some companies may outsource this service while others may own specialized transport systems or ports. The mode of transport used is dependent on the value and volume of the mineral products.

Mineral products with high value and low volume such as precious metals and selected gemstones like diamonds and emeralds may be airlifted from the mine site to the market. This mode of transport is efficient and safer due to security concerns. Bulk minerals that may be both of high value and low value may be transported via rail, trucks, and as shipments (sea freight) depending on the geographical location of the mine and the market.

2.3.5 Smelting, Refining, Solvent Extraction, and Electrowinning

During this phase of the value chain, minerals are recovered and extracted into their separate chemical elements. For instance, in the case of copper, the typical mineral products extracted are anodes, blisters, and cathodes that are produced depending on the applicable mineral processing methodology used.

Copper is most commonly present in the earth's crust in the form of copper-iron sulphides and copper sulphide minerals such as chalcopyrite, bornite, and chalcocite. There are low concentrations of these minerals in an orebody. Typical copper ore contains 0.5 % copper (open-pit mines) to 1 % or 2 % copper (underground mines). Pure copper metal is produced from these ores by concentration, smelting, and refining. Copper is also found in oxidized minerals (carbonates, oxides, hydroxyl-silicates, sulphates) but to a lesser degree. Copper metal is usually produced from these minerals by hydrometallurgical methods. This method is also used to produce copper metal from chalcocite. A third major source of copper is scrap copper and copper alloys. The production of copper from recycled objects/materials is 10 % or 15 % of mine production. In addition, there is considerable remelting and refining of scrap generated during fabrication and manufacture.

---

phosphate rock, and coal or; (ii) in the case of gemstones for which the valuable mineral is extracted through washing, sorting, cutting, grading, and polishing.

In summary, the mineral ore is usually a copper oxide or sulphide, and the steps of extraction include the following: (i) smelting and refining, and (ii) leaching, solvent extraction, and electrowinning.

Copper sulphide ore is normally found in both sedimentary and igneous rocks at appropriate depths and is typically won through open-pit or underground mining. The processing stage is illustrated in Figure 16.4.

Figure 16.4 Smelting and Refining

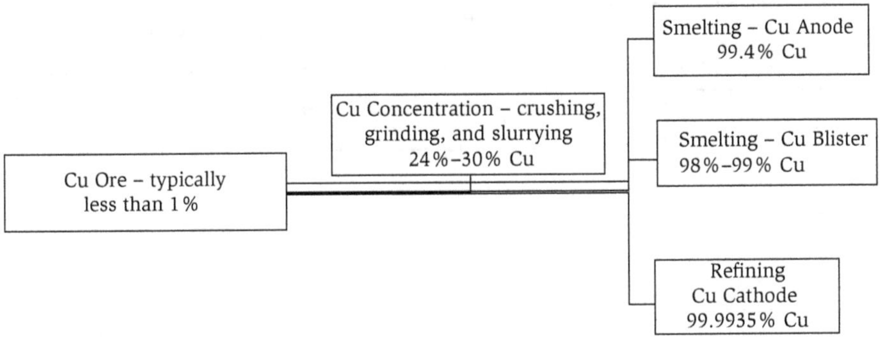

The process proceeds with the crushing and grinding of the ore to remove the gangue which will be composed of silica, iron, and other contaminants and is followed by slurring, thereby increasing the copper content in the concentrate to an average contained copper of 20%-30%. The concentrate undergoes smelting with two possible products depending on the extent of processing, specifically, copper anode that has 99.4% copper content or copper blister with approximately 98%-99% copper. The copper anode or blister can further be refined into copper cathode which is the purest form of copper with 99.9935% copper content. During the refining process, slimes and other valuable elements such as precious metals and cobalt are separated.

Copper oxide ore typically occurs near the earth's surface, can be at a depth of up to 600 metres in the ground, and is largely extracted through open-pit mining followed by leaching processes, solvent extraction, and finally electrowinning into copper cathode (Figure 16.5).

Figure 16.5 Leaching, Solvent Extraction and Electrowinning

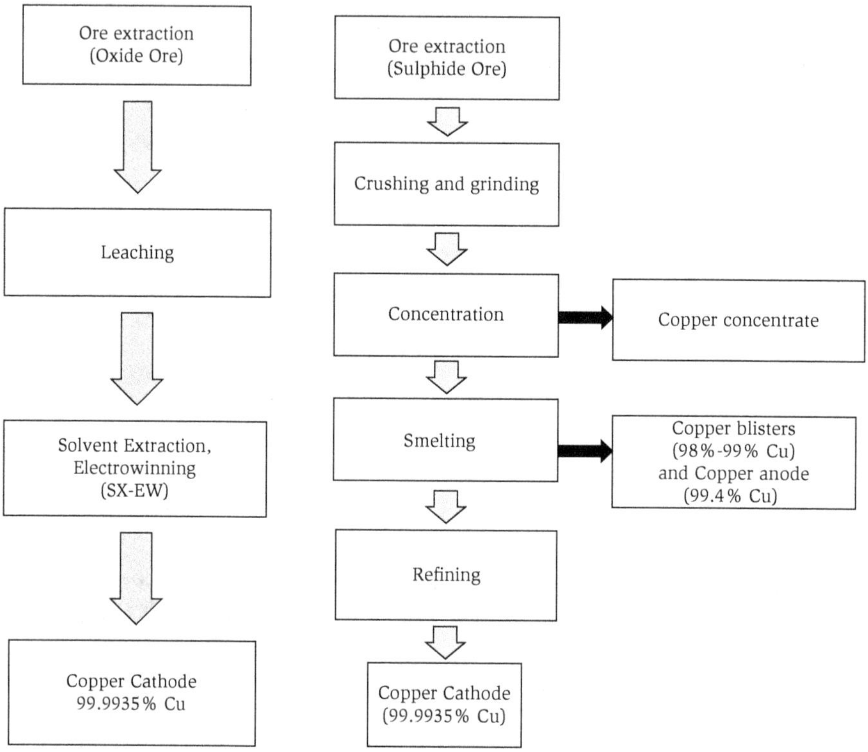

As shown above, copper can be refined into its final product as a copper cathode, copper anode, or copper blister with the latter two having a possibility of still containing valuable minerals such as precious metals and cobalt.

2.3.6 Sales and Marketing

This phase can involve several functions ranging from fulfilling orders, invoicing, devising, and implementing marketing strategies, market research depending on the commodity, and dealing with distribution regarding transportation of the product. Some of these functions are performed in-house, while others are done within a centralized MNE group company by what is commonly referred to as a marketing hub. The other phases of the mining value chain may involve other centralized group functions depending on the structure the MNE takes; these may be procurement hubs and other centralized entities for the provision of different services in administration, IT, accounting, etc. In some instances, the MNE may centralize some of these functions by splitting them into: (1) profit centres, (2) cost centres, (3) expenditure centres, and so forth. Each oversees its respective function such as the capital market, R&D, and logistics.[6]

2.3.7 *Mine Closure and Abandonment*

After the mineral resource is depleted or no longer economical to mine, the mine may be abandoned leading to its closure. Under this stage of mine closure, the assets and the mine are decommissioned mostly adhering to agreed environmental guidelines contained in the Environmental Impact Assessment commenced[7] prior to mine development and also the Environmental Management Plan undertaken during the course of the active life of the mine (production phase). The activities relating to environmental rehabilitation and restoration may impact a significant area of land depending on whether the mine was an open-pit or underground mine and the scale of mining assets that would require removal and disposal such as conveyor belts, railway tracks, and processing plants. Typically, open-pit mines require work that is much more extensive than underground mines largely due to the higher volumes of waste rock and tailings that need to be moved. It should be noted, however, that some of the activities relating to rehabilitation and restoration can be performed during the other stages of life cycle of the mine preceding the closure stage depending on the type of mining method employed. Table 16.1 highlights the activities that might be undertaken during mine closure.

Table 16.1 Mine Closure

- Backfilling by covering landfills with topsoil and planting vegetation thereafter
- Tailings dams left to evaporate, then covered with waste rock, clay, and soil in order to stabilize tailings waste
- Open pits filled with water creating dams and also fencing the pits to prevent access
- Waste dumps fenced off to prevent livestock denuding them of vegetation
- Waste dumps flattened to further stabilize them against erosion
- Mine is covered with a layer of clay to prevent exposure to rain and oxygen from the air that can oxidize the sulphides to produce sulphuric acid

Source: UN Handbook on Taxation of the Extractive Industries Issues for Developing Countries.

6. In some instances, the mineral product may be sold to commodity trading companies that are involved in complex activities throughout the value chain's different stages. This type of company is essentially in the business of transforming commodities such as copper, silver, and gold in space (logistics), in time (storage), and in form (processing). Their basic function has been described as performing physical arbitrages in order to enhance value through the various transformations mentioned above (Pirrong, 2014). For companies such as these and the mining entities discussed in this chapter, contribution to value creation is dependant based on not only the number of functions performed but also the economic significance of the functions in terms of their frequency, nature, and value created by the respective parties to the transaction is important.
7. *See* Phase one 'Explorations and Acquisition'.

Depending on the scale of assets to be disposed and scale of mining activities, mine closure activities may require deployment of significant financial resources. However, this is the stage when the mine is not generating any income and, therefore, it is key that developing countries have policies that ensure that financial resources are set aside during the production phase for future use at the point of decommissioning, environmental restoration, and rehabilitation. The cash outlay for this environmentally important exercise may therefore be provided by the government if the company had contributed funds into an environmental protection fund or escrow account during the production phase. If not, the company would use its own financial resources that it had reserved to cover the cost of decommissioning, environmental rehabilitation, and restoration.

Throughout the stages outlined above, the MNE strategically ensures that it oversees the processes and adjudicates relevant decisions to specific entities, including the entity in the host country. The MNE also assumes its degree of control and responsibility by ensuring that all matters of governance and regulations are dealt with accordingly in order to allow for the undisruptive operation of the mine.

In the part that follows, TP analysis is discussed in the context of the value chain in the commodity market. It is integral that the value chain is understood in this context under consideration. This is one of the key areas that tax authorities must pay keen attention to because industry knowledge will influence the analysis and conclusions drawn in each case, taking into consideration the specific facts and circumstances of every industry and business.

3 TP ISSUES IN THE COMMODITIES TRADE SECTOR

3.1 A Preliminary Overview of the Relevant TP Issues

Value chains in the commodity market in MNEs are normally integrated processes across its different entities. An MNE in this industry is likely to obtain services and products from both related parties and unrelated suppliers throughout the value chain. The mining value chain, as an example, rarely has all of its processes fully integrated into one mining company from exploration to production, marketing, and sale. This is owed to the fact that the activities of the mine throughout the mining processes are normally split between unrelated or related parties who may be performing the activities of one or more segments of the mining value chain. It is of paramount importance that companies in this industry, tax policymakers, and tax authorities fully comprehend the respective stages of the commodity value chain and the potential TP issues that the stages may create for both the resident company and its non-resident related parties. As earlier pointed out in the preceding chapters, the international standard established for transactions between related parties are that these transactions ought to be consistent with the ALP. The OECD TPG states the following with regards to these related party transactions:[8]

8. Paragraph 1.2, OECD TPG.

> When independent enterprises transact with each other, the conditions of their commercial and financial relations (e.g., the price of goods transferred or services provided and the conditions of the transfer or provision) ordinarily are determined by market forces. When related parties transact with each other, their commercial and financial relations may not be directly affected by external market forces in the same way, although related parties often seek to replicate the dynamics of market forces in their transactions with each other.

It is critical to analyse the flow of the fragmentation of the related party transactions, tracing the flow of the functions, risks, and assets to ensure that profits are taxed where economic activities generating the profits are performed and where value is created. The close analysis of these related party cross-border transactions therefore allows for conducting a thorough analysis of the TP policies governing the transactions which includes functional and comparability analysis of the related party transactions throughout the mining process, as was discussed in section 1. The comparability analysis involves a functional analysis aimed at identifying the economically significant activities.

Example[9]

Company A and Company B are residents of Country X and part of ABC Group. The company tax rate for income from mining operations in Country X is 40%, while the company tax rate for mining services is 25%. ABC Group operates in different industries in Country X, among which are mining services. Company A procures mining services worth USD 100 million from Company B which is in the mining service industry. Assuming taxable profits are 20% of the contract compensation, the amount of tax payable by the contract mining Company B will be CU 5 million (20% of 20 million). Taxed at 40%, the tax after profit would be CU 8 million which is CU 3 million more than the taxes paid through the contract mining Company B. Therefore, an incentive would arise to shift profits to Company B in this instance in order to take advantage of the tax savings.[10]

According to the OECD TPG,[11] the starting point of any TP analysis is in fact the contractual agreement between the related parties, which makes logical sense as it enables one to fully understanding the contractual obligations of each party to the transactions. The contractual agreements paint for the one evaluating them the clear contractual obligations of any related party that is engaged at all of the seven stages of mining discussed along with the entities contracted, if any, to provide support services. The OECD TPG, in line with BEPS Actions 8-10, further emphasized the importance of delineating the actual transaction between related parties in an effort to determine the functions performed, assets employed, and risks assumed at each stage of the value

9. Though domestic transfer pricing is unusual, it does occur in tax jurisdictions with preferential tax rates for different industries. An example of such a tax jurisdiction is Zambia, which has different tax rates for the agricultural sector, smelting in the mining sector, etc.
10. Though domestic transfer pricing is unusual, it does occur and possesses risks such as the one discussed in the example.
11. Subchapter D.1.1., OECD TPG.

chain. The determination of the actual nature of the transaction results establishing the economic substance and relevance of each transaction along the value chain. It is critical to analyse each transaction's legal form alongside the assessment of the inherent risk or assumption of the risk in each related party transaction. Risk evaluation typically involves establishing whether the entity that is contractually assigned to bear the risk has, in fact, the financial capacity to bear the risk and has control over the risk. An entity is said to have the financial capacity to bear the risk when it has access to funding to take on the risk or to lay off the risk, to pay for the risk mitigation functions and to bear the consequences of the risk if the risk materializes. Control over risk would involve the capability to make decisions to take on, lay off, or decline a risk-bearing opportunity and the capability to respond to the risk associated with the opportunity.

Typically, very few mining operations are fully integrated, i.e., vertical integration. Vertical integration in mining operation occurs when a mine is capable of and performs all of its functions relating to its mining operation throughout the entire mining process. In many cases however, the mining companies engage their related parties throughout the mining process to provide services (hubs) or perform different functions.

The following are some of the services in mining that are typically offered by hubs operating in the MNEs group:

- Corporate treasury hubs primarily offering financial management services, i.e., treasury functions, intra-group loans, cash pooling, hedging, guarantees for the local mining company.
- Procurement hub primarily offering procurement services of the mining equipment and other inputs.
- Marketing hub involved in establishing relations with customers and innovative marketing systems and strategies.
- Technical group service hub offering technical expert services in the mining field such as engineers and geologists.

Throughout the mining process, both intangibles and tangibles assets are transferred between related parties. Below are some examples of the intangible assets that may be transferred, especially during the exploration/acquisition of the mining explorations:

- exploration or production licences;
- intellectual property/innovations/patents.

Exploration or production licences, referred to earlier in this chapter, are licences issued by the host country's government that allow access to the mineral deposit in that country.

Intellectual property/innovations/patents may include computer programs/technology or databases for use in mineral production process or some industrial ingenuity or methods that may be significantly specialized to the mining operations and process. This asset guarantees the creation of value throughout the process and efficiency which leads to cost savings.

Table 16.2 illustrates the typical and most significant related party transactions that may occur at various stages of the mining value chain that effectuate TP issues.

Table 16.2 TP Issues in Mining Industry

Mining Phase	*Typical Activities/Related Party Transactions Giving Rise to TP Issues*
Acquisition /Exploration /Prospecting	- Sublicence of acquisition or exploration/mining rights. - Licensing of scientific studies, information, databases, and software used for exploration purposes. - R&D services for the development of IP used for exploration purposes (e.g., IP related to remote sensing, geochemical, and geophysical techniques). - Technical services such as secondments of geologist/geoscientists, engineers, and metallurgists and technical/financial expertise for the conducting of scoping and feasibility studies. - Leasing/purchasing of exploration plant and equipment. - Exploration tenement management and government approvals. - Legal advice for the drafting and management of farm-out/in and joint venture agreements, etc. - Treasury services to arrange the raising of equity funds through initial public offers and placements.
Mine Development	- Mine and processing plant design. - Engineering, procurement, construction, and project management services. - Procurement of earth moving, mining, and processing plant and equipment. - Establishment of off-lease transportation, road, rail, stockpiling/blending, and port facilities. - Logistics management services. - Treasury services relating to arrangement of project finance including capitalization of interest and lease of plant and equipment. - Provision of brokerage and captive insurance services. - Legal and contract management services.
Mining and Concentration & Transportation	- Contract R&D for the development of IP used for exploitation purposes. - Acquisition and/or leasing of 'sustaining' plant and equipment for extraction purposes. - Acquisition and/or leasing of transportation and other logistics assets. - Sales/transfers of ore or concentrates to smelters or trading entities. - Logistics management services. - Engineering and technical services and secondment of professional staff. - Treasury services, e.g., cash pooling, debt financing, guarantees. - Provision of brokerage and captive insurance services.

Mining Phase	*Typical Activities/Related Party Transactions Giving Rise to TP Issues*
	- Legal and contract management services. - Public relations, government, community, and stakeholder's liaison services. - Hedging and FOREX management.
Smelting and Refining	- Contract R&D for the development of IP used for processing purposes. - Secondment of professional and technical staff. - Acquisition and/or leasing of plant and equipment for the processing of minerals and/or their transportation and other logistics assets. - Sales/transfers of concentrates and/or intermediate or refined mineral products or metals.
Sales and Marketing	- Sales/transfers of concentrates and/or intermediate or refined mineral products or metals. - Marketing research and identification of opportunities for increasing sales volumes. - Negotiation of offtake agreements. - Distribution services, insurance, and shipping services. - Procurement services to production entities. - Hedging and FOREX management.

Source: Modified adaption from the Transfer Pricing in Mining with a Focus on Africa: A Reference Guide for Practitioners.[12]

As shown in the table, the related party transactions may involve the sale, purchase, or lease of tangible (mining equipment, processing equipment, mining products) and intangible assets (mining rights, exploration rights). The highlighted transactions are significant as they are of high value and involve the transfer of substantial amounts of money as consideration. The table also highlights the involvement of other group hubs for the provision of services such as procurement, marketing, and other technical services.

Risks associated with the different related party transactions are:

- credit risk;
- market risk;
- FOREX risk;
- regulatory risk;
- inventory risk;
- operational risk;
- processing risk;
- quality risk;
- product liability risk.

12. Guj, Martin, Maybee & Cawood, 2017.

3.2 Financing Arrangements in the Mining Industry

An MNE's financial hub typically provides varying treasury and financial services to the mine at all stages of the mining process discussed above from the start-up or acquisition to the exploration phase. As pointed out earlier, the mining process from exploration and acquisition to sales and marketing requires significant capital flows for start-up as well as expansion. This is especially so at the beginning of the mining expedition. MNEs argue that the level of risk involved at this stage of the mining operation make funding particularly difficult to access from third-party financing institutions, especially in developing countries. This being one of the reasons advanced for the preferences for the centralization of treasury functions through treasury or finance hubs. The capital intensity of mining activities may result in the mines or their investors assuming minimal or no profit for the longest time from exploration to such a time when the mine is fully operational. The centralized treasury functions hence are used to source funding from within the group or through one entity in the group whose many functions are investment and financing. These treasury departments are primarily focused on the transactions and management of the liquidity position of the mine using different financial instruments to support the mining operations.

Some of these treasury functions include cash pooling, captive insurance, debt financing, and guarantee services. The transactions of these treasury hubs being more complex compared to those of small independent businesses. The functions and structure of these financial hubs are, however, structured differently from business to business depending on the focus of the MNE. One of the integral functions is to ensure that the local mining entity has enough funds available for operation, i.e., start-up, or set-up of the mine, acquisitions, or exploration, etc. Other functions of the hub include rendering support to the mine in raising funds through debt and managing the relationships of the mine with external banks and other independent credit rating agencies.

The MNE has options to provide financial support to the mining investment either through contribution to equity or debt. While interest charged on the debt finance is a deductible expense for tax purpose and can hence be claimed as a deduction by the host mining company, dividends paid out from realised profits are not. This is because the return on equity is taxed on a preferential basis benefiting from a participation exemption, preferential tax rate, or taxation only on distribution.

The common tax treatment of debt is that the interest accrued in it is deductible and subject to a withholding tax on a cash basis. Dividends to shareholders or other equity returns are taxed as income on a realization basis and also subject to the same, but these payments are not deductible. As a result of the fluidity and fungibility of money, it is relatively easier to circumvent the mixing of related party funding as either debt or equity in a related party.

Financing arrangements thus give rise to TP issues due to the interest charged on the financing instrument to the mining operations. The financing related party entity may thus negotiate or set terms and conditions on the local mining operation debt that result in non arm's length pricing of the interest charged. The resulting excessive interest deduction, unless of course the domestic legislation restricts these interest deduction, results in TP risks. To evaluate the TP issues in the transactions between the treasury function and the related parties it transacts with, it is important to delineate the functions of the financial hub[13] and evaluate the TP policies governing the transactions carried out.

The excessive interest deductions in the local mining entity may erode the profits that would ideally be reported and taxed accordingly had the entity been financed by equity. When analysed in this context, it is clear that there is unfair competition between mining entities engaged in cross-border and domestic transactions. It also distorts the capital balance of a mining subsidiary. This creates an incentive for MNEs to have other entities in the MNE group hold mining assets or functions that would ideally be held by the subsidiary mining entity. This is typically an issue when the mining subsidiary is in a high tax jurisdiction, thereby increasing the incentive to increase interest expense deduction and shift profit to a more favourable/low tax jurisdiction.

The following are some of the considerations that an MNE should examine as TP issues that tax authorities are keen to examine:

- the capital structure of the mine, financial health (balance sheet) and its ability to repay the funds borrowed from its related party (debt service capacity);
- the interest rate analysis (i.e., the determination of the arm's length interest rate);
- analysis of comparable third-party debt financing agreements entered into by the mine;
- the financial capacity of the mine to bear the risks associated with the debt and the presence of guarantees from the related party;
- the tenor of the debt instrument; e.g., whether the interest rate on the debt will be reversed during the duration[14] or the inclusion of a conversion clause;
- market circumstances of the mine and the related party financing entity;
- funding the ORA to the mine.

Mining subsidiaries that have high-value mineral deposits are essentially in a more advantageous position not only to access funding but as well to service the interest and repayments on the debt.

The following are among the areas a third-party lender may examine in arising at a decision to advance funds to a mining entity:

- quality and grade of the mineral product;
- recovery cost of the mineral ore;
- metal price assumptions and markets for the product;
- return on the mining investment over a period of time;
- level of proven and probable reserves relative to resources;
- the stage of the mine's operation (e.g., greenfield in its start-up phase);

13. Paragraph 1.36, OECD TPG.
14. Mining companies may have the loan agreement running throughout production profile of the mine and may be as be spread across the mining period of the mine.

- the method of mining being employed;
- proximity to existing infrastructure;
- political, regulatory, environmental, and permitting issues.

In some countries, such as Zambia, domestic law allows for mines to carry forward their losses from mining operations for up to ten years.[15] It may therefore be practical to closely examine the funding obtained from related parties assessing the ORA to both the lender and the borrowing entity. It is important to evaluate the capital balance of the mine and the related financing entity and whether the advanced funds are indeed appropriately labelled as loans or whether they are to be treated as contribution to equity.[16]

The OECD's guidance on financial transactions[17] points to the importance of determining whether the borrower did indeed choose the best ORA for itself. The consideration is integral for a mining entity especially during the early stages of the exploration which is regarded as a high-risk venture; third parties in these investments are more likely to ensure that they protect their interest, ensuring the most rational investment decision.

The terms and conditions of the loan may be examined and the CUP method may be used to determine the arm's length interest rate where sufficient information on the comparable financial transaction is readily available. Otherwise, other approaches may be considered such as the cost approach that reflects the borrowing costs incurred by the lender in raising the funds which are then on-lent to the mining company within the group as debt funding.

The OECD TPG states the following:[18]

> The arm's length interest rate for a tested loan can be benchmarked against publicly available data for other borrowers with the same credit rating for loans with sufficiently similar terms and conditions and other comparability factors. With the extent of competition often present within lending markets, it might be expected that, given the characteristics of the loan (amount, maturity, currency, etc.) and the credit rating of the borrower or the rating of the specific issuance.

Additionally, many countries have thin capitalization rules in their domestic rules to limit the erosion of profits via interest payments.[19] Other countries such as Switzerland have safe harbour interest rates on related party loans.[20]

Action 4 of the OECD/G20 BEPS Project's recommendation is based on a fixed ratio rule that limits an entity's net deductions for interest and payments economically

15. https://www.parliament.gov.zm/sites/default/files/documents/acts/Income%20Tax%20Act.pdf.
16. *See* Chapters 2 and 10, Michael Lang and others (eds), *Fundamentals of Transfer Pricing: A Practical Guide* (Kluwer Law International 2019).
17. Chapter X, OECD TPG.
18. Paragraph 10.91, OECD TPG.
19. Prior to its introduction of the limited deductability rule recommended by BEPS Action 4, Zambia had a debt to equity thin cap rule for mining campanies of 3:1.
20. https://www.bing.com/search?q=safe+harbour+interest+rates+on+related+party+loans+ +in+switzerland%2C+france+and+us&go=Search&qs=ds&form=QBRE.

equivalent to interest to a percentage of its EBITDA. The action plan recommends a group and fixed ratio rule that allows an entity to deduct net interest expenses up to a benchmark net interest/EBITDA ratio within a corridor of 10%-30%. The group ratio rule permits deducting net interest expenses up to a group's net interest/EBITDA ratio when this is higher than the benchmark fixed ratio.[21]

A TP analysis in the mining industry should also examine the arm's length pricing of financial transactions such as hedging. Mitigating risk through hedging derivatives such as interest rate hedging and exchange rate hedging is especially common in the mining industry. Hedging transactions are complex to analyse, and therefore, at a policy level, some countries such as Zambia have a mining tax regime that separates the taxation of hedging income from the main mining operating income.

Example

Company A, located in Country X, and Company B, located in Country Y, are part of ABC Group. Company B is a parent company of Company A. Company A is a mining operations company. It is looking to finance drilling equipment for the mining operation. ABC Group functions as a centralized treasury, whereas Company B manages the treasury function. The corporate tax rate in Country X is 35%, while the corporate tax rate in Country Y is 15%. Both Countries X and Y have the standard treatment of debt and equity. Company A borrows CU 7 million from Company B at LIBOR plus 7%. The interest expense being deductible reduces the taxable profits of Company A.

Relevant TP considerations:

(1) What are the ORA to Company A with regards to borrowing? What was the purpose of the loan?
(2) Is the 7% interest rate at arm's length? Which parties negotiated the contract? Can Company A borrow with less cost from a third-party financial institution? How does Company B generate its funds? Are the group members such as Company A benefiting through an implicit guarantee or the lower rates at which Company B is able to procure funds from other entities?
(3) Would a third party advance that quantum of the loan to Company A at these terms and conditions? Is it likely that an independent bank would provide a loan of that quantum to Company A? Would an unrelated party be willing to lend to Company A with its mix of equity and debt finance? What is the capital balance of the entity (thin capitalization)? What is the creditworthiness of Company A?

Other relevant TP considerations:

(4) Has the taxpayer considered alternative sources of funding other than from the related party?

21. Action 4-Limited Deductibility of the OECD/G20 BEPS Project.

(5) Are the terms of the loan at arm's length (e.g., quantum, repayment period, subordination, currency, security)?
(6) Has Company A been charged a fee for the benefit that may arise from an implicit guarantee provided by the multinational group? The guidelines suggest that such an incidental benefit should not be charged.
(7) Was there an explicit guarantee provided to Company A, and what is the impact of that guarantee?
(8) Who is managing and controlling the risks associated with the provision of the loan and monitoring the collectability of the loan in the ABC MNE?
(9) If Company A has provided an independent bank quote is this a commitment considering that the bank transaction has not yet occurred? Are the terms committed? Such letters would not generally be regarded as providing evidence of arm's length terms and conditions although where a commercial lender has proceeded to make a formal offer to lend, a formal offer can provide useful information as to the terms and conditions which would be important to an independent lender.
(10) The currency of the advance of funds and the market circumstances of the mine and the lending entity.

Tax authorities will aim to ensure that the transaction is consistent with the ALP. In doing so, they will analyse each case's consistence with the ALP based on its merits as they relate to its facts and circumstances.

3.3 Transfer of Intangible Assets in the Mining Industry

During the production stage, the use of intellectual property such as technology for the smelter and other ICT infrastructure in the mining process is inevitable. These transactions involving the sale or transfer of intangible assets entail that the mining subsidiary incurs costs relating to the use of the IP and subsequent payment of royalties towards the exploitation of the IP. TP issues concerning the terms and conditions of these transactions have to be taken into consideration. Valuing IPs or assets, however, can be very complex as they are typically unique and hence hard to value. The sale or transfer of these intangibles in the mining sector merits close examinations as they create TP issues when determining the arm's length remuneration for the parties to the transaction.

Some intangibles that may be hard to value[22] include those exploited throughout the mining operations process. In fact, some intangibles that are taken into consideration for TP may not appear on the mining company's balance sheet. These include intangible assets such as unique technical, commercial, and managerial skills of key executives and professionals within individual firms that, particularly at the exploration and development stages, are very highly valued in the industry and by the stock

22. Paragraph 6.186, OECD TPG.

brokering community. These may, however, be included in the overall value of the mines.

Some of the issues to be addressed when analysing the transfer of intangibles include:

- the arm's length remuneration for the value created by the related party;
- legal ownership of the intangible and how that will affect the returns from intangibles;
- the exercising of control over the risks and having the financial capacity to assume the risk; the parties assuming risks in relation to intangibles actually do exercise; and
- risk-adjusted return depending on the functions performed, e.g., entities providing funding or assuming financial risks.

As discussed in this book, in a TP analysis, the entitlement to any profit or loss that is related to the differences between actual and expected profits will depend on who assumes the economically significant risk and performs the functions as well as whether the arm's length remuneration would be an included profit-sharing element. The legal ownership of the intangibles in the mining operations does not, in fact, determine automatic returns from the intangibles. When it is established that a related party entity only provides the funding and does not assume or control the other risks, only a risk-free return is warranted.

This analysis will inform the arm's length remuneration due to the MNE group entities involved in the specific transaction with the local mining entity.

3.4 Indirect Transfer of Mining Assets

Indirect transfer of mining rights in the mining industry occurs when the assets of a local mining company such as shares are transferred by the MNEs or its foreign shareholders. The transfer is referred to as indirect because it occurs in the tax jurisdiction of foreign shareholders, outside the borders of the mining company's tax jurisdiction.[23] This transfer may occur at any stage in the mining value chain. The indirect transfer of the mining asset gives rise to TP issues because it may and in most instances does escape the notice of the host country of the mining company. This results in the failure by the host country to capture and tax the gains from such a sale. In addition to this, the valuation of the sale to determine the accurate arm's length price in these transactions equally presents a challenge. It is of paramount importance therefore that MNE and the mining companies provide relevant information concerning such transactions. The tax administrations and policy makers equally ought to ensure that the tax jurisdictions protect their right to tax by effecting domestic laws that capture these transactions.

23. https://www.tax-platform.org/sites/pct/files/publications/PCT_Toolkit_The_Taxation_of_Offshore_Indirect_Transfers.pdf.

3.5 Group Shared Services in the Mining Industry

Most mining operations engage entities in the group to provide a wide range of services to be available throughout the mining process such as administrative, technical, financial, advisory and commercial services. This arrangement exists in the commodity trade sector throughout the value chain and the services mostly being technical or scientific.

Some of the technical services that would typically be provided are:

- sourcing and purchasing of mining assets such as drilling machines;
- management of the mining development and construction;
- feasibility studies during the acquisition and exploration;
- research and development in the mining industry, etc.

The fragmented activities in the mineral value-adding supply chain between related parties should ideally have profits allocated to functions performed during the different stages such as mineral processing, marketing and procurement, and treasury and hedging companies. In many instances, the supply of services, goods, or IPs that are necessary at every stage of the mining value chain are typically provided by related companies. The important factors to address when it comes to TP is whether intra-group services have actually been provided and, if so, whether the charges for such services are in accordance with the ALP. The OECD TPG states the following:[24]

> Under the arm's length principle, the question whether an intragroup service has been rendered when an activity is performed for one or more group members by another group member should depend on whether the activity provides a respective group member with economic or commercial value to enhance or maintain its business position. This can be determined by considering whether an independent enterprise in comparable circumstances would have been willing to pay for the activity if performed for it by an independent enterprise or would have performed the activity in-house for itself. If the activity is not one for which the independent enterprise would have been willing to pay or perform for itself, the activity ordinarily should not be considered as an intra-group service under the arm's length principle.

In analysing these transactions, the following factors have to be taken into consideration:

- correspondence between the mining subsidiary receiving the service and the entity in the group or the hub offering the service, e.g., reports from the different departments offering the services, minutes, feasibility studies on the mine undertaken by the technical assistants, etc.;
- the number, qualifications and experience of the individuals or stuff providing the services, e.g., the geologists, mining engineers, etc.;
- the availability of the specialized personnel in the hub providing the service;
- key performance indicators of the staff providing the services;

24. Paragraph 7.6, OECD TPG.

- the extent to which the local mine is supported by the stuff from the hub;
- when the hub is a procurement entity, whether the local mining entity benefits from the discounts on the procured mining equipment;
- when the hub is a marketing entity, when does the title to the goods pass after sale? Is it a flash title? Does the local mining subsidiary have contact with the final customers? Would the local mining subsidiary be able to sell its mineral product without the services of the marketing hub on the market?
- what assets are being employed by the entity providing the services and the one receiving the services? What are the economically significant risks assumed?

The considerations above help to determine the value of the services the local mining entity is receiving, if any, and the extent to which these were provided.

In the case of the services offered by group hubs such as the marketing or procurement hub, MNEs may centralize these functions to take advantage of the economies of scale such as bargaining power and volume discounts. However, it is important to note that, for TP consideration, the compensation to these hubs should be justified by the economic benefit to the local mining entity to which they are offering the services. The hubs need to therefore have a clearly defined role in the offering of services to the mine as well as have an economic and structural advantage.

In the mining industry, the CCA are very popular especially in mining countries with a history in this industry. In the event of these arrangements, the arm's length remuneration is expected to be in accordance with the contribution made and value added with respect to the service.

Table 16.3 shows some of the allocation keys that the mining operations may use for the intra-group services.

Table 16.3 Mining Operations and Some Applicable Allocation Keys

Activity	*Appropriate Allocation Key*
Human resource	Headcount with focus on the workforce directly involved in the provision of the services at the mine
Accounting/auditing	Time spent that can be determined using time sheets
IT services	Number of users determined by the accounts created and those in use
Technical services, e.g., geologist, mining engineers	Time spent that can be determined using time sheets

3.6 Sale or Purchase of Mineral Products

For a mining subsidiary, the sale of mining products may constitute the sale of both fully and partially processed mineral products and can take place at different stages of the mining process. The OECD TPG mentions the following with regards to commodity prices:[25]

> Under the CUP method, the arm's length price for commodity transactions may be determined by reference to comparable uncontrolled transactions and by reference to comparable uncontrolled arrangements represented by the quoted price. Quoted commodity prices generally reflect the agreement between independent buyers and sellers in the market on the price for a specific type and amount of commodity, traded under specific conditions at a certain point in time.

In some jurisdictions, pricing of commodities ordinarily follows the quoted price that is also referred to as the 'reference price'. The reference price is the price of commodities in a particular period obtained on an international or domestic exchange market as a reference by unrelated parties in the industry to set prices in unrelated parties' transactions. The price references are normally quoted on markets such as the LME and the London Bulletin Market as quoted in the reference publications. The quoted price also includes prices that may be obtained from recognized and transparent price reporting, statistical agencies, or governmental price-setting agencies for which such indexes are used as a reference by unrelated parties to determine their prices. The use of the reference price has been referred to as the sixth method that is, according to the CIAT,[26] a method that is a derivative of the first TP method – the comparable uncontrolled price method. The UN TPM states that the commodity rule is referenced as the sixth rule in Argentina where it seems to have originated.

Mineral products are normally sold on a CIF basis to the point of destination or final customer, or they can be sold FOB at the point of origin. The FOB price only includes transportation of goods to the main shipping point, whereas the CFR price includes transportation all the way to the destination port. The means of these sales are:

- offtake agreements are normally long-term contracts ranging from one month to three years or more. It normally includes the quotation period, quantities/quality sold, discounts, penalties, price reference, e.g., LME, LMB, etc.; and
- spot sales or over the counter agreements to commodity trading companies or merchants.

Offtake agreements are preferred as they bring a level of stability to revenue flows of the mining entities and mitigate price volatility risks, sales volume risk, market risks, etc.

25. Paragraph 2.19, OECD TPG.
26. https://mnetax.com/ciat-preparing-sixth-method-transfer-pricing-database-33316#:~:text=The%20sixth%20transfer%20pricing%20method,wide%20number%20of%20commodity%20producs (last accessed 30 January 2022).

The closer the mineral product is to the refined product, the less complex it is to price it. There is no standard price available like there is for finished mineral products because concentrates are partially processed mineral products. The price of concentrates is therefore arrived at by deducting the RC, freight cost, TC, etc., from the quoted price. The offtake contracts for concentrates are therefore arrived at by examining long-term contracts with smelters, refiners, etc. The NSR formula is traditionally applied by many in the mining industry to set concentrate prices. This price can be used to compare third-party transactions of mining entities and smelters or refineries. The net smelter payment is taken as a proportion of the value of the contained metal in the concentrate that is expected to vary depending on the quality of the mineral deposit.

The pricing of concentrates such as copper concentrates is based on standard terms in which the pricing is determined as follows:

Realized Concentrate Selling Price = LME Grade A Cathode – TC – RC – Penalties – Freight Costs – Price Participation Costs + Credits;

The TC/RC relate to the cost that will be incurred for smelting and refining the concentrate plus a margin for the smelter/refinery. These costs are normally benchmarked against what big smelters agree with their concentrate suppliers.

Penalties relate to charges for the removal of impurities and excessive moisture. They are levied when the deleterious elements exceed prescribed levels. The deleterious elements in copper concentrates can include nickel, silica, antimony, and arsenic and are charged when these elements exceed agreed thresholds. They are expensive to remove, may damage the smelter when in excess, and their disposal is very costly due to their potential damage to the environment.

Price participation costs have not been so common in recent years, though the practice is prevalent in times of higher metal prices when the smelters share in the price boom by levying a deduction on the LME price hence lowering the realized concentrate price.

In both the sale of the concentrates and the final mineral products, payments are made as a provisional payment covering 90% of the value and a second provisional payment covering the balance (10%) after assaying is carried out in the case of the concentrates or when then the mineral product reaches the port in the case of mineral products.

MNEs, at times, enter into sale and purchase agreements that provide for an advance payment of the commodity upon issuance of a provisional invoice with an advance payment fixed at a percentage of the provisional invoice value of up to 90%. The terms in such agreements normally include payment of interest on the advance payment (advance sales payment).

The inherent TP issues with regards to the sale of the mineral products include the price at which these minerals are sold at and the discounts applicable to the sale price. A TP analysis will therefore include the benchmarking of these discounts against what is prevailing in the market. CUP, if applicable, either by way of internal or external comparables, needs to satisfy the terms and conditions of sale in line with the ALP.

Example

Company A, located in Country X, and Company B, located in Country Y, are part of ABC Group. Company A sells its commodity, i.e., copper anode, to a related marketing hub, Company B, at LME prices less discounts on quality, freight, insurance, and refining charges.

The following is a summary of the terms and conditions in the Company A and Company B offtake agreement:

DURATION: Agreement expires on either the earlier of the lifetime of the mine or the tenth anniversary of the commencement.

QUALITY: As per the assay provided by Company A.

SHIPMENT: CIF, transportation arranged by Company B.

DELIVERY: Durban port or parity (as defined in INCOTERMS 2000).

PRICE: Shall be the sum of the metal payments less the deductions as specified below.

Metal payments will be averaged over the quotational period.

Copper: 99.50% of the final copper content, subject to a minimum deduction of 1.0 unit paid for at the official LME cash settlement quotation for Grade A copper as published in the Metal Bulletin in London in US Dollars.

Deductions:

Quality Discount: 550/Mt

Treatment and refining charges: shall be agreed mutually between the two parties.

QUOTATIONAL PERIOD agreed mutually between the Buyer and the Seller during the fourth quarter of each calendar year.

PAYMENT shall be in US Dollars by telegraphic transfer: 90% of the provisional invoice value paid, thirty days following the presentation of a full set of shipping documents for each shipment and balance of 10% paid promptly upon completion of all other formalities regarding the final agreed weights, assays, and prices.

TITLE within each shipment passes from the Seller to the Buyer upon his first provisional payment.

RISK passes from the Seller to the Buyer when the products pass over the ship's rail at the port of loading.

INSURANCE is covered by Buyer (Company B) from the time risk passes from the Seller (Company A).

TP considerations that arise in the given example are the following:

- What economic value does the marketing hub add to the supply chain? For instance, is there any further processing, blending, branding, or polishing to the product by the marketing hub among other value-adding activities that need to be investigated in forming a decision as to whether the remuneration due to the marketing hub is at arm's length?
- Are the discounts on quality at arm's length?
- Do the functions performed, assets employed, and risks assumed warrant the level of remuneration given to the marketing hub?
- What are the skills of the employees in the marketing hub? Do academic and professional qualifications demonstrate sales, customer relations, and marketing experience and expertise? Are these skills utilized to add economic value/benefit to Company A. Do those skills justify the remuneration earned?
- How does this compare with the capabilities of the marketing staff in Company A to the local mining entity?
- According to the offtake agreement, is the marketing hub Company B financially responsible for failure to comply with customers' quality specifications?
- Does Company B have long-term relationships with existing customers, processes for vetting new customers, and credit checks?

Example (continues from the previous example)

Company A is a mineral processing subsidiary that owns a smelter and refinery situated in Country X, a developing country. Company A produces copper anode, blisters, and cathodes with by-products of selenium and gold. Company A purchases copper concentrates for further processing from both unrelated parties and related parties (Company B and Company C). Company A also sells all of its products to both unrelated and related parties based in Europe and West Asia. An extract of its sale and purchase agreements for the year 2018 has the following terms and conditions:

Terms	*Company C Related Party Country H*	*Company B Related Party Country S*	*Unrelated Party Country C*
Copper Cathode Price	LME M + 2	LME +1	LME + 2
Premium	USD 95/Mt	USD 105/Mt	USD 110/Mt
Freight Cost	USD 120/Mt	USD 125/Mt	USD 120/Mt

Terms	*Company C Related Party Country H*	*Company B Related Party Country S*	*Unrelated Party Country C*
Commission	Nil	0.02 % of purchases	Nil
Copper Anode	LME M + 3 less Treatment or refining charges	LME M + 2 less Treatment or refining charges	LME M + 3 less Treatment or refining charges
TC/RC	USD 110/USD 80	USD 120/USD 90	USD 95/USD 70
Freight	USD 130/Mt	USD 140/Mt	USD 125/Mt
Payment	90 % of provisional invoice	90 % of provisional invoice	90 % of provisional invoice

In this context, the TP analysis will involve examining all aspects of the sale – the terms and conditions of the transaction taking into consideration the prices charged on freight, discounts given, quantities sold, etc., compared with the unrelated party transaction with the unrelated party:

(1) Compare the copper cathode premium price for both the related and unrelated party transactions. The premium price is notably lower for the two related parties compared to the unrelated party; the unrelated party transaction in this case can be used as a comparable.
(2) Analyse and compare the terms and conditions on the commission on sales. What are the functions performed and risks assumed by the company in country S to warrant commissions received? Are these different from the functions performed by the other entities? Generally, copper cathode requires little marketing, if any, considering its grade/quality. Is there a commission attached to the Swiss agreement?
(3) Analyse why the TC/RCs on intra-group transactions are higher than the unrelated party transaction. Is the quality sold to the tested transaction requiring further refining than that sold to the related party?
(4) Analyse the higher freight cost deductions on the intra-group transactions compared to those on the unrelated parties' transactions.

These transactions effectuate TP issues as it is critical to ensure that charges between the related parties are indeed at arm's length and are the charges that are prevalent between unrelated parties.

The TP issues identified above require policymakers and tax authorities to have in-depth knowledge on the operations of the mine at every stage such as the smelters, the pricing of the mineral product, and the valuable by-products that are contained in the concentrate. A lack of the relevant industry knowledge and skill on the part of the policy makers and tax authorities can be a source of revenue leakages for the source or host country from their mineral resources, primarily because it would lead to the passing of mining policies which may fail to capture or address the inherent issues in the industry adequately. A comprehensive study and review of the industry practices and norms, offtake agreements, contracts, assay reports on elements recovered and content, provisional and final invoices as well as the possible reference to commodity prices on global metal exchanges such as the LME and Fast Markets Metal Bulletin are key. This will evaluate whether the pricing of elements is at arm's length and in accordance with industry standards regarding penalties, credits, and other terms surrounding the sales and purchase agreements. The preferred TP method that can be used for adjusting the prices is the CUP method. However, from a policy perspective, for commodity industries that have reference prices obtained from independent commodity exchanges, a sixth method can be enacted in the tax laws. The sixth method may be used to price the sale of minerals between related entities as is the case in some countries such as Bolivia, Brazil, India, Peru, and Zambia.[27]

4 CONCLUSIONS

In order to protect the tax base of a source country in which the economic activity related to mining is created, it is important to thoroughly address the TP issues that arise at each stage of the mining process. This will ensure that resource mobilization is enhanced and sustained. Countries, especially those that are developing, should actively endeavour to design, legislate or update the appropriate domestic tax laws that protect the jurisdiction's right to tax the profits arising from economic activities taking place in its territory in the commodity sector. Particularly in the extractive industry for developing countries, the risk associated with the lack of improvement in the way investment agreements and legislation are drafted may lead to leakage of the much-needed revenues. Tax authorities must be well resourced with a supporting organizational structure in order to effectively and efficiently administer and collect revenue from the extractive industry that might be forfeited due to base erosion and profit shifting schemes. Some of the important considerations for tax jurisdictions, tax authorities, and policymakers are ensuring that there is an operational system in place to track all of the volumes of exports in the country.[28] In-depth knowledge of the extractive industry concerning the value-adding activities in the supply chain, industry practices in pricing commodities, activities that are expected under each stage of the life cycle, and the respective BEPS risk is key if countries are to fully audit the extractive sector in order to increase revenue collection.

27. Use of reference prices is found in section 97A(13) of the Income Tax Act Chapter 323 of the Laws of Zambia as Amended by Income Tax Act Number 1 of 2008.
28. Guj, Martin, Maybee & Cawood, 2017.

Annex

Below are some of the databases that can be used as comparable data in the commodity sector:

- Royaltystats offers royalty rates and licensing agreements worldwide compiled from the US Securities and Exchange Commission.
- Platts offers energy and metals information including price assessments and indices. Platts publishes the Mineral Valuation Service which compares price information for the sale of common iron ore products.
- Moody's Riskcalc offers credit rating tool which is useful in the analysis of related party debt.
- The Steel Index offers reference prices for iron ore fines imported into China, price differentials for iron and impurities, and estimates of freight cost, to allow the CIF price to be adjusted back to the FOB price.
- Metal Bulletin Research. Comprehensive database on base metal, coal, iron and related alloying minerals, minor metals and industrials. Includes information about related mining companies.
- Bauxite Price Index and Harbor Aluminium.
- US Geological Survey.
- Baltic Exchange. Bulk freight rates.
- LBMA. Publishes the daily AM and PM London fix spot gold prices.
- *Wall Street Journal.* Same as above, but data can be exported to MS Excel, CSV, XML, JSON.
- London Metals Exchange. Free data service providing daily prices; historical data available for purchase.
- Index Mundi. Monthly data with some lag time.

Source: Modified adaption from the Transfer Pricing in Mining with a Focus on Africa: A Reference Guide for Practitioners (Guj, et al., Transfer Pricing in Mining with a Focus on Africa, 2017).

CHAPTER 17

Transfer Pricing in the Fast-Moving Consumer Goods Sector

Martin Lagarden & Robert Risse

1 INTRODUCTION

This chapter provides a brief overview of the FMCG or CPG industry as a basis for subsequent TP considerations. The industry analysis outlined in the following sections establishes the context for evaluating general conditions and comparability factors, available business strategies, and TP approaches adopted by MNEs in the FMCG markets they serve worldwide.

The FMCG comprises products for everyday use or, more technically speaking, products with a useful life of less than approximately two years. These tangible goods are subject to high demand and will be sold quickly and recurrently at a relatively low cost.[1] Examples include non-durable household goods and convenience products such as packaged foods, snacks or sweets, beverages, cosmetics, toiletries, laundry and home care products, stationery, over-the-counter drugs,[2] and other consumables.[3]

Due to its consumer focus, this industry sector is targeted as one of the main contributors to expected additional taxable income generation in the 141 countries cooperating under the umbrella of the OECD/G20 Inclusive Framework on BEPS.[4] In October 2020, five years after the release of the final BEPS Project reports, the OECD published its 'blueprints' summarizing the then-current status of discussion on providing internationally aligned solutions vis-à-vis tax challenges arising from the digitalization of the economy in the shape of the so-called Pillar 1 and Pillar 2 measures.[5] One year later, this was complemented by an OECD policy statement on the two Pillars, addressing the tax challenges linked with the digitalization of the economy, with a view to implementing adequate and harmonized regulatory measures on a global scale in the years to come.[6]

From a typology perspective, the market structure in which the FMCG multinationals operate can be characterized as oligopolistic.[7] This implies few suppliers and a large number of purchasers. On the demand side, large retail multinationals usually function

1. *See* Werner Kaiser (2011) *Fast Moving Consumer Goods*, in: Gabriele Naderer, Eva Balzer (editors) *Qualitative Marktforschung in Theorie und Praxis*, 2nd edn, Gabler Verlag/Springer Fachmedien Wiesbaden GmbH, p. 605, https://en.wikipedia.org/wiki/Fast-moving_consumer_goods (last accessed 30 January 2022).
2. For example, health and wellness products in the food or non-food segment.
3. The product (or service) portfolio on offer has an impact on the production and sales site infrastructure and geographical location of MNEs operating in the FMCG industry as it may not always be cost-efficient to transport FMCG products cross-border over extended distances depending on their weight, perishability, or packaging quantities.
4. *See* OECD, *Inclusive Framework on Base Erosion and Profit Shifting*, list of participating countries, https://www.oecd.org/tax/beps/inclusive-framework-on-beps-composition.pdf (last accessed 25 March 2022).
5. *See* OECD, *International Community Renews Commitment to Address Tax Challenges from Digitalization of the Economy* (12 October 2020), https://www.oecd.org/tax/international-community-renews-commitment-to-address-tax-challenges-from-digitalisation-of-the-economy.htm (last accessed 23 March 2022); and, for example, PwC (2020) OECD releases Blueprints on Pillar One and Pillar Two, Updated Economic Analysis, 13 October 2020, https://www.pwc.com/gx/en/tax/newsletters/tax-policy-bulletin/assets/pwc-oecd-releases-blueprints-on-p1-and-p2-updated-economic-analysis.pdf (last accessed 22 March 2022).
6. *See* OECD, *Statement on a Two-Pillar Solution to Address the Tax Challenges Arising from the Digitalisation of the Economy* (8 October 2021), https://www.oecd.org/tax/beps/statement-on-a-two-pillar-solution-to-address-the-tax-challenges-arising-from-the-digitalisation-of-the-economy-october-2021.pdf (last accessed 25 March 2022).
7. *See* Joseph G. Nellis, David Parker (2004) Principles of Business Economics, Pearson Education Limited, Chapter 9; and John Thompson, Frank Martin (2005) Strategic Management, Thomson Learning, 5th edn, pp. 74-75.

as intermediaries between the FMCG producers and end consumers.[8] However, this may change to an extent going forward as the internet enables the development of new online business models for FMCG MNEs, and it also creates entry potentials for new competitors of established FMCG players. These may be start-ups covering niche positions or well-established MNEs from other industries like online retailing and trade that can extend their technological and/or capital resource base and existing market access into the FMCG industry realm with different types of diversification.[9]

Moreover, private label business that has been established by large retail chains for many years is putting pressure on FMCG MNEs.[10] Nonetheless, product differentiation exists, to some extent, in this industry either due to actual physical product differences, varying consumer perception, or both.[11] Therefore, barriers to market entry also play a relevant role in the FMCG industry. That may be evidenced by the anecdotal fact that most of the well-known MNEs mentioned below are looking back on a firm history of approximately hundred years or more.

In oligopolistic markets, companies have sufficient market power to avoid a mere price-taker role, and different price leadership strategies can be observed.[12] However, there is substantial competitive rivalry and, at the same time, mutual strategic interdependence between competing MNEs[13] as the actions of one firm are likely to provoke corresponding (counter) reactions of the other companies. This may lead to price war situations or even the opposite behaviour, that is, (explicit or tacit) collusion

8. From a transfer pricing perspective, this influences the operating margins that can be achieved in domestic markets by local affiliated manufacturers and/or sales as well as distribution companies belonging to an FMCG MNE.
9. That is, horizontal, lateral, or vertical diversification. Some general examples in this regard include, without being limited to: Amazon, Google, Mercado Libre, Pinterest, or Zalando.
10. FMCG MNEs could – and even do sometimes – operate to a limited extent as private label manufacturers themselves for large retailers with which they may cooperate in supplying their own branded products. This may be compared to generics production in the pharmaceutical industry. *See also*, Philip Kotler, Kevin Lane Keller (2006) Marketing Management, 12th edn, Pearson Education Inc., Upper Saddle River (NY), pp. 503-533, and Nellis, Parker (2004), pp. 173, 175, 184.
11. In fact, differentiation in the FMCG industry seems to be often times more reliant on advertising, marketing, and brand building and maintenance than on physical or technology-based product differences, which can have an implication for transfer prices for different intangibles within an MNE. *See also* Nellis, Parker (2004), p. 176.
12. For example, dominant firm, barometric, or collusive price leadership that can have an impact upon margins achieved by local affiliates in view of transfer prices paid or charged to other affiliated companies for intangible and tangible goods or services. *See* Nellis, Parker (2004), p. 184.
13. This is evidenced by the fact that most FMCG MNEs have adopted similar business models and strategic transformation initiatives over time. Examples include the: (i) establishment of shared service centres and consequential transfer pricing implications for corresponding intra-group service charging between involved affiliates; (ii) implementation of principal structures in the supply chain and/or beyond this functional area which has an impact on the selection and practical implementation of transfer pricing methods for tangible goods transactions and intangibles, the function and risk profiles of affiliated companies involved, and also on the margins earned by respective affiliates; or (iii) centralization of intellectual properties in the FMCG MNE which has an impact on intangibles' remuneration among affiliated companies.

between suppliers. Two central models of explaining firm behaviour in oligopolistic markets are the kinked demand curve and game theory.[14]

Top worldwide players in this industry sector in 2019 included Swiss-based Nestlé SA with sales of more than CHF 92 million;[15] Procter & Gamble Company (P&G) in the US with sales of more than USD 67 million;[16] the Anglo-Dutch conglomerate Unilever N.V. with sales of approximately EUR 52 million;[17] or the French family-owned L'Oréal group with sales of nearly EUR 30 million.[18]

The primary developed markets in which FMCG companies operate, that is, North America and Europe, including Russia, are highly competitive. Therefore, limited growth for multinationals in this sector is only possible either:

- in emerging markets;
- at the expense of other internationally established or local competitors; and/or
- via the acquisition of competitors.

Innovation has always been a major factor for companies in the FMCG industry. This refers to technologies and mass-market product or process innovation as well as advertising and marketing innovation, for example, in the frequent product launches and correspondingly high advertising spending levels in FMCG affiliates. To maintain customer loyalty, companies must continuously invest in these areas in order to differentiate themselves from competitors and provide an added value to their customers.

At the same time, operational efficiency improvement and cost control are also imperatives in the FMCG industry to steadily improve margins.[19] Therefore, companies operating in this industry are often leading organizational change and taking advantage of efficiency gains, for example, via the introduction of shared service centres that help to improve profitability by process standardization and harmonization, introduction of lean organizational structures, wage arbitrage exploitation, and a best-fit sourcing mix in procurement. As an example, the German-headquartered family-owned Henkel Group implemented an Eastern European shared service centre with three hundred employees in 2008. At the end of 2016, the number of employees in all of Henkel's five shared service centres worldwide had risen to almost three thousand.

Likewise, digitalization is heavily impacting the future development of MNEs in this sector with respect to their internal manufacturing and supply chain processes and

14. *See* Nellis, Parker (2004), pp. 176-188.
15. *See* Nestlé's Annual Report 2019, https://www.nestle.com/sites/default/files/2020-03/2019-annual-review-en.pdf (last accessed 23 March 2022).
16. *See* Procter & Gamble's Annual Report 2019, Form 10-K, https://www.pg.com/annualreport2019/download/PG-2019-Form-10k.pdf (last accessed 23 March 2022).
17. *See* Unilever's Annual Report 2019, https://www.unilever.com/Images/unilever-annual-report-and-accounts-2019_tcm244-547893_en.pdf (last accessed 23 March 2022).
18. *See* L'Oréal's Annual Report 2019, https://www.loreal-finance.com/system/files/2020-03/LOREAL_2019_Annual_Report_3.pdf (last accessed 23 March 2022).
19. *See* Sadun, R., Bloom, N., Van Reenen, J. (2017) Why Do We Undervalue Competent Management?, Harvard Business Review, Vol. 95, No. 5, September/October 2017 and Treacy M., Wiersema F. (1993) Customer Intimacy and Other Value Disciplines, Harvard Business Review, Vol. 71, No. 1, January/February, pp. 84-91.

automation under the currently fashionable headline 'Industry 4.0'. This is occurring in their transactions with suppliers and retailers, new business models regarding FMCG companies' sales channels, and their interaction with retail customers and end consumers.[20]

Competitiveness continues to increase due to growing new players from emerging markets or digital retail platforms such as Amazon or Alibaba and others that operate globally or are proceeding to do so. As major buyers of FMCG products are regionally or globally operating multinational retail chains with strong buying power, economies of scale are becoming increasingly important for FMCG companies, leading to increased merger and acquisition activities. Finally, sustainability requires substantial investments in R&D to reduce environmental and safety risks of FMCG products and processes in order to comply with increasing ecological standards and respective legislation, changing consumer demand in this direction.[21] At the same time, differentiation versus competitors is also pursued by the development of (more) individualized products and service offers enabled and enhanced by online information exchange with end consumers. Such investments can only be financed by higher economies of scale and increased profitability enabled by streamlined organizational structures.[22]

In summary, Porter's well-known five forces framework can be employed to illustrate the competitive situation in today's FMCG industry as outlined in Figure 17.1.

20. This may be part of the OECD's reasoning to address its guidance for future taxation of the digital economy under Pillar 1 to FMCG companies as prospective taxpayers in this regard.
21. This can have an impact on MNEs' production footprint and decisions on how to organize cross-border product supplies to affiliated sales and distribution companies. Recent examples in the FMCG industry include broad initiatives to reduce plastic waste in packaging or experimenting with new product dispensing approaches, for example, refill stations in supermarkets.
22. *See* Gregory Kelly, Udo Kopka, Jörn Küpper, Jessica Moulton (2018) Consumer Packaged Goods: The New Model for Consumer Goods, McKinsey & Company.

Figure 17.1 Porter's Five Forces Applied in the FMCG Industry[23]

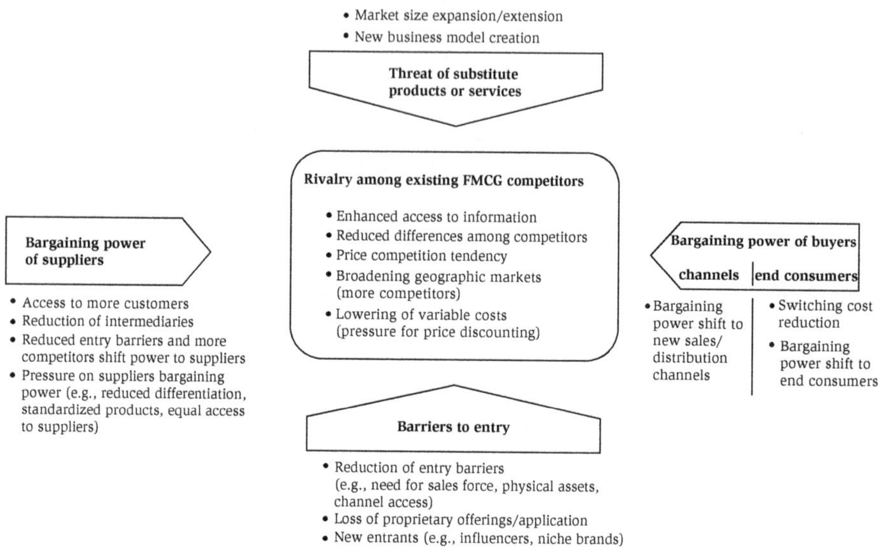

The threat of substitutes is emerging from potential market size expansion and extension as well as new business model creation enabled by the internet. Likewise, barriers to entry can be reduced by online sales (e.g., no need to establish or rely on a physical salesforce), and it becomes more challenging for FMCG companies to maintain their proprietary offerings over a longer time due to highly diversified online competition and rapid imitation of products or service offers. New entrants like influencers or start-ups may create their own (niche) brand (portfolio) that they market and sell entirely online. The bargaining power of suppliers is increasing by direct online access to more potential customers or even end consumers and the reduction of intermediaries in the supply chain. The reduction mentioned previously of entry barriers contributes to increasing supplier power. However, online access to more information also makes it more difficult for suppliers to differentiate their offerings vis-à-vis their own competitors. For the buyer, the bargaining power shifts to new online sales channels and also to end consumers who may directly contact the FMCG companies to provide their personal information for product or service personalization and also take advantage of low switching costs at the same time.

The combination of these factors is leading to a permanent and highly intense *rivalry among existing FMCG competitors*. Each company monitors the (re)action of its

23. Source: Martin Lagarden (author); *See also* Porter M.E. (2001) Strategy and the Internet, Harvard Business Review, Vol. 79, March, pp. 63-78.

competitors very closely as mentioned above in order to adapt their own strategic actions accordingly. Since information is readily available online, differentiation in often times well-established product categories becomes harder to sustain for FMCG MNEs, and price-driven competition is frequently observed. With the broadening of geographical markets, more local competitors enter the arena or become acquisition targets for global FMCG MNEs in order to nurture their growth. Finally, the reduction of variable costs by exploitation of economies of scale effects is contributing to margin-eroding price competition among FMCG MNEs as mentioned above.

Against this background, TP consequences arising from the business models chosen in the FMCG industry and their implications in view of current regulatory and technological trends will be outlined and analysed in the following sections.

2 VALUE CREATION IN THE FMCG SECTOR

This section will comprehensively examine the relevant value drivers and a generic value chain often encountered in the FMCG industry. Subsequently, the two prevalent business models in this sector will be explained, and their impact on the main intra-group transaction categories involving tangible goods, intangibles, and intra-group services will be discussed with a view to the four steps underlying the application of the arm's length principle.[24]

2.1 Value Drivers in the FMCG Industry

The identification of relevant value drivers is an important step for understanding the entire business of any company or MNE that is a complex interplay of major influencing factors. These include organizational structure hierarchies and managerial decision-making, work processes, flows of information, and (in)tangible goods and financial funds that interact with external customers, suppliers, and competitors in different geographical markets.

Example

ABC Group is in the business of providing a wide range of laundry and home care products to customers in different countries. Its affiliates' sales to end consumers are conducted via large internationally operating retail chains in more than eighty jurisdictions worldwide. Communication with prospective or actual end consumers is occurring not only via classical advertising channels, for example, television spots or various print media, but also increasingly via direct online communication with and advertising towards end consumers. ABC Group's economic success is reliant on its entire workforce; developing and driving its

24. *See* Michael Lang, Raffaele Petruzzi, Giammarco Cottani, Alfred Storck (2018) Fundamentals of Transfer Pricing: A Practical Guide, Kluwer Law International, Chapter 1, section 5.

brands; and technologies and supply chain processes. These influencing factors are reflected in its broad and continuously developing portfolio of branded cleaning products and detergents. In view of growing TPD and compliance requirements in different countries in recent years, ABC Group's management has decided to conduct a thorough analysis in order to better explain and argue relevant contributions to its value chain considering different categories of its affiliates. To do so, a series of interviews and workshops are conducted over a period of one year with various business representatives in different functions and roles and subsequently analysed by a central project team in the tax department at ABC Group's headquarters. The results are reviewed and adapted together with the interviewees when necessary and then presented to and finally confirmed by ABC Group's management leadership team.

Key value drivers have an impact in and on different business processes at certain points within an MNE. In addition, different affiliated legal entities will contribute to certain value drivers to a varying extent depending on their function and risk profile and on the assets employed to exercise their role in the MNE's overall value chain. The identification of key value drivers and an assessment of their relative importance is usually achieved with interviews conducted with various management leadership team members of an MNE in different business or administrative units. In conjunction with a business process analysis, the identified value drivers provide the basis for a quantitative value chain or value contribution analysis in an MNE.[25] As an example, key value drivers in an FMCG context are described below:

(1) Consumer insights
This value driver is about identifying and understanding emerging end consumer (and customer) demands or needs and preferences at an early stage either in a prospective or current product lifecycle. Mastering this value driver helps for developing new products and market or modify them effectively.

(2) Translating customer needs into products
This value driver paraphrases the ability to translate an identified idea or opportunity, for example, by market and trend research, competitive intelligence, or internal resources into a tangible product and related value proposition. It will strongly be influenced by the effectiveness and efficiency of existing processes and organizational structures in an MNE.

(3) Objective product performance and quality
This value driver describes the ability to manufacture performant products at the appropriate level of quality as experienced by end consumers and in a consistent manner. Living up to this value driver requires a thorough

25. *See* Martin Lagarden (2019) *Attribution of Intangible Related Returns*, in: Michael Lang, Alfred Storck, Raffaele Petruzzi, Robert Risse (editors), *Transfer Pricing and Intangibles*, Series on International Tax Law, Vol. 113, Linde Publishers, Chapter II.

understanding of the offered product, its manufacturing process, corresponding ingredients required, and their mutual interaction.[26] This allows for variations of certain elements that may enable product differentiation or variation without compromising a product's quality and value proposition.

(4) Perceived marketing and advertising excellence
This value driver deals with the ability to establish and enhance brand equity through development and execution of marketing and brand communication strategies and concepts that effectively strengthen and improve the value proposition of FMCG product and service offers. This driver is of particular importance as marketing and advertising are decisive areas of differentiation among competitors in this industry that help to sustainably maintain financial performance and business success.

(5) Sales effectiveness and CRM
This value driver is about striking an appropriate balance between customer demands as outlined under value drivers (1) and (2) and the costs to fulfil these in a sustainably manageable way. Success in this area is primarily dependent on establishing and maintaining good customer relationships.

(6) Reliability of product supply and customer service
This value driver is mainly related to the company's general responsiveness to customers' demands with a view to the ability to deliver products and/or services within the agreed service – and according to the promised quality level.

(7) Competitive direct and indirect material procurement
This value driver refers to the ability to maintain comparatively low procurement costs in the areas of raw and packaging materials, traded finished goods purchased from unrelated parties, contract and/or toll manufacturing services, and the provision of logistics and/or warehousing services which helps to provide a competitive advantage for FMCG MNEs.[27]

(8) Cost-efficient supply chain
This value driver describes the ability to maintain cost-efficient supply chain operations that remain responsive to changing market conditions. This driver is mainly related to organizational structures and processes associated with demand and supply planning, logistics, and manufacturing.[28]

---

26. Interaction in either a chemical or physical context within the product formulation itself (e.g., in beverages and foods, cosmetics or cleaning products regarding product efficiency, odour, stability, taste, warranty considerations, etc.) or with respect to their biological interaction with human metabolism, skin, or tissue upon product ingestion or external application (i.e., a product safety aspect).
27. *See*, for example, Minahan, A.T. (2005) Five Strategies for High Performance Procurement, Supply Chain Management Review, Vol. 9, September 2005, www.scmr.com, pp. 47-54; Keough, M. (1993) Buying Your Way to the Top, McKinsey Quarterly, Vol. 30, No. 3, pp. 41-62.
28. *See*, for example, Oberoi, J.S., Khamba, J.S. (2005) Strategically Managed Buyer-Supplier Relationships Across Supply Chain: An Exploratory Study, Human Systems Management, Vol. 24, No. 4, pp. 275-283; Pagell, M., Krumwiede, D.W., Sheu, C. (2007) Efficacy of Environmental

Not unexpectedly, some connections and interdependencies between the eight exemplary FMCG value drivers can be found as is illustrated in Figure 17.2.

Figure 17.2 Value Drivers and Their Relationships in an FMCG Context[29]

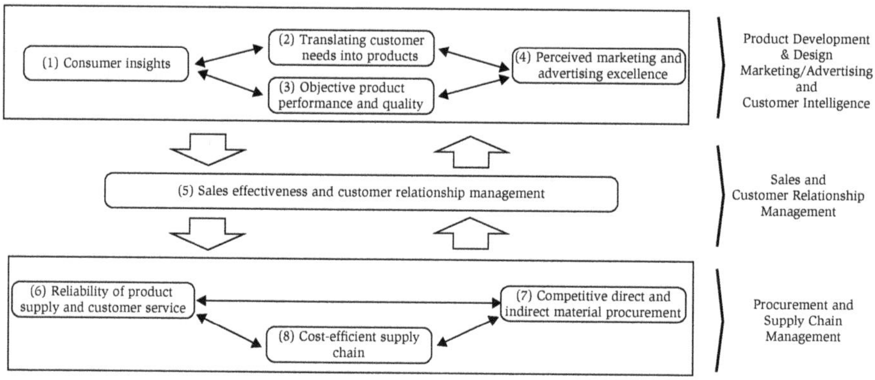

Nonetheless, these value drivers provide a more concrete basis for understanding and documenting details of value creation and distinct value contributors than an overly simplistic concentration on functions such as 'R&D', 'marketing/advertising' or 'sales' as generic value drivers in an FMCG MNE.

Moreover, the key value drivers may be conceptually categorized into three functional focus areas, specifically: (i) R&D, Design/Technology, (ii) Marketing & Sales, and (iii) Operational Excellence/Supply Chain. Within these areas, the value drivers relate to products, processes, and structures in an MNE. This analytical perspective provides additional insights with respect to distinct value contribution areas and the roles adopted by different types of affiliates[30] in an MNE. Table 17.1 depicts an overview of key value drivers in the FMCG industry, their relative importance, and the assignment to the three focus areas mentioned.[31]

and Supplier Relationship Investments: Moderating Effects of External Environment, International Journal of Production Research, Vol. 45, No. 9, May 2007, pp. 2005-2028.

29. Source: Martin Lagarden (author).
30. For example, production, distribution, supply chain entities or shared service centres.
31. Anonymized example based on an actual value driver analysis average over three different FMCG industry segments.

Table 17.1 Categorization of Key Value Drivers in the FMCG Industry by Focus Area[32]

Value Driver	*Relative Importance (%)*	*R&D, Design/Technology Focus*	*Marketing & Sales Focus*	*Operational Excellence/Supply Chain Focus*
(1) Consumer insights	13	✓	✓	
(2) Translating customer needs into products	10	✓	✓	✓
(3) Objective product performance and quality	13	✓	✓	✓
(4) Perceived marketing and advertising excellence	17		✓	
(5) Sales effectiveness and CRM	10		✓	✓
(6) Reliability of product supply and customer service	15		✓	✓
(7) Competitive direct and indirect material procurement	10	✓		✓
(8) Cost-efficient supply chain	12	✓		✓
Total	100%	28% (normalized)	38% (normalized)	34% (normalized)

While it could be argued that the distribution observed in Table 17.1 is relatively balanced, it is also obvious that there is a more pronounced relation of the eight value drivers to marketing and sales, followed by operational excellence/supply chain compared to R&D, design and technology in the third place.

It was mentioned in the introduction that differentiation is an important strategic success factor in oligopolistic markets. From the value driver assignment provided above, it can be concluded that such differentiation among FMCG competitors whose products often rely on similar (if not identical) technologies and designs seems to be more often achieved in the areas of marketing and sales as well as effective and efficient supply chain operations. This has an impact on the business models selected by major players in the FMCG industry and the corresponding TP implications as is explained in more detail below.

32. Source: Martin Lagarden (author).

In a preceding step, however, and in order to complement the value driver analysis, the following section will outline a generic value chain display for a typical FMCG MNE.

2.2 Generic FMCG Value Chain

In the FMCG industry, the generic value chain as shown in Figure 17.3 is geared towards external customers operating in the retail business sector,[33] on the one hand, and also to end consumers on the other which are the ultimate target of any marketing and advertising efforts in relation to the FMCG MNE's finished branded product portfolio offerings.

Figure 17.3 Generic FMCG MNE Value Chain[34]

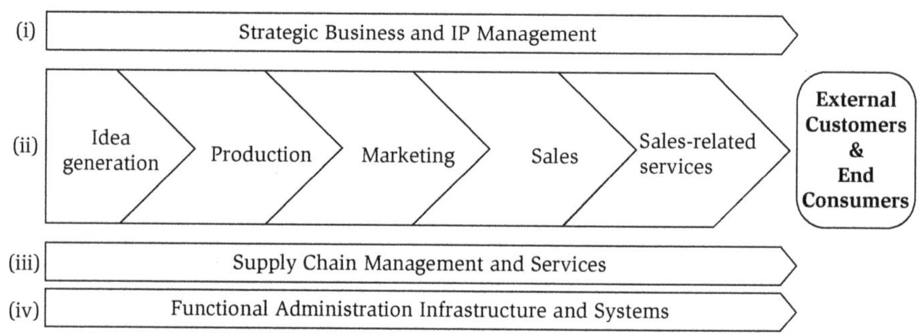

The value chain can be segmented into four different strands:

(i) strategic business management and IP management;
(ii) operative business functions;
(iii) supply chain management and supply chain services; and
(iv) functional administration infrastructure and functional administration systems.

Strands (i), (iii), and (iv) are overarching in view of the general operative business functions shown under strand (ii). In strand (i), corporate strategies and business models will be developed for the MNE, usually at the headquarters level.[35] However, in view of international management teams and situations like the COVID-19 pandemic where employees work from home for longer periods, the *actual location* of ultimate decision-making and corresponding value contribution or DEMPE functions becomes

33. That is, the traditional FMCG outlets such as a drugstore, pharmacy, supermarket, wholesale, and department store chains. Direct business models in which end consumers are supplied directly (D2C) by an FMCG MNE will be emerging in the future enabled by the enhanced digitalization of online sales channels and direct end consumer communication.
34. Source: Martin Lagarden (author).
35. This may be at a central (global) headquarters or also at regional headquarters levels.

less clearly defined.[36] With respect to IP management, a differentiation may be established between local IP[37] and global IP for which the latter is utilized throughout the MNE and needs to be made available to all affiliates. In that context, IP consolidation or decentralization strategies will have a TP impact as is further outlined in section 2.3 below.

The general operative business functions in strand (ii) range from idea generation derived from various internal and external sources[38] via production[39] and marketing to sales and sales-related services.[40] Additionally, sales-related services in the value chain can refer to pre- and post-sales services that may be targeted towards business customers[41] or end consumers.[42]

Despite the fact that individual steps in strand (ii) are displayed only in a linear fashion, several activities within these steps may take place in parallel as they are interdependent, for example, in production, marketing, sales, and sales-related services during a product launch process. Moreover, synergies between the steps cannot be adequately reflected in a linear value chain display nor the relative importance of certain steps compared to others. In essence, any value chain can only function as a holistic process if it remains uninterrupted and all steps operate successively and/or in parallel towards the common goal, that is, successful and sustainable sales transactions with third-party customers.

Finally, both supply chain management and related services (iii)[43] as well as the functional administration backbone including a supporting shared service centre infrastructure[44] and corresponding IT systems (iv) in an MNE are flanking the general operative business functions (ii). They are also indispensable contributors to the focus area of operational excellence which plays an important role as differentiator in the FMCG industry as outlined in the preceding section. While the qualitative generic value chain display presented here is beneficial for obtaining an overview about major value contributing activities and affiliated entities participating in the value contribution

36. *See*, for example, Heinz-Klaus Kroppen (2016) Behandlung Immaterieller Wirtschaftsgüter unter BEPS, in: Jürgen Lüdicke, Arne Schnitger & Christoph Spengel (editors) Besteuerung Internationaler Unternehmen: Festschrift für Dieter Endres, C.H. Beck Verlag, pp. 199-210.
37. For example, local trademarks that are only employed in geographically limited (i.e., certain domestic) markets.
38. Such sources may include, for example, R&D, marketing, sales, (retail) customers, end consumers or suppliers, or open innovation initiatives by FMCG MNEs.
39. To what extent production can be considered a more or lesser important value contributor in an FMCG MNE will depend on the level of product sophistication. For example, if production can be considered as a routine function involving only limited risks when raw materials are mixed, blended, heated, cooled, and finally packaged into product containers, this function may be also outsourced to third-party manufacturers insofar as deemed strategically appropriate and/or necessary by management in strands (i) or (iii).
40. The important role of marketing, sales, and sales-related services for branded FMCG MNEs has already been highlighted above.
41. That is, customer relationship management for retail chains purchasing from the FMCG MNE.
42. That is, providing advice to end consumers in product selection and application, for example, technical customer service.
43. Like contract manufacturing, toll manufacturing, warehousing, or logistics services, for example.
44. Providing general administrative services in areas such as HR, finance, or IT.

process[45] in an MNE, the relative value of individual functions and value drivers and their contribution to the overall FMCG MNE's value chain can only be established in a quantitative value chain analysis as is pointed out in section 2.1.

Example

Company A, located in Country X, is part of ABC Group. The company has been undergoing a tax audit for two recent fiscal years. In addition to its regular master file and local file documentation already provided to the tax authorities, Company A has also been asked to provide a value chain analysis with a focus on its role and responsibilities in the entire value chain of ABC Group. Together with the ABC Group's TP team at its headquarters, Company A is preparing a high-level analysis describing its functions, risks, roles, and responsibilities as a routine production and distribution company with no local IP ownership in Country X. Consequently, Company A's main contributions to ABC Group's value chain are centred around the areas of production, marketing, sales, and sales-related customer services in Country X. This is explained to tax authorities in writing and supported by a schematic visualization of ABC Group's value chain similar to the example provided in Figure 17.3.

On this basis of typical FMCG value drivers and the generic value chain, two main value-creating FMCG business models will be outlined in the next section.

2.3 Prevalent Business Models in the FMCG Industry

Business models have various features and affect intra-group transaction parties in different ways. This refers, for example, to functions exercised, risks borne, and assets employed as well as roles and responsibilities adopted by different affiliates in an FMCG MNE. The choice and managerial implementation of a particular business model designed to deliver on a business strategy should enable the MNE to achieve certain goals in economic, IP, or tax terms which subsequently affect the value creation and corresponding economic performance of the MNE and its affiliates.

Example

Company A, located in Country X, is the parent of ABC Group. It has been in the business of selling beauty care products to customers in Country X for more than one hundred years. Over time, Company A has been expanding its operations to other parts of the world. In the beginning, such foreign operations had been conducted employing third-party distributors or independent travelling sales

45. For example, the main value contribution provided by an affiliated (intercompany) manufacturing company could be located in Figure 17.3, row (ii), in the segment 'Production', while an affiliated sales company's value contribution will mainly be delivered in the corresponding segments 'Marketing' and/or 'Sales' and 'Sales-related services' in Figure 17.3, row (ii).

representatives. In later years, numerous affiliates had been established to conduct local production and/or sales activities with their own employees in domestic markets abroad. In recent years, ABC Group's business model has gradually been shifting from a central to a more regionally focused managerial steering in order to be closer to changing regional and local beauty and fashion trends and to provide product offers that are more individualized in local markets at decreasing time-to-market lead times. In parallel, the development of ABC Group's international online business presence is driven from Country X taking into account local market specifics and feedback provided by its affiliates in different countries.

In this respect, the degree of centralization can be considered as a prime differentiating factor among the two dominant FMCG business models presented in this section. However, it should be noted that different degrees of centralization will be encountered in actual situations with respect to the features mentioned previously (*see also* section 2.2). Therefore, the reader should not expect to observe either of the business models subsequently described in a 'textbook-like' fashion in real life.

2.3.1 Centralized Model

The centralization aspect in this business model refers to the FMCG MNE's legal entity structure and decision-making based on appropriate substance[46] with a view to three distinct perspectives:[47]

(i) functional;
(ii) IP; and
(iii) financing.

In this context, centralization implies that at least one of the three perspectives mentioned previously, two of these in a different combination or all three together, have been consolidated in one (or few) legal entity(ies) in the FMCG MNE. Such centralization is pursued by MNEs to take advantage of economies of scale and scope as well as strategic and operational synergies, for example, process standardization and simplification or cost savings that may result from the successful exploitation of

46. Substance in the context of significant people functions to enable decision-making upon and control of relevant risks and the financial capacity to bear such risks.
47. Strictly speaking, also IP creation and management as well as financing can be considered as 'functions' in an MNE to be subsumed under item (i) as a general headline. The IP perspective (ii) refers to intangible assets and corresponding DEMPE functions and the financing perspective (iii) is thought to be specifically related to intra-group financial funds management. Then, the functional perspective (i) is considered as being different from the other two insofar as it is considered to refer to operative strategic and transactional business management including international marketing, brand strategy and management, sales functions, new business development, or supply chain management functions including manufacturing, procurement, and purchasing. With respect to the latter distinction, procurement is considered to include the strategic part of sourcing and purchasing beyond transactional execution of sourcing tasks in the purchasing itself.

these aspects.[48] Corresponding centralization features and their TP impact in view of the mentioned three perspectives are subsequently discussed.

(i) Functional centralization

In this context, the FMCG MNE may centralize its (section i.1) administration functions, (section i.2) supply chain functions, and (section i.3) business management functions in one or a few affiliated companies.

Examples for section (i.1) are SSC organizations in which general administrative service functions such as HR, IT, finance (including tax and customs), purchasing, and corporate communications are bundled and consolidated to deliver standardized intra-group services to affiliated companies in an MNE. Usually, the transition to SSCs is accompanied by a sizeable personnel reduction of local administrative functions in the operative[49] affiliated companies of an MNE. Such routine intra-group services provided by SSCs are normally considered as 'low value adding' in the context of Chapter V of the OECD TP Guidelines and priced accordingly employing the cost-plus method in transfer prices. The arm's length character of the service prices charged by an SSC to its affiliated customers will customarily be tested after the fact in comparison to TNMM-based service benchmarking studies[50] considering independent third-party providers in different service sectors that reflect the service portfolio of the SSC in the MNE under consideration. As such, shared service centres are often located in low-cost countries, and FMCG MNEs take advantage of process efficiency gains, standardization, and cost reduction which contribute to their overall value chain as is mentioned in section 2.2.

In the case of section (i.2) supply chain centralization, strategic supply chain functions that are very often in combination with global procurement functions[51] will be centralized in an affiliated company with international or global responsibilities. These hubs manage, direct, and control a network of affiliated companies providing transactional supply chain and purchasing functions such as intra-group toll (or contract) manufacturing,[52] logistics and warehousing services, and local or regional sourcing and purchasing services. In such cases, intra-group services provided by

48. *See*, for example, John Thompson, Frank Martin (2005) Strategic Management, Thomson Learning, 5th edn., pp. 151-154.
49. In this context, the term 'operative' (alternatively: 'transactional') denotes manufacturing; marketing, sales, and distribution functions for different business units in an affiliated company dealing with external or intra-group customers in its domestic or export markets.
50. Considering, for example, the net cost-plus margin, operating profit margin, or Berry ratio as financial key performance indicators for benchmarking purposes in an intra-group service context.
51. If international or global procurement functions remain separated from the global strategic supply chain functions, both centres would act alongside each other, even potentially out of different jurisdictions. However, such a separation could be less effective and efficient from strategic, operational, and cost perspectives than an integrated approach with both strategic functions consolidated in one location. *See*, for example, Bonekamp, M., Dijkman, J. (2014) Transfer Pricing Aspects of Central Purchasing, International Transfer Pricing Journal, IBFD, Vol. 21, May/June, pp. 164-171.
52. In the case of contract manufacturing, the contract manufacturer will purchase materials needed for the manufacturing process from unrelated parties.

affiliated LSCCs[53] to the hub will be charged on a cost-plus basis to that central strategic SCPP. If the LSCC is functioning as a toll manufacturer for the SCPP, the latter will provide raw and packaging materials to the LSCC and remains the legal owner of the goods and inventories at all times.[54] Finished goods may then be transported to third-party customers by the LSCC, by third-party logistics companies on behalf of the SCPP, or picked up by external customers themselves.

Moreover, the SCPP will be licensing IP from the (central) MNE IP owner (or from unrelated parties) required to have finished branded goods manufactured by the affiliated LSCCs. The SCPP will be the central supplier for affiliated local distributors purchasing finished branded goods exclusively from the SCPP for subsequent sale to external customers in their domestic markets (or abroad). If a flash sale concept has been established between the SCPP and the LSMCs, the goods sold to external customers remain in the SCPP's ownership until 'one logical second' before the LSMC's sales transaction with its external third-party customer. The TNMM or resale minus method is most commonly employed to price the intra-group tangible goods transactions between the SCPP and its affiliated local distributors.

The local distributors, that is, the LSMCs, may operate as low-risk distributors in their home markets. However, depending on factors like local IP ownership or the scope of marketing and sales activities or even limited supply chain activities performed to an extent by LSMCs,[55] these affiliates may be considered as limited risk routine distributors that could be earning a profit margin according to benchmarked interquartile ranges of comparable independent full-fledged distributors. To explain more clearly, residual (or: 'excess') profits earned in transactions of LSMCs with their external customers can be derived by the SCPP via the transfer prices charged to the LSMCs. A certain share of these residual (or: 'excess') profits may have to be subsequently passed on by the SCPP to the central IP owner if the SCPP itself has only licensed but is not owning the relevant IP.

It should be noted that an internationally harmonized and standardized IT system (platform) is generally an indispensable prerequisite and decisive success factor in enabling centralized supply chain operations in an FMCG MNE. Such IT systems will usually be developed and implemented by a central strategic IT function at the MNE headquarters and supported by regional IT lead teams.

A specific variant of supply chain centralization may be observed in situations when a strategic intra-group production entity has been established in an MNE that exclusively manufactures and sells to all distribution companies in a certain region or even worldwide. In this case, the transfer prices charged by the producer to its affiliated distributors can be employed in a similar fashion as described under the flash sale concept described above. The corresponding residual profit will be allocated between the producer and the distributor depending on functions performed, risks borne, and

53. That is, local supply chain companies with a limited or low routine function and risk profile.
54. The goods will then be stored in SCPP or in third-party-owned warehouses that may be operated by the LSCC personnel, third-party logistics, or warehousing providers.
55. For example, stock-keeping, warehousing and/or logistics activities if no LSCC is located in the jurisdiction of the LSMC under consideration, and the SCPP is not employing a third-party provider for such services.

assets employed as well as the IP ownership and performance of the DEMPE functions among the intra-group transaction parties in that MNE.

Besides considerable administrative, operational, strategic benefits and synergies that the FMCG MNE can derive from the successful implementation of this business model, the MNE may also take advantage of a favourable tax treatment of SCPP profits in the jurisdiction where the SCPP is located.[56] However, pursuant to the OECD's BEPS Project, local tax advantages for this business model have been curbed in many jurisdictions over time, and mandatory disclosure rules require an immediate reporting of respective business model changes in an MNE provided the affiliated companies affected are located in Europe. Figure 17.4 illustrates this model.

Figure 17.4 Centralized FMCG MNE Business Model[57]

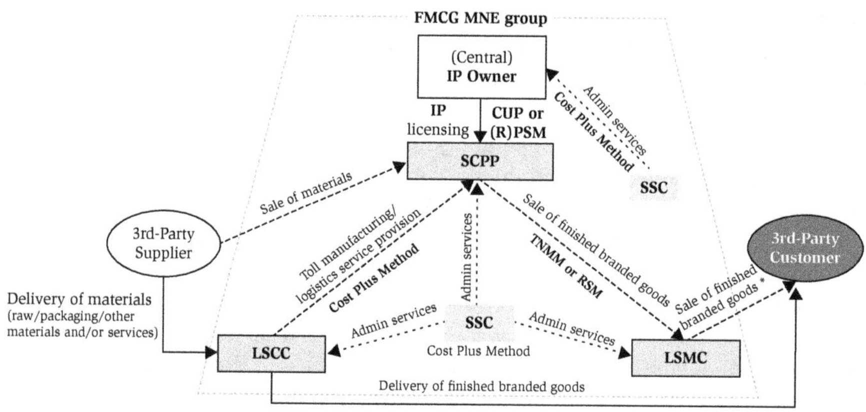

*Sale at domestic market price.

Finally, in the case of section (i.3), business management centralization, strategic functions in the areas of R&D, marketing and brand management, sales, and business development will be centralized in an affiliated company with global or at least regional (international) responsibilities, like an MNE's headquarters and parent company.

Contract R&D service provision by affiliated companies to the headquarters or parent company (principal) will often be encountered in such a set-up in order to enable IP centralization and consolidation[58] in an FMCG MNE as described in the subsequent section. The transfer prices charged by affiliates to the principal for such services will then be established on a cost-plus basis provided that the principal performs the strategic DEMPE functions related to the affiliates' R&D activities.

56. *See*, for example, Deloitte (2012) Centralised Entrepreneur/Principal Tax Structures, 2012/2013 edition, https://www2.deloitte.com/cn/en/pages/tax/articles/centralised-entrepreneur-principal-tax-structures.html (last accessed 25 March 2022).
57. Source: Martin Lagarden (author).
58. In terms of legal and economic IP ownership acquired by the principal.

(ii) IP centralization

In this context, the FMCG MNE's valuable IP may be developed and consolidated at the level of the parent company,[59] in the home country of the parent company, or in an IP-developing or IP holding subsidiary in another jurisdiction.

From a TP perspective, IP centralization advantages can be summarized as follows:

- strengthening the MNE's market position in accordance with its operating model;[60]
- strengthening the MNE's ability to market and defend its IP portfolio globally while adhering to generally accepted arm's length principles;[61]
- creating a platform to consolidate future IP acquisitions; and
- enhancing business units' IP strategies.

The second advantage mentioned refers to the establishment or maintenance of an intra-group licensing approach that may be a production-related[62] licence, a distribution-related[63] licence, or a combination of both provided to affiliated companies[64] which will have customs implications in different countries.[65] Alternatively, an IP-related remuneration for the IP owner can also be established via transfer prices charged to associated distributors if the IP owner is the producer itself and engaged in tangible goods transactions with these distributors as is explained above in section (i.2). If the central IP owner does not have these tangible goods transactions with its distributors, it will instead be charging royalties to the correlated IP users. Both approaches have a direct impact on the level of transaction values for customs purposes upon import by the distributor.

As mentioned under section (i.3), the level of IP centralization established in an FMCG MNE may also be reflected by the extent to which contract R&D services will be employed which can subsequently be linked to the third and fourth advantages mentioned above. Figure 17.5 illustrates this centralization feature in a simplified manner.

59. Assuming that that the parent company is the MNE's headquarters.
60. For example, creation of strategic and operational (including administrative) efficiency and effectiveness advantages due to IP ownership centralization and respective decision-making; consistent implementation of IP-related decisions across all business units; consistent communication of global brand, and technology messages (images) across all businesses and towards customers and end consumers.
61. For example, by intra-group IP licensing or in the case of tax and transfer pricing audit defence situations.
62. For example, a technology, design, formulation, process, or product licence.
63. For example, a trademark or brand licence.
64. That is, the IP users.
65. *See* Martin Lagarden (2019), *Attribution of Intangible Related Returns*, in: Michael Lang, Alfred Storck, Raffaele Petruzzi, Robert Risse (editors), *Transfer Pricing and Intangibles*, Series on International Tax Law, Vol. 113, Linde Publishers, Chapter II, pp. 73-74.

Figure 17.5 IP Centralization Supported by Contract R&D Service Provision in an FMCG MNE[66]

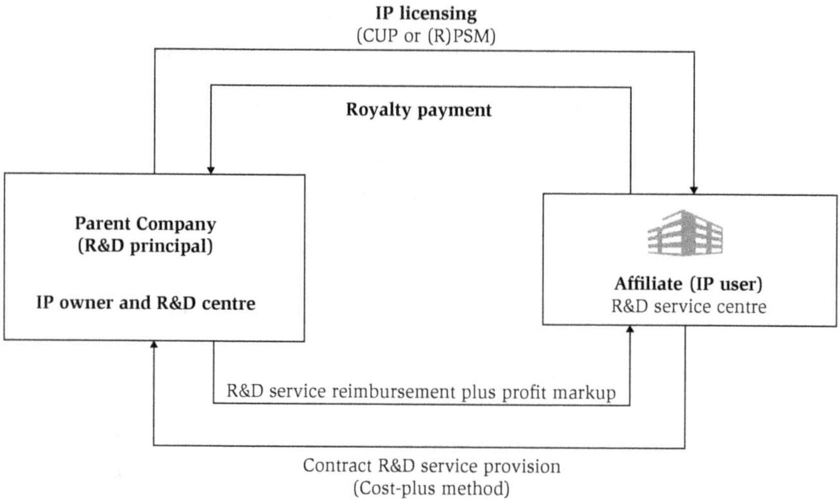

Depending on the jurisdiction where the IP is centralized, certain tax advantages or subsidies may be granted to the affiliated company owning the respective IP.[67] Moreover, centralization can provide synergy benefits in terms of developing, enhancing, maintaining, exploiting, and protecting the IP in question in accordance with the advantages mentioned above.

(iii) Centralized financing

If any excess cash is held on a sustainable basis at the level of MNE affiliates, that is, it is not required to settle ongoing payment obligations, such surplus funds will be passed along within the MNE through a cash pool facility, intra-group loans, dividend payments, or capital decreases. Affiliated companies in an MNE customarily cover their debt obligations and financing needs via intra-group financing, i.e.: (a) cash pool arrangements and (b) intra-company loans. If these instruments are centrally managed by a corporate treasury unit in the MNE's finance function, favourable financing conditions vis-à-vis external lenders or borrowers can be achieved from a group perspective. The centralization advantage emerges from the fact that economies of scale and scope can be realized when the corporate treasury function can bundle

66. Source: Martin Lagarden (author).
67. *See*, for example, Lisa Katharina Evers (2015) Intellectual Property Box Regimes, European Parliament, Directorate General for Internal Policies, IP/A/TAXE/2015-03, October 2015, https://www.europarl.europa.eu/RegData/etudes/IDAN/2015/563454/IPOL_IDA(2015)563454_EN.pdf (last accessed 30 January 2022); Elke Asen (2019) Patent Box Regimes in Europe, https://taxfoundation.org/patent-box-regimes-europe-2019/ (last accessed 30 January 2022); OECD, https://qdd.oecd.org/data/IP_Regimes (last accessed 30 January 2022); or the HNTE model in China.

affiliates' financing requirements and available funds with a view to capital market borrowing or investment.

Thus, the corporate treasury is in charge of deciding on the entire intra-group financing strategy and optimizing the liquidity across the MNE to ensure that the operative FMCG business has sufficient cash available in the appropriate place when needed and in the correct currency. The central treasury function will bear the risks for any differences between interest rates set with other affiliates and those that the treasury transacts with independent lenders. A corporate treasury screens banks and will decide upon the selection of those that are preferred for the FMCG MNE and on hedging transactions, for example, in the context of mergers and acquisitions. Therefore, risks for credit, liquidity, hedging, and currency for intra-group financing are borne centrally in this set-up.

From a transfer price-setting perspective, the CUP method will be employed to centrally establish interest rates for intra-group financing transactions via a cash pool facility or intra-group loans[68] as money can be regarded as a 'basic commodity' traded by banks and other financial institutions on domestic and international capital markets. Therefore, a considerable body of external comparable data is available online as reference for pricing intra-group financing transactions of different types. In that context, it should be borne in mind that intra-group interest rates, i.e., the transfer prices for financing transactions between MNE affiliates, consist of different price components. The latter include a risk-free rate of return,[69] a credit spread,[70] and a profit element[71] for the lender. A corporate treasury establishes these interest rates centrally as part of their intra-group financing strategy for the FMCG MNE.

Moreover, the choice of the central lead entity[72] providing intra-group financing facilities and in-house banking services to affiliates will also take regulatory, currency-related, or other business strategy considerations of the FMCG MNE into account.

However, the general centralization feature related to intra-group financing is by no means peculiar only to the FMCG industry sector. Rather, it may be encountered in all industries and countries where no legal or tax restrictions for such intra-company financing instruments exist – unless external financing alternatives that are likewise

68. Cash pools are primarily employed to accommodate short-term intra-group financing situations, for example, providing funds to or cash deposit facilities for affiliates for a time span of up to one or a few months. Consequently, intra-group loans will usually be used to cover longer term (e.g., beyond three months but that may also depend on the intra-group financing strategy established by the corporate treasury) or large volume intra-group financing transactions.
69. That is, a comparable short-term interbank rate, for example, EURIBOR, taking into account the term (duration) and currency of the intra-group financing transaction under consideration.
70. This transfer price component will take the credit default risk of the borrower from a lender's perspective into consideration; i.e., it is dependent on the affiliated borrower's credit rating performed centrally by the corporate treasury. Moreover, the credit rating of the central lender itself will also be considered when establishing the credit spread.
71. The profit element represents the remuneration for additional risks (i.e., beyond those covered by the credit spread) faced by the central financing entity in specific intra-group financing transactions. Such profit element can be determined adopting a transactional approach, i.e., for example, by analysing the bid-ask spreads for comparable transactions observed on capital markets.
72. For example, with respect to its legal form, location, substance, decision-making capacity, control over risk, and the capacity to bear corresponding financial risks.

negotiated by a central corporate treasury function appear to be more favourable for the MNE as a whole but not necessarily for an individual affiliate at all times.

In summary, functional and IP-related centralization aspects clearly play a dominant role in FMCG business models, with shared service centres (section i.1, *see* above) and centralized supply chain organizations (section i.2, *see* above) being the most important features observed in business practice. The main characteristics of an alternative approach, i.e., a more decentralized FMCG business model, will be discussed in the following section.

2.3.2 Decentralized Model

Following the reasoning introduced in section 2.3.1, the decentralization aspect in this business model may refer to the FMCG MNE's legal entity structure and decision-making based on appropriate substance with a view to the three distinct perspectives:[73]

(i) functional;
(ii) IP; and
(iii) financing.

Decentralization in this respect implies that affiliated companies in the MNE display a distinct full-fledged function and risk profile as well as corresponding asset ownership, predominantly in the areas of manufacturing, marketing, sales, and distribution. Corresponding decentralization features in view of the three perspectives mentioned are discussed subsequently.

(i) Functional decentralization

In these instances, the FMCG MNE may have deliberately refrained from centralizing its (section i.1) administration functions, (section i.2) supply chain functions, or (section i.3) business management functions within one or a few affiliated companies.

Examples for section (i.1) can be observed in affiliated companies that continue to perform the entire spectrum of administrative functions such as HR, IT, finance (including tax and customs), and purchasing either with their own personnel resources or often supported by outsourcing repetitive transactional activities in the administrative areas mentioned to respective third-party service providers. The external providers, their local service levels, and delivery will then be managed and controlled by responsible functional managers in the affiliated FMCG service recipients. From a historical standpoint, these entirely internal (or partially external supported) set-ups mark an organizational development stage before the advent of administrative shared service centre structures in MNEs. Due to the readily available full-fledged administrative infrastructure in each affiliate, respective intra-group service charges between affiliates appear to be minimized or entirely avoided. However, at the same time, economies of scale will not be realized by the FMCG MNE compared to the centralized business model pendant.

73. *See also* footnote 47.

In decentralized supply chain structures (section i.2), a significant number of full-fledged manufacturing affiliates can be found in the FMCG MNE, thus providing the (entire or at least partial) product spectrum required by the local affiliate for its domestic third-party business or respective sales to customers in neighbouring jurisdictions (export business). These full-fledged producers may also employ their own product development and marketing units.[74] Moreover, they may manage a network of third-party contract or toll manufacturers to complement their production capacities or to outsource more labour-intense production and packaging processes for efficiency and cost-saving purposes. As a consequence, cross-border deliveries between MNE affiliates will be limited as the individual affiliates can largely cater their own supplies of finished products. This can be relevant in situations in which transport costs constitute a high share in relation to product prices, for example, in products with comparatively higher water content and larger volume per unit. However, the manufacturing affiliates themselves may not necessarily own the IP required to produce and label their finished products. In that case, relevant IP could be licensed-in from the FMCG IP owners or from unrelated parties, as needed. Again, substantial economies of scale will not be realized by the FMCG MNE in that case compared to the more centralized business model.

Finally, under a decentralized business management structure (section i.3), the FMCG affiliates will operate as largely unrelated parties in their local and regional markets. The MNE structure could subsequently potentially be only a rather loose company network that may not be able to efficiently take advantage of synergy effects in terms of cost savings and process standardization compared to the more centralized business model framework described in section 2.3.1. However, a regional MNE structure[75] may serve as a reasonable compromise between either a fully centralized or decentralized set-up. In this manner, regional consolidation advantages with respect to the three perspectives mentioned above can be combined with market cultivation that is more individual, i.e., enabled and driven by local affiliates in countries.

(ii) IP decentralization

In the case of decentralization within the FMCG MNE, affiliated entities will either own the relevant IP that they need for the performance of their key functions, like manufacturing and sales and distribution.[76] Alternatively, the affiliates will have to licence-in the IP from other affiliates or unrelated parties if that IP has not been self-developed or acquired by the respective MNE itself at an earlier point in time.

74. To some extent, private label manufacturers may also be considered as examples in this context.
75. That is, for example, one leading regional administration affiliate managing and controlling individual production and sales affiliates in countries of the respective geographical region.
76. For example, technology and trademark IP is relevant for production affiliates and enabling them to manufacture and label the desired FMCG product portfolio in part or in its entirety and to sell it to other affiliates or unrelated parties. Trademark IP is relevant for sales and distribution associates as it enables these to sell their finished branded FMCG product portfolio on offer to other affiliates or unrelated parties. In either case, the IP may be self-developed or acquired (i.e., not licensed-in but purchased) from other affiliates or unrelated parties.

Consequently, this business model may imply the establishment of a licensing model between affiliates like in the case of the centralized model outlined in section 2.3.1 (ii). However, this would occur in a more fragmented and therefore less efficient way without entirely avoiding the same type of challenges by tax authorities in countries encountered under the centralized business model.[77] Additionally, assuming that the IP employed by the affiliates is similar in nature (if not identical) to establish and maintain a certain quality level and positioning of the branded FMCG products on offer, the risk of duplication of efforts among affiliates to obtain the IP required seems higher under a decentralized as opposed to a centralized business model.

On the other hand, depending on the jurisdiction where the MNE is located, certain tax advantages or subsidies may be exploited more easily by individual affiliates without jeopardizing the business strategy. This is compared to the centralized business model for which individual affiliates may be held responsible for refraining from establishing or maintaining 'core IP' themselves at the expense of the central IP owner in the FMCG MNE.

Example

Company A, located in Country X, is the parent of the ABC Group and Company B, located in Country Y, and Company C, located in Country Z, are affiliates of the same Group. ABC Group is an FMCG MNE specialized in the production of surface treatment and dyeing products for a wide range of different materials in home use applications and has affiliates in more than fifty countries around the world. Company A provides central guidance related to quality standards for raw materials, products, and respective testing procedures to its affiliates. Local affiliates in Country X customarily develop their product formulations, technology IP, and respective ingenuity themselves, employing their own personnel in their laboratories in order to ensure that the products are most effectively individualized and tailored to the specific end consumers' needs in the domestic markets where these affiliates operate. The products are then marketed under the well-known A logo that is owned and licensed by Company A to all connections worldwide. Company B has recently obtained the HNTE status which provides it with substantial, albeit temporary, tax benefits.[78] On the other hand, Company C takes advantage of the local IP box regime in Country Z as its product portfolio is different from Company B's so that the technology and product IP that is

77. At the level of the IP licensor, tax authorities often consider the applied royalty rates as 'too low' while, at the level of the affiliated licensees, these royalty rates may be challenged as being 'too high' by domestic tax authorities.

78. *See*, for example, Dai, X., Wang, F. (2019) Does the High- and New-Technology Enterprise Program Promote Innovative Performance? Evidence from Chinese Firms, China Economic Review, Vol. 57, October 2019, 101330, https://www.sciencedirect.com/science/article/pii/S1043951X19300914 (last accessed 30 January 2022); Zhao J., Zhang, V. (2018) Aligning China R&D Arrangements and Transfer Pricing in a Post BEPS World, Deloitte China, 17 September 2018, https://www2.deloitte.com/cn/en/pages/tax/articles/aligning-china-rnd-arrangement-and-transfer-pricing-in-a-post-beps-world.html (last accessed 25 March 2022).

independently self-developed in both companies is not identical and thus registered at the respective national patent office in either case.

As an alternative scenario, it is assumed that Company A itself has self-developed the majority of its relevant IP base and centralized the entire group's IP in Country A, correspondingly exercising the DEMPE functions with a view to its valuable technology and trademark intangibles. To do so, Company A is employing contract R&D service agreements with Company B and Company C that locally oversee customizing the centrally provided product formulations and technologies but only to a rather limited extent. Then, both Company B and Company C could not take advantage of the respectively available local tax incentive regimes as they most likely would not satisfy the corresponding domestic IP incentive programme requirements. Moreover, such an attempt by them would obviously be contrary to the Group's IP centralization strategy that Company A might have adopted earlier to better exploit the synergies from the larger and historically grown R&D resource base in its home country.

(iii) Decentralized financing

This approach could also be subsumed under the functional decentralization feature already described under section 2.3.2(i) above.[79] Consequently, each affiliate would have to establish its own treasury function in order to cater to and secure its local financing needs. This leads to a duplication of efforts in the MNE and correspondingly greater financing full costs[80] for the group overall if the internal costs could not be (over) compensated by significantly lower costs for external refinancing. Additionally, financial surpluses or requirements arising in individual affiliates (potentially only on short notice) might be balanced with less flexibility compared to a centralized intra-group financing approach. This would thus forgo the general synergy benefits that differentiate an aggregation of companies forming an MNE from a group of independent, stand-alone companies. Therefore, it seems quite unlikely that such set-up in an FMCG MNE would currently be observed.

In summary, while a decentralized business model may be observed in certain functional areas, for example, depending on the nature of products manufactured and transported to customers, currently, FMCG MNEs still somewhat prefer centralized business models regarding functional, IP, or financing related centralization. However, over the last years, steering models that are more regional have been emerging in FMCG MNEs, thus combining regional consolidation advantages with individual market cultivation more independently managed by local affiliates in the region's countries compared to the past.[81] Moreover, it seems likely that recent learning from

79. *See also* footnote 47.
80. That is, considering internal (their own personnel) and external financing costs (e.g., bank interest payment, hedging fees, etc.) together.
81. *See*, for example, Knight, E., Kumar, V., Wójcik, D., O'Neill, P. (2020) The Competitive Advantage of Regions: Economic Geography and Strategic Management Intersections, Regional

the COVID-19 pandemic will support this regionalization trend to particularly enhance the stability and resilience of global supply chains vis-à-vis unexpected business disruption.

Considering this, the following section will continue to explore various TP implications for FMCG MNEs in more detail.

3 TP ISSUES IN THE FMCG SECTOR

3.1 Transfer Pricing

This section outlines intra-group transactions frequently encountered in FMCG MNEs. At the outset, important transaction categories are described (section 3.1.1), followed by a delineation of TP methods commonly encountered in the context of the important transaction categories mentioned (section 3.1.2). Subsequently, VAT effects on customs values in relation to TP are discussed (section 3.2) and proceeded by a description of supply chain management and TP issues related to purchasing, production, distribution, and management functions (section 3.3).

3.1.1 Transaction Categories

In the FMCG industry sector, the most relevant intra-group transaction categories comprise:

- tangible goods;
- services;
- intangibles; and
- financing.

These categories and respective TP issues will subsequently be addressed.

(i) Tangible goods

Depending on the business model selected by an MNE, as described in sections 2.3.1 and 2.3.2, the total value (amounts) observed in each of the four transaction categories will vary. For example, the implementation of a centralized supply chain structure (c.f. section 2.3.1(i.2)) will lead to a considerable increase in the total amount and number of tangible goods transactions compared to a decentralized structure with a higher number of 'stand-alone' entities that produce and sell their FMCG portfolio in the home market or in other countries (export business) and to other affiliates cross-border (c.f. section 2.3.2(i.2)).

Studies, Vol. 54, No. 5, pp. 591-595, https://doi.org/10.1080/00343404.2020.1739262, https://www.tandfonline.com/doi/epub/10.1080/00343404.2020.1739262?needAccess=true (last accessed 26 March 2022).

(ii) Services

Likewise, the total amount of intra-group service charges will be higher if shared service centres have been established in the FMCG MNE (c.f. section 2.3.1(i.1)) compared to the decentralized set-up in which affiliates maintain their own administrative resources in-house. Both direct and indirect service charging models can be found between affiliated FMCG companies. The latter subcategory is prevalent in the area of central management services, that is, global or regional management cost allocation from an FMCG headquarters to its benefiting affiliates, duly excluding shareholder costs.

Public auditing of such management cost allocation models and their underlying rationale from a content perspective may be employed by the MNE. It can be used as an instrument to establish adequate TPD in view of the arm's length character of the chargeable cost basis taken into account, appropriate cost allocation keys being applied, and the correctness of calculations being performed. This is done to determine respective charging amounts by affiliate and corresponding accounting on either side. Such audit reports and supporting documentation samples collected by cost centre or service element provided[82] in the course of a public auditing process can help to evidence the benefit delivered to the affiliated service recipients in countries.

In the case of direct service charges, for example, technical or marketing services rendered by one FMCG affiliate to another, the supporting evidence for the benefit test[83] according to OECD TPG may be correspondingly easier to establish. Moreover, the spectrum of intra-group services delivered within the FMCG MNE may range from lower value-added services, for example, administrative services, to higher value-added services such as those for contract R&D. 'Lower value-adding', however, does not imply that these services are of little relevance only for an efficient functioning of the entire MNE's organization and process infrastructure.[84]

(iii) Intangibles

Intra-group transactions involving intangibles may be encountered as distinct licensing transactions on a regular basis in which relevant IP is provided by an affiliated IP owner to other FMCG affiliates performing production, sales, and marketing functions. Alternatively, tangible goods transactions and corresponding transfer prices charged may contain a remuneration increment for the IP employed to manufacture and label the products delivered to the affiliated buyer. Potential TP issues encountered in this context have been outlined above (cf. section 2.3.1(ii)). Intra-group IP asset sales will usually require a DCF[85] valuation or similar financial valuation techniques, i.e., no

82. For example, interviews conducted by public auditors with responsible service providing cost centre representatives, project presentations, meeting minutes, service reports, travel reports, trainings conducted and respective agenda, or training materials provided, etc.
83. *See* OECD TPG (2022), Chapter VII, section B.1. (paras 7.6 et seq.).
84. Compare Sadun, R., Bloom, N., Van Reenen, J. (2017) Why Do We Undervalue Competent Management?, Harvard Business Review, Vol. 95, No. 5, September/October 2017.
85. For a definition of DCF, *see* https://www.investopedia.com/terms/d/dcf.asp (last accessed 30 January 2022).

outright TP methods, in order to establish a fair market value for the IP asset in question in accordance with the arm's length principle. Potential issues in that regard have been highlighted in the OECD TPG.[86]

(iv) Financing

With respect to an intra-group provision of financial funds, different transactions can be distinguished that are, as such, not peculiar to only the FMCG industry sector.

a) Cash pooling (in-house banking)

Cash pools have increased in number and volume in recent years. They are observed within group associations, established under a *contract sui generis* in the context of an in-house bank set-up, and are always individually adapted to the needs of the MNE in question. The primary objectives of cash pools are the reduction of external refinancing costs, liquidity maintenance within the group, and creditworthiness improvement while maintaining financial flexibility of affiliated pool members.

Cash pools are a particularly beneficial intra-group financing instrument due to their flexibility (compared to loans) and the already existing contractual relationship (inclusive operational structures). In the event of a crisis, it is possible to increase limits or base amounts for cash pool participants. Furthermore, cash pools ensure that participants with liquidity surpluses can continue to deposit these in the pool while participants with cash requirements can cover these accordingly. This framework ensures the short-term distribution of cash within the FMCG MNE.

If there is external financing at the level of cash pool participants, e.g., a credit line obtained from a bank, this credit line should be further utilized, and liquid funds can be deposited into the cash pool at short notice. Deposits and loans should not remain largely unchanged in the cash pool for more than one year as longer-term deposits may entail the risk that cash pool amounts may be reclassified at a later date as medium- to long-term loans by tax authorities. Cash pool deposits should therefore be regularly monitored, adjusted, and documented in the same way as cash pool borrowing, taking into account base amounts and cash holdings at arm's length.

The cash pool leader or participants should be able to obtain liquid funds from the financial market/banks at all times and make them available in the cash pool. As a rule, credit lines are agreed with banks within the framework of implemented cash pools. From these credit lines, the cash pool and its participants can avail themselves up to a defined limit. External financing and investment conditions and also access to the cash pool by reducing entry limits can change in such a way that the respective conditions can be passed on to cash pool participants in a timely manner. In addition, changes in the risk position of the cash pool leader must be taken into account in the context of its compensation.

The remuneration of the cash pool leader depends on the characteristics of its functional and risk profile. Both the OECD TPG and the German tax authorities assume,

86. *See* OECD TPG (2022), Chapter VI, sections D.2.6.3. and 2.6.4.

in principle, that cash pool leaders have only a coordinating agent function.[87] If the cash pool leader does not prove that it performs a function beyond this and, above all, that it bears corresponding risks, this is detrimental to the amount of its cash pool remuneration.

The cash pool interest rate needs to be adjusted according to the risk profile of the cash pool leader. The amount of its remuneration is determined by: (i) a maturity premium, (ii) the increase (or decrease) in external financing costs, and (iii) an increased (or decreased) risk premium in line with correspondingly exercised functions and risks assumed. Existing contractual cash pool provisions and their potential for change must be observed. If there is no contractual opening clause or the conditions are not flexible, it is difficult to adjust the cash pool accordingly. Any changes to its conditions should be contractually regulated and documented for tax compliance and insolvency law purposes.

b) Guarantees/collateral

To reduce their credit risks, banks require their borrowers to provide collateral. Typically, loans extended by banks to individual group companies are secured by a guarantee from the financially stronger parent company. This enables group companies to obtain external loan conditions that are more favourable. The guarantee makes it less likely that the bank will default on its loan. In addition, financial guarantees will be issued instead of granting group loans if an internal group financing company or the parent company has a correspondingly good credit rating.

In the case of loans granted to a subsidiary by an external bank, a guarantee from the parent company can be beneficial. Such bank loans are often agreed in case of acquisitions by the subsidiaries, i.e., the so-called debt push down. If, in the case of a cash pool, the cash pool leader is not the parent company, an intra-group guarantee from the parent company should be possible nonetheless. If a benefit provided is proven, the parent company must be compensated for providing the guarantee. The benefit from a guarantee seems obvious if the risk position of the cash pool leader has changed significantly, i.e., deteriorated. In this case, the question arises whether an unrelated party would have agreed to a further allocation of funds in the cash pool or a loan under the existing circumstances.

The amount of a remunerable guarantee fee should be based on: (i) comparable guarantee fees if these can be observed among unrelated parties (CUP method); (ii) the interest saved by a lower interest rate due to the guarantee (yield method); (iii) the expected costs of the guarantor and the probabilities of default and recovery rates (cost approach, expected loss approach); or (iv) the additional capital required by the guarantee holder (capital support approach).[88] Currently, comparable and publicly traded credit default swaps can serve as a point of reference. The terms and conditions for intra-group guarantees must always be contractually defined. Changes in the credit market will change intra-group conditions for granting loans accordingly. This results

87. *See* OECD TPG (2022), Chapter X, section C.2.3.1.
88. *See* OECD TPG (2022) Chapter X, sections D.2. and D.3.

in adjustments to lending (borrowing) conditions. Intra-group guarantees must also be documented for compliance and possible insolvency law purposes.

c) Loans

In addition to the FMCG group's internal cash pools, the affiliated companies continue to have the option of granting intra-group loans. Whether and under what conditions an unrelated party would be prepared to grant a loan is the decisive criterion for the corresponding arm's length comparison. The interest rate level, the collateral provided, and the ability to repay the loan are to be considered as conditions for an arm's length comparison. Loans to affiliated companies with a weaker financial standing are subject to correspondingly higher interest rates. In such cases, the capital market would also demand higher risk premiums for lower credit ratings. This requires that the existing intra-group loans should be subject to a reassessment of the loan risks in comparable situations. An unrelated party would also make use of any special termination rights or renegotiation options for the provision of collateral and interest.

Whether it is possible to suspend debt servicing for a certain period of time is also being discussed among unrelated parties. However, this option is subject to certain important conditions that should be agreed in writing from the outset: (i) the period of the suspension of the debt service; and (ii) the extension of the term of the loan in order to agree on the suspended period or to subsequently arrange the adjusted repayment instalments.

Another measure to support subsidiaries could be a debt waiver by the lender to the subsidiary. Such a waiver, however, has the disadvantage that it is not recognized for tax purposes if it is based on the shareholder relationship. An unrelated party will not easily waive its claims. If a waiver of a financial claim is made with respect to a non-valuable part of the claim and the shareholder has incurred corresponding acquisition costs, this can lead to a loss to be taken into account for tax purposes. In addition, it is possible and even necessary to write off intra-group loans to the going concern value if it can be proven that they are no longer recoverable. However, these are only tax deductible to the extent that it can be proven that an unrelated party would also have granted the loan under otherwise identical circumstances.

d) Clearing accounts

In addition to the intra-group financing instruments mentioned above, intra-group clearing accounts for FMCG affiliates can offer a further possibility to provide short-term liquidity. Clearing accounts (which are similar to current accounts) provide an opportunity to group companies to receive cash and cash equivalents on a daily basis and to repay liabilities accordingly.

In contrast to cash pools in which several participants will regularly participate, internal clearing accounts represent an immediate relationship between two affiliates, and these accounts can also be available for longer-term financing if necessary.

Clearing accounts are subject to interest. Without interest, balancing payments may be qualified as a hidden profit distribution to the creditor that is usually subject to withholding tax. The interest on clearing accounts can be based on interbank interest rates similar to that on current bank accounts. These interest rates are currently on a daily basis if daily repayment has been agreed. Otherwise, a correspondingly higher term-specific interest rate must be taken into account in accordance with the repayment term. Clearing accounts must be contractually agreed. Regulations concerning the amount of the credit limit, interest rate, repayment date, currency, and securities must be agreed in writing in advance.

e) Hedging

FMCG MNEs have to manage a portfolio of currencies in different regions and countries. Therefore, hedging transactions are a common intra-group financing feature in these corporate groups. Usually, currency risks are managed centrally by a corporate treasury function in the FMCG MNE (*see* section 2.3.1(iii)).[89]

Transactional currency risk emerges from cash flows that are denominated in the currency of a foreign country that is different from the so-called group currency (reporting currency) of the respective FMCG MNE. The group-wide currency exposure can be derived from all external and internal cash flows in foreign currencies. This group exposure risk is centrally hedged, and the results of corresponding hedges are forwarded to affiliated FMCG companies with respective currency risks.

The business units in an FMCG MNE can plan currency exposures on an annual basis. This is then covered by respective hedge transactions. In essence, hedges reduce the P&L volatility for the FMCG MNE caused by fluctuating currency rates. For example, if imports denominated in a foreign currency become more expensive due to a devaluation of local currency, a hedge reduces that impact for the FMCG affiliate. The central treasury function will conclude the hedge with external banks and forward the result to the affiliate involved. In this way, a corporate treasury functions as an in-house bank for the FMCG MNE and ensures compliance in currency trading and favourable pricing conditions with external banks.

Three types of foreign currency risk can be distinguished. First, a transaction risk results from any cash flow position denominated in foreign currency (compared to group currency). Operative transaction risk (operative receivables and payables) can be distinguished, on the one hand, and financial transaction risk (e.g., IC loans, bank loans) on the other. Second, a translation risk emerges from foreign currency shareholdings as a foreign currency balance sheet, and P&L positions need to be converted into the base of currency of the FMCG MNE for consolidation purposes. Third, economic risk is the potential indirect impact of the development of currency rates – even without cash flows or positions being denominated in foreign currency. As an example, currency rate changes may affect the FMCG MNE's competitive position by providing its competitors with purchasing conditions that are more favourable or with lower production costs.

In general, currency hedges are entered into in order to minimize transaction risk. By contrast, hedging of translation risk is only applicable in exceptional cases for the

89. *See* OECD TPG (2022) Chapter X, section C.3.

FMCG MNE when the hedging costs are lower than the expected devaluation and the net investment would be entered into for only a limited period.

The market value for currency hedges may be allocated to the P&L of the respective FMCG affiliate and the business unit involved. That market value will depend on the hedging deal rate and respective spot rates, and the market value can be split into two components. The spot component is dependent on the difference between the hedge deal rate and the spot rate at maturity of the hedge transaction. The hedging cost component is dependent on the difference between the deal rate and the spot rate at the conclusion of a hedge.

Some FMCG MNEs apply hedge accounting. The main idea of this approach is to show the result of the hedge in the same period as the underlying transaction for which the hedge is made. In general, a differentiation can be made between a fair value hedge (i.e., the effective part of the hedge is reported in P&L) and a cash flow hedge (i.e., the effective part of the hedge is reported in OCI during the active hedge relationship and reclassified into the P&L after maturity). FMCG MNEs apply cash flow hedge accounting in hedges for COGS, for example. The reclassification of the hedge result will then be shown in the FMCG affiliate's earnings before interest and taxes.

3.1.2 TP Methods Employed

In order to answer the method selection question, the reader should keep in mind that a distinction must be made between the employment of a certain TP method for price setting and/or for outcome testing purposes. The methods applied may not necessarily be identical in either case. Transfer prices may very often be 'technically set up' in an FMCG MNE's accounting system employing the cost-plus or the resale minus approach on the intra-group manufacturer's side. However, the outcome testing for both the manufacturer and the receiving FMCG affiliate (tested party/distributor) upon year-end closing will most likely be done based on the TNMM, taking into account the function and risk profiles of both parties to the transaction.

Moreover, the manner in which the cost-plus or resale minus percentage as such may be determined by an intra-group manufacturer (sender) can also be reliant on the application of a (residual) profit split approach.[90] This depends, for example, on which incremental remuneration components need to be adequately reflected in the transfer price.[91] This approach will subsequently incur a certain remuneration or achieve a certain transactional net margin result (target profit) on the intra-group buyer's side

90. That is, a (residual) profit split approach may be used to establish an arm's length profit markup percentage for an intercompany transaction in a first step, which is then applied on the transaction cost base (i.e., subject to remuneration) in a cost-plus manner from a mere calculatory perspective in a second step.

91. For example, a remuneration for routine and/or non-routine functions on the intra-group manufacturer's side and/or a remuneration for the ultimate IP owner in the FMCG MNE which may not necessarily be identical with the intra-group manufacturer itself who may only have licensed the relevant IP from the affiliated IP owner. In the latter case, the manufacturer needs to cover his royalty payment to the IP owner via the transfer price charged to the intra-group buyer.

(receiver). These facts and circumstances should be addressed in the TPD of the FMCG MNE affiliates according to the OECD TPG.[92]

With respect to the four main intra-group transaction categories outlined in the preceding section, different TP methods can be employed to enable an arm's length pricing of the transaction in question.

(i) Tangible goods

In order to price tangible goods transactions between FMCG affiliates, standard methods such as cost-plus, resale minus, and the TNMM are the most widely employed. This choice is based on the underlying assumption that the nature of the receiving party's[93] function and risk profile can be characterized as routine. Whether transfer prices will be established on a cost-plus, resale minus, or TNMM basis will depend on the preference of the individual FMCG MNE and its IT system set-up.

The cost-plus method is straightforward in its application as relevant cost centre accounting data will be available in a high level of detail in most FMCG MNEs. Nonetheless, the TNMM will very often be applied in outcome testing to ensure that the manufacturing and receiving affiliates have earned an arm's length margin from their intra-group transaction.[94] In that context, the TNMM will be commonly applied based on the aggregated financial data of the sending (manufacturer) and receiving (distributor) affiliates as most FMCG MNEs do not have segmented P&L accounting available to differentiate between intra-group and third-party transactions. This is due to the obvious fact that the clear focus of any FMCG MNE is on the effective and efficient steering and control of its third-party business as this is the ultimate source of income for the FMCG as a whole.

In order to employ the resale minus method in a reliable manner, it should be considered that external selling prices (market prices) of all products sold in all respective domestic markets need to be known in order to apply the method in an arm's length manner. Contemporaneous price data and an appropriate IT infrastructure must be available in the FMCG MNE to satisfy this requirement accordingly.

Finally, the TNMM as a price-setting method will most likely be encountered in centralized FMCG supply chain structures where the receiving parties (local distributors/sellers) are directed by a central supply chain principal (intra-group supplier) with a view to a benchmarked interquartile range observed in the respective FMCG segment (*see* section 2.3.1(i.2)). Therefore, either the cost-plus markup or the resale minus percentage applied in the transfer prices for tangible goods on offer will be calculated. This will be accomplished in a manner that enables the receiving party to earn a benchmarked target net margin in view of its routine function and risk profile while the residual profit is incurred at the level of the central supplier.

92. *See* OECD TPG (2022) Chapter V, paras 5.22, 5.23 and 5.35.
93. That is, the intra-group buyer or 'tested party' in comparability analysis terms.
94. In most cases, independent comparables' gross margin data are not available for an immediate benchmarking of cost-plus or resale minus percentages applied in intra-group transactions.

(ii) Services

The pricing of intra-group services will primarily be reliant on a straightforward application of the cost-plus method. The service cost base should take into account full costs as derived from the underlying service providing cost centre's accounting data. General side costs not necessarily reflected in the service providing cost centre can be considered by applying a side cost-related markup on the immediate service cost in a first step in order to establish the service's full cost base.[95] In a second step, an arm's length profit markup for the service in question will then be applied on said full cost base to establish the final transfer price for the intra-group service in question, which has to be documented accordingly. In that context, the cost-plus profit markup may be employed to differentiate between higher and lower value-adding services.[96]

(iii) Intangibles

If intangibles are remunerated within the transfer price for tangible goods, the TNMM will be most commonly employed to establish arm's length transfer prices between FMCG affiliates, as outlined above (*see* section 3.1.2 (i)).

In the event of outright intra-group licensing transactions between affiliates, the CUP method is available as a price-setting and/or outcome testing method for companies operating in the FMCG sector. It has often been mentioned in TP literature that royalty rate benchmarking or the application of general principles such as Goldscheider's rule or the Knoppe formula do not constitute a valid basis for establishing arm's length prices for unique and valuable intangibles in those transactions.[97] However, such types of empirical evidence should not simply be waived as 'irrelevant' information as no entirely conclusive alternative can be offered instead – considering the well-known uncertainty challenges of pricing and valuing intangibles in business practice.[98] Then, it does make sense to collect any available information, for example, (preferably) internal and/or external CUP data in royalty benchmarking or applying different available pricing approaches to rationalize the establishment of transfer prices for intra-group transactions involving intangibles in FMCG MNEs.

95. According to the author's (Martin Lagarden's) understanding, such side costs cannot and do not include statutorily required goodwill amortization amounts. The latter do not influence the actually ongoing operative business conducted by an associated company under consideration in an MNE. That is, goodwill depreciation is not considered as a value contributor which can influence intra-group transfer prices and/or sales prices charged by the associated company vis-à-vis its external customers. Tax authorities, however, may adopt an opposing viewpoint.
96. For example, a higher markup percentage may be employed in the case of contract R&D services as compared to transactional HR or financial accounting services. *See also* OECD TPG (2022) Chapter VII, paras 7.61 et seq.
97. *See* OECD TPG (2022) Chapter II, para. 2.10 and Chapter VI, para. 6.144; Joerg Hanken, Guido Kleinhietpaß, Martin Lagarden (2020) Verrechnungspreise, Haufe Verlag, Freiburg, 3. Auflage, pp. 412-418; Nestler, A. (2013) Angemessene Lizenzbewertung anhand der Profit-Split-Methode: Was man von der Knoppe-Formel lernen kann, Betriebs-Berater, Vol. 68, No. 34, pp. 2027-2029 (English translation available in: Valnes Corporate Finance GmbH, Dr Anke Nestler, Comment Letter to the OECD Revised Discussion Draft on Transfer Pricing Aspects of Intangibles, 30 September 2013, pp. 3-7.).
98. *See* OECD TPG (2022) Chapter VI, sections D.3. and D.4.

Moreover, the (residual) profit split method can also be employed by FMCG affiliates to establish transfer prices (royalty rates) in order to ensure an arm's length remuneration of their valuable intangibles in intra-group licensing transactions.[99]

Finally, the application of financial valuation techniques in intra-group sales transactions involving intangible assets as such has been already addressed above (*see* section 3.1.1(iii)).

(iv) Financing

Due to the fact that financial funds can be regarded as a uniform commodity for which comparable capital market data is commonly available, the CUP method provides the prevailing approach to establish arm's length prices in intra-group financing transactions among FMCG affiliates, as described in the preceding sections 2.3.1(iii) and 3.1.1(iv).

3.2 VAT Effects on Customs Values and TP

As a rule, sales tax does not represent a cost burden for a company: The sales tax paid can be deducted as input tax, and only the end consumer is charged. This applies across borders, e.g., EU-wide for intra-community acquisitions (§ 1 paragraph 1 No. 5 in conjunction with § 1 a UStG and § 15 paragraph 1 sentence 1 No. 3 UStG) and import turnover tax (§ 1 paragraph 1 No. 4 in conjunction with § 21 UStG and § 15 paragraph 1 sentence 1 No. 2 UStG). The turnover tax becomes relevant for companies, on the one hand, because of their capital commitment and, on the other hand, if a definite charge is incurred due to errors in fulfilling the declaration and verification obligations. If business transactions are incorrectly assessed for VAT purposes, e.g., due to insufficient or incomplete information, a tax exemption or input tax deduction may be refused. This can also be the case with defective invoices or export certificates. An error rate can ultimately lead to a definite VAT charge particularly in the case of complex supply chains involving unrelated party transport companies. The comprehensive case law of the ECJ on intra-community deliveries with several companies shows the complexity: A correct VAT assessment is often only possible if it is known who is responsible for the transport (A 3.14 paragraph 10 UStAE)[100] and when the power of disposal is transferred. A further complicating factor is that the German special regulation for chain transactions in § 3 paragraph 6, sentences 5 and 6 UStG has no equivalent in the VAT Directive and is therefore difficult to reconcile with the findings of the ECJ. However, the relevant input tax deduction of the import turnover tax when importing into the EU can also be wrong in individual cases. The decisive factor is

99. *See*, for example, Martin Lagarden (2019), *Attribution of Intangible Related Returns*, in: Michael Lang, Alfred Storck, Raffaele Petruzzi, Robert Risse (editors), *Transfer Pricing and Intangibles*, Series on International Tax Law, Vol. 113, Linde Publishers, Chapter II, pp. 62-64.

100. Sales tax application decree 2020 (UStAE 2010) v. 1. 10. 2010 (BStBl I p. 846), last modified by BMF letter v. 16 November 2020 – III C 2 – S 7100-b/19/10001:004 (2020/1181130). This is an interpretation of the individual VAT regulations from the point of view of the tax authority, which reflects the opinion of the tax authority and takes into account the latest supreme court decisions.

always whether the import delivery is already deemed to have been carried out in the third country (§ 3 paragraph 6 p. 1 UStG) or in Germany (§ 3 paragraph 8 UStG). In the first case, the purchaser of the goods is usually entitled to deduct input tax from the import turnover tax; in the second case, it is usually the supplier. It is therefore relevant who has the power of disposal at the time of the import transaction for which the terms of delivery (Incoterms) can be an indication. An accompanying anomaly detection will uniformly consider these complex cases by means of an algorithm trained for these cases and will make deviations in the process steps clear.

Customs and VAT are closely related in legal terms. According to § 11 UStG, the customs value is the basis of assessment for the import turnover tax, and according to § 21 paragraph 2 UStG, the customs regulations for the import turnover tax are to be applied accordingly; this also applies if no customs duty is to be levied for customs reasons. The regulations mentioned above for determining the customs value thus directly influence the import turnover tax. This does not mean that the correct application of the customs regulations according to § 21 paragraph 2 UStG automatically leads to an import turnover tax liability. For example, this is the case if the customs debt is incurred only due to a breach of customs regulations (Article 79 UZK). Conflicts of qualification with regard to the duty to provide evidence for customs and turnover tax purposes may also arise in the case of exports on the basis of the definition of exporter in Article 1 No. 19 UZK-DA.[101] As a consequence, in certain situations, a tax exemption according to § 6 UStG can be denied. The interaction of the various legal requirements makes it clear that there is considerable potential for optimization in this area. The reconciliation of data and the transparent implementation of regulations can be best checked by process mining of the procedural steps. The control of the processes has the effect of achieving process management in compliance with the rules, savings in administrative costs and continuous improvement of the processes. The intersection between income tax and sales tax, on the other hand, is relatively small. However, the question arises, for example, whether subsequent corrections of the income tax-related transfer prices should also be considered as a change in the basis of assessment within the meaning of § 17 UStG. This is denied, at least for the EU VAT system, since subsequent off-balance sheet income corrections are not a subsequent agreement between the persons involved in the exchange of services. However, if there is an internal adjustment of the fees so that they are recognized as transfer prices, these must also be taken into account for VAT purposes from the time of the adjustment. In this case, the company modifies the actual charges to the legal circumstances in order to avoid a 'two sets of books'[102] system.

The digitalization of accounting and tax processes will be able to meet tax compliance requirements more effectively than before. Currently, many digitization methods

101. UZK-DA, UCC, Customs Code, Delegate Regulation (EU) 2015/2446 of the Commission of 28 July 2015 supplementing Regulation (EU) No. 952/2013 of the European Parliament and of the Council laying down provisions for the implementation of the Union Customs Code.

102. *See* Marcel Haak, Rebecca Reineke, Katrin Weiskricher-Merten, Stefan Wieleberg S., One Set or Two Sets of Books: The Impact of a Strategic Tax Auditor Retrieved On, https://pdfs.semanticscholar.org/a5d5/5b61c9767b9082c8011aeb282ae739f7f449.pdf (last accessed 30 January 2022).

such as robots (RPA), machine learning, deep learning with algorithms and process controls through process mining, and anomaly detection algorithms still seem overly inconclusive. With the increasing use of cloud data solutions, the likelihood of using these digital tools is increasing. The tools described below will also result in cost savings and a minimization of tax risks.

3.3 Supply Chain Management and TP Issues

In the FMCG industry, purchasing, production, and logistics are key success factors. As outlined in the introduction, economic factors that have influenced the actions of corporations are globalization, saturated buyer's markets, intense customer orientation and competition, individualization of products for customer orientation, and an accelerated technological development, i.e., digitalization of business models combined with a shortening of product life cycles.[103] In order to meet these requirements, the common claim 'process follows structure' is no longer relevant. Rather, processes shape the organizational structure of FMCG MNEs in a 'structure follows process' manner.[104] The corporate strategy is the basis for an organizational solution required to enable successful strategy implementation. This results in the extended premise 'structure follows process follows strategy'.[105] In the context of economic considerations made and potential TP implications, possible strategies and associated changes in corresponding value-added processes are discussed below. The overview employs a sequential view of the flows of goods and services. This orientation is made although, in the age of digitalization, the value chains targeted by the BEPS initiative are increasingly developing from one-dimensionally arranged to multidimensionally networked processes.

3.3.1 Purchasing

The goal of the procurement function is to maintain supply chain operations and to develop an external and internal supplier portfolio in order to avoid disruption of production processes and an overly strong dependency on individual suppliers. To realize these goals, a more comprehensive understanding of the purchasing process (source-to-pay) is required. The procurement organization can be divided into a strategic and an operational level. The strategic procurement process is concerned with the coverage of general material and service requirements in the FMCG group that are encountered in individual cases. Associated with this are aspects of strategy development and, derived from this, for example, decisions regarding global sourcing, single

103. J. Nevam Wright, Peter Race (2004) The Management of Service Operations, 2nd edn, Thomson Learning, p. 206.
104. Hans Strikwerda (2020) Organization Design in the 21st Century: From Structure Follows Strategy to Process Follows Proposition, available at SSRN, https://dx.doi.org/10.2139/ssrn.2002236 (last accessed 30 January 2022).
105. Bach, Norbert, Brehm, Carsten, Buchholz, Wolfgang, Petry, Thorsten (2012) Wertschöpfungsorientierte Organisation.

sourcing, or supplier portfolios. The operational procurement process comprises the entire process from an initial order to the corresponding payment. This process, known as source-to-pay, begins with the concrete determination of requirements and ends with creditor management. Both parts of the procurement are very important for the FMCG industry as the supply basis guarantees the high speed of innovation for new products; fast, cost-efficient, and automated production processes; and, ultimately, profitable sales.

The significance of the procurement process in the value chain, i.e., whether it is a strategic or an operational/supporting process, depends on the industry and the depth of value creation of the respective group.[106] In the FMCG industry, goods are manufactured and sold in a short timeframe; this circumstance affects the procurement process. A rapid production of goods and an accelerated sale with an annual goods turnover of ten to twelve times requires a functioning supply chain, including a fast procurement process. The global dependence on individual suppliers, such as that of global supply chains in China, can have a strong influence on the economic success of a company. FMCG companies need the security and stability of value chains.[107] It is therefore to be expected that the flexibility of procurement processes and the reduction of associated risks will come into focus going forward. One consequence is increased risk management for procurement sources. Strategic aspects include the identification and analysis of direct suppliers (Tier 1) as well as an analysis of the Tiers 2 and 3 supplier networks and the development of alternative procurement sources from various regions in addition. The so-called control towers of group-wide supply chain management together with procurement and digital solutions have been increasing for many years. The procurement function has therefore been increasingly performed centrally for some time now. This results in a centralized control of procurement in addition to the local purchasing functions that are only necessary to a limited extent. An optimized procurement reduces costs and promotes the rapid adaptation to market changes in the FMCG MNE.

From a transfer price perspective, possible adjustments of the procurement function must be evaluated. The analysis of facts and circumstances has to be examined case related, reviewing: (i) what relevance the procurement currently has and what it has in the future considering the reason for business success, (ii) who exercises the leading functions with a view to the procurement process and carries corresponding risks, and (iii) whether new intangible values such as digital procurement tools are added. With regard to any intangible assets, a complementary DEMPE analysis is advisable: Who performs key functions? Who makes essential decisions? Who controls risks?

If the strategic procurement function together with its risk management and the maintenance of relationships with suppliers is seen as a strategic competitive factor in the future, it should be reconsidered whether a cost-based compensation is appropriate or whether strategic procurement should be allocated at least part of the residual earnings of the FMCG group. With regard to the operational processing of procurement

106. J. Nevam Wright, Peter Race (2004) The Management of Service Operations, 2nd edn, Thomson Learning, p. 207.
107. *Ibid.*, pp. 209 ff.

transactions, it must be critically examined whether such processing justifies a residual remuneration. The question of remuneration can only be answered with an analysis of the implementation of the strategic procurement framework concept. Depending on the characteristics of such a concept, a small profit margin for the function is appropriate or a profit markup seems justified. If the operational processing performed by the purchasing department provides a significant added value, the invoiced transfer price for such a service should be adjusted. The centralization of the supply chain function coupled with digital standardization will create a new intangible value which will then have to be remunerated at a higher rate.

If there are adjustments in the allocation of revenue entitlements, for example, because a stronger central procurement function has been established or responsibility has been transferred from countries to a supply chain centre, the question of IP transfers or function relocation entailing corresponding transfer package valuations in the context of exit taxation as provided for by law, e.g., in Germany, shall be examined. Countries without comparable exit taxation will attempt to adjust transfer prices in the future accordingly. Provided that the local procurement function has merely been provided with routine remuneration and that, in the future, some of the functions that have also been taken over locally will be performed centrally, exit taxation is nevertheless unlikely to arise.

3.3.2 Production

The production process in the FMCG industry is significantly influenced by two goals: process and resource efficiency for an optimization of the COGS. The entire supply chain management in the area of operations/production is aimed at the cross-company coordination of material and information flows over the entire value-added process from incoming goods to outgoing goods. The compatibility of the order processing process with the supply chains of upstream and downstream partners is the strategic target for the optimization of the COGS.

In the context of risk distribution in the processes mentioned above, aspects such as the number of products, made-to-order production versus inventory production, tiered production (single-stage versus multistage), and the organization of production as well as the production quantities are now analysed and adjusted. This corresponds to the DEMPE analyses of participating functions. If production at a site is interrupted, for example, as a result of the corona pandemic, so-called start-up costs are incurred upon the return from a shutdown that are caused by insufficiently functioning supply chains, lack of demand, or the resumption of processes. In addition, as with procurement, the production process will also be reviewed in the medium to long term. To be discussed are the number of production sites, contract manufacturing versus inventory production, choice of location and production network, flexible production, and digitalization of production control. These are the strategic questions that companies must analyse against the background of costs and earnings. The global division of labour has advantages. Duplication of production sites is avoided. If production facilities are also set up directly in the countries of destination, freight traffic and the associated costs will decrease significantly. This is an opportunity for both the costs and the quality of the production process.[108] The World Economic Forum also notes that the ability to collect production data and use it for production control is becoming increasingly important for controlling a more flexible and modular production network.[109] In addition to increasing production, the next step is to consider the number of warehouses and their capital requirements. The reaction of continental European manufacturing companies to the Brexit is to establish additional warehouses in the United Kingdom. These warehouses were opened in order to be able to deliver immediately in the event of a hard Brexit in that country. The additional storage capacity will result in a considerable increase in costs that must also be reflected in the transfer prices.

In the short term, the resumption of production after a crisis such as COVID-19 or, e.g., after a hard Brexit in the United Kingdom leads to start-up and idle costs that are initially incurred by the production company. From a TP perspective, the current and future distribution of functions and risks must be assessed and adjustments described. Any adjustments and the introduction of new control systems are to be examined with regard to their value contribution and remunerated accordingly. In particular, the introduction of new value-creating software as an intangible asset will increase the profit entitlement of the investing function. Here, the DEMPE concept is used to identify the main decision, function, and risk carriers. The data models are of special importance. If production structures become more flexible, efficient control requires good production planning that should be data based and digitalized. In this respect, the development and maintenance of data models play a far greater role in value creation. The appropriate compensation of the digital models has to be checked and then adjusted using the DEMPE concept.

If production structures change in the short, medium, or long term, it will be necessary to examine the facts of relocation of functions and transfer of tangible or intangible assets. If the local production function is merely a routine task (production as a service, i.e., toll manufacturing), no situation will arise that requires a transfer package valuation for exit taxation. In this case, an individual valuation as a result of an escape clause such as that in German tax legislation is regularly considered. Nevertheless, it must be checked whether long-term acceptance commitments, valuable ingenuity, machines, inventories, or customer relationships are also transferred. In this case, individual transfer prices customary for unrelated parties would have to be determined.

The corona crisis has not only shut down production units but also interrupted logistics chains. Ports were closed, and passenger flights were cancelled that are used not only for business travel but also for freight. For various industry sectors outside the FMCG, the disruption in supply chains was a major problem. Production was meant to

108. Vitols, K., Schmid, K., Wilke, P. (2017) Digitalisierung, Automatisierung und Arbeit 4.0: Beschäftigungsperspektiven im norddeutschen Dienstleistungssektor, available, http://hdl.handle.net/10419/215964 (last accessed 30 January 2022).
109. World Economic Forum v. 6 April 2020, Supply chains have been upended. Here's how to make them more resilient, available, https://www.weforum.org/agenda/2020/04/supply-chains-resilient-covid-19/ (last accessed 30 January 2022).

continue; however, the necessary materials and preliminary products were not available. The various industries and also corporations expect a start-up phase of six weeks when the logistics hubs, such as those for ports and airports, are reopened. For the future, several companies have already announced that, in addition to the reactions to this global crisis already mentioned, they see warehousing policy as a decisive factor for a smooth supply chain organization. In that context, it is an additional argument that, at the current low-interest rate level, the capital commitment costs caused by higher inventory levels are considered a controllable financial indicator.

With regard to new warehouses, operating site risks must be examined. In many double taxation agreements, warehousing is considered a so-called auxiliary activity. This assessment will be questioned in the future against the background of anti-fragmentation rules through the Multilateral Instrument and in the context of a new classification of warehouses as 'non-auxiliary activities'.[110]

Any start-up and closure costs must be assessed on a case-by-case basis. Nevertheless, the specific allocation of functions and risks must be taken into account. In the current situation, an external third-party producer would also have to bear idle costs and start-up costs. As a market risk, the risk of idle capacity is generally not insured. It is therefore necessary to ask the FMCG group whether the production contracts provide for purchase obligations. If this is the case, an external unrelated party could also refer to this and claim acceptance as part of the commitment or at least use this as a negotiating argument in a hypothetical arm's length settlement. Furthermore, the current pandemic leads to an additional storage risk due to declines in the sales market. If it is assumed that the usual production volumes were produced at the onset of the crisis, an unrelated party would also bear such risks because it also would not have been able to react. Nevertheless, it is necessary to check whether the routine group unit produced like a normal company or whether it had a higher production volume due to the entrepreneur's specifications even before the pandemic. If this was the case, then the question would have to be asked whether the additional storage risk compared to an average market participant has to be borne by the entrepreneur.

3.3.3 Distribution

Due to the political guidelines on 'physical distancing', personal physical customer contacts and negotiations have currently come to a standstill. The focus of distribution is on so-called CRM systems, which have three main elements:

(1) operational CRM, i.e., the digital support of all processes at the point of sale;
(2) analytical CRM, i.e., the digital evaluation of data generated in the CRM process and its subsequent optimization; and
(3) communicational CRM, i.e., the control, support and synchronization of all communication channels to the customer.

110. Michael Wichmann Update DBA-Politik, IFA Symposium vom 6.Juli 2017, available: ifa-deutschland.de.

This development is driving the process forward of digitizing sales organizations. The proliferation of digital distribution channels is already occurring at the expense of stationary retail channels. New distribution channels and measures will increase. Digital interaction with customers via apps and new online chat campaigns can already be observed. Existing delivery models will be expanded which will lead to an increase in warehouse and logistics centres. As in the case of the production network, the use and evaluation of data and its application in sales, assortment planning, pricing, and marketing will change. The sales department will have to reassess functions, risks, and intangible assets. In this context, the DEMPE functions and, consequently, the external remuneration of new intangible assets, for example, through the development of web stores and apps, need to be discussed. With regard to possible additional stock-keeping, the question arises whether operating sites are established.

Furthermore, the data model must be analysed, i.e., who will collect, store, and process respective data? Usually, the customer requests on the front end (i.e., the web shop) are processed on a server in the back end. This server then forwards the sales order to the warehouse and at the same time the customer invoice to an external payment service provider. The data processing and data storage are done on a server of an unrelated party, e.g., Microsoft, Amazon, Apple, or Alibaba, that has access to the server in this functional chain and uses the data that are essential factors for a DEMPE analysis. Usually, only the central unit has access to the server. It extracts the data, evaluates these with business intelligence solutions and provides feedback to the product development department for an adaptation of the web store and the back end. The central unit controls the data strategy and the intangible assets such as the algorithms for processing the data. The local sales unit or web store often only receives summarized data in a dashboard format. The question from a TP perspective is how the central unit is to be remunerated for data processing, e.g., via a licence, if it is not already integrated into the payment flow of the web store. However, the question also arises whether the local unit is to be remunerated for 'its' customers ordering in the web shop and thus 'making local data available'. In this case, a transaction is likely to be missing, so that compensation is difficult to justify. However, at least against the background of the current OECD discussions on Pillars 1 and 2, it is to be expected that states will want to access such sales via the argument of 'local customers' on sales or earnings, for example.[111]

A special feature of web shops is the remuneration of the stationary sales units for generating sales via the web shop and the apps. In this model of 'mobile sales', the sales units are involved in brand development; however, the sales are generated in other companies or even abroad. In these cases, how are unrelated parties to be remunerated by the web shop operator for local activities? First of all, it will depend on the question of whether the sales company has exclusive distribution rights in the respective country. If this is the case, the question would be whether it can demand a user fee for the transfer of the distribution right or how the distribution right is to be

111. Heidecke, B., Lappe, S., Pandeya-Koch, A., Wilmanns, J. (2019) Quo vadis Verrechnungspreise der digitalen Wirtschaft nach 'Säule 1': Handlungsbedarf des deutschen Gesetzgebers, IWB, S. 941.

structured in order to exclude such claims. Ultimately, an unrelated party could also purchase the producer's goods and offer them online without the local distribution company being able to interfere and demand compensation for the effects of such competitive action. If a remuneration is nevertheless demanded, it could only be a broker's commission to be measured by a Berry ratio[112] or a service fee for local marketing support.

3.3.4 *Management Functions*

Additional risk control functions and control elements, for example, for the supply chain, can be implemented at the FMCG group headquarters. In many cases, controlling functions in the national units of a group and at group headquarters are duplicated to avoid future risks. This is followed by the question of how the resulting costs affect the group's allocation of costs to the headquarters and to the affiliates. According to the previous principle, costs are to be allocated to the beneficiaries according to the principle of causality. For costs that cannot be directly allocated, an appropriate cost allocation key is chosen. Shareholder costs – so-called stewardship costs – are not to be allocated to affiliates. Accordingly, the OECD countries:[113]

> Whether these activities [i.e., costs of management and control (monitoring) relating to the management and protection of the equity investment as such] fall under the term 'shareholder activities' defined in these guidelines depends on whether, in the case in question, it is an activity for which an unrelated party would be prepared to pay remuneration under comparable circumstances and conditions, or whether it would provide the services itself.

The first question to be asked is why the additional costs are incurred. For example, are there new legal requirements, the result of a shareholders' decision, or an additional measure to ensure the FMCG group's functionality and efficiency? Would an unrelated party be willing to remit compensation for such costs? As an arm's length measure to answer this question, the willingness of an unaffiliated company to invest in additional risk protection is considered. If such a willingness can be considered as something that can be relied upon on the basis of available risk assessments, an additional cost apportionment to the FMCG affiliates is justified.

4 OUTLOOK

4.1 COVID-19 Impact on Transfer Price Determination

Since the outbreak of the COVID-19 pandemic, depending on the business sector, some companies are facing massive challenges that will also have an impact on transfer price

112. The Berry ratio can be used in the context of determining a reasonable profit markup for transfer pricing. It is defined as the ratio of gross profit to operating expenses and determines a markup resulting from the use of operating expenses. The Berry ratio is a possible indicator for the determination of an appropriate profit markup as far as the operating expenses constitute the essential total expenditure, and it applies to sales companies in particular.
113. OECD TPG (2022), para. 7.10.

determination. However, the FMCG industry has proven to be very crisis resistant, e.g., in the areas of cosmetics and wellness, laundry and home care, or food and dietary supplements. Nonetheless, as a result of the subsequent lockdown in many countries, production and transport interruptions have occurred. Supply chains and logistics processes came to a standstill. Since then, the organizational units of companies in MNEs have been critically examined to determine the strategic value contribution that can be achieved by the function performed. The starting point is the short- and medium-term planning to be issued by each company within a group. This planning is supplemented by best-case and worst-case scenarios. The resulting effects on profit, cash flow, and capital structure demonstrate how transfer prices need to be flexibly adjusted.

At the beginning of the crisis, many market participants expect a rapid V-shaped recovery of the economy.[114] Figure 17.6 describes which scenarios are possible: Economists differentiate between several, usually three, typical courses of crisis that were already visible in the financial crisis of 2008/2009. A V-shaped situation shows a classic economic shock in which growth returns. In a U-shaped circumstance, part of the economic output is irretrievably lost after the first shock. An L-shaped scenario signals real structural damage with significant effects on future growth.

Figure 17.6 Recovery Scenarios after an Economic Crisis

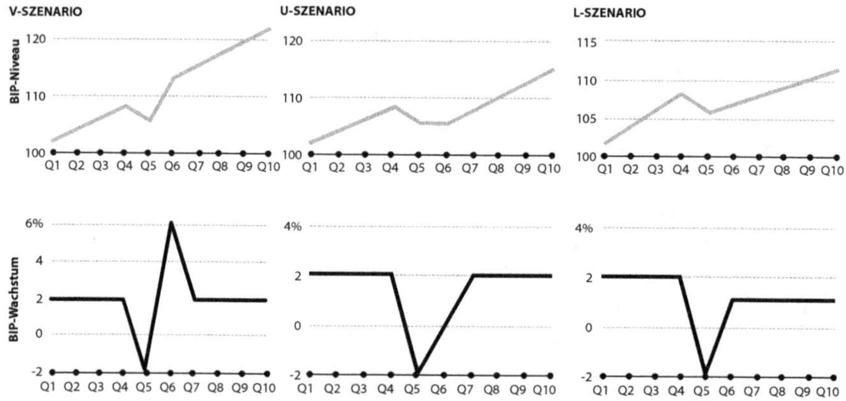

Quelle: BCG Center for Macroeconomics.

Other Ways That COVID-19 Is Changing Trade

The future of trade is also being redefined in other ways. For example, as part of its European Green Deal strategy to reduce greenhouse gas emissions, the European Commission is considering a proposal to introduce a carbon tax on imports. This tax could redefine global competitiveness in a number of industries.

114. COVID-19: Economic scenarios for the post-Corona-Zeit, www.deloitte.com 'blog' covid-19-briefings, covid dated: 26 March 2020.

The pandemic increases the urgency of efforts to restructure global supply chains as companies seek to make their production and procurement networks more resilient to shocks. It exacerbates the deteriorating trade relations between the US and China and puts more than USD 500 billion annually in mutual trade at risk, particularly in industries in both economies that will find it difficult to replace lost revenues and sources of critical components and materials. A possible decoupling of the US and Chinese technology sectors, which could lead to equipment and IT systems in both markets no longer being interoperable, could have even greater implications. These issues will be examined in more detail in forthcoming Boston Consulting Group publications.[115]

Companies should now begin to adapt to the new reality, for example, by reassessing their global production and supplier footprints and their approach to inventory as many of the changes are structural in nature and are likely to be long-lasting.

Forces Redefining the Future of Trade

The realignment of the world trade regime was already underway before COVID-19 emerged at the beginning of 2020. For much of the post-World War II period, world trade was a driving force of global economic growth, expanding three times faster than global GDP between 1950 and 2008 in an era of relatively continuous tariff reductions and new multilateral free trade pacts. In the 2010s, however, trade growth flattened relative to global GDP growth as new and deeper multilateral trade agreements came to a halt, the United Kingdom voted to leave the EU, and the US renegotiated existing trade treaties and relationships.

Customs wars between the US and major trading partners, especially China, contributed to a significant shift in US import sources. US imports from China fell in 2019 in almost all major industrial categories – most dramatically in energy products, semiconductors, machinery, and packaged food – but increased in most sectors in trade with the EU, Japan/South Korea, India, South East Asia, and Turkey. The full impact of US tariff increases was only partially felt in 2019. The COVID-19 crisis was another blow to trade. In addition to falling demand as countries slid into recession, trade was restricted by measures to contain the virus, such as factory closures and control of incoming shipments.

As stated, the probability for the different alternative scenarios of the 'L', 'U', or 'V' shaped recovery can be derived from the past financial crisis of 2008/2009 (Figure 17.7). Examples from different countries illustrate different courses of events that might be equally likely in the current COVID-19 crisis.

115. *See* BCG.com, How COVID-19 is reshaping industries, retrieved 10 November 2020.

Figure 17.7 Real Scenarios after the Financial Crisis 2000/2009[116]

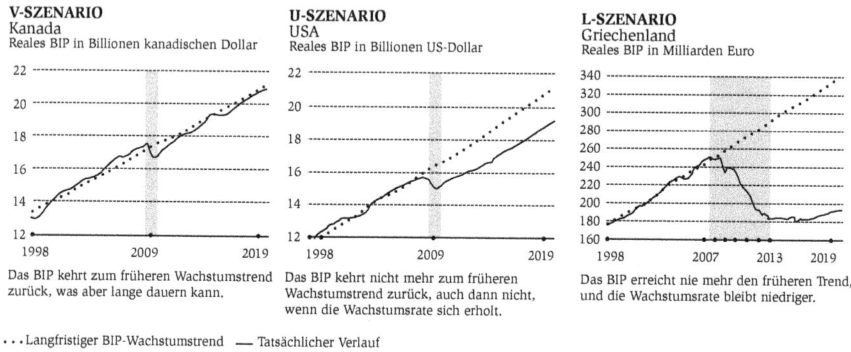

These different real developments allowed companies to make changes in their transfer prices already in 2020. This TP adjustment must not be a one-time action, but it must be anchored as a permanent process within the organization. The corresponding proactive measures could be:

a) Contractual provisions in an FMCG MNE

The OECD TPG states that there is often no conflict of interest between the related parties in intra-group contracts. Unrelated parties would ensure that: (i) terms and conditions are agreed that are in the best interests of both parties, (ii) the parties usually endeavour to ensure that the other party complies with the terms and conditions, and (iii) the terms and conditions are generally not changed but subsequently amended only when this is in the best interests of both parties.[117] The OECD TPG concludes that the contracts do provide a starting point for defining and determining the division of responsibilities, risks, and expected results of their cooperation as intended at the time of conclusion of the contract.[118] However, in addition to written contracts, further information will regularly be required for the contractual price analysis, and the knowledge of all agreements made for a certain business transaction is helpful in this regard.[119] If there are material differences between the contractual terms and conditions and the actual conduct of the related parties in their relationships with each other, the functions actually performed by them, assets actually used, and risks actually assumed in the context of the contractual terms and conditions should ultimately be decisive for determining the factual substance and the proper delineation

116. Statistics Canada, National Bureau of Economic Research, Bureau of Economic Analysis, Hellenic Statistical Authority (ELSTAT), available BCG Center for Macroeconomics, www.BCG .com, retrieved 10 November 2020.
117. OECD TPG (2022), Chapter I, para. 1.46.
118. *Ibid.*, para. 1.42.
119. *Ibid.*, para. 1.43.

of the actual business transaction.[120] This should clarify the international perspective that prevails in mutual agreement or arbitration proceedings at least between OECD Member States. The European directive ATAD will not change this. At best, it can only indicate a trend for the future treatment of transfer prices. The intra-group contracts are therefore to be considered both internationally from an economic point of view and domestically for the Member States of the OECD provided that the actual conduct does not deviate significantly from the content of the contract.

If this deviation occurs, the question will arise as to what unrelated parties would have agreed in the respective situation. The temporal context of the changes is thus decisive. If the actual conduct does not depart substantially from the contract and if this could have been agreed upon by unrelated parties, the contract is to be considered for tax purposes. If, however, the contract does not match the actual circumstances in essential parts, the former shall prevail. The change of transfer prices becomes necessary as far as the respective national legal situation allows it. It is also a conceivable scenario that the contract contains individual clauses that are not customary or the contract does not contain clauses that would normally have been agreed between unrelated parties. In these cases, the terms of the contract should be adjusted to take account of the arm's length principle. Inadequate or even missing (written) wording of intra-group contracts bears the risk that the tax authorities involved may judge a business transaction differently, i.e., disadvantageously, because of this. In the absence of clear contractual agreements, the tax authorities are not forced to recognize the transaction encountered. It is obvious that, in the case of an unclear contractual situation and an insufficient documentation of the facts, the tax authorities' scope for assessment and the associated susceptibility to dispute the facts of the case become much more probable.

In the context of the corona crisis, three main questions have arisen:

(1) Does the concluded agreement contain wording that is directly relevant during the corona crisis? This includes so-called force majeure clauses. Force majeure is an external event caused by elementary forces of nature or by the actions of outsiders. According to human insight and experience, this event is unforeseeable. Even the utmost care reasonably to be expected under the given circumstances cannot prevent this event by economically justifiable means. Force majeure must therefore be unforeseeable, unavoidable, and exceptional.[121] Such clauses are regularly found in purchase contracts with external suppliers of a company. In addition, acceptance commitments, delivery commitments, price guarantees, and price adjustment clauses are possible. Unless the clauses are unusual, they must be taken into account for tax purposes and form the framework for an economic analysis of realistic alternatives, so-called realistically available alternatives, from an OECD perspective.

120. Per the OECD's understanding, risks are associated with chances also; OECD TPG (2022), Chapter I, para. 1.46.

121. *See* an exemplary definition in German Federal Court of Justice, BGH v. 12 March 1987 – VII ZR 172/86, NJW 1987, 1938, 1939.

(2) Are there other legal possibilities or mandatory laws outside the contract that, due to the corona crisis, influence or even limit the realistic alternatives from an economic point of view?

    Examples are the disruption of the business basis, impossibility, and similar civil law legal institutions.

(3) How will the various contracts be structured in the future or existing contracts be adjusted in order to mitigate future risks comparable to the corona crisis?

In the case of the COVID-19 crisis, official declarations and announcements of state authorities such as the foreign ministry of a country and the official measures taken to contain the crisis are particularly important in this respect. The assessments and recommendations of the WHO also have an indicative effect. Current measures are:

- extensive border controls up to partial border closures;
- state curfews and the declaration of certain territories as restricted or risk areas;
- drastic restrictions on international air traffic; and
- state-imposed production restrictions or embargoes.

In a specific case, there must be an unavoidable event that cannot be eliminated by applying reasonable measures. Only then are legal consequences of force majeure effectuated. The reasonableness is to be determined by weighing the interests involved in each individual case.

The legal consequences of force majeure depend, first and foremost, on whether and with what content the parties to the contract have concluded a clause that contains regulations with regard to force majeure and its legal consequences. Thus, the force majeure clause can release parties alternatively from their contractual performance obligations for the duration of force majeure and indemnify the supplier from any claims for damages. Further, legal consequences can be agreed upon, for example, an exclusion of the withdrawal under civil law for merely temporary postponements of the delivery and service dates, the exclusion or agreement on an automatic termination of the contract, an extraordinary right of termination if the event of force majeure lasts longer than a certain period of time, or also an obligation to comprehensively inform the other related party about the expected duration of force majeure and all mitigating efforts undertaken.

With a view to the possible consequences under civil law mentioned above, the chosen TP system should be improved for the future. Existing intra-group contracts can be reviewed on the basis of current experience and adjusted promptly if necessary. Beyond measures to overcome the crisis, existing intra-group contracts should also be reviewed to determine whether they are suitable to regulate the facts actually realized by the related parties or whether adjustments are necessary. The contractual adjustments could also result in a changed functional and risk profile of an affiliated company. If this is implemented accordingly, groups can emerge stronger from the crisis, increase the stability of their TP system, and thus reduce the risk of a tax correction in a future tax audit. Many influencing factors will depend on the described 'curves' of economic recovery mentioned above. From the FMCG industry perspective, any change in the delivery and market conditions has a direct impact on the profit lines.

b) Digitalization

The term 'transformation' is defined as a 'process of change in companies, from the current as-is structure to a desired target state through a permanent change'.[122] With regard to the questionable automation of tax compliance, the statement: 'Anyone who does not deal with the topic of digitisation will perish' is initially implausible.[123] However, the signs of change for tax compliance in the FMCG sector and other industries are already visible.

The BEPS initiative and its implementation put digitization into a new spotlight. The implementation of BEPS Measure 1 for the recording of value-added contributions in the digital economy is exerting enormous pressure on change in national tax systems. France and Great Britain, for example, have already made changes to their domestic law that will tax the so-called GAFA[124] companies. However, what should a tax base for a new tax system look like? The discussions show that it is a matter of reorganizing tax law in an international sense. Current tax law is outdated and based on value creation concepts from the last millennium.[125] A final solution on how to tax what in a digital world will take some time of discussion and coordination between countries. It is clear that an increasing amount of data are being used and brought into a new network of relationships. Algorithms[126] will take over the 'calculation' of the tax base, and it is already apparent that the logic used in these algorithms will not necessarily be comprehensible to humans.[127]

The digitalization of tax processes is a must from the perspective of this development, and the above statement on digital transformation is a logical consequence. Only in this way can the current and future tax compliance requirements be mastered in an economically reasonable manner.

The necessary distinction to the compliance obligations from different tax laws results from the question of the effect of the obligation, among other things. The tax compliance obligations of the company must be a normative authority in its external relationship with the state. If it is clear that the management board has an organizational duty under internal rules and regulations, this duty should also have an effect in external relations. Smaller companies with manageable economic complexity are therefore, depending on the case, less affected by a requirement for a compliance

122. Christian Deuringer (2000) Organisation und Change Management, Wiesbaden, S. 38.
123. Tobias Kollmann, Blog Management Circle, available under, https://www.management-circle.de/blog/etablierte-unternehmen-scheitern-an-der-digitalisierung/ (last accessed 30 January 2022).
124. GAFA stands for the companies Google, Apple, Facebook and Amazon, available, https://www.bedeutungonline.de/was-bedeutet-gafa-abkuerzungbedeutung-definition/, retrieved on 25 July 2020.
125. Johannes Frey, Florian Schmid, FAZ on 17 July 2019, p. 16, Internationales Steuerrecht: Rechtsbruch durch Mindestbesteuerung? (faz.net).
126. *See* to the term available, https://wirtschaftslexikon.gabler.de/definition/algorithmus-27106 (last accessed 30 January 2022).
127. *See* Mario Martini, Blackbox Algorithmus, 2019, p. 194.

organizational obligation in the sense of the prevailing opinion. In this respect, the standards of what is necessary and reasonable in the fulfilment of tax requirements apply.[128] This statement contains the principle of economic proportionality that is decisive for the question of the compliance organization obligation: The greater the expected value of an impairment of legal interests, the more supervision is required to reduce the impairment probability. This concretization of reasonable measures is essentially aimed at insights into the economy.

The term 'organization' is a colloquial term with several meanings. Organizational theory should provide a guideline for economic action for every person and company active in the economy. Its purpose is to explain and understand the emergence, existence, and functioning of organizations. The theory thus serves to improve organizational practice and, in this context, it is also appropriate for finding approaches for interpretations of the indeterminate legal term 'compliance organization'.[129]

Business organization theory separates structure and process, thus distinguishing the organizational structure from the process organization. The organizational structure should regulate the division of departments, whereas the process organization should regulate the timing of working steps in relation to the subject matter.[130] This has led to the development of approaches to process organization that differentiate between structural and process organization and are based on a structured workflow. Ultimately, the overall task is broken down into processes.[131] With adequate tax compliance, costs and damages for the company are avoided. The economic concretization of compliance measures and organization, understood as process management, is measured by the efficiency of the compliance to be carried out combined with an effectiveness to achieve the measures required by corresponding compliance regulations.

The required use of resources in an economic sense is not considered. Instead, the two variable outputs are compared with the specific goal.[132] Ultimately, effective compliance includes the identification and analysis of a company's risks.

A tax and operational risk can be defined as 'a risk of loss caused by poor internal processes, employees, systems or external influences'.[133] In relation to a tax department, an operational tax risk arises from errors in processes within or outside the company's tax function. How legal risks, especially tax risks, can be controlled is ensured by means of guidelines for a risk management system. In this respect, compliance is part of a company's risk management system.[134] The requirements for

128. Fleischer, AG 2003,291, 300; M. Winter, F.S. Hüffer, 2010, SS 1103, 1106; Bürkle in Hauschka (Hrsg.), Corporate Compliance, 2007, § 8 Rn. 6.
129. Vgl. Scherer in Kieser/Ebers (Hrsg.) Organisationstheorien, 6. Aufl. 2006, pp. 19 ff.
130. Kosiol, Erich, Organisation im Unternehmen, 2nd ed. 1976, p. 32.
131. Georg. Schreyögg, Organisation -Grundlagen moderner Ogranisationsgestaltung, 5th edn, 2008, pp. 98 ff.
132. Susann Staats (2009) Metriken zur Messung von Effizienz und Effektivität von Konfigurationsmanagement- und Qualitätsmanagementverfahren, Bremen, pp. 29 ff.
133. Basel II: International Convergence of Capital Measurements and Capital Standards, revised version Juni 2006, abrufbar unter, http://www.bis.org/publ/bcbs128.pdf, Pkt. 644, S. 144 (last accessed 30 January 2022).
134. Compare DCGK Ziff. 3.4 Abs.2; Hauschka in Hauschka, § 1 Rn. 28.

such a system have increased considerably since the European Union published its Directive on Administrative Cooperation-DAC on 21 June 2017[135] as a consequence of the BEPS avoidance measures. The Polish tax authorities[136] have already implemented this directive into local law.[137] In addition to the requirements of the European Mandatory Disclosure Rules, VAT risks as well as local Polish facts and circumstances are also investigated. The tendency of the new risk management becomes clear from these developments. Risk management will increase in quality. The previous risk identification, e.g., according to the German IKS,[138] will gain heightened quality in accordance with the European measures.

c) Quantitative and qualitative classification of tax processes

Tax processes have different data sources according to different legal requirements. Data requirements, for example, in the area of sales tax, refer to incoming and outgoing invoices and their volume. The same applies to data for customs processes or for the TP area. The quantitative element for these tax assessment bases is determined from the various individual regulations. For the calculation of the corporate tax base, the data from the accounting system is modified. Thus, for example, those expenses that are to be qualified as non-deductible for tax purposes are determined accordingly for tax purposes and recorded in the off-balance sheet. The corresponding increase of the tax base to determine the taxable income therefore requires a qualitative tax law assessment of the costs of the FMCG affiliate.

The further differentiation of the classification of tax laws in digitizing process descriptions results from the contents of the regulations. Transfer prices are subject to both international regulations and national TP principles.[139] Such regulations are reflected in the design of the corresponding process descriptions.

The tax regulations that have transactions as their basis and are also based on international regulations (Figure 17.8) are mainly based on a large number of data.

135. Directive 2011/16/EU-DAC. 21 June 2017, 2017/0138 CNS.
136. EY-Ernst&Young, Poland to Implement Mandatory Disclosure Rules as of 1 January 2019, Global Tax Alert, 9 October 2018, available, https://www.ey.com/gl/en/tax/international-tax/alert--poland-to-implement-mandatory-disclosure-rules-as-of-1-january-2019 (last accessed 20 July 2020).
137. KPMG International Cooperative. Poland: Mandatory disclosure rules, cross-border tax planning arrangements, available, https://home.kpmg/xx/en/home/insights/2018/11/tnf.poland-mandatory-disclore-rules-cross-border-tax-planning.html (last accessed 20 July 2020).
138. Internes Risikontroll-System nach § 289 Abs. 5 HBG; Bungartz, O.: Handbuch Interne Kontrollsysteme (IKS) – Steuerung und Überwachung von Unternehmen. Erich Schmidt Verlag, Berlin, 2011, SS 58 ff., *see* the groundwork of the Committee of Sponsoring Organizations of the Treadway Commission (COSO) (eds): Internal Control – Integrated Framework. 2. Aufl. AICPA, Jersey NY 1994.
139. *See* German regulations in § 1 (3) AStG (Foreign Tax Code) and in: Verordnung zu Art, Inhalt und Umfang von Aufzeichnungen im Sinne des § 90 Abs. 3 der Abgabenordnung (Gewinnabgrenzungsaufzeichnungsverordnung – GAufzV) v. 13 November 2003 i. d. F. 26 June 2013; Verordnung zur Anwendung des Fremdvergleichsgrundsatzes nach § 1 Abs. 1 des Außensteuergesetzes in Fällen grenzüberschreitender Funktionsverlagerungen (Funktionsverlagerungsverordnung – FVerlV) v. 12 August 2008 i. d. F. v. 26 June 2013; Verordnung zur Anwendung des Fremdvergleichsgrundsatzes auf Betriebsstätten nach § 1 Abs. 5 des Außensteuergesetzes (Betriebsstättengewinnaufteilungsverordnung – BsGaV) v. 13 October 2014.

This is due to the main processes in a company. For example, the Source/Purchase-to-Pay or Order-to-Cash processes are the basis for determining the (sub-) process VAT.

Figure 17.8 Digital Data Versus Tax/Customs Types[140]

Digital transmission of data versus data content in traditional tax returns

	Quantitative data Master & transaction data Seller/customer details/invoice content import details/transactions between affiliated companies	**Qualitative data** Financial versus operational data Accounting data General ledger, charts of accounts Tax losses, capital contribution and dividend distribution
Global regulations	**Transfer Prices** **Customs regulations**	**Tax invoices, e.g., according to IAS 12**
Regional versus local rules	European VAT Indirect taxes Excise taxes	German trade tax US states taxes Wage withholding taxes

〉 **Cross-references to other data sources are increasingly possible**

Examples for the digitalization of tax processes

Based on the tax process understanding, the further question arises as to what extent the use of AI in these control processes will be possible. The current introduction and testing of a tax CMS in terms of the IDW Auditing Standard 980[141] offer support for automation. The basic elements of this system refer to processes that can be predominantly digitized. The use of AI takes place on different levels. The use of so-called robots causes an interaction with physical objects. Routine activities such as the collection of information from an invoice processing (ERP)[142] system and further processing for a monthly VAT return can be largely automated. The extension of classical rule-based approaches by learning concepts will be implemented as so-called machine learning to map human behaviour.

The ECJ in its decision of 'Senatex'[143] did not grant retroactive effect to the correction of an invoice with regard to a mandatory formal declaration. The basic principle of

140. Author's Illustration.
141. Institute of Public Auditors, IDW Prüfungsstandard 980 v. 31 May 2017, available, https://www.idw.de/idw/idw-aktuell/endgueltiger-idw-praxishinweis-1-2016-zu-tax-compliance-management-systemen/101304 (last accessed 30 January 2022).
142. Enterprise Resource Planning System.
143. ECJ (fourth chamber), 15 September 2016, *Senatex GmbH v. Finanzamt Hannover-Nord*, C 518/14.

value-added neutrality requires that the input tax deduction should be granted if the material requirements are met even if the company has not satisfied certain formal requirements. If a multiplicity of VAT-relevant calculations is put to the computation system, i.e., a machine for mechanical learning at disposal, this machine learns to recognize the formal and material conditions to identify errors independently and suggest changes. This occurs with all data made available and not only on the basis of samples as in human behaviour. Even if the ECJ judgment mentioned above appears positive for a company with a view to its input tax deduction, it is better to design the accounting process compliant in the legal sense following the tax regulations in such a way that all conceptual contents of tax compliance are fulfilled.

Machine learning takes place when the computer is able to 'learn' from data using statistical evaluation techniques without being specially programmed for this purpose. Learning in the field of human sensory perception means an incremental increase in performance in the execution of a specific task. Machine learning, on the other hand, causes patterns and regularities to be found in data sets. This enables the computer to apply the 'learned' to new data to predict potential risks and opportunities. Machine learning is not the only method as deep learning, advanced analytics, and robotics (RPA)[144] are other analytical techniques that are also used for tax compliance. These techniques are used, for example, to analyse patterns in historical data in order to identify risks and opportunities (predictive analytics), to analyse text to categorize and detect patterns and trends (text analysis), and to analyse data to locate networks in data and answer the question of how networks are connected (network analysis). Further examples of how digital technologies are used in practice are shown in the areas of sales tax, transfer prices, and the combination of both processes with customs clearance.

d) Conclusion

Since the finalization of the most important parts of the BEPS package, the implementation of countermeasures has been taken over by countries which accordingly affect the FMCG MNEs. One focus for practical implementation is the OECD's Inclusive Framework in which 141 countries (as of November 2021) and other international organizations work together on an equal footing to meet minimum standards when implementing BEPS countermeasures. The members of the Inclusive Framework have committed themselves to a rapid implementation of four minimum standards. One of these standards refers to TP, TPD, and CbCRs. According to the OECD, more than ninety countries have passed primary legislation to implement CbCR.[145]

What happens with the information? Understanding the information as an exclusive risk assessment is too narrow. The extended documentation for TP can also be used as a basis for further automated steps:

144. Robot Process Automation.
145. *See* Corporate Tax Statistics: Third Edition, as of 21 July 2021, https://www.oecd.org/tax/tax-policy/corporate-tax-statistics-third-edition.pdf (last accessed 30 January 2022).

(1) Benchmark studies can be considerably simplified. With the support of machine learning and algorithms, it will be easier to select appropriate comparables in the studies. The 'arm's length' principle is supported by a deeper logic.
(2) Transfer prices are calculated not only on the basis of products in their entirety but also taking into account the raw materials used in a product. This extension shows the elasticity of the product calculation with changing raw material prices. The transfer prices can be determined and adapted more accurately. Estimates by tax authorities will no longer be possible to the same extent as before.
(3) Comparative calculation of transfer prices according to different TP methods is enabled. The simulation of a transfer price calculation with a view to a given functional and risk profile results in a higher argumentation flexibility of companies versus tax authorities. Data sets are used by BI tools in multi-year calculations for comparison purposes.[146]
(4) Blockchain technologies can support the transmission of TP data to the various tax authorities.
(5) Digital support methods will provide tax authorities with real-time access to TP data that will support risk management approaches.

Consequently, the digitalization trend and growing transparency requirements will continue to shape the business and compliance environment for FMCG MNEs in the years to come.

146. Zöchling Plott, Rosar, Dziurd (2018) Digitalisierung im Steuerrecht, Digitale Transformation und Steuern, SS 1-18, 13.

CHAPTER 18

Transfer Pricing in the Insurance Sector

Velio Alessandro Moretti

1 INTRODUCTION

The insurance industry plays a crucial role in both social and economic terms. It facilitates risk transfer for both companies and individuals, thereby creating a more sustainable future for everyone.[1] In an age marked by an intense degree of unpredictability, whether global warming or emerging technologies, insurance provides a vital set of services.

From a social and economic perspective, insurance is a mechanism for alleviating the financial consequences of the risks involved in business or daily life. In law, insurance is an enforceable agreement between two parties that provides a certain type of benefit in return for a consideration.

The subject matter of insurance is *risk*. This term is frequently used by both theorists and insurance practitioners and defined as 'a condition in which there is a possibility of an adverse deviation from a desired outcome that is expected or hoped for'.[2]

TP in insurance has become an increasingly high-profile issue taking into account the following central principles:

- the insurance sector has seen significant recent consolidation resulting in post-integration restructuring with a strong focus on capital structure and capital management;
- analysts and stakeholders have increasingly begun to focus on insurance groups' management of effective tax rates and TP policies;
- multinational reinsurance programmes have formed an integral part of the insurance industry's drive towards maximizing shareholder value; and
- at the same time, TP has become an increasingly sensitive area for tax authorities seeking to protect their tax bases while remaining tax competitive.

The goal of this chapter is to focus particular attention – among others – on one of the main and most material transactions within insurance groups that are increasingly coming under greater scrutiny: reinsurance.

In doing so, first, it will be briefly explained how value is generated by the insurance companies and what are the main key drivers. Second, what constitutes reinsurance will be described and how TP regulations affect this phenomenon within the insurance sector with particular focus on the latest development of the OECD TPG.

2 VALUE CREATION IN INSURANCE SECTOR

Unique among businesses, an insurance company protects its customers – the unrelated policyholders – with a promise to pay in the future in the event of an insured loss. In particular, the founding factor of the insurance industry is what is known as 'inversion of the production cycle' which is the transposing of the expense-revenue cycle insofar as the insurance company first collects premiums for the promise to pay the claims if the insured event occurs in the future.[3] The promise to pay is supported by the capital of the insurance company and subject to strict regulations at country levels. While regulators and rating agencies generally push for more capital to support that

1. Torsten Rohlfs, *Solvency II in the Insurance Industry*, Springer, 2017.
2. Emmett J. Vaughan, *Fundamentals of Risk and Insurance*, John Wiley & Sons, 2018.
3. Paolo Zanghieri, *Business Cycle and Motor Insurance Profitability*, Department of Economics, University of Bologna, 2017.

promise, global insurance groups also face considerable pressure from investors with competing interests: shareholders seek distributions of any 'excess' capital which also helps to increase the insurers' ROE.

In more detail, insurance is a risk-spreading mechanism that allows buyers of insurance to transfer at least some of the risks associated with their business activities to insurance enterprises. In doing so, they exchange the uncertain cost of large potential future losses for the reasonably certain cost of the insurance premiums they pay. To create this security for consumers, insurers transfer to them some of the benefits of their ability to diversify risk by building a large portfolio of insurance consumers – referred to as the 'law of large numbers'[4] – so that the premiums charged are less than most risk-averse consumers are willing to pay.

In addition, insurers usually possess more information than consumers about the probability and likely severity of losses that might occur (e.g., the risk of earthquake or other natural events), and this knowledge also benefits consumers. However, the asymmetry of information is by no means one way. Only the customer can have full knowledge of his own circumstances. This situation has been recognized in law through the principle of utmost good faith.[5]

Finally, individual consumers benefit from a wide variety of ancillary risk-related services that insurance firms (including intermediaries and claims-handling firms) are able to offer. These include advice on safety and loss prevention, the mitigation of losses when they occur, and legal advice and support for dealing with compensation claims that might be made against them.

The ability of insurers to benefit consumers by spreading losses among a large group of policyholders and to additionally spread them over time also produces wider commercial and economic benefits. Business enterprises must take risks in order to make a profit and, by being able to transfer at least some of the risks associated with their business and investment decisions (such as the construction of a new factory or plant), the decision-making process itself is made less risky. This enables firms to contemplate more profitable enterprises that would otherwise be more risky. In this way, insurance markets allow the economy as a whole to be more enterprising and undertake longer-term capital expenditure decisions that might otherwise be delayed or rejected entirely.

The risk transfer and risk-spreading mechanisms provided by insurance companies can be viewed in terms of the efficient use of capital. Business firms would need to hold and retain a greater amount of precautionary capital to safeguard their enterprises if there were no insurance markets to absorb risk. Thus, insurance companies effectually supply contingent equity capital to industrial and commercial enterprises. This means that less equity capital is needed to support commercial activity across the entire economy.

4. The law according to which the probability density function of average loss tends to become concentrated around the mean as the sample number increases.
5. Under this, the customer has a duty to disclose all material facts to the insurer; otherwise, the insurer may avoid the policy.

Insurers also play a minor (but not insignificant) direct role in supporting international trade. The main contribution is made through MAT insurance, as well as motor and export credit insurance that support the financing and movement of goods (and people) internationally.

The demand for business insurance, and indeed insurance generally, obviously varies over time. It depends on a number of factors other than the degree of economic activity and economic growth in a specific market. These include:

- changes in the structure of the economy in a given market – this can reduce the demand for some types of insurance and/or increase it for others. For example, the switch from a manufacturing to a service economy may effectuate a reduction in the demand for industrial property and engineering insurance but increase the demand for professional indemnity insurance;
- the extent of compulsion to insure that may be imposed at the government level or through the demands of trade or professional bodies or the requirements of business partners;
- the influence of government in terms of taxation policy affecting insurance and also social security policy where a diminution in state provision (e.g., of workers' compensation benefits or health care) may stimulate increased demand for privately insured alternatives or vice versa; and
- social values and attitudes, including those based on systems of belief. For example, fatalism or the dictates of a particular religion may inhibit the demand for insurance.

Subject to the points made above, the demand for non-life insurance (unlike some forms of life insurance) is likely to be relatively inelastic.[6] Broadly defined, there are few close substitutes for insurance. Risk prevention and risk assumption (self-insurance) are not close substitutes as they do not involve risk transfer.

Concerning value creation, in general terms, a firm pursues projects in which the rate of return is greater than the firm's cost of capital in order to maximize the enterprise value.[7] Value creation particularly centres on the actual returns that can be obtained from corporate assets less the cost of capital needed to support those assets.[8] More in particular, shareholder value creation should be measured by the difference between the market value of the form's equity and the amount of equity capital that shareholders have invested in the firm. The former represents the financial market estimation of shareholders' investments in their firm, and the latter is associated with the actual amount of money they invested in it.[9]

An insurance company creates value when the net return from underwriting and investment activities – i.e., the two primary sources of income for insurers – is

6. Hiroyuki Nakata, *Demand for Non-life Insurance: A Cross-Country Analysis*, University of Tokyo, 2007.
7. Aswath Damodaran, *Applied Corporate Finance*, fourth edition, Wiley, 2015.
8. Pierre Vernimmen, Pascal Quiry, Maurizio Dallocchio, Yann Le Fur, Antonio Salvi, *Corporate Finance*, fourth edition, Wiley, 2015.
9. Gabriel Hawawini, Claude Viallet, *Finance for Executives*, fifth edition, Cengage Learning, 2015.

therefore greater than the cost of capital. Therefore, insurers focus their actions on two main drivers when making decisions that increase value creation:

- how to lower the cost of capital; and
- how to lower the volatility of underwriting results.

Thus far, the fact has been emphasized that value creation in insurance must take into account risk – i.e., the 'insurance risk' – that is transferred from the insured person who is referred to as the 'policyholder' to the insurer in exchange for a revenue (i.e., the 'insurance premium') that should therefore be higher than the cost of the firm's capital. From a legal standpoint, the risk transfer mechanism happens via the so-called insurance contract, i.e., the agreement between the insurer and the policyholder – also known as insured, beneficiary, or cedant – that exchanges a premium *ex ante* for a (potential) *ex post* claim.

Underwriting and investment are the primary functions that an insurer performs to seek value creation. These concepts will be explored in the following paragraphs to assist in understanding how insurers create value.

How value is created in insurance: The insurance value chains

The value chain[10] is a conceptual method for compartmentalizing a business and then examining each element separately in terms of the value added, its core drivers, and its relevance to the organization's key objectives. The key challenge presented by a value chain analysis is that each component is essentially driven by different success drivers.[11]

When it comes to the functions performed within insurance business, the following analysis will mostly make reference to the 2010 OECD Report, Part IV[12] in order to depict the general framework according to which the value is generated in insurance.

Product development

Product development involves:

- market research (i.e., analysis of the potential clients' segments);
- selection of the appropriate distribution channels;
- definition of fixed and variable compensation of the sales network;
- definition of the expected premium volume over time;
- gathering and maintaining (claims) statistics;
- legal stipulation of the extent of coverage;

10. The value chain analysis was developed in the 1980s by business schools, basically Harvard and Cranfield. 'Competitive advantage cannot be understood by looking at a firm as a whole. It stems from the many discrete activities a firm performs in designing, producing, marketing, delivering, and supporting its product.' Michael E. Porter, *Competitive Advantage: Creating and Sustaining Superior Performance*, Simon & Schuster, 1985.
11. Richard Lynch, *Corporate Strategy*, Pitman, 1997.
12. *Report on the attribution of profit to permanent establishment*, OECD, 2010.

- mathematical calculation of the premium depending on the features of insurance coverage (geographical, temporal, demographics, policy surrender, and settlement options, investment returns guaranteed or anticipated in the pricing of the premium, insurance excess options, etc.).

According to this function, the main features of the product are determined stemming from the legal to the mathematical framework of the product itself. These activities require a comprehensive analysis of the market and the specific legislations involved. With market research activities, insurers would seek to better understand consumers' behaviours and needs in order to develop an insurance product that is able to capture the quantitative, qualitative, geographical, and time-related features of the insurance coverage.

With this in mind, the main objective of this step is to be able to offer flexible pricing structures while seeking operational excellence: lower processing costs and expense-control management via promotion of reuse, best-practice sharing, and knowledge management. Flexibility is therefore a key driver in product development insofar as time-to-market is the central point regarding gaining the proper positioning and penetration in the market according to the specific target of clusters' consumers. This leads to the importance of appropriate market positioning and how products must be suitably segmented, i.e., higher-value customers are likely to desire greater amount of personalized attention, whereas mass affluent or commoditized products-oriented customers will only want to deal with direct distribution. As a consequence, a proper use of distribution channels is crucial for the purpose of understanding how to attract and retain the relevant customer base. This is why, among others, insurers tend to develop personalized insurance products to establish regular interaction with specific clusters of their client base utilizing the new digitalized channels, e.g., social media, internet, and blockchain.

Sales and marketing

Insurers seek to promote, place, and sell the insurance product to the relevant customer after the pertinent insurance product features are delineated with marketing and sales activities. In general, marketing and sales are interconnected insofar as sales activities are highly dependent on marketing, and the latter is also subsequently connected with product development due to the fact that it requires activities aimed at identifying, understanding, and analysing customer needs. As a consequence, advising clients as well as providing quotes and proposals are the main following steps to acquire them. With this in mind, one of the primary important tasks of insurers is to globally track the brand awareness of their products vis-à-vis local competitors. This is done in an attempt not only to understand the local reputation of the company and the specific products but also to plan marketing campaigns to expand local awareness and thus increase the customer base. This is done both directly by the insurer itself and in a combination with a relationship with external brokers that can be engaged to particularly benefit from their global network and client base relationship. Moreover, sales and marketing activities rely on the specific business model and product. The broker relationship is often a significant factor when it comes to global corporate and commercial insurance, whereas an agent relationship is more common in small commercial risks and personal lines. Lastly, CRM processes and tools are critical for insurers to maintain and foster client relationships over the long run.

Underwriting

Underwriting is at the core of the insurance value chain. It is the process of classifying, selecting, and pricing the insured risks that are subject to transfer to the insurer from the policyholder.[13] Classifying and selecting insured risks are the crucial aspects of underwriting insofar as the latter is ultimately a statistical observation modelling of classes of insured risks that will therefore be managed by insurers during the life cycle of the insurance policy. This is why underwriting is highly interconnected with the risk management function. It leads to risk pooling and diversification of risks by building a large portfolio of insurance consumers which, as previously mentioned, is the purpose of insurance value generation. It is thus worthwhile noticing that pricing comes after risk classification and selection, meaning that the acceptance of risks should not be mainly driven by profitability concerns. Rather, it is the appropriate actuarial selection of certain risks in light of the insurer's underwriting policy. This means that the focus is not on the selection of risks that will not generate losses but instead on avoiding the misclassification of insured risk according to the pricing of insurance contracts.

An appropriate classification of insured risk is sought by insurers to cope with moral hazard and adverse selection that are the prevalent founding concepts in the risk management markets. Moral hazard can be regarded as a change in behaviour arising from the presence of insurance or other forms of risk protection. It is generally associated with *ex ante* behaviour and might be considered an *ex ante* moral hazard in the context of failing to take actions to prevent losses knowing that insurance coverage exists. There is also a form of an *ex post* moral hazard that can arise from the presence of reinsurance where an insurer might relax its loss settlement and claims adjustment procedures in the aftermath of a loss knowing that it has reinsurance coverage. This can lead to an accumulation of claims or fraud. With underwriting activities, the insurer is therefore able to understand the nature of its portfolio in order to avoid adverse selection[14] situations in which the insurer supplies too much or too little risk coverage at a given price that ultimately leads to an excess of losses or dearth of business. This is why an underwriter requires proper resources to not only identify and classify risks but especially track the loss experience of each of the parties it is protecting. This enables him to properly stratify and then price the protection he is ultimately offering.

When it comes to underwriting profitability, a key feature of general insurance markets is that prices are subject to sharp swings. This is known as the 'underwriting cycle' or 'insurance cycle'. Since underwriting profitability is the difference between

13. *See Report on the attribution of profit to permanent establishment*, OECD, 2010, para. 34.
14. Adverse selection is defined as the mispricing of risk as a result of information asymmetries and occurs when a protection provider cannot clearly distinguish between different classes of risk. *See* Maria Heep-Altiner, Marin Mullins, Torsten Rohlfs, *Solvency II in the Insurance Industry*, Springer, 2017.

insurance premiums received (and earned) and claims and expenses that are incurred, the frequency and severity of claims during a period will be a core determinant of underwriting profitability. However, the term 'underwriting cycle' is usually defined in terms of a pattern of upward and downward movements in insurance prices that are broadly cyclical in nature and their subsequent impact on underwriting profitability which is similarly cyclical.[15]

Underwriting may also include a specific risk retention analysis. Concisely, when considering appropriate retention levels, insurers might decide to establish specific amounts of economic losses and impact in terms of capital. Passive retention can be the result of a failed or flawed governance process that causes an insurer to improperly identify or quantify its exposures. Active risk retention, in contrast, arises when an insurer properly identifies its risks and consciously decides to preserve some portion.[16] This activity may therefore lead to the decision to transfer a certain class of risks to another insurer via reinsurance.

Underwriting: What risks can be insured?

Underwriting is at the core of insurance insofar as the most important active decision-making functions relevant to the assumption of insurance risk typically fall within the category of underwriting activities (known as the KERT function)[17] in the insurance business. Therefore, it is crucial to further articulate this function in order to better understand when and to what extent a risk can be insured (e.g., insurability).[18]

Insurance techniques can be applied to many risks, but there are limits to what can be insured. This section will briefly examine the criteria of insurability which helps to illustrate a number of the basic principles of insurance. The criteria for insurability arise from the principles of actuarial science, business ethics, law, public policy, as well as technical and practical considerations. They include the following:

- the nature of the risk: for example, only 'pure' risks are easily insurable;
- the dimensions of the loss: in terms of randomness, size, and frequency;
- insurance premium;

15. One common empirical finding is that, while both the demand and supply for insurance varies over time, it is variations in supply that are more important than those in demand. This is because financial capital is the main determinant of supply. New financial capital can quickly come into a market to increase supply when premiums are high but can withdraw quickly from the market if it appears that the rate of return on capital is falling below a required rate. Again, new companies can come into the insurance industry fairly quickly provided there are no unusual delays in gaining regulatory approval. This contrasts with the manufacturing and agricultural sectors where supply is less elastic. However, there are many factors that might cause financial capital to increase or decrease, and the availability of capital does not mean that it will be used to provide underwriting capacity.
    See Sigma No. 5, Swiss Re, 2001.
16. Erik Banks, *Alternative Risk Transfer*, Wiley, 2004.
17. *See* 2010 OECD Report on the Attribution of Profits to Permanent Establishment, section B-2, Part IV.
18. *See* Eric A. Wiening, *Foundations of Risk Management and Insurance*, American Institute for Chartered Property Casualty Underwriters/Insurance Institute of America, 2002; Robert Mehr, *Principles of Insurance*, Homewood, 1985; Peter Nash Swishe, *The Insurable Interest Requirement*, Drake L. Rev. 477, 2004.

- moral hazard;
- public policy; and
- legal restrictions.

With regard to the nature of the risk, broadly speaking, only 'pure' (or 'one-way') risks are insurable. These are risks when there is a chance of loss or no loss and not 'speculative' (or 'two-way') risks when there is not only a chance of loss but also a chance of gain for which purpose the risk is deliberately taken.

Regarding the dimension of the losses, it must be measurable in monetary terms and not so large as to be beyond the insurers' capacity to pay. Ideally, insured risks should be independent of each other. A high probability of other risks in a portfolio being affected when a risk is impacted by a loss event may result in an accumulation of such losses, making risk spreading difficult. Independent losses that are high in frequency and relatively small in size are the most easily insured; in this context, the law of large numbers works most effectively. On the other hand, there are dangers in agreeing to insure very trivial losses. This is economically wasteful and may generate a 'moral hazard' (*see* below).

Insurance premiums must be calculable and reasonable, and there must be sufficient loss data to calculate the insurance premium with reasonable certainty; otherwise, an unacceptably high 'safety loading' will have to be included. The premium must not be so high in relation to the value of the insured object that it nullifies the business value of a transaction.

As explained above, a moral hazard is very relevant in insurance in the sense that the insured person may be incentivized to make a claim in certain situations that insurers would have to remunerate. Thus, in an insurance context, the charged market premiums may not be always the best proxy for moral hazard risk in insurance.[19] For example, being insured may make the policyholder more careless, encourage him to exaggerate his loss or, in an extreme case, encourage him to bring about a loss deliberately in order to receive the insurance payout. The problem of moral hazard lies behind the well-known principle that insurance can only operate properly in relation to losses that are 'fortuitous' or 'accidental' in nature.

The issue of public policy is closely connected with the question of moral hazard. Insurance should not be granted if doing so would tend to encourage crime, disorder, social unrest, or divisions in society. For example, the provision of insurance against criminal fines may encourage people to do something forbidden by law.

In turn, legality is closely connected with the question of public policy because a type of insurance that is harmful to the public interest may be declared illegal. However, legal restrictions may take other forms. For example, some forms of private insurance may be declared illegal if it is intended that the state alone should bear the risk. Again, the law may make coverage obligatory for some risks and precisely stipulate what the policy should and should not cover.

19. A moral hazard is the phenomenon whereby the granting of insurance has the effect of changing the behaviour of the insured or that of other people in such a way as to make the occurrence of the adverse insured event more likely. *See* Georges Dionne, Scott E. Harrington, *Foundations of Insurance Economics*, Springer Science & Business Media, 1992.

Risk management

Risk is the expected variance in profits, losses, or cash flows arising from an uncertain event.[20] Companies are exposed to a wide range of risks that must be managed if the market value of the company is to be increased – or, at a minimum, if the probability of financial distress is be decreased. Some of the risks can be retained as part of core business operations, while others are best transferred elsewhere when it is cost-effective to do so. In general terms, insurance companies need to manage the following risks: insurance risks, risks associated with investment activities, risks associated with risk management and reinsurance, operational risks, foreign exchange risks, liquidity risks, reputation risks, and other risks related to life and health insurance business lines. Other types of risks may also include strategic risks, contagion and related party risks, balance sheet and market risks, counterparty default risks, legal and regulatory risks.[21] To manage these, insurers have a comprehensive range of risk management tools, including claims adjustment policies, portfolio policies, reinsurance policies, and investment policies (such as the ALM policies).[22]

It is important to accentuate that the exercise of risk management activities aims at controlling risks and not eliminating them.[23] This is an important distinction because risk is not a variable that must be removed at any cost insofar as there are times when it is sensible for a company to retain and even increase its risk exposure because it helps to increase the value of the firm to shareholders. Thus, risk management's goal is understanding and closely managing risk exposure so that stakeholders are fully aware of how the firm might be impacted. Moreover, decisions on whether to use retain risks are of central importance to the risk management process, and this is why reinsurance can be used to manage the insurance risk exposure of an insurance company insofar as reinsurance involves the transfer of insurance risk to a reinsurer.[24]

With regard to the risk management process, it generally comprises a four-stage activity: risk identification, risk quantification, risk management, and risk monitoring.[25] This classification is beneficial for understanding its TP implications when it comes to the proper risk assumption qualification in light of the OECD TPG. Indeed, it is important to bear in mind that the objective of the identification process is properly identifying all of the relevant risks, and a failure in this stage may lead to surprise losses insofar as coming from an 'unknown source'. With risk quantification, the financial impact of the risk identified is determined using various quantitative tools. Pure risk management then comes after the identification and quantification of risks and is a process of active decision-making whereby an insurer decides whether it will control, retain, eliminate, or expand its exposure. Therefore – as per the OECD TPG's wording – he will decide to take on, lay off, or decline a risk-bearing opportunity together with

20. Erik Banks, *Alternative Risk Transfer*, Wiley, 2004. According to the author, it is important to distinguish risk from peril and hazard. A peril is a cause of loss while a hazard is an event that creates or increases peril.
21. *See* 2010 OECD Report, Part IV, paras 56-58.
22. *See* 2010 OECD Report, Part IV, para. 38.
23. G. Buck, P. Riches, *Risk Management: New Challenges and Solutions*, Reuters, 1999.
24. *See* 2010 OECD Report, Part IV, para. 40.
25. Erik Banks, *Alternative Risk Transfer*, Wiley, 2004.

the actual performance of that decision-making function.[26] After the insurer has decided how to manage his risk profile, he must actively monitor its exposure by tracking, reporting, and communicating information internally and externally to the stakeholders involved such as executive management, regulators, and investors.

Contract and claims management

Claims are the critical moment for both the insured and the insurer when the policyholder realizes what value there is in the policy he has been paying for and the insurer finds out the cost of providing that policy. It is therefore a crucial point in the value chain of insurance companies. Once a claim is raised, the team performing claim services is responsible for approving the payment of it in accordance with the terms of the policy. Typically, the claims team would receive invoices that are sent along with claim forms and once these are processed through the claims system, the amount payable is determined and the payment is settled (this is processed by the finance team). In the event that a policy holder challenges the insurer on the payment of a claim, the latter would open a case and review the claim with the team leader and/or would escalate the case to more senior individuals or specific internal committees. Claims management therefore begins after the filing of the policyholder's claim notification whereby the claim will be processed. It will be investigated by the insurer whose objective is understanding whether all of the terms and conditions of the insurance policy are met in order to further process the claim. After the investigation has been completed, the insurance company will formally open the claim and follow through with the process of its payment. At this stage, insurers may opt for cooperation with claims adjusters to assess, evaluate, and process the insurance claims. After the value of the specific claim is determined, the insurance company will issue the settlement check to finalize the payment.

Asset Management

Asset management has two primary functions:

(1) Investment Management – the investment management function comprises the short-term asset allocation, security selection, and investment accounting functions. Short-term asset allocation involves the execution of investment decisions within the boundaries of the investment guidelines established by the ALM function. Security selection is limited by both investment guidelines and local regulatory requirements. The investment account ensures proper recording and performance monitoring.

(2) ALM – establishes investment guidelines for a specific line of business or a specific product line. The investment guidelines generally define the longer-term asset allocation policy (security classes, credit, and other risk parameters maturities) by taking into account the nature and terms of liabilities, product guarantees and options, and regulatory requirements.

26. *See* OECD TPG, para. 1.61.

Within insurance groups, local insurance entities generally outsource their investment management to the in-house asset management entities of the group.

As a matter of fact, insurance undertakings must invest in and hold assets to adequately cover both their technical provisions and their required solvency margin. In order to ensure that an undertaking can meet its contractual liabilities to policyholders, such assets must be managed in a sound and prudent manner.[27] Insurance companies usually recognize the importance of separating the responsibility for managing their insurance businesses from that of managing the investments backing their reserves and capital. The management of these investments is a key function due to the scale of investments on an insurance company's balance sheet and the impact of investment results on its profitability. The nature of the insurance business requires significant capital that must be professionally managed. Insurance companies sell protection to their customers who pay premiums that are subsequently invested to cover future claims or benefits, administrative expenses, and profits to shareholders. Regulators generally require insurance companies to hold sufficient assets to back liabilities in every insurance business. The reserves must suffice to pay expected claims and benefits, even in the unplanned case that the insurer stops writing new business. Thus, regulators require that insurers do not rely on new premiums to pay for claims and benefits underwritten in the past. As insurers continuously underwrite new business, they normally hold significant and relatively stable amounts of investments on their balance sheet. Reserves generated by the insurance business are invested until they are needed for payouts. In addition, equity capital buffers help to ensure that the insurer has adequate funds to pay claims or benefits in scenarios in which actual payouts are larger than those reserved. Therefore, the investments on the insurer's balance sheets include reserves for expected claims and benefits as well as shareholder capital that functions as an additional buffer for unforeseeable events.[28] Thus, the main goal for insurance asset management is managing the potential mismatch in value of its assets and liabilities to ensure that it will not threaten the insurance company profitability and more in general as a going concern. Insurance investment risk is therefore when investments become insufficient to pay the liabilities due to adverse changes in the capital markets. Consequently, the analysis and the management of such relative movements in value - the ALM - are a crucial process for the purposes of insurance asset management. Moreover, it must comply with stringent regulatory requirements within the solvency framework according to which insurers have to follow strict investment strategies that are admitted by local regulators. Indeed, insofar as the assumption of risks results in the absorption of capital for insurance companies, careful consideration should be given to the fact that the assumption of financial risks may lead to the absorption of capital which might be otherwise used to cover insurance risks.

27. Guidelines for Insurance Undertakings on Asset Management, Central Bank of Ireland.
28. *See* Zurich Financial Services, 'Investment Management - a creator of value in an insurance company', March 2009, Second Edition, available online at, www.zurich.com.

Support functions

An insurance business will also have to undertake a number of support functions such as treasury, regulatory compliance, systems and development of intangibles, other back-office tasks, loss control, and credit analyses.[29] The treasury function is generally responsible for the liquidity management of the insurer that could be done via borrowing funds at the most advantageous terms possible or – for large insurance groups – acts as in-house bank via what is referred to as the cash pooling structure as a specific tool to manage short-term liquidity needs. The regulatory compliance function is responsible for advising the administrative, management, or supervisory body on compliance with laws, regulations, and administrative provisions adopted pursuant to the Solvency II Directive. Furthermore, another important support function concerns the IT and operations management that deals with the ongoing business operations and procedures of an insurance company with the intention of creating and maintaining an efficient operating platform. Among others, operations management includes the following activities: the management of the IT infrastructure, including coordinating the provisioning, capacity, performance and availability of the computing, networking and application environment; premises and facilities management; and the procurement and logistics management that deals with the sourcing of products and services essential for the ongoing business operations. The accounting function is responsible for providing all of the relevant financial information to all of the stakeholders involved via the so-called integrated reporting. The key areas in accounting are: technical insurance accounting – aiming in particular at calculating, validating, and reporting technical provisions according to the applicable regulatory framework – general and financial accounting, debt collection, preparation of the yearly financial statements, and other interim reporting packages.

HR is the support function that focuses on the recruitment, training, and development of employees in alignment with the group people strategy. Thus, HR is a key function when it comes to human development within MNEs via the implementation of global mobility initiatives – e.g., secondments and assignment arrangements between the subsidiaries of the group – and compensation and reward packages that incentivize and foster people performance.

Moreover, another important support function is the internal auditor whose role is the responsibility of internal control by providing independent evaluations of the adequacy and effectiveness of the internal control system and highlighting any need for updating, developing a common approach, methodology, methods, and organizational standards in compliance with the regulations.[30]

Legal is another support function aimed at managing the business operations in compliance with the local relevant laws.

29. *See* 2010 OECD Report, Part IV, para. 47.
30. *See* Article 47 of the Solvency II Directive.

3 THE MAIN TYPES OF INSURANCE

Insurance can be classified in a number of ways.[31] The various classifications discussed here are summarized at the end of this section.

– Classification 1: historical classification

As mentioned above, marine insurance was the first class to develop, followed by life insurance and fire insurance. Until the nineteenth century, these were the only classes, and insurance offices generally specialized in only one class. However, as has been seen, a somewhat miscellaneous collection of insurances was described as 'accident' business developed in the nineteenth century, thus adding a fourth class to marine, life, and fire. This classification is becoming obsolete and now has little relevance outside the context of the insurance industry. However, for the sake of completeness, it can be noted that, in the historical sense, insurance comprises marine, life, fire, and accident insurance. In the United States (and increasingly in Europe) 'casualty' insurance is an approximate equivalent to 'accident' business.

– Classification 2: Life insurance and general insurance

The term 'general insurance' is most often used in contrast with 'life' insurance (or 'assurance') to either describe non-life insurance contracts or in connection with insurers who transact non-life business. This basic division of insurance business into two large classes, life and general, is useful because there are a number of important differences between the two. For example, general insurance policies (in the United Kingdom at least) are usually annual renewable contracts, whereas life insurance is almost invariably for a much longer period of time. Again, general insurance is effected for the sole purpose of protecting the insured against loss, whereas life insurance is often also vehicle for personal investment to the extent that the life insurance protection provided may become subsidiary to the main function of the policy as a means of saving. Perhaps most obviously, life insurance contracts are primarily concerned with human life and hinge on its duration, whereas general insurance does not. Further differences become apparent if the organizations that provide insurance are examined. An insurer will normally restrict its activities to either life or general business. In fact, European law now forbids a new insurance company from transacting both life and general insurance. This specialization in one broad class or the other will be reflected in the structure of the firm, the way in which it is regulated by the government, its marketing and investment strategy, and how it generally operates. If an insurer transacts both life and general business (some insurers of this type, known as 'composite' companies, still exist in the United Kingdom), it will nevertheless effectively treat each as a separate activity, and the differences mentioned above will exist in the two divisions of the organization. Furthermore, the law will generally prevent the co-mingling of life and general insurance funds.

31. *See* E. Gurenko et al., Insurance Risk Transfer and Categorization of Reinsurance Contracts, Policy Research Working Paper, The World Bank, 2012.

Although commonly used, 'general insurance' and 'life insurance' are not technical terms and are not particularly precise. For example, pensions contracts, annuities, and permanent health insurance are certainly not general insurance, but they are not life insurance either. For this reason, the expression 'long-term insurance business' is often used in place of 'life insurance' since it is apt to include the types of contracts mentioned above. In particular, the statutory classification system adopted by all Member States of the EU (discussed below) employs the former term. Again, accident (or 'personal accident') policies are regarded as a form of general insurance business, although human life (and human limb) form part of the subject matter.

– Classification 3: the statutory classification

As suggested above, general insurance, and indeed all insurance, are subject to a statutory classification system that is common to all EU Member States. In the United Kingdom, it was originally embodied in the Insurance Companies Act 1982. This classification is primarily for authorization purposes. Insurers cannot operate without an authorization or licence from the appropriate government department or agency. In the United Kingdom, the Financial Services Authority is the licensing authority. The authorization (or licence) is only granted for defined classes or groups of classes. An insurer may therefore have authority to write some types of insurance business but not others. The statutory classification system, in this way, provides a method of defining fairly precisely what an insurer may and may not do. However, the system is not especially helpful for understanding the business of insurance since the various statutory classes do not necessarily correspond with the different types of policies that insurers actually offer or with the names that they use to describe them. The various statutory classes are listed at the end of this section.

– Classification 4: by type of user or buyer

Insurance may be purchased to protect the assets and earnings of a business or for the protection of private individuals. Policies of the first type are described as commercial insurance (or 'commercial lines') and the latter as personal insurance (or 'personal lines'). General insurance may fall in either category; a commercial fire policy is an example of the former, and a home insurance policy is an example of the latter. Most life policies are 'personal' insurance in the sense that they are usually purchased by individuals for their own protection and savings, although some life policies are arranged to protect business interests. Pension schemes are clearly intended for the benefit of individuals but are frequently arranged (and paid for) by employers.

This classification is a useful one. Personal insurance is usually a rather simple standardized product. For this reason, it can be marketed directly to the public through intermediaries who are not specialists in insurance (such as banks). A premium rating is usually based on a simple formula, and specialist underwriting skills are generally unnecessary. On the other hand, commercial risks are often substantial and complex so that a 'tailor-made' insurance programme is often necessary. This will usually be negotiated through a professional insurance broker and demands specialist underwriting skills on the part of the insurer. Finally, it can be noted that a personal insurance business is usually regulated more stringently than commercial lines with more measures for consumer protection. This is because the 'consumer' of personal insurance is regarded as being less sophisticated than the business buyer of insurance products and therefore in greater need of protection by the state.

– Classification 5: by subject matter or risk insured

The subject matter of a life insurance is, of course, human life, and the contract hinges in some way on its duration. The subject matter of a general insurance contract may be:

- some form of physical property that is exposed to the risk of loss or material damage and in which the insured has an interest;
- a potential financial or pecuniary loss; or
- an insured's legal liability to pay compensation to another person.

In many ways, this provides the most useful classification. Each category is briefly described below.

3.1 Material Damage (or Property) Insurance

These types of insurance cover some forms of tangible property and compensate the insured for loss of or physical damage to it. The property in question may be goods of one sort or another, buildings, crops growing on land, or any other material thing. The policy may cover a particular peril only (such as fire) or a number of specified perils. Alternatively, the contract may be written on an 'all risks' basis. In this case, the insurance covers loss or damage caused by any means other than perils that are specifically excluded (a number of perils are commonly regarded as uninsurable, and an 'all risks' insurance will always exclude some forms of loss despite the name). Instead of describing the risks that are covered, this type of insurance simply specifies those that are not.

Early insurance policies only covered specified perils. Marine policies covered fire and various other perils of the sea (such as pirates, men of war, sinking, and stranding), and policies on buildings and land-based property generally covered only fire (which was by far the most common and destructive source of loss). Cover against theft and (some other) perils developed surprisingly late in the United Kingdom. There is little evidence there of theft (or burglary) insurance of any sort being offered before the 1880s. In fact, the first policy providing burglary coverage on the contents of a private dwelling dates from probably about 1887 when a Lloyd's underwriter agreed to add the risk of burglary to a fire policy at the request of a broker who had asked 'more in fun than in earnest'.

The first 'all risks' contracts appeared around the beginning of the twentieth century. There is now an increasing tendency to insure against material damage on this basis. The insured has the benefit of the widest form of cover that is available and, at least in theory, the policy will be simple in its construction since only those risks that are excluded require definition (although, in a policy covering industrial property, the exclusions themselves may be extremely complex).

3.2 Financial Loss (or Pecuniary) Insurance

Damage to physical property obviously costs money to repair, hence the demand for the material damage insurance described above. However, when property is damaged, further financial loss may be incurred beyond the cost of restoring the property in question. Thus, if commercial or industrial premises are seriously damaged by fire, production may cease or reduce significantly for a period of time, resulting in the loss of profit for the proprietor. This potential financial loss can be insured and, although it is a direct consequence of material damage, it is most conveniently treated as a separate class of insurance (known as loss of profits or business interruption insurance).

Other types of pecuniary insurance exist to cover financial losses that do not result from any material damage to the insured's property. Credit insurance, for instance, covers losses arising from bad debts of the insured's customers who have become insolvent or have defaulted on their obligations. Alternatively, the insured may suffer financial loss (or at least incur heavy expenditures) as a result of his being drawn unexpectedly into litigation as either a plaintiff or defendant. Legal expenses insurance is available to meet this contingency. Various other types of financial loss can also be covered by insurance.

3.3 Liability Insurance

People who wrongfully cause harm to others by either injuring them or damaging their property become liable in law to pay compensation for any losses that have occurred. Individuals may become liable through careless behaviour connected with their personal activities, such as driving motor vehicles or playing a sport. Equally, business activity may be a source of liability. Employees may be injured as a result of inadequate safety precautions in the workplace or consumers can be harmed by defective products supplied by a firm. In these cases, liability to pay compensation normally falls on the firm rather than the individual. Given the increasing size of court awards and spiralling legal costs, the financial consequences for the wrongdoer in either case can be catastrophic, and the need to insure such risks has become paramount – the alternative being potential bankruptcy or, in the case of a firm, insolvency and closing the firm. Not surprisingly, liability insurance is mandatory in the United Kingdom and in many other countries in respect of the two main areas of activity where individuals are most likely to suffer harm at the hands of others: on the road and in the workplace. However, as shall be seen, the object here is not so much to protect the solvency of the wrongdoer as it is to ensure that the victim is not denied compensation simply because the offender himself is unable to pay.

Not all liabilities are insurable. For example, as a matter of public policy, insurance against the cost of meeting fines and other penalties imposed by the criminal law (such as those imposed for motoring offences) is not available. The very existence of insurance in such cases would undermine the deterrent effect of the penalties established by law, and claim payments would subsequently nullify any corrective effect that the penalty might have had on the wrongdoer. Again, while many forms of civil liability (especially tort liability) are insurable, there are exceptions. For instance, insurance can only provide against losses that are, broadly speaking, accidental. Liability policies are often described as 'third party' insurance. This is because the person who suffers injury or damage in the accident that results in a claim is not the insured who purchases coverage from the insurer but a third party who has suffered as a result of the insured's wrongdoing, such as the victim of a vehicle accident. The loss suffered by the insured (i.e., the liability to pay compensation) is an indirect consequence of the accident. By contrast, all other insurance is first-party insurance since they insure against some loss suffered directly by the insured himself, either to his life, limb, pocket, or property. The contrast between first-party insurance and third-party insurance is significant. The former, for instance, is generally regarded as providing mechanism that is more efficient for meeting losses. This is because the latter (third-party insurance) is only relevant when legal liability is established, and the cost of establishing this often adds substantially to the transaction, especially when it is necessary to take a dispute to court.

3.4 'Package' Policies and Combined Forms of Insurance

Not every insurance contract can be neatly classified into one of the basic categories outlined above. As new forms of insurance have developed and risks have become more complex, demand has arisen for policies that combine several types of coverage in one contract. In this way, most, if not all, of the insurance necessary for a particular vehicle, vessel, home, or business can be provided in one contract.

By way of example, motor policies, home insurance, and policies for small and medium sized businesses of various types typically provide coverage not only against material damage to the property in question but also insure various forms of liability and financial loss that can arise in connection with the property.

These contracts (and many others that could be mentioned) therefore differ from the simple classification outlined above and may provide two or even all three of the basic types of coverage mentioned in one document.

4 TP ISSUES IN THE INSURANCE SECTOR

Reinsurance is the most important intra-group transaction that insurance groups generally undertake in order to strategically manage insurance risk by ceding a greater or smaller share of the risk to reinsurance companies. A reinsurer is an insurer which deals with other insurers as policyholders.[32] This enables an insurance company to make substantial capital savings and attenuate the volatility of the technical results of the period.

32. *See* Robert Merkin, *A Guide to Reinsurance Law,* Informa London, 2007.

In particular, in a reinsurance contract, the ceding party, i.e., the direct insurer, cedes to the reinsurer all or part of the risk assumed with regard to the reinsured parties. As a result, the reinsurer assumes, within the limits of the specific reinsurance transaction, the risks and undertakings deriving from the insurance contracts of the ceding company. However, the obligation assumed by the reinsurer is solely towards the ceding company that remains solely responsible to the insured parties.

In reinsurance, the absorption of risk capital increases less in proportion to the increase of the operating result due to the level of diversification that the internal reinsurer manages to achieve. Reinsurance makes it possible to aggregate (geographically) diversified portfolios and thereby gain the benefits of this diversification.

Reinsurance represents the main mitigation technique for local insurance entities. Within insurance groups, the parent company generally acts as core reinsurer of the group legal entities and cedes or retrocedes part of the underwritten risks to external reinsurers.

The structure and the contents of the reinsurance agreements are defined between the group reinsurance function and the competent function of the group legal entities. The process includes the identification of the group legal entity's reinsurance requirements and areas of improvement, the evaluation of what-if reinsurance structures, and agreement on the final treaties. The features of reinsurance contracts are defined also on the basis of the outputs of stochastic models that are instrumental for identifying the most efficient reinsurance solutions. They also take into account the established underwriting risk tolerance limits of each group legal entity or on the basis of prudent actuarial principles.

There are two types of reinsurance with regard to the way in which the risk is ceded through reinsurance contracts: treaty reinsurance and facultative reinsurance. Treaty (or obligatory) reinsurance is a contractual arrangement that provides for the automatic placement of a specific type or category of risk underwritten by the primary insurer. Facultative reinsurance is the reinsurance of individual risks whereby the reinsurer separately rates and underwrites each risk. Thus, with treaty reinsurance, the reinsurer accepts a bulk of insurance policies underwritten by the primary insurers all pertaining to the same class of risk. It is therefore a standard approach to cede a sum of insurance policies having the same category of risk with one reinsurance contract. In treaty reinsurance, the reinsurer generally does not evaluate each individual risk but rather ascertains the overall profit potential of the business assumed from the ceding company. Facultative reinsurance is instead typically purchased by primary insurers for individual risks not covered by their reinsurance treaties, for excess losses on risks covered by their reinsurance treaties, and for 'unusual' risks.

Obligatory reinsurance exists in two forms: proportional and non-proportional reinsurance.

4.1 Proportional Reinsurance

In general terms, with proportional reinsurance, the reinsurer follows the coverage and the fortunes of the primary insurer (i.e., the cedant or the ceding company) for all of the reinsured insurance policies.[33]

The most common form of proportional reinsurance is quota share for which the reinsurer and the primary insurer share premiums and losses on a proportional basis. Furthermore, the reinsurer may pay the primary insurer the following commissions:

- a ceding commission due to the primary insurer in recognition of the costs of obtaining the business being reinsured (including commissions, local taxes, and miscellaneous administrative expenses); and
- a contingent commission known as a profit commission to the ceding company as an incentive to maintain the flow of profitable business to the reinsurer.

The main two types of proportional reinsurance are quota share and surplus share agreement.

With quota share treaties, the primary insurer cedes a pre-agreed fixed percentage of premiums and claims to the reinsurer. The most salient feature of quota share treaties is their administrative simplicity. Once the conditions have been agreed, the primary insurer (i.e., the cedant) does not need to control each of the risks individually neither for the distribution of premiums nor for the claim.

With a surplus share agreement, the cession to the reinsurer also consists of a proportion or percentage but only for those risks that exceed a predetermined amount. Once the cedant (or ceding company) sets its own retention risk level for a specific class of risk via a surplus treaty, the losses and premiums are shared between the company and the reinsurer proportionally with respect to the portion of risk undertaken. Surplus agreements allow the cedant greater flexibility than quota shares in ceding risk to the reinsurer. The reinsurer guarantees to cover the amount that exceeds the retention set for the direct insurer, while the risks that are individually worth less than the retention are wholly borne by the direct insurer. Unlike quota share arrangements, the reinsurer is not obligated to 'follow' each risk assumed by the ceding company but only those that result in so high an exposure that the overall amount of premiums paid to the reinsurer plus the commission to be paid to the ceding company are generally proportionally lower. This treaty is considered a proportional contract since each reinsurer receives the same percentage on the premium for each risk that exceeds the amount of retention and is involved in the same proportion in the settlement of any claim.

The advantage of proportional reinsurance for the primary insurer is that it allows establishing a balance in the risk portfolio retained for its own account as this is made

33. The so-called follow the fortune principle obligates the reinsurer to bear his contractually agreed share in the direct insurer's insurance and contractual risk arising out of the ceded business. *See* Dieter Arndt, *Reinsurance, Principles and State of the Art*, Verlag Versicherungswirtschaft, Karlsruhe, 2004.

more stable with a lower probability of deviation in the retained claims by generally fixing retentions that vary in amount according to the risk's level of hazard. Of course, therefore, the greatest difficulty for the insurer is to calculate the level of these retentions.

4.2 Non-proportional Reinsurance

With non-proportional reinsurance, the reinsurer only intervenes after a certain compensation amount is reached and covers the remaining share.

There are two main types of non-proportional reinsurance: excess of loss and stop-loss reinsurance.

With the excess of loss (XL) non-proportional reinsurance, the insurer and the reinsurer establish the reference amount which limits the costs of compensation related to the classes of business subject to the treaty shall be borne only by the insurer. The reinsurer shall bear in full loss in excess of the specified retention (so-called priority) until an agreed limit (so-called 'treaty limit'). Once the priority is established, the ceding company shall transfer to the reinsurer the risk or risks it does not retain and pay premiums calculated on the specific case as opposed to proportional reinsurance; thus, there is no commission to the ceding company.

For stop-loss non-proportional reinsurance, the reinsured is covered against the possibility that the overall claims/premiums earned ratio (loss ratio) exceeds an agreed percentage in a specific class of business. As such, the reinsurer is not required to compensate any claim until overall claims for the entire year do not exceed an agreed percentage on premiums, i.e., priority. This reinsurance method is different from other non-proportional reinsurance in the way that it determines the treaty limit and priority as they are not established as overall value but rather as a percentage on premiums.

Excess of loss treaties can be further divided into two main categories: per risk excess of loss and catastrophe excess of loss (Cat XL). The latter is focused on a specific natural event (e.g., storm, earthquake, etc.), and there must therefore be more than one claim caused by the same event and affecting more than one policy. With excess of loss per risk, this contract protects the insurer against claims exceeding the amount that it has decided to retain for its own account on a specific risk.

One of the main advantages for the cedant in dealing with non-proportional treaties is the higher retention of the premiums written insofar as XL protects the cedant above an absolute limit of retention and against the cost of a claim while the proportional insurance participates in the claim. Moreover, with non-proportional reinsurance, accounting operations and administrations costs are minimized vis-à-vis the proportional treaties. On the other hand, with non-proportional reinsurance, the cedant is largely dependent on developments in the reinsurance market, and prices can vary substantially from one year to the next depending on how the international claims experience goes. Additionally, the XL places the cedant in a negative cash flow situation insofar as most of the reinsurance premium is paid at the beginning of the contract in advance, and there is no profit commission. Thus, this type of reinsurance is not the best to support the start-up process of underwriting in an insurance company's particular class of business.

4.3 Why Reinsurance: The Commercial Rationale

As already mentioned, reinsurance can represent an alternative form of capital, allowing the company to write a greater volume of business than would otherwise be possible for the same level of capital. Through reinsurance, a ceding company will normally be able to reduce their capital requirements, thereby improving their solvency ratios or other capital-driven ratios. The driver may not necessarily be regulatory solvency but could be for rating agency capital adequacy or to meet group internal guidelines. The local subsidiary boards will normally articulate their own capital management policy, and this can also be a reason for seeking reinsurance. Although a company may have sufficient capital for the risks on its balance sheet, this could be an inefficient use of capital if the company has a single or a few peak risks that are out of balance with the other risks of the company. By reinsuring the peak risks, the ceding company may not only reduce its overall capital requirement under certain regulatory regimes but also gain proportionally more from diversification benefits and hence make more efficient use of its capital. The released capital can then be used, for example, to increase business or pay increased dividends. A more balanced portfolio from a risk perspective is also likely to reduce volatility in the profit and loss account, and this could be a further reason for reinsurance. Local subsidiary boards together with local management will normally determine the risk appetite for the local company. This will be based on numerous local factors and will also reflect the local company's views on the desirability of certain risks. Subsidiary companies often have their performance measured by the amount of profit generated within the company on a net retained basis. In this instance, the potential volatility of the profit and loss account may be of concern, and one way to reduce this volatility is to reinsure part or all of the risks that are the primary contributors to the volatility.[34]

The benefit of reinsurance can therefore be summarized in the following points:

- reduction of the volatility of underwriting results;
- capital relief and flexible financing;
- more underwriting opportunity thus improving the leading market position;
- financial security;
- accessing expertise and services insofar as the reinsurer can support in areas such as product development, pricing, and claims management; and
- profit & growth.

34. *See* Intra-Group Reinsurance Transactions, International Actuarial Association, October 2013.

4.4 TP Key Aspects in Reinsurance

4.4.1 *The Actuarial Pricing*

When related parties enter into cross-border intercompany reinsurance, TP regulations should apply. Thus, the conditions between the counterparties within the reinsurance agreement should be in accordance with the arm's length principle as per the latest version of the OECD TP Guidelines.

For excess of loss reinsurance contracts, 'price' is commonly expressed as the contract premium. In some cases, it is indicated as a percentage of underlying subject premium but, effectively, the price is still the final premium. However, in a quota share contract, the determination of price arises in effect from the ceding commission. Since premiums and losses covered under quota share percentages are determined as a contractually stated proportion of the underlying reinsured contracts, the contractual commissions are the actual determinant of the contract pricing. The higher that the expected ceding commission is, the lower the effective price of the contract.

In general terms, the approaches that actuaries typically use to determine the price of intercompany reinsurance contracts fall into three general categories of methods:

(1) Capital Based.
(2) Market Based.
(3) Contract Comparison (CUP Method).

As a starting point, for TP purposes, it is helpful to evaluate a reinsurance contract in the same manner that a pricing actuary in an actuarial department would price a reinsurance contract.[35] The TP actuary may derive a range of acceptable prices for which the width would vary depending on the type of business and the uncertainty in the market. There are also specific company considerations that may alter the price of the reinsurance contract. For example, a company may place more value on a contract because it contains a certain class of business that balances its portfolio. In addition, some of the methods used are hybrid methods utilizing market data, company data, and specific contract data and generally do not squarely belong to one of the four approaches.

The capital-based method is the most commonly used. It requires an estimate of capital associated with the policy and an estimate of what investors demand as a return on that capital.[36] This class of methods is useful for both excess of loss and quota share contracts. It tends to be an especially beneficial method for evaluating lines of business where the pricing tends to be highly dependent on the uncertainty and duration of cash flows. The three main determinants of the pricing are: the expected amount of covered

35. *See* Lynne Bloom, Marc Oberholtzer, *The Actuary's Role in Transfer Pricing*, Casualty Actuarial Society E-Forum, 2015.
36. ROC is commonly used when an estimate of the premium is made considering commissions paid to the ceding insurer, an estimate of losses that will be covered under the contract, and an estimated return on economic capital that is commensurate with the assuming company's target rate of return or opportunity cost of capital.

losses, the internal expenses, and the cost of capital that the reinsurer would keep for the risk reinsured.

Market-based methods are essentially industry comparisons of commonly used market benchmarks, such as combined ratios[37] from publicly available information. The benchmarked combined ratio can then be applied to the tested party's claims and expenses that are paid to arrive at an arm's length measure of annual premiums and thus underwriting profit (premiums receivable less claims and expenses).[38] The principal advantage of these types of methods is simplicity. They also reflect current market conditions and have 'real world' significance. A disadvantage to these methods is that they may not reflect the nuances of a particular contract and, as such, when more uncertainty occurs and/or there is a longer payout of claims, the less reasonable these methods are for TP purposes.

Another method to determine the arm's length price of a reinsurance transaction is to rely on internal comparables; i.e., an actuary may leverage insights gained from the pricing of contracts with unrelated parties. Of course, if this approach from one side has the advantage of providing clear and direct evidence that the pricing is consistent with actual contracts with unrelated parties, on the other hand, it might not consider the unique contract feature on the related transaction unless a reliable comparability adjustment could be made as per the OECD TPG.[39] However, this approach is generally applied in reinsurance treaties with cessions where the group reinsurer(s) operates as a follower with respect to a panel of independent third-party reinsurers, thus accepting a share of the risk under the same contractual terms and conditions applied by the panel of reinsurers. Since treaties managed by this panel are basically identical, the internal CUP Method can be considered the most reliable approach.

4.4.2 *The Multinational Programmes*

One of the most common TP issues within insurance groups is related to the arm's length conditions in the context of the so-called multinational programs according to which insurance groups provide their clients with insurance protection in multiple jurisdictions via the insurance subsidiaries of the insurance group.

With this model, insurance groups offer their clients multinational programmes that are established in the headquarters country of the customers where a 'master policy' insurance contract is issued. When the company has activities and requires insurance in other locations, the risks are covered via a 'local contract' through a local (fronting) representative (known as a 'fronting office') which cedes the risk back to the producing office (i.e., the entity who owns the relationship with the multinational client). Such an

37. A combined ratio (COR) is the measure of underwriting profitability in insurance that is calculated using the sum of incurred losses and expenses divided by earned premiums. Insurers can have an underwriting loss (a COR of more than 100%) but still be profitable because of investment income levels. *See* Anshuman Acharya, David Hamilton, Pradip Patiath, Zachary Surak, Grier Tumas Dienstag, Jasper van Ouwerkerk, *Insurance Resilience in a Rapidly Changing Coronavirus World*, McKinsey, 29 April 2020.
38. *See* OECD TPG, para. 10.220.
39. *See* OECD TPG, Chapter III.

operating model gives rise to a number of cross-border reinsurance flows. Thus, to simplify them, insurance groups generally establish a centralized clearing house model according to which all reinsurance flows relating to the reinsured business line will be ceded to one single entity acting as a 'pooler' usually via proportional quota share treaties.[40]

Multinational programmes are offered by some insurance companies in the market to provide solutions to clients seeking insurance in a number of jurisdictions, particularly in the non-life (property and casualty or P&C) sector. As stated above, P&C insurance protects against property losses and/or against legal liability that may result from injury or damage to the property of others. Insurers are faced with a number of challenges from both a regulatory and legal perspective due to the increasingly global marketplace in which they operate. In certain instances, insurance companies will be required to work together with third-party insurers to provide local insurance solutions to clients with operations in different jurisdictions. As indicated, insurance companies often offer multinational programmes to their customers via a centralized 'master' insurance policy that is issued in the headquarters country of the parent company and supported by a number of local insurance policies in each of the client's local markets.

4.4.3 *The TP Analysis*

This section will further articulate what are the main steps in order to comply with the TP regulations within reinsurance transactions and what are the main challenges considering the current TP framework and focusing in particular on a comparability analysis and economic analysis.

The application of the arm's length principle is based on a comparison of the conditions in a controlled transaction (i.e., between entities belonging to the same MNE group) with the conditions that would have been made had the parties been independent and undertaking a comparable transaction under similar circumstances. Therefore, a comparability analysis is at the heart of the application of the arm's length principle.[41]

For performing such an analysis, also in the case of a reinsurance transaction performed between insurance entities belonging to the same insurance group,[42] the first aspect is the accurate delineation of the actual transaction. It is aimed at identifying the commercial or financial relations (i.e., the comparability factors) between the associated enterprises, the conditions, and all economically relevant factors attached to those relations.

40. It is worthwhile mentioning that those types of multinational pooling schemes can occur via so-called ART reinsurance such as a loss portfolio transfer which is a particular type of quota share reinsurance called 'retrospective'. *See* Erik Banks, *Alternative Risk Transfer*, Wiley Finance, 2004.
41. *See* OECD TPG, paras 1.6 and 1.33.
42. According to the OECD TPG, Chapter X para. 10.195: 'The principles of accurate delineation of the actual transactions and allocation of risk detailed in Chapter I of these Guidelines apply to captive insurance and reinsurance in the same manner that they apply to any other intra-group transactions.'

A detailed analysis is required based on the following characteristics:

(1) contractual terms of the transaction that describe the allocation of responsibilities, obligations and rights, assumption of identified risks, and pricing arrangements;
(2) functions performed, assets used, and risks assumed by the respective associated enterprises are to be analysed through an appropriate functional analysis;
(3) specific characteristics of the property transferred or the services provided (i.e., of the reinsurance transactions envisaged);
(4) economic circumstances; and
(5) business strategies.

The functional analysis seeks to identify the economically significant activities and responsibilities undertaken, assets used or contributed, and risks assumed by the parties to the transactions.[43] It focuses on what the parties actually do and the capabilities they provide (also considering their decision-making activities). An essential part is also the risk analysis of the economically significant risks assumed by each party since the actual assumption of those risks and/or the control over them would influence the prices and other conditions of the intercompany transaction under analysis. Risk assumption means taking on the upside and downside consequences of the risk with the result that the party assuming a risk will also bear the financial and other consequences if the risk materializes. Specifically, according to the OECD TPG,[44] the control over risk involves the first two elements of risk management:

(1) the capability to make decisions to take on, lay off, or decline a risk-bearing opportunity together with the actual performance of that decision-making function; and
(2) the capability to make decisions on whether and how to respond to the risks associated with the opportunity together with the actual performance of that decision-making function.

The capability to perform and the actual performance of decision-making functions relating to a specific risk involve an understanding of the risk based on a relevant analysis of the information required for assessing the foreseeable downside and upside risk outcomes and the consequences for the business of the enterprise. Decision-makers should possess competence and experience in the area of the particular risk for which the decision is being made, have an understanding of the impact of their decision on the business, and also have access to and guide the elaboration of the relevant information.

Thus, the functional analysis within the reinsurance context aims at evaluating how and to what extent the control over the insured risk occurs and thus how actual

43. *See* OECD TPG, para. 1.51.
44. *See* OECD TPG, paras 1.61, 1.66-1.167.

decisions are made at the level of both the ceding companies and the reinsurer. In doing so, the negotiation process between the cedants and the reinsurer should be documented. Indeed, the process in which the negotiation occurs between the related parties is a crucial proxy for arm's length conditions insofar as it is expected to observe a certain level of commercial tension between two independent parties.

4.4.4 Negotiation

In general terms, the main steps to consider (and document) having in mind the actual conduct[45] of the related entities in a negotiation process within the functional analysis are as follows:

- the cedants prepare a business plan on a business line-by-business line basis setting out key metrics in respect of the ceded book (e.g., premium volume, expected losses, internal management expenses, combined ratio, etc.) which the cedants submit to the reinsurer for their review and consideration;
- the reinsurer will review each of the business plans submitted by the cedants and perform a preliminary analysis, testing the key assumptions (e.g., premium volume) proposed against their own key metrics, e.g., ROE, ROC;
- based on their review, the reinsurer will propose an initial ceding commission to the relevant cedant which usually results in back and forth discussions between the two of them before a ceding commission is agreed;
- from the perspective of the reinsurer, there must be evidence in the analysis that the maximum ceding commission it would be willing to pay is one that achieves a COR below 100% (i.e., break-even). Any ceding commission over and above this will result in the overall book being loss-making which will make the terms, in principle, unattractive and unacceptable from the perspective of the reinsurer;[46]
- from the cedant's perspective, there has to be evidence of the analysis for which the aim is to earn a ceding commission to cover any third-party acquisition expenses at cost and any administrative expenses at cost plus a

45. 'It is, therefore, particularly important in considering the commercial or financial relations between associated enterprises to examine whether the arrangements reflected in the actual conduct of the parties substantially conform to the terms of any written contract, or whether the associated enterprises' actual conduct indicates that the contractual terms have not been followed, do not reflect a complete picture of the transactions, have been incorrectly characterized or labelled by the enterprises, or are a sham. Where conduct is not fully consistent with economically significant contractual terms, further analysis is required to identify the actual transaction. Where there are material differences between contractual terms and the conduct of the associated enterprises in their relations with one another, the functions they actually perform, the assets they actually use, and the risks they actually assume, considered in the context of the contractual terms, should ultimately determine the factual substance and accurately delineate the actual transaction.' *See* OECD TPG, para. 1.46.
46. Unless there are very particular reasons for which at arms' length a reinsurer could and would accept to insure the book of business ceded even with a COR higher than 100%, considering other options realistically available, e.g., if it had reasonable expectations of future profits. *See* OECD TPG, para. 3.64 and para. 9.30.

markup. However, as explained in the paragraphs above, one of the primary drivers for the cedants to join a reinsurance scheme is to reduce volatility from a local perspective. Therefore, at arm's length, the cedant may be willing to accept a lower ceding commission that may not cover their forecasted expenses (both acquisition and administrative) on that particular book of business in order to meet their primary objective of volatility reduction;
- any analysis performed by the reinsurer within the overall reinsurance governance framework established by the group's head office;
- when a ceding commission cannot be agreed between the cedant and the reinsurer, the cedant may be required to provide a more detailed breakdown of the prepared forecast (particularly with respect to expenses). For example, when a cedant is in the start-up phase, expenses are likely to be higher, and additional granularity is required in these cases. In this case, the bargaining power is likely to rest with the reinsurer; and
- once the cedant and the reinsurer agree on a remuneration structure and terms of the ceded business that are commercially acceptable to both parties, a pricing addendum (containing correspondence and documentation of the negotiation process) is appended to the relevant reinsurance contract.

The negotiation process described above demonstrates that there is or is expected to be commercial tension in the negotiation process that demonstrates arm's length behaviour and that is in accordance with how third parties would negotiate the terms under comparable circumstances. The TP functional analysis should therefore describe the variations in the negotiation process for each of the cedants and the reinsurer taking into account all of the functions performed, assets used, and risks assumed[47] at both levels.

4.4.5 *Commercial Rationale for Reinsurance*

Another very important aspect of a TP analysis is to clearly document and explain the commercial rationale for the reinsurance arrangement under analysis from the perspective of both the reinsurer and the cedant. Indeed, demonstrating the commercial rationality of the intercompany transaction is a crucial aspect. Tax authorities could seek to disregard a transaction for tax purposes without necessarily engaging in the pricing analysis when the arrangements made for the transaction, viewed in their totality, differ from those that would have been adopted by independent enterprises behaving in a commercially rational manner in comparable circumstances.[48] This is further reinforced by Chapter IX of the OECD TPG on Business Restructuring which

47. The identification and analysis of the material risks assumed and the functions that are relevant to or affect the assumption or impact of these risks as well as their subsequent allocation between the parties to the transaction will directly affect how the profits or losses resulting from the transaction will be allocated through the arm's length pricing of the transaction. The OECD TPG has introduced a six-step process for analysing risks in transactions between related parties. *See* OECD TPG, para. 1.56.
48. *See* OECD TPG, para. 1.122.

includes extended guidance on issues relating to risks and to the recognition of transactions.[49]

Therefore, a key aspect in the TP analysis is to clearly demonstrate by providing evidence - having in mind the mentioned actual conduct principle - of the benefits of both of the counterparties in joining the reinsurance transaction.

In general terms, the benefits for the reinsurer can be grouped in the following:

- effective capital management: by pooling different risks, the reinsurer can benefit from the diversification of risks;
- economies of scale and synergies: when reinsurance flows are centralized - especially with multinational programmes - overall costs are reduced insofar as the administration of the multinational programme is simplified.

In general terms, the benefits for the ceding company can be grouped in the following:[50]

- volatility reduction: the adoption of a centralized model protects the net capital base of the ceding entities from depletion that may be caused as a result of extreme CAT events;
- capital improvement: from the perspective of the local ceding entities, the Intercompany transactions are expected to give rise to significant capital benefits locally.

Moreover, when it comes to commercial rationale, it is worthwhile noting that the OECD TPG introduced additional guidance aimed at assessing the 'genuineness' of captive insurance or fronting reinsurance arrangements via specific 'hallmarks'.[51] Although the guidance is not aimed at assessing the genuineness of 'reinsurance' per se but mainly provides guidance for MNE captive insurance and fronting reinsurance, for the sake of completeness, however, it could be advisable to have also performed the analysis of the transaction hallmarks that have been introduced.

The following features are indicators of what can typically be expected in an independent insurer:

(1) there is diversification and pooling of risk in the captive insurance;
(2) the economic capital position of the entities within the MNE group has improved as a result of diversification, and there is therefore a real economic impact for the MNE group as a whole;

49. Paragraph 9.10 of the OECD TPG emphasizes the importance of determining 'whether that allocation of risk is one that might be expected to have been agreed between independent parties in similar circumstances'.
50. Demonstrating and documenting the benefits for the ceding companies is crucial especially for reinsurance transactions where 100% for the premiums are reinsured to the reinsurer insofar as the ceding company is ceding 100% of the book of the business at stake and thus, at arm's length, a ceding company would do it only if it will receive clear and defined expected benefits, e.g., in terms of an improved capital position.
51. *See* OECD TPG, para. 10.199.

(3) both the captive insurance and any reinsurer are regulated entities with broadly similar regulatory regimes and regulators that require evidence of risk assumption and appropriate capital levels;
(4) the insured risk would otherwise be insurable outside the MNE group;
(5) the captive insurance has the requisite skills, including investment skills, and experience at its disposal; and
(6) the captive insurance has a real possibility of suffering losses.

As stated, the reinsurer benefits from a diversification effect given by the accepted pooling risks. This can be demonstrated via an empirical analysis that should be completed at the level of the reinsurer before entering into the transactions. Additionally, it should present various correlations by both geographical, business mix point of view and the correlation between the risk of the given segment and its total existing underwriting portfolio.

Empirical data backing the commercial rationale before entering into the reinsurance arrangement is therefore crucial for ensuring that the parties create arm's length conditions. Indeed, regardless of the TP methodology used to support the pricing of the transaction, there is an overriding need to be able to clearly articulate the commercial rationale behind entering into the reinsurance contract in the first place.[52] Moreover, it is worthwhile accentuating that the OECD TPG requires providing evidence of the requisite skills/experience related to underwriting, claims management, as well as actuarial and investment decisions. Thus, as a consequence, senior underwriting personnel at the reinsurer level have to be assessed in terms of whether people are in charge of taking key decisions in relation to all key aspects of the business reinsured on an actual conduct basis insofar as stated by the OECD TPG.[53]

4.4.6 *Economic Analysis*

The selection of an appropriate method to be used to test the arm's length character of a controlled transaction is based on a determination of the method which, under the facts and circumstances of the transaction under review, provides the most reliable or best estimation of an arm's length result. Factors used to determine the most appropriate method are the degree of comparability between the controlled and uncontrolled

52. Tax authorities are increasingly becoming less concerned with whether an insurer 'could' have entered into a transaction at a specific price than with whether it 'would' have done so with a third-party reinsurer. This raises the potential threat of recharacterization or disregarding the reinsurance transaction in the worst-case scenario. *See* Intragroup Reinsurance Transfer Pricing: A Risk-Based Approach, Transfer Pricing Report, Bloomberg BNA, 2008.
53. *See* footnote 46. Moreover, the actual transaction would need to be deduced from the evidence of actual conduct provided by identifying the economically relevant characteristics of the transaction. Indeed, if the pricing date specified in any written agreement between the associated enterprises is inconsistent with the actual conduct of the parties or with other facts of the case, tax administrations may determine a different pricing date consistent with those other facts of the case and what independent enterprises would have agreed in comparable circumstances (taking into considerations industry practices). *See* OECD TPG, paras 1.49, 1.89, 2.22.

transactions, the quality of the data, and the reliability of assumptions used in the analysis.

The appropriateness of each of the pricing methods (both traditional transactions and transactional profit methods) has to be evaluated to determine whether the pricing of the specific reinsurance transaction is consistent with the arm's length principle.

As per the latest OECD TP framework and best practice, in reinsurance transactions, the economic analysis must take into account the reinsurer's point of view and the ceding company on a two-sided approach. This section focuses in particular on the quota share reinsurance transactions for which the ceding commission is the key transfer pricing component that needs to be determined at arm's length.

From the reinsurer's perspective as part of this analysis, the items that may be considered are:

- the expected treaty loss ratio[54] under each reinsured business;
- the capital requirements and the financing cost associated with such capital;
- internal costs, including overhead and salaries; and
- the cost of retrocession[55] (if any).

These factors combined determine the maximum allowable treaty commissions that the reinsurer would be willing to pay out to each of the cedants in order to achieve its target combined ratio. As would be the case in a third-party context, the reinsurer would not be willing to pay out a ceding commission over and above this amount as it would have the effect of eroding its target ROC and potentially result in the book being loss-making which would ultimately make the terms of the reinsurance contract unattractive to accept for the reinsurer. The TP analysis performed from the reinsurer's point of view is further aimed at testing the target annualized ROC against the returns of third-party insurers via a TNMM benchmarking analysis.

The next step is to determine these commissions from the cedants' perspective. The CUP Method compares the amounts charged in controlled transactions with amounts charged in comparable third-party transactions. Comparable transactions may be between two third parties (i.e., an external CUP) or between one of the related parties and a third party (i.e., an internal CUP). A potentially comparable transaction would involve one of the following:

- a similar reinsurance arrangement entered into by the cedants or the reinsurer with a third-party reinsurer under similar circumstances;
- a similar reinsurance arrangement entered into by the cedants or the reinsurer with an unrelated party under similar circumstances; or
- identification of transactional data for similar reinsurance arrangements between third parties (uncontrolled entities) under similar circumstances.

54. Loss ratio is used in the insurance industry representing the ratio of losses to premiums earned. Losses in loss ratios include paid insurance claims and adjustment expenses. The loss ratio formula is insurance claims paid plus adjustment expenses divided by total earned premium. *See* https://www.investopedia.com/terms/l/loss-ratio.asp (last accessed 31 January 2022).

55. Retrocession is a transaction in which a reinsurer transfers risks it has reinsured to another reinsurer. *See* https://www.irmi.com/term/insurance-definitions/retrocession (last accessed 31 January 2022).

When both of the cedants and/or the reinsurer do not enter into an arrangement with third parties, a cost-plus approach is usually considered from the perspective of the cedant. An arm's length price is determined by applying an appropriate markup on costs incurred in the course of the transaction. The underlying rationale is that cost plus a suitable markup provides an appropriate profit for the functions performed, assets employed, and risks borne by the cedants in respect of the reinsurance transaction. Even when the cost-plus method is suitable from a theoretical perspective, there are often considerable practical obstacles to implementation due to the significant level of uncertainty and volatility associated with claims. The cost-plus method typically requires a transparent cost structure, and the cost base must be known with a degree of certainty; this is usually the case with proportional reinsurance. The cedants' cost base in this context would incorporate general expenses (e.g., salaries, overhead, etc.) that are incurred in administering the ceded book including acquisition expenses. The actual cost base depends on the management expenses of the insurer as it requires compensation for originating the business. This is reflected by the allowance for these expenses in the model in the form of a commission. Thus, with this approach - and in the absence of comparable arrangements with third parties - the arm's length markup on costs for the cedant will be determined via a benchmarking analysis in an application of the TNMM under the OECD TPG.

As already stated above, from the cedant's perspective, the main driver is to reduce volatility given the potential for one event to erode their capital base. As a consequence, they may be willing to accept a lower ceding commission in order to meet their primary objective of volatility reduction.

In conclusion, the final step of the economic analysis is therefore demonstrating how both the maximum ceding commission from the reinsurer's perspective and the minimum ceding commission from the cedant's point of view are within the arm's length ranges.[56] In particular, the maximum ceding commission from the reinsurer's perspective should take into account all the reinsurer target ratios as mentioned above and in particular with a target annualized ROC which is within an arm's length range of the third-party comparable insurers' ROC. The minimum ceding commission from the cedant's point of view is determined as the amount of commission that covers all the cedant's costs related to the book of business ceded via the reinsurance transaction plus an arm's length markup on costs related to the function the cedant performed, i.e., administering the ceded book. Finally, where the cedant may be willing to accept a lower ceding commission - thus, not covering (or partially covering) the costs generated in administering the ceded book - in order to meet their primary objective of reinsurance (e.g., volatility reduction), it will be therefore crucial that the functional

56. Within these mentioned reinsurance transactions, the reinsurer may generally enable the cedants to get a remuneration for funds withheld within the ceding company in the form of interest on deposits. In order to test the arm's length nature of deposit interest rate for transfer pricing purposes, since financial transactions are reasonably homogenous and reliable market data is readily available in public financial sources, reliable comparable uncontrolled transactions can regularly be identified in publicly available databases. Therefore, the external CUP Method is regarded as a reasonable and direct method to perform an arm's length analysis on deposit interest rates by identifying comparable yields on publicly traded debt issuances.

analysis shows it is an arm's length behaviour – taking into account the commercial rationale and the option realistically available, on an actual conduct basis – such as what would be done between independent parties.[57]

5 CONCLUSIONS

Insurance is a risk-spreading mechanism that allows buyers of insurance to transfer at least some of the risks associated with their business activities to insurance enterprises. In doing so, they exchange the uncertain cost of large potential future losses for the reasonably certain cost of the insurance premiums that they pay.

Among all of the functions of an insurance company, underwriting is at the core. It is the activity of statistical observation modelling of classes of insured risks that will therefore be managed by insurers during the life cycle of the insurance policy, and this is why underwriting is highly interconnected with the risk management function. Therefore, underwriting leads to risk pooling and diversification of risks by building an expansive portfolio of insurance consumers which, as already mentioned, is the purpose of insurance value generation. It is thus worthwhile noticing that pricing comes after risk classification and selection, meaning that the acceptance of risks should not be mainly driven by profitability concerns but, rather, it is the actuarial appropriate selection of certain risks in light of the insurer's underwriting policy.

Underwriting may also include a specific risk retention analysis. Concisely, in considering appropriate retention levels, insurers might choose to set them to specific amounts of economic losses and impact in terms of capital.

Reinsurance is the most important intra-group transactions that insurance groups generally undertake in order to strategically manage an insurance risk by ceding a greater or smaller share of the risk to reinsurance companies. In a reinsurance contract, the ceding party, i.e., the direct insurer, cedes to the reinsurer all or part of the risk assumed with regard to the reinsured parties. As a result, the reinsurer assumes, within the limits of the specific reinsurance transaction, the risks and undertakings deriving from the insurance contracts of the ceding company. However, the obligation assumed by the reinsurer is solely towards the ceding company which remains solely responsible towards the insured parties.

In general terms, reinsurance exists in two forms: proportional and non-proportional. With proportional reinsurance, the reinsurer follows the coverage and the fortunes of the primary insurer (i.e., the cedant or the ceding company) for all of the reinsured insurance policies whereas, with non-proportional reinsurance, the reinsurer only intervenes after a certain compensation amount is reached and subsequently covers the remaining share.

57. As explained, there are also very particular reasons for which at arms' length a reinsurer could and would accept to insure the book of business ceded even with a COR higher than 100%, considering other options realistically available, e.g., if it had reasonable expectations of future profits. *See* OECD TPG, para. 3.64 and para. 9.30.

The benefits of reinsurance can be therefore summarized in the following points:

- reduction of the volatility of underwriting results;
- capital relief and flexible financing;
- more underwriting opportunity thus improving the leading market position;
- financial security;
- accessing expertise and services insofar as the reinsurer can support in areas such as product development, pricing, and claims management; and
- profit & growth.

In general terms, the approaches that actuaries typically use to determine the price of intercompany reinsurance contracts fall into three general categories of methods:

(1) Capital based.
(2) Market based.
(3) Contract Comparison (CUP Method).

One of the most common TP issues within insurance groups is related to the arm's length conditions in the context of what is known as 'multinational programs' according to which insurance groups provide their clients with insurance protection in multiple jurisdictions via the insurance subsidiaries of the insurance group.

With this model, insurance groups offer their clients multinational programmes that are established in the headquarters country of the customers where a 'master policy' insurance contract is issued. When the company has activities and requires insurance in other locations, the risks are covered via a 'local contract' through a local (fronting) representative (referred to as the fronting office) which cedes the risk back to the producing office (i.e., the entity who owns the relationship with the multinational client). Such an operating model gives rise to a number of cross-border reinsurance flows. Thus, to simplify cross-border reinsurance flows, in general, insurance groups establish a centralized clearing house model according to which all reinsurance flows relating to the reinsured business line will be ceded to one single entity functioning as a 'pooler' via proportional quota share treaties.

In performing a comparability analysis, a detailed analysis is required based on the following characteristics:

- contractual terms of the transaction which describe the allocation of responsibilities, obligations and rights, assumption of identified risks, and pricing arrangements;
- functions performed, assets used, and risk assumed by the respective associated enterprises are to be analysed through an appropriate functional analysis;
- specific characteristics of the property transferred or the services provided (i.e., of the reinsurance transactions envisaged);
- economic circumstances; and
- business strategies.

One of the most important aspects is showing that the negotiation process described above demonstrates that there is or is expected to be commercial tension in the negotiation process which demonstrates arm's length behaviour and is in accordance with how third parties would negotiate the terms under comparable circumstances. Indeed, demonstrating the commercial rationality of the intercompany transaction is a crucial aspect. Tax authorities could seek to disregard a transaction for tax purposes without necessarily engaging in the pricing analysis when the arrangements made in relation to the transaction, viewed in their totality, differ from those that would have been adopted by independent enterprises behaving in a commercially rational manner in comparable circumstances.

Empirical data backing the commercial rationale before entering into the reinsurance arrangement is therefore crucial for ensuring that the parties create arm's length conditions. Indeed, regardless of the TP methodology used to support the pricing of the transaction, there is an overriding need to be able to clearly articulate the commercial rationale behind entering into the reinsurance contract in the first place.

Moreover, when it comes to commercial rationale, it is worthwhile noting that the OECD Report on Transfer Pricing Guidance on Financial Transactions introduced additional guidance aimed at assessing the 'genuineness' of captive insurance or fronting reinsurance arrangements via specific 'hallmarks'.[58] Although the guidance is not aimed at assessing the genuineness of 'reinsurance' per se but mainly provides guidance for MNE captive insurance and fronting reinsurance, for the sake of completeness, however, it could be advisable to have also performed the analysis of the transaction hallmarks that have been introduced.

For the economic analysis, it is crucial to conduct a two-sided analysis by which both the key metrics and target ratio of the reinsurer and the ceding company are taken into account such as what would be done between independent parties.

The appropriateness of each of the pricing methods (both traditional transactions and transactional profit methods) has to be evaluated to determine whether the pricing of the specific reinsurance transaction is consistent with the arm's length principle.

This chapter focused in particular on the economic analysis of the quota share treaties that take into account the reinsurer's point of view (i.e., the maximum level of commission it is willing to pay) and the ceding company (i.e., the minimum level of commission to cover its costs) on a two-sided approach.

In particular, the maximum ceding commission from the reinsurer's perspective should take into account all the reinsurer target ratios (e.g., expected treaty loss ratio, internal costs) and in particular with a target annualized ROC which is within an arm's length range of the third-party comparable insurers' ROC.

The minimum ceding commission from the cedant's point of view is determined as the amount of commission that covers all the cedant's costs related to the book of business ceded via the reinsurance transaction plus an arm's length markup on costs related to the function the cedant performed, i.e., administering the ceded book.

58. *See* OECD TPG, para. 10.199.

Particular issues arise where the cedant may be willing to accept a lower ceding commission and/or the reinsurer may be willing to accept to reinsure a book of business forecasting losses. In such cases, in this chapter it has been shown how and to what extent the functional analysis may show how it is an arm's length behaviour - taking into account the commercial rationale and the option realistically available, on an actual conduct basis - such as what would be done between independent parties.

CHAPTER 19

Transfer Pricing in the IT Sector

Niraja Srinivasan, Katarina Petovska, Tatiana Amba & Srini Lalapet[*]

1 INTRODUCTION

The IT industry has permeated every aspect of life; it has changed how life is lived, how work is done, and communication with others. It is also a key driver of industry

* The authors are grateful for reviews, comments and editorial changes from many IT industry leaders and transfer pricing experts, notably Lorraine Eden, Professor Emerita of Management and Research Professor of Law, Texas A&M University.

convergence and the foundation of the digital economy. The IT industry has extraordinary diversity, scale[1] and scope in terms of participants and the underlying technologies. It is also characterized by a rate of innovation that is unprecedented in history with new technologies spawning new business models and companies at an extraordinary rate.

The IT industry is a leading and top-performing sector within the S&P 500 Index[2] and comprises companies primarily engaged in the provision of IT-related and software development services; manufacturing of the technology hardware and storage; and the production of electronic equipment and components, including semiconductors and related equipment.[3] Premised on Moore's law,[4] the IT industry has experienced exponential growth over the past few decades. Currently, the world's top largest companies rated by market capitalization are the leading MNEs operating in the IT industry.

Considering the importance of the IT industry, tax authorities worldwide have taken a significant interest in how IT companies operate, how they generate revenues and, of course, how profits are taxed in their respective jurisdictions. In this context, a key concern for tax authorities is TP, especially when IT companies operate cross-border as they often do with relative ease. However, understanding TP within the IT industry is not a trivial exercise, especially given the wide variety of business models that are employed by companies in the industry. Furthermore, with the rate of innovation in this industry, business models are constantly changing and evolving, making it twice as difficult to precisely identify how value is being generated and how it should be taxed.

This chapter investigates the rudimentary elements of this challenge and reviews the fundamentals of how value is created in the IT sector in order to begin to attempt to effectively address the critical TP questions. To do so, section 2 discusses how value is created in the IT sector with a particular emphasis on the uniqueness of value creation in this sphere. Section 3 builds on this understanding of value creation and uses a stylized case study to illustrate this comprehension can help inform the TP analysis of IT business models. The last section concludes with a number of observations on the future of TP in the IT industry.

1. According to Gartner, Worldwide IT spending is expected to reach $ 4.5 trillion in 2022, https://www.gartner.com/en/newsroom/press-releases/2022-01-18-gartner-forecasts-worldwide-it-spending-to-grow-five-point-1-percent-in-2022 (last accessed 30 January 2022).
2. As of February 2021, IT industry companies had a total market capitalization of USD 18.9 trillion, S&P Capital IQ, Market Analysis, https://www.capitaliq.com/CIQDotNet/IndustryIntelligence/industryAnalysis.aspx (last accessed 27 February 2021).
3. Louis Bellucci, Jodie Gunzberg, *S&P Sector Primer Series: Information Technology*, 1 (2019).
4. Moore's law is a principle of exponential growth suggesting that computing speed and capability doubles approximately every two years.

2 VALUE CREATION IN THE IT INDUSTRY

2.1 History of Value Creation in the IT Industry

The value chain analysis as a concept was first introduced in the mid-1980s by Michael Porter.[5] He has argued that a company should be analysed through a sequence of the distinct activities that it performs and, to gain a competitive advantage over its competitors, a company must either perform these activities at a lower cost or perform them in a manner that leads to differentiation. In addition, he also introduced the concept of a value driver which can be viewed as either an input-output metric or a factor that results in a sustainable competitive advantage. The key value drivers and the sources of value creation in the IT industry - efficiency, productivity, and growth - can be analysed through two distinct yet consecutive time frames, i.e., pre- and post-internet eras.

Figure 19.1 Timeline of Innovations, Pre-internet Era[6]

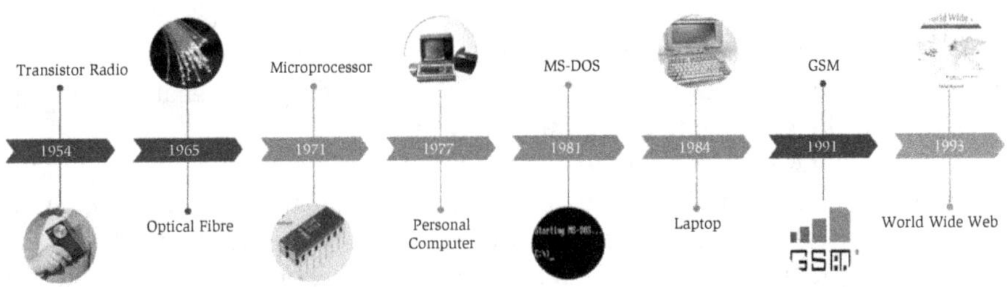

As shown in Figure 19.1, the pre-internet era is characterized by the parallel development of telecommunication and technological innovations that have converged with the internet's creation in 1993. The pre-internet's key value drivers were standardization, increase in processing power, and miniaturization of computing equipment, and a gradual replacement of mainframes with personal computers and laptops. The pre-internet era's key players, leading manufacturers of computing equipment – IBM, Apple, and Dell – competed in the market employing the customer-centric strategies that revolved around the democratization of processing equipment and their widespread use.

5. Michael E. Porter, Victor E. Millar, *How Information Gives You Competitive Advantage*, Harvard Business Review, 3 (1985).
6. The timeline depicted here has been adapted from Figure 1-9 Timeline of ICT Innovations in Harald Overby, Jan A. Audestad, *Digital Economics*, 21 (2018).

Figure 19.2 Timeline of Innovations, Post-internet Era[7]

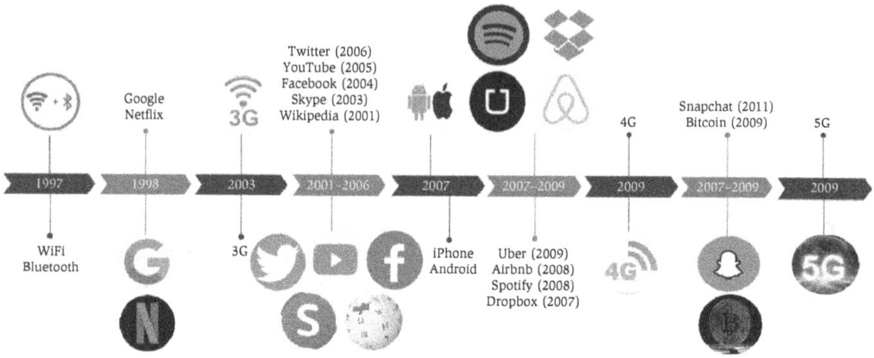

The invention and the introduction of the World Wide Web in the early 1990s transformed the IT industry since it enabled the emergence of a commercialized version of the internet as it is known today. Its impact was a watershed moment that radically changed the entire economic structure of the IT industry and can only be compared to the creation of the internal combustion engine that enabled the rapid development of the physical transportation network.[8]

As shown in Figure 19.2, the internet has been a primary driving force behind the evolution of the technology, solutions and market participants in the IT industry. It connected the world digitally, made jurisdictional borders indistinguishable, and enabled cross-border commerce of digital goods and services at a rate and scale unprecedented in history. It transformed the economic construct of international markets by reducing entry barriers for new market players, expanding access to a wider base of customers and suppliers, popularizing platform-based businesses, and creating a zero-marginal cost economy. Value creation in the post-internet era has also shifted from value chains to value shops and value networks.[9] Due to the internet, value is now generated in ways that were unimaginable even a few decades ago by transforming data in even more creative ways, innovating at an unprecedented pace, and leveraging network effects bolstered by the newly created economies of scale and scope.

7. The timeline depicted here has been adapted from Figure 1-9 Timeline of ICT Innovations in Overby, Audestad, *supra* n. 6.
8. The concept of radical change through the employment of new technology was first introduced by Russian economist Nikolai Kondratieff, a founder of the theory of the economic cycles, i.e., Kondratieff waves.
9. OECD, *Tax Challenges Arising from Digitalisation: Interim Report 2018: Inclusive Framework on BEPS*, OECD/G20 Base Erosion and Profit Shifting Project (Paris: OECD Publishing, 2018), 35.

2.2 Industry 4.0: Key Characteristics and Market Players

History repeats itself in cycles, and the world has already experienced tectonic shifts of paradigms and market constructs. The First Industrial Revolution dates back to the mid-eighteenth century and began with the invention of the steam engine. The Second Industrial Revolution occurred during the twentieth century with the introduction of electricity and the internal combustion engine. The Third Industrial Revolution aligned with the rapid development of communication and information technologies as described in Figure 19.1. Since the emergence of the internet, rapid advances in connectivity and accessibility of data have transformed the nature of the economy. The world economy is now increasingly digital and is based on automation and collaborative consumption. These new technological shifts are often referred to as the Fourth Industrial Revolution or Industry 4.0 (4IR).[10] It has three key features: mobility, network effects, and data usage. These are explained in more detail below:[11]

(1) Mobility: once the blueprint for a digital product has been developed, the marginal costs of producing, replicating, and providing a digital product to customers around the world are normally minimal. The main cost is thus the fixed cost of developing the blueprint, and the replication stage can be located wherever total costs are the lowest.
(2) Network effects: whenever the value of a product to its users increases with the number of other product users, demand-side economies of scale and scope are created through these network effects.
(3) Data usage: the third feature of 4IR is the growing usage of data that is 'continuously driving down the costs of collecting, storing and analysing data'. As the volume of data increases and the costs of generating and storing data decrease, the market-making costs (i.e., the costs of search, negotiations, monitoring, and enforcement) also decline, generating even more opportunities for domestic and cross-border trade.

As Porter predicted thirty-five years ago, access to data and the information revolution has affected competition in three vital ways:[12]

(1) It changed the industry structure and, in so doing, altered the rules of competition.
(2) It created sustainable competitive advantages by giving innovative companies entirely new ways to outperform their rivals.
(3) It spawned whole new businesses.

10. Klaus Schwab, *The Fourth Industrial Revolution*, 7 (2017).
11. Lorraine Eden, Niraja Srinivasan, Srini Lalapet, *Transfer Pricing Challenges in the Digital Economy: A Case Study of the Internet of Things (Part I of II)*, Tax Management International Journal, 48, 251 (2019).
12. Porter, *supra* n. 5, at 15-21.

The 4IR has also spurred the emergence of new technologies that have challenged the established market players' status quo in the IT sector. Progress in information technology characterized by digitization and servitization has led to a structural transformation of the economy. It has also modified the business strategies of the established market players who have been forced to innovate and determine new ways to continue competing effectively. As a consequence, the current IT market is shared by the two groups of companies that can be broadly described as follows:[13]

(1) 'Going Digital' – these companies are traditional IT 'brick-and-mortar' businesses adapting to the new business environment and market construct, and
(2) 'Born Digital' – 4IR 'millennials', i.e., businesses established in the post-internet era and operating based on digital economics principles.

The traditional IT companies are reinventing themselves and leveraging the power of new technologies to transform their business models to compete (going digital). These companies enjoy significant infrastructure and processing facilities at their disposal and most commonly compete via modification of their products into XaaS (infrastructure, platform, or software) offerings. The XaaS requires high initial set-up costs or a developed infrastructure – financial and physical assets – that is available to the established market players. These companies further provide access to their infrastructure, platform, or software on a subscription basis.[14]

The IT 'millennials' (born digital), i.e., companies that have emerged since the internet can be classified into the 'machine – platform – crowd' categories based on the emerging technologies they employ:[15]

- machine: companies competing through automation, algorithms, and use of big data, i.e., robotics, AI, machine learning, and big data analytics, e.g., Microsoft, Amazon, and Google;
- platform: large and influential young platform-based companies, key disruptors in the IT industry competing through network effects, e.g., Uber and Airbnb;
- crowd: start-up decentralized businesses utilizing and synthesizing accumulated human knowledge and expertise distributed worldwide to create significantly beneficial products, e.g., Linux, bitcoin, and blockchain.

2.3 4IR: Value Drivers

Pre-internet, value was generated through sales of products that benefitted from discrete product-specific innovations sold as upgrades/newer versions at higher profit margins. The key value drivers of that era were standardization, miniaturization, and an increase in processing power.

13. Eden, Srinivasan, Lalapet, *supra* n. 11, at 3.
14. Overby, Audestad, *supra* n. 6, at 64.
15. Andrew McAfee, Erik Brynjolfsson, *Harnessing Our Digital Future: Machine, Platform, Crowd*, 14 (2017).

However, the 4IR free-flowing streams of information made available through the internet have given rise to data as a new value driver utilized by companies to generate value. The International DataSphere Project measures the amount of data exponentially created and consumed in the world each year and forecasts data volume to reach 175 zettabytes (trillion gigabytes) by 2025 as shown in Figure 19.3.

Figure 19.3 Annual Size of Global Datasphere[16]

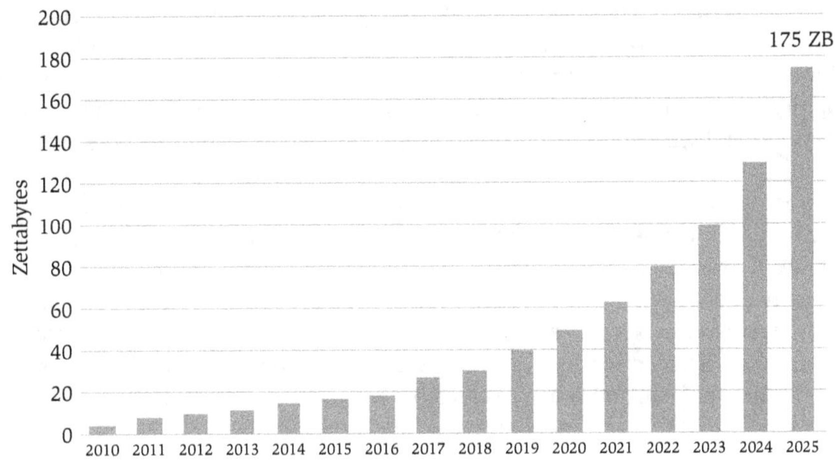

The volume of data is expected to increase with the popularization of 5G networks that would allow new technologies such as the IoT to create vast new data sets. Substantial volumes of data coupled with advances in processing technologies have now enabled the development of other associated emerging technologies such as data science, predictive analytics, and AI.

An increase in connectivity and access to data expanded the variety of choices presented to customers and brought forward agility and flexibility as the key value drivers. As a result, customers' expectations about ownership have evolved rapidly and created a new FCM. Customers expect to receive and use products as and when they need them, paying only for how much they use. Similarly, business decision-makers increasingly expect the pay-as-you-go services and require frictionless access to software and hardware without having to support and maintain it.[17]

With the creation of new value drivers generating revenues in the 4IR, the questions of if, how, and when value drivers can be treated as intangibles become important to answer. Unfortunately, there is no uniform definition of an intangible for TP, accounting, and valuation purposes.

16. David Reinsel, John Gantz, John Rydning, *An IDC White Paper: The Digitization of the World From Edge to Core*, 6 (2018).
17. Erik Day, *Why Everything as a Service Is a Game Changer for Small Businesses* (29 January 2020), https://www.business.com/articles/everything-as-a-service-gamechanger (last accessed 30 January 2022).

The value of data and when it might rise to the level of an intangible has been hotly debated. Indeed, not all data is created equal, and the volume of raw data cannot be a sole indicator of economic value. As long as data is unstructured and inaccessible for analysis or is unlinked and not aggregated, its potential value may remain unrealized.[18] Like other digital products and services, collection and cleaning of data require significant initial investments (in hardware, software, systems, and processes), low marginal costs of further reproduction and, most critically, human expertise.

In the context of a value chain analysis, data could begin generating value at the 'analytics' stage when it has been collected, cleaned, and processed. At this stage, data could potentially generate economic value as it can provide useful insights for the decision-makers, i.e., an effective allocation of existing resources or a formation of new capabilities. That stated, there is no real consensus on how this economic value should be measured and whether it can actually be considered an intangible asset in its own right.

Another important value driver within the 4IR is network effects. In economics, this arises when each element's value grows as the overall size of the network increases such that the whole is greater than the sum of the parts. With the increase in connectivity, network effects have become valuable drivers of economic value for platform businesses as the aggregation of network participants could potentially generate value. The networks are organized and driven by network orchestrators (owner of the platform) who are responsible for the growth of the network until it reaches a scale that brings benefits for network participants.

2.4 4IR: Trends

The McKinsey Global Institute has identified the following trends shaping the IT industry:[19]

- big data;
- Internet of (All) Things;
- XaaS;
- automation of work;
- integrated digital/physical experiences; and
- the evolution of commerce.

The trend of big data has emerged with an advance in processing capabilities coupled with an uninterrupted flow of large volumes of data. As the world becomes increasingly interconnected and digital, the abundance of data increases. Big data is harnessed to develop insights and new products through advanced and predictive analytics and inform decision-making.

18. HM Treasury, The Economic Value of Data: Discussion Paper, 4 (2018).
19. Jacques Bughin, Michael Chui, James Manyika, *McKinsey Global Institute: Ten IT-Enabled Business Trends for the Decade Ahead* (May 2013).

Internet of (All) Things is a technology that allows real-time remote monitoring and management of objects and systems across a network with the help of installed sensors bringing physical infrastructure into a connected digital space. The rapid advancement of this trend is driven by three key factors: a decrease in the price of the sensor equipment, the ability to connect the devices wirelessly, and an increase in the processing power of big data.

XaaS refers to the internet-enabled provision of digital services coupled with cloud computing that resulted in a trend to consume services online and receive access to assets on demand. The companies adopted a new way of business by providing solutions that are light on upfront investment and focus on flexible consumption.

Automation of work is enabled by the availability of big data combined with unprecedented computing power and connectivity that gave rise to significant advances in data analytics, AI, and natural user interfaces. This allows for automation of routine tasks, expansion of the knowledge workers' capabilities with machine learning, and expanded access to information systems through natural language interfaces.

Advances in connectivity and natural user interfaces allow giving the physical world digital characteristics and improving productivity and experience through tactile, mobile devices. The trend of integrated digital/physical experiences is expected to expand with the introduction of 5G networks and an increase in augmented and virtual reality devices.

An increase in mobile connectivity and a reduction in transaction costs resulted in the creation of digital marketplaces and platform businesses. This evolution of e-commerce enabled the inception of a 'sharing economy' that provides a platform to monetize unused assets and offer services to a wide pool of customers. A new type of multisided business model has emerged for which value is generated through interactions with multiple stakeholders.

The new complexities and varieties of business models form a highly fragmented and competitive market within the IT industry. In addition, an increase in processing speed, storage capacity, and data flow has given rise to the following key aspects of GVCs at the sectoral and firm levels. These are discussed in the subsection below.

2.5 Global Value Chains

Traditionally, GVCs in the IT industry are longer, more fragmented, and span across more jurisdictions than most industries. The latest trend, however, has a reverse trajectory. The GVCs are shortening (reducing their physical length, not the fragmentation) as a result of the following events:[20]

- trade tensions between the world's leading economies: the trade wars disrupted the established value chains and led to increased reshoring and regionalization;

20. United Nations Conference on Trade and Development, *World Investment Report* (2020).

- rapid digitalization of GVCs: the innovation-based 'megatrends' impact GVCs, and they become increasingly platform based and asset-light. As a result, they become less linear and transform into value networks; and
- servitization of the economy: the widespread use of digital technologies and the interaction of these technologies over the past decade led to a rapid upsurge in trade in services and the proliferation of intangibles in GVCs.

There is an increase in the pace of innovation *at a sector level*, a transition from analogue to digital, and a shift to acquiring innovation versus developing it internally.[21] Historically, the IT industry's innovation was driven by either in-house or outsourced technological R&D activities. The advent of the internet is enabling technology that transformed commercial and personal interactions and converged digital and physical worlds through instant access to the internet with smartphones. Consequently, data has emerged as a new variable that has led to the development of data-driven emerging technologies and new business models. The leading industry experts contend that data has formed a new type of capital that is similar to financial capital, and it is now widely used to create an assortment of products and services.

At the firm level, the 'going digital' companies are increasingly adopting their business models to compete in the new business environment. The B2B operating models are rapidly shifting to B2C models. The digital future requires agile IT supported by hybrid cloud operating models that enable data visibility and data management through a standardized infrastructure solution operating as a system.

Customers increasingly require flexibility, variety of choice, and simplicity, thus prefer the XaaS solutions that allow them to subscribe online for the pay-as-you-go products, tools, and technology services. The global market of the XaaS solution is predicted to steadily expand at a compound annual growth rate of 24%.[22] Its provider is expected to deliver a seamless and simple experience that allows customers to focus on their businesses.[23] The incumbent industry players, i.e., established manufacturers of hardware and software solutions, partner with the providers of cloud APIs to respond to new customer requirements, e.g., partnerships of Dell, HP, IBM with Amazon (AWS), Microsoft (Azure), and Google (Google Cloud) creating a multi-cloud hybrid business environment established on both public and private clouds.

2.6 4IR: Challenges

With the emergence of big data, a servitization trend, and the creation of numerous highly complex business models, multiple questions remain unanswered. There is an attempt to unbundle some of them below.

21. Andrew McAfee, Erik Brynjolfsson, *Harnessing Our Digital Future: Machine, Platform, Crowd*, 265 (2017).
22. Anything-as-a-Service Market: Global Industry Trends, https://www.businesswire.com/news/home/20190628005112/en/Anything-as-a-Service-Market-Grow-CAGR-24---Global (last accessed 30 January 2022).
23. Deepak Patil, Senior VP and General Manager of Dell's Cloud Platforms and Solutions Group: Dell's Strategy for Cloud and Delivering Data Centers as a Service by the Data Center Podcast (soundcloud.com) (last accessed 30 January 2022).

In the data-driven business models, value is generated with human expertise working in concert with software and hardware assets to collect and transform data. Therefore, a comprehensive understanding of the relative contribution of people versus physical assets is still critically important. Similarly, it is also important to acknowledge that, in certain business models, what is transacted itself, i.e., data, may also be a driver of economic value. For instance, the leading companies in the IT industry possess fewer physical assets but have a significant amount of data, e.g., Airbnb, Facebook, and Netflix. Like physical assets, data can have a long-term value and be defined as a good that is a non-rivalrous, non-fungible experience.[24]

Another interesting fact is the data circularity attribute. While physical assets generally exhibit decreasing returns to use, the quality of data increases the more it is used as it acquires additional attributes. For example, Google Inc.'s Waze navigation and traffic application integrate real-time crowdsourced data from drivers, so the Waze mapping data has increased value as more people use it.[25] Additional data improves predictive accuracy and enhances the information content, especially when combined with other data, including recommendations and customer feedback. Finally, it is also critical to acknowledge that even the best data in the world cannot replace the strategic insight that is necessary to use the data in a manner that actually generates economic value and sustains a company's competitive advantage for the long term.

The legal mechanisms set out below are the most common in data ownership management and could potentially give rise to economic value depending on how data is used:[26]

- data protection law grants individuals rights over their data;
- copyrights established over a database; and
- restrictions to data access at collection and storage, e.g., at a server level.

In this context, data privacy is an important aspect to consider within a data ownership framework as big data is often collected from personal data. At the EU level, new standards for protecting personal data are established through the EU's GDPR that provides people more control over the use of their data. The GDPR brings transparency about the personal data that is collected and allows customers to make a conscious choice on the 'trade-off' between disclosing their data and the benefits they receive from the personalized products and services. The rules of data ownership are still crystallizing at both the national and international levels. In most countries, there is no established comprehensive legal framework guiding data ownership and control.

2.7 4IR: Operating Models

The enhanced complexity in the IT industry has resulted in the emergence of a multitude of business models. In particular, the XaaS operating model is the focus of

24. MIT Technology Review, White Paper: The Rise of Data Capital, 4 (2016).
25. James E. Short and Steve Todd, *What's Your Data Worth,* MIT Sloan Management Review 3 March 2017 (Spring 2017).
26. HM Treasury, The Economic Value of Data: Discussion Paper, 11 (2018).

the analysis in this section since it is used by many of the so-called 'going digital' companies, and it can illustrate the complexity of emerging business models.

As discussed above, the IT industry has experienced a significant shift towards FCM. The FCM, often referred to as XaaS models, offers customers access to products as a service including different payment options aligning payment with actual use. FCMs are customer-centric models unlike traditional business models which are more product-centric.

With the XaaS offerings, customers, i.e., consumers, businesses, or governments, pay for what they use on demand. The customers pay for outcomes and not products which is a practical business model. By reducing their capital expenditure outlay, customers increase budget flexibility and decrease the risk of product failure or obsolescence. Instead, they pay for outcomes as needed which results in savings and the production of new revenue streams.[27]

Some of the key benefits of the FCM consumptions models are as follows:[28]

- Simplicity: Delivering turnkey and scalable solutions that are fully managed by providers. Customers usually have a single web interface enabling them to easily manage every aspect of their XaaS journey.
- Choice and Flexibility: For customers to decide what solutions to run as a service and pay for them the way they want (e.g., as they use it or pay for it as they go, leverage subscriptions, etc.) with all of the different options that ultimately provide operating expense flexibility. This may include everything from an infrastructure offering to the storage, server, networking, data protection, hyper-converged infrastructure, etc.
- Consistency: Consistent operating experience whether customers are running their XaaS experience on-premises, through the cloud, or moving and interacting with workloads at the edge.

3 TP ISSUES IN THE IT SECTOR

3.1 General Remarks

The previous section highlighted the pace at which the IT sector is innovating, transforming, and expanding. Complexity, uncertainty, and volatility mark the diversity of multiple hybrid business models and customer offerings within the same MNE, especially the going digitals. Revenue size and growth, profitability, intangible assets, capital invested, and risk across the business units can be markedly different.

It was also noted that the GVCs in the IT industry are transforming into shorter, more regionalized value chains. The combination of GVC changes as well as the diversity of product and service delivery models makes the TP policies and challenges of IT MNEs

27. Tasker O. Generes Jr., *Get Ready for the Product-as-a-Service Revolution*, https://www.forbes.com/sites/servicenow/2020/10/15/get-ready-for-the-product-as-a-service-revolution/?sh = 1042cd942267 (last accessed 30 January 2022).
28. 5 Keys to Dell's Revamped as-a-Service Strategy, https://www.crn.com/slide-shows/cloud/5-keys-to-dell-s-revamped-as-a-service-strategy-dell-svp/1 (last accessed 30 January 2022).

a complex and interesting study. As outlined in section 2, new IT industry business models have propelled a shift in value creation within MNEs.

The alignment of value creation with TP outcomes is firmly embedded in the OECD TPG, the US TP regulations,[29] the UN TPM and numerous local country TP guidelines and legislations. Any TP analysis should be undertaken from the perspective of value generation within the industry and country(ies) in which a multinational company operates.

This section will highlight the significant TP issues for key intra-group transactions within IT MNEs. With the help of a stylized case study of an FCM business model, the application of traditional TP methods to tangible, intangible, and services transactions will be reviewed. Whether the existing framework (and the likely legislative framework from the BEPS 2.0 and other local country tax reform initiatives) suffices for establishing an outcome that is both at arm's length and fair for both taxing authorities and MNEs will also be examined. Attention is paid to the significant trends in value creation that are discussed in the preceding section and the question of the adequacy of existing methods in valuing the transfer of IP and value-added or strategic service.[30] The section concludes by providing a brief overview of the major tax jurisdictions that have enacted or are contemplating DSTs and the impact that it will have on the global IT industry.

3.2 FCM TP Application and Challenges

The IT industry's myriad of business models is rapidly evolving and opening up another challenge for TP practitioners: do new service offerings such as the IoT and FCM or new delivery modalities such as multisided platforms change the functions, risks, and assets of the entities within the MNE that fulfil the customer contract? This is best illustrated with a case study of a newly developed FCM customer offering to customers.

Figure 19.4 provides a simplified view of the intra-group transactions that occur within a going-digital MNE that offers their customers the choice of either buying IT equipment and software outright in a single transaction or purchasing an as-a-service solution. The case study assumes that the MNE's existing customers have switched to a multi-year contract with the MNE's local sales and distribution subsidiary for access to an on-premise data centre[31] and software consumed as-a-service based on usage-based subscription. The value proposition to the as-a-service customer is rapid delivery

29. CFR 26, Internal Revenue Code section 482.
30. The analysis in this section refers to the current US Internal Revenue Code section 482 that governs transfer pricing in the US, the current TP legislation and practice around the world, and the OECD Inclusive Framework Pillar One Blueprint (OECD/IF). OECD/G20 Base Erosion and Profit Shifting Project, *Tax Challenges Arising from Digitalisation: Report on Pillar One Blueprint; Inclusive Framework on BEPS* (12 October 2020), https://www.oecd-ilibrary.org/deliver/beba0634-en.pdf?itemId=%2Fcontent%2Fpublication%2Fbeba0634-en&mimeType=pdf.
31. In reality, the MNE can simultaneously offer on-premise, off-premise, or a 'lease to buy' datacentre solution all based on the customer's needs. This example simplifies the case to on-premise equipment.

and deployment on customer premises as well as a usage-based consumption model. To illustrate the intra-group transactions and TP, the case assumes that the customer places an order to access ten terabytes of data centre storage and unlimited use of software.

Figure 19.4 TP in the FCM/As-a-Service Model: Illustrative

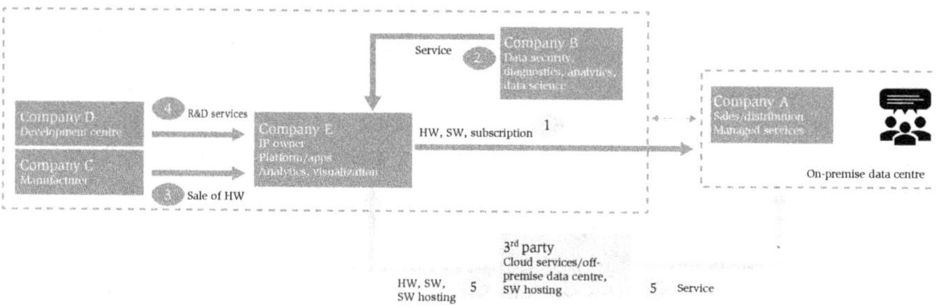

Example

Company A, located in Country X, Company B, located in Country Y, Company C, located in Country Z, Company D, located in Country V, and Company E, located in Country W, are part of the ABC Group. Company A is a sales, marketing, and installation services entity that sells the as-a-service offering to customers. For simplicity, it is assumed that all customers are located and use the FCM model in Country X. Company B is a provider of data security and diagnostic and analytical services related to the FCM solution. B's work is to transform the FCM usage data generated by customers into information and insights using proprietary algorithms. Company C manufactures data centre storage and edge devices. Company D designs software and hardware devices for Company E. Company E owns the legal and economic rights to the intangible assets that are generated by ABC Group's various development and design companies.

Inside the MNE's ecosystem of its 'order to fulfil' cycle, the customer's request effectuates a set of four distinct intra-group transactions between five related parties (Companies A through E in Figure 19.4). These four intra-group transactions that result in providing the end customer with their as-a-service solution are:

Transaction 1:	Company A purchases data centre equipment from Company E and instals it at the customer's site although maintaining the equipment on its balance sheet. It then leases access to the customer.

Transaction 2:	Company B employs engineers and data scientists who provide services under contract with E and work closely with Company E's R&D personnel and IP lawyers to develop the MNE's group intangible assets, such as patented machine learning algorithms.
Transaction 3:	Company C manufactures hardware devices under a contractual arrangement with Company E.
Transaction 4:	Company D designs and develops software under the contractual arrangement with Company E.

A fifth transaction shown in Figure 19.4 has Company E licensing unrelated party cloud hosting services to provide cloud/off-premise data centre services to Company A.

The first step in deciding what specific TP methods can be considered for each of these transactions, the functional analysis of the related parties should lead to the selection of the TP method and PLI. Again, for illustrative purposes, we present a summarized FAR matrix in Table 19.1.

Table 19.1 Illustrative FAR for an FCM Business Model[32]

Related Party	*Company A*	*Company B*	*Company C*	*Company D*	*Company E*
Key functions	Sales, marketing	Data security, diagnostics, analytical services	Manufacturer	Development centre	IP owner and ABC Group Headquarters
Assets – tangible (other than office space, leasehold)	Hardware sold as-a-service	IT equipment	Manufacturing PPE	R&D lab	IT equipment
Assets – intangible	Customer lists	None	None	None	Patented and unpatented SW, algorithms, know-how

32. This table has been created by the authors solely for the purposes of illustrating the functional profiles of the ABC Group companies in this example.

Related Party	*Company A*	*Company B*	*Company C*	*Company D*	*Company E*
Risks	Customer contracts cancellation Limited pricing risk Capex	Workforce retention	Workforce retention	Workforce retention	Workforce retention Technology obsolescence Quality, compatibility Capex, pricing risk Market risk
Characterization	LRD	Service provider	Manufacturer	Service provider	Global Principal

It is necessary to point out that the rapid innovation in the IT industry can mean that the functional analysis of related parties can also change rapidly, sometimes within a single year. This makes it problematic for the MNE TP practitioner to record the 'predominant' functions and risks borne by the entity in its local file submission for the fiscal year. For example, in a single year, the MNE's business leaders may decide to shift a service such as the monitoring of data generation from a local distribution subsidiary to the headquarters entity or to an R&D group, all located in different countries. This change in each entity's functional profile is the outcome of the MNE management decision to centralize or decentralize certain service operations to more effectively serve the customer. Considering the dynamic nature of digital solutions and relative flexibility in increasing efficiency of the operating model, characterization of the entities and resultant TP methods will be variable rather than long-term status quo.

3.3 Application of TP Methods to Specific Transaction Types

3.3.1 Tangible Property

The manufacturing and sale of tangible property such as IT hardware are typically priced using traditional transaction methods (CPM) or transactional profit methods (TNMM). Under these TP methods, the selection of appropriate PLIs for routine, full-fledged, contract, and toll manufacturing such as the return on sales, return on tangible assets, return on total assets, return on capital employed has been widely used by MNEs and taxing authorities and has acquired a certain familiar acceptance in the course of documentation and tax enquiries and audits.

Example (continues from the previous example)

In transaction 1, Company A purchases equipment from Company E. If no other comparable uncontrolled prices or transactions exist, the MNE may consider using a CPM or TNMM and ROS to benchmark Company A's return on marketing and distribution activity. In transaction 3, Company E purchases the equipment from Company C, the CPM or TNMM may also be appropriate to benchmark the arm's length return on Company C's manufacturing activity, and the return on assets or on capital employed are frequently used PLIs.

The approach that is discussed in the example is not without challenge in a going-digital MNE. As it has an increasing share of revenue arising from the FCM, several factors can increase or decrease the relative intensity of functions, risks and assets of the related parties. The MNE may bear more fixed asset risk (costs of holding the equipment), obsolescence risk (risk of tangible property becoming technologically obsolete), and commercial risk (risk of customer contractual cancellation, repricing, and renegotiation of terms with respect to duration, fixed fee versus pay-as-you-go models). As customers and big data multiply, the MNE stands to gain a competitive advantage from network effects and lower cost of managing big data. The question that need to be answered is what is the relative value of the effective management of the risk, and does that represent a new economically significant function? The familiar TP methods and/or PLIs may need to be reconsidered or amended for better comparability.

Box 3.1
Does Pillar One Amount B minimize marketing and distribution TP controversy for the IT sector?

The Amount B proposal in the Pillar One Blueprint released by the OECD/IF on 14 October 2020 and updated in October 2021 is designed to standardize the return to certain BMDA that takes place in a market jurisdiction. For going-digital and born-digital MNEs in the IT sector, can standard returns be defined, applied, and defended in a manner that minimizes controversy? The OECD/IF provide guidance on what does and does not constitute the BMDA by referring to negative and positive activities lists. However, (as of now) it has not elaborated further on the distinctions between LRDs that offer purely digital XaaS solutions such as Company A in this case study and those that are traditional sellers of tangible property. The IT sector has the largest concentration of digital services LRDs than any other industry, and the relatively narrow definition of Amount B activities do not qualify the as-a-service as clearly within or outside the scope of the BMDA. In fact, new compensation models for platforms and value shops create new functional profiles for the customer-facing entities. In the IT sector, digital sales LRDs are primarily engaged in technical market research, negotiating and generating advertising revenues, and acting as in-country liaison offices for regulatory/governance bodies. They do not manage 'supply chains' in the same manner as do the LRDs selling IT hardware. Higinbotham et al. (2021) contend that 'while CFB marketing and distribution models and operations are relatively well understood and their activities fall neatly into the positive or the negative list, this may not be true for marketing and distribution models in ADS'.[33]

3.3.2 *Intra-group Services*

Intra-group services are evolving into the most interesting and complex TP topics for the IT sector. These services span a wide range of service activities from headquarters management services provided by a parent company to operating subsidiaries to contract R&D and marketing services performed on behalf of principal or IP companies. The core of the TP challenges is the characterization of the activity as routine or non-routine and the consequent determination of the transfer price to apply. There are intra-group services that have no reliable third-party comparable benchmarks, and the complex nature of the activity and its value creation potential allows it to be characterized by the MNE as a service and the taxing authority as intangible, or vice versa. The definition of what constitutes routine and non-routine services is critical for determining the application of the appropriate TP method.

Example (continues from the previous example)

In transaction 2, Company B provides data analytics services to Company E. Company B's engineers have access to customer XaaS usage data and deploy AI and machine learning techniques to anonymize and sanitize the data as well as run it through MNE proprietary software and algorithms to extract information about customers' usage of the tax software and their error and learning patterns. The information can now be turned into ways to improve features of the software and to optimize the customer's cost of leasing datacentre storage. Company D's software development engineers will work with Company B's engineers and Company E's commercial strategists and IP lawyers to develop and exploit the improved XaaS offering. Further, as the number of customers increases and the MNE develops new metrics to capture even more differentiated customer data, the amount of data increases and information derived from data transformation and analytics becomes more valuable to the MNE's future products and XaaS revenue. The analysis of storage and software usage patterns converts the big data into information and enables the MNE to develop faster, more cost-efficient customized offerings for existing and new customers.

33. Harlow Higinbotham, Niraja Srinivasan, Vladimir Starkov, Nihan Mert-Beydilli, Lorraine Eden, *Amount B: Facts and Circumstances Matter – Even for Routine Distributors*, Bloomberg Tax, Daily Tax Report (5 February 2021), https://news.bloombergtax.com/daily-tax-report/amount-b-facts-and-circumstances-matter-even-for-routine-distributors.

At the outset, the MNE characterizes Company B as a routine data analysis services provider for which it is able to find broadly similar third-party analytical services companies. It applies a CPM or TNMM method to establish the intra-group price per hour service charge from Company B to Company E. As the various iterations and improvements described above take place, the inherent complexity of analysing 'bigger data' may require the MNE to make substantial investments in hiring additional highly skilled engineers and machines with extremely high computational speeds. Company B may possibly evolve in a different direction; it may begin to play a more strategic role in the type of advanced data analytics being performed and deciding how the resultant information is used in the MNE's strategic decisions. It could therefore transform into a value shop and a value driver for the entire MNE. Under these circumstances, the PSM, rather than CPM or TNMM, may be the most appropriate method to determine B's share of the total system profit. Another option is that Company B could simply continue to provide data transformation and analytical services. In this case, the MNE is fully entitled to continue using the one-sided TP method rather than the PSM. Depending on the asset intensity of the business, the PLI might also change from cost-plus to return on total assets.

In recent years, the character of intra-group services has come under heavy scrutiny as the basis for much of the TP controversy. When does the high-value service become a key value driver? The OECD TPG provides guidance for determining the arm's length pricing for transactions between related parties, including intra-group services. The arm's length profit is determined by considering functions performed, assets used, and risks assumed. From the perspective of the value generated by specific intra-group services, these can be grouped into two categories, i.e., routine and non-routine. Specifically, non-routine services bring a lot of complexity when considering the arm's length compensation. Due to the broad definition of intangible assets in the OECD TPG, embedded IP is likely to be found in a number of these transactions. To stipulate the arm's length compensation in some cases, a separate benchmarking analysis of embedded IP is necessary. This might not be a straightforward task leading to use of different IP valuation approaches. Specific guidance for taxpayers on how to approach these situations clearly does not exist.

A common feature of increasing efficiency within MNEs is the centralization of routine functions, particularly back office, which are then provided as intra-group service to other entities within MNEs. There is concern from tax authorities that there can be a tendency to overstate the functions performed or the fee charged which might result in tax base erosion. The OECD TPG addresses these issues in Chapter VII via a benefit test and a definition of the low value-adding services.

The US IRS' LB&I division announced the launch of the CSP Campaign on 16 April 2019. The CSPs are companies within MNEs for which their sole or primary function is to provide intra-group services to the parent company and/or other affiliates. The services they provide range from customer and technical support services, back-office services, software development and testing, document review and data entry, etc.

There is concern that excessive pricing for these services may result in shifting taxable income to the CSPs and erode the US tax base. The goal of this campaign is to ensure that US MNEs are paying their CSPs (usually based in India, Malaysia, China, and other skilled labour surplus locations) no more than arm's length prices.[34] However, are there situations when CSPs perform high-value non-routine services which may have intangibles embedded in them? This requires a deeper assessment and evaluation to minimize significant controversy.

3.3.3 Intangible Assets

Arguably, the most challenging and controversial area of IT industry TP is the pricing of the intra-group transfer of intangibles. At the core of the audits and litigation is the identification of what is a marketing or technology intangible asset. The TP analysis involving intangibles begins with an identification of intangible assets followed by specifying the legal and economic ownership of these assets leading to an identification of which entity within an MNE is entitled to returns generated by intangible assets. There are multiple regulations and guidance[35] that the taxpayer encounters while attempting to define whether an activity and its associated costs create an intangible asset.

When assessing the value of intangibles within their organizations, tax executives typically refer to their business leaders to define what activities and pools of expense are critical to the company's competitiveness and profitability and attempt to apply existing TP methods. TP audits almost always contain, as a central component, a disagreement about the business facts and circumstances as well as the relative value contributed by the parties. In the IT sector, with its rapid technological changes and dynamic redistribution of routine and complex work and organizations across jurisdictions, this fundamental disagreement takes on a higher magnitude, especially when it concerns questions of value creation and intangibles. Furthermore, the standard and periodic TP compliance documentation that is currently required by most tax authorities (local files, master files, country-by-country reports, ad hoc DEMPE analysis, etc.) is merely a starting point but certainly not conclusive evidence of where and how value creation occurs. Thus, who 'should' be defining value? The authors contend that the MNE business leaders who make the commercial decisions on where routine and non-routine work is performed and for what operational and financial reasons must be given the role of explaining this to the taxing authority. Regrettably, too often, this exchange occurs only at a contentious stage of an audit.

34. https://www.irs.gov/businesses/corporations/lbi-active-campaigns (last accessed 30 January 2022).
35. For transfer pricing purposes, an intangible asset as defined by the OECD TPG is (1) not a physical or financial asset and (2) is capable of being owned or controlled for use in commercial activities, aids in the commercial exploitation of a product or service, and has an important promotional value for the concerned product. In the US, taxpayers look to sections 197, 367(d) in addition to section 482. A review of tax court positions is also necessary. MNEs also consult the OECD Hard to Value intangibles guidance, the EU, and other regional and country guidelines or regulations.

Court Case

In the case of *Amazon.com*,[36] the US Court of Appeals agreed with the tax court's 2017 decision that the US tax authorities' inclusion of residual business assets (Amazon's culture of innovation, the value of workforce in place, going concern value, goodwill, and growth options) in the computation of the buy-in payment stepped beyond the prevailing § 482 cost-sharing regulations in force during the audit years. The dispute centred around the correct method for arriving at a fair market value of the pre-existing intangibles, and the court concluded that the definition is limited to independently transferable assets.

The second major challenge in setting transfer prices is the valuation of identified intangibles. Are financial appraisal techniques for intangible assets adequate for TP purposes, and are they being inadequately applied? The MNE, tax authorities, and their economists very often disagree on the appropriate discount rate to apply to IP cash flows, the economic useful life of the underlying intangible assets, and the market conditions at the time of the transfer between related parties. The market conditions also determine what *standard* of value must be applied to the intangible asset or economic right being transferred: fair market value, investment value, distressed sale value, or other standards of value. Whether it is marketing intangibles, technology hardware, or new platform models, the identification, character, and valuation are highly contested topics in almost every TP audit in the IT sector, and controversies often reach the US or EU Tax Court.

Court Case

In the case of *Veritas Software*,[37] the matter under contention was the calculation of the buy-in payment under the US company's cost-sharing arrangement with its Irish affiliate. To value the transfer of pre-existing intangibles, the US tax authorities' expert aggregated the intangibles under the synergy theory, treating it as a bundled sale rather than a sale of each separate intangible asset. The court rejected the US tax authorities' method on the grounds that it did not differentiate between the value of subsequently developed intangibles and pre-existing intangibles. The intangibles included access to marketing and R&D teams that are not among the intangibles recognized by the US TP rules. Furthermore, the US tax authorities incorrectly assigned a perpetual useful life for transferred intangibles that have a useful life of four years.

A third but nascent challenge is the significance and role of data in the identification and valuation of intangible assets. As discussed in section 2, large datasets that are proprietary to the MNE – either because it was the first mover to generate, collect, and

36. Ninth circuit US Court of Appeals, 16 August 2019, *Amazon.com, Inc. & Subsidiaries v. Commissioner*, 148 T.C. 108 (2017).
37. US Tax Court, 10 December 2009, *Veritas Software Company v. Commissioner* 125 T.C. 37 (2009).

clean data that existed in the public domain or because the data was generated in the course of its exclusive contract with a customer – are key value drivers for MNEs in the IT sector. The authors argue that, while raw unstructured data has no inherent value, it does become a source of competitive advantage for the MNE when it is transformed into insight. However, the challenge for TP lies in whether to ascribe value to proprietary datasets or to attribute it to the entities that create these datasets. Further research is required to analyse whether the existing IP valuation methods under financial standards or tax regulations can be applied to data if it was indeed considered a valuable asset.

3.4 Digital Services Tax

Considering an increased uncertainty around application of TP methods for the newly created business models and associated intangibles coupled with a fast-paced digitalization of the economy, countries around the world have launched unilateral measures to introduce additional taxes on certain types of digital payments, i.e., DSTs. The DSTs are similar to indirect taxes insofar that they are levied on turnover or transactions. The DSTs are heterogeneous; they take a variety of shapes and forms and are levied on different types of transactions. The non-uniform nature of the DSTs further intensifies the compliance burden for MNEs and brings a heightened uncertainty to their business operations. It is also worthwhile noting that one-sided measures such as these would be contrary to the OECD's Pillar One initiative.

Following a landmark Supreme Court ruling in the *South Dakota v. Wayfair. Inc* case that abolished a physical-presence nexus test for establishing taxing rights,[38] a number of the US states, e.g., District of Columbia, Maryland, and New York, launched unilateral taxation measures on revenues generated from digital activities. This includes the sale of digital products, online streaming, digital advertising, etc.

As of the writing of this chapter, the majority of the European countries have already either implemented or announced the introduction of some form of DSTs. The DSTs in Europe are primarily direct taxes with a tax rate from 1.5% to 7.5% levied on different types of tax bases, e.g., revenues generated from online advertisement, sale of user data, social media platforms, internet search engines, and online marketplaces.[39]

India was a pioneer in digital taxation with the introduction of an equalization levy in 2016 addressing revenues from online advertisement services. Since then, it has attempted to expand the scope with a replacement of a physical nexus with a significant economic presence test and eventually broadened the scope of a new DST on a wide range of digital services.[40] Following India's lead, a number of other countries in the region – Indonesia, Singapore, Malaysia, Pakistan, Taiwan, and

38. US Supreme Court, 21 June 2018, *South Dakota v. Wayfair, Inc.*, No. 17-494.
39. Elke Asen, *What European OECD Countries Are Doing about Digital Services Taxes*, https://taxfoundation.org/digital-tax-europe-2020 (last accessed 30 January 2022).
40. Office of the US Trade Representative, Report on India's Digital Services Tax, 3 (2021).

Vietnam – launched their own DSTs. China, Japan, New Zealand, and Thailand have announced the potential implementation of digital taxes.[41]

Multiple countries in the Latin American region have also introduced or announced an introduction of the DSTs. For example, digital tax legislation has been enacted in Argentina, Brazil (draft legislation), Costa Rica, Mexico, Paraguay, and Uruguay.

Similarly, in Africa, digital taxes were enacted in the local legislation in Kenya, Nigeria, Sierra Leone, Tunisia, and Zimbabwe.

This section has attempted to highlight the many challenges faced by MNE tax practitioners and tax authorities when trying to establish intra-group prices for dynamic and rapidly evolving 4IR models with the FCM case study. From entity characterization to the selection of the best TP methods and PLIs, the FCM case study illustrated how TP must be contemporaneously adjusted to reflect significant changes in where value is created. An important conclusion is that documentation is key for audit and controversy minimization in the IT sector, and documentation must exceed an updated local file and master file and include key reports and presentations from non-tax leaders in commercial and operational strategy.

4 CONCLUSION

As has been seen in this chapter, TP within the IT industry is a complex exercise that involves, first and foremost, a clear understanding of how value is created and sustained within a specific business model employed by a particular company. Given the plethora of IT industry business models that are continuously evolving, it is incredibly difficult to create a 'one-size-fits-all' TP approach that would be appropriate for the purpose of a single company, let alone an entire industry. This challenge is further exacerbated by the complexity of understanding the value of data and how it is used to generate revenue and profitability for IT companies in particular.

As this chapter has demonstrated, the most effective approach, at least from a TP perspective, is to review the sources of value creation within a specific business model and then seek to pry open the relative contribution of individual legal entities using a standard functional and risk analysis. Once this has been done, the subsequent challenge will be to apply TP methods to determine an arm's length remuneration for routine activities wherever possible. In cases when it is not possible to clearly demarcate a routine versus non-routine contribution, it may be worthwhile to consider alternatives such as higher routine margins or an application of profit split methods to ensure that various entities that contribute value are appropriately compensated. That stated, given the complexity of IT business models, areas of ambiguity will remain, and this will inevitably lead to tax disputes between MNEs and tax authorities.

In conclusion, as business models continue to evolve and new forms of value creation come to the forefront in the IT industry, the only given is that TP within the IT industry will continue to present new challenges for TP practitioners everywhere.

41. KPMG, *Developments summary – Taxation of the digitalised economy*, updated: 15 January 2021, https://tax.kpmg.us/content/dam/tax/en/pdfs/2020/digitalized-economy-taxation-developments-summary.pdf (last accessed 30 January 2022).

CHAPTER 20

Transfer Pricing in the Oil and Gas Sector

Barend Broen & Erik Jan van Sten

1 INTRODUCTION

In 2020, a year characterized by the significant impact of the COVID-19 virus outbreak on O&G companies, the world consumed approximately 90 million barrels of oil per day. At the beginning of that year, a barrel of Brent was priced at around USD 70. Four months later, it had dropped to USD 20 before crawling back up to USD 45.[1] In the US, the WTI futures price even dipped into the negative for a few days, driven by overproduction and a lack of storage capacity.[2] The fluctuations in the global demand for O&G resulted in extreme price volatility and, although 2020 proved to be exceptionally unstable, these numbers provide a glimpse into a number of the key risks managed within the O&G industry.

The O&G industry is adapting. Historically, it has essentially been locating and extracting hydrocarbons, processing them into gas and oil products, and selling these products to customers. Behind this simple overview lies a complex system of supply chains that are driven 'on the inside' by a wide range of organizational structures, processes, and value drivers. On the outside, it occurs by geopolitical and political factors, public opinion, globally diverse levels of market transparency, and supply and demand. Governments, public and private companies, and investors all participate in this industry and may be involved in only part of the chain or the chain in its entirety – the latter so-called integrated IOCs.

From the moment an oil and/or gas field is located until the first production typically takes many years, billions of USD of investments, and a high degree of technical risk – dry wells and spill containment – and non-technical risks such as changing public opinion and government policies as well as a changing market. Recouping the investment also takes a significant amount of time during which changes to market dynamics can have a profound impact on the project's financial performance. The O&G industry has therefore traditionally been characterized by substantial investments and a very high investment risk. These large risks have led companies and government organizations to work together in consortiums under a PSC or similar type of cooperative arrangement. In these consortiums, one of the partners, i.e., the operator, is usually assigned to be responsible for operational affairs.

The operator of the consortium is responsible for extracting the O&G molecules that are sold to processing plants and refineries that turn crude oil and natural gas into intermediates and refined products such as LNG, fuel, kerosene, marine diesel, base oils, and petrochemical feedstock. Subsequent chemical and manufacturing plants can process or combine the products and intermediates into final chemical polymers, lubricants, catalysts, etc. These products may be further processed or sold to business customers or consumers, for example, via fuel stations.

The extraction and production of raw molecules; transport of raw materials and manufactured products; refining and manufacturing; and marketing and sales processes may involve both related parties and third parties.

1. https://www.iea.org/topics/oil-market-report (last accessed 27 January 2022).
2. https://www.statista.com/statistics/326017/weekly-crude-oil-prices/ (last accessed 27 January 2022).

Today, the impact of global climate change on O&G companies is increasingly being recognized as one of the biggest challenges of the current times. They must now also deal with an energy mix that increasingly relies on clean energies (some of which are (still) based on hydrocarbons such as LNG and biodiesel); decarbonization and carbon taxation; and 'green' subsidies. As part of the energy transition, many O&G companies have pledged to invest in a reduced carbon footprint by increasing emphasis on clean energy solutions such as wind, carbon storage, and projects with a positive footprint to offset CO_2-intensive hydrocarbons.[3]

These developments are having a distinct impact on the traditional O&G value chain and on the TP models that accommodate these value chains. Altogether, the O&G industry is very diverse and complex and relies on an infinite range of supply chains and value chains. In this chapter on the O&G industry, the aim is to provide high-level insight by thoroughly investigating a typical value chain of an IOC that is involved in all stages of the industry (vertical integration) and explore some of the unique TP aspects and challenges of the industry.

2 VALUE CREATION IN THE O&G SECTOR

2.1 The O&G Value Chain

The O&G value chain encompasses a range of activities beginning with discovering O&G fields and ending with selling a variety of products to customers and consumers. Within the industry, three business stages are commonly distinguished:[4]

(1) Upstream, meaning the exploration, development, and production activities.
(2) Midstream, meaning the storage, trading, and transportation of crude oil and natural gas.
(3) Downstream, meaning refining and marketing.

The stages in the value chain are inherently linked with each other (conceptually, contractually, and physically) and are typically combined in the well-known O&G majors in different shapes and forms.

Figure 20.1 illustrates how the O&G value chain can be depicted based on the concept of Porter (1985).[5]

3. For example, https://reports.shell.com/annual-report/2019/ (last accessed 27 January 2022).
4. Peter D. Cameron, Michael C. Stanley, 2017. *Oil, Gas, and Mining: A Sourcebook for Understanding the Extractive Industries,* World Bank, 2017.
5. M.E. Porter, 1985. *Competitive Advantage: Creating and Sustaining Superior Performance,* Free Press, 1985.

Figure 20.1 O&G Value Chain

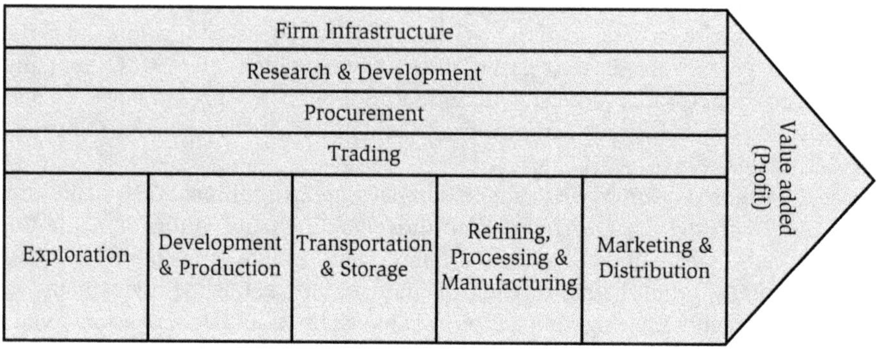

Porter distinguishes primary and support activities whereby the former directly relate to the product or service while the latter help in operating the primary activities.

2.2 Primary Activities in the O&G Industry

2.2.1 Exploration

Exploration in the O&G industry relates to the search for hydrocarbons (i.e., O&G) in the Earth's subsurface with the intent to discover commercially viable hydrocarbon reservoirs. It encompasses both geology and geophysics and requires specific knowledge and technological competence, including seismic analytical skills. The definitive confirmation of the availability of a hydrocarbon reservoir requires exploratory drilling which requires exploration licences and heavy equipment (including drilling rigs). After confirming the availability of O&G with an exploration well, an appraisal well is drilled for a more detailed analysis of the oil or gas field (including physical specs, pressure flow rate, etc.). The economic success of a field depends on the size and quality of the reservoir, investment cost to access the reservoir, and O&G prices. Wells are often ascertained to not be commercially viable and, therefore, the exploration activity has a substantial level of risk.

2.2.2 Development & Production

After an oil or gas reservoir has been raised, the development and production phase starts. Typically, exploration rights in the O&G industry also include the right to develop and produce, meaning that the same parties typically perform both functions. A field is developed by drilling the development well and installing the equipment and infrastructure necessary for production. Production relates to the extraction of O&G from the field for commercial use. Both of these functions require special ingenuity and equipment. Considering that new O&G reserves are typically more challenging to access, the necessary technology and equipment require substantial investments. This increases the production cost and exposure to O&G price fluctuations. Another apparent risk in the upstream relates to the environmental footprint of the O&G industry whereby oil spills have a detrimental impact on the environment and the party operating that field. Ultimately, when all useable O&G has been produced, the equipment needs to be dismantled and the surrounding location brought back to its natural condition. This final stage of production also comes with costs as well as environmental and reputational risks.

2.2.3 *Transportation and Storage*

The transportation and storage of oil products and related logistics play an important role in the O&G industry and provide the link between upstream and downstream. Transportation and storage can be divided into two stages for which primary logistics refer to the transportation (and related storage) from a production site to the oil refinery or gas processing facility while secondary logistics ensures that (semi) finished goods are transported to customers or retail sites. Crude oil, some of the refined oil products, natural gas, and natural gas liquids can be transported by pipelines while oil products and LNG can be carried by dedicated tanker trucks, trains, or ships. Supply and demand for O&G fluctuate heavily, and storage and transportation are valuable tools that are utilized to bridge the (price) gap between supply and demand.

2.2.4 *Refining, Processing, and Manufacturing*

Crude oil does not reach the end-user in the same form as it needs to be transformed in refineries before it is suitable for consumption by its various customers and consumers. Oil refining is the process of separating the hydrocarbon molecules present in crude oil and converting them into finished petroleum products. Refined oil is used to generate energy (transport, power generation, and heating) or as feedstock for the petrochemicals industry (source for, among others, industrial chemicals and plastic products). Due to heavy competition, refining margins are relatively narrow, therefore, profitability is very sensitive to changes in product supply and demand. Margins will also depend on the types of hardware that the site is meant to run vis-à-vis the available crude in the region (e.g., crude type and availability of that crude to the refinery).

With regard to natural gas, processing is usually required in order for it to become suitable for pipeline transportation and usage. Gas cannot be stored in its natural form. To move across longer distances than allowed by pipeline, natural gas is compressed and frozen into LNG close to the wellhead which allows it to be transported across the ocean or by road. At the other end, it is converted back into natural gas through heating (or regasification) and commonly transferred to the gas grid.

2.2.5 *Marketing and Distribution*

Ultimately, the O&G finished products are sold to customers and consumers. The various types of products are distributed through different channels and require other marketing strategies. Refined oil products for road transportation are typically sold through branded retail stations operated by an MNE or by a third party through franchising or licencing. Aviation and marine fuels are typically directly sold to airlines and shipping companies. Energy companies often purchase natural gas and other heating products to further distribute gas and power to residents and industry. Petrochemicals are sold directly to industrial customers.

2.3 Support Activities in the O&G Industry

2.3.1 Firm Infrastructure

Firm infrastructure consists of activities that usually benefit the entire value chain of the MNE. They are commonly performed at the head office or other central hub locations and typically include corporate functions such as strategic leadership, finance, HR, IT, legal, external relations, and safety. Firm infrastructure includes activities that are applicable to the entire group including the executive leadership team, (consolidated) accounting, and investor relations. It also encompasses corporate activities that are usually found efficient for centralizing the entire group to avoid duplications in local entities. It does not include activities that generate material value individually.

2.3.2 Research & Development

The O&G industry historically requires state of the art technologies for exploration, development, production, refining, processing, manufacturing, and transportation. O&G MNEs continue investing in R&D to improve the quality of products and the efficiency of projects, processes, and operations. R&D activities aim to find and develop new technologies to lower-carbon energy solutions for traditional O&G industries, and therefore, it is an important enabler of success. In the current matured O&G industry, technologies enable cost savings, productivity gains, cleaner and improved O&G products, access to reservoirs that were previously not accessible and new energy solutions. The ability to develop technology and innovate is often a differentiator that sets an O&G company apart from the competition.

2.3.3 Procurement

Procurement refers to the process of purchasing goods and services. Throughout the integrated O&G value chain, a broad variety of goods and services are used from floating production storage and offloading vessels to influencers on social media and everything in between. (Central) Procurement drives economies of scale, ensures security of supply, and generates working capital improvements. It operates in close connection with other value chain components such as R&D (sourcing of innovative goods and services), exploration, development, production, refining, processing and manufacturing (sourcing of materials, technical services, catalysts, etc.), transport and storage (sourcing of logistics services), and marketing and sales (sourcing of marketing materials, media, foods & beverages, etc.). Procurement also helps to deliver strategic themes of an MNE such as safety, sustainability, and/or cost savings. Overall, it typically provides quantitative and qualitative benefits to the MNE.

2.3.4 *Trading*

Crude oil, many refined oil products, chemical feedstocks, and natural gas markets are well established traded commodities. Increasingly, this also applies to the LNG and environmental credits which are relatively new products in a market that is not yet fully transparent. Traditionally, the trading process focused on managing demand and supply within an O&G company by buying and selling from the external market to avoid excesses and shortages throughout the supply chain. In view of market developments, trading centres increasingly act as a single face to the market for the majority of O&G products and as the primary organization to organize feedstock for refineries, chemical plants, and retail sites.

Several factors have contributed to trading becoming as such a key process for O&G companies to optimize their supply chain and manage the commodity and market risks. They are:

- large price volatility;
- markets changing dynamics between supply and demand due to customers' risk diversification and suppliers' reliance on long-term stable cash flow;
- the effects of the energy transition; and
- pressures to maintain margin.

Trading also performs a risk management role through hedging and can take on speculative trading positions. The extent and structure of portfolio trading may range from passive clearing houses to profit centres responsible for negotiations with suppliers and customers that actively buy and sell both physical and paper products. The value that is attributable to these trading models is, at this moment, a topic on which there is no global consensus.

2.4 Value Drivers in O&G Value Chain

2.4.1 *Strategic Choices*

The various components of the O&G value chain contribute differently to value creation from the exploitation of O&G resources whereby the relative value of the value chain components varies depending on the economic environment. In the very integrated O&G value chain, the relative value of activities is not necessarily the same for the three business stages of upstream, midstream, and downstream (e.g., R&D has a different relative value for upstream versus downstream). At a high level, the relative value contributions to the O&G value chain can be reasoned based on the inherent differences in functions, assets, and risks of the individual value chain components.

The sources for value creation in the O&G industry include exogenous context and conditions (including quality and quantity of the resource, availability of infrastruc ture, and the structure of the domestic economy), the companies participating in the sector (including cost efficiency, technical excellence, horizontal concentration, vertical integration, and strategic choices), and the sector's organization and institutional properties (i.e., merely specific policy decisions by governments including legal and regulatory frameworks, tax system, etc.). [6]

However, the O&G industry is experiencing turbulent times in which access to reservoirs requires an increasing amount of technology and investment, O&G prices become more volatile, public opinion more stringent, and the energy transition more pertinent. That requires IOCs to place more emphasis on other components of the value chain and reassess the relative contributions to value creation.

Such strategic choices of the IOC executive leadership, including investment decisions, are key to the success of an IOC. Furthermore, critical success factors to value creation can best be assessed by distinguishing between upstream, midstream and downstream activities.

2.4.2 Upstream

Historically, the access to O&G reserves in combination with the capability to extract the hydrocarbon molecules were decisive for the existence of an O&G company. Traditionally, the value in the O&G industry was therefore mainly driven by the exploration, development, and production activities that deliver access to scarce, high-quality natural resources. These two value chain components are very capital intensive and typically carry the highest level of risk throughout the value chain and therefore usually generate most of the value.[7]

It is therefore key for IOCs to obtain reliable data of a potential O&G field in order to locate commercially viable reservoirs and reduce the risk of impairing heavy investments for drilling (exploratory and appraisal) wells. In the next stage, the field becomes developed by drilling development wells and installing the necessary equipment. In this stage, a well can still be found non-commercially viable, and safety for personnel and the environment becomes more important with greater activity on site.

Once a well is in the production stage, production continuity is the key driver. A loss of production due to unscheduled maintenance or accidents drives substantial costs. As fields mature, production increases in volume until it reaches plateau production and then ramps off unless, through technology, field life can be extended.

The development of innovative technologies to operate the field efficiently can make or break the commercial viability of the production of a field. Additionally, R&D is key for developing technologies to efficiently access previously inaccessible reservoirs, like deep water technologies, to make them commercially viable and increase field recovery rates.

---

6. Silvana Tordo with Brandon S. Tracy, Noora Arfaa, 2011. *National Oil Companies and Value Creation.*
7. *Ibid.*

2.4.3 *Midstream*

Midstream relates to the storage and transport of crude oil and natural gas and serves as the link between upstream and downstream. As indicated previously, storage and transport are essential for bridging the gap between supply and demand whereby caution must be taken to manage environmental risks.

The management of supply and demand is often done by supply chain managers and traders. With upstream projects becoming riskier and more capital intensive, these projects require continuous production, low unused capacity, and a long-term stable cash flow to be commercially viable. On the other hand, customers increasingly diversify their portfolios using more suppliers and shorter duration contracts. Caught in the middle, shipping and storage become more relevant but, as proven by the COVID-19 crisis, can be oversupplied or constricted. All of these require careful balancing as any of the associated risk materializing would instantly result in significant material losses. A central trading desk has proven to be the optimal solution, and those companies with efficient trading activity and sufficient portfolio access have a competitive advantage. This is most visible for the LNG and oil products; however, it also applies to crude oil for which trading offers options to customers that 'just' a supplier would not have.

Trading is therefore increasingly becoming a central feature in the value chain of an IOC.

2.4.4 *Downstream*

The downstream activities are not necessarily typical for the O&G industry. The production of finished products and the marketing and distribution to customers and consumers are processes that are also found in, for instance, the FMCG as well as the automotive and pharmaceutical industries. Not surprisingly, these activities are often referred to as routine for TP purposes, which is not different for IOCs. Both, however, do require the use of intangibles (technology and/or brand) that can differentiate the company in competition.

Refining, processing, and manufacturing require production techniques that are specific to the O&G industry and continuously improve for efficiency purposes. Cutting edge technology (like for LNG processing) does provide an IOC with a major competitive advantage if 'discovered' first. The continuous R&D investments are proven to be valuable in the longer run.

Regarding marketing and distribution, branding can be a differentiator. When the retail activities in the O&G mainly create value for an IOC through volume, the brand can create the perception among consumers that the quality of the oil products is more assured. However, these price differences are generally minimal considering the highly competitive nature of the market while brand names are not considered dominant.[8] As

8. OECD, *Tax Challenges Arising from Digitalization: Report on Pillar One Blueprint* (OECD, 14 October 2020).

correctly stated by the OECD, the majority of O&G products are sold to customers and consumers who acquire them for their inherent characteristics.[9]

2.4.5 Conclusions

Overall, even in the developing O&G market, the upstream arguably remains the most significant value driver for O&G companies – the added value is generated from extracting a molecule that has little value when still part of the soil and becomes valuable once extracted.

However, to obtain economic access to reservoirs and for efficient field production, technology becomes increasingly important. The same is true for the trading activities that have demonstrated to be very necessary for an IOC to successfully compete in the matured O&G market.

If there is further exploration beyond the O&G, it is found that the entire industry is affected by the global energy transition. Although it is expected that the transition will take time, the pace is accelerating, and it requires the industry to adapt in order to remain relevant in an environment where cleaner energy solutions have become the standard. However, with a long and proven experience in the energy market as well as with the demand for O&G continuing to be significant for a long time to come, IOCs are well placed to take a leading role in that transition.

3 TP IN THE O&G SECTOR

3.1 Introduction

The O&G industry is relatively complex due to vertical integration and, as a result, is comprised of multiple supply and value chains. As a consequence, an IOC deals with a multitude of different intra-group transactions, and almost all TP themes that are relevant in relation to products, services, and intangibles are applicable to the O&G industry.

The two largest types of intra-group transactions relate to commodities and services:[10]

- commodity transactions regard the purchase and sale of crude oil, natural gas, and various oil products from upstream producers to the midstream and downstream sectors;
- intra-group service transactions are dominated by the provision of engineering and technical services to the upstream sector.

Figure 20.2 illustrates these key intra-group transactions in an example of a typical integrated O&G company whereby the bold black lines represent intra-group services, and the dotted black lines are the commodity transactions.

9. *Ibid.*
10. Deloitte Development LLC 2019, Transfer Pricing in the oil and gas sector.

Figure 20.2 Example of Organizational Structure of an Integrated O&G Company

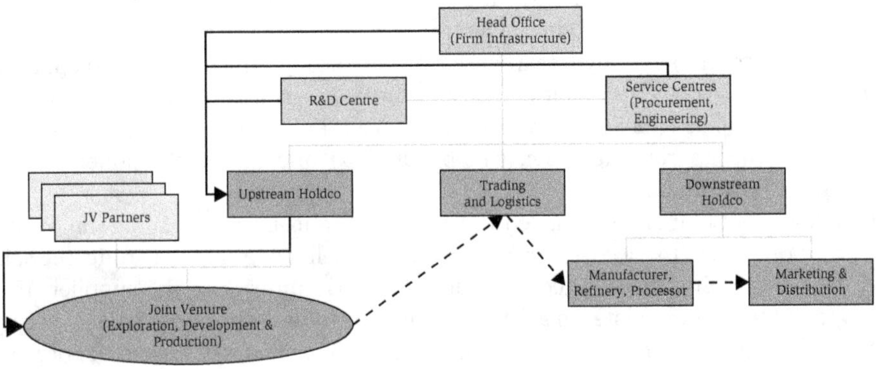

3.2 O&G Commodity TP

Oil is a globally recognized and traded commodity in a generally transparent market. The TP of O&G commodities adheres to the guidance in the OECD TPG and the UN TPM on the use of the CUP method, with commodities defined as physical products for which a publicly available quoted price is used as a reference. Although oil supply contracts may differ in respect of destinations, duration, volume delivered, transportation terms, demurrage and other factors, market quotes from government price-setting agencies or industry information publishers such as S&P Global Platts are widely used in the industry, and considered reliable CUPs.

For natural gas, LNG, and refined oil products such as naphtha and kerosene, the degree of market transparency varies. However, regional pricing data for these or similar products is usually available and can be used to derive an appropriate market price. As a result, there has traditionally been a little challenge in the use of market information to set TP for O&G commodities.

The OECD comments on the use of a quoted price as an arm's length reference in addition to the use of an actual internal or external CUP. Quoted commodity prices generally reflect the agreement between independent buyers and sellers in the market for a specific type and amount of commodity, traded under specific conditions at a certain point in time.[11] If the quoted price is 'widely and routinely used in the ordinary course of business', it can be considered a reference for the pricing of commodities between related parties.

The economically relevant characteristics that drive comparability for commodities include the physical features and quality of the commodity as well as contractual terms including traded volume, timing of arrangements, terms of delivery, transport terms, and currency. According to the general guidance on comparability, it is recommended to make adjustments so that the CUP better reflects the characteristics of the tested transaction if such an adjustment can reliably be made.

11. *See* para. 2.19, OECD TPG.

The general guidance on TP of commodities fully applies to O&G commodities. Three important indices used for crude oil across the globe are the WTI Crude Oil, North Sea Brent Crude Oil (Brent), and the East Asia index JCC. Similar global or regional indices exist for oil products (such as gas, LNG, heating oil), condensates (like naptha and kerosene), and hydrocarbon-based chemical products. When no appropriate index exists, it may be possible to take appropriate combinations of relevant indices – for instance, when a particular condensate from a refinery includes a certain per cent of naphtha, the appropriate index can be used as one of the components in an appropriate TP formula.

An adjustment that is often made to CUPs relates to insurance, loading, unloading, and transport. When these costs are assumed by the seller of a cargo of crude, the sales price is generally higher to reflect the additional cost and risk to the supplier. If an intra-group transaction relates to a sale for which the buyer bears these risks, it may be possible to take the quoted price and adjust it for the cost and risk involved. For many types of commodities, storage and vessel charter rates are publicly available and can be used for reliable transport cost adjustments.

As mentioned in section 2.3.4, the most visible change to the O&G value chain relates to the emergence of portfolio trading models that have evolved in view of increasing differences and volatility between demand and supply. The extent and structure of portfolio trading may range from passive clearing houses to centres responsible for negotiations that actively purchase and sell both physical and paper products.

The emergence of trading models has had an impact on the CUP method for O&G commodities in two fundamental ways. First, trading entities in the value chain require an arm's length compensation for their contributions – functions, assets, and risks. Second, to evidence, the added value of the trader, the use of identified comparable unrelated transactions as evidence of the traders' behaviour has become an important tool that complements the quoted price references.

Generally speaking, contributions in the form of functions, assets, and risks by trading entities in the supply chain should be compensated. Depending on the functionality of the trading entity, it may be the purchasing or selling party in an intra-group transaction. In these cases, its contribution may require an adjustment of the CUPs to reflect the functions, assets, and risks contributed by the trader, however, this is not always the case. For instance, a portfolio trader may buy commodities under various long-term supply contracts and sell these in short-term contracts with customers. It may be that the pricing difference between long-term and short-term reflects the commodity risk taken on by the trader in that case such that no adjustments may be required. The appropriate approach should be determined on a case-by-case basis.

The prominence of trading models has led to public and political debate concerning the perceived value erosion to other parts of the O&G value chain. For example, many companies have begun using their trading desks to centralize commodity price risk management, which may previously have exposed a refinery. By placing this activity on the trading desk, the refinery would typically require a lower but more stable margin. Of course, the trading desk will need to actually perform the control and risk mitigation functions and have the financial capacity to assume the risk. As evidence that this dynamic does not lead to artificial profit shifting to the trading desk, the pricing and other terms and conditions of actual third-party contracts have proven to be a beneficial tool. Such contracts can help clarify that the terms and conditions as agreed between the trading desk and the refinery happen in the market and could be considered at arm's length.

Example

Company A, located in Country X and Company B, located in Country Y, are part of ABC Group. Company A produces the LNG for sale to customers in South East Asia. The customers prefer to purchase with short-term contracts from many different suppliers. To allow its LNG production to operate on a continuous basis, all LNG is sold via Company B (trading entity) that acts as an intermediate between the supplier and customers of LNG. Company B has multiple long-term and short-term supplies from within and outside Company A, sufficient transport vessels, and adequate access to other customers to enable offering terms to its customers that differ from what the suppliers can offer directly.

As a true portfolio player, Company B should buy the LNG from Company A at the prices and terms it would do so from third parties and at which Company A could sell to third parties directly. As market evidence, multiple sources might be relevant, such as the Japan LNG Cocktail that gives the average price of long-term and short-term LNG sold into Japan, the Platts Japan-Korea Price Market which is a quoted price for spot LNG transactions in Asia, any LNG contracts for which the prices have been made public, and of course any available internal comparable transactions. Data from these sources should be adjusted for any differences with the intra-group transaction, for instance, in relation to shipping terms and, if relevant, for any risks assumed by Company B.

3.3 Cost Sharing Arrangements and Intra-group Services

In addition to commodities, a key aspect of TP in the O&G industry relates to the intra-group provision of services of CSA or CCA. Intra-group services and CSA have supported the O&G industry's business models for a long time.

As indicated earlier, the substantial investments and long lead times associated with projects; the significant operational, political, financial, and environmental risks facing companies in this industry; and the strategic nature of O&G projects for companies and countries have led to the emergence of large consortiums of O&G companies to develop and operate O&G reserves. These often include a government agency or national oil company.

The PSCs, JOAs, and other agreements that formalize such consortiums typically appoint an operator from among the participating companies. It is usually the partner with the largest interest in the partnership, manages the project on behalf of the consortium, and ensures that all costs and risks are shared with the consortium members. The operator typically relies on a wide range of research and development, technology, head office, technical, and functional services to allow it to carry out its responsibilities. The scale of these activities combined with the high investment risk in relation to the consortium's operations was such that, already as of the middle of the twentieth century, O&G majors began to cross-share risk and provide central access to technology and other resources among the affiliate entities within their groups that acted as an operator via cost-sharing arrangements.

CSAs and CCAs, which allowed the cost-sharing participants to share in the costs and risks and have access to the full suite of cost-shared technology, IT systems, and technical and non-technical services, were widely perceived as the most efficient means to provide access to technology and services. Currently, such arrangements are therefore commonplace in the O&G industry often in combination with intra-group services agreements.

In O&G CCAs, there is shared access to R&D, ingenuity, and expertise and the sharing of risks associated with rendering these activities, which is of significant importance for IOCs. Together with the other participants to the CSA, the investments and associated risks for technology development and (technology) services are shared.

CSAs also benefit the cross-fertilization of technology through the free flow of information among the participants of the CSA: the technology developed for use in one field can prove to be valuable for other fields. Thus, the sharing of costs and risks for technology development is valuable for all participants.

The operator's responsibilities include activities performed elsewhere in the MNE that may be centralized in the MNE's hub countries or specialist centres of excellence such as technical engineering, functional services, and corporate functions like IT, HR and investor relations, and back-office functions. By sharing the costs among the participants to the CSA, the model allows the centralization (economies of scale) and wider access to these services.

The need for increasingly specialized resources, capital constraints, and drive towards efficiency have, over the years, resulted in increased centralization of functions into service hubs and centres of excellence from which R&D and technical and non-technical services are rendered to CSA participants.

The set-up of dedicated service entities has not changed the fundamental nature of traditional O&G industry CSA and CCA models. However, it did highlight one particular aspect in which the O&G models increasingly diverged from the OECD view on pricing of intra-group services: the 'at-cost' principle.

In the O&G industry, it has been a common and longstanding practice that services to projects, especially in the upstream, are provided at fees that ensure recovery of costs without the inclusion of a profit margin for the service provider. This so-called at-cost principle is directly linked to a common characteristic of the O&G industry, specifically, that the operator is not allowed to benefit or lose from its position compared to the non-operating consortium members. As such, the PSCs or JOAs with consortium members commonly stipulate that the operator *and its affiliates* do not earn a profit or incur a loss from undertaking activities for the benefit of the consortium. The inclusion of affiliates in the 'at-cost' pricing clauses generally implied that dedicated service entities provided services to the consortium without a profit mark-up.

For a long time, the CSA and CCA structures with the at-cost principle remained intact with little change because an operator's obligations are generally established in long-term contracts and agreed with venture partners, which often include organizations that represent the government.

Only in recent years have updates to this structure been seen with, among others, more clearly defined distinctions between CCAs and intra-group services. There are two main reasons for this development:

- an increasing apparent discrepancy between historic practice and the post-BEPS view on TP as most clearly evidenced by the 2017 OECD TPG that included the outcome of BEPS Actions 8-10; and
- an increased use of remote service hubs and specialized third-party service providers.

The primary challenge in this respect relates to the fact that the operating entity has a direct economic interest in the consortium, however, its affiliate service provider that is historically providing services to the operator and consortium under the same conditions does not have such a direct economic interest.[12]

The OECD TPG clarified that:

- The participant's proportionate share of the overall contributions to a CCA must be consistent with its proportionate share of the overall expected benefits whereby the value of the contributions should be determined based on the guidance of the OECD TPG.
- Generally, contributions need to be compensated at value, and 'the compensation of the participants in a CCA should not differ (materially) from the compensation which the respective enterprises would receive if they would cooperate outside a CCA'.
- The dedicated group service entities are likely not considered as participants to the CCA: 'An enterprise that solely performs the subject activity but does not receive an interest in the output of the CCA, would not be considered a participant in the CCA but rather a service provider to the CCA. As such, it should be compensated for the services it provides on an arm's length basis external to the CCA.'

As a result of the developments noted above, services to an operator should now generally be regarded as Chapter VII services to a CCA and priced at arm's length, typically with a profit element.

This does not necessarily mean that there is no more room for the at-cost principle as a practical means to measure the relative value of current contributions. While the guidelines provide few arguments to support this case, it remains important to consider the comparability of all of the economically relevant characteristics of the transactions in the broader context of the arrangement, including the impact of any broader arrangement of economically related transactions which may exist between the parties

12. *Ibid.*

to the unrelated party transaction, and the sharing of risks. Furthermore, government policies should be treated as conditions of the market.

Note that one feature common to many CSA and CCA systems is that these models are based on the fundamental principle that not just the benefits but also all risks associated with the creation of R&D and the provision of services are shared among the CSA participants. Service companies are indemnified from any materialized risk associated with the performance of operator services, including the risk of non-performance or underutilization of staff. As such, even if the at-cost principle is not as advantageous especially when it is applied to dedicated group service entities, there are still good reasons for adjusting the profit margin to reflect the very limited operational risk associated with service companies that are dedicated to providing intra-group services to O&G operating companies.

Despite the commercial and legal situation that often prevents services from being priced other than at cost, the growing view that the O&G at-cost principle may not be fully compatible with the ALP has led to a situation in which O&G companies that heavily relied on at-cost for their internal services have had to accept a situation of double taxation. This was caused by the taxation of profit for the service entities and the inability to deduct the mark-up at the recipient or indeed the sharing of this mark-up with consortium members. This situation is unlikely to be resolved soon since parties in a consortium may not have the ability or desire to renegotiate the services clause in these contracts.

4 CONCLUSIONS

This chapter provides a glimpse into the characteristics of the O&G industry, its components for value creation, and its typical TP aspects. This chapter was written in turbulent times when the COVID-19 pandemic had a serious impact on the industry. At the moment of writing this conclusion, several of the large IOCs have announced reorganizations of an unprecedented scale reflecting the changed market circumstances and the effects of the energy transition on the O&G industry. The industry is adapting, and traditional aspects of the O&G industry are changing.

If the value chain of an O&G company is examined, three business sectors can be distinguished:

- upstream (exploration, development, and production activities);
- midstream (storage, transportation, and trading); and
- downstream (refining, manufacturing, processing, marketing, and distribution).

These activities are often combined in large IOCs where R&D activities, technical engineering, and corporate functions are typically centralized and accessible to all sectors.

In the developing industry, it is concluded that the upstream is arguably still the most significant value driver for O&G companies and that technology and trading activities (including demand and supply planning) are becoming increasingly important in an industry where efficiency is becoming a key driver to success.

These developments are having a distinct impact on the traditional O&G value chain and on the applicable TP. It has been explained that the two largest intra-group transactions in the O&G industry relate to commodities and services.

For commodity transactions, a CUP method is typically applied whereby prices are based on commodity indices or combinations of relevant indices. These prices are subject to comparability adjustments for activities performed by the trader which often include storage and transportation. It has been explained that the emergence of trading models and the more entrepreneurial role of trading and logistics entities in the value chain requires compensation for these activities to change accordingly.

With regard to intra-group services, it has been discussed that it is common practice in the O&G industry for affiliates to share investments and risks related to technology development, technical engineering, and other services through CCAs. Such agreements normally mirror the 'at-cost' pricing condition that is often dictated by the different types of agreements with third-party consortium partners to develop and operate O&G reserves but, following BEPS, is facing an increasing challenge.

CHAPTER 21

Transfer Pricing in the Pharmaceutical and Life Sciences Sector

Florian Zirnstein & Philipp Kaiser

1 INTRODUCTION

We are living in a highly dynamic world in which the life science sector addresses some of the most pressing global challenges. The following megatrends bring the life science industry into the spotlight to help provide solutions:

(1) Chronic and new diseases are on the rise and will place further pressure on healthcare systems, health resources, and scientific processes. Cardiovascular disease and cancer will continue to be the leading causes of death; currently, one in two people die from one of them.[1]
(2) The population is continuously growing and ageing. From an estimated 7.7 billion people worldwide in 2019, the global population could increase to approximately 8.5 billion in 2030 and 9.7 billion in 2050 with one in five people being 60 years of age or older.[2]
(3) Malnutrition (i.e., undernutrition, vitamin and mineral deficiencies, overweight and obesity) remains a global health concern. Today, one in three 11-year-old children in Europe is overweight. More than 2 billion people around the world show vitamin and mineral deficiencies. Malnutrition impacts the gut microbiome and is therefore linked to a number of diseases including cancer and autoimmune diseases.[3]
(4) Population and economic growth increase pressure on the ecosystem as humanity is consuming and emitting more than nature can recreate within a specific period of time. Going forward, resource-intensive industries including energy and agriculture will play a key role in using natural resources more efficiently and sustainably.[4]
(5) While many people in emerging economies still struggle to earn enough money to financially support themselves, the younger generations in developed countries have grown up in affluence. Many have seen the disadvantages of hard work with the example of their parents, i.e., limited room for self-actualization, divorce, and burnout.[5] The top 'good life factor' that everyone agrees on is good health.[6]
(6) Digital platforms will have an increasing impact, and the significance of e-commerce will expand. The success story of digital platforms is unprecedented; within a brief period of time, they have disrupted a myriad of

1. WHO Health statistics and information systems 2018: Projections of mortality and causes of death.
2. United Nations, Department of Economic and Social Affairs, World Population Prospects 2019.
3. WHO, Kane Dingh et al.: Childhood Malnutrition and the Intestinal Microbiome Malnutrition and the Microbiome, Pediatr Res., Vol. 77 No. 0, 2015, pp. 256-262; FAO 2018: The state of food security and nutrition in the world.
4. www.footprintnetwork.org (last accessed 27 January 2022), IPCC 2018, FAO 2017: The future of food and Agriculture. Trends and challenges, OECD.
5. Euromonitor, Zukunftsinstitut.
6. GfK 2017: Study involves more than 23,000 participants from seventeen countries.

businesses. Platforms are easy to scale and benefit from network effects so the pace of change is increasing exponentially.[7]

(7) Personalization and consumer experience have become the next competitive battleground. Digitalization allows for better and entirely new product and service offerings centred around the needs of the individual.

The life sciences sector is at the centre of the solution to health and resource challenges by contributing to better medicines, high-quality food in sufficient quantities, and further innovative solutions supported by major advances in digital technologies.

Life sciences encompass a broad range of different sectors from pharmaceutical, biotechnology, healthcare, and nutrition to chemical manufacturing organizations and data-centric health business-to-customer organizations. The life sciences sector is a pool of mostly innovation-based organizations that attempt to solve the challenges mentioned above.

The key value-adding enterprises in the life sciences sector are research-based companies searching for chemical and biological molecules and innovative breakthrough technologies. The most prominent research-based enterprises in this sector are pharmaceutical and biotech companies. This chapter is about this sector focusing on this industry's value creation and TP matters.[8]

Section 2 concerns value creation and describes the industry's key value drivers including R&D, complex manufacturing, marketing, and its key asset of IP. This section also deals with major industry trends such as mergers and acquisition-driven industry consolidation, market entrance of technology players including the risk of disruption and/or the chance of collaboration as well as technological leaps.

Section 3 regards important industry-specific TP matters. This section provides an overview of a typical centralized operating model focused on IP ownership with reference to the concept of DEMPE. Based on these fundamentals, the particularities of the pharmaceutical product lifecycle will be presented by discussing:

- the process from drug discovery to commercialization in the context of profit perception;
- the meaning of patent cliff and post-patent life concerning IP value;
- the industry-relevant concept of 'hard-to-value' intangibles and its unapparent difficulties, and
- the observation that high marketing expenses do not translate to marketing intangibles per se.

Additionally, this section addresses pricing controls and parallel imports as TP steering peculiarities of a highly regulated industry. The special impact of digital

7. World Economic Forum.
8. This excludes the generic pharmaceutical sector that refers to drugs that are produced and commercialized by competitors upon patent expiration. It also excludes often less prominently discussed life sciences sectors specifically referring to agriculture (i.e., agricultural chemicals as well as seeds and traits including digital solutions), animal health, health care, and nutrition.

technologies on the key value-creating functions described in section 2 and the meaning of digital disruption and changes from a TP perspective will also be examined in this section. A critical discussion about the tax concept of the OECD Pillar One in the context of research-based pharmaceutical and biotech companies will end this section. Section 3 also refers to important TP dedicated court cases, provides examples and includes references to the OECD TPG when appropriate.

Section 4 provides a summary of this chapter's key significant elements and discussion points.

2 VALUE CREATION IN THE PHARMACEUTICAL AND LIFE SCIENCE INDUSTRY

Innovation is critical to the success of research-based pharmaceutical and biotech companies. Drug discovery and development are time-consuming, expensive, and unpredictable. The purpose of conducting business in this industry is to deliver breakthroughs that improve the lives of customers. R&D is fundamental for fulfilling this purpose by translating advanced science and technologies into the therapies that are most relevant. This section refers to R&D, complex manufacturing, and marketing as the key value drivers with IP being the key asset for multinational companies operating in the research-based pharmaceutical and biotech industry.

2.1 Key Value Drivers and Assets

2.1.1 Research & Development

R&D in the pharmaceutical and biotech industry is intense and varies between areas but often has the same starting point which is, specifically, locating the correct molecule.

Research-based pharmaceutical companies invest considerable resources in the R&D of a new drug, with the objectives of improving patients' quality of life and also prolonging lives. It typically takes approximately ten to twelve years to develop a new drug. During this time, scientists from a variety of disciplines work on finding a suitable active ingredient from an enormous number of molecules. Between 5,000 and 10,000 molecules are rigorously studied in numerous laboratory tests, and the best of these are further optimized.[9]

From the four or five drug candidates that are subsequently tested on humans in clinical studies, often only one substance is approved and becomes available to physicians and patients. Cooperation in interdepartmental, multidisciplinary teams is an important requirement for success in the complex process of drug development (*see* Figure 21.1).[10]

9. Bayer: From Molecules to Medicine: A Journey Through Research & Development, 2013.
10. *Ibid.*

Figure 21.1 R&D Process in the Pharmaceutical Industry[11]

Drug Discovery

The development of every drug begins with the search for a target on which the drug can act. To determine this, scientists must have very precise knowledge of the biochemical processes that occur in the body and how these are changed by a disease. Once a target has been successfully identified, the scientists use a systematic test procedure to search for substances – known as lead candidates – that could be a suitable starting point for a new active ingredient. They must be able to bind well to the target protein, i.e., they must fit into the target like a key into a lock. In addition to compound screening, computer-based methods are used to find and develop suitable drug candidates. The compounds identified up to this point do not yet have all of the necessary properties of an active ingredient. At this stage, they might be compared with key blanks that can be inserted into the lock but not turned. Medicinal chemistry gives them the finishing that they need.

Pre-clinical Phase

In the pre-clinical development stage, pharmacologists and toxicologists test the new active compound under experimental conditions. They study the desired and adverse effects of the new drug candidate with the aim of precisely determining how it will react in the body.

Clinical Phases

Phase I clinical trials are the first stage in which physicians study the active ingredient in humans. They test its safety and tolerability as well as the way it affects the body. These studies are usually conducted on small groups of volunteers. In Phase II and III clinical trials, large patient groups are studied by physicians to determine the efficacy and safety of the new drug candidate. Independent hospitals or physicians' practices in many countries are involved in these phases of clinical development.

Registration

Drugs may only be launched if they have been given regulatory approval. The regulatory affairs department is responsible for preparing this final step of drug development. This department compiles the dossier that is submitted to the regulatory authorities and is the primary interface between the company and the authorities. As a rule, pharmaceutical companies strive to market their products worldwide. To do so, they require approval from each individual country.

11. *Ibid.*

In essence, finding a molecule and bringing a drug to market involves a high risk of failure and is a long journey from investment to return.[12] R&D expenditures can be a 100% sunk cost and may simply never produce a marketable product. From 2010 to 2018, the mean cost of bringing a new drug to market increased by approximately 70% to USD 2 billion with clinical trials comprising a substantial portion of this cost. Meanwhile, the average return on new R&D investments decreased to 1.8% in 2019 from 10.1% in 2010.[13] This signifies the pressure on the R&D pipeline and also evidences the industry-specific high risk that years-long R&D efforts can be useless, regardless of the R&D cost incurred. Therefore, ways to reduce the R&D failure risk are highly welcomed and sought.

Collaboration and Licensing Structures

A research-based pharmaceutical and biotech company typically performs a significant portion of R&D in-house and searches for promising chemical and biological lead molecules and innovative technologies developed by unrelated parties to use in its R&D processes. This insourcing of molecules and technologies can be done by acquisition or by entering into collaboration or licence agreements with other companies. These agreements allow focusing on strong in-house capabilities and acquiring, co-developing, or licensing promising compounds or technologies. There are also operating models in which a third party partially funds the development costs of pipeline products in return for rights to receive potential milestone payments, revenue-sharing payments, profit-sharing payments, or royalties. Collaboration, licence, and funding agreements allow companies to share risks and costs. Additionally, they enable access to external scientific and technological expertise and push their own or in-licenced products.[14]

2.1.2 Manufacturing

The manufacturing process is highly important for securing product supply in any industry. When it comes to creating value, the manufacturing process in the pharmaceutical and biotech industry is of less relevance when compared to R&D and marketing but is often underestimated related to complex manufacturing of large-scale biologics and biotech products.

Manufacturing procedures for small molecule active pharmaceutical ingredients without complex formulation and/or challenging manufacturing requirements may, upon product patent expiration, be replicated by generic manufacturers. Generally, replicating traditional tableted drugs is relatively simple.[15]

12. In 2019, the top ten pharmaceutical companies showed an R&D cost to revenue ratio of approximately 15%-28%, www.statista.com/statistics/309471/randd-spending-share-of-top-pharmaceutical-companies (last accessed 27 January 2022).
13. Deloitte: Ten Years on Measuring the Return from Pharmaceutical Innovation 2019, 2020, 2020. This analysis focuses on the R&D in the biopharma sector.
14. Pfizer, Form 10-K, 2019, p. 6.
15. AstraZeneca, Annual Report & Form 20-F Information 2019, p. 15.

In contrast, manufacturing large-scale biologics is a high market entrance barrier itself since these large molecules are much more complex to produce and cannot be relatively easily replicated.[16] Such production is subject to immense capital expenditure and extremely sensitive to product loss due to contamination, oxidation, equipment failure, improper installation, or operator error. Slight deviations from standard manufacturing processes typically result in product defects and other supply disruptions. If there are microbial, viral, or other contaminants ascertained in products or manufacturing sites, manufacturing facilities may need to be temporarily closed to solve the problem.[17] Therefore, even if a biotech product is off-patent, the complexity of its manufacturing process can be a barrier to entry for generic biosimilar manufacturers. This allows companies to avoid competition for biologics even though the product patent has expired.

In addition to meeting the requirements for regulatory marketing approval of a medicine, there is the need for manufacturers to meet stringent quality control and manufacturing procedures such as the GMP regulations used in many jurisdictions. In complying with the standards established in these regulations, manufacturers must continue to expend time, money, and effort in the areas of production and quality control to ensure ongoing technical compliance. Regulatory agencies regulate and inspect equipment, facilities, and processes used in the manufacturing and testing of pharmaceutical and biologic products prior to approving a product.[18] If a company received approval from regulatory authorities and subsequently materially changes the manufacturing equipment, location, or process, additional regulatory review and approval may be required.[19]

2.1.3 *Marketing*

The research-based pharmaceutical and biotech industry can be defined through prescription pharmaceutical products and speciality therapeutics. Products are generally marketed to healthcare providers and patients.[20] Healthcare providers are typically doctors, nurses, pharmacists, and insurance organizations.

Research-based pharmaceutical and biotech companies have to effectively market their products considering the relatively short patent life after approval. This requires substantial initial marketing spending in order to rapidly gain market share to boost returns on investment in the lifecycle of a patent. It also requires actions to establish an environment that could allow the company to continue to sell the product even after

16. *Ibid.*
17. Biogen, Form 10 K, 2019, pp. 43ff.
18. T. Jung in D. Fischer, J. Breitenbach (Hrsg.): Die Pharmaindustrie, 2013, pp. 160ff.
19. *Ibid.*, p. 23.
20. Promotion activities are set by country-specific regulations. In most countries, direct patient promotion is not allowed. It is only allowed in the United States and New Zealand; this still makes direct patient promotion highly important since the United States is the largest market for the industry, D. Fischer, J. Breitenbach (Hrsg.): Die Pharmaindustrie, 2013, p. 270.

patent protection has lapsed.[21] Not all pharmaceutical and biotech companies are in a position to continually launch new products in key markets around the world. An unrelated party in a country is unlikely to have the financial power and stamina to run respective product campaigns. In particular, start-up biotech companies often form a collaboration with multinational pharmaceutical companies to access their experience and infrastructure for conducting an expensive marketing strategy.

In addition to the material capital needed to execute marketing strategies, experience and expertise with the medical profession's practices in each country and compliance with various different regulatory requirements are needed to enable a constant flow of product supply in the countries. The medical professional who prescribes the product is the main point of contact for describing the benefits of the product to the patient (end-user) while sales by the company are made indirectly through wholesalers to pharmacists and hospitals. This marketing effort, also referred to as detailing, is typically labour intensive and involves highly trained sales representatives who demonstrate the additional value of new products in face-to-face communication with medical professionals.[22]

Competition is intense. Generally, products of research-based pharmaceutical and biotech companies compete with other branded or generic drugs or biosimilars that treat comparable diseases. The principal forms of competition include efficacy, safety, ease of use, and cost-effectiveness. The manner of competition differs among product categories and segments, but demonstrating the value of products is a critical success factor for them. Competitors are other research-based pharmaceutical and biotech companies, smaller research companies with targeted therapeutic areas, and generic and biosimilar manufacturers.[23]

Research-based pharmaceutical and biotech companies typically spend between 15% and 35% (launch phase) of sales for the provision of scientific and medical information, selling, and other distribution activities to gain a sufficient market share when entering a new market.[24] These expenditures are significant and comparable to expenditures for R&D activities in any specific period.[25]

After the launch of new products, there is still a material risk of not gaining a sufficient market share by marketing efforts before other products are created and offered as competition. Even considering this risk, a second-to-market product can still

21. Branded generics can be an integral part of research-based pharmaceutical and biotech companies. The idea is to keep marketing spending relatively high even after patent expiration and make use of a strong brand to defend market shares.
22. Karl Wündisch: Pharmaceutical Industry and Transfer Pricing: Anything Special, ITPJ, Vol. 10, No. 6, November/December 2003, pp. 204ff.
23. Pfizer, Form 10-K, p. 12.
24. Small start-up biotech companies might not have sales or royalty income in their development phase and, even if they do, the need for high initial marketing expenditures might heavily imbalance any marketing expense/sales ratio as described above in this section. This is why start-up biotech companies join forces with multinationals; they gain access to marketing know-how and infrastructure.
25. Karl Wündisch: Pharmaceutical Industry and Transfer Pricing: Anything Special, ITPJ, Vol. 10, No. 6, November/December 2003, pp. 204ff.

be successful. Therefore, upon launching a product, the highest risk has been overcome.[26]

2.1.4 Patents and Brands

IP in the research-based pharmaceutical and biotech industry is mainly centred around patents resulting from R&D and brands resulting from marketing strategies. There is a focus on patents in this section as their lifetime is the period when research-based pharmaceutical and biotech companies yield financially from high-risk and high-cost drug discovery as described in the previous sections.

Research-based pharmaceutical and biotech companies typically own patents around the world that protect the pharmaceutical and other products and their application, formulations, product manufacturing processes, and precursor chemical compounds used in manufacturing. The patents for individual products remain in force for varying periods beginning with the date of filing or approval. The patent protection depends on the patent type, scope coverage, and local availability of legal remedies which differs from country to country. In the event of regulatory delays in a country, patent term extensions might be available.

The loss, expiration, or invalidity of patents, related litigations, and the expiration of co-promotion and licensing rights can have material downside effects on sales. Many branded products have multiple patents that expire on different dates. If the patent protection has expired or its defence has been legally lost before expiration, the exclusivity on these products will typically be lost, resulting in the production of identical or highly similar products by generic or biosimilar manufacturers sold cheaper. Such price competition can heavily and rapidly reduce sales for the affected products.[27]

Generally, brands are of minor importance to this sector compared to the consumer health industry sector. However, particularly blockbuster products of research-based pharmaceutical and biotech companies that are globally sold under the brand (name and logo) and product design trademarks are of importance to the business. Branded generics can be an integral part of these companies. The idea is to maintain relatively high marketing spending even after patent expiration and make use of a strong brand to defend market shares.[28]

A lack of effective IP protection in a country may limit research-based pharmaceutical and biotech companies' operations in such countries.

2.2 Trends

Mergers and acquisitions are of key importance for the research-based pharmaceutical and biotech companies as they leverage value creation. Industry consolidation is

26. *Ibid.*
27. Pfizer, Form 10-K, p. 10.
28. *Ibid.*

steadily progressing with a specific focus on promising platforms or biotechnology solutions in development but not yet marketed. In particular, large multinational companies attempt to make the first move to commercialize breakthrough drugs and customer solutions as described in this section. Tech players try to disrupt certain areas of the life sciences industry and are also keen to enter into collaborations with multinational pharmaceutical companies.

2.2.1 Mergers and Acquisitions

Pharmaceutical companies have been motivated to perform mergers and acquisitions for three main reasons:[29]

(1) Innovation is the engine of the industry. It is specific and detailed as molecules and processes must generally come together to make a single successful drug. In addition, new platform technologies, digital ingenuity, and regulatory and policy expertise are required to meet the latest challenges. Innovation will continue to motivate pharmaceutical companies to acquire smaller, more creative firms – inside and outside the industry.
(2) Economies of scale are key as R&D, manufacturing, and commercialization of drugs are expensive. There has been always pressure on industry players to reduce costs, streamline production and distribution, or reduce in other areas. Acquisitions, mergers, joint ventures, and strategic partnerships are productive ways for companies to efficiently reach economies of scale.
(3) Portfolio realignment is needed to manage product pipelines and mitigate patent cliff risk. Continuous monitoring and calibration of product portfolios are very critical. For example, there might be a need to divest non-core assets to enter into new or adjacent therapeutic areas.

In 2019, the M&A activity in the pharmaceutical sector peaked at USD 414 billion worth of deals around the world. Figure 21.2 shows the deal value in billion USD with an all-time high in 2019 and a sharp drop in 2020 because of the COVID-19 pandemic.[30]

29. Jan Ascher, Roerich Bansal, Ajay Dhankhar and Edward Kim (McKinsey): A New Prescription for M&A in Pharma, September 2020.
30. Includes announced biopharma deals (not withdrawn) with more than USD 25 million in deal value. As of 24 August 2020. Source: Dealogic.

Figure 21.2 Impact of COVID-19 on M&A in Pharmaceutical Sector

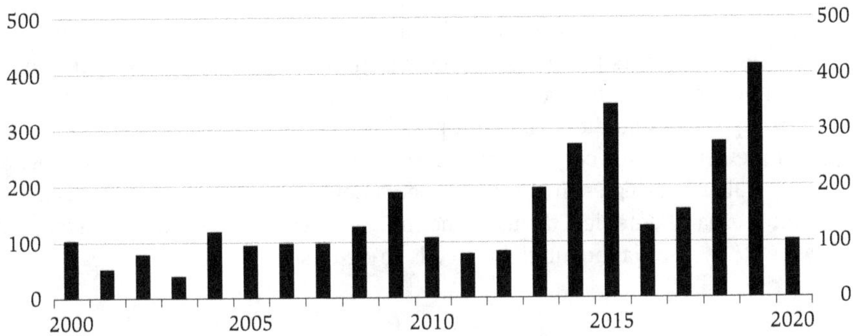

The pharmaceuticals sector more than doubled its global M&A from 2005 to 2019. There is no evidence that this course will slow or change. Despite the sharp pandemic-caused decline in M&A in 2020, the sector is likely to resume its M&A activity sooner rather than later as there is sufficient 'dry powder'. This term refers to the availability of excess cash reserves. Currently, according to various sources, the top dozen global pharmaceutical companies have more than USD 170 billion in M&A dry powder – USD 76 billion in excess cash and USD 94 billion in debt capacity.[31]

2.2.2 *New Market Entrants: Tech Players*

The pace of innovation is being accelerated exponentially through the convergence of scientific disciplines with data science and digital technology. Scientists are increasingly able to address issues directly at the genetic or cellular level by using nature's own techniques. In human and animal health, approaches are proceeding from symptomatic treatment to prevention and cure. Treatments will be increasingly tailored to an individual's condition and genetic makeup.[32]

The following tech players (examples) help to drive innovation:

(1) Alphabet broadly engages in healthcare with its branches:[33]
   - Verily focuses on using data to improve healthcare. It currently works on sensors for continuous monitoring, interventions (e.g., advancing surgical robots), platforms and analytical tools (e.g., for diabetes), precision medicine (e.g., via baselining of genetic data).
   - Calico focuses on learning about and then combating ageing and age-related diseases. The subsidiary uses AI to make sense of large datasets and to automate certain lab processes.

31. McKinsey, A New Prescription for M&A in Pharma, 10 September 2020.
32. MIT, McKinsey, Deloitte.
33. Company website.

- DeepMind is expanding its mobile streams app to become an AI-powered assistant for nurses and doctors to deliver faster, better care everywhere.[34]

(2) Amazon introduced Amazon Pharmacy on the sales channel side which allows customers to purchase prescription medications through the Amazon online store, and PillPack[35] by Amazon Pharmacy helps customers manage multiple daily medications with presorted doses.[36]

(3) Apple sees health care and wellness as a core part of its app, services, and wearables strategies. It has developed a personal health record and is delving into research, medical devices, and more. To what extent Apple will enter into the R&D and diagnostic fields needs to be observed.

2.2.3 Technological Leaps

Technology leaps or radical technological changes describe the replacement of existing technology with a new or game-changing improvement in technology.[37] The following examples are technological leaps in the research-based pharmaceutical and biotech industry that are also digitally impacting the companies operating in that industry.

Computational science is a multidisciplinary field that uses advanced computing capabilities to understand and solve complex problems. At its core, it applies advanced analytics and AI and uses models and simulations to understand non-obvious patterns in complex systems, generate insights, and predict outcomes. Computational science plays a key role in enabling and accelerating novel data-intense technologies. It rationalizes decision making and increases overall R&D process efficiency. It can identify new targets, predict the most effective molecule structures and outcomes, e.g., in humans/plants based on prior in silico, in vitro, and in vivo tests. In the future, differentiation will not be whether computational science is being applied but how well it is being applied (*see* Figure 21.3). Therefore, access to high-quality data and the right talent are key prerequisites.[38]

34. Economist, The World in 2020, Demis Hassabis, Co-Founder and CEO, DeepMind, on the potential of AI.
35. https://techcrunch.com/2018/06/28/amazon-buys-pillpack-an-online-pharmacy-that-was-rumored-to-be-talking-to-walmart/ (last accessed 27 January 2022).
36. Company website and businesswire.com.
37. Schuh, Guo: Technology Leaps: Definition and Framework for Assessing the Potential of Technology Leaps, EJRRMS, Vol. 3 No. 5, 2015.
38. Emerj.com.

Figure 21.3 Computational Science and Its Potential Across the Value Chain

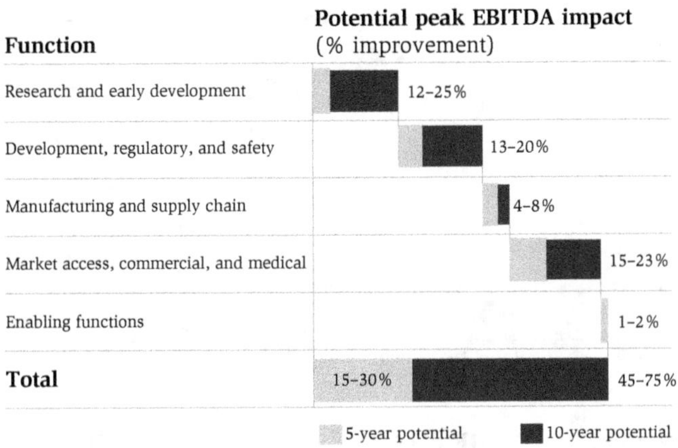

Source: McKinsey analysis (2018) based on blinded client data.

The vision statement of Atom, a public-private consortium, aims to create a paradigm change in drug development: 'Our goal is to transform drug discovery from a slow, sequential, and high-failure process into a rapid, integrated, and patient-centric model. [...] From target to patient-ready in < 1year.'[39]

Bioprinting could address the shortage of human organ transplants. It describes the 3D printing of living tissues and organs with the objective of addressing the global organ transplant shortage in human health but also providing alternative test media in R&D.

Genome editing uses genetic precision tools to make specific changes to a cell's DNA. It has the ability to transform the entire life science industry. In addition, it drives basic research: Switching genes on and off helps to improve the understanding of the role of different genes. CRISPR is currently the leading technique. It is faster, cheaper, and more precise than conventional methods, and does not require other species' genes.[40]

In human health, gene therapy currently focuses on conditions that are caused by a single gene mutation. Today, sixteen cellular and gene therapies are approved by the Food and Drug Administration and many further such as treating several cancer conditions, retinal blinding disorder, immune deficiencies, or haemophilia are in clinical development.[41]

Figure 21.4 shows that the gene therapy world market is expected to grow dramatically (market size in million USD and average growth rate 2017-2028).[42]

39. atomscience.org.
40. SingularityHub, Lux Research, Nature, curia.europe.eu.
41. Alliance for Regenerative Medicine, FDA.gov.
42. Visiongain: Gene Therapy R&D and Revenue Forecasts 2018-2028.

Figure 21.4 Gene Therapy Growth Prediction

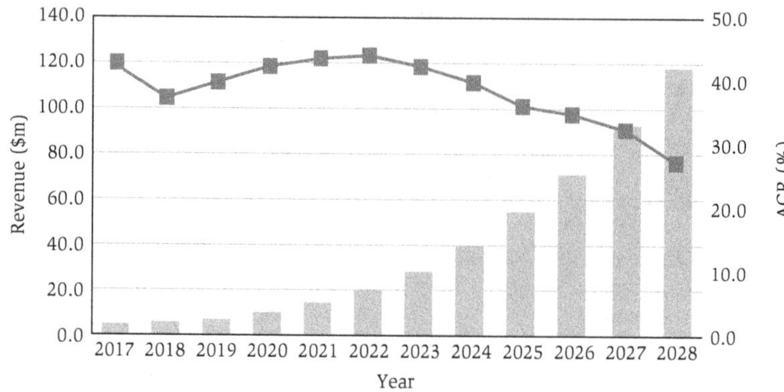

3 TP MATTERS IN THE PHARMACEUTICAL AND LIFE SCIENCE INDUSTRY

This section specifically addresses the key TP aspects of the research-based pharmaceutical and biotech industry, including the operating model and IP ownership, the TP relevant uniqueness of a drug's lifecycle, TP steering peculiarities, and the special digital impact on R&D, marketing, and manufacturing. This section also includes references to TP dedicated court cases and provides examples and context considering the OECD TPG.

3.1 Typical Centralized Operating Model and IP Ownership

Multinationals in the research-based pharmaceutical and biotech industry typically conduct their internal and external R&D in various locations around the world. The primary reasons for this decentralized approach are regulatory requirements, local expertise, and access to the global talent pool. Nevertheless, many companies apply the principles of centralized IP ownership with one or more entrepreneurial legal entities and utilize internal operating business models with one or more local distribution and/or manufacturing entities. There are several non-tax reasons and benefits for using a centralized IP and operating model, e.g., synergies and cost reductions in registrations and in the patent litigation area. It further significantly simplifies unrelated party licensing arrangements (*see* Figure 21.5).[43]

43. *See* section 2.1.1 and Seppo Penttilä & Anita Isomaa-Myllymäki: Centralization of Intangibles and Transfer Pricing under BEPS and Finish Tax Law, Eur. Taxn. Vol. 58 No. 2/3, 2018, Journal Articles & Papers IBFD.

Figure 21.5 Simplified Centralized Operating Model in Pharmaceutical Sector

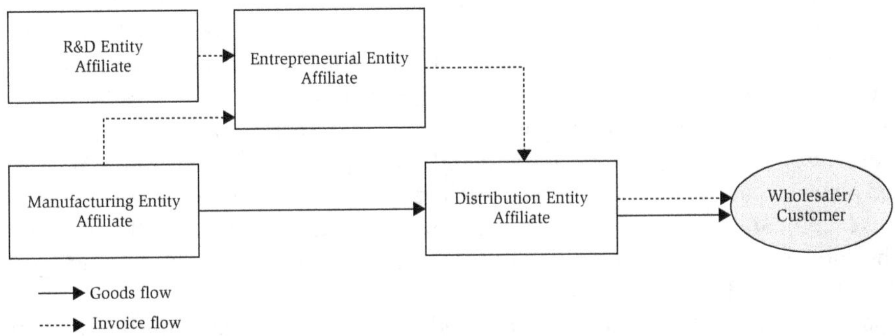

The entrepreneurial legal entity performs and controls key functions (e.g., end-to-end R&D, key decision making, global marketing strategy including product launch plan with all information about the product, and training materials for the local sales force). This central, or often called principal entity, performs and controls all major functions and takes all major risks, especially, e.g., the front-loaded financing risk for R&D (successful and unsuccessful). By that, it economically owns all relevant IP (e.g., patents and brands)[44] and, based on the TP design applied, assumes the residual profit or loss within the supply chain.

The local manufacturing or distribution entity is typically characterized as a low-risk manufacturer or distributor by not bearing any significant risks and therefore earning a low but stable return which is commonly derived based on the TNMM and/or the CPM.[45]

Action 8 of the OECD BEPS Project[46] and Chapter 6 of the OECD TPG have focused on these centralized IP ownership and operating models. The OECD introduced a new concept into the functional analysis that focuses on the DEMPE of IP. The economic ownership of IP in centralized operating models is one of the most controversial topics and often brought scrutiny by tax authorities around the world even before this focus on DEMPE.

3.2 Particularities of the Pharmaceutical Product Lifecycle

3.2.1 From Drug Discovery to Commercialization and the Perception of Profitability

Income statements of research-based pharmaceutical and biotech companies often show very substantial levels of profitability as they 'only' include the results of

44. *See* section 2.1.4.
45. For details about transfer-pricing methodologies, reference is made to, e.g., Chapter II, OECD TPG.
46. OECD, *Action 8-10: Transfer Pricing*, https://www.oecd.org/tax/beps/beps-actions/action8-10/.

successfully approved and launched products. This neglects the fact that R&D expenditures can be a 100% sunk cost and simply may not produce a marketable product at all.[47] Neither past R&D expenses for successful products nor sunk R&D expenses for failed pipeline products can be directly allocated to revenues of marketed products in a single year due to the asynchrony of R&D and commercialization expenses with product sales based on basic accounting principles. The failure of developing marketable products is widely ignored. This is, of course, true for many other industries, however, due to the long R&D lead time and the high expense ratios in the research-based pharmaceutical and biotech industry, the 'distortion effect' of past and sunk R&D cost is incomparably significant. This circumstance could contribute to the perception of the industry as always highly profitable and typically results in scrutiny by tax authorities around the world.[48]

It is worth mentioning that research-based pharmaceutical and biotech companies can have up to one-third of their current expenses not directly allocated to the products currently sold. Consequently, all current R&D expenses need to be continuously covered by all current product sales. Therefore, especially small or start-up biotech companies with limited or no commercialized products are very much dependent on venture capital or other forms of collaboration to fund their R&D programs.[49] In the worst cases, a highly profitable blockbuster product (annual sales of above EUR 1 billion) cannot recoup all R&D costs over the time it is patent-protected and sold on the market.

Example

Company A, located in Country X and Company B, located in Country Y, are part of the ABC Group. Company A continuously funds R&D in the cardiovascular therapeutic area with approximately CU 500 million p.a. Its commercialized product 'Magic' is a p.a. CU 1 billion blockbuster that has been on the market for three years and sold around the world. 'Magic's' patent expires in seven years, and the risk of generic manufacturing is significant. Past R&D expenses for 'Magic' cumulated over twelve years were CU 1.5 billion whereas the sunk cost over the same period for failed products was CU 4.5 billion, resulting in a total loss of CU 6 billion in the cardiovascular area before commercialization of 'Magic'. Taking an oversimplified consolidated view (i.e., without marketing and other expenses), over the twenty-two years from the start of R&D to the patent

47. *See* section 2.1.1 and Deloitte: Ten Years on Measuring the Return from Pharmaceutical Innovation 2019, 2020, 2020.
48. For example, the Australian tax authorities established a cluster where specialized tax authorities focus on the review of transfer-pricing practices of Australian based multinational subsidiaries in the pharmaceutical industry (so-called Pharmaceuticals Cluster). It is worth mentioning that this is the only industry-specific cluster the ATO has established thus far, https://www.ato.gov.au/Business/International-tax-for-business/In-detail/Pharmaceuticals-Cluster/ (last accessed 27 January 2022).
49. Karl Wündisch: Pharmaceutical Industry and Transfer Pricing: Anything Special, ITPJ, Vol. 10 No. 6, November/December 2003, pp. 204ff. and section 2.1.1.

cliff without further commercialization of new products results in a total loss for 'Magic' of CU 1 billion (= Total income of CU 10 billion minus total R&D expenditure of CU 11 billion).

3.2.2 *Patent Cliff and Post-Patent Life*

Patent cliffs refer to the point in time when the patent granted for a product expires. Patent cliffs in the research-based pharmaceutical and biotech industry place enormous pressure on the R&D organization as new product launches are required but rather limited. Patent cliff concerns are common in cases when generic manufacturers enter the market. They are less common for biologics and biotech as large molecule drugs are much more difficult to replicate.[50]

It might be argued that the patent cliff may motivate companies to more closely examine the value drivers of their business as patent expiration might reduce the value of IP and manufacturing. Typically, it is not required to have such a closer review when operating centralized internal business models for which entrepreneurial entities execute key functions, take major risks, and use valuable assets (such as IP). The reason is that entrepreneurial entities continuously fund R&D and receive the residual income from all products in the commercial pipeline. Hence, the principles of residual income allocation are basically not affected by patent expirations.

3.2.3 *Hard-to-Value Intangibles*

Multinationals in the research-based pharmaceutical and biotech industry are typically operating centralized IP structures.[51] To apply such a centralized structure, it is sometimes needed or beneficial to transfer IP between different legal entities in more than one jurisdiction, e.g., as a consequence if IP was acquired from an M&A transaction. Furthermore, these transfers will most likely become even more frequent due to the impact of digitalization and the fact that value chain models are changing faster than ever before.

In terms of BEPS Actions 8-10, the OECD 'invented' the concept of so-called HTVI and provides special guidance.[52] As described in section 2, in the research-based pharmaceutical and biotech industry, it is typically very difficult to predict if currently developed products fail or succeed. This makes the valuation of the underlying IP in development in case of a transfer very difficult, and it is therefore likely that, in many circumstances, IP in this industry must be categorized as HTVI. In its guidance for HTVI, the OECD abandons its principle of applying an *ex ante* perspective at the valuation date and entitles tax authorities to use *ex post* information as a 'pointer' about

50. *See* section 2.1.2.
51. *See* section 3.1.
52. OECD, *Guidance for Tax Administrations on the Application of the Approach to Hard-to-Value Intangibles: BEPS Actions 8-10*, OECD/G20 Base Erosion and Profit Shifting Project (Paris: OECD, 2018).

the arm's length nature of the *ex ante* valuation and proposes to apply a price adjustment clause.[53]

Example (continues from the previous example)

Company A has concluded pre-clinical tests for the compound and has successfully taken it through Phases I and II of the clinical trials. Company A moves the legal and economic ownership of 'Magic' to Company B, in 2021. Company B will be responsible for the Phase III trials following the transfer. In order to determine the price for the patent on the partially developed drug, the parties projected the expected cash flows generated upon commercialization of the drug over the remaining life of the patent. Taking into account the functions performed, risks assumed, and assets used in relation to the compound by Company A and Company B before and after the transaction and by applying the discounted cash flow method, a net present value of CU 700 million was determined and paid in the year of transfer.

The parties assumed sales would not exceed 1,000 doses per year and that commercialization would not commence until 2025. The discount rate was determined by referring to external data showing the risk of failure for drugs in the cardiovascular therapeutic area at the same stage of development. Even if the tax authorities of Country X had been aware of these facts relating to the transfer of the patented drug in 2021, it would have had little means of verifying the reasonableness of the taxpayer's assumptions relating to sales.

Scenario A: In 2024, the tax authorities in Country X audit Company A for the period 2020-2022. The authorities obtain information that commercialization was initiated in 2023 since Phase III trials were completed much earlier than expected. At the time of transfer, sales in 2023 and 2024 were originally projected to be achieved in 2025 and 2026. Company A cannot demonstrate that its original valuation took into account the possibility that sales would begin in earlier periods and cannot demonstrate that such a development was unforeseeable.

The tax authorities use the presumptive evidence provided by the *ex post* outcome to determine that the valuation made at the time the transaction took place did not consider the possibility of sales occurring in earlier years. Company A's original valuation is revised to include the appropriately risk-adjusted possibility of earlier sales resulting in a revised net present value of the drug in 2021 of CU 1 billion instead of CU 700 million. For the purposes of the example, the net present value of CU 1 billion in 2021 is deemed arm's length and results in an additional income of CU 300 million (i.e., +43%).

Scenario B: Like Scenario A, however, CU 800 million instead of CU 1 billion is deemed at arm's length. This results in an additional income of CU 100 million

53. Paragraphs 6.187-6.193, OECD TPG.

(i.e., +14%). The exemption to the income adjustment provided by item (iii) in paragraph 6.193 of Chapter VI applies since the adjusted sales price is within 20% of the compensation determined at the time of the transaction. Hence, under the OECD TPG for the HTVI, Country Y's tax authorities would not be allowed to adjust the income from CU 700 to EUR 800 million. Even if the revised sales price was CU 840 million, the 20% exemption would remain valid.

In order to mitigate the situation of Scenario A, the use of the suggested price adjustment clauses can typically be observed and, if the transfer of IP has a significant value, the application of a bilateral or multilateral APA can also be considered although, in many jurisdictions, it can be time- and resource-consuming while providing a risk mitigation measure.[54]

Overall, it can be expected that, even after the additional guidance, the transfer of IP in the research-based pharmaceutical and biotech industry remains a hot and controversial topic in tax audits around the globe. In addition to the challenge of how to deal with uncertainty and risks, it can be difficult to balance specific valuation rules in the country of the seller and in the country of the buyer as different valuation standards may apply. Emphasis should therefore be placed on the argumentation and documentation of certain key valuation parameters that have been chosen (e.g., internal or external WACC, WACC to WARA) and ensure conceptual consistency regarding *ex ante* income expectations, reflection of risks/uncertainty, discount factors, and *ex post* oriented measures such as price adjustment clauses.[55] The HTVI regulations are still quite new, and practical experience is limited. There is a concern that tax authorities will likely attempt to classify a significant portion of intangibles as HTVI and will adjust these transactions in hindsight by disregarding past and sunk R&D costs linked to a successfully approved and launched product.[56] This would add to additional controversy including mutual agreement procedures.

3.2.4 *Marketing Intangibles*

Discussions around marketing intangibles in the research-based pharmaceutical and biotech industry refer to a peculiarity of the industry, specifically, that the customer is not typically the patient who purchases the drugs. Marketing compiles the following key activities:[57]

- highly skilled and educated scientific sales forces visit doctors to describe the added value of pharmaceutical products (so-called detailing); and
- promotional spending in the medical community (e.g., by sponsoring congresses) and direct consumer promotional campaigns.

54. Paragraph 6.193, 2017 OECD TPG.
55. Andreas Riedl, Kai Schwinger: How to Deal with Risk in the Context of Two-Sided IP Valuations after BEPS?, ITPJ, Vol. 25 No. 6, November/December 2018, p. 454.
56. *See* sections 2.1.1 and 3.2.1.
57. Reference is made to digital Impact on the marketing function, section 3.4.

This type of marketing is very expensive in relation to the amounts spent in other industries. This is also why some tax authorities tend to qualify such local marketing activities as marketing intangibles. From an industry-specific viewpoint, such marketing and promotional activities are required based on how the pharmaceutical business model is embedded in the regulatory framework of a country. Therefore, relatively high local budgets for marketing and promotion are routine costs of conducting business in this industry. This typically translates into the following key TP considerations for distribution entities:

- functional profile: Local know-how and promotional plans derive from globally existing resources and usage but not ownership of product-related IP (e.g., patent, brand, and know-how) and mere responsibility to sell the product locally; and
- TP methodology: the TNMM guarantees local distribution entities a low but stable profit (despite the risk of post-commercialization failure of the product).

Accordingly, based on the functions performed, risks taken, and assets used by the entrepreneur and local low-risk distribution entity, if marketing intangibles existed, they would not belong to the local distribution entity although this entity employs a strong and highly academic sales force, has local executives who decide on local marketing and promotion spend, and negotiations with local health organizations' bodies. Still, in order not to neglect local value add compared to mere wholesalers, important people functions and market access are key considerations to synthetically include an additional profit element in a standard benchmarking analysis to determine an arm's length return under the TNMM. A so-called synthetic approach can take into account the marketing cost/sales ratio to calculate a profit element to be added to the standard wholesaler profitability. This is a generally accepted approach as the set of comparable entities deriving from benchmarking studies typically do not list specific pharmaceutical distribution entities that include the marketing activities referred to above in this section.

Court Case[58]

On 11 September 2006, GlaxoSmithKline announced the settlement of a long-lasting dispute with the IRS involving a payment of USD 3.1 billion. Glaxo attempted to solve the dispute via alternative means but was refused an APA with the IRS and relief from the IRS and UK Inland Revenues. During the years at issue, Glaxo US was the distributor of certain Glaxo products in the US patented by the Glaxo Group in the UK. In terms of intra-group transactions, Glaxo US was purchasing the active ingredients from Glaxo UK and licensed-in the right to distribute the Glaxo products. Transfer prices for the goods and licence were established by applying the resale minus methodology. The IRS argued that

58. BNA, 14 April 2004, Glaxo fights USD 7.8 billion in Allocations, Seeks USD 1 Billion Refund for Discrimination.

trademarks and marketing intangibles were developed by Glaxo US in the US since the Glaxo products were first sold there, and such trademarks and marketing intangibles were provided at no cost to Glaxo UK. Therefore, the IRS used a profit split methodology applied to the residual profit by assessing the contributions of Glaxo US and Glaxo UK. There is no information about how the IRS applied the profit split method. The case was settled with a compromise by not fully following the argumentation of the IRS nor the argumentation of Glaxo. The critical success factor, on the one side, was the argument that the outstanding sales performance of the Glaxo product, Zantac, was largely attributable to the marketing performed in the US and, on the other side, Zantac as a pioneer drug should have been allocated to the success of R&D.

'Marketing intangibles' continue to have the potential for TP disputes arising between the taxpayer and tax authorities with respect to different interpretations, misunderstandings, and perspectives on what creates value. The Glaxo case is a good example of incongruent opinions of what drives value in the taxpayers' group of companies and more generally in the pharmaceutical industry. From the authors' perspective, applying a profit split methodology would require a full value chain contribution analysis, particularly including R&D, manufacturing, and marketing. Only considering the value of marketing seems unbalanced. A significant amount of marketing expenses per se or the industry-specific detailing does not justify the qualification as a marketing intangible. The synthetic approach applied in benchmarking studies is a pragmatic way to locally appreciate the added marketing value.

Referring to 'marketing intangibles', the OECD TPG do not specifically name pharmaceutical specific detailing nor the synthetic approach as instruments for higher remunerations but generally acknowledge that, 'in some cases, a distributor may perform functions, use assets or assume risks that exceed those an unrelated party distributor with similar rights might incur' and also refer to 'higher distribution profits' in such cases.[59]

3.3 TP Steering Peculiarities

Steering transfer prices in regulated markets is difficult as internationally accepted and applied TP methodologies may clash with prices set by governmental bodies.

Increasing public healthcare costs because of gradually realized megatrends such as population growth, ageing, and an increase in chronic diseases continuously places pressure on the research-based pharmaceutical and biotech industry. Healthcare reforms targeting the reduction of overall pharmaceutical spending are even increasing the pressure. Many governments use price controls to reduce drug prices and, with this, manage and balance expenditures of their healthcare system,[60] however, these

59. Paragraph 6.78, OECD TPG.
60. *See* exemplary and, most recently, China: Bloomberg News, Drugmakers Agree to Halve Prices to Secure Access to China, 28 December 2020.

controls decrease a pharmaceutical company's revenues and profits.[61] The OECD TPG do acknowledge, 'nevertheless, it is quite obvious that a country with price controls must take into account that those price controls will affect the profits that can be realized by enterprises selling goods subject to those controls'.[62]

Price controls in the research-based pharmaceutical and biotech industry effectuate another industry peculiarity referred to as parallel imports. These occur when pharmaceutical patent-protected and branded products are sold into one country with a low product price and then imported through third-party wholesalers into another country with a higher product price in the same market (e.g., EU). Parallel imports are a consequence of the principle of free movement of goods and services agreed on between countries to strengthen the markets of an entire region (i.e., economic zones) such as the European Union.[63] These imports have a considerable effect on the market share of sales by the MNEs of the same medicine in one country (*see* Figure 21.6).

Figure 21.6 Share of Parallel Imports in Pharmacy Market Sales in the EU in 2018[64]

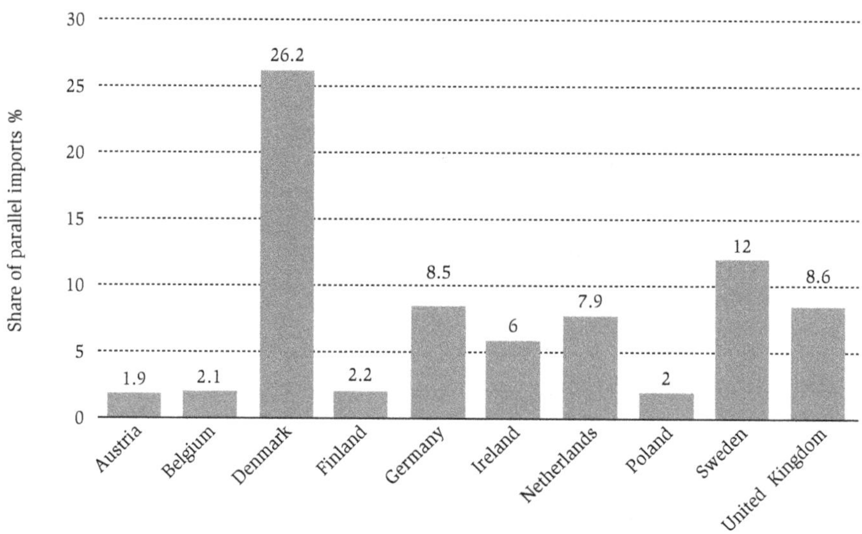

Parallel imports can have the following major impacts on TP:

- reduction of residual profitability on the level of entrepreneurial group entities when the internal business model qualifies the local distribution entities as low-risk distributors; and

61. Wündisch: Pharmaceutical Industry and Transfer Pricing: Anything Special, ITPJ 2003, pp. 204ff.
62. Paragraph 1.132f, OECD TPG.
63. Wündisch, Pharmaceutical Industry and Transfer Pricing: Anything Special, ITPJ 2003, pp. 204ff.
64. Statista 2020, Share of parallel imports in pharmacy market sales in selected European countries in 2018. Note that UK left the EU.

- application of the comparable uncontrolled price methodology as the third-party wholesaler imports the same product as the local affiliate distribution entity from the same company.

3.4 Digital Impact

Digital technology has enabled the healthcare industry to provide solutions that are more targeted and effective to patients worldwide. Digitalization will most likely impact and change the entire value and supply chain of pharmaceutical and biotech companies. This includes the enhancement of the R&D process, detection of diseases through screening, image diagnostic based on AI, and machine learning. This is coupled with digital at-home diagnostics, remote patient support by telehealth and digital communities, supply of therapies to customers through digital pharmacies, and supply-chain solutions for medical supply.[65]

Internal business models need to be calibrated and potentially changed to integrate digital technology and its value contribution. Therefore, TP in the research-based pharmaceutical and biotech industry is increasingly impacted by digital technology. The availability of big data, market entry of digitally creative start-ups, and the rapid growth of digital marketplaces particularly impact R&D and marketing. A critical success factor to expand digital technology in this industry is the protection of patients' data.

R&D

As referred to in section 2.1.1, R&D costs have been sharply increasing over the last ten years with declining ROI rates. This is an unsustainable trend. The integration of digital technology into the R&D process, specifically the designing and conducting of clinical trials, can help to improve R&D productivity, bring its costs under control, and generate returns on investments on a sustainable level. Relevant digital technology includes automating processes, efficiently using big new data sets, and powerful predictive analytics as well as statistical models to support early decision making.[66]

Data generated by numerous clinical trials performed worldwide can be very useful for scientific purposes. Patients can voluntarily grant access to their health records for scientific purposes. If allowed by data protection rights such (anonymized) personal data could be centrally stored via cloud solutions on servers abroad.[67] Such central storage of worldwide patient data would be highly beneficial for R&D productivity as highly skilled central R&D and technology teams can use big population data sets to run predictive analytics to already target a drug candidate's registration in as many countries as possible. Basically, data is subject to the laws and governance structures within the country where it is collected. Therefore, making use of, for instance, a set of

65. Daniel Cohen, Amy Hung, Eli Weinberg and Dandi Zhu (McKinsey): Healthtech in the Fast Lane: What Is Fueling Investor Excitement?, December 2020.
66. ICON, How digital transformation can reverse declining ROI, 2019 and *see* section 2.2.3, computational science.
67. Oestreicher, Muntermann, Schwager, ifst-Schrift 537, 2020.

data from Japanese and Korean patients in the US typically fails based on data protection rights. Hence, the usage of personal data, as long as it is not voluntarily shared by patients, remains local and, for the time being, has no TP relevance.

Outlook: What Could Be the Consequences from a Tax and TP Perspective?

As described, digital transformation might significantly impact the speed and efficiency of R&D. This could change the traditional value driver landscape in the industry such as if the value contribution analysis within R&D needs to be distinguished between elements that can be traced back to the traditional activity in the lab and the digital component of the development process.

In addition, if the digital transformation is able to significantly reduce the R&D lead time, the 'distortion effect' in the P/L described in section 3.2.1 regarding past and sunk R&D costs might be reduced.

A third interesting concern in the R&D area could be the question of IP ownership. The digital transformation will make the R&D activity and the availability of data more location independent. For example, simulation in the computational science field and centrally available data do not require localization of activities to detect differences in specific populations. Breaking this nexus of localization might reduce the functional profile of a local affiliate entity engaging in R&D as it is more difficult to define its contribution to the overall drug candidate success. The reduced local functional contribution to value creation typically distributes profit to where the control and use of centrally available data take place. Besides assessing the value of captured data, questions such as who owns the data, develops and controls advanced analytics and AI, uses models and simulations to understand non-obvious patterns in complex systems, generates insights, and predicts outcomes would need to be determined. Digital technology might be able to fully centralize IP relevant functions in one country and make the just recently implemented DEMPE concept[68] somewhat redundant.

Marketing and Sales

The digital disruption of the marketing and sales channels in the market for prescription drugs is less advanced compared to other industries. However, in a market that is increasingly driven by outcomes and personalized therapies, the mastery of digital technologies will be essential for generating sales.[69] Direct patient engagement is a critical success factor for enabling a positive outcome for e-commerce and digital marketplaces that allow selling prescription drugs to customers. The most prominent example where disruption of established sales channels through online pharmacies can be seen in the US where following, the acquisition of Pillpack,[70] Amazon most recently launched Amazon Pharmacy.

In many countries, there are strong barriers to entering the B2C market for prescription drugs because of extensive regulation and lobbying power of established

68. *See* section 3.1.
69. ICON, How digital transformation can reverse declining ROI, 2019.
70. *See* section 2.2.2.

organizations (e.g., pharmacy associations).[71] Nevertheless, the e-commerce giant Amazon building a digital pharmacy marketplace in the US allows rapid roll-out to other markets as soon as regulatory authorities allow opening such markets. This should not be underestimated. Cost pressure on health systems might motivate authorities to open markets for more price competition potentially leading to a significant change in the structure and value drivers in the marketing and sales area. In addition, increased online sales for prescription drugs would afford an opportunity for ordering drugs in County A with a ship-to destination in Country B.[72]

Manufacturing

In general, there is no specific differentiation in the manufacturing process of the research-based pharmaceutical and biotech industry compared to other industries regarding digital technology. Direct machinery communication (internet of things) allows for making manufacturing processes more efficient and further developing relatively new existing technologies already in use to the next level (e.g., bioprinting using 3D printing) will increase efficiency. Supply security is a key value proposition in the research-based pharmaceutical and biotech industry. This is particularly true for large and complex manufacturing processes. Fully integrated supply chains are fundamental and manufacturing sites are already partly fully connected. The impact of digitalization on manufacturing is relatively low compared to R&D and marketing from a TP perspective.[73]

3.5 OECD Pillar One: Should the Pharmaceutical Industry Be in Scope?

The pharmaceutical industry is prominently discussed in the tax policy debate around the new OECD Pillar One taxation concept for digital business.[74] It is generally highly debatable if the industry in its current form qualifies as customer-facing as there is no cross-border digitalized sales channel directly to patients. Marketing and sales for prescription drugs are performed through local distribution entities directly engaging with doctors. This section will not discuss the elements of the Pillar One concept in detail, however, it will highlight a flaw of the allocation-based concept that partly moves away from the arm's length principle. The idea that is conceptually based on a partial reallocation of the residual profit in a specific year fully neglects the front-loaded and lengthy R&D process and the described distortion of the income statement of pharmaceutical companies.[75]

Cutting the returns of the investment but not its cost is against any economic investment principle. Assuming the application of a centralized operating and IP

71. Depending on local regulatory conditions. Currently, Amazon Pharmacy offers in the US only. *See also* section 2.2.2, tech players.
72. With potentially similar consequences as for parallel imports described in section 3.3.
73. Oestreicher, Muntermann, Schwager, ifst-Schrift 537, 2020.
74. OECD (2020), *Tax Challenges Arising from Digitalisation: Report on Pillar One Blueprint: Inclusive Framework on BEPS*, OECD/G20 Base Erosion and Profit Shifting Project (Paris: OECD Publishing, https://doi.org/10.1787/beba0634-en).
75. *See* section 3.2.1.

ownership model with one entity that controls and funds the entire R&D process, the formulary apportionment of the residual profit based on the logic of the Pillar One concept negatively impacts this central entity in an unbalanced manner and places additional pressure on the ROI ratio.

In addition, it could be argued that, in the pharmaceutical industry, there is no 'need' to apply an additional reallocation of residual profit measure towards the distribution entities as many companies apply the so-called synthetic approach that essentially already provides an extra profit element to the market jurisdictions.[76]

4 CONCLUSION

This chapter provided insight into the value creation and TP in the research-based pharmaceutical and biotech industry by introducing how important this innovative industry is for providing solutions for the challenges of tomorrow. The industry can be considered a spotlight industry regarding TP matters because of its laser focus on IP and often erroneously perceived overall profitability. This chapter concludes by highlighting the key significant elements and discussion points.

Value creation in the industry has been introduced by describing why the following key value drivers are of special importance and how they contribute to IP for patents and brands as the industry's key asset:

- continuous and relentless R&D with very limited breakthrough success;
- highly skilled and expensive marketing efforts to accelerate time to maximize sales in a limited patent-protected period; and
- complex manufacturing practices.

Further industry consolidation through intense M&A targeting a promising platform or biotechnology solutions in development but not yet marketed and new market entrance of tech players will very likely disrupt certain areas and show the high degree of competition within the industry.

TP matters in the industry have been introduced by providing an overview of how multinationals in the research-based pharmaceutical and biotech industry typically construct the internal operating and IP model. Applying the principles of centralized operating internal business models with one or more entrepreneurial legal entities and local low-risk distribution and/or manufacturing entities where the TNMM and/or CPLM are applied allows consolidating economic IP ownership and residual profit allocation for the entrepreneurial legal entities.

Based on these fundamentals, it has been analysed why the following specific and controversial topics are key transfer-pricing matters for the research-based pharmaceutical and biotech industry:

76. *See* section 3.2.4.

(1) The 'distortion effect' of past and sunk R&D costs keeps the R&D risk for entrepreneurial entities incomparably high and justifies pocketing the relatively substantial residual profit upon product commercialization. The idea of reallocating the residual profit in a specific year under OECD Pillar One fully neglects the 'distortion effect' and is therefore widely disregarding how value in this industry is created.
(2) The significant relevance of continuously overcoming the patent cliff and the relatively low relevance that the same has for the construction and operation of centralized operating models.
(3) The potential characterization of IP as HTVI, valuation risk-mitigating measures, and the additional controversy risk that the OECD TPG on the HTVI might bring.
(4) The Glaxo case as the most prominent in TP case law history highlights the controversy around marketing intangibles. Applying a 'synthetic benchmarking approach' allows low-risk distribution entities to earn comparably more for performing industry-specific detailing and promotional activities.

It has been further identified what the TP steering peculiarities in the industry are and how governmentally enforced pricing controls override the concept of the most appropriate TP methods. The problem resulting from pricing controls around parallel imports has been analysed.

An outlook of why and how digital technology can impact the industries' key value-driving functions has also been provided. Digital technology might accelerate the speed and efficiency of R&D which could positively impact the 'distortion effect', challenge the status quo of IP ownership, value contribution, and the DEMPE concept. Currently, there are less disruptive consequences on marketing with digitally enabled technology compared to other industries because of market regulations. However, targeting therapies that are more personalized and outcome-based will likely bring disruptive changes in the future. In the US, Amazon Pharmacy has recently begun selling prescription drugs online but not yet cross-border, however, if regulations allowed, this would effectuate similar digital tax questions that the tech giant is confronted with already today.

This chapter concludes by critically challenging the current inclusion of pharmaceutical companies into the scope of the new OECD Pillar One taxation concept.

Regions

CHAPTER 22
Transfer Pricing in Brazil

Andrea Costa Chaves[*] & *Gabriela Capristano Cardoso*[**]

* The chapter was written in the author's personal capacity and does not reflect any official opinion or position of the Brazilian Tax Authority.

** This chapter was finalized before the author joined the OECD and the opinions expressed in it are the author's and do not reflect those of the Organisation, or its Member countries.

1 INTRODUCTION

TP in Brazil is known for the use of fixed margins. The purpose of this chapter is neither to defend nor criticize Brazil's tax policy but rather to provide technical material to assist in comprehending Brazilian TP rules and how they operate in its integrality beyond the fixed margins. The overview of the country's practice is well presented in the UN TPM including a section on Strengths and Weaknesses of The Brazilian Methods with Predetermined Profit Margins. It is a relevant source of information on the rationale for Brazilian TP policy.[1]

The aim of the chapter is to provide a broad perspective of Brazilian TP legislation. It presents the scope and concepts attached to the law and its regulations and includes examples of how to apply the different TP methods. Accordingly, section 2 summarizes the rationale for adopting TP rules and for its subsequent evolution; section 3 presents Brazilian TP rules and provides examples of how they operate; section 4 presents rules that apply instead of TP control; section 5 provides a brief description of Brazil's TP position on DTCs; and, finally, section 6 draws conclusions from Brazilian TP rules.

2 RATIONALE AND EVOLUTION OF TP RULES

In 1996, Brazilian TP rules were introduced with a law proposal that intended to complement Laws 9,249 and 9,250, both from 1995, that aimed to modernize the income tax legislation.[2] More specifically, Articles 18-24 of Law 9,430[3] of 1996 are the legal basis for TP legislation in Brazil. The explanatory statement[4] clarifies that the law was introduced to modernize the Brazilian legislation to be better suited for globalization. It further states that TP rules aim 'to avoid the practice, harmful to national interests, of transferring results abroad, by manipulating the prices agreed upon in the importation or exportation of goods, services, or rights, in operations with related persons, residents or domiciled abroad'.

At the time that Law 9,430/1996 entered into force in January 1997, the OECD had not yet published the OECD TPG in the format as it is currently known. The 1979 OECD Report on Transfer Pricing and Multinational Enterprises[5] (the 1979 OECD Report) was

1. *See* Aurélio Pereira Valadão, M., Brazil Country Practices (Part D: Country Practices of the UN TPM), pp. 527-545.
2. *See* Explanatory Statement of the law proposal, paras 2 and 3 (in Portuguese), p. 113, available at, https://www.camara.leg.br/proposicoesWeb/prop_mostrarintegra;jsessionid=3E191F1E955D0EE13B0A33FA27FE0135.proposicoesWebExterno2?codteor=1132081&filename=Dossie+-PL+2448/1996 (last accessed 30 January 2022).
3. Law 9,430/1996 (modified by Law 12,715/2012), (in Portuguese), available at, http://www.planalto.gov.br/ccivil_03/leis/l9430.htm (last accessed 30 January 2022).
4. *Supra* n. 2, paras 111-123.
5. OECD, *Transfer Pricing and Multinational Enterprises* (Paris: OECD Publishing, 1979), https://doi.org/10.1787/9789264167773-en (last accessed 30 January 2022).

approved by the OECD Council in July 1995 and supplemented by the Report on IP and Services that was adopted in April 1996.[6] Therefore, it is likely that the Brazilian TP legislation was inspired by the 1979 OECD Report considering the legislative process timeline to the approval of Law 9,430/1996 and the OECD work regarding TP up to the publication of the first version of the OECD TPG in 2009. This could explain the reason for the Brazilian law only having traditional methods and its regulation being focused primarily on tangible goods. It is worth noting that Brazilian tax law already had the longstanding limitation for deductions on outbound expenses of royalties and technical, scientific, administrative, or similar assistance which explains why these transactions are out of the scope of TP rules in Brazil.[7]

Since 1996, there had been no change in TP law aimed to keep pace with the evolution of the OECD TPG. However, a number of modifications in the Brazilian TP framework were introduced mostly in connection to disputes submitted to the administrative tax court. Taxpayers in Brazil have the constitutional right to submit to the judiciary any violation of a right,[8] including if such violation derives from the Brazilian tax authorities'[9] tax assessments. In addition to this constitutional right, the tax law has a two-level dispute resolution process that judges appeal to cases involving federal taxes or contributions, including TP cases. The first level consists of specialized units within the tax administration, while the second level is within the Ministry of Finance.[10] The tax appeal, both in the first and second levels, suspends tax collection which may create an incentive for the taxpayer to always appeal to the administrative court against every tax assessment.

The second level is the Administrative Council for Tax Appeals, known by its Portuguese acronym CARF, a collegiate body that judges the most relevant cases. It is important to note that most pertinent TP cases judged by the CARF from 2004 to 2018 corresponded to disputes related to tax assessments of the taxable years from 1997 to 2010. Consequently, there is no CARF decision until 2018 involving the TP law as it currently stands, including no case on the use of the commodities method (*see* section 3.2.5), as the last legal change in this regard entered into force in 2013. Further, there were very few disputes involving loans and a smaller number on export transactions. In contrast, most disputes brought before the CARF (which influenced later changes in TP legislation) related to the freedom to select the PRL[11] method for the sale of

6. *See* Foreword, p. 3, OECD TPG.
7. *See* Articles 52 and 71 of the Law 4,506/1964 (in Portuguese), available at, http://www.planalto.gov.br/ccivil_03/LEIS/L4506.htm#art71 (last accessed 30 January 2022).
8. *See* Article 5, item XXXV, Constitution of Federative Republic of Brazil, available at, https://www2.senado.leg.br/bdsf/bitstream/handle/id/243334/Constitution_2013.pdf?sequence = 11&isAllowed = y (last accessed 30 January 2022).
9. *Secretaria Especial da Receita Federal do Brasil*, in Portuguese, is the Brazilian Tax Administration (in English, The Special Secretariat of the Federal Revenue of Brazil), and is a Secretariat belonging to the structure of the Ministry of Finance.
10. *See* Article 25 of Decree 70,235/1972 (in Portuguese), available at, http://www.planalto.gov.br/ccivil_03/decreto/D70235cons.htm (last accessed 30 January 2022).
11. Acronym for *Preços de Revenda menos Lucro* in Portuguese, Brazil's equivalent to the RPM for import transactions.

imported goods that were processed in Brazil prior to resale (*see* section 3.2.4.2) and to the burden of proof associated with the selection of the method (*see* section 3.2.1).

In this respect, Law 9,959/2000 introduced a change to the PRL providing for a new fixed profit margin for goods imported to serve as raw material for production in Brazil, while maintaining the existing margin for resale without any processing in Brazil. Similarly, Law 12,715/2012 also attempted to resolve issues arising from disputes, including a new change on the PRL, and more target rules regarding freight, insurance, and import taxes.[12] However, its main innovation was the introduction of the commodities method equivalent to the CUP method (*see* section 3.2.5).

Finally, it is worth mentioning that in December 2019, Brazil and the OECD published an assessment of similarities and divergences between the Brazilian TP framework and the OECD TPG, including options for the alignment of the Brazilian TP rules with the OECD TPG.[13] Notwithstanding, no change in legislation has yet happened.

3 DESCRIPTION OF THE RULES

TP rules in Brazil deviate from the OECD TPG mainly because it uses (i) the freedom of selection of the method instead of using the most appropriate method approach, (ii) the methods equivalent to the RPM and CPM make use of fixed margins, and (iii) there are prescriptive rules for loans. In addition, only traditional methods are available, and they differ for import and export transactions.

3.1 Scope of TP Legislation

TP in Brazil applies to cross-border transactions involving goods, services, and rights which are three distinctive and broad concepts in the legal framework of Brazil. Notwithstanding the broad nature of the scope, outbound expenses of royalties and technical, scientific, administrative, or similar assistance are excluded from TP control and, instead, special rules apply to limit the deduction of those payments. Additionally, there is a specific rule for loans based on publicly available interest rates.

Example

Company A, located in Country X, is the parent company of the ABC Group, and Company B, located in Brazil, is a subsidiary of the same group. Company B

12. In this regard, between 2009 and 2013, the CARF consolidated the view that those expenses, when supported by the Brazilian importer, should be included in the transfer pricing calculation.
13. *See* Transfer Pricing in Brazil Towards Convergence with the OECD Standard: A Joint Assessment of the Similarities and Differences Between the Brazilian and OECD Frameworks, pp. 238-286, available at, http://www.oecd.org/tax/transfer-pricing/transfer-pricing-in-brazil-towards-convergence-with-the-oecd-standard.pdf (last accessed 5 August 2020).

receives technical assistance from Company A. The payment for this service is not subject to TP rules in Brazil but to special rules limiting its deductibility. If instead, Company B would provide technical assistance to Company A, this transaction would be subject to TP in Brazil as inbound technical services fees are not excluded from TP control.

Regarding the related party concept, Brazilian law provides for hypotheses when there are control, participation and decision powers and for others when there is implied power to influence pricing policy. More specifically, for Brazilian TP purposes, the concept of a related party regarding the corporate income taxpayer resident in Brazil consists of a taxpayer resident abroad that:

(i) controls it, direct or indirectly, including its parent company;[14]
(ii) participates in its interest and has a significant influence on its decisions. A significant influence is presumed if the participation is 20% or more of interest share with voting rights;[15]
(iii) is controlled by the taxpayer resident in Brazil;
(iv) the taxpayer resident in Brazil participates in its interest and has a significant influence on the decisions of the taxpayer resident abroad;
(v) are under common control or at least 10% of the interest of each taxpayer belongs to the same individual or entity;
(vi) participates together with the corporate income taxpayer resident in Brazil in the capital of a third entity, and their participation characterizes them as controllers or having a significant influence on the decisions of this third entity;
(vii) is an associate in a consortium or condominium in any business, as defined in Brazilian law;[16]
(viii) enjoys exclusivity as its agent, distributor, or concessionaire for the purchase and sale of goods, services, or rights;
(ix) the taxpayer resident in Brazil enjoys exclusivity as its agent, distributor, or concessionaire for the purchase and sale of goods, services, or rights.

Moreover, the related party concept includes the subsidiaries and branches of the corporate income taxpayer resident in Brazil that are located in foreign countries. An individual resident abroad in the situations described in items i, ii, vi, vii, viii, and ix is considered a related party. In addition, any individual relative to the third degree,

14. For the concept of control, *see* Article 243(2) of the Law 6,404/1976 (in Portuguese), available at, http://www.planalto.gov.br/ccivil_03/LEIS/L6404consol.htm (last accessed 30 January 2022).
15. For the legal concept of participation with significant influence and the legal presumption, *see* Article 243(1)(4)(5) of the Law 6,404/1976, available at, http://www.planalto.gov.br/ccivil_03/LEIS/L6404consol.htm (last accessed 30 January 2022).
16. For the consortium concept in Brazilian Law, *see* Articles 278 and 279 of the Law 6,404/1976, *Ibid*. For the condominium concept, *see* Articles 1314-1358-U, Chapter VI, of the Law 10,406/2002, Brazilian Civil Code (in Portuguese), available at, http://www.planalto.gov.br/ccivil_03/LEIS/L6404consol.htm (last accessed 30 January 2022).

including by affinity, spouse, or companion of directors or a direct or indirect controller of the corporate income taxpayer resident in Brazil is a related party for Brazilian TP purposes.

Finally, cross-border transactions between an individual or an entity resident in Brazil and an individual or an entity located in a jurisdiction with a favourable income tax or a privileged tax regime beneficiary are subject to TP control. The law considers a country or its dependency as a favourable income tax jurisdiction when the income tax rate is less than 20% or its legislation forbids access to information related to participation and ownership of entities or identification of the beneficiary of non-resident income. The legal concept of privileged tax regime encompasses at least one of four features, two of which are identical to the definition of a jurisdiction with favourable income tax. The additional features prescribed in the law to qualify a privileged tax regime are the following: (i) the granting of tax advantages to a non-resident without substantive economic activity in the jurisdiction; or (ii) the taxation of income earned abroad with a tax rate of less than 20%. The Brazilian Tax Administration[17] publishes a list of jurisdictions with favourable income tax[18] and a list of privileged tax regimes.[19]

3.2 TP Methods and Selection of the Method

TP methods in Brazil are designed for export and import transactions. Import transactions use the following methods: *Preços Independentes Comparados* (PIC), *Preço sob Cotação na Importação* (PCI), *Preços de Revenda menos Lucro* (PRL) and *Custo de Produção mais Lucro* (CPL). For export transactions, the following methods may apply: *Preço de Venda nas Exportações* (PEVEX); *Preço sob Cotação na Exportação* (PECEX), *Preço de Venda por Atacado no País de Destino Diminuído do Lucro* (PVA), *Preço de Venda a Varejo no País de Destino Diminuído do Lucro* (PVV) and *Custo de Aquisição ou de Produção mais Tributos e Lucro* (CAP). Although nine methods are available in the Brazilian TP legislation, they are similar to the three traditional methods recognized by the OECD TPG and by the UN TPM, as presented below in Table 22.1 – Correspondence of OECD and UN Traditional Methods and Brazilian TP Methods.

17. The Special Secretariat of Federal Revenue of Brazil (RFB).
18. *See* Article 1 of the RFB Normative Instruction 1,037/2010 for the list of jurisdictions with favourable income tax (in Portuguese), available at, http://normas.receita.fazenda.gov.br/sijut2consulta/link.action?visao=anotado&idAto=16002 (last accessed 30 January 2022).
19. For the list of jurisdictions with favourable income tax regime (in Portuguese), *see* Article 2 of the RFB Normative Instruction 1,037/2010, available at, http://normas.receita.fazenda.gov.br/sijut2consulta/link.action?visao=anotado&idAto=16002 (last accessed 30 January 2022).

Table 22.1 Correspondence of OECD and UN Traditional Methods and Brazilian TP Methods

OECD Traditional Methods	*Import Methods*	*Export Methods*
CUP	PIC	PEVEX
	PCI	PECEX
RPM	PRL	PVA
		PVV
CPM	CPL	CAP

3.2.1 *The Freedom of Selection of Methods*

Taxpayers applying TP in Brazil are free to select any applicable method even if it will result in the lowest adjustment of the taxable base. The freedom of selection of methods differs from the OECD and UN's most appropriate method approach. As an exception, this freedom does not apply to commodities transactions for which the methods PCI for import transactions and PECEX for export transactions are mandatory (*see* section 3.2.5) or for loans (*see* section 3.2.6) for which the law specifies the reference tax rate, and the Ministry of Finance establishes the acceptable spread.

It is important to note that the first normative instruction in this respect in Brazil,[20] which has the status of secondary legislation, established some guidance on the appropriateness of the methods and stated that the equivalent to the RPM for importation (i.e., PRL) was not applicable for import transactions whenever the final product was produced using the imported good, service, or right. However, there were many disputes brought before the administrative court in this respect, and the jurisprudence confirmed the position that, as the secondary legislation could not contradict the law that did not impose any restriction on the methods or preference among them, the taxpayer could select any TP method.

The choice of the method needs to be on the tax return and all of the calculations and supporting documents must be available in the case of a tax assessment. If a choice is made by the taxpayer, the tax authorities should restrict the analysis to the calculation presented and determine if it conforms to the TP legislation.[21] Moreover, the tax authorities bear the burden of proof that the taxpayer failed to substantiate the application of the chosen method. If that is the case or if the taxpayer's tax return does

20. *See* Article 4 of the SRF Normative Instruction 38/1997 (in Portuguese), available at, http://normas.receita.fazenda.gov.br/sijut2consulta/link.action?idAto = 13658&visao = original (last accessed 30 January 2022).
21. For example, *see* CARF of 18 April 2008, CSRF/01-05.734, *Sanofi-Aventis Farmaceutica Ltda v. RFB*; CARF of 18 April 2008, CSRF/01-05.784, *Merck Sharp & Dohme Farmaceutica Ltda v. RFB*; CARF of 23 April 2008, CSRF/01-05.782, *Merck Sharp & Dohme Farmaceutica Ltda v. RFB* (all in Portuguese), available at, http://carf.fazenda.gov.br/sincon/public/pages/ConsultarJurisprudencia/listaJurisprudencia.jsf (last accessed 30 January 2022).

not contain any choice or the taxpayer does not present any calculation or supporting documents, the tax authorities can apply any method without the need to test all methods to prove that the chosen one applied results in the best outcome for the taxpayer.[22]

3.2.2 General Rules

General rules apply to import and export TP methods equally. According to them, only upward adjustments are allowed under the Brazilian framework. In this regard, the taxable base will not be adjusted if a TP method calculates higher expenses or lower income compared to the related party transaction value. In addition, if there is a primary adjustment, it will only impact the taxable base of corporate income tax and have no effect on, e.g., customs duties or indirect taxes.

Some methods use the concept of similar goods as defined by Normative Instruction 1,312/2012.[23] Accordingly, similarity happens if two goods have the same nature and function, one can mutually replace the other in its functionality, and they have equivalent specifications.[24] Moreover, in applying any method for which the arithmetic mean of prices composes the method, only purchases and sales among unrelated party sellers and buyers are considered.

The rules regarding the exchange rate[25] used to convert the value of expenses that are in a foreign currency into Brazilian currency (Real) have minor differences between import and export transactions. In the case of goods, the rate of the second working day before the import declaration registration will be used or, in the case of export transactions, the day of shipping will be considered. For services and rights, the rate of the second working day before the expenses or revenue is accrued should be utilized.

Finally, the Brazilian TP regulations establish that if the related party transaction price diverges up to 5% from the price established by one of the import or export

22. For example, *see* CARF of 18 July 2012, 1202-000.822, *Johnson Matthey Brasil Ltda v. RFB*; CARF of 23 August 2012, 1401-000.800, *Philips Eletronica Da Amazonia Ltda v. RFB*; CARF of 29 August 2012, 1401-000.801, *Philips Eletronica Da Amazonia Ltda v. RFB*; CARF of 21 December 2012, 1402-001.028, *Siemens Ltda v. RFB*; CARF of 11 January 2013, 1402-001.209, *Siemens Eletroeletronica Ltda v. RFB*; CARF of 22 June 2013, 1402-001.342, *DSM Produtos Nutricionais Brasil Ltda v. RFB*; CARF of 23 August 2013, 1402-001.418, *Robert Bosch Limitada v. RFB*; CARF of 18 November 2013, 1402-001508, *Valeo Sistemas Automotivos Ltda v. RFB*; CARF of 10 December 2013, 1402-001.493, *Dow Brasil S.A v. RFB*; CARF of 1 October 2014, 9101-001.340, *Kodak Brasileira Comercio De Produtos Para Imagem E Servicos Ltda v. RFB*; CARF of 23 March 2016, 9101-001.341, *Kodak Brasileira Comercio De Produtos Para Imagem E Servicos Ltda v. RFB* (all in Portuguese), available at, http://carf.fazenda.gov.br/sincon/public/pages/ConsultarJurisprudencia/listaJurisprudencia.jsf (last accessed 30 January 2022).
23. RFB Normative Instruction 1,312/2012 is the secondary legislation that regulates transfer pricing in Brazil (in Portuguese), available at, http://normas.receita.fazenda.gov.br/sijut2consulta/link.action?visao=anotado&idAto=39257 (last accessed 30 January 2022).
24. *Ibid.*, Article 42.
25. The purchase rate should be considered in the case of exports or the sale rate in the case of imports; these are fixed in the opening bulletin of the Central Bank of Brazil. *See* Articles 7 and 29 of the RFB Normative Instruction 1,312/2012, http://normas.receita.fazenda.gov.br/sijut2consulta/link.action?visao=anotado&idAto=39257 (last accessed 30 January 2022).

methods, the taxpayer is not requested to make any adjustment. For transactions with commodities, the acceptable divergence is up to 3%.[26]

3.2.3 TP Methods for Export Transactions

There are five available methods to evaluate the income derived from exports to related parties if safe harbours do not apply (*see* section 3.3). Although they have similarities with the CUP method, the RPM, and the CPM included in the OECD TPG and UN TPM, as presented in Table 22.1, the PVV, PVA and CAP (comparable to the RPM and the CPM) make use of a fixed margin for gross profitability. Except for the commodity method (PECEX, *see* section 3.2.5), all of those methods (PEVEX, PVA, PVV, and CAP) refer to the arithmetic mean that considers prices (or cost) of the entire taxable period.

The comparison between the related party transaction price with the price from the application of any method (called parameter price) consists of comparing the arithmetic mean price practised on the export (on the related party transaction) and the parameter price. The arithmetic mean consists of multiplying each transaction price by the respective quantities. The result will be added and divided by the quantities sum, resulting in the weighted arithmetic mean price.

If it is not possible to identify sales from the same period of the related party transactions, sales carried out in previous or subsequent periods can be used and are subject to an adjustment for a variation in the exchange rate during the period between the sales and the related party transaction. When applying the PEVEX, PVA, PVV, and CAP, comparability adjustments to the value of goods, services, and rights are permitted to account for differences in commercial terms, physical nature, and content. Comparability adjustments can also be performed for similar goods, services, or rights due to differences in physical nature and content considering, for this purpose, the costs related to the production of the good, the execution of the service, or the constitution of the right. Nevertheless, comparability adjustments are only allowed to the extent that the differences in relation to the good, service, or right affect the comparison.

However, when comparing identical goods, services, or rights, Normative Instruction 1,312/2012[27] reduces the scope of the allowed comparability adjustments. Accordingly, the following adjustments are allowed: (i) payment term; (ii) traded quantities; (iii) guarantee related to the functioning of the good or the applicability of the service or right; (iv) promotion to the public through advertising and publicity; (v) inspection costs relating to quality, the standard of services, and hygiene conditions; (vi) intermediation costs in purchase or sale operations performed by the unrelated parties considered for comparing prices; (vii) packing; (viii) freight and insurance; (ix) credit risks; and (x) costs of unloading at the port, internal transportation, storage and customs clearance including import taxes and fees; these are all in the destination

26. *Ibid.*, Articles 51 and 51-A.
27. *Ibid.*, Article 22(1).

market of the asset. Moreover, Normative Instruction 1,312/2012 provides guidance on some of those adjustments.

Regarding differences in payment terms, the amount of interest calculated based on the interest rate commonly used by the taxpayer considering the period between the terms granted for the payment of the obligations under analysis will adjust the value for TP. If such a rate does not exist, the interest rate applicable for loans will be used (*see* section 3.2.6). Moreover, adjustments regarding variances in quantities must be based on documents from sellers demonstrating the practice of applying higher discounts for higher quantities purchased by the same buyer.

Regarding the guarantee related to the functioning of the good or the applicability of the service or right, the value embedded in the price cannot exceed the result of the division of total guarantee expenses in the previous fiscal year by the total quantity of goods, services, or right in the local market during the same period. The cost corresponding to the same guarantee practised in another country will be accepted and converted to the national currency if there has never been a sale in the local market.

Some costs can only be deducted from the price if the buyer in the related party transaction does not support those costs but the buyer in comparable independent transactions bears the burden of such expenses. This rule applies to the promotion to the public through advertising and publicity, inspections relating to quality, the standard of services and hygiene conditions, and intermediation. In addition, differences in the costs of the packaging materials, freight, and insurance are subject to adjustments.

Finally, credit risk adjustments will be admitted exclusively to transactions carried out between a buyer and a seller in Brazil. It should be made based on the percentage resulting from the comparison of total losses and credits from the previous fiscal year.

The following sections describe each applicable method for export transactions except for commodity or loan transactions which are covered in sections 3.2.5 and 3.2.6, respectively.

3.2.3.1 PEVEX (Brazil's Equivalent to the CUP Method)

Brazil's equivalent to the CUP method for export transactions is called *Preço de Venda nas Exportações* in Portuguese and is known by its acronym PEVEX. It consists of using the arithmetic mean of the export sale prices considering identical or similar goods, services, or rights exported during the same taxable period and with similar payment conditions. The export sale prices used in the method can only be those from the Brazilian taxpayer or from another Brazilian exporter to unrelated parties. Stated differently, it only uses domestic comparables which can be internal or external.

Example

Company A located in Brazil produces and exports cutlery to Company B located in Country Y; both are subsidiaries of the parent company of the ABC Group. Company A sells the same cutlery to unrelated parties in Country Z. If Company A applies the PEVEX to evaluate the related party transaction with Company B, it could use the mean of export prices to unrelated parties in Country Y.

Example

Company A located in Brazil produces and exports bedding to Company B located in Country Y; both are subsidiaries of the parent company of the ABC Group. Company C located in Country Z is unrelated to Companies A and B and also exports similar bedding to unrelated parties in Country W. In applying the PEVEX, Company A cannot use Company C's export prices as comparables to evaluate the related party transaction with Company B because Company C is not exporting from Brazil to Country W.

However, if Company C was instead located in Brazil, Company A could use Company C's export prices to unrelated parties in Country Y as comparables in applying the PEVEX.

Example

Company A located in Brazil exports cars to Company B located in Country Y, both being subsidiaries of the parent company of the ABC Group. Exports in Year 0 were the following:

Export from A to B	*Quantity*	*Price*	*Value Exported*
January	1,000	USD 10,000.00	USD 10,000,000.00
May	1,600	USD 9,000.00	USD 14,400,000.00
August	3,000	USD 8,000.00	USD 24,000,000.00
Export Revenue in Year 0			**USD 48,400,000.00**

The arithmetic mean of export prices from Company A to Company B (the price of the related party transactions) in Year 0 is Prelated party = USD 8,642.86.

$$\boldsymbol{Pcontrolled} = \frac{\mathbf{1,000 \times USD\ 10,000 + 1,600 \times USD\ 9,000 + 3,000 \times USD\ 8,000}}{\mathbf{1,000 + 1,600 + 3,000}}$$

$$= \mathbf{USD\ 8,642.86}$$

Company A also exported to an unrelated Company F located in Country W. Exports in Year 0 were the following:

Export from A to F	*Quantity*	*Price*	*Value Exported*
March	100	USD 12,000.00	USD 1,200,000.00
July	110	USD 14,000.00	USD 1,540,000.00
October	530	USD 13,000.00	USD 6,890,000.00

The arithmetic mean of export prices from Company A to Company F (the price of comparable transactions referred to as the parameter price) in Year 0 is:

$$parameter = \frac{100 \times \text{USD } 12{,}000 + 110 \times \text{USD } 14{,}000 + 530 \times \text{USD } 13{,}000}{100 + 110 + 530}$$
$$= \text{USD } 13{,}013.51$$

Considering that there was no need for comparability adjustments, Company A could use the PEVEX method that would compare the related party price to the parameter price which is greater than the former, leading to the following addition to the taxable profit of Year 0:

Difference between Pparameter and Prelated party = USD 13,013.51 – USD 8,642.86 = USD 4,370.65, which is the TP adjustment to the related party transaction price.

The additional taxable profit in Year 0 is as follows:

Quantity	*Adjustment to Related Party Transaction Price*	*Addition to the Value Exported*
1,000	USD 4,370.65	USD 4,370,650.00
1,600	USD 4,370.65	USD 6,993,040.00
3,000	USD 4,370.65	USD 13,111,950.00
Additional Taxable Profit in Year 0		**USD 24,475,640.00**

Example (continues from the previous example)

If the facts were the same as in the previous example except that the parameter price ascertained in the application of the PEVEX is USD 8,997.00. In that case, there would be no TP adjustment to the related party transaction because the divergence from the parameter price in less than 5% (Pparameter to Prelated party = USD 8,997.00 – USD 8,642.86 = USD 354.14 < 5% × USD 8,997.00 = USD 449.85). This divergence margin is also applicable to the other export methods (except on the export of commodities for which the acceptable divergence from the parameter price is up to 3%).

3.2.3.2 PVA (Brazil's Equivalent to the RPM)

There are two methods for export transactions in Brazil that are equivalent to the RPM. The first is called *Preço de Venda por Atacado no País de Destino Diminuído do Lucro* in Portuguese and known by its acronym PVA. It consists of using the arithmetic mean of the wholesale prices in the destination foreign market considering identical or similar goods, services, or rights and similar payment conditions minus taxes included in the price in that foreign country and a 15% profit margin.

The Brazilian taxpayer can select this method whenever its related party transaction is an export to a related party that is a wholesaler in the foreign market and sells to unrelated party retailers. In this case, it will consider internal comparables to apply the method. It can alternatively use the sales of any wholesaler to unrelated party retailers in the same foreign market. Thus, the PVA may take into consideration the function of the related company as a wholesaler; however, it does not matter if it performs more functions or assumes additional risks. Additionally, the method only accepts foreign comparables of the importer country.

Example

Company A located in Brazil produces and exports bedding to Company B located in Country Y; both are subsidiaries of the parent company of the ABC Group. Company B resells that bedding in the wholesale market in Country Y. Exports in Year 0 were the following:

Export from A to B	*Quantity*	*Price*	*Value Exported*
January	1,000	USD 100.00	USD 100,000.00
May	1,600	USD 90.00	USD 144,000.00
August	3,000	USD 80.00	USD 240,000.00
Export Revenue in Year 0			**USD 484,000.00**

The arithmetic mean of export prices from Company A to Company B (the price of the related party transactions) in Year 0 is Prelated party = USD 86.43.

Company B sells to unrelated party retailers in Country Y and to related party retailers.

Sales from B to Related and Unrelated Retailers in Country Y		*Quantity*	*Price*
February	Related	1,300	USD 120.00
	Unrelated	1,250	USD 130.00
July	Related	1,600	USD 97.00
	Unrelated	950	USD 140.00
October	Related	3,000	USD 76.00
	Unrelated	2,700	USD 133.00
Wholesale Revenue in Year 0	**USD 1,193,800.00**		

Assuming the values above are discounted from taxes included in prices in Country Y, the arithmetic mean of resale prices from Company B to unrelated party retailers in Country Y minus the fixed profit margin provided by the legislation (the price of comparable transactions, the so-called parameter price) in Year 0 is:

$$\boldsymbol{Pparameter} = \left(\frac{\mathbf{1,250 \times USD\ 130 + 950 \times USD\ 140 + 2,700 \times USD\ 133}}{\mathbf{1,250 + 950 + 2,700}}\right) \times \mathbf{(1 - 0.15) = USD\ 113.55}$$

Considering that there was no need for comparability adjustments, Company A could use the PVA method to compare the related party price to the parameter price which is greater than the former.

Difference between Pparameter and Prelated party = USD 113.55 – USD 86.43 = USD 27.12, which is the TP adjustment to the related party transaction's price. The additional taxable profit in Year 0 is as follows:

Quantity	*Adjustment to Related Party Transaction Price*	*Addition to the Value Exported*
1,300	USD 27.12	USD 35,256.00
1,600	USD 27.12	USD 43,392.00
3,000	USD 27.12	USD 81,360.00
Additional Taxable Profit in Year 0		**USD 160,008.00**

3.2.3.3 *PVV (Brazil's Equivalent to the RPM)*

The second Brazilian export method equivalent to the RPM is called *Preço de Venda a Varejo no País de Destino Diminuído do Lucro* in Portuguese and is known by its acronym PVV. It consists of using the arithmetic mean of the retail sale price in the destination foreign market considering identical or similar goods, services, or rights and with similar payment conditions minus taxes included in the price in that country and a 30% profit margin.

Example

Company A located in Brazil produces and exports sparkling wine to Company B located in Country Y; both are subsidiaries of the parent company of the ABC Group. Company B resells the sparkling wine to final consumers in Country Y. Exports in Year 0 were the following:

Export from A to B	*Quantity*	*Price*	*Value Exported*
January	1,000	USD 10.00	USD 10,000.00
May	1,600	USD 9.00	USD 14,400.00
August	3,000	USD 8.50	USD 25,500.00
Export Revenue in Year 0			**USD 49,900.00**

The arithmetic mean of export prices from A to B (the price of the related party transactions) in Year 0 is Prelated party= USD 8.91.

Company B sells to final consumers in Country Y.

Sales from B to Final Consumers in Country Y	*Quantity*	*Price*
February	300	USD 14.10
July	600	USD 13.70
October	300	USD 12.60
December	270	USD 13.30
Wholesale Revenue in Year 0	**USD 19,821.00**	

Assuming the values above are discounted from taxes included in the prices in Country Y, the arithmetic mean of sales prices from Company B to final consumers in Country Y minus the fixed profit margin provided by the legislation (the price of comparable transactions called the parameter price) in Year 0 is:

$$\textbf{\textit{Pparameter}} = \left(\frac{\mathbf{300 \times USD\ 14.10 + 600 \times USD\ 13.70 + 300 \times USD\ 12.60 + 270 \times USD\ 13.30}}{\mathbf{300 + 600 + 300 + 270}}\right) \times (\mathbf{1 - 0.30}) = \mathbf{USD\ 9.44}$$

Difference between Pparameter and Prelated party = USD 9.44 – USD 8.91 = USD 0.53, which is the TP adjustment to the related party transaction's price. The additional taxable profit in Year 0 is as follows:

Quantity	*Adjustment to Related Party Transaction Price*	*Addition to the Value Exported*
1,000	USD 0.53	USD 530.00
1,600	USD 0.53	USD 848.00
3,000	USD 0.53	USD 1,590.00
Additional Taxable Profit in Year 0		**USD 2,968.00**

3.2.3.4 CAP (Brazil's Equivalent to the CPM)

The Brazilian TP method for export transactions equivalent to the CPM is referred to as *Custo de Aquisição ou de Produção mais Tributos e Lucro* in Portuguese and is known by its acronym CAP. It consists of using the arithmetic mean of the cost of acquisition or production of exported goods, services, or rights plus taxes in Brazil and a 15 % profit margin.

Example

Company A located in Brazil manufactures and sells titles to Company B located in Country Y according to the specifications and design of Company B. Both companies are subsidiaries of the parent company of the ABC Group.

Exports in Year 0 were the following:

Export from A to B	*Quantity*	*Price*	*Value Exported*
January	1,000	USD 20.00	USD 20,000.00
May	1,600	USD 19.00	USD 30,400.00
August	3,000	USD 18.50	USD 55,500.00
Export Revenue in Year 0			**USD 105,900.00**

The arithmetic mean of export prices from Company A to Company B (the price of the related party transactions) in Year 0 is Prelated party = USD 18.91.

The cost of production of the goods exported was:

Cost of Exports from A to B	*Quantity*	*Cost of Production*	*Total Cost of Production*
January	1,000	USD 17.21	USD 17,210.00
May	1,600	USD 17.32	USD 27,712.00
August	3,000	USD 17.50	USD 52,500.00
Cost of Production of Goods Exported in Year 0			**USD 97,422.00**

Assuming the values above include taxes in Brazil, the arithmetic mean of the unit production cost of goods exported from Company A to Company B added to the fixed profit margin provided by the legislation (the price of comparable transactions called the parameter price) in Year 0 is:

$$\boldsymbol{Pparameter} = \left(\frac{\mathbf{1,000 \times USD\ 17.21 + 1,600 \times USD\ 17.32 + 3,000 \times USD\ 17.50}}{\mathbf{1,000 + 1,600 + 3,000}}\right) \times \mathbf{(1 + 0.15) = USD\ 20.01}$$

Considering that there was no need for comparability adjustments, Company A could use the CAP method to compare the related party price to the parameter price, which is greater than the former.

Difference between Pparameter and Prelated party = USD 20.01 – USD 18.91 = USD 1.10, which is the TP adjustment to the related party transaction's price. The additional taxable profit in Year 0 is as follows:

Quantity	*Adjustment to Related Party Transaction Price*	*Addition to the Value Exported*
1,000	USD 1.10	USD 1,100.00
1,600	USD 1.10	USD 1,760.00
3,000	USD 1.10	USD 3,300.00
Additional Taxable Profit in Year 0		**USD 6,160.00**

3.2.4 *TP Methods for Import Transactions*

There are four available methods to evaluate the expenses in import transactions between related parties. Although they have similarities with the CUP method, RPM and CPM are included in the OECD TPG and in the UN TPM, as presented in Table 22.1 (PIC, PCI, PRL, and CPL), the PRL and the CPL make use of a fixed margin for gross profitability.

In the case of the PRL, the Brazilian method equivalent to the RPM for import transactions, it differs from the methods used for export transactions because the law contains three different margins depending on the economic sector in which the Brazilian entity operates. Additionally, it consists of a formula that accommodates both situations when the Brazilian entity resells the final product without processing or it manufactures and subsequently sells the final product.

The following sections describe each applicable method for import transactions except for commodity and loan transactions which are covered in sections 3.2.5 and 3.2.6, respectively.

3.2.4.1 *PIC (Brazil's Equivalent to the CUP Method)*

Brazil's method for import transactions equivalent to the CUP method is called *Preços Independentes Comparados* in Portuguese and is known by its acronym PIC. It consists of using the weighted arithmetic mean of the purchase and sale prices of identical or similar goods, services, or rights with similar payment conditions.

This method can consider purchases from and sales to unrelated parties of the Brazilian taxpayer as well as unrelated party purchases and sales that could be on the Brazilian or foreign markets. Finally, all purchases and sales have to be from the same taxable period of the related party transaction.

There are, however, some limitations on the transactions that can be considered for calculating the arithmetic mean. In this regard, they should: (i) represent at least 5% of the related party transaction value in the taxable period in the case of internal comparables of the Brazilian taxpayer; and (ii) correspond to unrelated party transactions of the same taxable year of the related party ones or, in the absence of such transactions, transactions from the previous taxable year can be used and adjusted by the variation on the exchange rate.

Moreover, there were disputes in Brazil relating to the use of secret comparables (mostly the import declarations of unrelated parties) by the tax authorities in calculating the PIC method. The CARF decided that the tax authorities' burden of proof included not only calculating the PIC but also proving that the secret comparables used in such a case were identical or similar to the product imported in the related party transactions.[28]

Example

Company A located in Brazil and Company B located in Country Y are both subsidiaries of the parent company of the ABC Group. Company A imports an active principle to produce pharmaceutical products from Company B and unrelated parties. Imports of Company A in Year 0 were the following:

Import from B	*Quantity*	*Price*	*Value*
February	130	USD 10.00	USD 1,300.00
July	160	USD 9.70	USD 1,552.00
October	90	USD 7.60	USD 684.00
		Total	**USD 3,536.00**

Import from Unrelated	*Quantity*	*Price*	*Value*
January	1	USD11.00	USD 11.00
November	6	USD11.50	USD 69.00
December	3	USD10.00	USD 30.00
	Total		**USD 110.00**

Although it has had unrelated party transactions during the year, Company A could not use the PIC method in Year 0 because these transactions represent less than 5% of the value of the related party transactions $\left(\frac{\textbf{USD 110}}{\textbf{USD 3,536}} = \textbf{3.11\%}\right)$.

28. For example, *see* CARF of 1 June 2005, 101-94.888, *Astrazeneca Do Brasil Ltda v. RFB*; CARF of 14 December 2007, 105-16.472, *Boehringer Ingelheim Do Brasil Quimica e Farmaceutica Ltda v. RFB*; CARF of 19 August 2008, 107-09.411, *Kodak Brasileira Comercio De Produtos Para Imagem e Servicos Ltda v. RFB*; CARF of 19 August 2008, 107-09.412, *Kodak Brasileira Comercio De Produtos Para Imagem e Servicos Ltda v. RFB* (all in Portuguese), available at, http://carf.fazenda.gov.br/sincon/public/pages/ConsultarJurisprudencia/listaJurisprudencia.jsf (last accessed 30 January 2022).

This method operates similarly to the PEVEX for exports (*see* example in section 3.2.3.1).

3.2.4.2 PRL (Brazil's Equivalent to the RPM)

Brazil's equivalent to the RPM for import transactions is called *Preços de Revenda menos Lucro* in Portuguese and is known by its acronym PRL. Besides its application to the resale of products imported in a related party transaction, it differs from the RPM because it also applies if there is a manufacturing process applied to the imported products in Brazil. This feature of the method was introduced by the first amendment in the TP law in Brazil,[29] Provisional Measure 2,013/1999, converted into Law 9,959/2000 in response to disputes claiming the illegality of SRF Normative Instruction 38/1997, the secondary legislation that stated that the taxpayer could only choose PRL for resale of products without any processing. The cases against the tax authorities alleged that the freedom of selection of methods was violated; this position was supported by the jurisprudence of the CARF (*see* section 3.2.1).

The interpretation of Law 9,959/2000 incited many disputes regarding the wording of the provision that created the PRL to manufacturing (60% fixed margin). A grammatical interpretation of the provision would imply that the method always included 60% of the value added by the Brazilian production in the parameter price. However, the logic of the PRL 60% was to depart from a market price excluding the value added by the manufacturing activity in Brazil and then discount the 60% fixed margin to calculate the price to compare with that of the related party transaction. In this respect, SRF Normative Instruction 32/2001[30] applied the grammatical interpretation and remained in force for more than one year. It was then revoked by SRF Normative Instruction 243/2002[31] which applied a systematic interpretation.

Again, many disputes were brought before the CARF questioning the legality of SRF Normative Instruction 243/2002. In most cases,[32] the CARF decided in favour of its

29. The original fixed 20% gross profit margin for resale became two different fixed profit margins: 60% for import transactions of goods applied in manufacturing activities and 20% for all other cases. This change was introduced by Provisional Measure 2,013/1999, converted into the Law 9,959/2000 (in Portuguese), available at, https://www2.camara.leg.br/legin/fed/medpro/1999/medidaprovisoria-2013-4-30-dezembro-1999-370114-publicacaooriginal-1-pe.html (last accessed 30 January 2022).
30. For PRL, *see* Article 12 of the SRF Normative Instruction 32/2001 (in Portuguese), available at, http://normas.receita.fazenda.gov.br/sijut2consulta/link.action?visao=anotado&idAto=13539 (last accessed 30 January 2022).
31. For PRL, *see* Article 12 of the SRF Normative Instruction 243/2002 (in Portuguese), available at, http://normas.receita.fazenda.gov.br/sijut2consulta/link.action?visao=anotado&idAto=15119 (last accessed 30 January 2022).
32. For example, *see* CARF of 29 February 2012, 1102-00610, *LG Electronics Da Amazonia Ltda v. RFB*; CARF of 14 June 2013, 1301-001.096, *Do Brasil Ltda v. RFB*; CARF of 22 June 2013, 1402-001.342, *DSM Produtos Nutricionais Brasil Ltda v. RFB*; CARF of 20 August 2013, 1402-001.379, *Elevadores Atlas Schindler Ltda v. RFB*; CARF of 24 October 2013, 1302-001.162, *Electronics Do Brasil Ltda v. RFB;* CARF of 24 October 2013, 1302-001.167, *Yazaki Do Brasil Ltda v. RFB;* CARF of 30 October 2013, 1302-001.163, *Alcatel-Lucent Brasil S.A v. RFB*; CARF of 27 November 2013, 1402-001.467, *Astrazeneca Do Brasil Ltda. v. RFB*; CARF of 10 December 2013,

legality, later issuing Precedent 115[33] that is binding on CARF judges[34] and effectively puts an end to disputes on this matter. Moreover, in a couple of cases, the tax authorities attempted to apply the new interpretation retroactively, however, this approach was not accepted because it violated the trust in the secondary legislation in force at the time of the taxable fact.[35] Partially due to these disputes, TP law changed again in 2012 with the introduction of Law 12,715/2012. Among the new provisions, it implemented the present version of the PRL which is very similar to the systematic interpretation disputed in the CARF cases.

The present version of the PRL consists of the following methodology:

(a) net sale price: the weighted arithmetic mean of the sale prices in Brazil to unrelated parties of the good, right, or service produced with similar payment conditions minus the granted unconditional discounts, taxes, and contributions on sales and commissions and brokerage fees;
(b) percentual participation of goods, rights, or services imported in the total cost of the good, right, or service sold: the percentage ratio between the weighted mean cost of the imported good, right, or service and the weighted mean total cost of a good, right, or service sold calculated based on the company's cost spreadsheet;
(c) participation of the goods, rights, or services imported in the sale price of the good, right, or service sold: application of the percentual participation of imported goods, rights, or services in the total cost calculated in item b on the net sale price calculated in item a;
(d) profit margin: the application of the percentual fixed profit margin corresponding to the economic sector in which the taxpayer operates in Brazil on the participation of the goods, rights, or services imported in the sale price of the good, right, or service sold calculated in item c; and
(e) parameter price: the difference between the participation of imported goods, rights, or services in the sale price of the good, right, or service sold calculated in item c and the value of the profit margin calculated in item d.

Item b above includes the cost of freight and insurance paid by the importer on its calculation only if it is not contracted with related parties or residents in low tax

1402-001.493, *DOW BRASIL S.A v. RFB* (all in Portuguese), available at, http://carf.fazenda.gov.br/sincon/public/pages/ConsultarJurisprudencia/listaJurisprudencia.jsf (last accessed 7 October 2020).

33. CARF precedents are available in Portuguese at, http://idg.carf.fazenda.gov.br/jurisprudencia/sumulas-carf (last accessed 30 January 2022).

34. *See* Article 72 of the CARF Bylaws (in Portuguese), available at, http://idg.carf.fazenda.gov.br/acesso-a-informacao/institucional/regimento-interno/reg-outros/ricarf-multi-11072016.pdf (last accessed 30 January 2022).

35. For example, *see* CARF of 30 May 2012, 1401-000.684, *Yazaki Do Brasil Ltda v. RFB*; CARF of 27 June 2012, 1201-000.658, *Delphi Automotive Systems Do Brasil Ltda v. RFB*; CARF of 16 July 2014, 1301-001.275, *LG Electronics Da Amazonia Ltda v. RFB* (all in Portuguese), available at, http://carf.fazenda.gov.br/sincon/public/pages/ConsultarJurisprudencia/listaJurisprudencia.jsf (last accessed 30 January 2022).

jurisdictions or a beneficiary of a privileged tax regime. It does not include the cost of import taxes and customs clearance.

The Brazilian taxpayer subject to TP control should use the fixed profit margins corresponding to the economic sector in which it operates to calculate item d above:

Gross Profit Margin (%)	*Economic Sector*
40%	(i) manufacture of pharmochemical and pharmaceutical products; (ii) manufacture of tobacco products; (iii) manufacture of optical, photographic, and cinematographic equipment and instruments; (iv) manufacture of machines, devices, and equipment for dental-medical and hospital use; (v) extraction of oil and natural gas; and (vi) manufacture of petroleum products.
30%	(i) manufacture of chemical products; (ii) manufacture of glass and glass products; (iii) manufacture of cellulose, paper, and paper products; and (iv) metallurgy.
20%	Others.

The profit margin to be adopted if the taxpayer operates in more than one economic sector must correspond to that applied for the imported goods. It can be the case that the same imported goods could be resold or applied in the production of one or more products. If such a situation arises, the final price will be the weighted mean of the values from the application of the PRL according to their respective destination (resale or production).

The application of the method uses the sales prices of the period in which the imported goods comprised the COGS if it is only resold or the cost of production if it is a raw material used for manufacturing in Brazil.

Example

Company A located in Brazil and Company B located in Country Y are both subsidiaries of the parent company of the ABC Group. Company A imports cars from Company B and resells them to the Brazilian market (consumers). Imports of Company A in Year 0 were the following:

Imports from A to B	*Quantity*	*Price*	*Value Imported*
March	1,000	USD 9,500.00	USD 9,500,000.00
April	1,600	USD 8,700.00	USD 13,920,000.00
November	1,500	USD 9,900.00	USD 14,850,000.00
Imports Expenses in Year 0			**USD 38,270,000.00**

In Year 0, Company A's sales of cars to Brazilian consumers were the following:

Sales to Final Consumer	*Quantity*	*Price*	*Net Sales Revenue*
April	308	USD 10,000.00	USD 3,080,000.00
May	300	USD 10,500.00	USD 3,150,000.00
June	201	USD 10,300.00	USD 2,070,300.00
July	407	USD 11,000.00	USD 4,477,000.00
August	201	USD 10,900.00	USD 2,190,900.00
December	409	USD 11,100.00	USD 4,539,900.00
Net Sales Revenue in Year 0			**USD 19,508,100.00**

The arithmetic mean of prices of import by Company A from Company B, the related party transactions price in Year 0, is Prelated party = **USD 9,138.12**, calculated below considering the following values:[36]

COGS	*Quantity*	*Imported Price*	*Expenses*
April	308	USD 9,500.00	USD 2,926,000.00
May	300	USD 9,500.00	USD 2,850,000.00
June	201	USD 9,500.00	USD 1,909,500.00
July	191	USD 9,500.00	USD 1,814,500.00
	216	USD 8,700.00	USD 1,879,200.00
August	201	USD 8,700.00	USD 1,748,700.00
December	409	USD 8,700.00	USD 3,558,300.00
Sales Revenue in Year 0			**USD 16,686,200.00**

36. For purposes of this example, assume the initial stock in Year 0 of Company A is zero and it uses first-in, first-out for evaluating the COGS.

$$\textbf{Pcontrolled} = \left(\frac{(308 + 300 + 201 + 191) \times \text{USD } 9{,}500.00 + (216 + 201 + 409) \times \text{USD } 8{,}700.00}{1{,}000 + 826}\right)$$

$$= \text{USD } 9{,}138.12$$

Step a, calculating net sale price:

Sales to Final Consumer	*Quantity*	*Price*	*Discounts*	*Taxes on Sale*	*Sale Commission Fee*	*Net Sales Revenue*
April	308	USD 10,000.00	USD 100.00	USD 10.00	USD 30.00	USD 3,036,880.00
May	300	USD 10,500.00	USD 105.00	USD 10.50	USD 31.50	USD 3,105,900.00
June	201	USD 10,300.00	USD 103.00	USD 10.30	USD 30.90	USD 2,041,315.80
July	407	USD 11,000.00	USD 110.00	USD 11.00	USD 33.00	USD 4,414,322.00
August	201	USD 10,900.00	USD 109.00	USD 10.90	USD 32.70	USD 2,160,227.40
December	409	USD 11,100.00	USD 111.00	USD 11.10	USD 33.30	USD 4,476,341.40
Net Sales Revenue in Year 0						**USD 19,234,986.60**

$$\textbf{net sale price} = \left(\frac{\text{USD } 19{,}234{,}986.60}{308 + 300 + 201 + 407 + 201 + 409}\right) = \text{USD } 10{,}533.95$$

Step b, calculating the percentual participation of the imported goods in the total cost of the goods sold.

In the case of resale, the cost of the imported goods is equal to the cost of the goods sold:

$$\textbf{\% participation of the goods imported in cost of goods sold} = \left(\frac{\textit{cost of the imported cars}}{\textit{cost of the cars sold}}\right) = \left(\frac{\textit{cost of the imported cars}}{\textit{cost of the imported cars}}\right) = 100\%$$

Step c, calculating the participation of the goods imported in the sale price of the goods sold:

$$\textbf{participation of imported goods in the sale price of goods sold} = (\textbf{step a}) \times (\textbf{step b}) = (\textbf{net sale price}) \times \left(\begin{matrix}\textbf{\% participation of the imported goods in} \\ \textbf{the total cost of the goods sold}\end{matrix}\right) = \text{USD } 10{,}533.95 \times 100\% = \text{USD } 10{,}533.95$$

Step d, calculating the profit margin. Company A operates in the distribution of cars in Brazil, so the fixed profit margin applicable to this economic sector is 20%.

$$\boldsymbol{profit\ margin = (fixed\ profit\ margin) \times (step\ c) = 20\%}$$
$$\boldsymbol{\times (participation\ of\ imported\ goods\ in\ the\ sale\ price\ of\ goods\ sold)}$$
$$\boldsymbol{= 20\% \times \text{USD } 10{,}533.95 = \text{USD } 2{,}106.79.}$$

Step e, calculating the parameter price in Year 0:

$$\boldsymbol{Pparameter = (step\ c) - (step\ d)}$$
$$\boldsymbol{= \begin{pmatrix} participation\ of\ the\ imported\ goods \\ in\ the\ sale\ price\ of\ goods\ sold \end{pmatrix} - (profit\ margin)}$$
$$\boldsymbol{= \text{USD } 10{,}533.95 - \text{USD } 2{,}106.79 = \text{USD } 8{,}427.16}$$

Difference between Prelated party and Pparameter = USD 9,138.12 - USD 8,427.16 = USD 710.96, which is the TP adjustment to the related party transaction's price.

The additional taxable profit in Year 0 is as follows:

Quantity	*Adjustment to Related Party Transaction Price*	*Reduction to the Value Imported*
308	USD 710.96	USD 218,975.68
300	USD 710.96	USD 213,288.00
201	USD 710.96	USD 142,902.96
191	USD 710.96	USD 135,793.36
216	USD 710.96	USD 153,567.36
201	USD 710.96	USD 142,902.96
409	USD 710.96	USD 290,782.64
Additional Taxable Profit in Year 0		**USD 1,298,212.96**

Example (continues from the previous example)

The facts are the same as the previous example except that Company A imports Product Y that is a raw material in the manufacturing of Product X, which is subsequently sold for the same values as the previous example. Additionally, in this example, Company A manufactures equipment for medical and hospital use in Brazil, therefore, the fixed profit margin applicable to this economic sector is 40%.

In applying PRL, all of the calculations will be the same as in the previous example until step b. Thus, the Prelated party is **USD 9,138.12** and the Net Sale Price is **USD 10,533.95**.

Step b, calculating the percentual participation of the imported goods in the total cost of the goods sold. As Company A manufactures Product X using the imported good Product Y in the process, there are other costs of production (e.g., other raw materials, indirect costs). Therefore, the cost of imported goods will be different from the COGS. Assume that the Product X cost of production is USD 13,054.46, which is the COGS:

$$\boldsymbol{\%\,participation\ of\ the\ imported\ goods\ in\ cost\ of\ goods\ sold}$$
$$= \left(\frac{\boldsymbol{cost\ of\ the\ imported\ goods}}{\boldsymbol{cost\ of\ the\ goods\ sold}}\right) = \left(\frac{\boldsymbol{cost\ of\ imported\ Products\ Y}}{\boldsymbol{cost\ of\ Products\ X\ sold}}\right)$$
$$= \left(\frac{\textbf{USD 9,138.12}}{\textbf{USD 13,054.46}}\right) = \textbf{70\%}$$

Step c, calculating the participation of the imported goods in the sale price of the goods sold:

$$\boldsymbol{participation\ of\ the\ imported\ goods\ in\ the\ sale\ price\ of\ goods\ sold}$$
$$= \boldsymbol{(step\ a) \times (step\ b) = (net\ sale\ price)}$$
$$\times\ \boldsymbol{(\%\ participation\ of\ the\ imported\ goods\ in\ the\ total\ cost\ of\ the\ goods\ sold)}$$
$$= \textbf{USD 10,533.95} \times \textbf{70\%} = \textbf{USD 7,373.77}$$

Step d, calculating the profit margin. The fixed profit margin applicable to the economic sector in which Company A operates is 40%.

$$\boldsymbol{profit\ margin = (fixed\ profit\ margin) \times (step\ c)}$$
$$= \textbf{40\%} \times \left(\begin{array}{c}\boldsymbol{participation\ of\ imported}\\ \boldsymbol{goods\ in\ the\ sale\ price\ of\ go}\\ \boldsymbol{od\ sold}\end{array}\right)$$
$$= \textbf{40\%} \times \textbf{USD 7,373.77} = \textbf{USD 2,949.51.}$$

Step e, calculating the parameter price in Year 0:

$$\boldsymbol{Pparameter = (step\ c) - (step\ d)}$$
$$= \left(\begin{array}{c}\boldsymbol{participation\ imported\ of\ goods}\\ \boldsymbol{in\ the\ sale\ price\ of\ good\ sold}\end{array}\right) - \boldsymbol{(profit\ margin)}$$
$$= \textbf{USD 7,373.77} - \textbf{USD 2,949.51} = \textbf{USD 4,424.26}$$

Difference between Prelated party and Pparameter = USD 9,138.12 - USD 4,424.26 = USD 4,713.86, which is the TP adjustment to the related party transaction's price.

The additional taxable profit in Year 0 is as follows:

Quantity	*Adjustment to Related Party Transaction Price*	*Reduction to the Value Imported*
308	USD 4,713.86	USD 1,451,868.88
300	USD 4,713.86	USD 1,414,158.00
201	USD 4,713.86	USD 947,485.86

Quantity	*Adjustment to Related Party Transaction Price*	*Reduction to the Val-ueImported*
191	USD 4,713.86	USD 900,347.26
216	USD 4,713.86	USD 1,018,193.76
201	USD 4,713.86	USD 947,485.86
409	USD 4,713.86	USD 1,927,968.74
Additional Taxable Profit in Year 0		**USD 8,607,508.36**

3.2.4.3 CPL (Brazil's Equivalent to the CPM)

The method equivalent to the CPM for import transactions in Brazil is the *Custo de Produção mais Lucro* in Portuguese and is known by its acronym CPL. This method consists of using the weighted arithmetic mean of the cost of production of identical or similar exported goods, services, or rights plus export taxes in the country of their origin and a 20% profit margin. This method operates similarly to the CAP for exports (*see* example in section 3.2.3.4).

3.2.5 Commodities Methods

The import and export transactions of commodities are subject to mandatory TP methods that are equivalent to the CUP method. For import transactions, the applicable method is called *Preço sob Cotação na Importação* in Portuguese and is known by its acronym PCI. For export transactions, the method is referred to as *Preço sob Cotação na Exportação* in Portuguese and is known by its acronym PECEX.

Although the law defines the PCI and PECEX[37] as two different methods, both consist of using the average daily quote of goods or rights subject to public prices on internationally recognized commodities and futures exchanges. The PCI and PECEX are mandatory in the case of the existence of publicly available prices. They consist of comparing the related party commodity transaction price with the commodity average quote on internationally recognized commodity and futures exchanges and adjusted by the average market premium on the date of the transaction. If no quote is available for the transaction date, the one from the first date available before the transaction date will be used.

In the event that the taxpayer fails to identify the date of the transaction for the commodities methods, the date of registration of the import declaration or the date of shipping, respectively, will be considered for import and export transactions.

37. For the PCI and PECEX, *see*, respectively, Articles 18-A and 19-A of the Law 9,430/1996, *supra* n. 3.

Table 22.2 Commodities and Future Exchange Accepted by the Brazilian Tax Authorities

Country	*Commodities & Future Exchange*	*City of Location*
Australia	Australian Securities Exchange (ASX)	Sydney
Brazil	Commodities & Futures Exchange (BM&F)*	São Paulo
China	Beijing Iron Ore Trading Center Corporation (COREX)	Beijing
	China Beijing International Mining Exchange (CBMX)	
	Hong Kong Commodity Exchange (HKE)	Hong Kong
India	National Commodity & Derivatives Exchange Limited (NCDEX)	Bombay
	Multi Commodity Exchange (MCX)	
Japan	Tokyo Commodity Exchange (TOCOM)	Tokyo
	Tokyo Grain Exchange (TGE)**	
Singapore	Global ORE	Singapore
	Singapore Commodity Exchange (SICOM)	
South Africa	JSE Safex APD (SAFEX)	Johannesburg
South Korea	Korea Exchange (KRK)	Busan
Thailand	Agricultural Futures Exchange of Thailand (AFET)	Bangkok
United Kingdom	Intercontinental Exchange (ICE Europe)	London
	Life NYSE Euronext (LIFFE)	
	London Bullion Market Association (LBMA)	
	London Metal Exchange (LME)	
United States	Intercontinental Exchange (ICE USA) - Atlanta EUA	Atlanta
	Chicago Board of Trade (CBOT)***	Chicago
	Chicago Mercantile Exchange (CME)	
	Commodity Exchange (COMEX)***	New York
	New York Mercantile Exchange (NYMEX)***	

Source: Elaborated by the authors based on Annex II, RFB Normative Instruction 1,312/2012.[38]

* As it is read in the Annex but it is actually B3.

**Acquired by TOCOM.

***Merged with CME.

38. Annexes (in Portuguese) can be downloaded from RFB Normative Instruction 1,312/2012, *supra* n. 23.

If the commodity does not have a quote on an internationally recognized commodities and futures exchange, the prices obtained from independent data sources provided by internationally recognized sectoral research institutions will be used as a source of comparison with the related party transaction. However, if a commodity does have a quote in both of them, the reference quote of the commodities and futures exchange should be used.

The tax administration has the legal power to establish the acceptable internationally recognized commodities and futures exchanges and the sectoral research institutions for the application of the PCI and PECEX. In this regard, Table 22.2 presents the commodities and futures exchanges, and Table 22.3 depicts the sectoral research institutions that are accepted by the Brazilian tax authorities. They also set a list of commodities subject to both methods as long as they have publicly available prices, as stated in Table 22.4.

Table 22.3 Sectoral Research Institutions Accepted by the Brazilian Tax Authorities

Sectoral Research Institutions Internationally Recognized
PLATTS *
ARGUS
CMA
ESALQ
TSI*
THE METAL BULLETIN
CRU MONITOR
CIS
CMAI*
POTEN&PARTNERS
BLOOMBERG
ICIS HEREN

Source: Annex III, RFB Normative Instruction 1,312/2012.[39]

* Presently, S&P Global Platts, that merged with HIS Markit.

39. *Ibid.*

Table 22.4 List of Commodities Subject to PCI and PECEX

Harmonized System (HS) Codes	*HS Description*
02	Meat and edible meat offal
0901	Coffee, whether or not roasted or decaffeinated; husks and skins; coffee substitutes containing coffee in any proportion
1001	Wheat and meslin.
1101	Wheat or meslin flour
1201	Soya beans, whether or not broken
1507	Soya-bean oil and its fractions, whether or not refined, but not chemically modified
1701	Cane or beet sugar and chemically pure sucrose, in solid form
18	Cocoa and cocoa preparations
2009.1	Orange juice
2304	Oil-cake and other solid residues; whether or not ground or in the form of pellets, resulting from the extraction of soya-bean oil
2602	Manganese ores and concentrates, including ferruginous manganese ores and concentrates with a manganese content of 20 % or more, calculated on the dry weight
2603	Copper ores and concentrates
2604	Nickel ores and concentrates
2605	Cobalt ores and concentrates
2607	Lead ores and concentrates
2608	Zinc ores and concentrates
2609	Tin ores and concentrates
2701	Coal; briquettes, ovoids and similar solid fuels manufactured from coal
2702	Lignite; whether or not agglomerated, excluding jet
2703	Peat; (including peat litter), whether or not agglomerated
2704	Coke and semi-coke; of coal, lignite or peat, whether or not agglomerated; retort carbon
2709	Petroleum oils and oils obtained from bituminous minerals, crude

Harmonized System (HS) Codes	*HS Description*
2710	Petroleum oils and oils obtained from bituminous minerals, other than crude; preparations not elsewhere specified or included, containing by weight 70 % or more of petroleum oils or of oils obtained from bituminous minerals, these oils being the basic constituents of the preparations; waste oils
2711	Petroleum gases and other gaseous hydrocarbons
52	Cotton
7108	Gold (including gold plated with platinum) unwrought or in semi-manufactured forms, or in powder form
72	Iron and steel
74	Copper and articles thereof
75	Nickel and articles thereof
76	Aluminium and articles thereof
78	Lead and articles thereof
79	Zinc and articles thereof
80	Tin; articles thereof
8105	Cobalt mattes and other intermediate products of cobalt metallurgy; cobalt and articles thereof, including waste and scrap
8111	Manganese and articles thereof, including waste and scrap

Source: Elaborated by the authors based on Annex I, RFB Normative Instruction 1,312/2012,[40] and on the World Customs Organization Harmonized System Nomenclature 2017 edition.[41]

Finally, the following examples illustrate how the commodities methods operate.

Example

Company A located in Brazil and Company B located in Country Y are both subsidiaries of the parent company of the ABC Group. Company A exports coffee beans to Company B. Exports of Company A in February of Year 0 were the following:

40. *Ibid.*
41. The WCO HS Nomenclature can be consulted at, http://www.wcoomd.org/en/topics/nomenclature/instrument-and-tools/hs-nomenclature-2017-edition/hs-nomenclature-2017-edition.aspx (last accessed 30 January 2022).

Export from A to B	Quantity (60 kg Bag)	Price	Value Exported
5 February	1,300	USD 200.00	USD 260,000.00
10 February	1,600	USD 199.00	USD 318,400.00
15 February	900	USD 201.00	USD 180,900.00
	Total		USD 759,300.00

As the coffee beans exported by Company A are one of the commodities subject to the commodity method (HS code 0901.11), Company A must use this method for calculating the parameter price. The coffee market in Brazil uses the São Paulo Commodities and Futures Exchange (currently B3) as the reference price for their negotiations. Company A and Company B negotiated the transactions approximately five days before the export dates, and the quote on B3 was the following:

Date	Price
1 February	USD 260.00
5 February	USD 271.00
10 February	USD 268.00

The negotiated coffee future contract in B3 has the following specifications:

	Future Contract Negotiated in B3
Product Negotiated	Coffee beans, not roasted, produced in Brazil, coffea arabica, type 6-25 (6/7) or better, hard drink or better
Quotation	United States Dollars per bag
Place of Delivery	São Paulo

Source: Elaborated by the authors based on the actual B3 coffee future contract.[42]

These specifications of the standard contract negotiated in B3 are compared to the characteristics of the related party transaction (Company A exportation of coffee to Company B) to verify if there is a difference that may affect the price of the commodity. Assume that the coffee exported by Company A is exactly the one above (coffee beans, not roasted, produced in Brazil, coffea arabica) but of

42. The B3 Coffee Future Contract (in Portuguese) is available at, http://www.b3.com.br/pt_br/produtos-e-servicos/negociacao/commodities/ficha-do-produto-8AE490CA6D41D4C7016D45F3CA71386A.htm (last accessed 30 January 2022).

lower quality (lower quality than type 6-25). Additionally, the market pays a negative premium of USD 1.50 per bag of lower-quality coffee, implying that a comparability adjustment by the market premium is required in order to consider the quality differences.

Therefore, taking all of this information into consideration to apply the commodity method, the TP adjustment that Company A should make will be calculated as follows:

Quantity (60 kg Bag)	Quote of the Date of Transaction	Premium	Value of the Export (Commodity Method)
1,300	USD 260.00	–USD 1.50	USD 336,050.00
1,600	USD 271.00	–USD 1.50	USD 431,200.00
900	USD 268.00	–USD 1.50	USD 239,850.00

Date of Transaction	Export Revenue of the Tested Transaction (a)	Value of the Export (Commodity Method) (b)	TP Adjustment to Export Revenue (b-a)
1 February	USD 260,000.00	USD 336,050.00	USD 76,050.00
5 February	USD 318,400.00	USD 431,200.00	USD 112,800.00
10 February	USD 180,900.00	USD 239,850.00	USD 58,950.00

It is important to note that conversion to the local currency of the adjustment calculated above was omitted for simplification of the example but, for tax purposes, the TP adjustment is at the end of the fiscal year (31 December Year 0) and variation of the exchange rate may affect the tax base.

Example

If the facts were the same as in the previous example except that the quoted prices for the application of the PECEX were different, the results would change as shown below:

Date of Transaction	*Export Revenue of the Tested Transaction (a)*	*Value of the Export (Commodity Method) (b)*	*TP Adjustment to Export Revenue (b-a)*
1 February	USD 260,000.00	USD 266,050.00	USD 6,050.00
5 February	USD 318,400.00	USD 327,010.00	USD 8,610.00
10 February	USD 180,900.00	USD 185,040.00	USD 4,140.00

In that case, there would be no TP adjustment to the related party transactions because they diverge from the value of the commodity method by less than 3%.

It is important to note that the PCI method works similarly to the PECEX with an acceptable deviation margin for import transactions also of up to 3% of the value of the commodity method (PCI).

3.2.6 *TP Method Applicable for Loans*

The interest applicable to related party loans is only deductible for tax purposes in Brazil if it does not exceed the amount calculated based on the reference rate established by law (*see* Table 22.5) plus a spread rate defined by the Ministry of Finance based on the market average that is proportional to the period to which the interest refers. The same rule applies to recognizing the income of interest from related party loans which has to be at least the amount calculated based on the same reference rate plus a spread.

Table 22.5 Loan Market Rate Reference

Contract's Characteristics	*Market Rate of Reference*
Loans in Dollars with fixed rate	The market rate for sovereign bonds of the Federative Republic of Brazil issued abroad in United States of America dollars
Loans in local currency (*Real*) with fixed rate	The market rate for sovereign bonds of the Federative Republic of Brazil issued abroad in local currency (*Real*)
Others	The rate of London Interbank Offered Rate – LIBOR for a period of 6 months

Source: Article 22, § 6 of Law 9,430/1996.[43]

The interest deduction limit will be calculated based on the amount of the obligation or right for the date of the final loan term and expressed in the currency of the contract

43. *Supra* n. 3.

converted into local currency at the BCB exchange rate. In the case of a loan with contractual characteristics that impose the use of the LIBOR, but it is in a currency to which there is no LIBOR rate available, the reference rate should be the LIBOR rate for deposits in US dollars. Finally, since 2013, the spread fixed by the Ministry of Finance[44] is 3.5% for deductibility of interest and 2.5% for recognition of a Brazilian taxpayer's income.

3.2.7 *Alteration of Fixed Profit Margins*

The Brazilian TP law[45] delegated the possibility to alter the fixed profit margins applicable to some export and import TP methods to the Ministry of Finance. Any alteration has to be motivated and can only reduce the fixed profit margins for the import methods and increase them for the export methods due to the constitutional principle of legality that no tax can be imposed or increased without a law.[46]

The alteration of the fixed margin was regulated by the Ministry of Finance Ordinance 222/2008.[47] The request to alter the fixed margins can be general, for sectors, or a specific taxpayer by the initiative of the government, a national economic sectoral representative, or the taxpayer. To date, there is no evidence of an application of this possibility.

3.3 Safe Harbours

All three safe harbours in Brazilian TP rules only apply to export transactions except for transactions involving commodities (*see* section 3.2.5).

The first safe harbour provides that the income derived from the related party transactions of goods, services, or rights in the fiscal year will only be subject to TP legislation if the arithmetic mean price in exports in the taxable period is less than 90% of the arithmetic mean of the sale price in Brazil of the same goods, services, or rights during the same period and under similar payment conditions. Compliance with this safe harbour occurs by comparing exports with sales performed by the taxpayer or, if there were no sales during the period, with sales of other companies.

Additionally, to compare the same level of prices, the price of sales in Brazil will take into account discounts and taxes embedded in the sale price.[48] Freight and insurance

44. *See* Ministry of Finance Ordinance 427/2013 (in Portuguese), available at, http://normas.receita.fazenda.gov.br/sijut2consulta/link.action?visao=anotado&idAto=44409 (last accessed 30 January 2022).
45. *Supra* n. 3, Article 20.
46. *Supra* n. 8, Article 150(I).
47. Ministry of Finance Ordinance 222/2008 (in Portuguese), available at, http://normas.receita.fazenda.gov.br/sijut2consulta/link.action?visao=anotado&idAto=25066 (last accessed 30 January 2022).
48. As Brazil does not have a VAT but some taxes that can have features of a VAT, transfer pricing legislation is included the ICMS, ISS, Cofins, and PIS (abbreviations in Portuguese for Brazilian taxes with VAT features). *See* Article 19(2)(I) of the Law 9,430/1996, *supra* n. 3.

costs that are paid by the exporter should be excluded from prices for comparison purposes.

Example

Company A located in Brazil and Company B located in Country Y are both subsidiaries of the parent company of the ABC Group. Company A sells the same chicken to unrelated parties in Brazil. In a taxable period, Company A exported 10,000 kilos of chicken to Company B and sold 1,000 kilos of chicken to unrelated parties in Brazil. The arithmetic mean sale price in Brazil to unrelated parties was USD 2.00 per kilo. TP legislation will apply if the arithmetic mean price of the export to Company B was less than USD 1.80 (= 0.9 x USD 2.00) per kilo in the same period. Thus, if the arithmetic mean price of Company A exports to Company B was USD 1.83 per kilo, TP legislation in Brazil would not apply, however, it would apply if the arithmetic mean price is USD 1.77 per kilo.

The other safe harbours consist of a test that, whenever it is met, exempts the taxpayer from providing any evidence of TP other than the regular documents of the commercial transaction. In this regard, the second safe harbour considers a minimum level of profitability of the related party export transactions that satisfy a test of low materiality. Accordingly, if the Brazilian taxpayer proves that the taxable income (profit before taxes) resulting from the revenue of exports to related parties represents at least 10% of the total export revenues, the safe harbour applies. The total export revenues consider the annual average of the two previous years. In addition, the related party export transactions cannot exceed 20% of the total net export revenue.

According to the last safe harbour, if the net export revenues do not exceed 5% of the total net revenues in the same period, the safe harbour applies. For calculating the net export revenues, revenues from sales made to individuals or legal entities resident or domiciled in a country with favourable taxation must also be included.

Finally, neither of the last two safe harbours above apply to sales to a resident in a jurisdiction with a favourable income tax regime.

4 OTHER RELATED RULES

Since 1958, royalties for the exploitation of industry marks and trademarks, invention patents, and technical, scientific, administrative, or similar assistance payments can be deducted up to the maximum limit of 5% of the gross revenue of the manufactured or sold product.[49] Additionally, in 1964, a law established additional conditions for the deduction. Accordingly, royalty expenses are only deductible if they are necessary to

49. *See* Article 74 of the Law 3,470/1958 (in Portuguese), available at, http://www.planalto.gov.br/ccivil_03/leis/L3470.htm. The actual limits vary among industries, and is fixed by the Ministry of Finance Ordinance 436/1958 (in Portuguese), available at, https://www.gov.br/inpi/pt-br/assuntos/contratos-de-tecnologia-e-de-franquia/arquivos/legislacao-transferencia-de-tecnologia/portaria436.pdf (last accessed 30 January 2022).

maintain possession, use, or enjoyment of the good or right that produces the royalty.[50] Further legal limitations also apply to specific situations.[51]

The royalties' contract should be registered with the INPI and BCB[52] for deductibility in the following situations: (i) royalties for the use of invention patents, manufacturing processes, and formulas or the use of industry marks or trademarks paid by the Brazilian entity to its controller resident abroad (who exercises direct or indirect control); and (ii) royalties for the use of invention patents, manufacturing processes, and formulas or the use of industry marks and trademarks paid or credited to a beneficiary resident abroad. If any of those situations arise without satisfying the conditions, the payment will not be deductible.

Furthermore, the following situations are also not deductible: (i) royalties paid to shareholders, individuals, or legal entities or managers and their relatives or dependents; (ii) royalties for the use of invention patents, manufacturing processes, and formulas or the use of industry or trademarks paid by the Brazilian subsidiary to its foreign parent company.

Regarding the expenses for technical, scientific, administrative, or similar assistance, they should have a contract registered with the BCB and INPI[53] corresponding to services rendered to the company through technicians, drawings, or instructions sent to Brazil and technical studies carried out abroad on behalf of the company in any situation. Expenses for those types of assistance are not deductible when paid or credited by the Brazilian subsidiary to its foreign parent company.[54]

Finally, TP legislation will not apply to transactions among related parties subject to that legislation.

5 TP IN DTCs

While TP rules in Brazil differ from the OECD and UN guidance, Brazil has concluded DTCs containing a provision similar to Article 9 of the OECD MTC and UN MTC. To date, Brazil has concluded a total of thirty-six DTCs. DTCs currently in force are with: Argentina, Austria, Belgium, Canada, Chile, China (Mainland), Czechoslovakia (now applicable to both Slovak and Czech Republics), Denmark, Ecuador, Finland, France, Hungary, India, Israel, Italy, Japan, Korea (South), Luxembourg, Mexico, the Netherlands, Norway, Peru, Philippines, Portugal, Russian Federation, South Africa, Spain, Sweden, Switzerland, Trinidad and Tobago, Turkey, Ukraine, United Arab Emirates

50. *Supra* n. 7, Article 71.
51. In 1991, the law altered those limitations. *See* Article 50 of the Law 8,383/1991 (in Portuguese), available at, http://www.planalto.gov.br/ccivil_03/leis/L8383.htm (last accessed 30 January 2022).
52. The need of contract registration in BCB was revoked, entering into force at the end of 2020 due to alteration on Article 9 of Law 4,131/1964, available at http://www.planalto.gov.br/ccivil_03/leis/L4131.htm (last accessed 27 March 2022), by Law 14,286/2021, available at http://www.planalto.gov.br/ccivil_03/_ato2019-2022/2021/lei/L14286.htm (last accessed 27 March 2022).
53. *Ibid.*
54. *See* Article 52 of the Law 4,506/1964 (*supra* n. 7), Article 50 of the Law 8,383/1991 (*Ibid*), and Article 12 of the Law 4,131/1964 (in Portuguese), available at, http://www.planalto.gov.br/ccivil_03/LEIS/L4131.htm#art12 (last accessed 30 January 2022).

and Venezuela.[55] The DTC with Germany has not been in force since 1 January 2006. Moreover, a DTC was signed in 2018 with Singapore,[56] however, it is not yet in force.

The first treaty to enter into force in 1967 was that with Japan and, after the first version of the OECD TPG in 2009, only five new treaties entered into force. Nevertheless, taxpayers raised the question to the CARF of whether the Brazilian TP law was adhering to Article 9 of the DTCs signed by Brazil. The CARF understood that there was no contradiction.[57] Moreover, it expressed the opinion that Article 9, paragraph 1, authorizes a country to make adjustments when related parties do not transact in accordance with the arm's length principle.[58]

None of Brazil's DTCs has a provision in line with Article 9(2) of the OECD MTC or UN MTC. However, Brazil has clarified that a corresponding adjustment may be performed regardless of such a provision.[59] Finally, Brazil's MAP guidance provides access to a MAP in TP cases.[60]

6 CONCLUSION

This chapter has discussed the TP rules applicable in Brazil. Section 2 outlined the motivation for introducing TP rules in the country and its evolution over the more than twenty years since the first TP rules entered into force. This section notes that the adoption of the first of these rules in Brazil in 1996 found inspiration from the 1979 OECD Report[61] and that its evolution was mainly based on responses to recurrent disputes in the Brazilian administrative court (CARF).

Section 3 then provided a detailed description of the Brazilian TP rules, including its main features which are the freedom of selection of the method and the application of the fixed margins. It provided examples on the application of the various TP methods and also described the TP safe harbours available in Brazil.

55. *See* Double Taxation Conventions signed by Brazil that are in force, or were in the case of Germany (all in Portuguese), available at, https://receita.economia.gov.br/acesso-rapido/legislacao/acordos-internacionais/acordos-para-evitar-a-dupla-tributacao/acordos-para-evitar-a-dupla-tributacao (last accessed 9 October 2020).
56. Brazil; Singapore – Treaty between Brazil and Singapore approved by Brazilian Chamber of Deputies (6 March 2020), News IBFD (last accessed 9 October 2020).
57. For example, *see* CARF of 29 January 2009, 108-09.763, *Boehringer Ingelheim Do Brasil Quimica e Farmaceutica Ltda v. RFB*; and CARF of 29 August 2012, 1401-000.801, *Philips Eletronica Da Amazonia Ltda v. RFB* (all in Portuguese), available at, http://carf.fazenda.gov.br/sincon/public/pages/ConsultarJurisprudencia/listaJurisprudencia.jsf (last accessed 30 January 2022).
58. *See* CARF of 30 March 2012, 1103-00.608, *Comercial Sao Nicolau Ltda v. RFB* (in Portuguese), available at, http://carf.fazenda.gov.br/sincon/public/pages/ConsultarJurisprudencia/listaJurisprudencia.jsf (last accessed 30 January 2022).
59. OECD, *Making Dispute Resolution More Effective: MAP Peer Review Report, Brazil (Stage 1): Inclusive Framework on BEPS: Action 14*, OECD and G20 Base Erosion and Profit Shifting Project (Paris: OECD Publishing, 2019) https://doi.org/10.1787/12acb5ea-en. (last accessed 30 January 2022).
60. Ministry of Finance, Secretariat of the Federal Revenue of Brazil (RFB), Manual Mutual Agreement Procedure (2018), available at, http://receita.economia.gov.br/acesso-rapido/legislacao/acordos-internacionais/map/manual-map_en.pdf (last accessed 30 January 2022).
61. OECD, *supra* n. 5.

The longstanding limitation for deductions on outbound expenses of royalties and technical, scientific, administrative, or similar assistance is described in section 4 as those transactions are excluded from the TP control in Brazil.

As noted, Brazilian TP rules were introduced and inspired by the 1979 OECD Report and thus presented the arm's length principle in Brazil. However, the rules that only include methods similar to the traditional methods were not updated to follow the changes in the international TP framework recommended in the recent versions of the OECD TPG and UN TPM. The evolution of TP rules in Brazil was instead heavily influenced by recurring disputes. As noted in section 2, the cases decided by the CARF from 2004 to 2018 refer to the taxable years of 1997 to 2010 prior to changes introduced by Law 12,715/2012. In this respect, it will be interesting to see the CARF understanding once cases based on more recent taxable years are decided.

Finally, Brazil and the OECD published a joint assessment of similarities and divergences between the Brazilian TP framework and the OECD TPG, including options for the alignment of the rules with the OECD TPG.[62] To date, there have been no changes introduced in Brazilian legislation as a result of the Brazil/OECD Project.

62. OECD, *supra* n. 13.

CHAPTER 23

Transfer Pricing in China

Shimeng Lan

1 INTRODUCTION

China's TP legislation was initiated in the 1990s and went through major changes in 2016 and 2017 following the OECD BEPS Project. The arm's length principle is the cornerstone of TP in China, which is reflected in the Chinese domestic law and the DTCs.

As with other developing countries, China faces several challenges in its TP practices including the lack of reliable comparables, quantification and allocation of LSA, and the identification and valuation of intangibles.[1] Though China's current TP rules largely accord with the OECD TPG, through years of practice, the STA[2] has developed its own approaches to respond to the challenges and unique questions arising from China. It has shared some of its views and experience in the China Country Practice Chapter in the UN TPM (2013, 2017 and 2021 versions).

This chapter provides an overview of the theoretical and practical framework of TP in China. It begins with an introduction of the TP legal framework and continues with the explanations of important notions, TP methods and documentation requirements under Chinese law. Next, it sheds light on the STA's views and practices on specific issues related to LSA, intangibles and intra-group services. It further presents the STA's experience on the TP administration and dispute prevention and resolution. Last, but not least, it analyses the potential impact of the Unified Approach on China before recapturing the major findings.

2 LEGAL FRAMEWORK

China's first TP legislation can be traced back to 1991 under the Income Tax Law for Enterprises with Foreign Investment and Foreign Enterprises. This relatively late start can be explained by its economic background. China previously had a planned economy until the reform and opening up in 1978.[3] During the 1980s and 1990s, the main economic policy of the Chinese Government was to attract FDI by granting tax incentives with a tax exemption or reduced rate.[4] Tax revenue from foreign-invested

1. UN TPM D.2.4.1.1.
2. The name of the national taxation authority used to be 'State Administration of Taxation (SAT)', but it was changed to STA in 2019. The author refers to the STA throughout the chapter for consistency.
3. Justin Yifu Lin, Fang Cai and Zhou Li, *The Lessons of China's Transition to a Market Economy*, Cato Journal, Vol. 16, No. 2, 201, 201 (Fall 1996).
4. Shanwu Yuan, Jinghua Liu and Glenn DeSouza, *Changing Transfer Pricing Landscape: 'Like It or Not'*, Bulletin for International Taxation, July/August, 259, 260 (2013).

companies at that time was minimal.[5] This situation was changed in 2008 when China adjusted the tax rate and tax base between foreign and domestic companies so that there would be no difference. Against this backdrop, many foreign-invested companies are becoming profitable after years of operations in China.[6] On the other hand, more Chinese companies began to invest abroad, especially in other developing countries.[7] The concern of base erosion and profit shifting motivated the tax authorities to enhance the TP rules.[8]

Currently, the legal basis of TP in China consists of four parts:

(1) EITL.
(2) EITL Rules.
(3) The Law of Tax Administration and Collection.
(4) Announcements/Circulars from the STA (mainly) and MoF.

The first three laws and regulations provide a general framework for TP rules in China. For example, Articles 41-44 of the EITL concern TP rules. They are placed under the chapter 'Special Adjustments to Tax Payments'. These articles broadly set out principal rules of TP.

A summary of the articles is as follows (*see* Table 23.1).

Table 23.1 Key Articles in the EITL Concerning TP Rules

Article 41	Provides a legal basis for tax authorities to make special adjustments to transactions between related parties that are not in accordance with the arm's length principle based on reasonable TP method, and to allocate cost based on the arm's length principle. Provides a legal basis for CSA
Article 42	Provides a legal basis for APAs
Article 43	Provides a legal basis for enterprises to submit TPDs in the event of an investigation by the tax authorities
Article 44	Provides a legal basis for the tax authorities to assess taxable income if an enterprise refuses to provide information regarding its related-party transactions or provides false or incomplete information

Similar to the EITL, the EITL Implementation Rules and the Law of Tax Administration and Collection also set out general principles regarding TP implementation and

5. Claire (Xue) Peng, *A Rethink of Location-Specific Advantages with an Analysis of the Chinese Approach,* Bulletin for International Taxation, November/December, 482, 492 (2017).
6. *See* Yuan et al., *supra* n. 4.
7. *Ibid.*
8. *See* Yuan et al., *supra* n. 4, and Peng, *supra* n. 5.

administration. They are also quite brief but do not contain detailed practical guidelines. In practice, the announcements/circulars issued by the STA are most frequently referred to by taxpayers and tax practitioners.

In 2009, the STA issued the Implementation Measures of Special Tax Adjustments – Guoshuifa No. 2 (Circular 2).[9] This was the most important TP legislative document in the pre-BEPS era.[10] However, many rules under this circular became obsolete due to the announcements that were introduced later.

From 2016, the STA began to revamp the TP rules taking into account the BEPS Actions.[11] Three announcements became particularly important. Announcement 42[12] details the concepts of related parties and the TPD requirements. Announcement 64 updated the APA rules set forth in Circular 2.[13] It also includes an exchange of information clause in accordance with the BEPS Action 5.[14] Announcement 6,[15] in March 2017, marked the completion of the BEPS-inspired TP framework.[16] It sets out specific tax audits procedures[17] and penalties applicable to TP adjustments. It provides practical guidance on the comparability analysis[18] and different TP methods.[19] In addition, it also specifies the MAP procedures reflecting BEPS Action 14.[20] It is also worth mentioning that Article 24 provides that the tax authorities should prioritize public information when doing a comparability analysis but may also use non-public information thus establishing the legal basis for tax authorities for the so-called secret comparable.[21]

Table 23.2 provides a brief summary of the three Announcements' contents.

9. Notice of the State Administration of Taxation on Issuing the Measures for the Implementation of Special Tax Adjustments (for Trial Implementation) (No. 2 [2009] of the State Administration of Taxation) (unofficial translation).
10. For example, it provides guidelines on related-party filing, contemporaneous documentation management, TP methods, TP investigation and adjustments, APA, CSA.
11. Cheng Chi, Patrick Lu, Choon Beng Teoh and Kelly Liao, *Now That China Has Data, What Is It Going Do with It?*, https://www.internationaltaxreview.com/article/b1fydc6pd5rw7c/now-that-china-has-data-what-is-it-going-do-with-it (last accessed 29 January 2022).
12. The Public Notice on the Enhancement of the Reporting of Related Party Transactions and Administration of Contemporaneous Documentation (Public Notice of the State Administration of Taxation [2016] 42) (unofficial translation).
13. The Public Notice of the State Administration of Taxation on the Issues Concerning Improving the Administration of Advance Pricing Arrangements (The Public Notice No. 64 [2016] of the State Administration of Taxation) (unofficial translation).
14. Article 20 of the Announcement No. 64.
15. Public Notice of the State Administration of Taxation on Issuing the 'Administrative Measures of Special Tax Investigation and Adjustment and Mutual Agreement Procedure' (SAT Public Notice [2017] No. 6) (unofficial translation).
16. Cheng Chi, Xiaoyue Wang, Kelly Liao, Mimi Wang and Rafael Miraglia, *TP in China: All the Data in the World*, International Tax Review, 28 November 2017, https://www.internationaltaxreview.com/article/b1f7nb15cznbhk/tp-in-china-all-the-data-in-the-world (last accessed 29 January 2022).
17. Articles 5-13 of the Announcement 6.
18. Articles 15 and 27 of the Announcement 6.
19. Articles 26-22 of the Announcement 6.
20. Articles 47-60 of the Announcement 6.
21. Article 24 of the Announcement 6.

Table 23.2 Brief Summary of STA Announcement Nos 42, 64 and 6

Announcement 42	Related parties (Article 2)
	Related transactions (Article 4)
	TP contemporaneous documentation requirements (the rest of the articles)
Announcement 64	Specific procedures and requirements of APA (the rest)
	Exchange of unilateral APA (Article 20)
Announcement 6	Specific tax adjustments (Articles 2-14) (Articles 23-29) (Articles 37-46)
	Comparability analysis (Article 15, Article 24)
	TP methods (Articles 16-22)
	Intangibles (Articles 30-33)
	Intra-group services (Articles 34-36)
	MAP (Articles 47-61)

3 IMPORTANT CONCEPTS, TP METHODS AND DOCUMENTATION

3.1 Important Concepts

3.1.1 Related Parties

Announcement 42 provides a rather broad definition of 'related parties' under Article 2. An enterprise may be considered related to other enterprises, organizations, or individuals in any of the following seven scenarios:

(1) Share ownership
This is the most common relationship between related parties. If one party directly or indirectly holds 25% of the other party or a common unrelated party holds both parties' shares, the two parties are related parties.[22] Announcement 42 further clarifies that, if the shareholder holds the shares of the other party through an intermediary, the percentage of shares held by the intermediary will be considered as being held by the shareholder as long as the shareholder holds 25% or more of the shares of the intermediary. If two natural persons with a spousal relationship, lineal consanguinity, sibling, or maintenance or support relationship jointly hold the shares, the percentage of their holdings should be combined.[23]

22. Article 2(1) first paragraph of the Announcement 42.
23. Article 2(1) second and third paragraph of the Announcement 42.

(2) Debt relationship
Under this scenario, the proportion of shareholding does not exceed the 25% threshold. However, if one party grants a loan to the other party taking up 50% or more of the paid-in capital or guarantees 10% or more of the total debts of the other party, the two parties are also regarded as related.[24]

Court Case

In a case published by the China Taxation News in 2017, the Chang Zhou tax authorities determined related parties according to their debt relationship.[25] Construction Company A has transferred the shares it held in Bank J to Company B for a total amount of CNY 46.8 million. Company A did not declare the transfer of shares in its tax return and was audited by the tax authorities. During the investigation, they realized that Company A has a debt amounting to CNY 42 million that was lent by Company B. The paid-in capital of Company A was CNY 70 million. Since the debt from Company B exceeded 50% of Company A's paid-in capital, the two companies were determined as related parties. Tax authorities made TP adjustments on this basis.

(3) Control over licensing of intangibles
This situation arises when the shareholding proportion does not reach the 25% threshold, but one party can only conduct production or business if the other party provides the patent, non-patent technologies, trademark, copyright, or any other franchised right.[26]

---

24. Announcement further clarifies how to calculate the proportion of total amount of loans to paid-in capital. Article 2(2) provides:

> Where both parties have the shareholding relationship or their shares are held by a same unrelated party, if, although the shareholding proportion fails to comply with the provisions of item (1) herein, the total amount of loans received by one party from the other party accounts for 50% or more of the first-mentioned party's paid-in capital, or 10% or more of total amount of loans received by the first-mentioned party are guaranteed by the other party (excluding loan or guarantee with independent party financial institutions).

Proportion of total amount of loans to paid-in capital = annual weighted average amount of loans/annual weighted average paid-in capital, among which:
Annual weighted average amount of loans = book amount of loans in i transactions × actual number of borrowing or lending days for loans in i transactions in a year/365.
Annual weighted average paid-in capital = book amount of paid-in capital in i transactions × actual number of days involved in paid-in capital in i transactions in a year/365. (Unofficial translation by en.pkulaw.cn).

25. In China, most TP cases investigated by the tax authorities are not published. A small number of cases are published in the local or national newspaper with anonymous information on taxpayers. This case was published by the China Taxation News on 18 July 2017. The authors of this news are Guohua Yang, Jishan Jiang, and Yingying Zhu.
26. Article 2(3) of the Announcement 42:

> Where both parties have the shareholding relationship or their shares are held by a same unrelated party, although the shareholding proportion fails to reach that as specified in item (1) herein, the production and business operations of one party can be normally conducted

(4) Control over procurement and sales
Similar to the previous situation, the shareholding proportion in this scenario does not reach the 25% threshold. One party controls the other party's procurement and sales including goods and services or any other business operation.[27]

(5) Control over appointment of senior personnel
If more than half of the directors or senior executives of one party are appointed or assigned by the other party or serve as the other party's directors or senior executives concurrently, the two parties are regarded as related. Further, if more than half of the directors or senior executives of both parties are appointed or assigned by a common unrelated party, the two parties are also regarded as related.[28]

Senior executives include the secretary of the board of directors, manager, deputy manager, chief financial officer of a listed company and other personnel prescribed in the company's bylaws.[29]

(6) Natural persons
Two natural persons who are spouses, relatives, siblings or because of custodianship or family maintenance and support relationship are related to each other if any of the conditions described above under 1-5 is fulfilled;[30]

(7) If the two parties have any other common interest in nature, they may also be regarded as related to each other.[31] This is the catchall clause that provides tax authorities with discretions in the event of any situations outside the scope of the first six scenarios.

3.1.2 Related-Party Transactions

There are mainly five types of related-party transactions:[32]

(1) transfer of the right to use or ownership of tangible assets;
(2) transfer of the right to use or ownership of intangibles;

---

only if the other party provides the patent right, non-patent technologies, trademark right, copyright or any other franchised right. (Unofficial translation by en.pkulaw.cn).

27. Article 2(4) of the Announcement 42:

> Where both parties have the shareholding relationship or their shares are held by a same unrelated party, although the shareholding proportion fails to reach that as specified in item (1) herein, the procurement, sale, receipt of labour services, provision of labour services, or any other business operation of the first-mentioned party is controlled by the other party.

The aforesaid control means that one party has the right to decide the other party's financial and business policies, and obtains benefits from the other party's business activities on such as basis. (Unofficial translation by en.pkulaw.cn).

28. Article 2(5) of the Announcement 42.
29. *Ibid.*
30. Article 2(6) of the Announcement 42.
31. Article 2(7) of the Announcement 42.
32. Article 4 of the Announcement 42.

(3) transfer of financial assets;
(4) financing services; and
(5) labour service.

Among others, financial assets include assets originating from accounts receivables, notes receivables, other receivables, equity investment, and derivative financial instruments. Financing services include all types of long- and short-term loans including a capital pool of the group, guarantee expenses, all types of prepayments with accrued interest, and delayed receipts and payments, among others.[33]

3.2 TP Methods

Taxpayers and tax authorities could choose from the following six methods for their TP study: CUP, RPM, CPM, TNMM, PSM, and other appropriate methods.[34] Other appropriate methods include asset valuation methods applying a cost approach, market approach, or income approach and methods that reflect the basic principle that profit attribution aligns with economic substance and value creation.[35] It is worth mentioning that China does not rule out formulary apportionment as an alternative method in TP.[36] Furthermore, there is no order of priority among the methods.[37]

In practice, the TNMM is the most popular method used by both taxpayers and tax authorities in TP audits; with the FCMU being the most used PLI.[38] In recent years, the tax authorities have also actively explored other methods such as the PSM, especially when significant marketing intangibles and LSAs are involved.[39]

The tax authorities are also keen on assessing the profits of the tested Chinese entity in light of the GVCA of the entire MNE, especially when there are practical difficulties finding appropriate comparables.[40] As *Li* states, China 'supports a holistic, "family-oriented" approach to the allocation of MNEs' profit among jurisdictions where value-creation activities take place'.[41] It allows the tax authorities to allocate profits to the Chinese entities based on important value drivers (e.g., LSAs and intangibles)

33. *Ibid.*
34. Article 16 of the Announcement 6.
35. Article 22 of the Announcement 6.
36. UN TPM D.2.4.7.3.
37. UN TPM D.2.3.6.1.
38. Tony Dong, Daisy Duan, Alice Zhang and Xuerong Bai, *Transfer Pricing in China: Overview* (King & Wood Mallesons 2022), https://uk.practicallaw.thomsonreuters.com/w-007-8954?transitionType=Default&contextData=(sc.Default)&firstPage=true#co_anchor_I60a29376523d11e89bf199c0ee06c731 (last accessed 29 January 2022); Baker & McKenzie, Newsletter: Transfer Pricing (People's Republic of China) p. 5 (January 2013). Also *see* Jin Yan Li, *International Taxation in China: A Contextualized Analysis*, section 10.5.6.3, P.424 (IBFD 2016).
39. *See* Dong et al., *supra* n. 38 and Baker & McKenzie Newsletter. *See also* Li, *supra* n. 38, section 10.5.7.3, P.427. *See also* the UN TPM D.2.4.6.13.
40. *See* Li, *supra* n. 38, in section 10.4.2.3, P.409. *See also* Article 21, 2nd paragraph of the Announcement 6.
41. Jinyan Li and Stephen Ji, *Location-Specific Advantages: A Rising Disruptive Factor in Transfer Pricing*, Bulletin for International Taxation, Vol. 71, 259, 261 (May 2017).

created in China by either applying the PSM or reducing the 'royalties' or 'service fee' payments to the foreign-related party.[42]

3.3 Transfer Pricing Documentation

Under Chinese tax law, taxpayers bear the burden of proof that their related-party transactions are in accordance with the arm's length principle. Taxpayers shall comply with the annual reporting obligations and provide relevant information upon the request of tax authorities in the case of a TP audit.[43]

Announcement 42 regulates the reporting obligations of enterprises that consists of three major parts: the contemporary documentation, the CbCR, and the annual reporting form on related-party transactions.

3.3.1 Contemporary Documentation

Contemporary documentation includes the master file, local file, and special issue file.[44]

Master File

A company must prepare a MF if it fulfils one of the two conditions below:[45]

(1) it has cross-border transactions and belongs to a group in which the ultimate holding company with consolidated financial statements has prepared the master file; or
(2) the total amount of related-party transactions exceeds CNY 1 billion.

The reporting information required in the master file is mostly the same as that for the OECD TPG except for the following extra information not required in the OECD TPG:[46]

(1) For the description of business, it requires enterprises to report business restructuring including industrial structure adjustments and the transfer of corporate functions and risks or assets within the group.
(2) For the intangibles, it requires to report not only the location of principal R&D facilities and location of R&D management but also their primary functions, risks, assets, and personnel.

42. *See* Li, *supra* n. 38, in section 10.4.2.3, P.409 and section 10.5.7.3, P.427.
43. Article 43 of the EIT law.
44. Article 10 of the Announcement 42.
45. Article 11 of the Announcement 42.
46. Article 12 of the Announcement 42.

(3) For financial and tax positions, it requires not only unilateral APA but also bilateral APAs to be disclosed. In addition, the name and location of the reporting entity for the CbCR need to be reported.

Local File

A company has to prepare a LF if the value of its related-party transactions exceeds one of the following thresholds:[47]

- CNY 200 million for the transfer of tangibles;
- CNY 100 million for the transfer of intangibles;
- CNY 100 million for the transfer of financial assets; and
- CNY 40 million for the transfer of other assets.

The requirements of the local file under Announcement 42 are also largely consistent with the OECD TPG with more detailed explanations on each item of information that is required to be disclosed. For example, for tested transactions, it specifies that the factors affecting the pricing may include intangible assets, cost savings, market premiums, and other location-specific factors.[48]

An important deviation from the OECD TPG is the inclusion of the GVCA in the local file. It requires information at every stage of the business flow, logistics, and capital flow within the entire group, including the design, development, manufacturing, marketing, sales, delivery, settlement, consumption, after-sales service, recycling, and the financial statements of each of the above participants of the recent financial year.[49] It also requires an analysis of the impact of LSA on the value creation of the enterprise.[50] This bears the underlying assumption that the LSA generates additional profits for the MNE.[51] Furthermore, the enterprise also needs to present the allocation principle and result of the profit allocation of the group in the global value chain.[52] These requirements are more stringent than the OECD TPG.[53]

In addition, Announcement 42 also has detailed rules on the disclosure of information related to intra-group services, intra-group share transfers, and outbound investments.[54] These requirements are more specific and detailed than the OECD TPG.

For the selection of the most reasonable TP method, Announcement 42 requires the enterprise to demonstrate its contribution to the overall profit or residual profit of the

47. Article 13 of the Announcement 42.
48. Article 14(3)-1 of the Announcement 42.
49. Article 14(3)-2 of the Announcement 42.
50. *Ibid.*
51. *See* Li and Ji, *supra* n. 41, p. 264.
52. *Ibid.*
53. KPMG, *State Administration of Taxation (SAT) Issued Announcement on the Enhancement of the Reporting of Related Party Transactions and Administration of Contemporaneous Documentation*, China Tax Alert – Issue 23, July 2016, https://home.kpmg/cn/en/home/insights/2016/07/china-tax-alert-23.html (last accessed 29 January 2022).
54. Article 14 of the Announcement 42.

entire group no matter which method is chosen.[55] This is also beyond the requirement in the OECD TPG.

Special Issues File

A special issues file includes information on CSAs and thin capitalization.[56] The CSA file requires enterprises to present the basic information of the CSA, e.g., the entry/exit of participants in the year in question, the comparison between the expected and actual profit, and the adjustments made thereafter.[57] The thin capitalization file essentially examines whether unrelated parties are able and willing to accept the debt with the same terms under similar circumstances.[58]

3.3.2 CbCR

A Chinese enterprise is required to file the CbCR when it is the ultimate holding company of a group with annual consolidated group revenue in the immediately preceding fiscal year of more than RMB 5.5 billion (approximately EUR 678 million) or when it is appointed by the MNE as the reporting entity of the group.[59] Tax authorities may also request a CbCR even without fulfilling the conditions above. This occurs when the subordinate MNE prepares a CbCR in accordance with relevant regulations of other countries but meets one of the following conditions:[60]

- The MNE has not provided country reports to any country.
- Although the MNE has provided country reports to other countries, the country has not yet established an exchange of information mechanism with China.
- Although multinational enterprise groups have provided a CbCR to other countries and that country has established an exchange of information mechanism with China, the CbCR has not actually been successfully exchanged with China.

It also provides an exemption for a total or partial CbCR obligation when the ultimate holding enterprise of the MNE is a Chinese resident company and its information involves national security.

Other requirements of the CbCR are broadly consistent with the BEPS report including the definition of ultimate holding company and the format of the report.

55. *Ibid.*
56. Article 15 of the Announcement 42.
57. Article 16 of the Announcement 42.
58. Article 17 of the Announcement 42.
59. Article 5 of the Announcement 42.
60. Article 8 of the Announcement 42.

3.3.3 *Annual Reporting Form on Related-Party Transactions*

The annual reporting form on related-party transactions consists of the following 22 sub-forms (*see* Table 23.3).

Table 23.3 Overview of the Annual Reporting Form on Related-Party Transactions

1. Information sheet for the reporting entity
2. Summary table of annual related business transactions of enterprises of the People's Republic of China
3. Related-party relationship table
4. Tangible assets ownership transactions table
5. Intangibles ownership transactions table
6. Tangible asset user right transactions table
7. Tangibles user right transactions table
8. Financial asset transactions table
9. Financing form
10. Related-party services table
11. Equity investment table
12. CSA table
13. Foreign payments table
14. Foreign-related party information table
15. Annual related business transactions financial statement table (reporting the information of the individual enterprise)
16. Annual related business transactions financial statement (reporting the consolidated information on enterprises)
17. & 18. CbCR – Overview of allocation of income, taxes and business activities by tax jurisdiction (in Chinese and English)
19. & 20. CbCR – List of all the constituent entities of the MNE included in each aggregation per tax jurisdiction (in Chinese and English)
21. & 22. CbCR – Additional Information (in Chinese and English)

Previously, the annual reporting form contains only nine sub-tables.[61] Comparatively, the new table under Announcement 42 includes more details. For example, it added the financial assets transaction information, CSA information, and the financial statement of annual related business transactions. It is also more specific. For example, the tangible and intangible assets were split into two parts emphasizing ownership and user rights.

61. The requirements were set out in the Guoshuifa [2008] No. 114 which is invalid now.

4 PRACTICAL SOLUTIONS TO UNIQUE CHALLENGES IN CHINA

4.1 Location Saving Advantages

4.1.1 Theoretical Framework

The LSAs are defined as advantages for production arising from assets, resource endowments, government industry policies and incentives, etc., which exist in specific localities' in the UN TPM China practice chapter.[62] It includes advantages from location savings and market premium. The STA initially proposed the concept of location savings in 2009[63] and that of market premium in 2011.[64]

Location savings are defined as 'the economic benefit arising from moving operations to a low-cost jurisdiction'.[65] In the case of China, net cost savings may derive from low costs on raw materials, labour, rent, infrastructure, etc.[66] The UN TPM provided an example: 'Household electronics manufacturers invest in China to take advantage of a large pool of well-educated low-cost labour and a well-developed network of suppliers, or global automotive companies set up JVs in China to assemble automobiles locally to be close to the market and the customers and to take advantage of lower costs.'

The concept of market premium is less concise and not as widely accepted as location savings.[67] Under the UN TPM, it is defined as 'the additional profit derived from a jurisdiction with unique qualities impacting on the sale and demand for a service or product'.[68] Typical examples of market premiums in China arise from luxury goods, pharmaceutical, and automotive industries.[69]

Several unique characteristics of the Chinese market may contribute to the market premium.[70] The continuously high demand from that market is the most important contributing factor to the market premium. Some Chinese consumers, especially young consumers with strong purchasing power, tend to buy foreign brands over those that are domestic. This preference drives the price upward. Further, the Chinese market faces more ethical issues (e.g., food safety issues) and information asymmetry compared to developed countries. Chinese consumers tend to be willing to pay a higher premium to ensure a better quality of goods and services.

From the supply end, several sectors have industry access systems that entail first-mover advantages for those that enter early. Furthermore, for certain industries,

62. UN TPM D.2.4.4.1.
63. Notice of the SAT's Work on the Anti-Tax Avoidance in 2008, Guo Shui Han [2009] 106, 6 March 2009.
64. Notice of the SAT's Work on the Anti-Tax Avoidance in 2010, Guo Shui Han [2011] 167, 14 July 2011.
65. UN TPM B.1.10.14.
66. UN TPM D.2.4.4.3.
67. *See* Li and Ji, *supra* n. 41, p. 261.
68. UN TPM D.2.4.4.4.
69. UN TPM D.2.4.4.10. For a specific example of the automobile industry, *see* D.2.4.4.7.
70. The following points are all summarized by the Research Group of Tax Bureau Directly under Guangzhou National Tax Bureau, *Research and Practice Exploration on Market Premium in Special Tax Adjustment*, International Taxation in China, 9th issue, 49, 50 (2015).

especially luxurious goods, the quality and brand awareness of domestic products develop comparatively less rapid than those that are foreign. The watch industry can be used as an example. In China, the high-end (over CNY 5,000) and mid-end (CNY 1,500-2,000) markets are dominated by Swiss-brand watches with domestic brands only accounting for approximately 25% of the market.[71] These factors contribute to higher prices and consumption of the same goods and services in China compared to other markets which results in additional profits for MNEs.[72]

4.1.2 Application of the Location Saving Advantages in a TP Analysis

The STA attaches substantial importance to the role of the LSA in a TP analysis. This can be seen from the frequency of its appearance in the legislation. It was mentioned three times in Announcement 6 for the purpose of comparative analysis and selection of the TP methods.[73] Furthermore, Announcement 42 requires the analysis of the impact of the LSA on the value creation in the local file. Announcement 64 also requires taxpayers to prepare an LSA analysis in the application documentation for the APAs. The general assumption behind those rules is that the LSA generates additional profits for MNEs through the activities of the Chinese local entities.[74] Therefore, the Chinese entities should receive reasonable compensation for such contributions.[75]

STA applies a four-step approach on the issue of LSAs:

(1) identify if an LSA exists;
(2) determine whether the LSA generates additional profit;
(3) quantify and measure the additional profits arising from the LSA; and
(4) determine the TP method to allocate the profits arising from the LSA.

In practice, this approach is relevant for a comparability analysis, selection of TP method, and allocation of profits. In terms of the comparability analysis, the STA accounts for the LSAs by making comparability adjustments to the foreign comparables

71. Analysis of the development pattern of China's watch industry in 2019, four favourable development factors and market trends, https://www.chyxx.com/industry/202002/833534.html (last accessed 29 January 2022).
72. *See* Research Group of Tax Bureau Directly under Guangzhou National Tax Bureau, *supra* n. 70, p. 51.
73. Article 15 requires taxpayers to consider the LSA as part of the economic environment element when conducting a comparative analysis. Article 21 requires considering the LSAs for a comparability analysis under the PSM to determine the reliability of information and assumptions used to evaluate the contribution of each related party to the residual profit. Article 27 requires to consider the LSA when the selected comparables are in different economic environments and to select an appropriate transfer pricing method to determine the contribution to profits derived from the location-specific factors.
74. *See* Li and Ji, *supra* n. 41, p. 264. The LSAs do not necessarily generate location rents. However, Chinese law does not have the concept of 'location rent' and generally assumes there is location rent from the LSAs. For more analysis on the location rent, *see* this Article. *See also* Peng, *supra* n. 5, p. 485.
75. *See* Li and Ji, *supra* n. 41, p. 265.

when local comparables are not available.[76] One example was provided in the UN TPM China practice chapter. Companies in the Asia Pacific region, especially Korea and Japan, are often used for benchmarking when applying profit-based methods.[77] The STA often makes adjustments to the comparables to reduce the differences in the geographical markets.[78]

In terms of the TP method, when significant LSAs are identified, the STA attempts to factor them by applying the PSM or performing comparability adjustments when the TNMM is used. For example, if the median operating expense to sales ratio for the comparable set was only 7%, and the same ratio for the taxpayer was 40%, to the extent there are location savings, the Chinese tax authorities would first adjust the cost base. They would then calculate the additional return required for the extra efforts made by the Chinese taxpayer to derive the total return for that individual.[79]

Furthermore, in the STA's view, the LSA is also a distinct value-creating factor that affects the allocation of profit to the Chinese entity. Its contribution to value creation is 'no less than' intangibles.[80]

In the UN TPM, the allocation of profits taking into account location savings was explained with an example. The Chinese subsidiary provides contract R&D services to the foreign parent company. The cost base of the Chinese entity for the service is 100. Had foreign companies in a developed country conducted the same service, the base would have been 150. The CPM is applied assuming the median FCMU based on foreign comparables (mostly in developed countries) is 8% (*see* Figure 23.1).

Figure 23.1 Pictorial Representation of the Example

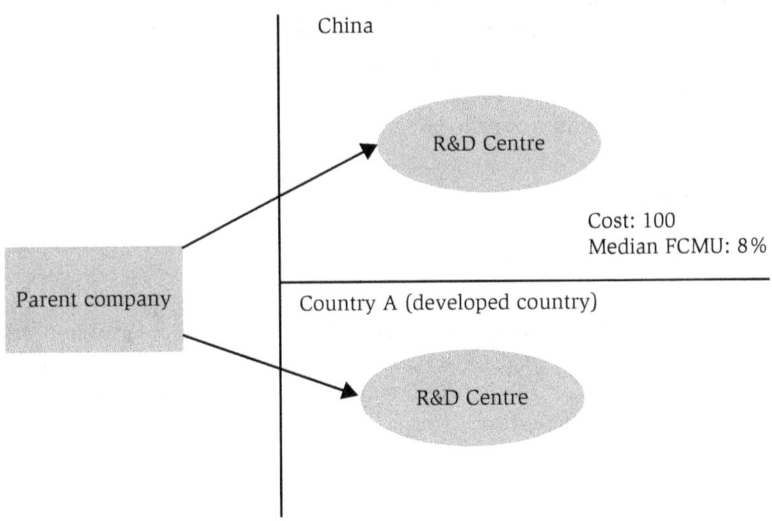

76. UN TPM D.2.4.6.12.
77. UN TPM D.2.4.3.5.
78. UN TPM D.2.4.3.6.
79. UN TPM D.2.4.6.13.
80. *See* Li and Ji, *supra* n. 41, p. 263. *See also* A Research Group of Tax Bureau Directly under Guangzhou National Tax Bureau, *supra* n. 70, p. 52.

The steps and calculations of the Chinese tax authorities are as follows (*see* Table 23.4).

Table 23.4 The Steps and Calculations of the Chinese Tax Authorities

	Steps	*Calculations*
i	Calculate the arm's length range of FCMUs based on foreign comparables, mostly in developed countries	Assume the median FCMU is 8%
ii	Calculate the difference between the cost base of the Chinese taxpayer (e.g., 100) and the average cost base of the foreign companies (e.g., 150)	150 – 100 = 50
iii	Multiply the arm's length FCMU (e.g., 8%) with the difference in the cost bases (50)	0.08 × 50 = 4
iv	The resulting profit is the additional profit (i.e., 4) attributable to China for location savings	4
v	Determine the total arm's length profit for the Chinese taxpayer	4 + 0.08 × 100 = 12
vi	Determine the adjusted arm's length FCMU for the Chinese taxpayer	12/100 = 12%

The STA reached the additional profit attributable to the LSA by multiplying the FCMU by the difference in the cost base. This example is quite self-explanatory. However, in the event of a market premium, the identification and quantification are less straightforward and require both an industrial and quantitative analysis.[81] Currently, there is no further guidance from the STA on how to conduct such an analysis.[82] Neither are there safe harbour rules. Therefore, taxpayers may face uncertainty in allocating the profits arising from the LSAs.

4.2 Intangibles

4.2.1 Theoretical Framework

According to the Implementation Rules of the EITL, intangibles refer to non-monetary long-term assets without physical substance that are held by an enterprise for use in the manufacturing of goods or the rendering of services, for lease to others, or for administrative purposes, including patents, trademarks, copyrights, land use-rights,

81. In an interview with Transfer Pricing Weekly, Liao Tizhong, Deputy Director General of International Taxation of the SAT, cautioned that it is more difficult to apply the analysis to market premiums. Liao suggested that economic modelling and potentially an econometric analysis and game theory should be explored in ascertaining the profits generated by market premiums. *See* Sophie Ashley, *SAT's Liao Tizhong Discusses China's Transfer Pricing Position: Part One*, Transfer Pricing Weekly (30 April 2013).

82. *See also* A Research Group of Tax Bureau Directly under Guangzhou National Tax Bureau, *supra* n. 70, p. 52.

non-patented technologies, goodwill, etc.[83] There is no explicit reference to trade intangibles and marketing intangibles under the law although these terms are being used.

Court Case

In a case published by the STA,[84] the multinational company A fully owns Chinese Subsidiary B. To help Company B expand its business in the Chinese market, Company A provides the data of its clients from all over the world to Company B on a long-term basis. Company B characterizes this as client-introduction and transaction facilitation services and therefore pays 5% service fees to Company A. However, the STA thinks the client data owned by Company A is a marketing intangible. Therefore, the STA made special adjustments and charged a 10% withholding tax to royalties. This is in accordance with the OECD definition of marketing intangibles that include customer lists, customer relationships, and customer data that is used or aids in marketing and selling goods or services to customers.[85]

4.2.2 Practice

While acknowledging that MNEs in developed countries often develop superior technical intangibles and provide them to Chinese related parties, the STA places more emphasis on the contribution of the Chinese entities to the value creations of the intangibles and discusses whether local activities generate unique intangibles.[86]

For example, the STA is often sceptical about royalties with a fixed rate for multiple years and thinks they should be periodically adjusted to reflect real economic value for the Chinese entity.[87] This often relates to manufacturing businesses. The primary reasons are twofold. First, throughout the manufacturing process, if there is no improvement or innovations to the technologies, the economic benefits brought by the intangibles may decrease with the passing of time.[88] Second, Chinese entities may enhance technology through trial and error thereby increasing the value of the intangibles.[89] In addition, the STA also investigates whether the local manufacturers

83. Article 65 of the EITL Implementation Rules (Unofficial translation from Deloitte).
84. International Taxation Department of the STA, *Case collection of the tax administration of non-resident enterprises*, Case 2 under the Chapter of the royalty cases, China Taxation Publishing House (2012).
85. Jing Wu and Qing Xia, *International Perspectives on the Practical Application of Transfer Pricing on Marketing Intangibles*, International Taxation in China, 8th issue, 29, 34 (2019).
86. UN TPM D.2.4.5.1 and D. 2.4.5.4.
87. *See* Chi et al., *supra* n. 16, p. 39. Also *see* Li, *supra* n. 38, section 10.6.4.2, p. 435.
88. *See* Chi et al., *supra* n. 16, p. 39. *See also* Wei Liu and Jian Li, *The Analysis on the Tax Risk Assessment and Management on Royalties* (author translation), International Taxation in China, 3rd issue, 78, 79 (2020); Ling Su, *The Intangibles' Special Tax Adjustments Should Pay Attention to the Profit Attribution Issues Concerning MNE's R&D Institution in China,* International Taxation in China, 10th issue, 61, 64 (2018).
89. *Ibid.*

actively develop and maintain relationships with local customers thus generating intangibles in the form of local customer relationships.[90]

With regard to distributions, the STA often examines if the local distributor generates local marketing intangibles.[91]

Article 30 of the Announcement 6 provides:

> When determining the contribution made by an enterprise and its related parties to the value of intangibles and the corresponding allocation of returns, it is necessary to conduct a comprehensive analysis of the global operation process of the group to which the enterprise belongs, and fully consider the value contribution of each party in the development, enhancement, maintenance, protection, exploitation and *promotion* of the intangibles, how the value of intangibles is realized, and the interaction of the intangibles with business within the enterprise group with respect to functions performed, assets used and risks assumed. (emphasis added by the author)

Compared to the OECD, the STA not only focuses on the DEMPE functions but also on the 'promotion' function (DEMPEP). It is of the view that local distributors play a major role in promoting the recognition of foreign brands in the Chinese market and generate unique marketing intangibles in the course of such promotional activities which is witnessed by the incurred extraordinary expenses on advertisement, marketing, and sales activities.[92] The STA believes such marketing intangibles should be reasonably compensated.[93] It often applies the PSM to make such a compensation or to adjust the royalty rates that the Chinese entities pay to the foreign entities.[94] Furthermore, the STA also believes that marketing intangibles and the LSAs are often closely integrated for developing countries and should be comprehensively taken into account when calculating the compensation.[95]

Contract R&D is another model that attracts the attention of the STA. Under this model, Chinese entities typically undertake contract R&D services and are remunerated based on cost plus a 5%-10% mark-up.[96] The STA may argue differently if it believes that these entities should have economic ownership over the intangibles by performing the R&D activities in China.[97] This argument may be supported on the following grounds.

First, as the STA proposed in the UN TPM, in some cases, the alleged owner of the intangibles does not possess the technical expertise nor the financial capacity to

90. Deloitte Tax Comments, *The OECD Publishes guidelines on Intangibles: several issues need to be solved*, Issue P199/2014, 29 September 2014.
91. *Ibid.*
92. *See* Deloitte, *supra* n. 90. *See also*, Wu and Xia, *supra* n. 85, p. 34 *See also*, Lina Ye, *Marketing Intangible's Tax Base Division: From the Arm's Length Principle to the Market Premium Theory*, Social Science Journal, 7th issue, 90, 95 (2019).
93. *Ibid.*
94. *See* Deloitte, *supra* n. 90.
95. UN TPM D.2.4.5.1.
96. Xiaowei Shi, Qilei Peng and Yan Xue, *A Rethink of the Transfer Pricing Model of MNEs' R&D Function in China*, International Taxation in China, 2nd issue, 58, 59 (2020).
97. *See* Li, *supra* n. 38, in section 10.6.2, p. 432.

contribute to the value of the intangibles.[98] Second, the STA indicates that some of the Chinese contract R&D entities acquire the 'high and new technology status' in China and enjoy tax incentives on the basis of owning valuable core technology. This contradicts the claim that they merely perform a routine R&D services function that does not generate intangibles. Third, empirical research shows that most of the Chinese R&D centres have been upgraded to perform new production process design and new product development rather than simple technical support functions.[99] Chinese entities have generated valuable intangible assets in this process, and the CPM does not adequately reflect the upgraded functions performed and the value created by them.[100]

Furthermore, in the past, the following structure often appeared: the parent company of the MNE signed a CSA with a related party in a low-tax jurisdiction that serves as a 'cash box' company and enjoyed the economic rights of the intangibles. The parent company would consequently become the legal owner of the intangibles. On the other hand, the Chinese R&D entities that contributed to the development of the core intangibles were often regarded as mere R&D service providers instead of CSA participants and were not entitled to participate in the distribution of excess profits.[101]

Announcement 6 attempts to effectively address this situation. It provides:[102]

> The enterprise that only has legal ownership of the intangibles, but has made no contribution to the value of the intangibles should not be allocated with income derived from the intangibles. The enterprise that only provides funding during the development and exploitation of intangibles, but does not undertake relevant functions and assume relevant risks, should only be entitled to a reasonable return on the funding cost.

This adheres to the principle established in the TPG. However, due to a lack of knowledge and experience, it is often difficult for tax authorities to determine whether the related party has the ability to manage and control the financial risks related to the CSA.[103]

Under Chinese law, it is possible for a Chinese company to participate in a CSA in accordance with the arm's length principle.[104] Prior to 2015, Chinese entities that did so should have reported to the STA within thirty days from the date when the CSA was reached. Local tax authorities should have reviewed whether the CSA was in accordance with the arm's length principle and reported it to the STA for review and approval.[105] Announcements 27 and 45 in 2015 renounced this review and emphasized more on the post-conclusion supervision of the CSA.[106] This provided convenience for

98. UN TPM D.2.4.6.5.
99. *See* Shi et al., *supra* n. 96, p. 59. *See also* Su, *supra* n. 88, p. 62.
100. *See* Su, *supra* n. 88, p. 62.
101. *See* Shi et al., *supra* n. 96, p. 61.
102. Article 32 of the Announcement 6.
103. *Ibid.*
104. Article 41 of the EITL: 'Costs associated with the joint development or transfer of intangible assets, or with the provision or receipt of labour services shall be allocated based on the arm's length principle when computing taxable income.'
105. Article 69 of the Announcement 2.
106. Announcement on Regulating the Administration of Cost Apportionment Agreements, Announcement No. 45 [2015] of the State Administration of Taxation.

taxpayers to participate in a CSA, however, the current legal framework merely provided compliance rules for it without sufficient practical guidance on some of the key issues.[107] For example, there is no guidance on the allocation of expected benefits from the CSA and the pricing method for the buy-in and buy-out payments.[108] Therefore, taxpayers still face uncertainties in respect of certain technical issues.

4.2.3 *Case Study*

In 2011, the Guangzhou tax authorities published a case related to intangibles and the application of the PSM.[109] Company G, a tax resident in Guangzhou (China), is a subsidiary of Company C, a Chinese resident company jointly owned by a company resident in Hong Kong (China) and a company resident in Shenzhen (China). Since its establishment in 1994, Company G had steady sales revenue of approximately CNY 500 million each year. Since 2000, the revenue has rapidly increased to almost CNY 700-CNY 800 million. However, the company has always maintained a low-level profit with the average rate from 1996 to 2004 at only 3.51%. The Guangzhou tax authorities suspected the level of profit did not correspond with its sales performance and conducted a tax audit (*see* Figure 23.2).

Figure 23.2 Pictorial Representation of the Case Study

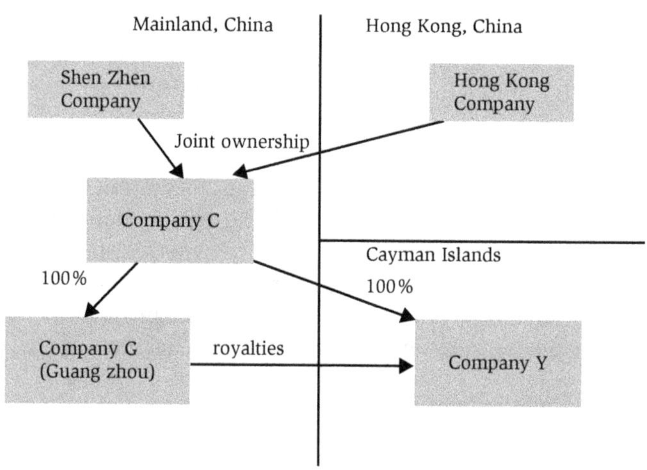

107. Article 16 of the Announcement 42 sets outs the documents to be reported in respect of CSAs.
108. *See* Deloitte Tax Comments, China promulgated new regulations on Cost Sharing Arrangements, Issue P225/2015, 13 August 2015.
109. ShenZhen Smart Finance&Tax Consulting Co., Ltd, *[Special attention] Classic case of profit split method of transfer pricing*, https://www.sohu.com/a/146703504_611489 (last accessed 29 January 2022).

The tax authorities found that Company G incurred significant sales expenses, among which, the royalties paid to Company Y for the use of trademark accounted for almost half of the total sales expenses. Company Y was the sister company of Company G, resident in the Cayman Islands with only CU 200 registered capital. Company G accrued CNY 480 million in royalties from 1996 to 2004 while its total profit over the years was only CNY 270 million. Company G initially paid 3.5% of its total sales revenue as royalties which was subsequently increased to 5% in 1996 and 7% in 1997 without relevant explanations on the basis for such increase.

Company G contended that it was a mere low-risk distributor and thus had a limited profit. However, the tax authorities ascertained that Company G performed an entire range of functions including the procurement and wholesale of products, planning and promotion of advertising across the nation, and coordination of the business development in different parts of the country. It was also responsible for establishing branches or franchise stores in various places and in charge of the management and supervision of such branches and stores to implement the group policies. It assumed the risks for all of the above functions and was not a low-risk distributor.

Tax authorities maintained that the increased value of the trademark was indispensable for Company G's endeavour in the local business development and promotion of the brand. However, none of the marketing expenses of Company G was remunerated. For this reason, the tax authorities determined that the 7% royalties were too high and adjusted the profit of Company G using the PSM.

The total profit used for the purpose of the split was CNY 480 million in royalties accrued by Company G. The operating profit rate of 15 comparable companies that performed routine distributor functions was between 3.87%-7.61%, and the median value was 6.43%. After negotiations and compromises from both parties, the company's routine profit rate from 1997 to 2004 was finally set at 6%. After adjusting the routine profits, the remaining profits were split between Company G and its related companies according to their respective functions and contributions. From 1997 to 2004, the taxable income increased by more than CNY 200 million, and more than CNY 60 million in additional corporate income tax was paid. After the adjustment, the average profit rate from 1997 to 2004 was 7.5%. Despite the undisclosed details of the calculation of the PSM, this case reflects the STA's position that Chinese entities' contribution to the value creation of intangibles through local business development and promotional activities should be reasonably compensated, and the PSM is a reasonable method under this circumstance.

4.3 Intra-group Services

4.3.1 Theoretical Framework

Intra-group services are regulated under Articles 34-36 of Announcement 6 which requires them to be in accordance with the arm's length principle; specifically, they should be beneficial services and the price should be at arm's length. Beneficial services are those that could bring direct or indirect economic benefits to the service recipient, and unrelated parties would have been willing to pay for or perform them in-house for themselves under the same or similar circumstances.[110] Announcement 6 also proposed direct- and indirect-charge methods for determining the pricing of the intra-group service. These are consistent with the definition under the OECD TPG.

One important deviation from the OECD TPG is that: 'Finance, tax, human resources, legal and other service activities carried out for the decision-making, monitoring, control and compliance purposes of the enterprise group' are regarded as non-beneficial services as opposed to the LVAS under the TPG. The service fees for such non-beneficial services are non-deductible. Announcement 6 also did not adopt the simplified method to determine the arm's length charges for the LVAS proposed in the TPG.

4.3.2 Practice

Service fees have become a major target for tax authorities' investigations in recent years, and they examine the service fee payment from multiple perspectives.[111] On the one hand, they examine the reasonableness of outbound payments from Chinese entities to those that are foreign.[112] On the other hand, with more Chinese companies investing abroad, they also investigate whether there is any service provided by the Chinese parent company to foreign subsidiaries outside China and, if so, whether a service fee has been charged.[113]

First, the tax authorities examine the contractual arrangements between the related parties, unveiling the substance rather than the form of the contract. This is usually the starting point and an important step for determining whether the service is a beneficial service and whether the pricing is reasonable. Second, they conduct tests from multiple perspectives to determine whether a service is a beneficial service. The below scenarios are regarded as non-beneficial services:[114]

110. Article 43 of the Announcement 6.
111. PWC tax insights from transfer pricing, *China's SAT issues new measures for special tax investigations adjustments and mutual agreement procedures*, 14 April 2017.
112. *Ibid.*
113. *See also* Xiaoyue Wang and Choon Beng Teoh, *Outbound Investment and TP: A More Robust Framework Emerges*, ITR, No. 131, 59, 59 (2020), Accessible via, https://www.internationaltaxreview.com/article/b1j8y77w953x5t/we-need-to-talk-about-platforms-ongoing-tax-challenges-in-china last (last accessed 29 January 2022).
114. Article 35 of the Announcement 6.

- services that are mere duplications of what has been purchased or performed by the recipient entity itself;
- services performed by the related party for the purpose of protecting its direct or indirect equity interest. Such services are controlling, managerial, and supervisory in nature and may include shareholder activities, the preparation of business and financial reports of the head office of the group, financing operations of the head office, and tax, accounting, human resource and legal services provided for the benefit of the head office's decision, management, supervision and control. Under this circumstance, tax authorities may recharacterize the 'service fee' to 'management fee' which is non-deductible for the subsidiaries;[115]
- services not specific to the recipient and merely an incidental benefit gained through group synergies, e.g., resource optimization and scale effect from the group reorganization and lower financing expenses due to a higher credit rating of the group;
- services that have been compensated in other related transactions, e.g., patent-related services for which the service provider has been remunerated through royalties and loan-related services for which the service provider has been remunerated through interest payments;
- services unrelated to the functions performed and risks assumed by the recipient entity or are not necessary for the operations of the service recipient; and
- services that do not bring any direct or indirect economic benefits for the recipient, or the recipient would not have been willing to pay under independent circumstances.

Third, the tax authorities also check the authenticity of the service. The deductions will be denied should the tax authorities determine that the foreign-related party without substance is not able to provide services to the service recipient.[116] Since 2014, tax authorities have increased the focus of tax audits on the payment of services fees to low-tax jurisdictions or low substance overseas companies, and it remains a current major focus of the tax authorities.[117]

Furthermore, tax authorities are often alerted when the services are provided to other related parties at the same time but with a different pricing policy. They may also challenge the reasonableness of the service fee being charged proportionately to the sales revenue and income of the related party.

115. The EITL Implementation Rules Article 49.
116. Article 37 of the Announcement 6.
117. *See* Chi et al., *supra* n. 16, P.39.

4.3.3 *Case Study*

Case study 1

In one case published in the China tax newspaper in 2016, Beijing tax authorities recharacterized service fees charged within a group as management fees and denied the deduction. The service in question mainly involved investment projects evaluation, fund planning, and other research and guidance on financial management, information system management, and cost management. Tax authorities concluded that the outcome of the services was not identifiable. There were no project evaluation reports or any form of deliverables by the parent company as an outcome of the services. Consequently, the tax authorities determined that the transactions between the parent company and the subsidiaries did not have a reasonable commercial purpose. The nature of the fee was not a service fee but the management fee charged by the parent company to the subsidiary which was non-deductible.

Furthermore, the tax authorities have also challenged the fee arrangement which was proportionate to the annual income of the subsidiaries. They argued that it was not reasonable to have significant differences among the fees charged to different subsidiaries since the content of the services was the same.

Case study 2

Zhejiang Quzhou tax authorities published a case in which technical service fees and royalties for trademarks were paid by Company M, a Chinese company, specializing in paper production, to its foreign-related party Company F in 2004-2014.[118] The technical service fees amounted to 4% of the sales revenue each year. Meanwhile, another company in Shanghai (Company S) related to Company F also paid for the same type of technical services at 2% of the sales revenue of Company F (*see* Figure 23.3).

Figure 23.3 Pictorial Representation of the Case Study

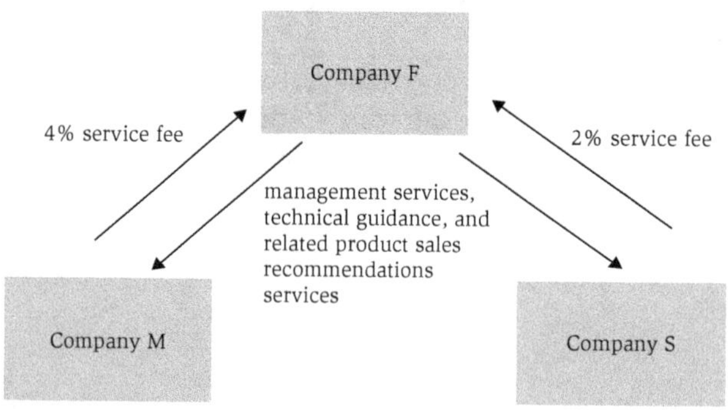

118. Rendong Yu and Weijian Lin, *Anti-tax Avoidance Investigation Reveals the Secret of Large Payments by Foreign Companies* (author translation), China Taxation News, 16 May 2017.

Company M was an enterprise engaged in the production, procurement, management, R&D, sales, and other businesses of paper products. Company F was the overseas holding company of Company M. In its daily operations, it primarily provided management services and technical guidance in relation to technologies used for production.

The focus of the investigation was on the authenticity of the transaction and the reasonableness of the pricing. First, the tax authorities found that, although the technical service agreement seemed to have a broad coverage from its form, it was essentially a mere reproduction of the internal management policy of the group without much substance on the provision of services.

Second, the tax authorities challenged the necessity of the service. They argued that Company M had full command of the production process and technology of the paper product over the last ten years. Further, domestic competitors have generally mastered and used the same technology, and the relevant technical information is publicly available in China. Therefore, it was not necessary for Company M to obtain the technical service from Company F.

With regard to the amount of the service fee, Company M argued that Company F held different percentages of shares in Company M and Company S. That was the reason why Company S paid only 2% of the revenue to Company F while Company M pays 4%. The tax authorities regarded this as a disguised pre-tax allocation of dividends since the amount of payment is dependent on the percentage of share ownership. Consequently, the tax authorities denied the deduction of the technical service fees of Company M and charged tax on this amount.

5 THREE-PRONGED TAX AVOIDANCE PREVENTION AND CONTROL SYSTEM

The STA has constructed a three-pronged tax avoidance prevention and control system focusing on administration, service, and investigation.[119] Concerning administration, the STA has established a profit monitoring system to routinely review MNEs' profits. With regard to the services, the STA not only provides seminars and training to update taxpayers about the most recent tax regulations and policies but also enhances dispute prevention and resolution through APAs and MAPs. Last, but not least, the STA conducts both isolated and coordinated anti-avoidance audits to investigate the profitability of taxpayers. These investigations enable the STA to detect and deter non-compliance or tax avoidance behaviour.

119. UN: E/C.18/2020/CRP.40 Add.1 The updated China Country Practice. Published as the documentation for the UN Committee of Experts on International Cooperation in Tax Matters Twenty-First Session.

5.1 Administration

Among other administrative measures, Chinese tax authorities have implemented a profit monitoring system for MNEs in China using mainly the annual tax returns and the related transaction forms filed by taxpayers.[120] They also analyse the profit level of the industry or specific sector and combine it with individual screening to ascertain outliers using the CTAIS.[121]

In April 2018, Jiang Su tax authorities launched a new profit monitoring system that is expected to be gradually implemented national wide.[122] The new system has a broader data source that includes not only data from the TPDs but also external data from other government departments such as the State Administration of Foreign Exchange, enterprises' financial reports, securities analyst reports, and online public information collected via web crawling. All of the information will be input into the system of the tax authorities for big data analysis. The system conducts tax risk assessments and tax compliance level assessments. Tax authorities take corresponding measures for different taxpayers based on the risk level classification. High-risk taxpayers' profits will be continuously monitored and may attract investigations from the tax authorities.

5.2 Services: Dispute Prevention and Resolution

5.2.1 Advance Pricing Agreements

China's APA practice began in the 1990s.[123] However, at that time, there were no standardized guidelines applicable national wide. The local tax authorities had discretion, therefore, the APA standards varied across regions.[124] In 2005, the STA implemented standardized APA rules, and it has been well-regulated since that time.[125] Currently, Announcement 64 provides the most updated rules on APAs taking into account the OECD TPG.

China allows all three types of APAs: unilateral, bilateral, and multilateral. However, no multilateral APA has yet been signed.[126] The negotiation and execution of an APA are divided into six stages: preparatory meeting, expression of intention, analysis and

120. UN TPM D. 2.2.12.
121. *Ibid.*
122. *See* Chi et al. *supra* n. 16.
123. STA, China Advance Pricing Arrangement Annual Report, P.10 (2020). The Regulation on the Taxation of Transactions between Related Parties (Trial) (Guo Shui Fa [1998] No. 59) provided the first legal basis for the APAs.
124. *Ibid.*
125. First legal basis was the Guoshuifa [2004] No. 118, later the SAT replaced it with Guoshuifa [2009] No. 2.
126. Article 2 of the Announcement 64.

assessment, formal application, negotiation and signing, and monitoring of execution.[127] Taxpayers should prepare abundant information before the preparatory meeting including the information on production and business operations, financial accounting reports, audit reports, contemporaneous documentation, etc., for the most recent three-five years and whether there are cost savings, market premiums, and other LSAs.

If in agreement, tax authorities will approve for the enterprise to submit the expression of intention together with extensive documentation including the pricing principles and calculation methods used in APAs as well as the functional analysis, comparability analysis, and assumptions. Furthermore, it is required to submit a value chain or supply chain analysis and consideration of LSAs. During the analysis and assessment stage, tax authorities may also request supplementary information.

Therefore, taxpayers are expected to be well prepared before filing the application. This helps the tax authorities to optimize their resources and focus on reviewing complete and accurate application materials.[128]

An APA is applicable to a related transaction within three-five years after the tax authorities accept the taxpayer's expression of intention. It may also be retrospectively applied to similar transactions. The maximum rollback period is ten years. Tax authorities may levy or refund taxes from previous tax years accordingly.[129]

There were 156 APAs concluded in China from 2005 to 31 December 2020, including 116 unilateral and 90 bilateral APAs.[130] This is lower than other large economies.[131] There might be various reasons for the low number of APAs, e.g., concerns that information provided for an APA could be used in future audits[132] and the deficiency of personnel capacity at the tax authorities.[133] Furthermore, as there has been a continued interest of taxpayers for a bilateral APA to gain certainty and avoid double taxation, the workload of the tax authorities has also increased.[134] Since 2016, the STA has established an additional unit assisting in the APA and MAP cases;[135] however, the capacity of tax authorities should be further enhanced.

The numbers of unilateral and bilateral APAs signed during each year are as follows (*see* Figure 23.4).[136]

127. *Ibid.*
128. KPMG, *China Tax Authority APA Report highlights commitment to taxpayer certainty*, China Tax Alert - Issue 2, January 2019. *See also*, *See* Wang and Teoh, *supra* n. 113, p. 64 (2020).
129. Article 3 of the Announcement 64.
130. STA, China Advance Pricing Arrangement Annual Report, p. 23 (2018).
131. For example, the US executed 1,820 APAs from 1991-2018. In 2018 itself, 107 APAs were executed. (IRS, Announcement and report concerning APAs, 22 March 2019). The UK has agreed to 134 APAs during 2013-2018. *See* Dong et al., *supra* n. 38.
132. Na Li, *Advance Pricing Agreements in China*, Bulletin for International Taxation, Vol. 70, No. 5, 273, 275 (May 2016).
133. *See* KPMG, *China Tax Authority APA Report highlights commitment to taxpayer certainty*, China Tax Alert - Issue 2, January 2019, *supra* n. 128.
134. *See* STA, China Advance Pricing Arrangement Annual Report, P.5 (2018).
135. *See* KPMG, *China Tax Authority APA Report highlights commitment to taxpayer certainty*, China Tax Alert - Issue 2, January 2019, *supra* n. 128.
136. The information is updated to 2020.

Figure 23.4 Data Regarding APAs Executed

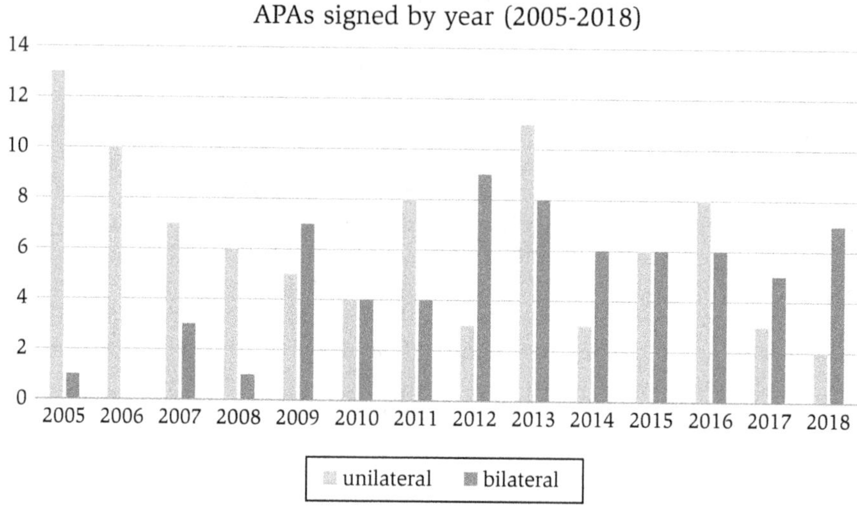

Over 90% of the unilateral APAs were concluded within two years. Bilateral APAs generally take longer due to the involvement of another jurisdiction. Approximately 55% of them were finalized within two years and around 70% within three years (cumulatively).[137] APAs about the transfer of the right to use or ownership of tangible assets comprised 58.11%, 23.31% were about services, and 18.58% about the transfer of the right to use or ownership of intangibles.[138] Asian countries accounted for the most counterparties for bilateral APAs. From 2005 to 2020, fifty-nine APAs were made with Asian countries, nineteen with European countries, eleven with North American countries and one with an Oceania country.[139]

The TNMM was the dominant method used among all of the APAs (199 times) of which the FCMU was the most popular PLI (124 times), and the EBIT operating margin was also often used (73 times) as the PLI. The CPM was the second most popular method which was used 21 times. Comparatively, other methods such as the CUP, RPM, and PSM were used less than ten times. However, the tax authorities actively explore the use of other methods such as the PSM. This is especially the case when parties have made significant contributions to the value creation or have shown location-specific advantages such as market premium or cost savings.[140]

Manufacturing was the dominant industry covered by the APAs. There were 165 APAs concluded in this regard which comprised circa 80% of the total number. Wholesale trade and retail, as well as leasing and commercial services, were involved in twenty-one and eight APAs, respectively, ranking second and third.

137. *See* STA, China Advance Pricing Arrangement Annual Report, P.5 (2020). *Supra* n. 126, p. 59.
138. *See* STA, China Advance Pricing Arrangement Annual Report, P.5 (2020). *Supra* n. 126, p. 55.
139. *See* STA, China Advance Pricing Arrangement Annual Report, P.5 (2020). *Supra* n. 126, p. 55.
140. *See* STA, China Advance Pricing Arrangement Annual Report (2020). *Supra* n. 126, p. 61.

5.2.2 *Dispute Resolution*

In China, most tax disputes are resolved between taxpayers and tax authorities amicably via administrative procedures.[141] If taxpayers do not agree with the tax adjustment by the local tax authorities, they could file an administrative review to the upper-level tax authorities, however, they must first pay the additional tax determined by the local tax authorities before the initiation of the review procedure.[142] Taxpayers are also granted the right to file a lawsuit in court although, in reality, they rarely do so for various reasons.[143]

Disputes involving another jurisdiction are usually resolved through a MAP. A MAP on TP cases is regulated under Articles 47-61 of Announcement 6. Taxpayers could file an application directly with the STA head office with the 'Application for Initiating Mutual Agreement Procedures Concerning Special Tax Adjustments' and relevant information related to the special tax adjustments within the timeframe stipulated in the treaty.[144] The STA can also initiate the MAP upon receiving the formal notification from the other country requesting a MAP.[145] When the STA decides to do so, it will inform the relevant local tax authorities where the taxpayer resides and the competent authority of the other country.[146] If an agreement is reached between the two competent authorities, the relevant local tax authorities will be responsible for delivering the agreement to the taxpayer.[147] They will also deliver the notice of additional payment and refund, if applicable, and supervise its implementation.[148]

China has 107 DTCs all of which contain a MAP clause broadly consistent with Article 25 of the 2017 OECD MTC. According to the OECD MAP peer review report on China, the country's treaty network is 'almost entirely consistent with the requirements of the Action 14 Minimum Standard' except that 'some of its tax treaties (around 10%) neither contain a provision stating that mutual agreements shall be implemented notwithstanding any time limits in domestic law (which is required under Article 25(2), second sentence), nor the alternative provisions for Article 9(1) and Article 7(2) to set a time limit for making transfer pricing adjustments'.[149] In this regard, a number of the treaties will be automatically modified upon entry into force of the MLI. As for treaties that are not modified by the MLI, China will conduct bilateral negotiations and amend the treaties accordingly.

141. *See* Dong et al., *supra* n. 38.
142. Article 88 of The Law of Tax Administration and Collection.
143. Wei Cui, *An Empirical Study of China's Tax Administrative Litigation*, Tsinghua University Law Journal, 3rd issue 2015. Available at, http://fzzfyjy.cupl.edu.cn/info/1063/5006.htm (last accessed 29 January 2022).
144. Article 48 of the Announcement 6.
145. Article 49 of the Announcement 6.
146. Article 50 of the Announcement 6.
147. Article 56 of the Announcement 6.
148. *Ibid.*
149. OECD, *Making Dispute Resolution More Effective: MAP Peer Review Report, China (Stage 1): Inclusive Framework on BEPS: Action 14*, OECD and G20 Base Erosion and Profit Shifting Project (Paris: OECD Publishing, 2019), p. 9.

With regard to dispute resolutions clauses under the MLI, China has opted-in both Articles 16 and 17 except for one reservation on the first sentence of Article 16 that allows taxpayers to present the case to the competent authority of either country. China did not opt-in to the mandatory arbitration clauses presumably due to sovereignty and resources concerns.[150]

Based on the OECD MAP statistic report, the numbers of the MAP inventory until 2020 are as follows (*see* Table 23.5).

Table 23.5 China's MAP Inventory till 2020

Cases Started Before 1 January 2016	*2020 Start Inventory*	*Cases Started*	*Cases Closed*	*2020 End Inventory*
TP cases	12	0	2	10
Other cases	20	0	2	18
Cases started as from 1 January 2016	2020 start inventory	Cases started	Cases closed	2020 end inventory
TP cases	40	18	3	55
Other cases	49	28	8	69

More than half of the MAP cases are in relation to TP issues, i.e., profit attribution and allocation. The main partners for the TP MAP cases are Japan, Korea, Korea, and the US.[151] Around 40% of cases were withdrawn by the taxpayer and in 20% of cases partial agreement was reached.[152]

The average time for closing a TP case during 2016-2018 for China was 31.66 months.[153] Although this exceeds the 24-month average timeframe specified under BEPS Action 14, the average time taken to close a TP case in 2017 and 2018 was 3.51 and 17.76 months, respectively, which is shorter than 24 months and the average time taken by the members of the inclusive framework.[154] The 31.66-month average time is due to the longer period taken to resolve cases initiated in 2016.[155] A trend of a

150. *See* PWC, A new landscape of China's tax treaties: China signs the Multilateral Convention and reveals her positions, June 2017, issue 22. *See also*, Yongwei Liu, *The Absolute Nature of Tax Sovereignty: From the Perspective of Dispute Resolution Mechanism of International Tax Treaty*, Studies in Law and Business, 5th issue, 85, 87 (2010).
151. OECD MAP Statistics 2020 China (People's Republic of), https://www.oecd.org/tax/dispute/2020-map-statistics-china.pdf (last accessed 27 September 2020).
152. *Ibid.*
153. *See* OECD, *supra* n. 151, para. 152. Note the statistics here refers to cases started and closed during 2016-2018.
154. OECD MAP Statistics 2017, https://www.oecd.org/tax/dispute/mutual-agreement-procedure-statistics-2017-per-jurisdiction-transfer-pricing.htm (last accessed 27 September 2020) and 2018 China (People's Republic of), *supra* n. 151.
155. OECD MAP Statistics 2016 China (People's Republic of), https://www.oecd.org/tax/dispute/mutual-agreement-procedure-statistics-2016-per-jurisdiction-transfer-pricing.htm (last accessed 27 September 2020).

shortened timeframe could be observed. In addition, the STA has indicated an enhancement of capacity for a MAP concerning TP cases.[156] It has also been proactive in improving the efficiency of the MAP and discussing other possible avenues for dispute resolution in light of the Belt and Road Initiative proposed by President Xi, which is in accordance with the interests of Chinese companies investing abroad.[157] The efficiency of resolving TP disputes is expected to be continuously improved.

5.3 Investigation

Regarding the third aspect of the three-pronged system, the STA focuses on the investigations of specific taxpayers through TP audits. According to Announcement 6, tax authorities particularly target the following scenarios:[158]

- enterprises with substantial related-party transaction amounts or multiple types of related-party transactions;
- enterprises with long-term losses, thin profit margins, or fluctuating profit;
- enterprises with profits lower than the industry level;
- enterprises with a profit level that does not align with its functional and risk profile or with returns shared that do not align with cost allocated;
- enterprises that enter into transactions with related parties located in low-tax countries (regions);
- enterprises that fail to report the related-party transaction or prepare required contemporaneous documentation;
- enterprises with a related-party debt-to-equity ratio exceeding the prescribed threshold;
- controlled or jointly controlled by Chinese resident enterprises and Chinese resident individuals established in a country (region) with an effective tax rate lower than 12.5%, enterprises that do not distribute or under-distribute profits without reasonable business needs; and
- enterprises that implement other tax planning schemes or arrangements without proper commercial purposes.

Among all of the above, the second and third scenarios are most frequently observed in the cases published by the authorities in newspapers. The fact that a company has continuously growing sales while maintaining low profitability or incurring loss is prone to attract special attention from the tax authorities.[159]

In recent years, they have conducted coordinated nationwide industry-specific audits. Each year, tax authorities select a few industries as the primary target for TP

156. *See* OECD, *supra* n. 151, para. 159.
157. *See* Wang and Teoh, *supra* n. 113, p. 64.
158. Article 4 of the Announcement No. 6 (Unofficial translation).
159. *See* Dong et al. *supra* n. 38; also *see* Gang Dong from King & Wood Mallesons, *Overview of Hong Kong and China Transfer Pricing Issues*, https://cmkwmlive.kwm.com/en/knowledge/insights/overview-of-transfer-pricing-in-hk-and-china-20151126 (last accessed 29 January 2022); and other cases published on China Taxation News.

audits. Industries including luxury goods, pharmaceuticals, and automobiles are frequently under review.[160]

In addition, as mentioned in sections 4.2 and 4.3, intra-group service fees and royalties have been focal points of tax audits. This is especially the case when there are excessive amounts of outbound services fees or a fixed percentage of royalties to foreign-related companies throughout the years with any changes.[161] Furthermore, tax authorities also attend to the application of LSA to the GVCA and the DEMPEP contributions to the value of intangibles.[162]

6 POTENTIAL IMPACTS OF THE UNILATERAL APPROACH ON CHINA

The digital economy has been experiencing a steady increase in China in recent years. In 2019, its scale hit a record high which accounted for 36.2% of the national GDP.[163] In Beijing and Shanghai, it accounted for more than 50% of the GDP.[164]

The taxation of the digital economy has instigated numerous discussions over the years. The OECD released the Unified Approach in October 2019. It includes three major components. Amount A is a share of deemed residual profit allocated to market jurisdictions. Amount B is a fixed remuneration for baseline marketing and distribution functions. Amount C includes any additional profit when in-country functions exceed the baseline activity compensated under Amount B.[165] The Unified Approach is expected to have an impact on China, although some of the current Chinese TP rules may achieve similar effects.

For the purpose of Amount A, two types of businesses have been identified as applicable: automated digital services, e.g., online search engines, social media platforms, and consumer-facing businesses that generate revenues from sales of goods or services to consumers, e.g., personal computing products and luxury goods.[166]

The impact of Amount A on automated digital services may be limited from the Chinese perspective. On the one hand, many foreign digital companies do not directly operate in the Chinese market due to a market speciality. For example, Google and Facebook have limited users in China where their main business is to provide online advertising services to Chinese advertisers to help them target foreign users. Similarly, Amazon closed its China marketplace business in 2019. As such, the Unified Approach

160. UN TPM D.2.2.14.
161. *See* Chi et al. *supra* n. 16.
162. *Ibid.*
163. China Academy of Information and Communications Technology, Digital Economy Development in China (2020).
164. *Ibid.*
165. OECD, *Public Consultation-Document Secretariat Proposal for a 'Unified Approach' under Pillar One* (2019).
166. OECD, *Statement by the OECD and G20 Inclusive Framework on BEPS on the Two-Pillar Approach to Address the Tax Challenges Arising from the Digitalisation of the Economy: January 2020*, OECD and G20 Inclusive Framework on BEPS (Paris: OECD, 2020), www.oecd.org/tax/beps/statement-by-the-oecd-g20-inclusive-framework-on-beps-january-2020.pdf.

will have limited or no impact on them.[167] Amount A's impact may be limited to cross-border e-commerce, Kindle, and AWS business in China.[168]

On the other hand, several Chinese digital companies have successfully expanded their business abroad. For example, Alibaba (Alipay) and Tencent (Wechat) have launched mobile payment services outside China. This initially targeted only Chinese tourists in foreign countries but has gradually been expanded to other groups of users, especially in South East Asia.[169] These two companies and other similar companies have a broad customer base in foreign countries; therefore, it is likely that part of their Amount A profit will be allocated to foreign market jurisdictions. Nonetheless, Chinese digital companies also face stringent reviews and supervision from foreign governments (e.g., TikTok) which poses challenges for their expansion.[170] Overall speaking, the vast majority of the companies still have their primary customer base and derive revenues from within China.[171] Therefore, Amount A's impact on them may also be limited.

The second type of consumer-facing business may have a more significant impact on China since it has a large market and consumer base. A classic example is the consumption of luxury products. It is estimated that Chinese consumers will contribute to nearly 50% of the global luxurious goods consumption by 2025.[172] However, as discussed above in section 4.1, since China already takes market premium and marketing intangibles concepts into account for the allocation of profits, the effect will overlap with the Amount A profit.[173] The interplay between these concepts and the Unified Approach still remains to be seen.

For Amount B, China already has a similar rule asserting that toll manufacturers, baseline distributors, and contract R&D performers should maintain a reasonable level of profit.[174] If such enterprises incur a loss, they should prepare contemporaneous documentation of local files for the loss-making years regardless of whether it exceeds the thresholds for preparing it, and the tax authorities will review the local files and

167. Conrad Turley and Sunny Leung, *BEPS 2.0: What Will It Mean for China?*, ITR, No. 131, 83, 86, 2019. Accessible via, https://www.internationaltaxreview.com/article/b1j8y67b715tb6/beps-20-what-will-it-mean-for-china (last accessed 29 January 2022).
168. *Ibid.*
169. Conrad Turley and Sunny Leung, *We Need to Talk about Platforms: Ongoing Tax Challenges in China*, ITR, No. 131, 88, 89, 2019. Accessible via, https://www.internationaltaxreview.com/article/b1j8y77w953x5t/we-need-to-talk-about-platforms-ongoing-tax-challenges-in-china (last accessed 29 January 2022).
170. Li Liu & Gaohua Chen, *On OECD's 'Two-Pillar' Reform and Its Impacts on China*, International Taxation in China, 8th issue, 14, 20 (2018).
171. David Watkins and Daljit Kaur from Deloitte, *Asia-Pacific's Response to the Proposed OECD Reforms*, https://www.internationaltaxreview.com/article/b1l9lmjgt33bpf/asia-pacifics-response-to-the-proposed-oecd-reforms (last accessed 29 January 2022). The McKinsey Global Institute's China and the world report of July 2019 countries that 19% of China's corporate revenue was earned overseas in 2017, as compared to 44% of revenue earned outside the US by US firms.
172. Bain & Company, *Global personal luxury goods market set to contract between 20 – 35% in 2020*, https://www.bain.com/about/media-center/press-releases/2020/spring-luxury-report/ (last accessed 29 January 2022).
173. *See* Turley and Leung, *supra* n. 169, P.87.
174. Article 28 of the Announcement 6.

strengthen monitoring and administration.[175] The concept behind this rule adheres with the Unified Approach.

For Amount C, the STA already has similar claims that many Chinese distribution companies are not exactly comparable with simple distributors performing limited functions in a mature market.[176] Many of them perform significantly more functions that are manifested by more incurred operating expenses relative to sales.[177] Furthermore, as discussed above, the STA usually factors market difference, any LSAs, and marketing intangibles created by the Chinese entity into a comparability analysis, the selection of TP method, and profit allocation.[178] It is not certain how much additional tax revenue will be accumulated due to Amount C.

7 CONCLUSIONS

The previous analysis demonstrates several distinctive trends of the TP in China. China emphasizes the contribution of the LSA and marketing intangibles to the profit of MNEs and believes it should be reasonably compensated. To do so, China has been actively exploring the use of the PSM and GVCA in assessing the profit of Chinese entities.

In recent years, the STA has increasingly focused on outbound payments for royalties and service fees to related parties. For royalties, it often opposes those determined as a fixed rate for multiple years. For intra-group services, the STA often examines the benefit, authenticity, and pricing arrangements of large outbound transactions.

With the continuous growth of outbound investment, China is no longer a pure source state but increasingly functions as a resident state. The source countries (especially developing countries) where Chinese companies invest may use similar arguments, e.g., the LSA and marketing intangibles, to contend that more profit should be allocated to their jurisdictions. Highly digitalized Chinese companies might also have more tax presence in other jurisdictions in accordance with the Unified Approach. Therefore, effective dispute prevention and resolution mechanisms are imperative for Chinese investors. The country is committed to improving the efficiency of the MAP and is expected to continue exploring other avenues for dispute prevention and resolution to provide more certainty for taxpayers.

175. *Ibid.*
176. UN TPM D.2.4.6.11.
177. UN TPM D.2.4.6.12.
178. *Ibid.* and D.2.4.6.13.

CHAPTER 24

Transfer Pricing in the European Union

Jérôme Monsenego

1 INTRODUCTION

This chapter aims at describing the different aspects of EU law that concern TP. To do so, its structure follows the different sources of EU law relevant to the field of TP. First, TP will be considered from the perspective of the primary law of the EU, i.e., the fundamental freedoms and the state aid rules (section 1). The focus is then on the secondary law of the EU that is of relevance for the field of TP; this concerns mainly certain compliance rules and the resolution of TP disputes (section 2). Third, different instruments of soft law in the area of TP are presented (section 3).

Given the breadth of this topic and the limited space of this chapter, the developments contained herein cannot be exhaustive. Moreover, as this book is a handbook, no critical analysis is made of the more controversial issues related to this topic.

2 EU PRIMARY LAW APPLIED TO TP RULES

The most relevant legal sources in the field of TP are domestic law and tax treaties, as there is little harmonization of TP rules within the EU. However, domestic laws and tax treaties must abide by its primary law. Both the fundamental freedoms and the state aid rules have implications for the design and application of TP rules. The interaction between TP rules and the fundamental freedoms will first be discussed (section 1.1) before subsequently presenting the application of the state aid rules to the field of TP (section 1.2).

2.1 TP from the Perspective of the Fundamental Freedoms

At the time of writing this chapter, the most important questions about the interaction between TP rules based on the arm's length principle and the fundamental freedoms had been answered by the CJEU. This concerns the general compatibility of the fundamental freedoms with adjustments to the tax base of related parties in order to align the prices of intra-group transactions with arm's length prices. The CJEU found such adjustments potentially compatible with the fundamental freedoms (section 1.1.1). However, certain questions remain with respect to both the interaction between the fundamental freedoms and the arm's length principle as well as the potential issues of compatibility with the fundamental freedoms of the OECD/G20 Pillar One project (section 1.1.2).

2.1.1 Existing Case Law and Questions Answered by the CJEU

There is an inherent conflict between TP rules and the European fundamental freedoms. This is because, on the one hand, TP rules are only relevant in a cross-border context given that the pricing of intra-group transactions between entities resident of different countries may affect their respective corporate tax base. On the other hand, the purpose of the fundamental freedoms is to ensure the realization of the internal market by removing obstacles to the mobility of individuals and corporations, something that would normally suppose that similar treatment is provided in domestic and cross-border contexts. Therefore, the application of TP rules, when they lead to tax consequences in a cross-border context that are less favourable than in a domestic situation, give rise to a conflict with fundamental freedoms.

Despite the difference in treatment that TP rules imply for domestic and cross-border situations, the CJEU has found that such rules are generally compatible with the European fundamental freedoms under the circumstances relevant in the cases it had to deal with. Two court cases are particularly relevant in this respect: the *SGI* case and the *Hornbach* case. The former case concerned the compatibility of the Belgian TP rules with the fundamental freedoms, in particular in the event of the grant of an interest-free loan.[1] The latter case was about the German TP rules when they are applied in relation to the gratuitous provision of comfort letters.[2] These cases were later confirmed by the CJEU in the *Impresa Pizzarotti* case[3] that concerned the attribution of profits to permanent establishments. In *Impresa Pizzarotti,* a branch had concluded two 'loan agreements' as a 'lender'[4] with its parent company that did not contain any clause concerning the charging of interest by the branch thus leading to a reassessment of its income with an interest rate at arm's length.

1. *See* Case C-311/08, *Société de Gestion Industrielle SA (SGI).*
2. *See* Case C-382/16, *Hornbach-Baumarkt v. Finanzamt Landau.*
3. *See* Case C-558/19, *Impresa Pizzarotti & C SPA Italia Sucursala Cluj v. Agenția Națională de Administrare Fiscală – Direcția Generală de Administrare a Marilor Contribuabili.*
4. *See* Case C-558/19, *Impresa Pizzarotti & C SPA Italia Sucursala Cluj v. Agenția Națională de Administrare Fiscală – Direcția Generală de Administrare a Marilor Contribuabili,* para. 7.

As a starting point, the CJEU considers that TP rules imply a restriction on the freedom of establishment because of the difference in treatment they imply between domestic and cross-border intra-group transactions.[5] Counterarguments such as the possibility to obtain a corresponding adjustment on the basis of the arbitration convention and thus remove the additional tax burden resulting from the primary adjustment did not preclude the existence of a restriction.[6] The restriction was nevertheless justified as the CJEU observed that permitting resident companies to transfer their profits to foreign related parties (in the event that TP rules would be inapplicable) would undermine the balanced allocation of the power to impose taxes between the Member States and enable tax avoidance. The two justifications were accepted when being 'taken together' in the *SGI* case,[7] while the sole preservation of the allocation of powers of taxation between the Member States sufficed in *Hornbach*[8] and in *Impresa Pizzarotti*[9] to justify the restriction implied by the domestic rules. The *Impresa Pizzarotti* is consistent with the *SGI* and *Hornbach* cases, and the fact that the court ruled without an opinion from the advocate general and with a formation consisting of three judges points to the continuity between this case and the previous cases, although a few nuances seem to exist. Conceptually, it is mainly the principle of territoriality that made the court accept the justification of TP rules,[10] considering the need of the Member States to exercise their tax jurisdiction in relation to activities carried out in their territory.[11]

TP rules, when they are justified, must nevertheless be in accordance with the principle of proportionality. To do so, the CJEU has found that they must meet two requirements. First, the taxpayer must be afforded an opportunity, without being subject to undue administrative constraints, to provide evidence of any commercial justification that there may have been for that transaction.[12] This should prevent, for instance, tax reassessments decided by tax authorities without engaging in a dialogue with the taxpayer. It should nevertheless be observed that the concept of 'commercial justification' is not precisely defined; in this respect, in the *Hornbach* case, the CJEU interestingly ascertained that the position of a shareholder may justify the gratuitous provision of comfort letters. Second, the corrective tax measure must be confined to the part that exceeds what would have been agreed between the related parties under

5. *See* Case C-382/16, *Hornbach-Baumarkt v. Finanzamt Landau*, para. 35.
6. *See* Case C-311/08, *Société de Gestion Industrielle SA (SGI)*, para. 54.
7. *See* Case C-311/08, *Société de Gestion Industrielle SA (SGI)*, para. 69.
8. *See* Case C-382/16, *Hornbach-Baumarkt v. Finanzamt Landau*, para. 47.
9. *See* Case C-558/19, *Impresa Pizzarotti & C SPA Italia Sucursala Cluj v. Agenţia Naţională de Administrare Fiscală – Direcţia Generală de Administrare a Marilor Contribuabili*, para. 34.
10. For a general study of the principle of territoriality in EU tax law, *see* Jérôme Monsenego, *Taxation of Foreign Business Income Within the European Internal Market: An Analysis of the Conflict Between the Objective of Achievement of the European Internal Market and the Principles of Territoriality and Worldwide Taxation* (IBFD 2012).
11. *See* Case C-311/08, *Société de Gestion Industrielle SA (SGI)*, para. 64; Case C-382/16, *Hornbach-Baumarkt v. Finanzamt Landau*, para. 40; Case C-558/19, *Impresa Pizzarotti & C SPA Italia Sucursala Cluj v. Agenţia Naţională de Administrare Fiscală – Direcţia Generală de Administrare a Marilor Contribuabili*, para. 33.
12. *See* Case C-311/08, *Société de Gestion Industrielle SA (SGI)*, para. 71; Case C-382/16, *Hornbach-Baumarkt v. Finanzamt Landau*, para. 49.

market conditions.[13] Stated otherwise, TP rules must respect the arm's length principle when they are relied on to reassess the prices of intra-group transactions; an adjustment cannot go beyond the arm's length principle. The content of such an arm's length principle, however, may be subject to controversies. Based on these requirements, the Belgian and German TP rules tested in the *SGI* and *Hornbach* cases were found potentially proportionate, subject to the assessment of the respective referring courts concerning the fulfilment of the two criteria mentioned previously. A similar conclusion was reached in the *Impresa Pizzarotti* case concerning the Romanian legislation on the correction of the profits attributed to permanent establishments.[14]

Last, TP rules should be carefully designed to ensure fulfilment of the principle of proportionality. For TP rules to be considered proportionate to the objectives pursued, they must meet the requirements of the principle of legal certainty according to which 'rules of law must be clear, precise and predictable as regards their effects'.[15]

2.1.2 Unsolved Questions and Potential Compatibility Issues of the OECD Pillar One Project

Despite the answers brought by the CJEU in the cases mentioned above, certain unanswered issues remain. As emphasized by the Confédération Fiscale Européenne task force:[16]

> The Hornbach decision leaves open important issues for consideration relating to the applicable freedom, the comparability analysis, the proportionality analysis of the accepted justification criteria, the implications attached to the evidence and the meaning of 'commercial reasons', as well as the scope of the decision (either limited to the specific circumstances of comfort letters or related to a more general alternative approach).

With respect to the choice of freedom of movement, it can be observed that the analysis conducted by the CJEU in the *SGI* case enables the application of the free movement of capital to TP rules.[17] This raises the question of the rules' potential limitations that may be implied by the free movement of capital when such rules apply in relation to third countries.

In addition to the elements mentioned above, TP rules that provide for certain compliance obligations (primarily TPD requirements and CbCR) as opposed to TP rules

13. *See* Case C-311/08, *Société de Gestion Industrielle SA (SGI)*, para. 72; Case C-382/16, *Hornbach-Baumarkt v. Finanzamt Landau*, para. 49. *See also* Case C-318/10, *Société d'investissement pour l'agriculture tropicale SA (SIAT)*, para. 52.
14. *See* Case C-558/19, *Impresa Pizzarotti & C SPA Italia Sucursala Cluj v. Agenția Națională de Administrare Fiscală – Direcția Generală de Administrare a Marilor Contribuabili*, paras 37 and 38.
15. *See* Case C-318/10, *Société d'investissement pour l'agriculture tropicale SA (SIAT)*, paras 58 and 59.
16. *See* Confédération Fiscale Européenne, *Opinion Statement ECJ-TF 1/2019 on the ECJ Decision of 31 May 2018 in Hornbach-Baumarkt (Case C-382/16) Concerning the Application of Transfer Pricing Rules to Transactions Between Resident and Non-Resident Associated Enterprises*, 59 European Taxation, 2019-9, p. 449.
17. *See* Case C-311/08, *Société de Gestion Industrielle SA (SGI)*, para. 30.

that are of a substantive nature are yet to be tested in light of the fundamental freedoms.

Finally, the OECD Pillar One project, in particular the allocation of Amount A to market jurisdictions, may raise issues of compatibility with the fundamental freedoms.[18] Indeed, the increased tax burden in the country of destination that is implied by the allocation of Amount A results in a difference in treatment between companies with a foreign connection that are in the scope of Amount A and domestic companies with no such association that are, per definition, not subject to higher tax liability. The question of whether these two categories of companies are in a comparable situation would first need to be answered. In *SGI*, the CJEU considered that resident companies were in a comparable situation even if they were owned by foreign shareholders. Permanent establishments have also been deemed to be in a comparable situation to resident companies in several respects.[19] However, in cases when Amount A is levied with no physical presence but only on the basis of a digital presence, comparability is less obvious. The question is also raised whether it may be justified and, if so, if it is proportionate to levy Amount A only on certain companies that are members of a multinational enterprise but never on domestic companies. Contrary to the arm's length principle which is indeed necessary to prevent tax avoidance, Amount A aims at amending the balance between residence-based and source-based taxation by granting new or additional taxing rights to the market jurisdictions. Since the arm's length principle was determined by the CJEU to be an appropriate means for ensuring a balanced allocation of the power to impose taxes, it can be wondered if the court may consider that, in certain cases, the lack of taxation due to the absence of physical presence may jeopardize such a balanced cross-border allocation of taxes. If this occurs, a reallocation may be necessary to remedy the inadequacies of the old tax system. If indeed the levy of Amount A may be justified, the question is raised whether the extent of the difference in treatment is proportionate to the objective to reallocate part of the corporate tax base to the market jurisdictions. Since the choice of the size of Amount A is not objective, but rather subjective, it may be difficult to justify the levy of Amount A. It must be demonstrated that it does not go beyond what is necessary to attain a balanced allocation of the taxing rights between the Member States since the CJEU found in *SGI* and *Hornbach* that the corrective tax measure must stay within the boundaries of the arm's length principle.[20]

After considering the interaction between TP rules and the fundamental freedoms, the section below is dedicated to the application of the state aid rules to the field of TP.

18. *See* OECD, *Tax Challenges Arising from Digitalisation: Report on Pillar One Blueprint: Inclusive Framework on BEPS* (2020); OECD, *Statement on a Two-Pillar Solution to Address the Tax Challenges Arising from the Digitalisation of the Economy* (1 July 2021); OECD, Statement on a Two-Pillar Solution to Address the Tax Challenges Arising from the Digitalisation of the Economy (8 October 2021).

19. *See, e.g.*, Case C-311/97, *Royal Bank of Scotland plc v. Elliniko Dimosio (Greek State)*.

20. *See* Case C-311/08, *Société de Gestion Industrielle SA (SGI)*, para. 72.

2.2 TP from the Perspective of the State Aid Rules

The interaction between the state aid rules and TP is, at the time of writing this chapter, far from being precisely determined. What is clear, is that the fiscal autonomy of the Member States is not a valid argument for TP rules or measures to escape State aid control: even in non-harmonized areas where the Member States can design the characteristics constituting each tax such as the tax base or the tax rate,[21] the fiscal competence of the Member States has to be exercised in conformity with EU law, including the State aid rules.[22]

Several cases initiated and decided by the European Commission and appealed before the European courts raise questions in relation to both the design (section 1.2.1) and the application (section 1.2.2) of TP rules. The potential interaction between the state aid rules and the OECD Pillar One project is also considered (section 1.2.3).

2.2.1 The Design of TP Rules from a State Aid Perspective

It was established by the CJEU already in 2006 that the design of rules that affect the computation of income earned by related parties may be subject to state aid control.[23] However, the *Forum 187* case did not concern general TP rules per se, and it did not attract significant attention at the time it was ruled. It was only with the launch by the European Commission of investigations against several advance tax rulings granted by the Member States in matters of TP that the question of the interaction between state aid and TP became more debated.

One of the main questions relates to the possible existence of an obligation under the state aid rules for the Member States of the EU to tax the members of multinational enterprises according to a certain method irrespective of the content of their domestic law. The problem is also raised in relation to the attribution of profits to permanent establishments. The European Commission has suggested the view according to which the arm's length principle 'necessarily forms part of the commission's assessment of tax measures granted to group companies under Article 107(1) of the Treaty, independently of whether a Member State has incorporated this principle into its national legal system and in what form'.[24] The content of such an arm's length principle would, to a great extent – although not necessarily fully – overlap with the arm's length principle as it is described in the OECD TPG.[25]

This question is particularly at stake in the *Apple* case in which the European Commission argued that the legislation of Ireland should have included a provision

21. *See* Case C-562/19 P, *European Commission v. Republic of Poland*, para. 38.
22. *See* Case C-337/19 P, *Commission v. Belgium and Magnetrol International*, paras 161-166.
23. *See* Joined Cases C-182/03 and C-217/03 (*Kingdom of Belgium and JTPF 187 ASBL v. Commission of the European Communities*).
24. *See* Commission Notice on the notion of State aid as referred to in Article 107(1) of the Treaty on the Functioning of the European Union (2016/C 262/01), para. 172.
25. *See* Commission Notice on the notion of State aid as referred to in Article 107(1) of the Treaty on the Functioning of the European Union (2016/C 262/01), para. 173, in particular the last sentence and the use of the word 'unlikely'.

implementing the arm's length principle. It also contended that the absence of such a provision in the domestic law did not relieve this Member State from the obligation to attribute profits to a PE in accordance with the arm's length principle.[26] At the time of writing of this chapter, the case had been ruled on by the General Court of the EU (General Court),[27] and an appeal was pending before the CJEU.[28] The General Court did not uphold the view of the European Commission according to which the state aid rules, as such, imply a general obligation to apply the arm's length principle. Instead, the reference system that determines the normal level of taxation in the state aid analytical framework was ascertained to be primarily comprised of domestic law and not of rules that would directly originate from state aid law.[29] The General Court had made a similar statement in earlier cases considering that 'the Commission does not (...) have the power autonomously to define the "normal" taxation of an integrated undertaking, disregarding national tax rules'.[30]

If this position is to be confirmed by the CJEU, the choice of the TP rules of a Member State would remain within its sovereignty; only the application of such rules would be subject to state aid control. Nevertheless, the arm's length principle was still found by the General Court to constitute a 'tool'[31] or a 'benchmark'[32] for assessing whether favourable treatment has been granted. Similar views were expressed in the *Fiat*[33] and *Starbucks*[34] cases which were ruled on by the General Court before the *Apple* case. It is yet to be determined what meaning to attribute to a 'tool' or 'benchmark' if these terms were confirmed by the CJEU.

In addition, it must be observed that the General Court found that related parties and unrelated parties are in a comparable situation when the comparison is made in light of the objective of a corporate income tax system.[35] Although not fully supporting the

26. *See* Commission Decision of 30 August 2016 on State aid SA.38373 (2014/C) (ex 2014/NN) (ex 2014/CP) implemented by Ireland to Apple.
27. *See* Cases T-778/16 (*Ireland v. Commission*) and T-892/16 (*Apple Sales International and Apple Operations Europe v. Commission*).
28. *See* Case C-465/20 P (*Commission v. Ireland and Others*).
29. *See*, in particular, paras 184 and 219 of the *Apple* case in which the General Court accepted the reliance on domestic law, including court cases, to determine the material content of the reference system. For a similar view, *see* Jérôme Monsenego, *Selectivity in State Aid Law and the Methods for the Allocation of the Corporate Tax Base* (Wolters Kluwer 2018), pp. 34-54.
30. *See* Cases T-755/15 and T-759/15 (*Grand Duchy of Luxembourg and Fiat Chrysler Finance Europe v. European Commission*), para. 112.
31. *See* Cases T-778/16 (*Ireland v. Commission*) and T-892/16 (*Apple Sales International and Apple Operations Europe v. Commission*), para. 214.
32. *See* Cases T-778/16 (*Ireland v. Commission*) and T-892/16 (*Apple Sales International and Apple Operations Europe v. Commission*), para. 215.
33. *See* Cases T-755/15 and T-759/15 (*Grand Duchy of Luxembourg and Fiat Chrysler Finance Europe v. European Commission*), para. 143.
34. *See* Cases T-760/15 and T-636/16 (*Kingdom of the Netherlands and Others v. European Commission*), para. 151.
35. *See* Cases T-778/16 (*Ireland v. Commission*) and T-892/16 (*Apple Sales International and Apple Operations Europe v. Commission*), paras 155 and 161. The possible comparison between unrelated and related parties is a key element in the reasoning of the European Commission. Should they not be in a factual and legal comparable situation for state aid purposes, the claims of the commission would fail as the Member States would have the right to treat these categories of enterprises differently.

views of the commission in the *Apple* case, the General Court did rule consistently with its argumentation on the question of comparability. This is an important aspect of the first round of cases ruled by the General Court which excludes a fundamentally different method of taxation for multinational enterprises compared to unrelated parties unless differences in treatment are justified by the logic of a corporate income tax system.

In any case, there will be a wait for the appeals against the judgments of the General Court to be ruled on by the CJEU. This will provide a better understanding of the interaction between the state aid rules and the design of TP rules.[36] Depending on how the CJEU will rule, alternative methods to the arm's length principle may or may not appear as legally compatible with state aid law.

2.2.2 The Application of TP Rules from a State Aid Perspective

The application of TP rules may, as any tax rule, be subject to state aid control in order to ensure a non-discriminatory application of the law. The purpose of state aid control is to assess whether TP rules have been applied in a particular case that is consistent with their normal operation. According to the General Court, this is also the case if the taxation of related parties or permanent establishments has been subject to an advance tax ruling or an APA.[37] The argument justifying this position is based on the traditional view that, although direct taxation has not been harmonized, the Member States must nevertheless exercise their competence in this field consistently with EU law. At the same time, the cases ruled by the General Court reveal a high burden of proof on the European Commission to bring evidence that the application of TP rules has resulted in the grant of a selective advantage.[38]

Several aspects of the application of the arm's length principle have been subject to the state aid control of the European Commission. Three of these are particularly important to emphasize and are discussed below: the possibility to use an arm's length range, the choice of a TP method, and the possibility to apply soft law instruments for the purpose of state aid control, including retroactively.

36. *See*, in particular, the forthcoming cases: Case C-337/19 P (*Commission v. Belgium and Magnetrol International*); Case C-898/19 P (*Ireland v. Commission and Others*); Case C-465/20 P (*Commission v. Ireland and Others*); Case C-457/21 P (*Commission v. Amazon.com and Others*).
37. *See* Cases T-778/16 (*Ireland v. Commission*) and T-892/16 (*Apple Sales International and Apple Operations Europe v. Commission*), para. 123; Cases T-755/15 and T-759/15 (*Grand Duchy of Luxembourg and Fiat Chrysler Finance Europe v. European Commission*), paras 134 and 135; Cases T-131/16 and T-263/16 (*Kingdom of Belgium and Magnetrol International v. European Commission*), paras 62 and 63.
38. Evidence of transfer mispricing might be difficult to show in matters that are, to a great extent, dependent on the interpretation of previous facts. It might be discussed whether this burden is reasonable when the question is about a possible deviation from the reference system that has been accepted by a Member State at the initiative of a taxpayer.

The General Court acknowledged the imprecision that is inherent to the arm's length principle,[39] i.e., its 'approximate nature'.[40] This is consistent with the view expressed in the OECD TPG that the arm's length principle is not exact science.[41] Therefore, the General Court concluded that the European Commission 'can identify an advantage for the purposes of Article 107(1) TFEU only if the variation between the two comparables goes beyond the inaccuracies inherent in the methodology used to obtain that approximation'.[42] This implies that a margin of error should be accepted before considering that illegal state aid has been granted. It also means that the General Court does not reject the concept of range that has been advocated for a long period of time in the OECD TPG.[43] Therefore, if the notion of range is accepted under the state aid rules, there cannot be a claim that only a certain value within the range, e.g., the median, would be the 'right' market value for which a deviation from it would necessarily imply illegal state aid. Nevertheless, the General Court is not clear on how to determine the arm's length range in a manner that is compliant with the state aid rules, i.e., how to distinguish between an inaccuracy 'inherent in the application of a method designed to obtain a reliable approximation of a market-based outcome' and one that constitutes an incorrect application of the arm's length principle and potential illegal state aid.

The General Court has also provided guidance as to whether the choice of a TP method may, as such, imply illegal state aid. The court made it clear in the *Starbucks* case that 'choosing the transfer pricing method is not an end in itself, but is done with a view to the intra-group transaction for which the arm's length level must be determined and not the other way around'.[44] Indeed, what matters is the actual transfer price or profit margin and not the method that has been used to determine it or even to test it. As stated by the General Court, 'the various methods for setting transfer prices - whether it be the CUP method or the TNMM - endeavour to attain profit levels reflecting arm's length transfer prices'.[45] Accordingly, the court found that 'it cannot be concluded, as a rule, that one method does not allow a reliable approximation of an arm's length outcome to be reached'.[46] A similar view was expressed in the *Amazon* case.[47] The General Court also considered this question in the *Apple* case and

39. *See* Cases T-760/15 and T-636/16 (*Kingdom of the Netherlands and Others v. European Commission*), para. 199.
40. *See* Cases T-755/15 and T-759/15 (*Grand Duchy of Luxembourg and Fiat Chrysler Finance Europe v. European Commission*), para. 207.
41. *See* paras 1.13, 3.55, and 4.8 of the 2022 OECD TPG.
42. *See* Cases T-778/16 (*Ireland v. Commission*) and T-892/16 (*Apple Sales International and Apple Operations Europe v. Commission*), para. 216.
43. *See* Cases T-760/15 and T-636/16 (*Kingdom of the Netherlands and Others v. European Commission*), para. 218, second sentence.
44. *See* Cases T-760/15 and T-636/16 (*Kingdom of the Netherlands and Others v. European Commission*), para. 209.
45. *See* Cases T-760/15 and T-636/16 (*Kingdom of the Netherlands and Others v. European Commission*), para. 202.
46. *See* Cases T-760/15 and T-636/16 (*Kingdom of the Netherlands and Others v. European Commission*), para. 202.
47. *See* Case T-816/17 (*Grand Duchy of Luxembourg, Amazon EU Sàrl and Amazon.com, Inc. v. European Commission*), para. 500.

determined that the mere non-observance of methodological requirements, in particular in connection with the OECD TPG, is not sufficient grounds for concluding that the calculated profit is not a reliable approximation of a market-based outcome.[48] The position of the General Court, which is yet to be confirmed by the Court of Justice, is reasonable since the methods described in the OECD TPG all aim at implementing the same principle.[49]

Last, the question may be raised of whether soft law instruments, in particular, the OECD TPG and the authorized OECD approach for the attribution of profits to permanent establishments may or should be used for the purpose of state aid control. It is quite clear that the General Court did take into account the OECD TPG;[50] it even referred to both the 1995 and 2010 versions of them.[51] However, this does not mean that the General Court found the guidelines binding on the Member States or necessary to use as part of state aid control.[52] Rather, the General Court ascertained the guidelines as an important, yet not binding, interpretative source:[53]

> even though the Commission correctly observed that it cannot be formally bound by the OECD Guidelines, the fact remains that those guidelines are based on important work carried out by groups of renowned experts, that they reflect the international consensus achieved with regard to transfer pricing and that they thus have a certain practical significance in the interpretation of issues relating to transfer pricing.[54]

Similarly, the General Court determined, with respect to the attribution of profits to permanent establishments, that:

> the Authorised OECD Approach is an approach that is based on work carried out by groups of experts and which reflects international consensus regarding profit allocation to permanent establishments. It is, therefore, certainly of practical significance when interpreting questions relating to that profit allocation.[55]

The problem, however, is the meaning that should be attributed to the 'practical significance' of such soft law instruments for the interpretation of the reference system. It is ambiguous to what extent a Member State may or even should rely on the OECD

---

48. *See* Cases T-778/16 (*Ireland v. Commission*) and T-892/16 (*Apple Sales International and Apple Operations Europe v. Commission*), para. 319.
49. *See* Jérôme Monsenego, *Selectivity in State Aid Law and the Methods for the Allocation of the Corporate Tax Base* (Wolters Kluwer 2018), p. 125.
50. *See* Cases T-760/15 and T-636/16 (*Kingdom of the Netherlands and Others v. European Commission*), para. 461.
51. *See* e.g., Cases T-760/15 and T-636/16 (*Kingdom of the Netherlands and Others v. European Commission*), para. 335.
52. *See* Cases T-760/15 and T-636/16 (*Kingdom of the Netherlands and Others v. European Commission*), para. 433.
53. Similarly, *see* Jérôme Monsenego, *Selectivity in State Aid Law and the Methods for the Allocation of the Corporate Tax Base* (Wolters Kluwer 2018), pp. 132-136.
54. *See* e.g., Cases T-760/15 and T-636/16 (*Kingdom of the Netherlands and Others v. European Commission*), para. 155; Cases T-755/15 and T-759/15 (*Grand Duchy of Luxembourg and Fiat Chrysler Finance Europe v. European Commission*), para. 147.
55. *See* Cases T-778/16 (*Ireland v. Commission*) and T-892/16 (*Apple Sales International and Apple Operations Europe v. Commission*), para. 237.

TPG and the authorized OECD approach for the purpose of taxing related parties and permanent establishments. Perhaps the CJEU will provide more guidance with respect to this question.

The question may also be raised whether later amendments to the OECD TPG may be taken into account retroactively to assess a possible deviation from the reference system. Clearly, the General Court does not preclude the consideration of later material as evidenced by the reliance on the authorized OECD approach in the *Apple* case.[56] It also took into account the 2010 OECD TPG in the Starbucks case while the ruling was granted prior to the 2010 amendments.[57] However, when it comes to the consideration of facts that reveal the substance of a transaction, the General Court made it clear that only information existing at the time of an APA should be taken into account.[58] This should reasonably be valid for both arguments in law and for those in facts since an appropriate TP analysis implies the determination of a certain set of facts to which certain rules are applied. It would then be the reference system as it was at the time of the enactment or the issuance of a tax measure that is used as a benchmark to determine 'normal' taxation. This should preclude, among others, the use of a later version of the OECD TPG to assess the correctness of an earlier TP measure, at least if it is established that there is a material difference between different versions of the guidelines, as clearly emphasized in the *Amazon* case with respect to the DEMPE functions.[59]

2.2.3 Potential Interaction Between the State Aid Rules and the OECD Pillar One Project

In essence, the Pillar One project aims at shifting part of the residual profits (such residual profits being computed according to the arm's length principle) to the market jurisdictions on the basis of a formula.[60] This would decrease the tax burden in the country of origin and increase it in the countries of destination. Relief from tax in the country of origin would, per definition, not apply to unrelated parties or to domestic groups. Certain multinational enterprises would also be out of the scope of Amount A. Therefore, it can be wondered if the Pillar One project amounts to a selective advantage in the country of origin to the benefit of certain multinational enterprises that export goods or services or have users abroad. The aid would correspond to Amount A which is to be taxed in the market jurisdictions instead of the country where the residual profits would be taxed. Such a tax relief would hardly be motivated by the logic of the

56. The General Court found that there is 'some overlap' between Irish tax law and the Authorized OECD Approach: *See* Cases T-778/16 (*Ireland v. Commission*) and T-892/16 (*Apple Sales International and Apple Operations Europe v. Commission*), para. 239.
57. *See* Cases T-760/15 and T-636/16 (*Kingdom of the Netherlands and Others v. European Commission*), para. 12.
58. *See* Cases T-760/15 and T-636/16 (*Kingdom of the Netherlands and Others v. European Commission*), para. 251.
59. *See* Case T-816/17 (*Grand Duchy of Luxembourg, Amazon EU Sàrl and Amazon.com, Inc. v. European Commission*), para. 155.
60. *See* OECD, *Tax Challenges Arising from Digitalisation: Report on Pillar One Blueprint – Inclusive Framework on BEPS* (2020).

tax system of the country of origin. This is because the problem that is attempting to be effectively addressed lies in market jurisdictions where a multinational enterprise might be lacking a tax liability because of the absence of a physical presence.

At the same time, a state aid issue may also exist in the countries that are allocated an Amount A. In the countries of destination, the proposed new nexus rules will mostly target certain business models, and thresholds are suggested. This may result in a selective advantage to the benefit of undertakings that will not have a taxable presence or for which little or no income will be allocated to the newly created taxable presence. The advantage that companies not within the scope of the Pillar One project would benefit from seems hardly justified by the logic of the corporate income tax system. Certain multinational enterprises may be lacking a nexus as a simple consequence of the choice to levy Amount A on certain types of businesses or if certain thresholds are passed. This is not imposed by the intrinsic functioning of the corporate income tax system. Stand-alone enterprises with domestic activities would, per definition, not be in the scope of the new nexus rules.

Potential conflicts with the state aid rules may not be not surprising due to the purpose of the Pillar One project. Its objective is to design tax rules that compensate for the lack of tax liability for certain enterprises under the traditional framework of Articles 5, 7, and 9 of the OECD MTC. This will be accomplished by introducing a new tax liability that only targets such enterprises.

3 EU SECONDARY LAW RELATING TO TP

In the field of TP, EU secondary law has gained importance with respect to several administrative, as opposed to substantive, aspects. This concerns certain compliance obligations (section 2.1) and the resolution of cross-border tax disputes (section 2.2).

3.1 Compliance Obligations

The DAC in the field of taxation contains several provisions that are relevant from a TP perspective:[61]

- CbCR (section 2.1.1);
- the presence of tax officials in administrative offices;
- the participation in administrative enquiries and simultaneous controls (section 2.1.2);
- the automatic exchange of information on advance cross-border rulings and APAs (section 2.1.3); and
- the mandatory automatic exchange of information on reportable cross-border arrangements (section 2.1.4).

61. *See* Council Directive 2011/16/EU of 15 February 2011 on administrative cooperation in the field of taxation and repealing Directive 77/799/EEC, OJ L 64, 11 March 2011, pp. 1-12.

3.1.1 *Country-by-Country Reporting*

The DAC contains provisions on CbCR. The CbCR within the EU is not public but may become so in the future. The directive applies to groups located in or with operations in the EU with total consolidated revenue equal to or higher than EUR 750 million. It is in the Member State of residence of an MNE's ultimate parent entity that the CbCR is filed. The competent authority of a Member State where the CbCR was received will then, by means of automatic exchange, communicate it to any other Member State in which one or more entities of the group are either a resident or have a permanent establishment.

A template for the CbCR is found as an appendix to the DAC and shall be used for reporting a group's allocation of income, taxes, and business activities on a country-by-country basis. The report includes information on the revenue, the profit before tax, the income tax paid and accrued, the number of employees, the stated capital, the retained earnings, and the tangible assets of the entities concerned by the report. The template found in the Appendix also contains a list of all of the constituent entities of the multinational enterprise included in each aggregation per tax jurisdiction.

3.1.2 *Presence in Administrative Offices, Participation in Administrative Enquiries, and Simultaneous Controls*

The DAC contains provisions concerning the presence of tax officials in the administrative offices of the other Member States and their participation in administrative enquiries.[62] By agreement between the requesting and the requested authorities and in accordance with the arrangements established by the latter, officials authorized by the requesting authority may, with a view to exchanging information, either be present in the offices where the administrative authorities of the requested Member State carry out their duties or be present during administrative enquiries performed in the territory of the requested Member State. Further, the DAC affords officials of the requesting authority present in another Member State the possibility to interview individuals and examine records if this is permitted under the legislation of the requested Member State.

When it comes to simultaneous controls (the DAC does not use the term 'joint audits'), the DAC provides for certain rules when the tax authorities of two or more Member States agree to audit one or more related parties in their own territory.[63] To do so, the competent authority in each Member State shall independently identify the persons for whom it intends to propose a simultaneous control. It shall notify the competent authority of the other Member States concerned of any cases for which it proposes a simultaneous control and offer reasons for its choice. The competent authority of each Member State concerned shall decide whether it wishes to take part

62. *See* Article 11 of the DAC.
63. *See* Article 12 of the DAC.

in simultaneous controls, and it shall confirm its agreement or communicate its reasoned refusal to the authority that proposed a simultaneous control.

3.1.3 *Automatic Exchange of Information on Advance Cross-Border Rulings and APAs*

In 2015, the Member States agreed on an amendment to the DAC, introducing a mechanism for the automatic exchange of information on advance cross-border rulings and APAs.[64] This mechanism is not specific to TP but is highly relevant in this area of tax law. According to the DAC, the competent authority of a Member State where an advance cross-border ruling or an APA was issued shall, by automatic exchange, communicate information thereon to the competent authorities of all other Member States and to the European Commission.

The information to be communicated by a Member State shall include, in particular, a summary of the content of the advance cross-border ruling or APA. This includes the TP methodology accepted in a ruling, the size of the cross-border transactions, and a description of the relevant business activities or transactions provided in abstract terms without revealing business secrets. In certain circumstances, the Member States may request additional information including the full text of an advance cross-border ruling or an APA.

Bilateral or multilateral APAs with third countries may, in certain cases, be excluded from the scope of automatic exchange of information. Whether such agreements may be exchanged would normally depend on the possibility given in the applicable tax treaty to disclose information to third parties. When the exchange of information is prevented by a tax treaty, the information that should have been exchanged is normally registered in a database. Information contained in this database is not publicly available.

3.1.4 *Mandatory Automatic Exchange of Information on Reportable Cross-Border Arrangements*

The DAC contains provisions on the mandatory disclosure and exchange of information on reportable cross-border arrangements.[65] This amendment, enacted in 2018, implies rules for increased transparency that apply to intermediaries defined as 'any person that designs, markets, organises or makes available for implementation or manages the implementation of a reportable cross-border arrangement'.[66]

The reporting obligation applies in the presence of cross-border arrangements that contain one or more of the 'hallmarks' listed in the directive. These hallmarks have a broader scope than just TP. There are three types of TP hallmarks that are within the scope of the reporting obligation that effectuate mandatory disclosure with no need to

64. *See* Article 8a of the DAC.
65. *See* Article 8ab of the DAC.
66. *See* Article 3(21) of the DAC.

meet the main benefit test.[67] Stated differently, these three hallmarks do not require that a cross-border intra-group transaction is tax-motivated to instigate the reporting obligation. The first TP hallmark concerns arrangements that involve the use of unilateral safe harbour rules. The second relates to arrangements involving the transfer of 'hard-to-value intangibles'.[68] The third specific hallmark concerning TP relates to arrangements involving an intra-group cross-border transfer of functions and/or risks and/or assets if the projected annual EBIT, during the three-year period after the transfer, of the transferor or transferors, are less than 50% of the projected annual EBIT of such transferor or transferors if the transfer had not been made.

The reporting obligation may also be borne by the taxpayer. This would especially be the case when the intermediary is not located in the EU, when the intermediary is bound by professional privilege or secrecy rules, or when there is no recourse to an intermediary.

Sanctions apply to intermediaries that do not report the arrangements in accordance with the directive. However, the sanctions are not harmonized: the directive solely requires that the Member States implement penalties that are 'effective, proportionate and dissuasive'.[69]

3.2 The Resolution of Cross-Border Tax Disputes

3.2.1 The Arbitration Convention

In 1990, the Member States concluded an inter-governmental convention on the elimination of double taxation in connection with TP adjustments.[70] This convention was intended to provide an arbitration mechanism in the case that double taxation in TP matters and issues on the attribution of profits to permanent establishments that cannot be eliminated by the competent authorities. The Member States have also adopted a non-binding code of conduct to implement the arbitration convention effectively and consistently.[71]

The procedural aspects are regulated by the convention and the code of conduct and share several features with the procedure suggested in the commentary on Article 25(5) of the OECD MTC. A case is examined by the competent authorities as part of a MAP

67. The main benefit test is contained in Part I of the Annex IV of the DAC.
68. *See* Part II, point E(2) of the Annex IV of the DAC, in which hard-to-value intangibles are defined as intangibles or rights in intangibles for which, at the time of their transfer between associated enterprises, a twofold requirement is fulfilled. One such stipulation is that no reliable comparables exist. The second is that, at the time the transaction was entered into, the projections of future cash flows or income expected to be derived from the transferred intangible or the assumptions used in valuing the intangible are highly uncertain, making it difficult to predict the level of ultimate success of the intangible at the time of the transfer.
69. *See* Article 25a of the DAC.
70. *See* Convention 90/436/EEC on the elimination of double taxation in connection with the adjustment of profits of associated enterprises, OJ 20 August 1990, L 225/10.
71. *See* the Revised Code of Conduct for the effective implementation of the Convention on the elimination of double taxation in connection with the adjustment of profits of associated enterprises, 2009/C 322/01, Official Journal of the EU (30 December 2009).

initiated within three years of the occurrence of double taxation. The authorities then have two years to attempt to solve the case as part of the MAP. In the event of failure, the taxpayer normally has the right to have the case submitted to an advisory commission. Yet the taxpayer does not have the right to initiate the arbitration procedure which is a prerogative of the competent authorities. Once the advisory commission has been established, it must deliver an independent opinion within six months (the arbitration method is the independent opinion approach and not the baseball arbitration approach). The competent authorities have a final opportunity to solve the case within six months before the opinion of the advisory commission becomes binding.

The arbitration convention was an ambitious tool that aimed at generally implementing mandatory binding arbitration within the EU. However, several obstacles prevented it from being an efficient tool to prevent or resolve international tax disputes. Its entry into force was problematic, and its effective implementation suffered from the lack of compulsory delays in many cases. The JTPF has found that it was frequent that taxpayers waived the two-year time limit as provided for in Article 7(4) of the convention, thus reducing its effectiveness. The scope of the arbitration convention was also limited to TP matters and the attribution of profits to permanent establishments.

Moreover, even after the MLI's entry into force and the growing number of countries that signed it, numerous double taxation conventions concluded between the Member States did not include an arbitration provision. Therefore, an obvious need for improved dispute resolution mechanisms remained even after the signature of the MLI. This is particularly the case in the aftermath of the BEPS Project since several amendments to the OECD TPG are likely to increase the complexity and the number of TP disputes.

3.2.2 The Dispute Resolution Directive

In view of the points mentioned above, the Member States agreed on a dispute resolution directive in 2017 that did not affect the existence of the arbitration convention. The dispute resolution directive builds on several features of the arbitration convention and improves some of its defects, resulting in a complex instrument containing far-reaching obligations on the Member States to effectively eliminate situations of double taxation. The main novelty of the directive is the possibility offered to taxpayers to refer to domestic courts if the competent authorities of the Member States do not timely follow the different steps and comply with the various obligations provided in the directive.

The European Commission first issued a draft directive in 2016 that was eventually amended before its adoption by the Member States in 2017.[72] The instrument chosen by the Member States, a directive issued on the basis of Article 115 of the TFEU,

72. *See* Council Directive (EU) 2017/1852 of 10 October 2017 on tax dispute resolution mechanisms in the EU, OJ L 265, 14 October 2017, pp. 1-14.

supposes that the Member States interpret it in accordance with the principle of conforming interpretation that is subject to the control of the CJEU. The compatibility of the directive with the primary law of the EU may also be assessed by this court.

The scope of the directive is broader than in the initial draft that only applied to 'income from business'. The directive contains mechanisms to resolve disputes that arise from the interpretation and the application of DTC. Therefore, the directive provides rights and obligations to taxpayers when they are affected by such disputes.[73]

The directive contains several mechanisms that aim at effectively resolving a cross-border tax dispute. These mechanisms are complex because of the different participants that may be affected by the resolution of it and considering the numerous chances that are given to the competent authorities to solve a case by mutual agreement. The directive contains three main stages: the complaint, the MAP, and the dispute resolution phase. The different steps of these three main stages are summarized in the following figure:

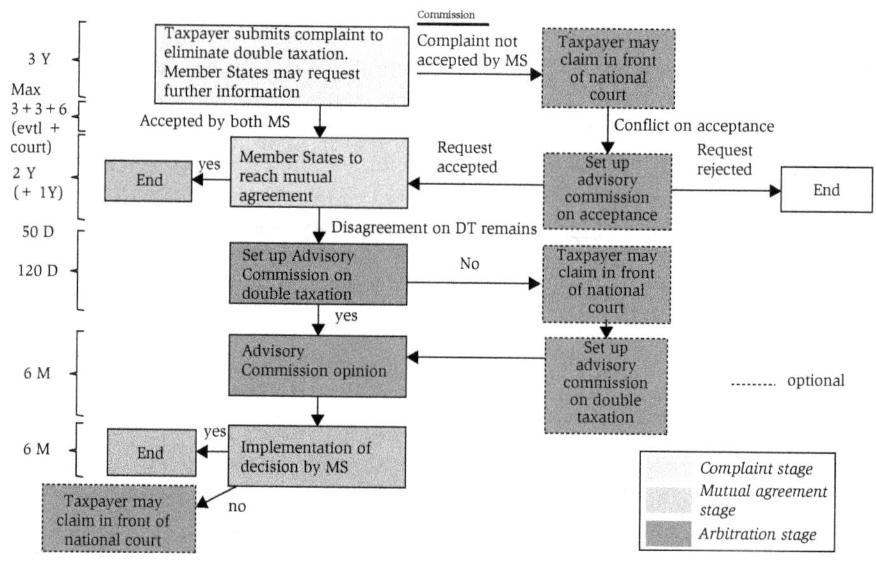

Source: European Commission.[74]

The complaint phase affords the taxpayer an opportunity to bring a case before the competent authorities of the Member States concerned in order to request the resolution of a cross-border tax dispute concerning the interpretation or the application of a DTC. At the same time, this phase aims at ensuring that the request is receivable which, in most situations, consists of verifying that the taxpayer has been subject to international double taxation. The complaint must be submitted to the competent authorities

73. *See* Article 1 of the dispute resolution directive.
74. *See* https://ec.europa.eu/taxation_customs/sites/taxation/files/jtpf_presentation_on_drm.pdf (valid until 23 February 2021).

within three years from an action resulting in a question in dispute. Thereafter the request must be accepted or rejected with a motivated decision. The absence of the competent authorities' decision on the receivability of the request is deemed as an implicit acceptance. What is particularly novel in the dispute resolution directive is the possibility given to the taxpayer to challenge the refusal of the complaint. On the one hand, if all competent authorities reject the complaint, the taxpayer may appeal these decisions under national rules. On the other hand, if they disagree with the acceptance of the request, the dispute resolution phase is initiated in order to allow an advisory commission to reassess the admissibility of the request.

During the MAP phase, the competent authorities shall endeavour to resolve the dispute within two years. This period may be extended by up to one year upon a written justification. If the dispute is not solved during this phase, they need to inform the taxpayer who can then initiate the dispute resolution phase.

The dispute resolution stage may occur both with respect to the receivability of the complaint and the resolution of the dispute. On the one hand, if the competent authorities disagree with the acceptance of a complaint, the taxpayer may initiate the dispute resolution phase to obtain the opinion of an advisory commission on the receivability of the case. This opinion is to be issued within six months. If the case is deemed receivable, the competent authorities have a last chance to enter the MAP phase. If they do not wish to enter the MAP phase, the advisory commission, which has already been constituted, provides an opinion within six months (possibly extended by another three months) on how to resolve the dispute. The case then returns to the competent authorities who have a last opportunity to decide how to resolve the dispute. Should they not agree, they will have to implement the opinion of the advisory commission.

The second situation in which the dispute resolution stage takes place is when the competent authorities have accepted the complaint but failed to resolve the dispute during the time of the MAP phase. Similar to what was described above, an advisory commission provides an opinion on how to do so. This opinion is not binding unless they fail to reach a consensus.

The set-up of the advisory commission also contains interesting guarantees provided to the taxpayer by the directive. The request to set up the advisory commission is made by the taxpayer to the competent authorities. Not only are the delays to establish the advisory commission relatively short. The directive also provides a right for the taxpayer to initiate a domestic procedure to ensure that the advisory commission is effectively appointed in situations when the competent authorities have not set up the commission within the prescribed delays.

Among the various features of the dispute resolution directive, it can be observed that the competent authorities participate in the advisory commission which can be perceived as an incentive to encourage mutual agreements between the former and may generally promote effective cooperation between them. The taxpayer does not formally participate in the procedure but may appear or be represented before the advisory commission. The chair of the advisory commission shall be a judge unless all parties agree otherwise. It is also important to note that the dispute resolution directive makes it possible to set up an alternative dispute resolution commission that may consist of a standing committee of a permanent nature.[75] An alternative dispute resolution commission may apply, when appropriate, any dispute resolution processes or techniques to resolve the question in dispute (e.g., baseball arbitration) as long as this is done in a binding manner.

Last, the directive emphasizes that the final decision shall not be a precedent but nevertheless requires the publication of the decision, or at least an abstract thereof. Overall, the dispute resolution directive is a complex, yet well-balanced, tool to promote the prevention and, when necessary, the resolution of cross-border tax disputes.

The table below provides a high-level comparison of Article 25 of the OECD MTC, the EU arbitration convention, and the dispute resolution directive:[76]

	Article 25 OECD MTC	*EU Arbitration Convention*	*EU Arbitration Directive*
Scope	All types of taxation not in accordance with a DTC	TP issues	All types of disputes arising from the interpretation and application of agreements and conventions
Taxpayer initiative	Yes	Yes	Yes
Taxpayer participation	Limited	Yes[77]	Limited
Time limit	Yes	Yes	Yes
Compulsory solution	Yes	Yes	Yes

4 EU SOFT LAW ON TP

The soft law of the EU that applies to TP stems mainly from the work of the EU JTPF, the objective of which is to achieve a more uniform application of TP rules within the EU. The JTPF is not an organ that competes with the OECD or promotes a different approach to TP. Rather, it provides practical recommendations to effectively implement the OECD TPG and achieve some uniformity in the application of TP rules.

75. *See* Article 10(1) of the dispute resolution directive. *See also* Sophia Piotrowski et al., *Towards a Standing Committee Pursuant to Article 10 of the EU Tax Dispute Resolution Directive: A Proposal for Implementation*, 47 Intertax, 2019-8/9, pp. 678-692.

76. For a more detailed comparison, *see*, e.g., Sriram Govind and Jérôme Monsenego, *Multilateralism in Dispute Resolution: Some Thoughts on the OECD Multilateral Instrument and the EU Dispute Resolution Directive*, in Ana Paula Dourado (ed.), *International and EU Tax Multilateralism: Challenges Raised by the MLI* (IBFD GREIT Series 2020), pp. 295-315.

77. Taxpayers have the right to request to appear or be represented in front of the commission. *See* more detailed explanations below.

Several of the reports issued by the JTPF have gained the support of the European Commission in its communications. By supporting the work of the JTPF, the commission would normally invite the European Council to endorse the recommendations and the Member States to implement them. It is to be observed that the reports of the JTPF are not systematically updated, while the OECD TPG are subject to regular updates. Therefore, there might be issues for which the recommendations of the JTPF become, with time, less aligned with the OECD TPG.

The communications issued by the European Commission in the area of TP (section 3.1) will first be presented. Second, the focus will be on the reports issued by the JTPF that had not (yet) received the support of the European Commission in a communication at the time of writing of this chapter (section 3.2). The communications and reports presented below follow the chronological order of their publication.

4.1 Communications from the European Commission

The communications from the European Commission in the field of TP are based on the work of the JTPF. These communications are not binding as they solely express the support of the commission for the work of the JTPF. The following topics are considered below: transfer pricing documentation (section 3.1.1), APAs within the EU (section 3.1.2), low value-adding intra-group services (section 3.1.3), non-EU triangular cases (section 3.1.4), TP and SMEs (section 3.1.5), cost contribution arrangements on services not creating IP (section 3.1.6), secondary adjustments (section 3.1.7), TP risk management (section 3.1.8), and compensating adjustments (section 3.1.9).

4.1.1 Transfer Pricing Documentation

To mitigate the differences between the TPD requirements of the Member States and to limit compliance costs, the JTPF suggested a coordinated approach to documentation, the EU TPD. It is composed of two parts, i.e., the master file and country-specific files. The EU TPD is not fully aligned with the latest recommendations of the OECD on TPD, in particular, Chapter 5 of the 2017 OECD TPG.

The master file is a compilation of standardized documentation relevant to all EU group members of a multinational enterprise. It should contain a description of the economic reality of the multinational enterprise and of its TP system in a way that is relevant to all EU Member States concerned. The country-specific files contain information specific to each country where the multinational enterprise is present. The content of the country-specific documentation supplements the master file. Together, the two files constitute the TPD for the relevant EU Member State. The two documents would provide tax authorities with the information necessary to conduct their audit activities while reducing the compliance costs of multinational enterprises. The EU TPD should contain enough details to allow the tax authorities to make a risk assessment for case selection purposes or, at the beginning of a tax audit, ask relevant and precise questions regarding the groups' TP, and assess the transfer prices of the intra-group transactions.

Based on the work of the JTPF, the European Commission suggested the adoption of a code of conduct on TPD for related parties in the EU.[78] The code of conduct was subject to a resolution of the council which is not legally binding on the Member States but represents an important commitment.[79] Therefore, the use of the EU TPD is only optional for a multinational enterprise.

In addition to the EU TPD, the code of conduct contains several political commitments with no binding effect on the Member States. Among other commitments, the Member States undertake not to require smaller and less complex enterprises to produce the amount or complexity of documentation that might be expected from larger and more structurally complicated enterprises; the Member States should also refrain from imposing unreasonable compliance costs or administrative burden on enterprises in requesting documentation to be created or obtained, and they should ensure that there is no public disclosure of confidential information contained in the documentation. Finally, the Member States commit not to impose documentation-related penalties when taxpayers comply in good faith, in a reasonable manner, and within a reasonable time with standardized and consistent documentation whether it is prepared in accordance with the EU TPD standard or with the Member State's own documentation requirements.

4.1.2 Guidelines for APAs Within the EU

APAs may be an interesting tool to prevent disputes and provide certainty by agreeing in advance on a set of criteria for the determination of the TP methodology applicable to certain intra-group transactions. APAs concerned with the methodology rather than the actual profit earned from a specific transaction. Considering the potential advantages of entering into APAs, the commission adopted a communication on the work of the JTPF in the field of dispute avoidance and resolution procedures including guidelines for APAs within the EU.[80] They are based on the best practices identified by the JTPF, establish procedures for an efficient APA process, and detail the stages usually found in an APA.[81]

In addition, several important recommendations are provided. Among such recommendations, the following can be emphasized:

(1) Bilateral APAs are preferred over unilateral APAs mainly because they ensure a greater level of certainty and compliance with the arm's length principle. Therefore, tax authorities are deemed entitled to refuse requests for unilateral

78. *See* COM(2005) 543 final.
79. *See* resolution of the council and of the representatives of the governments of the Member States, meeting within the council of 27 June 2006 on a code of conduct on transfer pricing documentation for associated enterprises in the European Union (EU TPD), OJ C 176, 28 July 2006, pp. 1-7.
80. *See* COM(2007) 71 final.
81. According to the guidelines, an APA application should typically have four distinct stages: (a) Pre-filing stage/informal application; (b) formal application; (c) evaluation and negotiation of the APA; and (d) formal agreement. These stages are described in points 21 to 47 of the guidelines.

APAs when they consider that a bilateral or multilateral APA is more appropriate or when none at all is appropriate.

(2) The withdrawal by a taxpayer of an APA application should not automatically instigate a tax audit.

(3) In the event that a Member State introduces fees for entry into its APA programme, such fees should not be set so high that they are a disincentive for applying for one of them.

(4) When the tax authorities come to an agreement with respect to the TP methodology of an intra-group transaction, the APA will become effective only once the taxpayer provides its consensus to its terms and conditions.

(5) Critical assumptions are deemed 'vital' to an APA. They should be tailored to the individual circumstances of the taxpayer and the type of the transaction covered but still be wide enough to ensure certainty to the parties and avoid unnecessary renegotiations.

(6) To mitigate the number and extent of renegotiations, the APA agreement should include parameters for an acceptable level of divergence for some of the critical assumptions.

(7) Rollbacks are accepted when they are provided for in domestic legislation when they are adopted as a secondary result of the APA, and only when it is appropriate to the facts of the case. The previous facts and circumstances relevant to a rollback must be similar to those of the future years covered by an APA.

(8) Tax authorities should attempt to facilitate access to APAs for SMEs when APAs are useful for dispute avoidance or resolution.

4.1.3 *Guidelines on Low Value-Adding Intra-group Services*

In a communication from 2011, the European Commission gave its support to the guidelines on low value-adding intra-group services drafted by the JTPF.[82] As a starting point, the JTPF observed that the compliance burden and the situations of double taxation had been increasing for intra-group services. The chapter on intra-group services included in the OECD TPG at that time was also deemed partly insufficient. Therefore, the JTPF issued guidelines intended to gain efficiency when dealing with this category of intra-group transactions while remaining consistent with the OECD TPG. The report makes also the important statement that all costs should normally be allocable to a group member from a TP perspective, however, without guaranteeing their deductibility from a domestic law perspective.

First, it is considered in the report that, given the routine nature of low value-adding services, it should normally be possible to describe such services in a 'relatively modest document'. It would indicate that it can be assumed that a service has been rendered and that it provides a benefit to the recipient if the recipient indeed would have paid for

82. *See* COM(2011) 16 final.

the activity or performed the service itself had it been independent.[83] The report enumerates different items that may need to be included in this document such as indicative ratios,[84] explanations on the rationale and the benefit of the services, and a description of the allocation key used and whether profit markups are being applied.

The report contains an interesting appendix that provides a non-exhaustive and non-prescriptive list of various shareholder costs that would normally be deemed to be incurred for the benefit of the parent company, thus not being allocable to other group companies.[85] This list is quite detailed and includes comments and recommendations by the JTPF regarding how to deal with different categories of costs. For example, costs of the parent company's audit of the accounts of a subsidiary, if the audit is conducted exclusively in the interest of the parent company, are deemed to be shareholder costs; however, if the audit is also in the interest of the subsidiary, the activity is deemed to be partly an intra-group service.[86] At the same time, the JTPF concluded that the analysis will always require that certain questions be raised in relation to each cost listed, in particular, whether or not the cost benefits the entire group, certain subsidiaries, or only the parent company. Considering the need to answer these questions, it is considered that a case-by-case approach is necessary.

With respect to allocation keys, it is considered in the report that, although any allocation key can be justified, its choice must also be upheld, and the key must be applied consistently.[87] The report also contains a non-exhaustive list of allocation keys that are of common usage.[88]

Finally, the report emphasizes that low value-adding services will typically only attract a 'modest' markup. According to the JTPF, 'experience shows that typically agreed mark ups fall within a range of 3-10%, often around 5%'.[89]

4.1.4 Non-EU Triangular Cases

In the same communication as that relating to low value-adding services, the commission expressed its support to the JTPF's report dedicated to non-EU triangular cases. The report provides some non-prescriptive suggestions regarding dispute resolution without any prejudice to whether such cases may be covered by the EU arbitration

83. *See* COM(2011) 16 final, Appendix 1, point 22.
84. For example, a ratio of the costs incurred for intra-group services compared to overall operating expenses.
85. *See* COM(2011) 16 final, Appendix 2, pp. 23 and following.
86. In such a case, the JTPF considers that this is the case when the audit is compulsory under the law of the state of incorporation of the subsidiary, when the audit report is published with the financial statement of the subsidiary or published on the website of the subsidiary or, in general, is used by the subsidiary (e.g., provided to a bank when the subsidiary applies for a loan or used by the management of the subsidiary itself): *see* COM(2011) 16 final, Appendix 2, point d.1.
87. *See* COM(2011) 16 final, point 52.
88. *See* COM(2011) 16 final, point 53, referring to specific keys for the following types of services: '(a) IT: number of PCs; (b) Business management software (e.g., SAP): number of licenses; (c) Human Resources: headcount; (d) Health and safety: headcount; (e) Management development: headcount; (f) Tax, Accounting, etc: turnover or size of balance sheet; (g) Marketing services: turnover; (h) Vehicle fleet management: number of cars'.
89. *See* COM(2011) 16 final, point 65.

convention. In this context, it should be observed that at the time this report was issued, the dispute resolution directive had not yet been adopted.

Triangular cases are defined as cases involving an intra-group transaction between group companies established in two Member States while, at the same time, another related party resident of a third state had a significant influence that resulted in a pricing outcome, not in accordance with the arm's length principle.[90] In such cases, the two Member States engaged in a MAP cannot fully resolve a double taxation situation in a TP case by applying the arm's length principle. This is because a related party situated in a third state had a significant influence in contributing to a non-arm's length result in a chain of transactions. Therefore, the elimination of double taxation is conditional upon the involvement of the relevant third state.

The report suggests several approaches that might be helpful in solving such triangular cases without, however, recommending a particular method; this is mainly because of the complexity and lack of binding dispute resolution mechanisms that characterize this type of dispute. Among various approaches, the report recommends considering the improvement and extension of the tax treaty network of the Member States, the use of rollbacks in conformity with the guidelines on APAs, and the extension of the arbitration convention on a case-by-case basis to third countries according to Articles 35 and 36 of the Vienna Convention on the law of treaties. It is also considered that the taxpayer plays a central role in resolving such triangular cases, although the MAP is primarily a procedure between tax authorities.

4.1.5 TP and SMEs

The JTPF issued a report on TP and SMEs that was welcomed and supported by the European Commission in a communication.[91] The primary issue concerns the administrative burden that TP may represent for SMEs and the potential need for simplification of various compliance obligations. The JTPF observed that, within the EU, there is no common definition of SMEs for tax purposes and no common tax treatment of SMEs. Relieving measures for SMEs, if there are any, tend to vary between the Member States which explains the goal set by the European Commission to achieve a more uniform application of TP rules within the Union.

The JTPF generally recommends an approach based on proportionality when considering the needs of SMEs, the requirements of tax authorities, and the ability of SMEs to meet these requirements. Although the arm's length principle is neutral and applies equally to enterprises of all sizes, it is recognized in the report that the application of the arm's length principle may prove relatively more difficult for SMEs. To formulate recommendations, the report distinguishes between the pre-audit, audit, and dispute resolution stages.

With respect to the pre-audit phase, the report insists on improving the communication and relations between SMEs and tax authorities, including by providing means

90. *See* COM(2011) 16 final, p. 28, point 6.
91. *See* COM(2012) 516 final.

for SMEs to gain certainty before a transaction takes place. The report also encourages voluntary compliance which would suggest that the Member States ensure that SMEs have access to up-to-date information and advice. In addition, Members States are invited to develop simplification measures to reduce the administrative burden of SMEs.[92]

For the audit stage, the JTPF considers that it would be inappropriate to impose documentation-related penalties arising from an audit requirement to provide documentation that was not required pre-audit if the taxpayer was acting in good faith, relying on the streamline approach, and is not able to supply the required documentation. To ensure that SMEs receive appropriate treatment when they are audited and, at the same time, achieve this objective in a cost-efficient manner, the report suggests setting up internal peer group reviews or a structural organization of audit resources within tax authorities. Similar to the pre-audit phase, it is recommended to consider the introduction of simplification measures, possibly by drawing on the best practices of other Member States. The Member States are also encouraged to implement the recommendations of the JTPF formulated in its other reports.[93]

Finally, the JTPF observed that the burden of double taxation and of the resources necessary to eliminate it might be quite substantial for SMEs. Therefore, it is recommended that tax authorities act unilaterally to solve cases of double taxation and introduce fast track dispute resolution processes that do not fully align with the steps of the MAP for resolving the less complex cases of double taxation of 'low value'. What is deemed as a 'non-complex transaction with a relatively low monetary value', however, is not defined in the report.[94]

4.1.6 Cost Contribution Arrangements on Services Not Creating IP

The report of the JTPF concerning cost contribution arrangements on services not creating IP emphasizes the need for such an arrangement to be in accordance with the arm's length principle. To do so, the JTPF provides a list of features that are deemed to characterize a cost contribution arrangement on services not creating IP that is consistent with the arm's length principle:[95]

(1) The arrangement should make business sense.
(2) The economic substance should be consistent with the terms of the cost contribution arrangement.
(3) The terms of a cost contribution arrangement should be generally agreed upon prior to the beginning of the activity.
(4) The terms of a cost contribution arrangement should be at arm's length taking into account the circumstances known or reasonably foreseeable at the time of entry into the arrangement.

92. *See* COM(2012) 516 final, Appendix I, points 17-28.
93. *See* COM(2012) 516 final, Appendix I, points 29-35.
94. *See* COM(2012) 516 final, Appendix I, points 36-39.
95. *See* COM(2012) 516 final, Appendix II, point 16.

(5) Each participant should have a reasonable expectation of a benefit.
(6) The participant's share of the costs should be consistent with its share of the expected benefits.
(7) Reasonably expected benefits can be assessed in terms of efficiency or effectiveness in quantitative or qualitative terms.
(8) Contributions by a participant can be in cash or in kind and, therefore, active participation is not a requirement. The level of influence on decision-making will vary depending on the type of cost contribution arrangement, the expertise of the participants, and the amount of costs being allocated to the respective participants.
(9) When a service subject to a cost contribution arrangement is also provided to or received from nonparticipants in the cost contribution arrangement, it has to be valued at arm's length.
(10) If participants join or leave the cost contribution arrangement, shares should be adjusted/rebalanced in accordance with the arm's length principle.

The report also contains a description of the information that may need to be provided to evidence that a cost contribution arrangement is consistent with the arm's length principle. This includes general information about the cost contribution arrangement, expected benefits from it, contributions to the arrangement, how to monitor and adjust the cost contribution arrangement, and a list of the entities (related or not) who benefit from services included in the arrangement, including the fees charged and the allocation keys used.[96]

It can be observed that, while the value of each participant's contribution must be consistent with the value that unrelated parties would have agreed to in comparable situations, for cost contribution arrangements on services not creating IP, it is considered in the report that there is often a small difference between the use of costs and the use of market prices for the purposes of measuring the value of the contributions. Therefore, for practical reasons, it is recommended in the report to generally value the contributions at costs. Although Chapter 8 of the OECD TPG has been updated since the publication of this report by the JTPF, similar recommendations are found in paragraph 8.28 of the OECD TPG.

The document contains a table with elements to help differentiate between shared intra-group services – including cost pools – and cost contribution arrangements on services not creating IP.[97]

4.1.7 *Secondary Adjustments*

Although secondary adjustments (e.g., a withholding tax on a deemed dividend) are normally reversed if the primary adjustment is reversed, double taxation may arise

96. *See* COM(2012) 516 final, Appendix II, points 25-26.
97. *See* COM(2012) 516 final, Appendix II, point 12.

when the other state does not provide a corresponding tax credit for the withholding tax or does not recognize the deemed dividend as a transaction.

To mitigate situations of double taxation, the JTPF recommends that, if secondary adjustments are not compulsory according to the domestic law, Member States refrain from making secondary adjustments when they lead to double taxation. If, in contrast, secondary adjustments are compulsory under the legislation of a Member State, it is recommended that the Member States provide ways and means to avoid double taxation. This can be achieved, for example, by endeavouring to resolve it through a MAP or by allowing the repatriation of funds at an early stage when possible.[98]

The report then contains guidance specifically applicable to secondary adjustments that occur within the EU. In this context, a distinction should be made between situations when there has been a repatriation of funds (i.e., effectively reversing the funds so that the accounts of the parties involved are in line with the economic intent of the primary adjustment) and situations when no such repatriation has occurred. When there is no repatriation of funds and, given the complications and risks for double taxation raised by secondary adjustments, the JTPF recommends that, within the EU, secondary adjustments are characterized as constructive dividends or constructive capital contributions rather than as constructive loans. The reason for this is that the parent-subsidiary directive would normally prevent the levy of withholding taxes upon deemed dividend payments or capital contributions made between a parent company and a subsidiary resident of a Member State.[99]

When there has been a repatriation of funds, two options are envisaged in the report based on the time at which the repatriation is made. In situations in which repatriation is part of the settlement of a MAP, it is recommended in the report that the agreement states that no withholding tax will be applied by the Member State out of which the repatriation is made and no additional taxable burden will be imposed in the Member State to which the repatriation is made. When repatriation is considered at an earlier stage than the MAP, for example, as part of a tax audit, it is recommended to ensure that the other Member State is informed concurrently based on an exchange of information procedure or by the taxpayer if the taxpayer agrees. It is also indicated in the report that a repatriation agreement reached at the audit stage should not preclude a request by the taxpayer for a MAP nor should it indicate agreement or disagreement with an audit statement.

Concerning penalties, the main recommendation of the report is that, when a secondary adjustment is required, Member States should refrain from imposing a penalty with respect to the secondary adjustment. This means that penalties should only be applied in connexion to the primary adjustment. Yet, when penalties on secondary adjustments are nevertheless applied, it is recommended to address them in

98. *See* COM(2014) 315 final, Appendix I, point 6.
99. *See* COM(2014) 315 final, Appendix I, point 8. *See also* Articles 4 and 5 of the Council Directive 2011/96/EU of 30 November 2011 on the common system of taxation applicable in the case of parent companies and subsidiaries of different Member States.

a MAP to ensure the removal of double taxation resulting from secondary adjustments.[100]

Finally, the question is raised whether double taxation issues resulting from secondary adjustments are encompassed within the arbitration convention and the dispute resolution directive. In a survey conducted by the JTPF, most Member States that applied secondary adjustments expressed the view that double taxation issues resulting from secondary adjustments are not covered by the arbitration convention. However, most Member States applying secondary adjustments also responded that they would be willing to address secondary adjustments in the course of a MAP. Therefore, in cases when it is not possible to avoid double taxation at the outset, the report emphasizes that a taxpayer would be required to file a request under the arbitration convention and a request for a MAP under the relevant tax treaty. Member States that do not consider that secondary adjustments can be treated under the arbitration convention are thus encouraged to highlight in their public guidance the fact that a separate request under a treaty may be needed to remove double taxation. Here, it can be observed that this guidance has not been updated since the adoption of the dispute resolution directive.

4.1.8 TP Risk Management

This report addresses not only the risk that transfer prices are not established in accordance with the arm's length principle but also the risk that resources are not allocated efficiently.[101]

Consistently with other reports, the JTPF recommends here to take a cooperative approach based on dialogue and trust for each phase of a normal TP process (pre-audit phase, audit phase, and dispute resolution phase). This requires communication at an early stage as well as sufficient transparency on the facts and circumstances relevant to the case. The report recommends prioritizing resources allocated to areas with a high TP risk which suggests that the actions envisaged are well-targeted and appropriate to the circumstances of the case.

To assess whether there is a TP risk and if the tax authorities should dedicate resources to a particular case, the report recommends an appropriate organizational framework. This may include, as is present in certain Member States, setting up a group of TP experts that may decide on how to proceed with a specific case or an approach based on cooperative compliance arrangements. To improve the efficiency of the allocation of resources, the report recommends the exchange of information on the basis of the DAC, the performance of simultaneous audits, and the implementation of simplification measures in certain cases.

100. *See* COM(2014) 315 final, Appendix I, point 21.
101. *See* COM(2014) 315 final, Appendix II, point 4.

4.1.9 *Compensating Adjustments*

Compensating adjustments refer to adjustments made before the tax return is filed in which the taxpayer reports a transfer price for tax purposes that is deemed by the taxpayer as being at arm's length even though it differs from the amount actually charged. Compensating adjustments are recognized by a few countries based on the fact that 'the tax return should reflect the actual transactions'.[102]

To address the practical issues arising from compensating adjustments, the report indicates that the Member States of the EU agreed to two guiding principles. On the one hand, the Member States consider that the profits of the related enterprises with respect to the commercial or financial relations between them need to be calculated symmetrically, i.e., enterprises participating in a transaction should use the same price for respective transactions. On the other hand, a compensating adjustment initiated by the taxpayer should be accepted if certain conditions are fulfilled.[103]

The report further indicates that, in the case that the actual result is beyond the range of arm's length results targeted when setting the price at the time of the transaction, the adjustment should be made to the most appropriate point in an arm's length range.[104]

4.2 Reports from the EU JTPF

The JTPF assists and advises the European Commission on certain TP matters. It is appointed for a limited period of time, but its mandate has been regularly renewed. The JTPF has issued numerous reports on particular TP issues, often beginning with the OECD TPG and providing concrete guidance for the practical application of the arm's length principle within the EU. As mentioned on the website of the European Commission, the JTPF 'operates on the basis of consensus to propose to the Commission pragmatic, non-legislative solutions to practical problems posed by transfer pricing practices in the EU'.[105] The JTPF also compiles statistics on pending MAPs under the arbitration convention.[106]

Reports on the following topics had been drafted by the JTPF but not (yet) adopted by the commission at the time of writing this chapter: the use of comparables in the EU (section 3.2.1), the use of economic valuation techniques in TP (section 3.2.2), a

102. *See* para. 4.39 of the OECD TPG.
103. *See* COM(2014) 315 final, Appendix III, point 16, where it is indicated that the conditions are the following: before the relevant transaction or series of transactions, the taxpayer made reasonable efforts to achieve an arm's-length outcome. This would normally be described in the transfer pricing documentation of the taxpayer; the taxpayer makes the adjustment symmetrically in the accounts in both Member States involved; the taxpayer applies the same approach consistently over time; the taxpayer makes the adjustment before filing the tax return; the taxpayer is able to explain for what reasons his forecast did not match the result achieved when it is required by internal legislation in at least one of the Member States involved.
104. *See* COM(2014) 315 final, Appendix III, point 17.
105. *See* https://ec.europa.eu/taxation_customs/joint-transfer-pricing-forum_en (last accessed 24 March 2022).
106. *See* e.g., JTPF/007a/2018/EN.

coordinated approach to TP controls within the EU (section 3.2.3), and the application of the profit split method within the EU (section 3.2.4). The content of these reports is briefly described in the sections below.

4.2.1 *Report on the Use of Comparables in the EU*

The report establishes best practices and pragmatic solutions by issuing various recommendations for both taxpayers and tax authorities. It aims at increasing the objectivity and transparency of comparable searches for TP purposes.[107]

The report recommends that taxpayers and tax authorities apply a principle of transparency when they respectively conduct or control a comparable search, however, at the same time, it emphasizes that this burden should be proportionate.

The report also briefly examines the use of internal comparables and accentuates that, as they are less expensive to search for than external comparables, they could particularly be explored to achieve proportionality when used for small transactions and SMEs. In any case, the report makes clear that internal and external comparables should be treated in the same manner regarding the degree of comparability required, i.e., there is no systematic preference towards using internal or external comparables. When it comes to external comparables, a process to select them, including both a quantitative analysis and a qualitative review, is suggested in the report.

In cases when interquartile ranges are used, it is considered in the report that every point situated in the range should be considered as being at arm's length. However, if a transaction is priced outside the range, the report suggests that the median of the range should be considered as a reference point.[108]

Useful recommendations are also provided with respect to comparability adjustments which should generally follow the principles advocated by the JTPF in terms of quality, transparency, consistency, and proportionality. This last point may nevertheless be difficult to enforce given the high expectations placed on the quality and the documentation supporting comparability adjustments.

Finally, an important clarification is made with respect to pan-European comparables. It is mentioned in the report that conducting a pan-EU comparable search requires referring to the relevant geographic market that generally includes the territory in which the multinational enterprise operates, as long as it is homogeneous. Therefore, when using foreign or pan-European data, it is emphasized that taxpayers should document the reasons underlying the choice of the region on which the comparable search is based.

4.2.2 *Report on the Use of Economic Valuation Techniques in TP*

Economic valuation is often undertaken for determining the TP consequences of intra-group transactions related to intangibles or going concerns. Considering that

107. *See* JTPF/007/2016/FINAL/EN.
108. *See* JTPF/007/2016/FINAL/EN, p. 12.

valuation is also performed outside the field of TP, the objective of the report is to 'build a bridge between general practice of economic valuation and transfer pricing'.[109]

Valuation is a highly complex area, and it is acknowledged in the report that the opportunity for simplification or standardization of economic valuation techniques is limited. Taxpayers and tax authorities thus need to face the complexity of this field which is why the report insists on promoting common theoretical grounds for performing valuation as well as communication and transparency between the parties involved.

The first recommendation is that, in the case that an economic valuation is used for TP, its consistency with the arm's length principle and the principles of the OECD TPG should be documented. Methodologies, assumptions, and sources on which the economic valuation is based should be 'comprehensible to a reviewer'. Given that a number of economic valuation techniques build on inputs (e.g., cash flows) that are TP sensitive, the report insists that it is important to ensure that there is coherence between economic valuation techniques relied upon in a related party context and the method relied upon to determine transfer prices.[110] Moreover, while international standards are deemed preferable, it is emphasized in the report that using a certain valuation standard should not, by itself, lead to rejecting a result provided that it is at arm's length.[111]

Transparency and communication between taxpayers and tax authorities are strongly encouraged in the report. It is particularly recommended that, when using a discount rate, both taxpayers and tax authorities should demonstrate features such as how the discount rate was calculated, why the calculation is regarded as appropriate, and what information was used to calculate it.

The report also contains four practical and particularly useful appendices. The first appendix contains a description of several economic valuation techniques for TP purposes together with their respective strengths and weaknesses. The second appendix describes various internal and external sources of parameters for valuation purposes together with their respective source, challenges, and proposed solutions to such challenges. The third appendix contains a non-exhaustive list of examples on how to calculate the required return on equity. Finally, the fourth appendix mentions factors that may be considered for assessing the bargaining power of the parties to a transaction involving an intangible that may be subject to valuation. These factors are based on a decision of a US court in which fifteen factors were relied upon to determine the type of monetary payments that would compensate for a patent infringement.

4.2.3 Report on a Coordinated Approach to TP Controls Within the EU

The need to coordinate the approach to TP audits is important as, while multinational enterprises act globally, tax audits are conducted on a domestic basis. In addition, it is considered in the report that TP is potentially more subjective than other areas of direct

109. *See* JTPF/003/2017/FINAL/EN, point 2, p. 4.
110. *See* JTPF/003/2017/FINAL/EN, recommendation 1, p. 5.
111. *See* JTPF/003/2017/FINAL/EN, recommendation 3, p. 7.

and indirect taxation and, for this reason, sensitive to disputes.[112] The report acknowledges that, in the TP field, tax authorities do not share a common interest. Therefore, the report begins from the premise that a coordinated approach to TP controls would 'contribute to a better functioning of the internal market on two fronts: it would offer tax authorities a transparent and efficient tool to facilitate the allocation of taxing rights and also prevent the occurrence of double taxation and less than single taxation'.[113] Already in an earlier report, it was recommended to take simultaneous controls or joint audits into consideration in appropriate cases while it was recognized that the capacity and experience of tax authorities were limited at that time.[114]

To enhance the cooperation between tax authorities, it is recommended that exchange of information and cooperation between tax authorities be used 'where they are expected to assist in the identification of transfer pricing risks and to contribute to an efficient audit'.[115] At the same time, to improve the cooperation between tax authorities and taxpayers, it is recommended that they take a cooperative approach based on dialogue and trust through promoting communication, information, and transparency.

The report also mentions that Member States are encouraged to implement legislation that permits the active presence of visiting foreign officials in accordance with Article 11 of the DAC Directive since it was found that this article had not been implemented in a uniform fashion at the national level.

With respect to simultaneous controls, which are allowed in the EU according to Article 12 of the DAC, it is found in the report that, while most of the Member States had taken part in simultaneous controls since the entry into force of the directive, the Member States did not always have the legal framework that would allow them to perform corresponding downward adjustments as a result of a common understanding of the facts and circumstances and of the application of the arm's length principle. Therefore, the report recommends that the Member States enact the appropriate legal framework to perform such corresponding downward adjustments. Although it is acknowledged in the report that the term 'joint audit' as such does not feature in the DAC, it is considered that it would still be feasible for tax authorities to carry out TP controls in a way that, 'in essence', is very similar to the concept of a joint audit. This is based on the combination of the right to perform simultaneous controls under Article 12 of the DAC and be present in tax audits of other countries according to Article 11 of the DAC: tax authorities may be sent to another Member State to form a joint audit team with domestic officials and examine the facts and the circumstances of a case.

The second part of the report provides a set of best practices for a coordinated approach to TP controls during the initial phase (which includes the selection process), the audit phase, and the dispute resolution phase. Among other recommendations, the report emphasizes the twofold need to communicate and, at the same time, respect the confidentiality of information. Tax authorities should also guarantee the due respect of

112. *See* JTPF/013/2018/EN, p. 3.
113. *See* JTPF/013/2018/EN, p. 2.
114. *See* JTPF/007/FINAL/2013/EN.
115. *See* JTPF/013/2018/EN, recommendation 1, p. 3.

taxpayers' rights derived from national law (including the constitution) and the EU Charter of Fundamental Rights.

4.2.4 *Report on the Application of the Profit Split Method Within the EU*

While the profit split method – in the OECD TPG – is no longer a TP method of last resort, guidance on its application has long been limited, especially regarding the actual operation of this method. Therefore, the programme of work of the JTPF included the provision of output in order to address the problems in the practical application of the profit split method, especially with respect to the high degree of subjectivity encountered when stakeholders determine how to share profits. The aim of the JTPF's exercise was thus 'to take stock of how the PSM is applied within the EU and work towards a common approach to addressing the relevant challenges arising under the current OECD framework'.[116] The JTPF's report is to be regarded as 'complementary to, and supportive of' the text of the OECD TPG on TPSM.[117]

Providing clarification and standardization on the application of the profit split method is difficult considering the need to still take into account the facts and circumstances on a case-by-case basis as part of the accurate delineation of a transaction from the perspectives of all parties. As a starting point, the JTPF ordered a survey on the experiences of its members in the practical application of the profit split method. The survey revealed that, although the profit split method had been used in different industries, there was still only limited experience of it. Experience shows that the profit split method has been mostly used as part of APAs. Therefore, the report concludes that the profit split method 'may not necessarily ensure tax certainty and may be exposed to risks of litigation'.[118]

The report confirms the useful interpretations of the OECD TPG. The following points are particularly worth emphasizing. For the profit split method to apply, it is considered in the report that it would normally be required that the contributions of the parties are both unique and valuable. Nevertheless, the report indicates that in the presence of highly integrated business operations, the profit split method is likely to be applicable regardless of whether both parties also make unique and valuable contributions. This means that, when there is a significant degree of integration, the profit split method might be applicable even without unique and valuable contributions. In order to determine that the integration between different parties is of a high degree, the report suggests that operations would be 'highly integrated' when two or more legal entities share and/or combine functions, assets, and risks while jointly achieving a common objective.

The report contains also a flow chart tree that visually explains the profit split selection process with the different questions that must be asked that would lead to the conclusion that the profit split method is or is not likely to be the most appropriate method.

116. *See* JTPF/002/2019/EN, p. 2.
117. *See* JTPF/002/2019/EN.
118. *See* JTPF/002/2019/EN, p. 15.

Finally, the report provides indications on how to share the profits, in particular by providing a non-prescriptive list of splitting factors with a brief analysis of the pros and cons of each splitting factor, circumstances, and value drivers. The splitting factors are grouped into several categories: people-based factors, sales/volume-based factors, asset-based factors, cost-based factors, and other factors.

CHAPTER 25

Transfer Pricing in India

Rahul Mitra, Nitin Narang & Tarini Nijhara

1 TP IN INDIA

1.1 Introduction and Overview of TP in India

Vide Finance Act, 2001, section 92 of the Income Tax Act, 1961 (the Act) was substituted by sections 92-92F with effect from 1 April 2001 to include TP compliance in the calendar of the taxpayers having international transactions with overseas related parties (referred to as 'associated enterprises' in the Act). With its promulgation, a clear and binding statutory framework was included to undertake the related compliances, computation based on arm's length principle, and the role of tax officers to verify and recompute the arm's length result if the circumstances so required. The Indian TP regulations have evolved and have gained maturity over the past two decades and are now proceeding towards being in coherence with global best practices. Being a G-20 member, India has participated, confirmed broad consensus, and implemented with dedication the recommendations comprised in various action points of the BEPS Project, including those on TP. Overall, the Indian TP regulations are akin to the OECD TPG except for some unique features that distinguish them from the general TP guidelines followed worldwide.

1.2 TP Evolution in India

Below are the important milestones in the evolution of TP in India over the decades:

Year	Milestones
2001	– Detailed regulation for transfer pricing compliance regulation was introduced in India
2002	– Introduction of tolerance limit of ± 5% to satiate normal variations – Clarification on non-applicability of transfer pricing if such application results in downward revision in income
2006	– Extension of non-availability of deduction in respect of income enhanced by the AO for profits and gains derived from exports by newly established units in special economic zones, similar to units registered under STPI or other export-oriented units
2009	– Constitution of DRP – Empowerment of CBDT to formulate SHR
2011	– Amendment in provision of tolerance limit of ± 5%– central government to notify such allowable percentage of variation for different industries from time to time – TPO's powers extended to determination of arm's-length price in respect of international transactions other than referred by AO and to exercise the power of survey
2012	– Retrospective amendment made to terms 'international transaction' and 'IP' – Scope of transfer pricing extended to certain SDTs covering payments made under Section 40A(2)(b) and tax holiday entities/units. Threshold limit for applicability of SDTs set at INR 5 crores. – Introduction of the APA program – Allowance of appeal by AO against directions of DRP – Notified upper ceiling of 3% as tolerance range in the case of arithmetic mean application
2013	– Notified upper ceiling of 1% as tolerance range in the case of wholesale traders and 3% in all other cases – The safe harbour rates/margins were introduced for the first time
2014	– Introduction of rollback provisions in APA – Introduction of range concept and multiple-year data concept – Deemed international transactions concept clarified
2015	– Domestic transfer pricing threshold limit increased from INR 5 crore to INR 20 crore – Introduction of risk-based selection of cases for transfer pricing audits
2016	– Adoption of three-tier transfer pricing documentation structure as prescribed by the OECD BEPS Action 13 – Restrained revenue authorities to have no right to appeal against DRP directions – Time limits for assessment completion involving transfer pricing reduced by 3 months to 33 months
2017	– Introduction of secondary adjustments – Reduction in scope of SDTs to exclude payments made under section 40A(2)(b) – Time limits for assessment completion involving transfer pricing further reduced to 30 months for fiscal year 2017-2018 and to 24 months for fiscal year 2018-2019 onwards – Introduction of interest deduction limitation (30% of earnings before interest and taxes, depreciation and amortization)
2019	– Clarifications and rationalization regarding secondary adjustments including provision of one-time payment option of 18% (plus surcharge of 12%) – Master file to be filed by CEs even when there are no international transactions
2020	– Due date of maintenance of transfer pricing documentation and filing of Form 3CEB advanced by one month; however, due to COVID-19, due dates extended to 31 December 2020 for FY 2019-2020 – Introduction of new MAP rules in accordance with recommendations of OECD peer review report on India (such as MAP cases to be resolved within 24 months) – SHR and APA scope expanded to cover income attributable to a business connection or a PE of a non-resident

The detailed Indian TP regulations contained in Chapter X of the Income Tax Act, 1961 (the Act), including comprehensive information on related rules, circulars, instructions, notifications, etc. can be accessed on the website maintained by the Government of India. The Indian TP regulations include the following:

- TP Concept.
- Computation of income from international transactions having regard to arm's length price.
- Meaning of associated enterprise.
- Meaning of international transaction.
- Meaning of SDT.
- Computation of arm's length price.
- Reference to TPO.
- SHR.
- APA.
- Secondary adjustments.
- Documentation requirements (local file and master file).
- Report from an accountant to be furnished.
- Relevant definitions.
- Limitation of interest deduction.
- CbCR.
- Penalty provisions.

The upcoming sections of this Chapter have endeavoured to elaborate on significant and unique aspects of the TP regime in India in detail.

1.3 Salient Features of Indian TP Regulations

1.3.1 Related Parties

Consistent with the globally accepted rules, two persons are considered 'associated enterprise' if one enterprise actively participates in the capital, control, or management of the other organization with specific thresholds governed by section 92A(2) of the Act.

1.3.2 International Transactions

The Indian TP provisions apply when an international transaction has occurred between two or more related parties. As per section 92B(1) of the Act, an international transaction is defined as a transaction between two or more related parties, either or both of whom are non-residents for goods, services, intangibles, etc.

Further, the Indian TP regulations have the concept of *'deemed international transaction'* vide section 92B(2) of the Act wherein a transaction entered into by an enterprise with an unrelated party can also be deemed to be an international transaction if either of the following condition is satisfied:

- there is a prior agreement in relation to the relevant transaction between such unrelated party and the related party; or
- the terms of the relevant transaction are determined in substance between such unrelated party and the related party.

Example

Company A, located in India and Company B located in Australia are related parties. Company C is not a related party of Company A or Company B. However, Company B enters into a global supply agreement with Company C to supply goods to all of its global subsidiaries. Accordingly, Company B and Company C determine the terms of the transaction of the supply of goods undertaken between Company A and Company C.

In such a case, even though Company A and Company C are unrelated parties, the said transaction is deemed to be an international transaction to which Indian TP provisions are applicable.

In the authors' view, section 92B(2) does not create any additional charge in the matter of TP, and the concept was always latently present in the overall scheme of TP in India concerning dealings between two related parties. This impacts erosion of the tax base of the country. Section 92B(2) was inserted by the government since the inception of the formal TP regulations in India out of abundant precaution. It was done so that no taxpayer could claim immunity from TP on the grounds that its transactions were with an unrelated party irrespective of the role that its related party might have played in the transactions. However, the manner in which the safeguard has been introduced by the government and as also resultantly understood and administered by the Indian Revenue Board has been unfortunate, leading to controversies and impediments in compliance.

1.3.3 Specified Domestic Transactions

Domestic intra-group transactions have a bearing on the tax base of the country in cases when one of the transacting parties is liable to pay tax at a lower rate in comparison to the other party, such as with transactions regarding tax holiday units. The issue of parking additional profits in tax holidays by taxpayers through arranging transactions either with its related parties or other undertakings within the same legal entity for achieving the above objective came up for debate before the tax tribunals in a number of cases.

The Indian Government, in FY 2012-2013, expanded the scope of Indian TP regulations to cover SDTs to carve out a specific nature of transactions to ensure that both the outflow and inflow transfer of goods and services in such circumstances are at arm's length. This is so that no unreasonable amounts of profits are deliberately parked in such low tax bracket undertakings by taxpayers in order to gain tax breaks. However, the applicability of the SDT provisions is regulated to a *de minimis* monetary limit of the aggregate value of such transactions to INR 20 crores in order to restrict these provisions to significant risk areas.

Since such tax holiday units were already governed by fair market value provisions under different statutes and other non-TP provisions of the Act, the introduction of the concept of SDTs under Indian TP provisions seems merely to bring in TP compliance provisions for such transactions under the Act. Additionally, the introduction of the SDT formalized the computation mechanism of the fair market value.

Accordingly, the author considers the extension of such domestic TP compliance requirements to tax holiday due to the following two reasons:

(1) first of all, the obligation or mandate to ensure adherence to such arm's length transfer of goods and services, as referred to above, was already cast upon the 'accountant' who was entrusted with the overall mandate to certify the quantum of profits derived by the tax holiday undertaking. This would take into account *inter alia* transfer of goods and services between other ventures with the same legal entity and other legal entities of the same group, to be effected at market value, which is nothing but adhering to the principles of the arm's length price; and

(2) the government could never quite conceive how leaks of taxes actually occurred in tax holiday undertakings, albeit unconsciously and without any mala fide intent whatsoever on the part of taxpayers. Revenue officers are also not able to articulate the mystery in as many terms, in the context of the role played by such undertakings in the overall supply chain either within the same legal entity or different legal entities within the same group. The solution does not rest in merely ensuring that the transfer of goods and services involving the undertaking and other parts of the same legal entity and/or other legal entities of the group are at arm's length.

The answer to such a problem actually lies in a much broader understanding of the overall fundamentals of TP. This is specifically the overall supply chain of the business, functions performed and assets owned by the various constituents. This lies in the very connotation of the phrase 'profits derived from the undertaking' if understood in its proper economic form on the bedrock of the principles of TP. It can thus be eliminated even in its existing form or else, in the event that the government would look at ring-fencing the issue through explicit enactment of law, then different sets of legislative amendments would be required to meet the end objective.

1.3.4 TP Methods

Instead of specification of any hierarchy of the methods, the Indian TP regulations advocate the use of the most appropriate method that provides the best reliable measure of an arm's length result under the particular set of facts and circumstances of each case.

Generally, five TP methods are widely used as per global practices, viz. CUP, CPM, RPM, PSM, and TNMM. In addition to these, the CBDT India prescribes the use of a sixth TP method, i.e., the other method, vide notification number 18/2012 dated 23 May 2012 for computing the arm's length price under the Indian TP regulations to be effective from 1 April 2012 and, accordingly, to apply from the fiscal year 2011-2012 onwards. The use of the other method as the sixth method allows the utilization of 'any method' that takes into account (a) the price that has been charged or paid or (b) would have been charged or paid for the same or similar tested transaction with or between unrelated parties, under similar circumstances, and considering all of the relevant facts.

The other method offers more flexibility particularly in cases when the application of the five specific methods is not possible based on documented reasons. These could include difficulties in obtaining comparable data due to the uniqueness of transactions such as intangibles or business transfers, transfer of unlisted shares, etc. This would thereby allow the use of bona fide quotations, bids, proposals as comparable transactions or prices, and also economic and commercially justifiable models and similar approaches.

Further, it is noteworthy that in the case of Global One India P. Ltd.,[1] the judiciary advocated the use of the other method as retroactive and, thus its applicability is also valid in earlier years. This retroactivity is also considering that the aim and object of introducing a rule are to allow the taxpayer to adopt any other method for determining the arm's length price in order to remove unintended practical difficulties and enable proper determination of the arm's length price.

1.3.5 Use of Multiple Year Data

Indian Finance (Number 2) Act 2014 introduced a multiple year data concept in Indian regulations. It prescribes that in the case when the RPM, CPM, or TNMM is used as the most appropriate method for determination of the arm's length price of an international transaction/SDT, the comparability analysis will be conducted based on data relating to the current year. In a case when data relating to the current year is not available while maintaining the TPD by the prescribed due date, then data relating to the FY immediately preceding two FYs can be considered on the condition that the company has also carried out the same or similar comparable tested transaction in those preceding two years.

Some important facets of the application of this concept are listed below:

- No cut-off date is specified to restrict the use of data available up to a particular point in time. Consequently, if the current year data becomes available during the assessment proceedings, then the same shall be considered irrespective of the fact that such current year data was not available at the time of furnishing the return of income.

1. *Global One India Pvt. Ltd. v. ACIT* (ITA Nos 5571/Del/2011, 5896/Del/2012), pp. 56-57 (ITAT, 2014).

- In the case that a company is found to be comparable based on the preceding two years' data, it does not qualify to be a comparable for the current year for either quantitative or qualitative reasons, then such company would need to be rejected from the comparables data set.
- When an enterprise has undertaken comparable tested transactions in more than one FY, then the weighted average of the prices of such transactions is to be considered for the purpose of computing arm's length price.

Notwithstanding the usage of multiple year data for comparables in the above cases, the single-year data (i.e., for the current year) of the tested party is used for comparison.

1.3.6 Range Concept

Prior to 1 April 2014, the arithmetic mean of comparable prices/rates was considered as the arm's length price with a prescribed tolerance range/band considered to determine the arm's length nature of each transaction. However, along with the introduction of multiple year data, the range concept was modified in India to align it with the international best practices. However, the concept of range in India continues to differ compared to the global rules on the following counts:

(1) It can be availed only when the most appropriate method is either the CUP, RPM, CPM, or TNMM, i.e., not in the case of the PSM and the other method.
(2) The range available and its computation differ based on the number of comparable companies identified as explained below:
   (a) If comparable companies are below six: a transaction will be considered to be at arm's length if the actual transaction value falls within a tolerance range approximate to the arithmetic mean of the comparable price/profit level indicator with a tolerance range benefit for wholesale trading activities[2] and/or for all other activities, as the case may be, and as per the range prescribed for the year. If the actual transaction price does not fall within the prescribed range, then the arm's length price shall be taken to be the arithmetic mean of the data set.
   (b) If comparable companies are six or more: Regarding the permissible range, globally accepted inter-quartile range of the results derived from the uncontrolled comparables is permissible in general. However, under the Indian regulations, a comparatively restricted bandwidth is allowed with an arm's length range from 35th to the 65th percentile of the comparable dataset. The crucial points to be considered for the application of the range concept are summarized below.

2. The definition of wholesale trading has been defined in the regulations. *See* https://www.incometaxindia.gov.in/communications/notification/notification_83_2020.pdf.

An arm's length range beginning from the 35th percentile of the dataset and ending at the 65th percentile will be considered after arranging them in ascending order. If the value arrived is not a whole number, the value shall be rounded off to the next higher value which shall be considered so as to cover at least 35%/65% of the value below it. If these values are whole numbers, then the value shall be the arithmetic mean of such value and the immediately succeeding value in the data set.

Refer to the below illustrations to understand the application of the range concept as detailed above:

Illustration 1: When the data set comprises nine data points (arranged in ascending order) and the percentiles computed are not whole numbers

Percentile	*Formula*	*Result*	*Value to Be selected*
35th	Total No. of data points in set × 35% = [9 × 35%]	3.15	4th value*
65th	Total No. of data points in set × 65% = [9 × 35%]	5.85	6th value*
Median	Total No. of data points in set × 50% = [9 × 50%]	4.50	5th value*

* Value here means respective weighted average profit level indicator of the comparable in the data set as arranged in ascending order.

Illustration 2: When the data set comprises twenty data points (arranged in ascending order) and the percentiles computed are whole numbers

Percentile	*Formula*	*Result*	*Value to Be selected*
35th	Total No. of data points in set × 35% = [20 × 35%]	7.00	Average of 7th and 8th value*
65th	Total No. of data points in set × 65% = [20 × 65%]	13.00	Average of 13th and 14th value*
Median	Total No. of data points in set × 50% = [20 × 50%]	10.00	Average of 10th and 11th value*

* Value here means respective weighted average profit level indicator of the comparable in the data set as arranged in ascending order.

If the actual transaction price falls beyond the prescribed range, then the arm's length price shall be taken to be the median of the data set.

1.3.7 Documentation

India has adopted the three-tier structure (which entails master file, CbCR, and local file) as mandated by BEPS Action Plan 13 in order to further align with global practices. In this action plan of the BEPS report, it recommends adopting a standardized approach to TPD. This consists of:

- Maintenance of prescribed local file/TPD (section 92D of the Act read with Rule 10D of the Income Tax Rules 1962) if the aggregate value of international transactions of the taxpayer exceeds the *de minimis* threshold of INR 1 crore. However, even if the aggregate value of the international transactions is below INR 1 crore, the taxpayer is still required to maintain sufficient documents/information (if not prescribed documentation) to demonstrate that its transactions are compliant with the arm's length principle as prescribed in the Indian regulations. In the case of SDTs, the value of transactions should exceed INR 20 crores for its applicability. The documentation is required to be maintained by the taxpayer for each year on a contemporaneous basis for a period of nine years from the end of the relevant fiscal year.
- Obtain and file an accountant's report/TP certificate (under prescribed Form No. 3CEB) as per section 92E of the Act. This is required to be e-filed by the taxpayer each year as per the prescribed due date (currently, one month prior to the due date of filing the return of income with the income tax authorities). There is no threshold limit prescribed for this and should be e-filed if there are any international transactions. However, for the SDT, the prescribed threshold of INR 20 crores applies for its applicability.
- Compliance with new rules for the master file and CbCR (i.e., sections 286 and 92D of the Act, respectively) depending on the fulfilment of certain conditions and thresholds prescribed by the Indian regulations as summarized below:

Compliance	*Form No.*	*Applicability*
Master File	Part A of Form No. 3CEAA	Applicable to every CE of an international group (even if the value of international transaction is nil)
	Part B of Form No. 3CEAA	The CE of an international group, satisfying: (a) Consolidated revenue of such international group of which the CE is a part as reflected in its consolidated financial statements for the accounting year exceeds INR 500 crores; *and* (b) The aggregate value of international transactions of the CE: - during the reporting accounting year, as per books of accounts, exceeds INR 50 crores, *or*

Compliance	*Form No.*	*Applicability*
		- aggregate value of international transactions of the CE in respect of purchase, sale, transfer, lease, or use of IP during the reporting accounting year, as per books of accounts, exceeds INR 10 crores.
	Form No. 3CEAB (intimation)	International groups having multiple CEs resident in India - intimation to the authorities concerned in respect of the designated CE that would be filing the master file in India
CbCR is required to be filed if the consolidated group revenue (of the preceding accounting year) exceeds INR 6,400 crores[3]	Form No. 3CEAC (intimation)	Indian CE of foreign international group to furnish the particulars of parent entity/alternate reporting entity *[section 286(1) of the Act]*
	Form No. 3CEAD (detailed form)	The requirements of CbCR are applicable to: (a) Parent entity, or alternate reporting entity (section 286(2) of the Act) resident in India. (b) CE of an international group resident in India whose parent is non-resident [and if conditions of section 286(4) of the Act are satisfied i.e., parent entity is not obligated to file the CbCR, no agreement for exchange of CbCR or systemic failure].
	Form No. 3CEAE (intimation)	The designated entity, when there are multiple CEs resident in India of an international group whose parent is non-resident [and if conditions of section 286(4) of the Act are satisfied]

1.3.8 *Stringent Penalties*

The regulations prescribe penal provisions for default in compliance, which are summarized below:

Default	*Penalty Prescribed*
Failure to furnish information/documents during audit	2% of value of international transaction or the SDT
Adjustment to taxpayer's income	50%-200% of tax on adjustment amount
Failure to furnish accountant's report	INR 100,000

3. As per Notification No. 31/2021 dated 5 April 2021 issued by CBDT.

Default	*Penalty Prescribed*
- failure to maintain prescribed information/documents; or - failure to report a transaction in the accountant's report; or - maintaining or furnishing incorrect information or document.	2% of value of international transaction (or SDT)
Failure to furnish master file report	INR 500,000
Furnishing a false piece of documentary evidence	Sum equal to the aggregate amount of such false or omitted entry
Failure to furnish CbCR by the due date of filing of return of income	INR 5,000 per day for delay up to one month INR 15,000 per day for delay beyond one month INR 50,000 per day for delay in payment of penalty after receipt of instructions to pay
Failure to furnish additional information/documents sought by Revenue authorities	INR 5,000 per day from the day on which the period for furnishing the information/document expires INR 50,000 per day for delay in payment of penalty after receipt of instructions to pay
Inaccurate information filed under CbCR	INR 500,000

2 DISPUTE RESOLUTION MECHANISMS

To enhance the focus on complex issues, India recently shifted from a quantitative approach to a risk-based system for selecting cases for TP scrutiny in accordance with the OECD and other international guidance.

Once the case is selected for scrutiny, the arm's length value of the transactions encompassed within the TP regulations can, as per the provisions of the Act, be determined by the AO or it can make a reference to the experts referred to as the TPO. The order of the TPO is subsequently merged with the order of the AO, in order to propose/confirm the total adjustments to the case. The AO and TPO form the first level of the assessment proceedings under the Indian TP regulations. The time limit for assessment completion involving a TP matter is twenty-four months from the end of the relevant assessment year for the fiscal year 2018-2019 onwards. Once the order proposing/confirming the adjustment is passed by the AO, the taxpayer can opt to resolve the issue by either pursuing traditional or alternate dispute resolution mechanisms.

Below, the traditional dispute resolution mechanisms and some of the more acceptable dispute resolution mechanisms are discussed.

2.1 Traditional Dispute Resolution Mechanism

The traditional TP dispute resolution mechanism in India across the hierarchy of various forums has been briefed in the below table:

Stage of Litigation Process	*Authority*	*Brief Overview*	*Time Estimate for Order Pronouncement*
I	Option 1: DRP Option 2: Commissioner of Income Tax (Appeals) ['CIT(A)']	First level of appeal: The taxpayer has an option to file objections before DRP against draft order of AO or appeal before CIT(A) against the final order of AO	Nine months from the end of the month in which AO's draft order is received by the taxpayer No prescribed timelines Recommended time is one year from the end of FY in which appeal is filed. However, since no stringent timeline is defined, this results in prolonged litigation often spanning 2-5 years
II	Income Tax Appellate Tribunal (ITAT or Tribunal)	Second level of appeal and Last fact-finding authority: DRP route: The taxpayer has an option to file an appeal against the final assessment order of AO (post-DRP directions) CIT(A) route: Both the taxpayer and department have an option to file an appeal against the order of CIT(A)	No prescribed timelines On average, it takes 2-4 years from the end of FY in which appeal is filed

Stage of Litigation Process	*Authority*	*Brief Overview*	*Time Estimate for Order Pronouncement*
III	High Court (HC)	Only question of law – both the taxpayer and tax department have an option to file an appeal against the order of the ITAT	No prescribed timelines On average, it takes 2-5 years from the end of the FY in which appeal is filed
IV	Supreme Court of India (SC)	Apex Court in India and assesses only question of law – both the taxpayer and tax department have an option to file an appeal against the order of HC	

The above-explained traditional mechanism of litigations in India has also been evolving over time. One recent significant makeover is the introduction of e-assessments and e-appeals before the ITAT by the government with the objective to ease the compliance burden and minimize the physical interface between the taxpayers and the tax officials in order to achieve the objective of providing seamless, paperless, and faceless tax assessment.

2.2 Alternate Dispute Avoidance and Resolution Mechanisms

In order to reduce TP disputes in regular/traditional dispute resolution mechanisms and to ease the administration of the TP law in India, the Government of India has taken a number of initiatives such as the APA program, Vivad se Vishwas scheme, Settlement Commission, SHR, MAP, etc. for avoidance/mutual resolution of TP disputes. Elucidated below are the three prominent options promulgated by the Indian Government.

2.2.1 SHR

Introduced by the Indian Government vide Finance Act 2009 for the first round of the SHR with respect to eligibility, threshold, and coverage of transactions, safe harbour rates/margins were introduced in August 2013 for a period of five years. This was followed by a revision in 2017 for a period of three years that have been further notified to continue to apply for FY ended March 2020, followed by a revision in 2021 for a period of one year, i.e., FY ended 2021.

Section 92CB of the Act defines the term 'safe harbour' as circumstances in which the tax authorities shall accept the transfer price declared by the taxpayer to be at arm's length. Some of the salient aspects of the Indian safe harbour scheme are stated below:

- non-eligibility to invoke a MAP if the transfer price declared by the eligible taxpayer under the SHR is accepted;
- if the safe harbour is opted for, the eligible taxpayer is not entitled to make any comparability adjustments nor avail the benefit of the prescribed variation/range to the transfer price;
- compliance with prescribed TPD and Form 3CEB maintenance and filing requirements are necessary even if the SHR is selected; and
- the SHR is not to apply in respect of transactions entered into with a related party located in a country or territory notified under section 94A of the Act or in a no/low tax country/territory.

The SHR in India covers transactions (with insignificant risks) in the nature of provision of software services, IT-enabled services, knowledge process outsourcing services, contract R&D services for software development, etc.

The Indian judiciary, at times, in the case of regular non-SHR proceedings, deviates from the detailed definitions of the terms provided in the SHR. For example, the ITAT, Delhi, characterized operational outsourcing services as low-end IT-enabled services by referring to the definition provided in the SHR in the case of IHG IT Services (India) Pvt. Ltd.[4] However, in some cases, such a reference has also been denied such as in the cases of Vaildor Capital India Pvt. Ltd,[5] Optum Global Solutions (India) Private Limited[6] etc. The tribunal rejected reliance on the SHR to conclude that forex fluctuations are operating expenses as opposed to its nature being specified as non-operating in the SHR. The SHR is a separate regime where arm's length price is not really computed and the pre-determined margin percentages are adopted based on a different set of rules. Therefore, in the author's view, the principles of SHR should not ideally be adopted in the cases of regular TP assessments wherein in-depth functional analysis and detailed arm's length analysis are to be performed based on the fundamentals of TP.

Though SHR in India has not been the preferred dispute resolution mechanism for taxpayers primarily due to a limited coverage of transactions, high rates/margins, and non-availability of compliance relief. However, a calculated decision to select SHR can enable a taxpayer to adopt an appropriate TP policy that mitigates TP risks.

2.2.2 APA

APA provisions were brought into effect in India on 30 August 2012. In the context of Indian TP regulations, an APA is an agreement between the CBDT India and any person for the determination of the arm's length price. It can also specify the manner in which the arm's length price is to be determined in relation to an international transaction.

4. *IHG IT Services (India) Pvt. Ltd v. DCIT* [ITA No. 397/Del/2017], pp. 9-10 (ITAT, 2017).
5. *Vaildor Capital India Pvt. Ltd v. ITO* (ITA No. 1961/Del/2015), pp. 7-8 (ITAT, 2018).
6. *Optum Global Solutions (India) Private Limited (Formerly known as United Health Group Information Services Pvt. Ltd) v. DCIT* (ITA No. 473/Del/2016), p. 44 (ITAT, 2020).

Terms of an APA generally, among other things, include international transactions covered by the agreement, agreed TP methodology, determination of the arm's length price, and critical assumptions.

The salient features of an APA scheme in India are elucidated below:

- taxpayer can opt for either a unilateral APA, bilateral APA, or multilateral APA;
- valid for the periods specified in the agreement with a cap of a maximum period of five consecutive years;
- provision for roll back mechanism for up to preceding four years;
- Indian tax authorities, as part of their commitment to the OECD, have begun accepting bilateral APA applications for countries where Article 9(2) of OECD MTC is absent; and
- versatility to compute the arm's length price using an unspecified method, adjustments, or variations as required.

As can be observed from various judicial pronouncements (such as Ranbaxy Laboratories Ltd.,[7] Springer [India] Pvt. Ltd,[8] Metal One Corporation India Pvt. Ltd,[9] Bundy India Limited,[10] to name a few), the approach to arm's length price determination of a prior year that is outside the scope of the agreed APA has been adopted from the APA signed by the taxpayer for subsequent years. This is provided that the analysis of functions performed, assets used and risks assumed, and other factual circumstances remain the same. The saga of such judicial pronouncements has set a very rational trend to allow taxpayers and the tax authorities to place reliance on principles adopted in APA for years that are subject to factual similarity that is not actually covered by the scheme.

The status of APA applications in India till 31 March 2019 can be seen in the table below:[11]

Unilateral APA Applications Filed	*Bilateral APA Applications Filed*	*Total Applications Filed (A)*	*Agreements Signed out of (A)*	*Applications Disposed of out of (A) Due to Other Reasons*	*Applications under Processing out of (A)*
944	211	1,155	271	82	802

7. *Ranbaxy Laboratories Ltd. v. ACIT* [ITA No. 196/Del/2013], pp. 28-31 (ITAT, 2016).
8. *Springer [India] Pvt. Ltd v. ACIT* [ITA No. 6708/Del/2016], p. 6 (ITAT, 2020).
9. *Metal One Corporation India Pvt. Ltd v. DCIT*, [ITA No. 1761/Del/2015], pp. 6-7 (ITAT, 2020).
10. *Bundy India Limited v. DCIT* [ITA No. 720/Ahd/2017], etc., pp. 9-10 (ITAT, 2019).
11. For further details on statistics regarding the execution of the APA scheme in India, the annual report on it that was published in November 2019 by CBDT India for FY 2018-2019 can be accessed via, https://www.incometaxindia.gov.in/Lists/Latest%20News/Attachments/360/FINAL_ANNUAL_REPORT_29_11_19.pdf (last accessed 30 January 2022).

2.2.3 *MAP*

The MAP has been instrumental in resolving various disputes and has helped MNEs to avoid economic double taxation by allowing corresponding adjustments in the other country. It gained more traction in an Indian context when, vide the Press Release on 27 November 2017, the CBDT India issued clarification for relaxing India's position on the acceptance of TP applications for MAP cases and bilateral APAs in cases of countries when Article 9(2) of the OECD Commentary is absent. Further, relief through a MAP is conceivable regardless of remedies available under domestic tax laws.

There have been significant developments in the Indian MAP regime recently as elucidated below.

To address the recommendations in the OECD's Peer Review Report so as to align with the minimum standard as laid down in BEPS Action 14, in May 2020, the Indian Government merged Rule 44H with Rule 44G of the Income Tax Rules, 1962 governing the MAP provisions and made certain amendments therein, some of which are given below:

(1) Detailed guidelines along with timelines are to be provided in the Indian Income Tax Rules from the invocation of a MAP to giving effect to the MAP resolution by the AO.
(2) The Indian Competent Authority shall convey its acceptance or otherwise for taking up the reference under a MAP to the foreign competent authority.
(3) The Indian Competent Authority shall endeavour to achieve a MAP resolution within an average time period of twenty-four months.

Moreover, as per the amended Indian Income Tax Rules 1962, in the case that the competent authority resolution leads to an outcome that is beneficial (e.g., lower mark-up for TP cases) than the going-in position, that benefit shall not be allowed to the taxpayer.

Following up close on the above, in August 2020, the CBDT India introduced detailed guidance on the MAP which prominently establishes the situations and procedures for accessing it, clarification on technical issues, and the implementation process in this regard. The said guidance will assist all stakeholders in this regard, i.e., the taxpayers, tax practitioners, tax authorities in India, and the competent authority of India. However, it is pertinent to note that the provisions of domestic legislation, rules, instructions, and circulars or the tax treaties shall prevail in the event of any clash with the MAP guidance.

The recent developments highlight the government's initiative to create a non-adversarial tax regime in India and provide a more promising outlook of the MAP regime in India.

On a practical note, in various cases, the Indian Tribunals have also permitted the application of margin approved under the MAP resolution with a particular country to related party transactions with non-MAP countries subject to a similar functional analysis. One case with such a verdict is Amazon Development Centre (India) Pvt.

Ltd.[12] The adoption of such an approach similar to that in the case of the APA also augurs well for clearing the long-pending cases and building a conducive business environment for growth.

On 18 November 2020, the OECD released the 2019 MAP statistics and the winners of the MAP awards for several categories, such as average time to close MAP cases, age of inventory, caseload management and cooperation. In one category, India with Japan won the collaborative award for the highest agreement ratio of 64% as the pair of jurisdictions dealt with their joint caseload of TP cases most effectively.

Although the MAP mechanism ideally covers disputes related to TP, PEs, and characterization of income, in the Indian context, the majority of disputes until now have been in relation to TP adjustment cases.[13]

The below table juxtaposes various features of the SHR, APA and MAP schemes in the Indian TP framework:

S. No.	*Point of Comparison*	*SHR*	*APA*	*MAP*
1.	Post compliance requirement	The taxpayer has to file the return of income as per the minimum profits required to be declared in the SHR for the eligible transaction	The taxpayer has to file an annual compliance report and revised return of income (for each year covered under the APA)	After the taxpayer provides consent to the agreement reached between the competent authorities of the two countries, then the AO has to pass a revised order incorporating the MAP resolution and issues a demand notice accordingly
2.	Binding nature	Binding on taxpayer and tax officer unless disputed otherwise by AO	Binding on taxpayer and tax authorities unless there is a change in law/facts	Not binding on taxpayer and tax authorities if taxpayer does not give consent to the agreement reached between the Competent authorities of both countries

12. *Amazon Development Centre (India) Pvt. Ltd v. ITO* (ITA Nos 76/Bang/2014, 78/Bang/2014, 1387/Bang/2014), pp. 7-10 (ITAT, 2018).
13. Detailed statistics on the Indian MAP regime can be accessed at, https://www.oecd.org/tax/dispute/2020-map-statistics-india.pdf (last accessed 30 January 2022).

S. No.	Point of Comparison	SHR	APA	MAP
3.	Withdrawal	For 2019-2020, it is only for one year and, once applied, cannot be withdrawn	Can be withdrawn any time before the APA is concluded	Taxpayer has the option not to give their consent to the agreement reached between the competent authorities of both countries
4.	Impact of secondary adjustment	Taxpayer to receive balance differential money within prescribed timeline if the books of accounts are not as per the margin/rate prescribed in the SHR	Taxpayer to receive the balance differential of money for each year unless a refund is in process	Taxpayer to receive the balance differential of money for each year if resolution is lower than existing mark-up, no benefit available
5.	Transactions covered	Only eligible international transactions and SDTs as covered in the Act	Only international transactions covered by the taxpayer in its application	Only international transactions under dispute and covered by the taxpayer in its MAP application

3 OTHER SIGNIFICANT DEVELOPMENTS

3.1 Secondary Adjustments

The secondary adjustment provisions (section 92CE of the Act) were introduced in Indian regulations vide Finance Act 2017 in order to align the economic benefit of the transaction with the arm's length position. Otherwise stated, it was done in order to make the actual allocation of profits consistent with the primary adjustment thereby removing the imbalance between the cash account and the actual profit of the taxpayer.

Vide Indian secondary adjustment provisions, the Indian authorities have adopted the scheme of imputing interest on the amount of primary adjustment inflicted upon the taxpayer which is rechristened as a deemed loan extended to the overseas related party that is the counterparty to the relevant transaction. The incidence of tax on interest is effectuated if the amount of the primary adjustment is not repatriated by the overseas related party in favour of the Indian taxpayer within a period of ninety days/the prescribed time. It must be either in the form of a suo moto action on the part of the taxpayer in offering an adjustment in the tax return or through the intervention of the Revenue authorities in the form of assessments, specifically, having reached finality in appeals or resolution of MAPs or APAs. However, the secondary adjustment provisions are not applicable if (a) the amount of the primary adjustment made in the case of a taxpayer in any previous year does not exceed INR one crore and (b) the primary adjustment is made in respect of a fiscal year commencing on or before 1 April 2015.

Both the OECD TPG and UN TPM recognize three forms in which a secondary adjustment may be instigated – constructive dividends, constructive equity contributions, and constructive loans. In most cases, the countries that have introduced secondary adjustments in their domestic tax legislations generally adopt the deemed dividend route for collecting tax on the primary adjustment rather than the imputation of interest on the same. This is achieved by recharacterizing the same as a deemed loan as adopted by the Indian regulations that made the regulations rigid. They required mandatory imputation of interest irrespective of whether the relevant overseas related party was a part of the group of descendants of the taxpayer. Further, the imputation of interest till perpetuity in the event that the amount of primary adjustment would have never been repatriated was too punitive to the taxpayer. To rationalize the secondary adjustment provisions, the Finance (Number 2) Act 2019 attempted to address the issues stated previously by proposing two alternatives to the taxpayers in this regard as detailed below:

(i) provide an option to the taxpayer to pay a 'one-time' and final income tax at the rate of 18% (to be further increased by surcharge and cess thereon) on the amount of primary adjustment. This pardons the taxpayer from the precisions of being taxed on notional interest on the same amount till eternity or until the said sum was repatriated in favour of the taxpayer by the overseas related party. Further being counteractive, the finance act clarifies that the taxpayers would neither be able to claim any credit for such a one-time tax nor a deduction with respect to the amount of principal adjustment. Thus, going forward, taxpayers facing primary adjustments would need to choose between one of two options. They could decide to pay tax at the rate of 30% on interest on a notional loan until the amount of the principal adjustment is repatriated. On the contrary, they could pay the one time and final tax thereon at the rate of 18% (since the rate of tax in either case would be enhanced with the levy of surcharge and cess, no reference is made to such elements for the sake of convenience); and
(ii) enable the taxpayer to repatriate excess money from any of the related parties of the taxpayer that is not resident in India. This would resolve the undue hardship of taxpayers in repatriation of money owing to reasons such as cessation of a related party relationship, non-existence of a related party at the time of a secondary adjustment, primary adjustment relating to multiple related parties, related party facing financial difficulties in repatriating the money, etc.

The steps taken by the Indian Government to clarify various aspects in the context of secondary adjustments and rationalization of these provisions in India will certainly enable effective implementation of this concept in India and further the goal of alignment of Indian regulations with international best practices.

4 SIGNIFICANT LITIGATED TP ISSUES IN INDIA

Although the move headed for risk-based assessment has resulted in a substantial reduction in the number of TP assessments, the TP adjustments have largely endured the same. The evolution of key litigated issues is provided below.

4.1 Marketing Intangibles

With India as a new emerging market, it has very distinctive market-specific characteristics such as location advantages, market accessibility, large customer base, etc. which has propelled subsidiaries/related parties of MNEs to devise distinct and significantly extensive and accelerated marketing strategies to establish a stronghold in India. This has made the issue of marketing intangibles one of the prominently debated TP topics in India.

4.1.1 Issue

In a number of cases, the tax authorities in India adopt an aggressive approach by alleging that the AMP related activities and expenses add value to the trade mark/brand legally owned by the foreign-related party by way of brand building. This thereby concludes that the local subsidiary must be compensated by the legal brand owner (i.e., the foreign-related party) for the benefit bestowed on an arm's length basis.

However, apart from defining IP as part of an 'international transaction', the Indian TP regulations do not provide any specific guidelines on intangibles. Moreover, there is no specific inclusion of AMP expenses in the definition of the term 'international transaction'. This gave rise to the controversial question of whether the AMP should even qualify as an international transaction at all. Further, the issue in this context pertains to the allowance of such AMP expenses in the hands of the taxpayer, considering the commercial rationale or the legal ownership. According to the tax authorities, legal ownership of intangibles is relevant under the TP regulations. However, the taxpayers contend that being the economic owner of such intangibles, the Indian subsidiary should not be required to recover the AMP expenses from its related parties as it is the direct beneficiary of the benefits from the incurrence of these expenses.

For computing the arm's length price of such alleged international transaction, the tax department, in most cases, adopts the 'bright line test' in accordance with the concept laid down in one of the US tax court cases. In accordance with the test, the AMP expense incurred by the taxpayer that exceeds the average AMP expense incurred by comparable companies in India should be considered a non-routine AMP expense (i.e., expenses incurred for enhancing the value of foreign-related parties' brand in India) and should be benchmarked in accordance with the arm's length principle.

In the above backdrop, the pertinent questions that arise on this vexed issue are:

- Should the AMP expenses be construed as an international transaction?
- Should the Indian distributor, even if not the 'legal owner', be held to be the 'economic owner/developer of the brand/trademark' and hence not recover the AMP?
- If construed to be an international transaction, then how can the arm's length price be determined, and what is the validity of the 'bright line test'?
- As alleged, what is the enhancement in the value of the brand, and how has the same only been attributed to the Indian subsidiary's AMP expenses?

4.1.2 View of Judiciary

The matter is currently pending adjudication before the SC with both taxpayers and the Indian Revenue Board having filed appeals against different dictums contained in rulings of various HCs of the country.

The most notable of such rulings are those having been delivered by the Delhi HC in the cases of Sony Ericsson Mobile Communications India Pvt. Ltd.[14] and Maruti Suzuki India Ltd.[15]

Brief synopses of the two rulings of the Delhi HC are as follows:

(1) In the case of Sony Ericsson, the Delhi HC held that, since taxpayer distributors had argued that the rewards of their excessive AMP expenses were subsumed within the profit margins of distribution, the taxpayers could not contend that AMP expenses were not 'international transactions' at the same time. However, having held as above, the HC hastened to add that, while a taxpayer distributor who may perform additional functions on account of the AMP as compared to similar companies would generally require additional remuneration for such functions. Such additional rewards may be granted through pricing of products or distribution margins. If so received, the revenue officer cannot demand a separate remuneration through reimbursement of excess AMP expenses along with a mark-up, as such action would clearly result in double addition or taxation, which does not have any sanctity.

(2) In the case of Maruti Suzuki, optically being of the character of an entrepreneurial licensed manufacturer, the HC dismissed the attempt on the part of the revenue officer to impute TP adjustment of the above nature while

14. *Sony Ericsson Mobile Communications India Pvt. Ltd. v. CIT* (ITA No. 16/2014), pp. 136 and 139 (HC, 2015).
15. Delhi High Court, 11 December 2015, *Maruti Suzuki Ltd. v. CIT* (ITA Nos 110/2014, 710/2015), pp. 39-44 (HC, 2015).

adjudicating the case. The excess AMP spend of Maruti Suzuki India, as a percentage of its turnover was over the average of those of its comparable companies selected under TNMM. The main reasoning of the HC, while concurring with the arguments of the taxpayer, was that the AMP spend on a stand-alone basis could not be treated as an 'international transaction' under the provisions of the Indian TP regulations, in the context of licensed manufacturers of the type of Maruti Suzuki India. Thus, the TP adjustment with respect to any part thereof, in the manner proposed by the revenue officer, namely reimbursement of the 'so-called' excess amount of the AMP spend, by the foreign licensor of the brand, was clearly not sustainable.

Appeals arising from both the said rulings of the Delhi HC along with the other rulings following the ratio of such rulings filed both by taxpayers and the Indian tax authorities are currently pending adjudication before the SC. It is worthwhile to note that the main ground, which is being contested by both the parties before the SC, is whether AMP expenses are an 'international transaction'.

Until any resolution is provided by the SC, the available antagonistic HC and tribunal judgements at present do not provide clear direction to proceed on the matter.

4.1.3 *Key Takeaways*

The question that arises is, would the issue of the AMP expenses, which is a subset of the overall concept of marketing intangibles, be fully resolved only through the SC answering such a question, albeit in the backdrop of the facts of different types of taxpayers?

The SC may render justice only with respect to the limited issue before itself which is created by the manner in which TP adjustments have been made by the tax authorities in such cases wherein reimbursement of excess AMP expenses of a licensee with a mark-up has been proposed. Therefore, there is uncertainty as to how and to what extent would the larger issue around marketing intangibles be addressed by the SC. Additionally, doubts arise whether the SC would actually be laying down detailed guidance around the same in the context of different classes of taxpayers in the absence of the SC being seized of such matter. Only time will unfold the SC's view.

However, on their part, it is imperative for the taxpayers to undertake a comprehensive and detailed analysis of the supply chain, functional profile of the transacting entities in terms of the DEMPE related to marketing intangibles, legal contracts, economic substances, etc., to substantiate the arm's length nature of their business models.

4.2 Profit Attribution to PEs in India

The definition of a PE included in tax treaties is crucial for determining whether a non-resident enterprise must pay income tax in another state. In the Indian context, the business profits of a non-resident enterprise are subject to income tax in India if it is satisfying the threshold conditions of having a business connection in India and the threshold prescribed in the applicable tax treaties. On satisfaction of the taxable threshold nexus of a business connection under the Act along with the taxable threshold nexus of a PE under the applicable tax treaty, profits of a foreign enterprise become taxable in India to the extent that they are attributable to its business manoeuvres in India. Briefly, such taxpayers may pay taxes on business income from India on a gross or net basis as per prescribed rules. In the event that a taxpayer opts to pay on a net basis, it is required to maintain books of accounts and financial statements for this purpose. During the audits of PEs in India, in the case that such books of accounts are either not maintained or it is not feasible to ascertain the actual profits from such books of accounts, the AO has often taken recourse to secondary options prescribed in Rule 10 of the Income Tax Rules 1962. As an outcome, the attribution has been done, in many cases, by either considering the profits as per the percentage of revenue accruing or arising considered reasonable by the tax authorities or those derived as a proportion of the total business profits of the non-resident based on the ratio of revenue accruing or arising in India to total revenue.

4.2.1 *Issue*

The critical dilemma in PE profit attribution is the establishment of the profits that should be attributed to specific functions in a business model involving cross-border operations. The present methodology being adopted in litigation by the tax authorities considers the discretion to determine such profits without any clear or specific guidance owing to which the computations in this regard are carried out in an arbitrary manner in various forums. The outcomes being based on high-level conjectures, the resulting subjective, or arbitrary judgments prolong the ongoing litigations. Being away from the principles of TP, the outcome is far from reality and leads to protracted litigation. In essence, the profits, for the purposes of attributing to the PE, would be those that the PE might be expected to make if it were a separate and unrelated party engaged in the same or similar activities under the same or similar conditions, considering the enterprise's functional analysis through the PE and other parts of the enterprise.

4.2.2 *View of Judiciary*

The landmark verdict regarding this topic is the decision of the SC in the case of Morgan Stanley & Co[16] which establishes that, once Indian PE is remunerated on an arm's length basis, no further profit is attributable to it. However, it is worthwhile to note the additional statement of the SC that, in cases when a TP analysis does not reflect functions performed/risks assumed adequately, then further profit attribution will certainly be required in such cases.

16. *Director of Income Tax (International tax) v. Morgan Stanley & Co* (292 ITR 416), pp. 19-20 (SC, 2009).

Nonetheless, with the evolving nature of the Indian economy, the disputes on PE profit attribution have been refuted to abate, and tribunals and courts continue to apply this principle variably based on an arbitrary manner of evaluating the facts and circumstances of each case.

4.2.3 *Significant Developments*

(1) The CBDT India's Draft Guidelines on Attribution of Profits to PEs

The CBDT India issued a recommendatory report on attribution of profits to PEs on 18 April 2019 prepared by a committee formed by the CBDT India for the said purposes. It invited comments from various stakeholders, post which the CBDT India might have finalized its views on this issue that could be introduced through amendments to the provisions of the Act and the Income Tax Rules 1962.

In summary, the committee stated that arm's length principles under TP cannot be applied for the attribution of profits to PEs under the Indian model tax treaties. It also indicated that a formulary approach must be adopted for such an attribution by applying the global operating profit margin of a foreign enterprise to the revenue derived from India and further adjusted with reference to certain weightage relating to various factors, e.g., assets, employees, wages, etc. The report also explicitly negated the AOA (the guidance developed by the OECD to explain how it intends Article 7 on profit attribution to be applied) which requires profits to be attributed on the basis of the functional analysis.

Thus, the said draft guidelines attracted significant criticism from the various TP experts on numerous grounds. Consequently, the draft guidelines could not currently conclude and continue to be a draft.[17]

(2) The APA and SHR provisions to cover determination of attribution of profit to a PE

In absence of any certainty in this regard, in order to provide an option for certainty and clarity to the taxpayers in relation to the attribution of profits to a PE, the Indian Government vide Finance Act 2020 extended the scope of the SHR and APA to include within its ambit the determination of profits attributable to a PE by amending section 92CB and section 92CC of the Act.

4.2.4 *Key Takeaways*

The common wordings of Article 7 of the pre-2010 OECD MTCs, the UN MTCs and the Indian model tax treaties, barring certain exceptions – namely where any treaty signed by India contains the Force of Attraction clause. Also, in the matter of allowability of deductions in the hands of the PE for payments made to the Head Office or other parts

17. The detailed draft report of the CBDT India can be accessed via, https://www.incometaxindia.gov.in/news/public_consultation_notice_18_4_19.pdf (last accessed 30 January 2022).

of the foreign enterprise, of which it is a PE, for receipt of services, license of intangibles, etc., beyond the actual cost incurred by the foreign enterprise on such services, intangibles, etc., clearly provide that profits, for the purposes of attributing to the PE, would be those, which the PE might be expected to make if it were a distinct and separate enterprise, engaged in the same or similar activities under the same or similar conditions and dealing wholly independently with the enterprise of which it is a PE.

Now, the determination of such profits under the hypothesis of the PE being a distinct and separate enterprise dealing wholly independently with the enterprise of which it is a PE is nothing but adherence with arm's length principles under the TP. It aims at analysing how unrelated parties would have dealt with each other in uncontrolled conditions which is the very philosophy of the arm's length principles under the TP.

With a view to providing greater certainty in the matter of attribution of profits to a PE, the OECD released a detailed report or guidelines for attribution of profits to PEs in 2008. It relied upon the principles of arm's length under the TP through resorting to the functional analysis which is incidentally the very lifeline of arm's length principles under the TP without which the same cannot simply operate.

Accordingly, in the author's view, when the committee proceeded to adopt the 'mixed approach' for the purposes of the attribution of profits to PEs that purportedly allocate profits partly to the jurisdiction where consumers are located and partly to the jurisdiction where supply activities are undertaken. Assuming for once that such a 'mixed approach' is correct, there is no basis to come to the conclusion that arm's length principles under TP shall not be able to achieve such avowed objective of allocating profits to the jurisdictions of market and supply in a judicious and fair manner. Further, it is also unfair to assume that the only way to achieve such objective is to adopt a formulary approach, whether or not the same may be modified in any manner with the coinage of 'fractional apportionment', as above. Thus, the committee's conclusion completely lacks a basis.

Over the years, the issue of attribution of profits to PEs is under active consideration of the Indian Revenue Board. Various representations have been made before it to accept the arm's length principles under TP for the purposes of attributing profits to PEs under traditional business models. Such an approach, subject to minor differences of opinions, would be consistent with the majority of the countries that accept the authorized approach of the OECD in this regard.

As stated earlier, the recommendations of the committee of the CBDT India, as discussed above, have not yet seen fruition even after the expiry of over a year since its issuance in April 2019. The publication of a position paper or additional regulations by the Indian Revenue Board in this regard would be particularly helpful for providing greater certainty, consistency, and predictability to the process of profit attribution. However, it must be based on a proper TP analysis and take into consideration attribution based on the FAR of the PE and not on any arbitrary approach that deviates from the arm's length standards.

4.3 Location Savings

Location savings are net savings in cost obtained by an MNE through relocating its core operations from a high-cost jurisdiction to a low-cost jurisdiction such as India with the motive of earning extra profits through certain benefits. These could include labour and material cost savings; cheaper or subsidized availability of capital, production, distribution, technology, and logistics support; enhanced customer base; increased spending capacity; etc., that may support the MNE in gaining a competitive advantage. Accordingly, significant profits could arise for the group in such a scenario as a result of relocating its operations to India.

4.3.1 Issue

The major dispute with regard to location savings is based on the premise set up by the Indian revenue that the price determined on the basis of local comparables does not adequately allocate location savings. This comes along with further challenges of quantification of such location savings/extra profits and attribution of the same among the Indian subsidiary and the related party. On account of such location savings, Indian revenue tends to make upward TP adjustments wherein they measure the location advantage with reference to the variance of costs in the high-cost jurisdiction vis-à-vis the costs incurred in the low-cost jurisdiction.

Further, prior to revision of the Indian revenue's stand in the UN TPM-India Chapter, the TPO also placed reliance on the position taken by the Indian tax authorities in UN TPM that stated that the price determined on the basis of local comparables does not adequately allocate location savings and accordingly, applied PSM for attribution of the location savings among the related parties.

4.3.2 View of Judiciary

The claim for a TP adjustment due to location saving has been relinquished in most of the cases by the judiciary in India. A liberal and pro-taxpayer stand has been embraced by the Indian courts. In this regard, principles laid down by the landmark rulings of the GAP International Sourcing India P Ltd[18] and Watson Pharma Pvt. Ltd[19] (which have later been relied on in several cases) are listed below:

- the advantage of location savings is passed on to the end customer due to a competitive environment;
- since the taxpayer and its related parties function in a perfectly competitive market and hence, the location savings are not a unique advantage to the taxpayer over competitors and do not qualify as an intangible for the taxpayer;

18. *GAP International Sourcing India P Ltd v. ACIT* (ITA Nos 5147/Del2011 & 228/Del/2012), pp. 43 and 44 (ITAT, 2012).
19. *Watson Pharma Pvt. Ltd v. DCIT* (ITA No. 1423/Mum/2014), pp. 24-26 (ITAT, 2015).

- the location savings benefit, if any, would be subsumed in the profitability earned by comparables if the taxpayer benchmarks the transaction using local (Indian) comparables;
- the reliance placed on Action Plan 8 of the BEPS Project which provides that, where local market comparables are available, specific adjustments for location savings are unnecessary; and
- the tribunal made it clear that it is not obligated to abide by the views presented in the UN TPM – India Chapter by the Indian Revenue Board.

4.3.3 *Significant Developments/India Chapter in UN TPM*

Irrespective of the fact that decisions of the appellate authorities were unimpaired by the prior stand of the Indian tax authorities in the UN TPM-India Chapter, it is worthwhile to note that the Indian Revenue Board has amended its earlier position as reflected in the previous version of the country chapter in UN TPM. It now recognizes that the location savings would be embedded in the results of appropriate local comparables selected for the determination of the arm's length price of transactions entered into by the Indian subsidiary companies with their related parties.

The above revision to the UN TPM-India Chapter is much appreciated as *inter alia* it brings homogeneity with the position of the BEPS Actions 8-10 Report and adapts that the location savings loses its significance for arriving at an arm's length price in the case of availability of local comparable companies.

4.3.4 *Key Takeaways*

From the above discussions, it is clear that in perfect competition, the location savings may not actually result in premium profits as the savings in costs are generally passed on to customers owing to market competitiveness. Further, location savings are not possessed by any specific taxpayer ahead of other similarly placed players in the market so as to make a proper comparability analysis fruitless for recognizing the benefits arising out of unique intangibles.

The issue of whether or not to make upward adjustments on account of location rent might arise when comparable companies of more developed economies are selected to determine an arm's length price with respect to taxpayers residing in developing economies. This generally provides benefits of location savings, given the growth curve of such buoyant low-cost economies, as opposed to the relative stagnation or low growth rate faced by developed economies, where the profit margins of companies in general, with reference to higher cost bases, would be relatively low, as compared to developing economies. As were the situations experienced in China and Mexico, when taxpayers, in the absence of robust databases for local comparables, used to select comparable companies based in Japan and the US respectively, to determine arm's length prices for contract manufacturing and other services, performed for their overseas headquarters. Such an approach was found to be at fault by Chinese and Mexican tax authorities on the ground of not having captured location rents arising out of location savings provided by the developing economies of China and Mexico respectively.

However, both taxpayers and the Indian revenue have been selecting comparables from local databases all along, e.g., Prowess, ACE TP, and Capitaline, the coverage of each of which has only increased and improved with every passing year. Thus, the issue of location rent arising out of location savings ideally should not arise in TP assessments in India if proper local comparables can be identified.

4.4 Contract R&D Centres

MNEs should usually shift their R&D operations either wholly or partly to developing/low-cost jurisdictions like India in order to reduce their R&D cost. The R&D activities are generally performed per a contract that stipulates that the foreign-related party will be the legal owner of any intangible arising out of such R&D activities. Additionally, the Indian affiliate provides routine services by acting as a contract service provider and accordingly does not employ valuable assets and bear significant risks. Consequently, Indian companies are remunerated with a mark-up on the cost incurred.

4.4.1 Issue

The Indian tax authorities have objected that, notwithstanding the formal structures of a contract R&D service provider model being put in place, high value-adding and sophisticated services are performed by the Indian contract R&D centres. This subsequently leads to the generation of valuable and unique intellectual property from the work undertaken in India. Accordingly, the tax authorities allege that the Indian R&D centre becomes the economic owner of the intellectual property that is transferred without adequate compensation. Such activities require substantial investment and highly skilled personnel and, therefore, significant risk lies with the Indian entity. In such circumstances, routine and low cost plus mark-up does not reflect a correct arm's length result and thus the Indian centre should be rewarded commensurate to the risk assumed in the association of the development of intangibles.

Based on the alleged mismatches between form and substance with respect to the structures around contract R&D services, the Indian tax authorities disregarded such contract R&D structures. It generally proceeded to adopt the PSM to assign rewards to Indian researchers on the purported grounds of conceptualizing and monitoring the R&D functions and, accordingly, economically owning trade intangibles emanating therefrom.

Further, in the case that a foreign-related party is located in a no-tax/low-tax jurisdiction, then it is presumed that such a foreign-related party is not assuming the risk.

4.4.2 *View of Judiciary*

In several cases, the judiciary upheld to disregard the TP study prepared by the taxpayer in light of differences in the actual functional analysis such as in the case of GE India Technology Centre Pvt. Ltd.[20] The tribunal made the pertinent observation to the concept that risk can be controlled remotely by the parent company and that the Indian subsidiaries engaged in core functions, such as carrying out R&D activities or providing services, are risk-free entities. This is something that needs to be demonstrated by the taxpayer. Thus, the judiciary called for evidence and facts to be substantiated to establish the extent of risk associated with the Indian entity.

4.4.3 *Indian Regulations on Contract R&D*

Albeit India does not have any formal rules in place, however, in 2013, CBDT India adhered to the rules of the OECD and issued a circular[21] to provide a set of qualitative criteria. They were to aid in the decision-making on characterization with an emphasis on the substance of an arrangement and not merely on the contractual terms of the arrangement arising out of the contract. This guidance specified the classification of R&D centres under three categories (entrepreneurial in nature, cost-sharing arrangements, and contract R&D) on the basis of their functional analysis. It provided specific guidelines for identifying a development centre as a contract R&D service provider with insignificant risk and stated that the same principles will be considered for the selection of the most appropriate method.

4.4.4 *View of Indian Tax Authorities in UN TPM: India Chapter*

It appears that the Indian tax authorities are otherwise fine with accepting the concept of a contract R&D service provider structure with a cost-plus remuneration model for the researcher based in India. However, India has observed in the UN TPM country chapter that in cases when, as against the formal contract R&D model, the Indian researchers carry out strategic functions, they are entitled to rewards commensurate to the assumption of risks around the development and exploitation of intangibles, as associated with such performance of enhanced strategic functions. It further stated that such researchers should therefore not be entitled to a routine and low cost-plus remuneration model.

Currently, 'low' is a relative term. The question is whether, having regard to a proper functional analysis, a structure can be validly accepted to be one of contract R&D services? If the answer is in the affirmative, then the remuneration model would ideally need to be cost-plus. The 'plus' or 'mark-up' would need to be arrived at by adhering to necessary factors of a comparability analysis with neither the taxpayer nor the

20. *GE India Technology Centre Pvt. Ltd v. DCIT* (ITA No. 789/Bang/2010 and ITA Nos 487 & 925/Bang/2011), pp. 31 and 32 (ITAT, 2012).
21. Circular No. 06/2013 [F No. 500/139/2012], dated 29 June 2013.

revenue board having any right to a preconception with respect to the end result, specifically, 'low' or 'high', respectively.

The benchmarking exercise is performed in a proper manner by accepting comparable companies with a similar functional profile as that of the taxpayer. It should specifically result in identifying companies that do not carry unique intangibles. An appropriate arm's length mark-up would automatically unfold that should not carry the stigma of either 'low' or 'high'.

The nature of services rendered by a contract service provider cannot or should not determine the percentage of 'mark-up'. On the other hand, the selection of comparables with a commensurate functional profile would, in a normal course, lead to the determination of an appropriate arm's length mark-up.

4.4.5 Key Takeaways

Due to ambiguousness and subjective interpretation, contract R&D has been an area of high litigation in India that depends on the facts and circumstances of each case.

However, the guidelines provided by CBDT India in the circular discussed above were helpful to clarify the confusion in many cases. A primary onus should be laid on efficient global documentation catering to the analysis and the documentation associated with TP of R&D operations. It is crucial that the actual functional analysis for R&D operations align with the contractual agreement that stipulates ownership of intangibles with the foreign-related party and the Indian affiliate with a routine service provider.

It can be noted that similar to the above, the characterization issue and comparables selection are the most disputed TP aspects also in the case of other contract service providers.

4.5 Financial Transactions

4.5.1 Background and Evolution

Financial transactions are a prerequisite for obtaining funding across MNEs. The most common financial transactions undertaken by MNEs in India are in the form of intra-group loans, corporate guarantees, and trade receivables. The retrospective amendment in Finance Act 2012 in the definition of 'international transaction' as per section 92B of the act enhanced the focus of the tax authorities on these and financial transactions such as purchase or sale of marketable securities, etc. They thereby nullified the cumulative effect of prior judgements that closed the cases on the rationale that these transactions did not constitute international transactions.

4.5.2 *Issuance of Guarantee*

– Issue

In situations wherein the Indian parent entities extend corporate guarantees to their overseas related parties, the Indian tax authorities are of the view that the latter are obligated to pay a service charge to the Indian entity. Accordingly, the tax authorities allege that the Indian entity should charge a guarantee fee in such circumstances. However, the challenge arises when determining the arm's length price. Generally, this arm's length price of such guarantees is determined using the CUP method. In most cases, interest rate and guarantee rate quotes available from banking companies are taken as the benchmark rate to arrive at the arm's length price. However, non-availability of specialized databases and comparable transfer prices for cases of complex inter-company loans as well as an implicit element of guarantee from the parent company in securing debt pose potent challenges.

– View of Judiciary

The Delhi ITAT in the case of Bharti Airtel Limited[22] came up with a rational position that, even after the retrospective amendment of the definition of 'international transaction' by the Finance Act 2012 with effect from 1 April 2002, provision of corporate guarantee still does not constitute an international transaction, unless the same had a bearing on the profits, income, losses or assets of the taxpayer. This would thereby imply that, unless the taxpayer had himself incurred any cost to provide the guarantee, benefitting the overseas subsidiary company, such provision of guarantee would not constitute an international transaction, so as to be covered by the ambit of TP regulations. In coming to such a conclusion, the Delhi Tribunal drew inspiration from the manner in which the aspect of the provision of guarantee was phrased in the definition of the term 'international transaction'.

The above ruling was followed by the Ahmedabad Tribunal in the case of Micro Ink Limited.[23] Incidentally, the Ahmedabad Tribunal also brought an altogether new dimension to the issue of corporate guarantees, to hold, by referring to the 2010 OECD TPG. It stated that where a parent company provided a corporate guarantee with respect to loans obtained by the overseas subsidiary for augmenting its funds for business, the same constituted 'shareholder's function' being performed by the Indian parent, not necessitating charging of any guarantee commission.

Accordingly, the issuance of corporate guarantees in the nature of quasi capital or shareholder activity does not amount to a service in respect of which an arm's length adjustment can be done.

22. *Bharti Airtel Limited v. ACIT* (I.T.A. No. 5816/Del/2012), pp. 13-26 (ITAT, 2014).
23. *Micro Ink Limited v. ACIT* (I.T.A. No. 2873/Ahd/10), pp. 9-54 (ITAT, 2015).

4.5.3 *Intra-group Loans*

– Issue

The two major issues with respect to intra-group loans are (a) imputation of interest on free-of-cost loans; and (b) when interest is imputed, the basis of charging interest in the case of INR loans and foreign currency loans.

– View of Judiciary

The entire issue involving interest imputation on intra-group loans revolves around the correct delineation of funds as equity or debt funding and the determination of the arm's length interest. India has already witnessed a spate of rulings providing contrary views on the said issue. On the one hand, the free-of-cost loan has been considered to be of a special character such as in the nature of quasi-equity/shareholder activity, etc., or held no interest chargeable on other grounds like commercial expediency, etc., in several cases including Cadila Healthcare Limited,[24] Micro Inks Limited,[25] etc. On the other hand, in the absence of a carve-out of the special character of the arrangement, the contentions of the taxpayers to treat the arrangement as a quasi-equity has been rejected in many cases such as Perot Systems TSI Ltd[26] and Soma Textile & Industries Limited.[27] Accordingly, the facts of each arrangement need to be examined to appropriately characterize the arrangement and, accordingly, undertake a benchmarking analysis to determine its arm's length price.

Further, as discussed above, for interest imputation, a question arose that incidentally intrigued several tribunals of India. The question being that for the purpose of computing the interest on an outbound loan granted by an Indian MNE or parent in favour of its overseas subsidiary, being denominated in foreign currency, should the comparability analysis be either carried out with reference to the currency in which the loan was granted or with reference to INR, by taking the prime lending rate of Indian banks?

The Indian Revenue Board has, in most cases, adopted the latter path, contending that the arm's length price must be computed with reference to the rate of interest, that the taxpayer, as the Indian parent, would have earned if the money was lent or deposited in INR in India. The majority of the tribunals in India had ruled that, in such situations, the arm's length price of the interest income had to be computed with reference to the currency in which the loan was granted, i.e., in foreign currency. This is because the correct approach was to examine what an unrelated party placed in similar circumstances outside India, would have been willing to pay on a similar nature and amount of the loan advanced by the Indian MNC. The Delhi HC ruled on similar

24. *Cadila Healthcare Limited v. ACIT* (IT (TP) Nos 898/Ahd/2014 and 694/Ahd/2015), pp. 2-15 (ITAT, 2017).
25. *Micro Inks Limited v. ACIT* (ITA No. 1668/Ahd/2006), pp. 6-24 (ITAT, 2013).
26. *Perot Systems TSI Ltd v. DCIT* ([2010] 37 SOT 358 [DELHI]), pp. 2-8 (ITAT, 2009).
27. *Soma Textile & Industries Limited v. ACIT* (I.T.A. No. 262 [Ahd] of 2012), pp. 2-7 (ITAT, 2015).

lines as those in the case of M/s. Cotton Naturals (I) Pvt. Ltd.,[28] thus approving the fundamental approach of the tribunals and bringing relief for taxpayers.

4.5.4 *Key Takeaways*

It is noteworthy that the SHR in India encompasses the transactions in nature of guarantee and intra-group loans to offer some certainty in this regard. However, while the interest rates in relation to foreign currency loans as per jurisprudence and the SHR have been discussed, the descent of the LIBOR cannot be overlooked.

In the authors' opinion, the issue of a corporate guarantee should be dealt with as per the fundamentals of TP instead of seeking protection behind the shield of legal interpretation of the term 'international transaction'. The government has attempted to expand this from time to time in an overzealous effort to counter several attempts made by taxpayers to extricate themselves from the provisions of TP by resorting to the definition of the said term under varying circumstances. Further, the issue of TP relating to financial transactions covering guarantees, loans, etc., is a very niche area. It requires significant expertise in the execution and deployment of sophisticated databases, e.g., Moody's RiskCalc, Loan Connector, Bloomberg, etc., for ascertaining credit ratings of companies, identifying comparable loan agreements with reference to similar credit ratings, comparison of rates of interest, etc.

Accordingly, the current need would be for tax authorities to issue detailed regulations in this area similar to how globally this critical subject has attracted traction with continuous development. This has occurred with the inclusion of Chapter 9 to the UN TPM as well as Chapter X in OECD TPG.

Further, the provisions of section 94B of the act thereby restricting an interest expense exceeding INR 1 crore to 30% of EBITDA for the year must be evaluated alongside being the supplement to thin capitalization rules in India.

5 IMPACT OF COVID-19 ON TP IN INDIA

The Coronavirus pandemic has not only terribly impacted human lives but has also led to severe economic breakdown and market chaos. The measures taken by the Indian Government to control this pandemic (including nationwide lockdowns) have created other economic issues. These include those such as impacting liquidity, rejigging organizations' supply chain operations, and restricting the cross-border and in-border movement of people creating inequities in demand and supplies leading to a diminishing effect in output and consumption. While liquidity, the operationalization of the supply chain, and sustainability are the immediate focus, MNEs are also reinvestigating the existing modus operandi and acclimatizing their TP policies and design to the post-COVID-19 environment.

28. *CIT v. Cotton Naturals (I) Pvt. Ltd* (ITA No. 233/2014), pp. 28-34 (HC, 2015).

Outlined below are some of the key TP related aspects emanating from COVID-19:

- existing supply chain redesign;
- impact on intra-group financial transactions;
- global TP policy redesign;
- revision/termination of inter-company agreements;
- re-evaluation of APAs;
- analysis of PE risk emerging from virtual working and significant people functions undertaken via digital means from remote locations; and
- impact on TPD and profitability.

The Indian Government has not yet introduced any specific guidance to deal with various TP challenges arising due to COVID-19. However, since it broadly adheres to the OECD guidelines, it is expected that the awaited OECD guidance in this regard would be broadly adopted by the Indian Government.

Meanwhile, taking guidance from the global principle issued thus far, the taxpayers must embrace the measures listed below to assess and document the economic impacts of COVID-19 on TP arrangements:

- Functional Profile – conduct a functional analysis before and after COVID-19.
- Economic Circumstances – outline and evidence the actual economic impact of COVID-19 on the relevant industry juxtaposed with the impact on taxpayer's operations.
- Contractual Arrangements – regarding contractual arrangements between transacting parties, maintain reliable evidence and documentation to defend if any obligations or material terms and conditions have been varied, amended, or terminated.
- Impact Analysis – evidence of COVID-19 on the specific product and service offerings and consequential financial results including variance analysis of budgeted (pre-COVID-19) versus actual results.
- Business Strategies – evidence changes in business strategies due to COVID-19 including decisions made, types of outcomes, and actions taken to give effect to those strategies.
- APA Impact – evaluate whether any critical assumptions of the agreement have been impacted. If so, the taxpayer must proactively seek an early resolution instead of subsequent litigation.

All of the above measures ultimately call for a 'but for COVID-19 test' and clearly reinforce the fact that the key to mitigating TP risk lies in maintaining adequate evidence and ensuring that TP positions are well-documented.

As discussed above, the Indian Government has not introduced any specific guidelines concerning the above. However, considering the difficulties faced by the taxpayers in adhering to the deadlines for compliance under various laws, the Indian Government has extended the due dates of various compliance requirements for the fiscal year 2019-2020 as well as 2020-2021 including the annual compliance requirements for TP in India. Further, the use of digital means for communication between the taxpayer to undertake TP assessments is another step undertaken to facilitate safe and efficient proceedings during these times. Moreover, from the last two years, the SHR announced by the Indian Government are extended for a single year only. It seems that it had wisely made this announcement considering that the pandemic lockdown in India and underlying economic factors would begin to negatively impact businesses from the start of the pandemic. Accordingly, in future years, the government may consider special rates and factors for the pandemic impact on businesses.

In light of the above discussion, the guidance from the OECD and the Indian Government to address TP challenges originating from COVID-19 is much awaited and will be appreciated.

CHAPTER 26
Transfer Pricing in the United States

H. David Rosenbloom & Neal M. Kochman

1 US TP PRINCIPLES

Section 482 of the IRC[1] authorizes the IRS to shift income, deductions, credits, or allowances between or among controlled parties in order to avoid evasion of taxes or clearly reflect income. Changed only minimally and in very specific ways since 1934, this broad authority has evolved into a comprehensive set of TP regulations[2] governing all cross-border transactions of MNEs doing business in the US. Working from the presumption that transactions between unrelated parties produce prices that are acceptable for tax purposes – i.e., are at arm's length – these rules are designed to measure the results of tested transactions[3] and determine whether those results are consistent with the arm's length pricing of comparable unrelated party transactions.

In general, the US rules are consistent with the OECD TPG, particularly as the latter have incorporated US concepts such as abandoning a hierarchy of TP methods in favour of selecting the best or most appropriate method. Moreover, as with the OECD, much of the focus of the IRS on TP in recent years has been on intangible transfers. There had been some speculation that the passage of the TCJA would reduce pressure on US TP through a substantial reduction in the US corporate tax rate and other changes designed to discourage foreign activities; however, it remains to be seen whether that will, in fact, be the case.

US TP law and practice differ from those of other countries in several important ways. First, as a general matter, the US rules are more prescriptive and detailed than those of the OECD TPG and contain many more specific examples. The US rules endeavour to communicate not only the sorts of considerations that need to enter into a TP analysis but also how the analysis should conclude in specific circumstances.

Second, the US relies on a penalty regime for TP compliance coupled with a defence to penalties if the taxpayer has adequate documentation of its TP in its possession by the time it files a tax return. The penalties are linked to prices reported on the return which will often be filed long after a tested transaction has occurred, at a time when more information is available and the taxpayer has had the benefit of a careful review of its TP positions. As a consequence of the US focus on the return as the basis for penalties, the regulations afford taxpayers the opportunity to 'self-initiate' TP adjustments if such adjustments are necessary to report an arm's length price. The US thus effectively judges whether a tested transaction was at arm's length based on the price reported on the tax return as opposed to the price used in the transaction. This differs from the practice of other countries and can lead to misunderstandings, especially in the application of the MAP of tax treaties.

A third important difference is the US concept of the CSA which has given rise to TP issues apparently known only to the US. A CSA is different from the OECD TPG's cost contribution agreement and is limited to the development of IP. US taxpayers have

1. The Internal Revenue Code of 1986, as amended (Title 26 of the U.S. Code). Section references in this chapter are to the IRC or the regulations promulgated thereunder.
2. Sections 1.482-1 through -9 of the U.S. Treasury Regulations (Treas. Reg.) found in title 26 of the Code of Federal Regulations.
3. The term 'controlled transaction' is substituted by 'tested transaction' throughout the book except for quoted texts.

used CSAs not merely to share the cost of developing intangibles but as a means of expatriating the non-US enjoyment of intangibles so that the income from such enjoyment escapes a US taxing jurisdiction. This practice has led to many large TP disputes over the past fifteen years and is likely to be a source of disputes well into the future. It does not appear that the issues presented in these disputes have surfaced in other jurisdictions.

1.1 Controlled Parties

For the IRS to make allocations under section 482, the parties involved in the transaction under review must be under common control. Only then is a transaction a 'tested transaction' subject to potential TP adjustment. There is a presumption of control, however, whenever income or deductions have been arbitrarily shifted. 'Controlled' includes any kind of control, direct or indirect, whether legally enforceable or not, and however exercisable or exercised, including control resulting from the actions of two or more taxpayers acting in concert or with a common goal or purpose. It is the reality of control that is decisive, not its form or the mode of its exercise.[4]

Control is predominantly an ownership test. The US Supreme Court has held that control depends upon the presence of the power to shift income from one controlled entity to another.[5] Courts will generally examine the reality of control and not record ownership.[6] Usually, though, control means majority ownership or, in the case of brother/sister rather than parent/subsidiary transactions, majority ownership by a common parent. Indirect control may exist when there are agreements that permit a party to control an entity.[7]

Control for section 482 purposes also includes two or more taxpayers acting in concert or with a common goal or purpose. In Revenue Ruling 2003-96, the IRS indicated that a 'common goal or purpose' will be found in factual situations, such as *B. Forman v. Commissioner*[8] and *South Texas Rice Warehouse v. Commissioner*.[9] The ruling provides that an example of common interest control would be three equal and, otherwise, unrelated shareholders in a corporation that, acting in concert, individually purchase from or sell items to the corporation at prices that differ from those that would be charged by unrelated parties in similar circumstances. Even though none of the shareholders individually have actual or effective control of the corporation, when the shareholders act in concert with a common goal of shifting income or deductions from or to the corporation, each shareholder is considered to control the corporation for purposes of section 482.

---

4. Treas. Reg. § 1.482-1(i)(4).
5. *Commissioner v. First Sec. Bank of Utah*, 405 U.S. 394 (1972).
6. *Grenada Industries v. Commissioner*, 17 T.C. 231 (1951).
7. *Charles Town, Inc. v. Commissioner*, 372 F.2d 415 (4th Cir. 1967). Control existed when there was an agreement that two brothers who controlled Fairmount Steel Co. would be the directors of Charles Town Co., and they would make all of the major decisions in the management of Charles Town. *R.T. French v. Commissioner*, 60 T.C. 836 (1973).
8. *B. Forman Co., Inc. v. Commissioner*, 453 F.2d 1144, (2nd Cir. 1972).
9. *South Texas Rice Warehouse Co. v. Commissioner*, 366 F.2d 890 (5th Cir. 1966).

In *B. Forman Co. v. Commissioner*, two corporations formed a third corporation, Midtown, to operate a shopping centre and each had a 50% interest in the issued and outstanding shares of Midtown. The two shareholders, Forman and McCurdy, entered into a shareholder agreement that required each party to vote its Midtown stock for three directors nominated by McCurdy and three directors designated by Forman. The shareholders each made a three-year interest-free loan of USD 1 million to the company. The deduction of the interest expense by Midtown was not tax-efficient because it was a loss corporation, and the interest income would have increased McCurdy's and Forman's taxable income. The US Second Circuit Court of Appeals upheld the allocation of interest to the shareholders, finding that each acted in concert in making loans without interest to Midtown because their identical interest in the company gave each the reality of control. The court based its finding on the grounds that Forman and McCurdy 'were not competitors in their dealings with one another or with Midtown as to Midtown'.

In *South Texas Rice Warehouse v. Commissioner*, a corporation and partnership were owned equally by four families.[10] The partnership entered into an agreement to rent the operating assets of the corporation. The lease agreement separated the entity that was depreciating the assets from the entity receiving income from the operation of the assets. The rent was insufficient to cover the book expenses of the corporation, and the corporation claimed a loss carry back and a refund. The court held that section 482 was applicable because the purpose of forming the partnership was to effectuate a short-term reallocation of income without affecting long-term ownership or control. The purpose of leasing the operating assets to the partnership was to shift income to the shareholders' children. The taxpayers in question had a common interest in shifting income.

Other cases addressing 'acting in concert' include *Dallas Ceramic Co. v. United States*[11] in which the US Fifth Circuit Court of Appeals found that section 482 did not apply to transactions between a corporation that was wholly owned by a taxpayer and a corporation in which the taxpayer and his immediate family had approximately a 37% interest. The concerted action principle did not apply because the shareholders of each corporation did not have a common interest since income shifted from one corporation would disproportionately benefit shareholders of the other. The court found, 'there must be a common design for the shifting of income in order for different individuals to constitute the "same interest". Here, the two businesses were owned and controlled by different individuals, and it is clear there was no design to shift income among them. Any overpayment made by Dallas Ceramic to Ceramica would have been completely contrary to Robert and his family's financial interest since they had no interest in Ceramica and would have received no benefits from such overpayments'.[12]

10. Each family had a 25% interest in each entity, however, the intra-family breakdown differed between the corporation and the partnership.
11. *Dallas Ceramic Co. v. U.S.*, 598 F.2d 1382 (5th Cir. 1979).
12. *Brittingham v. Commissioner*, 66 T.C. 373 (1976).

In *Bransford v. Commissioner*,[13] the US Tax Court rejected the IRS's concerted action argument because the parties had competing interests. A group of individuals formed Peabody Properties to purchase real property. Peabody Properties sold portions of the property to MIP Corporation, an entity partially owned by shareholders of Peabody Properties. The US Tax Court found that the parties were not acting in concert to shift income to Peabody Properties because an allocation of income would not benefit all of the shareholders of MIP Corporation.

1.2 Arm's-Length Standard

As noted above, section 482 allows the IRS to adjust the results of tested transactions to 'clearly reflect income'. That phrase has long been interpreted to mean that the results of the transactions satisfy the ALS, i.e., that the tax results of a tested transaction are consistent with those of an equivalent transaction conducted between unrelated parties. Accordingly, Treas. Reg. § 1.482-1(b)(1) provides:

> In determining the true taxable income of a controlled taxpayer, the standard to be applied in every case is that of a taxpayer dealing at arm's length with an uncontrolled taxpayer. A controlled transaction meets the arm's-length standard if the results of the transaction are consistent with the results that would have been realized if uncontrolled taxpayers had engaged in the same transaction under the same circumstances (arm's-length result). However, because identical transactions can rarely be located, whether a transaction produces an arm's-length result generally will be determined by reference to the results of comparable transactions under comparable circumstances.

The ALS is an IRS sword, not a taxpayer shield. Adjustments made by the IRS to satisfy the ALS are presumptively correct and the burden is generally borne by the taxpayer to prove otherwise. A taxpayer is bound by its tax filing position and may not amend its return to reflect a lower arm's length result. That is, a taxpayer may not reduce the taxable income reported on its originally filed return (*see* Treas. Reg. § 1.482-1(a)(1)(3)). On the other hand, since it is results as reported that matter, a taxpayer may report taxable income that is different from that of the actual pricing of a tested transaction. Neither the method used to price the transaction nor the taxpayer's intent is of relevance. If the IRS makes an adjustment, it must apply the ALS even if it is taxpayer-favourable.[14]

To guard against underreporting of results in tested transactions, the IRC has incorporated a 20% 'transfer pricing' penalty that, in certain circumstances, is doubled to 40%. The only way for a taxpayer to avoid this penalty when a TP adjustment is sustained is to have contemporaneous TPD demonstrating that it reasonably applied the regulations. 'Contemporaneous' for this purpose means completed by the time the original return is filed.

13. *Bransford v. Commissioner*, 36 TCM 1262 (1977).
14. *See Pikeville Coal v. U.S.*, 79 AFTR 2d 97-502 (Ct. Cl.) (the court could consider the value of the coal transferred and the reasonableness of the IRS determination).

1.3 Best Method

In 1968, the US Department of the Treasury (Treasury) issued regulations that included a hierarchy rule for selecting the method for assessing whether pricing of a tested transaction satisfied the ALS. In 1994, new regulations abandoned that rule, adopting instead the 'best method rule'. The best method is summarized in section 1.482-1(c)(2) of the regulations which states:

> The arm's-length result of a controlled transaction must be determined under the method that, under the facts and circumstances, provides the most reliable measure of an arm's-length result. Thus, there is no strict priority of methods, and no method will invariably be considered to be more reliable than the others. An arm's-length result may be determined under any method without establishing the inapplicability of another method, but if another method subsequently is shown to produce a more reliable measure of an arm's-length result, such other method must be used. Similarly, if two or more applications of a single method provide inconsistent results, the arm's-length result must be determined under the application that, under the facts and circumstances, provides the most reliable measure of an arm's-length result.

The regulations further state that in determining which method provides the most reliable result, 'the two primary factors to take into account are the degree of comparability between the controlled transaction (or taxpayer) and any uncontrolled comparables, and the quality of the data and assumptions used in the analysis'.[15]

Determining the best method is an iterative process that begins with an analysis of the functions, assets, and risks associated with the transaction under review and how they are allocated to the controlled parties. The availability of information on comparable untested transactions and companies is then assessed. The ability to apply a possible method is next assessed along with the likely reliability of the result of applying that method. In making this assessment, it may be appropriate to aggregate or segment multiple transactions. The process is repeated for each potential method, and the one that will provide the most reliable result is selected as the best method.

Factors for assessing the reliability of a method include the level of comparability between the controlled and untested transactions or taxpayers, the availability of complete and accurate data on comparable transactions or companies, and the sensitivity of results to assumptions. It is often difficult to identify and find data on truly comparable transactions so, often, the best method approach focuses on profits earned by comparable companies. The regulations include examples demonstrating the selection of the method. In some cases, the best method will not be clear, and it may be appropriate to combine results of more than one method.

1.4 Comparability

A tested transaction satisfies the ALS when its results are consistent with those of comparable transactions conducted between unrelated parties. This standard provokes

15. Treas. Reg. § 1.482-1(c)(2).

questioning of when an untested transaction is sufficiently similar to a tested transaction to provide a reliable arm's length measure. Guidance for conducting a comparability analysis and selecting reliable 'comparables' is provided in section 1.482-1(d) of the regulations. That guidance is applied in assessing the reliability of the various potential methods for determining the arm's length results.

A comparability analysis should consider all of the factors that may impact pricing. These include functions performed, contractual terms, risks assumed, economic and financial conditions, and the nature of property or services transferred. An untested transaction does not have to be identical to a tested transaction to be comparable but must be sufficiently similar to provide a reliable measure. The requisite degree of similarity varies for different TP methods as does the importance of the different comparability factors.

The functional analysis identifies and compares the activities performed and resources used that are economically significant to the controlled and untested transactions under review. These activities may include research and development; product design and engineering; product fabrication, extraction, and assembly; procurement; marketing and distribution functions; transport and warehousing; and managerial, legal, accounting and finance, credit and collection, training, and personnel management activities. Consideration of the types of assets used includes plant and equipment and valuable intangibles.

The contractual terms analysis involves a comparison of significant features that could affect the results of the controlled and untested transactions. Such terms include the form of consideration; volume; warranties; rights to updates; duration and termination rights; collateral transactions and ongoing business relationships; and credit and payment provisions. Terms entered into through a written agreement executed prior to a transaction, including allocating of risk, will generally be respected. In the absence of a written agreement, the IRS may impute terms of an implied agreement based on a course of action consistent with the economic substance of the transaction.

The risks analysis compares the significant risks that could affect the price of or profit earned in the controlled and untested transactions. Risks to consider include the market and its fluctuations in cost, demand, and inventory; success or failure of research and development; financial risk with foreign exchange and interest rates; credit and collection; product liability; and general business risks related to ownership of property, plant, and equipment. Contractual terms allocating risk to a related party will generally be respected unless they are inconsistent with the economic substance of the transaction and the conduct of the controlled parties.

Economic conditions that could affect the comparability of controlled and untested transactions include geographic markets, the size of the market and level of economic development in the market, the level of the market, e.g., wholesale versus retail, market share, location, specific costs or factors, competition, economic condition of the relevant industry, and alternatives realistically available to the buyer and seller. In assessing the comparability of intangibles, key considerations include the existence of embedded intangibles such as brand, quality, sales volume, geographic market, class of intangible, and profit potential.

It is rare to find untested transactions that are truly identical to the tested transaction. The regulations provide that an untested transaction is comparable when it is a reliable measure of the arm's length result. Adjustments must often be made to compensate for material differences between controlled and untested transactions. A material difference is one that would materially affect the arm's length result under the method being used. For example, in testing whether the price charged by a related party distributor is at arm's length, the party that bears inventory risk could be material, and adjustments would need to be made to the pricing of comparable sales if the allocation of inventory risk is different for the untested transaction.

The regulations also recognize that there are special circumstances that may affect comparability and the determination of an arm's length result. These include:[16]

(1) Market share strategies used to gain entry into a market or to increase the share of an existing market. When implementing such a strategy, the controlled parties would be expected to temporarily incur additional market development costs or to temporarily charge lower prices as compared to mature participants in the market.
(2) Different geographic market. Ordinarily controlled and untested transaction data should be derived from the same geographic market, however, when sufficient comparable data is not available, data from different markets may be used to measure arm's length results.
(3) Location savings. When an uncontrolled taxpayer operates in a different geographic market than a controlled taxpayer, adjustments may be necessary to account for different costs of operating in the different markets. In general, any location savings realized by the controlled taxpayer must be allocated among controlled parties consistent with how they would be allocated among unrelated parties.
(4) Legal restrictions. Such restrictions under the US or foreign law may restrict the ability of controlled taxpayers to price consistently with the ALS.

Transactions that are not conducted in the ordinary course of business or for which the principal purpose was to establish an arm's length price may not ordinarily be used as comparables. Such transactions do not provide a reliable measure of an arm's length result.

16. *See First Security Bank of Utah*, 405 U.S. 394 (1972), *Proctor & Gamble*, 961 F.2d 1255 (6th Cir. 1992), *Texaco/Exxon*, 98 F.3d 825 (5th Cir. 1995). The impact of foreign restrictions on arm's-length pricing is the subject of a case pending in the US Tax Court: *3M v. Commissioner*, TC No. 005816-13. The case has been fully briefed, however, as of 1 May 2022, a decision had not been rendered. The case involves Brazilian limits on royalties paid to foreign related parties; limits that the IRS considers less than what would be paid at arm's length for the licensed manufacturing intangibles, trademarks, and copyrights.

1.5 Arm's-Length Range

In some cases, the application of a TP method will indicate a single arm's length result. Typically, though, a method will produce multiple 'comparable' results. In these circumstances, the regulations authorize the development of an arm's length range. When it is properly constructed, the results of a tested transaction are considered at arm's length if they fall within the range. If they fall outside the range, the IRS may make an adjustment, at its discretion, typically to the median result but sometimes to an endpoint of the range or even by deciding that a particular uncontrolled result is the best comparable.

An arm's length range is developed from two or more uncontrolled results of similar reliability and comparability. Adjustments are made to the uncontrolled observations to account for material differences between the controlled and untested transactions. If it is not possible to adjust the results of a particular comparable to account for all such differences, that observation is generally discarded and not used to construct the range. On the other hand, all comparables for which all necessary adjustments can be made are used.

Once a set of comparables has been determined, there is a question of how to actually set the range. In some cases, the results of all of the comparables are used. However, use of the full range is limited to cases in which (1) information is sufficiently complete so that it is likely that all material differences have been identified, (2) each such difference has a definite and reasonably ascertainable effect on price or profit, and (3) an adjustment is made for each such effect. When these conditions are not met, which is typically the case, a statistical technique must be used to adjust the range to make it more reliable.

The regulations generally provide for use of an interquartile range when the conditions for using the full range are not met. The interquartile range is a range for which there is a 75% chance of a result falling above the lower end of the range and a 75% chance of a result falling below the upper end. This narrower range that eliminates comparables outside these limits increases reliability that a tested transaction falling within the range satisfies the ALS. The regulations permit other statistical techniques to narrow the range if they produce a more reliable result than the interquartile range.

Provided there is an agreement between the IRS and the taxpayer on the best method for determining whether a tested transaction satisfies the ALS, the selection of comparables and development of the arm's length range tend to be the main sources of controversy. Factors that come into play include whether to use single-year or multi-year data, screening criteria for determining that a potential comparable is sufficiently comparable and reliable to use, and the types of adjustments to be made to each comparable's results.

1.6 Scope of Review

The IRS's authority to determine true taxable income extends to any case in which taxable income of a controlled taxpayer is different than it would have been had the taxpayer been dealing at arm's length with an uncontrolled taxpayer. The intent of the taxpayer is irrelevant; there is no prerequisite that the taxpayer planned to avoid tax or engaged in a sham transaction. All that is relevant is that the taxable income reported differs from what it would have been at arm's length. Allocations may be made even if income has not actually been realized,[17] the transaction at issue is covered by non-recognition provisions, or the transaction is between members of a US consolidated group.

In evaluating a transaction, the IRS will respect the structure arranged by the taxpayer unless that structure lacks economic substance. In determining whether the terms of a tested transaction would be acceptable at arm's length, the IRS may consider alternatives realistically available to the controlled taxpayers. When conditions are appropriate for consideration of realistic alternatives, arm's length results will be deemed to be those consistent with those of the alternatives.

Usually, the assessment of whether a transaction satisfies the ALS is based on comparable transactions occurring in the same taxable year. However, in many cases, it is appropriate to consider data from multiple years, including years before and after the year of the actual transaction. Circumstances warranting the use of multiple-year data vary depending on the TP method being used. In general, though, they include situations in which complete and accurate data is not available for the taxable year under review, the business cycle affects the tested transaction, or there are significant product life cycle effects. When the use of multiple-year data is appropriate, the average results for the tested transaction over those years are compared to an arm's length range constructed from comparable results over the same period.

Although many of the TP methods envision a single transaction, it is often difficult to isolate an individual tested transaction. In such cases, it may be appropriate to evaluate an entire product line or other grouping. In other cases, it may be suitable to use sampling or other statistical techniques.

2 US TP AUTHORITY

The statutory authority for the IRS to make TP adjustments consists of a single IRC section. To apply that authority fairly and consistently, the IRS and Treasury have issued a comprehensive set of regulations that are generally accepted as authority. How those regulations should be applied in a particular circumstance, however, is not always clear which leads to disputes between the IRS and taxpayers that often find their way to the courts. The main sources of authority for US TP are thus the statute,

17. *See Central De Gas De Chihuahua S. A. v. Commissioner*, 102 TC 515 (1994) (where no rent was charged between controlled parties for trucks leased and used in the US; the deemed arm's-length rent determined by the IRS under section 482 was treated as an amount actually paid and received).

regulations, and case law. In addition, the IRS often issues notices and rulings regarding particular issues, and income tax treaties entered into by the US often impact the country's TP.

2.1 Section 482

Section 482 consists of three sentences; the first has essentially been unchanged since 1934 and the other two subsequently added to deal with perceived abuses associated with transfers of IP. It states:

> In any case of two or more organizations, trades, or businesses (whether or not incorporated, whether or not organized in the United States, and whether or not affiliated) owned or controlled directly or indirectly by the same interests, the Secretary may distribute, apportion, or allocate gross income, deductions, credits, or allowances between or among such organizations, trades, or businesses, if he determines that such distribution, apportionment, or allocation is necessary in order to prevent evasion of taxes or clearly to reflect the income of any of such organizations, trades, or businesses. In the case of any transfer (or license) of intangible property (within the meaning of section 367(d)(4)), the income with respect to such transfer or license shall be commensurate with the income attributable to the intangible. For purposes of this section, the Secretary shall require the valuation of transfers of IP (including IP transferred with other property or services) on an aggregate basis or the valuation of such a transfer on the basis of the realistic alternatives to such a transfer, if the Secretary determines that such basis is the most reliable means of valuation of such transfers.

The second sentence provides the CWI standard. It was added in 1986 to address situations in which taxpayers transferred intangibles with high-profit potential at an early stage of development into low tax jurisdictions. The CWI standard allows the IRS to make backward TP adjustments based on future results from the use of the transferred IP. Guidance for applying the standard is provided in section 1.482-4(f)(2) of the regulations and is discussed in section 4.1 below.

The TCJA made two changes to section 482. First, it changed the definition of intangibles for section 482 purposes from that contained in section 936(h)(3)(B) which did not include goodwill, going concern value, or workforce in place to that contained in section 367(d)(4) and amended section 367(d)(4) to include goodwill, going concern value, workforce in place, or any other item the value or potential value of which is not attributable to tangible property. Second, it added the third sentence to make it clear that, when appropriate, the IRS may value IP on an aggregate basis or by reference to realistic alternatives. These concepts have long existed in the regulations; however, the court in the *Amazon* case[18] rejected the IRS's application of an aggregate approach.

18. *Amazon.com v. Commissioner*, 148 T.C. 108 (2017), *aff'd* 934 F.3d 976 (9th Cir. 2019). *See* discussion in section 4.4 below.

2.2 The Regulations

In 1994, the IRS and Treasury issued comprehensive regulations interpreting the broad principles of section 482. They have been amended and supplemented in the years since then and provide guidance for analysing tested transactions and methods for determining whether the results of those transactions satisfy the ALS. They contain many examples demonstrating the application of key concepts and the various methods.

In general, taxpayers have the discretion to arrange their affairs including the prices they charge in tested transactions, however, the regulations require taxpayers to file returns that reflect arm's length results even if those results differ from the prices actually charged.[19] This means taxpayers should apply the regulations to their tested transactions before finalizing their original US tax returns. If they later determine adjustments should have been made to satisfy the ALS, they are precluded from making downward adjustments to taxable income on amended returns; it is therefore important that any adjustments that will decrease US taxable income be identified and implemented on the original return.[20] Amended returns that increase US taxable income are, of course, permitted at any time and may serve to prevent the imposition of certain penalties.[21]

Treasury regulations interpret and provide guidance for applying the IRC. They receive substantial deference in court and are generally treated as authority.[22] Courts, however, will disregard a regulation if it is clearly inconsistent with congressional intent. The Treasury generally issues two types of regulations: legislative that are authorized by a specific section of the IRC and fill in gaps in the legislation and interpretive that are promulgated under section 7805(a) to provide necessary rules and regulations. The Administrative Procedure Act provides procedures for issuing regulations and, for legislative regulations, in particular, requires notice and comment as well as 'reasoned decision making'.

Prior to 2015, courts uniformly treated the section 482 regulations as valid interpretations of US law and adhered to them in deciding cases. Then, in *Altera v. Commissioner*,[23] the US Tax Court held that section 1.482-7(d)(2) of the regulations[24] that involved a question of the costs to be shared in a CSA was invalid because it violated the ALS. During the comment period for the regulation, evidence had been provided that a type of the costs at issue (stock option expenses) was not shared in arm's length transactions. The court found that because the IRS had adopted the ALS, it was precluded from requiring controlled taxpayers to compensate what uncontrolled taxpayers would not, and the regulation did not reflect 'reasoned decision making'.

The decision probably would have had a limited direct impact because new cost-sharing regulations had been issued and relatively few taxpayers would have been

19. Treas. Reg. § 1.482-1(a)(3).
20. *Ibid.*
21. *See* Treas. Reg. § 1.6662-6(a)(4).
22. *See Mayo Foundation v. United States*, 562 U.S. 42 (2011).
23. *Altera v. Commissioner*, 145 T.C. 91 (2015).
24. Now Treas. Reg. § 1.482-7A(d)(2).

able to apply the decision to their CSAs. The decision, however, caused concerns that challenges would be mounted to other provisions of the TP regulations and other Treasury regulations, and the IRS appealed to the Ninth Circuit Court of Appeals which initially reversed the Tax Court decision in *Altera v. Commissioner.*[25] However, following the death of one of the panel members, the Ninth Circuit withdrew its opinion, convened a new panel, and scheduled a rehearing. In *Altera v. Commissioner,*[26] the Ninth Circuit again reversed the Tax Court, holding the regulations to be valid and consistent with the ALS which, according to the court, is more about reaching a result than applying a particular method.[27] The court further held that the Treasury did not violate the Administrative Procedure Act when promulgating the regulation noting, '[w]hile the rulemaking process was less than ideal, the APA does not require perfection' and they were 'able to discern Treasury's path'.[28] In November 2019, the Ninth Circuit denied a petition to rehear the case *en banc* and, in June 2020, the US Supreme Court denied the taxpayer's petition for a writ of certiorari.

Under US jurisprudence, the Ninth Circuit's decision only binds cases brought within its jurisdiction. This means taxpayers could challenge provisions of the TP regulations in other circuits, hoping that the Tax Court would accord with its earlier reasoning and that, on appeal, a different circuit would not follow the Ninth's reasoning. However, in the face of *Altera*, such future challenges to the regulations seem unlikely.

The TP regulations consist of nine sections plus an outline.[29] They are:

(1) Section 1.482-1 containing general principles and guidelines, many of which were discussed in section 1 above, for determining whether a tested transaction is at arm's length. This includes selecting the best method for analysing the results of a particular transaction and assessing the comparability of untested transactions and taxpayers.
(2) Section 1.482-2 providing rules for determining arm's length interest rates and rental charges.
(3) Sections 1.482-3 identifying the methods that may be used to determine if the prices charged in controlled tangible property transactions produce arm's length results.
(4) Section 1.482-4 containing permissible methods for IP transfers and providing guidance for applying the CWI.
(5) Section 1.482-5 explaining and providing rules for applying the comparable profits method a specified method for tangible, intangible, and services tested transactions.
(6) Section 1.482-6 providing rules for the application of the two profit split methods – the comparable profit split and residual profit split – which, like the

25. Nos 16-70496, 16-70497 (9th Cir. 2018).
26. 926 F.3d 1061 (9th Cir. 2019).
27. 926 F.3d at 1087.
28. *Ibid.*, at 1087.
29. Treas. Reg. § 1.482-0.

comparable profits method, are specified methods for tangible, intangible, and services transactions.

(7) Section 1.482-7 containing rules for qualified CSAs and specified methods for determining the value of pre-existing intangibles contributed to a CSA. Section 1.482-7A contains the previous cost-sharing regulations.

(8) Section 1.482-8 illustrating through examples the application of the best method rule for determining which of the available specified approaches will provide the most reliable result for a particular tested transaction.

(9) Section 1.482-9 identifying and providing rules for applying the specified methods for evaluating whether charges in controlled services transactions are at arm's length.

In 1998, regulations were proposed covering allocations of profit for global dealing transactions;[30] however, those regulations have remained in their proposed form and have not been finalized or issued as temporary regulations.

2.3 Supplemental Guidance

In addition to regulations, the IRS occasionally issues supplemental guidance. This guidance does not bear the same weight of authority as the regulations but often provides valuable insights. It includes revenue procedures for seeking assistance from the IRS, applying for certain programs, or taking certain permissible actions; revenue rulings that analyse situations that may be applicable to multiple taxpayers and explain the IRS's view of the appropriate tax treatment; private letter rulings issued to individual taxpayers; informal internal communications expressing views regarding various tax situations that often explain intent prior to the initiation of a regulation project; and training materials for IRS agents and analysts. Key TP documents include Rev. Proc. 2015-40 that provides guidance for applying for competent authority assistance; Rev. Proc. 2015-41 that governs the APA program; and APMA training materials.

US TP rules and methods are generally consistent with the OECD TPG. Therefore, OECD guidance is often a valuable supplemental source for interpreting key TP concepts. In addition, the US has income tax treaties with many foreign countries. The associated enterprise article requires arm's length dealing between related parties located in the countries. The business profits article generally requires branch allocations of income consistent with what would have occurred had the branch been an unrelated party operating at arm's length. These are valuable tools for use by taxpayers when controversies arise either in the US or the foreign treaty partner (*see* MAP discussion in section 4.4).

30. Prop. Treas. Reg. § 1,482-8.

2.4 Case Law

Most TP adjustments proposed by the IRS are resolved at the audit level through agreements by the taxpayer and IRS agents. If consensus is not achieved, the IRS generally issues a notice of proposed adjustment that allows the taxpayer to reach a resolution through an internal IRS appeals process or, if there is an applicable income tax treaty, through the treaty's MAP. Only a small number of cases remain unresolved following the appeals process and result in court proceedings.

TP cases are typically very fact-intensive and usually focus on the selection of the best method and its application, including the selection of appropriate comparables. Accordingly, decisions in these cases are often of limited precedential value with respect to other taxpayers and other tested transactions. Some cases, however, do establish or give substance to key principles, such as those discussed above in section 1.1 on the definition of control. Recent important cases have included *Altera*, discussed above, and *Amazon*, discussed below in section 4.4.

3 TP METHODS

The regulations contain specified methods for assessing whether the results of three major categories of tested transactions - tangible property, IP, and services - are at arm's length and guidance for analysing controlled loans and leases as well as rules for CSAs. A method other than the specified approaches, i.e., an unspecified method, may be used when it can be shown that it provides the most reliable measure under the best method rule. The specified methods include transactional methods that determine arm's length results by comparing prices charged in tested transactions to those charged in comparable untested transactions and profit-based methods that compare the profits earned by a related party through tested transactions with the profits earned by unrelated parties that engage in similar transactions.

Comparability standards vary for the methods with some requiring close product comparability while others focus more on functional comparability. Close product comparability is particularly important for the CUP and CUT methods whereas close functional comparability is more important for methods such as the RPM and CPM. The comparable profits method and the profit split methods, on the other hand, generally require only broad product and functional comparability.

In selecting and applying a method, a key question is which party to analyse, i.e., which party should be the related party? For methods other than the profit split methods, only the results of the related party are assessed for conformity with the ALS. If the related party's results are at arm's length, all residual profit from the tested transaction flowing to the other party is considered to also be at arm's length. Only the profit split methods consider the profitability of all controlled parties. The selection of the related party in the 'one-sided' methods depends on what is being analysed, the complexity of the controlled parties, and the availability of reliable data.

3.1 Profit-Based Methods

Each of the transactional methods specified in the regulations is linked to a particular category of transactions and generally requires a high degree of comparability, making these methods difficult to apply in many cases. As a result, profit-based methods often prove to be the best. The regulations specify two profit-based methods, each of which may be used to analyse tangible, intangible, or services tested transactions. In the US, a profit-based method proves to be the best method for the vast majority of tested transactions.

3.1.1 Comparable Profits Method

Introduced in the 1994 regulations and similar to the TNMM, the comparable profits method indirectly measures transfer prices by testing the operating profit resulting from tested transactions against the operating profit realized by unrelated parties that perform similar functions. When selecting comparable companies, functional comparability is more important than product comparability. The related party whose operating profits are tested is the party with the most reliable data requiring the fewest adjustments. Typically, this is the least complex party and the one that does not possess any non-routine intangibles.

The comparable profits method is most often used to test routine functions such as distribution and manufacturing. With its emphasis on functional comparability, it can be used when product comparables are not available. Even so, it may be difficult to find close comparables, and reliably applying the method requires adjustments for material differences between the related party and unrelated parties selected as comparables. Differences in functions, assets, and risks that may need to be adjusted include business or product life cycle; resources employed such as property, plant, and equipment; size of the business; asset mix; inventory valuation method; pensions; amortization expenses for intangibles; working capital; and currency risk.

To compare the operating profit of controlled and unrelated parties, a PLI is selected. Typical PLIs include operating margin, return on assets, return on invested capital, the Berry ratio, and markup on total cost; the operating margin is the most commonly used. Applying the method involves developing an arm's length range of PLIs from the financial data of comparable companies and determining whether the PLI for the related party falls within the range. Data for comparable companies are drawn from public financial reports that are accumulated in a database such as Compustat. The comparable profits method is typically the best method when product comparables cannot be found or accounting comparability cannot be assured. It is usually limited to transactions in which one party performs only routine functions.

3.1.2 Profit Split Methods

The profit split method allocates the total profit or loss from a tested transaction between the controlled participants based on their relative contributions to the combined activity. As a specified method for tangible, intangible, and services transactions, its use is typically limited to situations in which two or more controlled parties make non-routine contributions to the combined enterprise and, because of the complexity of the arrangement, other methods cannot reliably be applied. It is most often employed in vertically integrated MNEs when non-routine activities are not isolated in single locations.

There are two profit split methods, i.e., the comparable profit split and the residual profit split. The former is not often used because comparable profit split data is rarely available. The residual profit split first allocates operating profit between the controlled parties based on their routine activities and then allocates the residual profit or loss based on the parties' intangible contributions. Intangible contributions are usually measured by relative R&D expenditures, external benchmarks, or capitalized R&D expenditures.

3.2 Tangible Property

In addition to the profit-based methods, the regulations include three transactional specified methods that may be used for analysing tested transactions involving tangible property: the CUP method, the RPM, and the CPM. These methods generally require a higher degree of comparability than the comparable profits method and are therefore often difficult to apply.

The CUP method compares the prices charged in related party transactions to the prices charged in comparable market-based untested transactions. The method is generally the best approach when close comparable transactions can be identified, and reliable price information for those transactions is available. The major limitation to applying the method is the high degree of comparability required between the controlled and untested transactions. Factors often making it difficult to apply the CUP method include the need for product comparability design; embedded and other intangibles; volume, timing, contract terms, function, and geographic market differences that affect price and are difficult to adjust for; and availability of reliable and complete pricing and related data. Product comparability requires sales occurring under almost the exact same circumstances and no material differences. Direct evidence of prices charged for comparable transactions is generally required.

The CUP method is the easiest to apply when a related party sells or purchases an identical or a similar product to or from both related and unrelated parties. To illustrate, a tested transaction involving the manufacture of a component as an input to an assembly process with the sale of the finished product to unrelated customers will be used as an example. The CUP method may be applied if the controlled component manufacturer supplies a similar component to an unrelated customer. It can also be employed if the controlled assembler purchases similar components from an unrelated supplier. However, this is only if any material differences can reliably be adjusted for or the conditions of sale or purchase are similar. In either case, there would be reliable data at an arm's length price for the component.

The RPM looks at the gross profit margin earned in untested transactions to determine an arm's length transfer price. It does not require as close product comparability as the CUP method; instead, the emphasis is on functional comparability, i.e., ensuring that the functions being compensated are similar in the controlled and untested transactions.

The gross profit margin from untested transactions as a percentage of sales is subtracted from the resale price to arrive at the transfer price. General industry data may be used if transactional comparables are not available. Adjustments must be made for functional differences such as advertising undertaken, warranties provided, product liability risks assumed, inventory levels and risks, scale of operations, terms of sale, accounting conventions, services provided, credit arrangements, and embedded intangibles included in the products sold. The RPM typically is used when a distributor purchases products from both related and unrelated party manufacturers and resells them to unrelated parties without adding value.

The CPM compares the gross profit markup on a tested transaction to the markup realized by unrelated parties performing similar functions and bearing similar risks under corresponding contractual terms. It is most often used for a routine manufacturer that sells goods to both related and unrelated party distributors. The manufacturer need not supply identical products to both related and unrelated customers. Instead, the key is that the functions performed are comparable and any material differences can be reliably adjusted for or the sales terms are much the same.

Prices are based on gross profit markup on fully absorbed costs earned by functionally comparable companies. The comparables must be similar in terms of functions performed, risks borne, intangibles possessed, production processes used, and cost structure. Any material differences in accounting conventions between the related party and comparable companies must be capable of reliable adjustment. General industry gross profit markups may be used absent comparable transactional data. Gross profit data is typically difficult to obtain for non-US based companies. When applied to a routine manufacturer, the manufacturer receives the arm's length return expressed as a percentage of costs, and the related party distributor bears market and business risks associated with the sale of the product to unrelated customers.

3.3 Intangible Property

An enterprise's non-routine returns are generally attributable to the non-routine intangibles it possesses. Accordingly, IP transfers comprise the most complex and contentious area of TP with potentially substantial differences in taxpayer and IRS views of the value of the IP and which jurisdiction is entitled to the non-routine returns.[31] Unlike tangible property transactions that generally require physical property or services that usually require people in place, intangibles are highly mobile and

31. For example, in the case of *Coca-Cola v. Commissioner*, TC No. 31183-15, the IRS increased royalties due to Coca-Cola from foreign bottling subsidiaries by nearly USD 10 billion for its 2007 through 2009 taxable years. In this case, the IRS and Coca-Cola had entered into a closing agreement setting royalty rates for earlier years, and Coca-Cola had continued to apply those

can be placed in any jurisdiction through a paper transfer. In 1986, section 482 was amended to add the CWI standard allowing the IRS to take a backward look at the value of a controlled intangible transaction and make periodic adjustments to the allocation of income generated by the use of the intangible.

Section 1.482-4(b) of the regulations defines an intangible as an asset that comprises any of the following items and has substantial value independent of the services of any individual:

- patents, inventions, formulae, processes, designs, know-how;
- copyrights and compositions;
- trademarks, trade names, or brand names;
- franchises, licenses, or contracts;
- methods, programs, systems, procedures, campaigns, surveys, studies, forecasts, estimates, customer lists; or technical data; and
- other similar items that derive value not from physical attributes but from intellectual content or other IP.

The IRS has long interpreted this definition as broad enough to encompass items such as goodwill and workforce in place even though those items are not mentioned in the regulation or in the section 936(h)(3)(B) definition referenced in section 482 prior to the amendment by the TCJA. Any questions of whether such intangibles are subject to section 482 should now be completely answered with the TCJA amendments that define intangibles for section 482 purposes by reference to section 367(d)(4). This now explicitly includes goodwill, going concern value, and workforce in place (including its composition and terms and conditions (contractual or otherwise) of its employment) in the definition of IP.

Factors that make a TP analysis of controlled IP transfers difficult include: the unique nature of many of the intangibles transferred, the fact that many types of intangibles are rarely transferred to unrelated parties, the appropriateness of valuation versus pricing methods, and differences in terms and conditions under which intangibles are transferred to related versus unrelated parties, including bargaining asymmetries, for which adjustments may be difficult. An intangible transferred to a related party may bring with it a business opportunity that would not be transferred to an unrelated party barring a sale of the associated business. Intangibles are often transferred in conjunction with other tested transactions; they may be embedded in tangible property or

rates. The IRS asserted that it is not bound by the closing agreement and its acceptance of the use of the agreed rates in a subsequent audit cycle and performed a new comparable profits method analysis supporting its adjustments. In November 2020, the Tax Court found that the IRS did not act arbitrarily or capriciously in reallocating the royalties and upheld the IRS's massive adjustment, which resulted in additional tax of over USD 3 billion. According to the Tax Court, '[w]here controlled transactions implicate high-value intangibles, therefore, the most reliable transfer pricing method is often one that avoids any direct valuation of those intangibles' and the facts in this case were particularly susceptible to an application of the comparable profits method (155 T.C. 145 (2020)). The Tax Court denied Coca-Cola's motion for reconsideration. Nevertheless, the dispute continues on as Coca-Cola has indicated that it plans to appeal.

associated with the performance of services. When this occurs, the intangible that is transferred must usually be analysed separately from the primary tested transaction,[32]

The only specified method for controlled intangible transactions, other than the profit-based methods, is the CUT method. Similar to the CUP method, it compares the amount charged in a controlled transfer to the amounts charged in similar unrelated party transfers. Like the CUP method, it provides a direct measure of an arm's length price and is generally the best method when it can be reliably applied. Unfortunately, it is even more difficult to find a dependable CUT than definitive CUPs. The method is most applicable when the same or a similar intangible is transferred in almost the exact same circumstances to controlled and unrelated parties.

The regulations do permit the use of 'comparable intangibles' when applying the CUT method which are intangibles related to a similar product or process in the same market and industry and that have corresponding profit potential.[33] Profit potential is generally measured by the net present value of the expected future returns from the exploitation of the intangible. This calculation is highly dependent on assumptions and the need to isolate returns to the intangible from returns to other assets and functions. A residual approach is often required under which returns to routine functions and assets are isolated, and the remaining returns are assumed to be from the transferred intangible.

Section 1.482-4(c)(2)(iii)(B)(2) of the regulations lists comparability factors for selecting CUTs. They include: terms of transfer (exclusivity, use restrictions), update rights, uniqueness of intangibles, contract duration, economic and product liability risk, collateral transactions, functions undertaken by each party, and completeness and accuracy of data.

The difficulties in reliably applying the CUT method as well as those associated with using the comparable profits method and profit split methods with respect to intangibles often result in an unspecified method, such as the income method or discounted cash flow that values the intangible rather than pricing the transfer, being the best method for evaluating controlled intangible transactions. Taxpayers often use a guidepost that the transferee must receive 65%-75% of the profits from the intangible in order to be incentivized to maximize its use. The IRS tends to reject this approach.

An unspecified method for evaluating the arm's length nature of an intangible transfer may include the consideration of realistic alternatives available to the transferor. For example, whether a royalty charged by a related party to license product intangibles that will be used to produce and sell a product is at arm's length may be evaluated by comparing the return to the licensor to what it could have earned had it manufactured and sold the product itself.[34]

32. *See* Treas. Reg. § 1.482-3(f).
33. *See* Treas. Reg. § 1.482-4(c)(iii)(2)(B)(1).
34. *See* example in Treas. Reg. § 1.482-4(d)(2).

3.4 Cost-Sharing Arrangements

A CSA is a means for controlled parties to share in the development of intangibles and gain access to those intangibles without having to concern themselves with future payments of arm's length compensation for use of the intangibles. Under a CSA, each participant bears a portion of the costs and risks of development equal to its share of RAB from the exploitation of the intangibles. A CSA is similar to a CCA under the OECD TPG except that it is limited to intangibles whereas a CCA may also be used for tangibles or services. The service regulations provide for SSAs that have some similarities to CSAs. Additionally, the requirements for qualifying for a CSA are much more developed and complicated. Its key feature is that participants gain access to the subject intangibles by sharing in costs without markup as would be required if they contracted for development services.

When Congress added CWI to section 482 in 1986, it noted in the legislative history that it did not intend to preclude taxpayers from entering into CSAs by doing so. In 1995, the Treasury and the IRS finalized cost-sharing regulations that provided requirements for an agreement to qualify as a CSA and rules for sharing costs. The regulations also provided for buy-in payments under which a participant making pre-existing intangibles available to the CSA would be compensated by other participants because an intangibles development activity often builds on previous development activities. These buy-in payments were required to be at arm's length, however, the regulations did not include methods for making that determination. Instead, they relied on the general IP TP rules.

As companies adopted CSAs, two key issues soon emerged: the value of pre-existing intangibles and corresponding required buy-in payments and the definition of costs, specifically, whether stock-based compensation should be included in the costs to be shared. The former issue led to a significant amount of controversy and eventually new regulations and a legislative initiative. Most of those disputes were resolved through the IRS appeals process, but two cases were brought before the Tax Court under the 1995 regulations, resulting in decisions in favour of the taxpayer (*Verita*[35] and *Amazon*). On the cost-sharing issue, two cases also made it to the Tax Court – *Xilinx*,[36]

35. *Veritas v. Commissioner*, 133 T.C. 297 (2009). The case involved the buy-in for a storage software CSA with an Irish subsidiary. The taxpayer used a standard declining royalty licence over a four-year period while the IRS applied the income method assuming a perpetual life for the pre-existing intangibles. The taxpayer's valuation was based on royalties for the right to produce or sell software versus the intangibles. The Tax Court rejected the IRS method and determined that the buy-in for intangibles was to be valued at the time the CSA was entered into and not based on future value, and a four-year rather than perpetual useful life was appropriate for valuing the pre-existing intangibles.
36. *Xilinx v. Commissioner*, 105 AFTR 2d 2010-1490 (2010). The issue in the case was whether an employee stock option expense should be included as part of the costs to be shared under a CSA. The applicable 1995 regulations were silent on the matter but did require that 'all costs' be shared. The case revolved around an apparent inconsistency between this requirement in the cost-sharing regulations and the Treas. Reg. § 1.482-1 general requirement that the ALS requires testing against what unrelated parties would do. The Tax Court held for the taxpayer. The Ninth Circuit initially reversed, but then reversed itself after *amici* briefs argued persuasively that resolving the inconsistency in favour of the cost-sharing regulations would undermine the ALS.

a win for the taxpayer, and *Altera*, a challenge to the validity of the regulations added in 2003 to provide that stock option costs must be included in costs to be shared, in which the IRS was eventually successful.

Court Case

In the case *Amazon.com v. Commissioner*,[37] the issue, as in *Veritas*, was the buy-in payment for pre-existing intangibles contributed to a CSA under the 1995 cost-sharing regulations. The CSA was with Amazon's Irish subsidiary, and the IRS asserted more than a USD 3 billion adjustment based on its application of a DCF method. Under the DCF, the IRS valued Amazon's entire European business, factored out the value of routine assets, and treated the entire residual value as the value of the pre-existing intangibles. The Tax Court rejected this method and instead agreed with Amazon that the best method for valuing the intangibles was the CUT method because the intangibles could be isolated and valued separately. Moreover, although the regulations permit an aggregate analysis, the residual approach used by the IRS captured the value of intangibles not included in the then applicable definition of intangibles for section 482 purposes, such as goodwill and going concern.

The Ninth Circuit affirmed, holding that residual business assets are not the same as intangibles as defined in the other applicable statute. The case is an important example of the application of the best method rule in the context of intangible transfers and how to interpret key aspects of the regulations. It may be of limited practical impact, though, for two reasons. First, it involved the 1995 cost-sharing regulations which have since been revised with much more stringent requirements for valuing pre-existing intangibles. Second, the TCJA amendments to section 482 codified the aggregate and realistic alternative aspects of the regulations that were rejected by the courts.

Owing to the substantial controversies surrounding CSAs under the 1995 regulations, on the last day of 2008, the Treasury and the IRS issued new temporary and proposed cost-sharing regulations. In 2011, those regulations were finalized. Under the new regulations, to qualify as a CSA, the arrangement must be contemporaneously recorded in a written agreement that contains specific provisions such as duration, identity of the intangibles to be developed, and the method for calculating the RAB shares of participants with an adjustment mechanism.

The regulations contain a host of administrative requirements for a CSA to be bona fide. When this occurs and it has economic substance, IRS adjustments are limited to the intangible development cost pool, RAB share computations, and the determination of buy-in payments. The IRS may review CSTs that cross payments by the participants so that each ends up bearing its appropriate share of total intangible development costs and platform contribution transactions (PCTs) that involve compensating participants

37. *Amazon.com v. Commissioner*, 148 T.C. 108 (2017), *aff'd* 934 F.3d 976 (9th Cir. 2019).

that provide pre-existing intangibles for use in the CSA. CSTs are fairly straightforward, however, PCTs can present difficult valuation issues. Therefore, the regulations incorporate specified methods that must be used for PCTs.

A platform contribution is 'any resource, capacity, or right ... reasonably anticipated to contribute to developing CSA intangibles'.[38] A platform contribution is presumed to be exclusive to the CSA, although this presumption can be rebutted, and failure to account for platform contributions can result in the loss of CSA status. Platform rights are viewed as perpetual and separate form making or selling rights. Section 1.482-7(g) of the regulations provides the specified methods for valuing platform contributions. They are the CUT method, the income method, the acquisition price method, the market capitalization method, and the residual profit split method; as for other tested transactions, unspecified methods may be used if they provide the most reliable result. The core principle of a platform contribution valuation is the investor model which is essentially a realistic alternative concept; an investor would not make an investment that is less advantageous than its realistic investment alternatives. That is, the participant making a platform contribution always has the option of retaining the asset and using it to develop intangibles that it could then license to other participants. Accordingly, the participant should not be in a less advantageous state by entering into the CSA than it would have been under the sole development and licensing alternative.

The CUT method is the same method specified in section 1.482-4 of the regulations but is even more difficult to apply in the CSA context because comparables are rare and licences to make or sell rights are not considered comparable to licences of platform rights by the IRS. The income method is essentially the investor model approach. It compares the net present value of a participant from participating in the CSA to the net present value of its alternative to participating in the CSA. The amount charged for a PCT is at arm's length when the two values are equal. In general, the best alternative for a payor of a PCT is to licence the intangibles to be developed under the CSA from an uncontrolled licensor that undertakes the commitment to bear the entire risk of intangible development that would otherwise have been shared under the CSA. The best realistic alternative for a payee of a PCT, i.e., a participant making a platform contribution, is to bear the entire risk of developing the intangibles and subsequently licence the intangibles to uncontrolled licensees.

The income method is generally applicable only if there is only one platform contributor. If there are multiple contributors, the residual profit split method is used. Inputs used to calculate the present values, such as discount factors, may have their own arm's length ranges. Accordingly, the regulations acknowledge that the application of the income methods may result in a range of arm's length PCTs.

The acquisition price method evaluates the arm's length price for a PCT by reference to the stock or asset acquisition price of an entire organization (or a portion thereof) in an untested transaction. The method may be used when a substantial amount of all of an acquired company's non-routine intangibles are contributed to the CSA. The arm's length price is equal to the adjusted acquisition price as divided among the controlled

38. Treas. Reg. § 1.482-7(c).

participants based on their RAB shares. The adjusted acquisition price is the acquisition price plus liabilities assumed and less the value of any tangible property and rights, resources, and capabilities not covered by the platform contribution.

The market capitalization evaluates the arm's length price by reference to the average market capitalization of a controlled participant making a platform contribution for which stock is regularly traded on an established securities market. The adjusted average market capitalization is an average daily value measured over a sixty-day period increased by liabilities assumed and decreased by resources, capabilities, or rights not covered by the platform contribution. The arm's length price for the PCT is the adjusted average market capitalization apportioned among PCT layers in accordance with their RAB shares.

The residual profit split is potentially applicable when there is more than one platform contributor. Residual profit is the present value of expected profits from the exploitation of the intangibles to be developed under the CSA decreased by market returns for routine contributions, decreased by operating cost contributions, and decreased by cost contributions. That arm's length measure of the value of all platform contributions is then divided among the platform contributors based on their relative contributions, and PCTs are then determined for PCT payers according to their RAB shares.

It is doubtful that the new cost-sharing regulations will bring an end to CSA-related disputes between taxpayers and the IRS. In fact, the first post-1995 regulation buy-in case is now working its way through the US Tax Court.[39]

3.5 Services

In 2009, the Treasury and the IRS finalized new regulations that specify TP methods for use with controlled services transactions. A service is subject to regulations when it results in an identifiable increment of economic or commercial value, and the recipient of the service would be willing to pay for that increment at arm's length. The specified methods for analysing such transactions are the SCM which permits certain controlled services to be charged at cost, and several methods approximately analogous to the tangible property methods to be used when the SCM does not apply. These other methods include the two profit-based methods – the comparable profits method and profit splits – along with the comparable uncontrolled services price, the gross services margin, and the cost of services plus methods. As for other tested transactions, the regulations also permit the use of an unspecified method if it will provide the most reliable result.

In general, a service is subject to regulations if it provides a commercial benefit to the recipient of the service. Certain activities performed by a parent company, such as

39. *Facebook v. Commissioner*, TC No. 21959-16. The case involves the temporary cost-sharing regulations. The notice of deficiency includes an adjustment to the value of the pre-existing intangibles and the determination of RAB shares expected to inure to Facebook's domestic and foreign operations which is relevant to the division of intangible development costs and the buy-in issue.

stewardship, are excluded because they are conducted for the benefit of the provider or are considered to remotely benefit the recipient. Similarly, a service that duplicates what a related party does for itself is not included because the recipient would not pay for such a service at arm's length. It is common for controlled services transactions to occur in conjunction with transfers of tangible or IP, and the application of the services regulations may require coordination with the rules for those transactions and isolation of the services transaction and its associated costs which often require the use of allocation techniques.

The SCM is an elective method under which the service provider may charge based on the total costs of providing the service without markup. Only certain services are eligible for it, i.e., those listed in Rev. Proc. 2007-13 and other low margin services which are services with a median markup based on an arm's length interquartile range of 7% or less. Categories of eligible services include payroll; unemployment, disability, and workers compensation; accounts receivable; accounts payable; general administrative; corporate and public relations; meeting coordination and travel planning; accounting and auditing; taxes; and purchasing.

The SCM may not be applied to manufacturing, production, extraction, construction, distribution, R&D, engineering, guarantees, insurance, or any other service even if listed in Rev. Proc. 2007-13 for which the taxpayer 'reasonably concludes in its business judgment that the service does not contribute significantly to key competitive advantages, core capabilities, or fundamental risks of success or failure in one or more trades or businesses of the controlled group'.[40] This business judgment rule is applied based on all of the facts and circumstances, and the judgment of the taxpayer may be challenged by the IRS on audit. In addition, certain documentation requirements must be met before a service can qualify as an SCM-covered service.

If a service satisfies the business judgment rule and the taxpayer elects to use the SCM, the IRS is limited on audit to reviewing and adjusting the associated 'total services costs' as that term is defined in section 1.482-9(j) of the regulations. If a taxpayer decides it does not want to use the SCM, the taxpayer must determine the best method for determining the arm's length price from among the other available services methods. The taxpayer may change the elections to use the SCM with respect to a particular eligible service from year-to-year without IRS approval and may use the method for some eligible services and not for others. For example, a taxpayer could pay an arm's length price on an eligible service provided to it by its foreign subsidiaries while charging its foreign subsidiaries the cost for a similar service provided to it by its foreign subsidiaries.

The services regulations provide for an SSA which is similar to a CSA. However, although included in the section of the regulations dealing with the SCM, it is clear that the SSAs are not restricted to SCM-eligible services. When used for a service not eligible for the SCM, an SSA will be required to incorporate arm's length charges, unlike a CSA that provides for sharing of costs without markup. An SSA requires two or more participants and must include all taxpayers that reasonably anticipate a benefit from

40. Treas. Reg. § 1.482-9(b)(5).

one or more services covered by the SSA. Each shared service must confer a benefit on at least one participant and adequate contemporaneous documentation must be maintained.

The three transactional service methods that may be used when SCM does not apply are similar to their tangible property counterparts. The comparable uncontrolled services price and the cost of services plus methods are applied in the same manner as the CUP and CPM, respectively. The gross services margin method is analogous to the RPM. It evaluates whether the amount charged in a controlled services transaction is at arm's length by reference to the gross profit margin realized in comparable untested transactions. The method may be used when a controlled taxpayer performs services for another member of the controlled group in connection with that other member's transactions with uncontrolled taxpayers. It may also be employed when a related party conducts a portion of a service performed by the controlled group for unrelated parties.

3.6 Loans and Leases

The regulations include rules for determining an arm's length interest charge. The rules include a safe harbour under which eligible loans may bear interest at a rate between 100% and 130% of the appropriate applicable federal rate based on the term of the loan. For loans not eligible for the safe harbour rules, benchmarking based on the credit rating of the borrower and the maturity of the loan generally is used.

The regulations also include guidance for determining arm's length rents. Section 1.482-2(c)(2)(i) of the regulations provides that:

> an arm's length rental charge shall be the amount of rent which was charged, or would have been charged for the use of the same or similar property, during the time it was in use, in independent transactions with or between unrelated parties under similar circumstances considering the period and location of the use, the owner's investment in the property or rent paid for the property, expenses of maintaining the property, the type of property involved, its condition, and all other relevant facts.

Accordingly, establishing arm's length rent generally requires identifying closely comparable lease agreements between unrelated parties for the use of similar property.

4 COMPLIANCE

Taxpayers that fail to report income on their US returns that reflects arm's length dealings with related parties may be subject to substantial penalties. Corporate taxpayers with assets exceeding USD 10 million must include Schedule UTPs with their return on which they list tax positions for which a reserve was taken on audited financials or a reserve that was not utilized because of an intent to litigate the issue. UTP issues often include TP positions. Taxpayers are not required to submit TP studies with their returns, however, the preparation of contemporaneous TPD is the only way to avoid TP penalties.

Many large taxpayers are under continual audit, i.e., every tax year is reviewed by an IRS audit team. Other taxpayers may go many years between audits. At the beginning of an audit, the initial information document request submitted by the IRS is usually for the taxpayer's TPD. The audit team may include IRS economists and counsel in addition to international examiners. For high-value TP cases involving difficult issues, outside economists may sometimes be added. TP examinations generally fall within the purview of the Treaty and TP office within the IRS Large Business & International Division, and audit teams may be supplemented by TTPO personnel. The settlement of a case sometimes requires a taxpayer to enter into an APA or competent authority deliberations under a treaty; in those circumstances, personnel from the APMA within TTPO will also be involved.

4.1 TP Adjustments

At the conclusion of an audit, the IRS may propose TP adjustments that may include primary adjustments and conforming adjustments. A primary adjustment is an increase in revenue or decrease in deductions on account of allocations required to conform the results of the taxpayer under review in a tested transaction to an arm's length result. A conforming adjustment is an adjustment necessary to conform accounts, consistent with the primary adjustment, to explain how cash that would have been granted to one entity had a transaction been conducted at arm's length is now possessed by a different entity. Conforming adjustments generally involve deemed dividends or capital contributions which can create additional tax consequences. However, for certain situations, the IRS has procedures for making conforming adjustments without the deemed payment of dividends or capital contributions. Under Rev. Proc. 99-32, a taxpayer may establish an account receivable or account payable for the amount of the secondary adjustment.

A US primary adjustment implies an offsetting correlative adjustment in the jurisdiction of the controlled counterparty. If that correlative adjustment is to a related party in a foreign jurisdiction, its allowance for foreign purposes is a matter for the foreign government to decide. If the US has a tax treaty with a foreign jurisdiction, the taxpayer may request competent authority assistance under the treaty MAPs to avoid paying double tax. A TP adjustment can also have customs impacts and state tax effects.[41]

When the IRS enforces section 482, the taxpayer may, in certain circumstances, claim a set-off against the allocation. Under section 1.482-1(g)(4) of the regulations, a set-off will be allowed for other non-arm's length transactions between the same controlled parties in the same year provided that the taxpayer (a) establishes that the transaction that is the basis of the set-off was not at arm's length and the amount of the appropriate arm's length charge; (b) documents all correlative adjustments resulting from the proposed set-off; and (c) notifies the IRS of the basis of any claimed set-off within thirty days after the IRS formally notifies the taxpayer of the proposed

41. *See* section 1059A.

adjustment either through the transmission of an examination report or a notice of deficiency.

TP adjustments for controlled tangible property and services transactions are straightforward involving an allocation of income or deductions for the year under review. IP adjustments, on the other hand, may be complicated by an application of the CWI standard that permits backward-looking adjustments based on income realized from exploitation of the transferred IP. The CWI requires that the profit actually realized from the use of the intangibles be considered when determining whether the transfer was priced at arm's length.

The CWI essentially means that, if the results over time from exploitation of an intangible are inconsistent with the projected results used in setting the transfer price for the intangible, the transfer price was presumptively not at arm's length, and adjustments must be made to reflect the differences between the projected and actual results. These backward-looking adjustments are referred to as 'periodic adjustments' and may only be made by the IRS; taxpayers may not adjust for results that turn out to be less favourable than expected. This disparity is considered fair by the IRS because of information asymmetries. Moreover, taxpayers may include forward-looking contingent adjustments in their intangible transfer agreements. They can rebut periodic adjustments by showing their original assumptions were valid based on the available information at the time of the transfer.

Guidance for determining periodic adjustments is in section 1.482-4(f)(2) of the regulations. The rules apply to intangibles that are transferred for use over a period greater than one year. Whether periodic adjustments are warranted because the income earned from exploiting an intangible is inconsistent with projections is based on all of the facts and circumstances over the entire period of use. A determination in one year that the amount charged for the transfer was at arm's length does not preclude adjustments in later years nor does the expiration of the statute of limitation on adjustments for the year of transfer.

Compensation for intangible transfers typically takes the form of periodic royalty payments for which case periodic adjustments are based on a comparison of royalties paid under the transfer agreement and royalties that would have been paid at arm's length. If the intangible is transferred for a lump sum or there is an upfront payment in addition to periodic royalties, it is necessary to convert that lump sum to a series of equivalent royalties over the period of use of the intangible. Those equivalent payments are then compared to arm's length royalties to determine whether periodic adjustments are required. The conversion occurs through a present value analysis based on the amount of the lump sum payment, an appropriate discount rate, and projected sales over the term of the transferred intangible's use.[42]

There are several exceptions to the IRS's ability to make periodic adjustments. They are:

42. *See* Treas. Reg. § 1.482-4(f)(6).

(1) Transactions involving the same intangible. If the same intangible was transferred to an uncontrolled taxpayer under almost the same exact circumstances and the uncontrolled CUT was used to set compensation for the first year for which a substantial periodic adjustment would otherwise be required, no allocation will be made.
(2) Written agreement and results within range. The regulations include two exceptions, one for when the CUT method was used and the other for when a different method was used to set the transfer price. In general, both require the transfer to be covered by a written agreement, that there has been no substantial change in the functions performed by the transferee, the consideration in the first year for which substantial consideration was required was arm's length, and profit actually realized or costs saved in the examination year and all past years in the aggregate are not less than 80% or more than 120% of the projections at the outset. The requirements for the content of the written controlled agreement are more stringent if the CUT method was used to determine the transfer price.
(3) Extraordinary events. No allocations will be made if the taxpayer can demonstrate that differences between projected and actual results were due to extraordinary events that could not reasonably have been foreseen, and the written agreement and requirements for the written agreement exceptions are otherwise met.
(4) Five-year period. If the taxpayer meets the requirements of either of the written agreement exceptions for a period of five years beginning in the first taxable year in which consideration was required to be paid, no subsequent allocation will be made.

The cost-sharing regulations include a periodic adjustment provision for PCT payments.[43] The IRS may make adjustments in open tax years and any subsequent tax years if the AERR is outside the PRRR. The AERR is the ratio of the present value of total profit divided by the present value of investment for which investment is the value of cost contributions and PCT payments. The PRRR range is 0.667-1.5 unless the taxpayer has failed to comply with the documentation requirements, in which case the range diminishes to 0.8-1.25. If the AERR is outside the range, the PCT payment is adjusted.

4.2 Penalties and Documentation

When a TP adjustment results in an increase in income tax liability, an additional penalty may apply. Section 6662(e) valuation misstatement penalties are imposed if the net TP adjustment exceeds the lower of USD 5 million or 10% of a taxpayer's gross receipts. In general, section 6662 penalties can be avoided for a reasonable cause but, in the case of the TP penalty, the only acceptable reasonable cause is to have contemporaneous TPD. A TP adjustment is excluded from the pool of TP adjustments

43. Treas. Reg. § 1.482-7(i)(6).

subject to penalty if (1) it is established that prices were set in accordance with a specific method set forth in the section 482 regulations, (2) the taxpayer has documentation that was in existence at the time the return was filed, sets forth the determination of the price in accordance with a described method, and establishes that the use of the method was reasonable, and (3) the taxpayer provides the documentation within thirty days of an IRS request for it.[44]

The contemporaneous documentation required to avoid TP penalties is similar to an OECD master file and includes ten principal documents plus background documents. The principal documents are:

- overview of taxpayer's business;
- description of organizational structure;
- documentation explicitly required under section 482 (such as licence agreements);
- description of the method selected and reason for selection;
- description of alternative methods not used and reason for not using them;
- description of tested transactions and internal data;
- description of comparables and adjustments (if any);
- explanation of economic analysis and projections used;
- description of data obtained after tax year and before filing return; and
- general index of documents.

The principal documents usually are packaged as a TP study and are often prepared by an outside advisor.

4.3 Advance Pricing Agreements

In the early 1990s, the IRS initiated an APA program as a means to settle TP issues in advance, eliminating the need for often lengthy and contentious TP audits. Since then, over 2,600 APA requests have been filed with more than 121 in 2019. The process to negotiate and finalize an APA can take years but, eventually, a successful APA can have significant taxpayer and IRS benefits.

An APA is a binding written agreement[45] between the taxpayer and the IRS that identifies the covered tested transactions, the TP method to be used for each such transaction. It also ascertains the target results and testing mechanisms; the term; critical assumptions that, if violated, could require an adjustment to the APA or release the IRS or the taxpayer from the agreement; and annual report requirements to demonstrate compliance with the agreement. An APA may be unilateral between the

44. Section 6662(e)(3)(B).
45. Taxpayers generally view an APA as a contract, but in *Eaton Corporation and Subsidiaries v. Commissioner*, 140 T.C. 410 (2013), the Tax Court determined that an APA is an administrative determination by the IRS rather than a contract. As a result, the IRS is entitled to great deference, subject to an abuse of discretion standard, in administering the APA. In subsequent litigation, the Tax Court held that the IRS's cancellation of Eaton's APAs was arbitrary and capricious. *Eaton Corporation and Subs. v. Commissioner*, TC Memo 2017-147.

IRS and taxpayer with no involvement of a foreign jurisdiction, bilateral (agreement between the IRS and a foreign treaty partner in addition to the agreement between the IRS and taxpayer), or multilateral (separate agreements between the IRS and more than one treaty partner). Current rules for requesting and administering APAs appear in Rev. Proc. 2015-41. If a taxpayer complies with the terms of the APA, the IRS will treat the covered transactions as satisfying the ALS.

4.4 Controversy

The IRS generally has three years to audit a taxpayer's return and propose adjustments. All returns of very large taxpayers are subject to audit, usually on a three-year cycle, however, smaller taxpayers may go many years between audits. If the IRS identifies a TP issue during an audit, it will typically collect relevant information through information document requests and, very often, reach a resolution with the taxpayer during the audit. If it does not, the IRS will issue a notice of proposed adjustment that enables the taxpayer to access the IRS appeals process to resolve the issue or, in some cases, a notice of deficiency that requires the taxpayer to appear before the court if it objects. The IRS Appeals is an independent body within the IRS that attempts to resolve disputes, often on the basis of hazards of litigation.

A TP adjustment in the US means there should be a correlative offsetting adjustment in the jurisdiction of the foreign counterparty. If there is an income tax treaty between the US and a foreign jurisdiction, the taxpayer may, in addition to or as a substitute for IRS Appeals, seek resolution through the competent authority process. Bilateral income tax treaties allocate taxing jurisdiction thereby avoiding the imposition of double tax on items of income. Key provisions for TP purposes are the related party and the MAP articles. The related party article establishes the arm's length principle. The MAP article allows 'competent authorities' to endeavour to resolve cases of taxation not in accordance with the treaty, e.g., a double taxation that results from a primary TP adjustment without a corresponding correlative adjustment.

Revenue Procedure 2015-40 governs US requests for competent authority assistance. This request may be filed at any time once an adjustment can be quantified. If a taxpayer resolves its US TP adjustments by written agreement (an Appeals Form 870AD or a closing agreement), the US competent authority will only negotiate for a correlative adjustment in the foreign jurisdiction; it will not compromise the agreed-to US adjustment.

Competent authority requests are filed in both jurisdictions, and the two governments subsequently enter into negotiations. The process can be lengthy with no guarantee that the two governments will achieve consensus. Any inter-governmental agreement reached is non-binding on the taxpayer. Several US treaties now provide for binding 'baseball' arbitration after a two-year stalemate (Belgium, Canada, France, Germany, Japan, Spain, and Switzerland).

5 CONCLUSIONS

The US has a comprehensive set of rules that are generally consistent with the OECD TPG but more detailed and prescriptive for ensuring that transactions between controlled parties are conducted at arm's length. Determining arm's length prices, though, is highly dependent on facts and circumstances. Controversies between the IRS and taxpayers are common, particularly in the areas of intangible transfers and CSAs. Recent court cases have established important principles, however, issues remain, including the limits of IRS regulations, interpretation of the 2011 cost-sharing regulations, the meaning of arm's length and the role of actual dealings between unrelated parties, the role of economic substance and realistic alternatives in selecting and applying TP methods, the appropriate use of an aggregate analysis, and the application of the services regulations.

New Technologies

CHAPTER 27

Use of New Technologies in Transfer Pricing by Taxpayers

Dorottya Kovács

1 INTRODUCTION

For a long time already, TP has been a focus area for (tax) technology. As an interdisciplinary field, TP has gained importance not only from a corporate income tax perspective but also impacted numerous other tax areas such as VAT and customs. In addition, from a MNE's perspective, TP functions are often shared among many departments such as tax, controlling, finance, treasury and supply chain, with decisions, tasks, and impact often spread along the global value chains. This has led to some aspects of TP being automated either as part of tax functions or part of an MNE's overall IT concept while other areas are still subject to quite manual processes. In all areas, technological developments promise new solutions to further support the TP function. This article aims to shed light on current available technology to support different fields of TP as well as associated challenges and to provide an outlook on future potential use cases.

Several factors have increased the focus on technological solutions. TP is subject to various expanding regulations, increasing compliance requirements, as well as an expanded focus on audits by tax authorities in many jurisdictions around the globe, with tax authorities more and more looking into the use of the technologies themselves. In addition, due to evolving globalization, the complexity of cross-border transactions is becoming more elaborate, leading to raised expectations on having an efficient and structured TP role from within an MNE. Furthermore, new technological developments influence global business models in core digital businesses and also allow for more possibilities to support the TP function in the future. These global changes intensively affect multinational companies which are therefore looking for effective solutions. Technology-based disentanglements can help overcome difficulties, and these solutions have growing popularity. This chapter provides theoretical and practical guidance on how the application of technologies can help companies in TP.

The purpose of this chapter is to give a general overview of the available technologies to support TP compliance for multinational companies and also highlight the possible challenges that multinationals need to take into account when implementing a technology-based solution to simplify their TP processes. Thereby, section 2 provides an introduction to intelligent automation relevant for TP with a focus on the most recent developments in this field. Section 3 presents the use of technologies in TP. It describes the drivers for the use of technologies and highlights the main factors that MNEs need to consider before using a TP software. The life cycle of TP is also described by linking the processes in TP and the parts that can be simplified with the usage of technologies. Examples of TP technologies are examined in this part as well. Section 4 discusses the limitation of technologies that pose challenges to the effective conduct of technology implementation. Section 5 provides an outlook of the future issues and developments in the discussed areas. The conclusions and remarks are summed up in the final section.

2 INTELLIGENT AUTOMATION

2.1 Technological Development

The status of digitalization is different in every company; therefore, the degree of maturity of the intelligent automation of tasks moves on a range with increasing complexity from simple process automation through the use of bots and advanced process automation to cognitive automation using AI (*see* Figure 27.1).

Figure 27.1 Different Stages and Processes of Automation

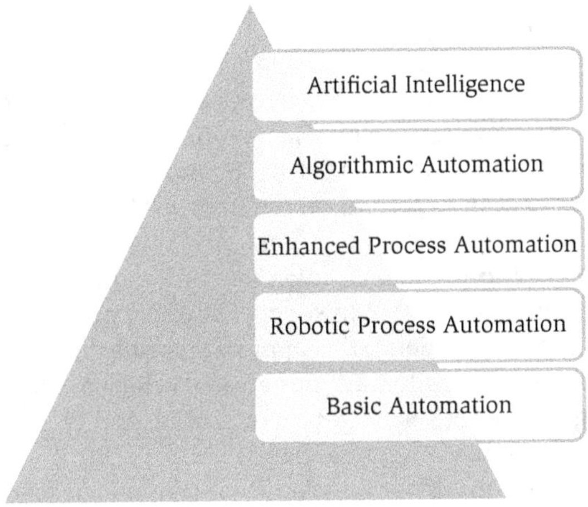

The current basic requirement for the intelligent automation of tasks is the implementation of clearly defined, standardized processes. In the context of simple process automation (also referred to as RPA), bots are a useful solution for automating highly standardized and repetitive tasks. The area of advanced process automation includes tools and methods for the collection and intelligent analysis of data. The term 'artificial intelligence' (AI) is used as a generic term for technologies that include machine learning. With the help of machine learning methods, algorithms based on historical data are trained to predict certain target variables, or they search independently for regularities in large amounts of data. These types of machine learning are also referred to as supervised or unsupervised learning. Finally, cognitive automation is at the other end of the complexity scale and sometimes requires significant investments in terms of time and budget. The aim here is to put an algorithm in a certain field of knowledge in a state from which it can continue to learn independently and is able to solve problems in the relevant area on the basis of observation, hypothesis formation, factual analysis, and conclusions based thereon.[1]

All of the approaches mentioned are ultimately based on the analysis of structured and unstructured output data. While structured data is available in a formalized form and is easier to evaluate, unstructured data does not follow a fixed structure. (These are, for example, the text files in natural language that can be converted into vectors with the help of word embedding methods and then analysed.) The level of automation is very different in different industries. In the area of TP, the use of intelligent technologies is still relatively new. Empirical studies currently show a high need for digitization but, at the same time, very low potential for future developments in the area of TP. Today, there are mainly applications of simple process automation, for

1. Michel Braun & Dr Jenny Köppe, Die Verrechnungspreis-Funktion der Zukunft, Owlit, June 2019.

example, with bots or software solutions. Advanced process automation and cognitive automation are largely still in the making.[2]

Technologies to develop IT applications in use today can broadly be categorized into two groups: classical rule-based software and AI. Both have different use cases in tax technology.[3]

In rule-based software, it is the task of the software developer to translate existing rules and regulations such as a code of law into an algorithm. The advantage of this approach is the use of regulations based on quantifiable criteria. However, many regulations in tax law and, in particular, in the field of TP are subject to interpretation for which a strict rule-based software seems less suitable. This type of software, however, can be utilized to provide an overview of the different interpretations of a regulation which can be a useful tool to support advisors and practitioners in coming up with their conclusions. In general, this approach is closer to a civil law perspective where the code of law is the ultimate basis rather than a common law/case law perspective which gives more weight to former law cases that can be used to predict probable future outcomes and interpretations.[4]

Notwithstanding, the main driver for the recent technological advancements is the developments in the area of AI. While there is no broadly accepted definition of AI, it generally describes software that develops and identifies rules based on big data input sets. In analogy to the human brain, so-called neuronal networks are trained based on the data determining the rules mostly based on probability. An overview of different types of AI with potential use in tax technology is given below. Both broad groups of software are used in tax technology either separately or in combination.[5]

2.2 Blockchain

It is simply impossible to talk about intelligent automation without mentioning blockchain technology. Nowadays, blockchain is completely associated with cryptocurrencies since blockchain is a platform on which the bitcoin network runs. However, blockchain is wider than bitcoin and has several applications that can go beyond cryptocurrencies. In order to understand blockchain technology, it is important to understand DLT as the two terms, 'blockchain' and 'DLT', are often used interchangeably. DLT is a decentralized database managed by multiple participants across multiple nodes, and blockchain is a type of DLT where transactions are recorded with an immutable cryptographic signature so-called hash. The transactions are grouped in

2. *Ibid.*
3. Christopher Burr & Nello Cristianini, 'Can Machines Read Our Minds?' (SpringerLink, March 2019), https://doi.org/10.1007/s11023-019-09497-4 (last accessed 18 February 2022).
4. Jessica Morley et al., The Debate on the Ethics of AI in Health Care: A Reconstruction and Critical Review, SSRN, November 2019.
5. Christopher Burr & Nello Cristianini, 'Can Machines Read Our Minds?' (SpringerLink, March 2019).

blocks and each new block includes a hash of the previous one, chaining them together, therefore, distributed ledgers are often called blockchains.[6]

A key characteristic of blockchain enables value to be exchanged at the moment a transaction occurs and does this without intervention from other parties and without a centralized governing authority. The distributed ledger is dependent upon its stakeholders who support its accuracy, reliability, and immutability. Therefore, blockchain technology enables companies involved in a transaction to know what happened and when it happened, as well as confirm that other parties in the transaction are seeing the same data flow without the need for an intermediary providing assurance and without a need to reconcile data afterwards.[7] Visibly, blockchain technology has enormous potential and a transformational effect on all industries.

Following the introduction of blockchain technology, it did not take long for tax to recognize the benefits of the platform. Among other applications, the technology could transform the current approaches and solutions to various tax issues, both domestic and cross-border.[8] Blockchain technology can be a good platform for facilitating indirect tax compliance since the distributed ledger platform creates transparency and overcomes the lack of trust through its ability to create unalterable records of transactions and contracts.[9] Moreover, a blockchain decentralized ledger can be used for smart contracts. Smart contracts are self-executing digital agreements in the form of software in which the terms and conditions of an agreement can be preprogrammed and designed to execute themselves when predetermined conditions are met. Also, the payments for transactions can be automated in case the programmed conditions are satisfied. The ability to execute smart contracts and enable smart payments will be the major application for MNEs in their cross-border TP.[10] In this chapter, the author will further analyse the benefits and limitations of using blockchain to improve TP processes.

2.3 Artificial Intelligence

The term AI has been broadly used in academics since the 1950s; however, there is no generally accepted definition or classification for its many sub-areas. An often-used grouping is done based on the underlying methods and technology as presented below:

6. Blockchain technology explained. *See* https://www.r3.com/blockchain-101/ (last accessed 26 January 2022).
7. S. Wagh, 'Potential Application of Blockchain in Multinational Transfer Pricing' (March 2017), available at, https://www.linkedin.com/pulse/potential-application-blockchain-multinational-transfer-sagar-wagh (last accessed 18 February 2022).
8. S. Sim et al., Blockchain, Transfer Pricing, Customs Valuations, and Indirect Taxes: Transforming the Global Tax Environment, 26 Bloomberg BNA (June 2017).
9. B. Kuijper, T. Cameron & Z. Szatmari, Technology-Enabled Tax Compliance, 74 Bull. Intl. Taxn. 10 (2020), Journal Articles & Papers.
10. S. Wagh, 'Potential Application of Blockchain in Multinational Transfer Pricing' (March 2017), available at, https://www.linkedin.com/pulse/potential-application-blockchain-multinational-transfer-sagar-wagh (last accessed 18 February 2022).

Machine learning: computer algorithms improve through experience and by use of data. If several layers of neuronal networks are used, this is referred to as 'deep learning'. Different types of learning are differentiated such as the following: In a supervised learning environment, the software engineer monitors and gives guidance to the learning process. This means that input is provided to the data in terms of classification or labelling of data points. In an unsupervised learning setting, no such input is provided and the algorithm identifies structures like grouping or labelling from the data. Reinforced learning means that the machine received feedback in the course of the learning if the identified grouping or labelling is correct.
Knowledge representation and reasoning: information is presented in a way that is machine-readable and allows for conclusions.
Process mining is used to identify real processes from event logs. With different techniques used under this term, one example is the BPMN which models business processes within a company. Thereby the real processes, not idealized should-be processes, are identified and made visible. The discovered de facto processes can then be compared to the planned (de jure) processes showing the improvement potential of the process.[11]
Anomaly detection means that data is analysed to identify unexpected and inconsistent data points in a data set. It is used mostly for VAT and customs.
Natural language processing leverages deep machine learning techniques to derive meaningful insights and relationships from huge amounts of texts.[12]
RPA is a software technology that makes it easy to build, deploy, and manage software robots that emulate human actions interacting with digital systems and software.[13]

3 THE USE OF TECHNOLOGIES IN TP

Due to the growing complexity of cross-border inter-group transactions, MNEs are facing challenges in their daily work processes. Technology-based solutions might be the support needed for documenting intra-group transactions to enhance end-to-end traceability and to meet regulations, compliance, and audits across their global network.

3.1 Drivers for the Use of Technology in TP

The growing complexity of intra-group transactions and changing regulations are only two of the many drivers for using technology-based support in TP. Notwithstanding, many other factors, both internal and external, should still be mentioned.

11. Constantin Houy, Maarten Hamberg & Peter Fettke, Robotic Process Automation in Public Administration, Conference Paper, 2019.
12. Rsystem explanation.
13. UiPath explanation.

The main external driver is the regulatory framework. The entities of the MNEs are subject to local regulations as well as compliance and audit rules in their jurisdiction, not to mention that international TP rules have evolved significantly in recent years. Due to increased investigation and media attention on MNEs with a focus on whether they pay insufficient tax in jurisdictions where they operate, transparency has become crucial for both countries and international organizations such as the OECD and the EU. Therefore, the development of TPD rules under the OECD BEPS Project, including the local and master files as well as CbCR requirements, put a disclosure obligation on MNEs. Moreover, many countries have implemented additional disclosure requirements in local tax audits.[14] Auditors in each location expect entities to have appropriate controls over each intra-group transaction, match it to its respective underlying financial flow, and trace end-to-end for the supporting documentation. The arm's length principle applies across all intra-group transactions and is a significant source of dispute between MNEs and tax authorities. If an MNE is not able to trace and demonstrate compliance with the TP rules, then it has to expend considerable resources defending audits and be subject to TP adjustments or even face penalties for violating foreign exchange controls.[15] Complying with the regulatory framework can be time-consuming and expensive; consequently, MNEs need to improve efficiency and implement a standardized approach in their TP process. The consistent approach supported with well-prepared documentation and correct figures can help in a situation when a large amount of information needs to be provided to the tax authorities in a certain timeframe. A well-developed TP technology can also support MNEs to meet the disclosure requirements. In addition, tax authorities have been focusing on digitalization as well which puts additional pressure on MNEs to utilize TP technology.[16]

The tasks of the TP department show a high degree of complexity and have always placed high demands on employees. The basic task of the TP department is to ensure that the remuneration of transactions between related parties within a group is at arm's length and prove this to the tax authorities. From an organizational point of view, the challenges in fulfilling these duties start with collecting information. The conversion of data for tax purposes, its use for the fulfilment of declaration obligations, as well as the efficient implementation of coordination processes and division of labour between different units and areas are challenges that are put on the TP department.[17]

Due to the highly connected intra-group supply chains that may involve hundreds of entities across the world, the size and complexity of the intra-group transactions are

14. Emanuel Baptista et al., Tax Technology Applied to Supply Chain, OECD/International, October 2020.
15. IBM Research Whitepaper, Blockchain/DLT: A Game-Changer in Managing MNCs Intercompany Transactions, June 2017.
16. Emanuel Baptista et al., Tax Technology Applied to Supply Chain, OECD/International, October 2020.
17. Michel Braun & Dr Jenny Köppe, Die Verrechnungspreis-Funktion der Zukunft, Owlit, June 2019.

becoming increasingly complicated therefore anticipating cash flow, exercising control, and instituting proper governance are becoming likewise difficult.[18] Moreover, tax departments need to provide insights for the benefit of other units of the organization regarding monitoring of costs, profitability, effective tax rate, and the value of people and assets.[19] Obtaining information related to coordination and communication with domestic and foreign departments can create various difficulties for companies. Information from foreign companies is sometimes not available in the system and must be requested from colleagues abroad. In addition, the data provided are often not tailored to the needs of the TP department and have to be modified. Personnel changes, namely, huge fluctuation, also raise difficulties if details on certain issues are to be answered years later as part of a tax audit. System changes and deletion of data could cause additional challenges and exacerbate the potential for lost information. Even if the information can be traced, the manual gathering and analysis process can be inefficient and expensive. Moreover, the time lag between the actual transaction, the financial billing, and payment cycle as well as the time of TP, accounting, and foreign exchange control authority audits could be as far apart as years.[20]

Domestic and foreign communication and the transfer of information to the tax authorities are sometimes not coordinated and can therefore show inconsistencies. This is partly due to personnel bottlenecks that prevent information from undergoing an adequate risk assessment before it is passed on to the tax authorities. Furthermore, settlements between local and foreign units are often determined manually using spreadsheet programs which quickly become more complex and therefore more susceptible to errors, especially in the case of special issues. Another challenge for TP departments is the submission of documents that support the nature of the service relationships, in particular, the proof of the benefit of providing intra-group services from the perspective of the receiving unit.[21] In addition, shareholders also demand MNEs' management and, through them, the tax functions to properly monitor, manage, and control intra-group transactions.[22] Monitoring, managing, and controlling intra-group transactions as well as collecting the relevant documents require complex, structured processes that are not implemented accordingly in many companies. Furthermore, the increased disclosure requirements put internal burdens on multinationals as well. Companies either accept the additional costs of hiring new staff or the same number of employees need to work more and deal with the additional disclosure requirements. By implementing a TP technology, companies could increase efficiency

18. IBM Research Whitepaper, Blockchain/DLT: A Game-Changer in Managing MNCs Intercompany Transactions, June 2017.
19. Emanuel Baptista et al., Tax Technology Applied to Supply Chain, OECD/International, October 2020.
20. IBM Research Whitepaper, Blockchain/DLT: A Game-Changer in Managing MNCs Intercompany Transactions, June 2017.
21. Michel Braun & Dr Jenny Köppe, Die Verrechnungspreis-Funktion der Zukunft, Owlit, June 2019.
22. IBM Research Whitepaper, Blockchain/DLT: A Game-Changer in Managing MNCs Intercompany Transactions, June 2017.

and probably could do the extra work with fewer employees therefore with less cost.[23] Moreover, the challenges for the TP departments bear an increasing risk potential that can be effectively reduced through the use of technology, therefore, implementing technology-based support for TP will become more important in the future.

3.2 What to Consider Before Using a TP Technology?

After demonstrating the various driving factors for introducing technologies for TP processes, it is not a surprise that MNEs are increasingly interested in using TP software solutions insofar as possible. While the right TP automation solution can be highly beneficial for an organization, it still requires adequate preparation from companies. The non-exhaustive parameters considered when taking into account the use of technologies for TP purposes are summarized as follows:[24]

> The scope of the technology is needed to be defined, namely, the business process or problem where the TP technology could help. The scope can be to implement an efficient and cost-effective TP policy. (Technology can support the collection of the intra-group data for TP purposes, calculate adjustments, and process the TP analysis.) Insofar as the aim of the TP software is to save costs on external advisors in relation to TP, MNEs should find a software that can enable the company to build and manage TP reports on their own.

In the practical conduct of the TP planning, diagnosing the contributing departments to the TP process is essential. TP reports are commonly managed by tax or TP departments although accounting departments' contributions might be relevant as well. In contrast, TP policy implementation is integrated ownership between tax and TP (policy owners) and finance (data owners), and thus finance will be part of the decision process. The organization should enable the information flow between the departments in order to have a clear and transparent TP process which supports the implementation of a TP software.

The value of the TP software needs to be defined considering all of the relevant factors. Companies should not forget to take into account the acquisition cost, ongoing cost, and the FTE required to implement and manage the TP software. Specifying the major expected benefits of implementing a TP software can support the planning process. Technologies can improve data quality, save time, and reduce the cost of external advisors, just to name a few advantages. Although some of the factors might be hard to be quantified, the calculation of the pay-back period estimation can support the decision.

The readiness of the organization to automate the TP process should be reviewed. Namely, intra-group data should be available at an appropriate level of detail in order to be able to implement a TP software. Therefore, technology requires the involvement

23. Emanuel Baptista, et al., Tax Technology Applied to Supply Chain, OECD/International, October 2020.
24. John Farooque Dar, Interested in TP Software? Four Things to Consider, June 2017, available at, https://www.linkedin.com/pulse/interested-transfer-pricing-software-four-things-consider-dar/ (last accessed 26 January 2022).

and commitment of the whole organization as the information flow between the departments should work without interruption and obstacles when implementing an efficient TP software solution.

The ownership of the project should be defined in advance since implementation requires transparency at every level of the organization. As for a TP software leadership commonly means tax and/or finance, therefore in most organizations, the ultimate sponsor is the Head of Tax or the CFO.

Data needs to be structured for the implementation of a technology. This is a crucial point of the implementation. If the data is incorrect or invalid, the outcome of the process will not give us a correct result, and the whole process will not support the new system.

The different IT governance regulations in the various companies can cause other obstacles during the implementation process. The company should be aware of the IT security regulations before implementing a new technology.

Implementation of a new technology can cause employee and management challenges in the company. To cure and overcome these barriers, the companies need to engage their employees in the project and should show them the benefits of the new solution.

3.3 TP Life cycle

The division of the TP life cycle can be made into four separate stages. It is not a surprise that the TP function has gradually started pursuing the ambition to automate parts of the TP life cycle through technology-enabled solutions.

Figure 27.2 TP Life cycle

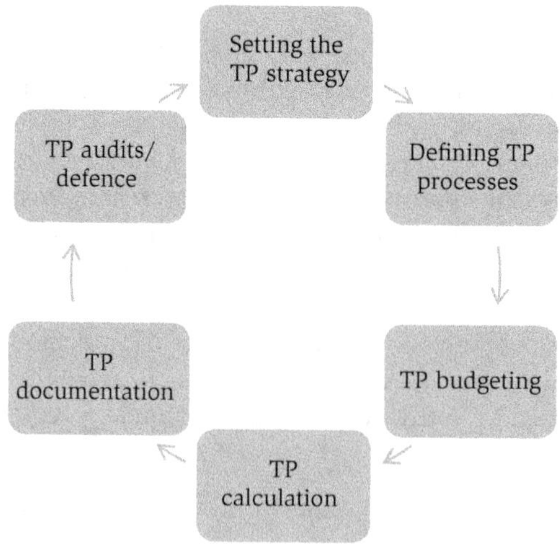

The TP life cycle begins with setting the TP strategy which is essential to the successful creation of company's TP policy (*see* Figure 27.2). The key components of the planning should include streamlining a process to identify individuals within the organization that are knowledgeable about new intra-group transactions and are able to gather the information necessary to perform an economic analysis that will form the basis of an arm's length price. Once the arm's length price has been determined, the planning phase should be supported with an established set of rules to ensure the policy is implemented consistently throughout the company.[25] The TP budgeting is part of the planning phase. The whole financial structure should be defined for TP purposes.

Documentation is a retrospective exercise in which intra-group transactions are tested to determine whether or not related parties conducted their intra-group activities at an arm's length price. The importance of documentation has proliferated in recent years as the number of countries requiring TPD has grown rapidly as tax authorities continue to review TP strategies when it comes to tax audits.[26]

Once the TP policy is set, monitoring becomes the central focus of the TP department to ensure that prices result in the desired arm's length outcome. If the monitoring system is properly implemented, it can result in substantial efficiencies like lower compliance costs and, more importantly, fewer financial statements and tax risks.[27]

There are significant benefits to properly managing all phases of the TP life cycle. Besides TP risk reduction and tax savings, organizations can expect improved communication and overall efficiency growth. Companies are encouraged to build a precise process to mitigate risks to TP compliance and realize the benefits of a comprehensive TP life cycle.[28]

3.3.1 *Which TP Processes Are Suitable for (Intelligent) Automation?*

For setting the TP policies, the knowledge and interpretation of TP rules and law play a major role. In this regard, TP is often not a classical field for rule-based software as many aspects depend on the specific facts and circumstances of the case. However, when it comes to providing an overview of existing rules and their interpretations as a guidance to advisors and practitioners, such tools are useful support.[29]

The determination of transfer prices is either done directly by the in-house tax/TP department or spread among different functions throughout the company such as controlling, finance, treasury, and supply chain. In the second case, the challenge for the TP function is to ensure that information on the correct setting of the prices is known to the relevant employees and to gather the data afterwards. In this regard,

25. https://www.cpapracticeadvisor.com/accounting-audit/news/12055983/how-to-manage-the-4-stages-of-the-transfer-pricing-life-cycle (last accessed 26 January 2022).
26. *Ibid.*
27. *Ibid.*
28. Michel Braun & Dr Jenny Köppe, Die Verrechnungspreis-Funktion der Zukunft, Owlit, June 2019.
29. Christopher Burr & Nello Cristianini, 'Can Machines Read Our Minds?' (SpringerLink, March 2019).

solutions in the field of simple robot process automation and workflows can prove very helpful.[30] Also, techniques such as process mining can be applied to identify the real processes behind the setting of transfer prices and improve the structures behind the process. Further, the setting of prices can be supported by machine learning if the algorithm is trained to predict future transfer prices based on historic data sets.[31]

The monitoring of transfer prices is a major focus area in the field of operational TP, in particular, if an MNE applies margin monitoring with regular adjustments, an investment in software will be given extended consideration.

In order to compile the documentation and fulfil the disclosure requirements, information from many stakeholders are gathered. Documentation creation is an administrative challenge for many business groups which, in current discussions, is a major concern for technology solutions. The use of a combination of possibly already existing and new tools can be quite useful. The process approach is assumed that combines central documentation creation with local input such as the relevant data that is requested from the local companies by the central tax department, and the local TPD is created centrally on the basis of this information. This is followed by a review by the local companies which may also include an adjustment to local requirements. Significant efficiency gains can be generated here in the area of simple process automation through the use of bots and workflow solutions. Bots are useful at this point because, unlike macros that can automate steps in the context of spreadsheet programs, they act across the software. Corresponding RPA software is now available with intuitive user interfaces that allow users without programming knowledge to do so with little training time. The starting point of the documentation process is the collection of data whereby the local data are requested from foreign companies. This includes, for example, the transaction volumes per transaction group, the existing contracts, or the most important competitors. This is where a workflow solution can achieve significant efficiency gains. This refers to tools that can be used, for example, to send automatic e-mails, assign responsibilities, and monitor processing deadlines. They can help whenever several people are working on the same work results and need a uniform central data collection system for this purpose.[32]

The next step is to create documentation reports based on the collected data and transfer the data into standardized templates. This process can be automated by populating the template with placeholders, adding the appropriate attributes to the information query file, and having a bot insert the collected and matched data into the template and generate the local files for each company. The bot can then send these to the local companies for checking and organizing the storage of the final documentation reports.

One of the challenges of TP is to steer companies within a certain margin target range using at least partially budgeted values. In this context, it is important to monitor transaction volumes during the year and, if necessary, adjust prices if potential

30. Michel Braun & Dr Jenny Köppe, Die Verrechnungspreis-Funktion der Zukunft, Owlit, June 2019.
31. *Ibid.*
32. *Ibid.*

deviations are detected in the relevant period that are not expected to balance out. Here, automation of the relevant processes can provide essential support. For this purpose, solutions are offered on the market that are often sold under the name 'operational transfer pricing'. Standardized extraction programs exist for widely used ERP systems; for others, appropriate interfaces can be developed. It is advisable to extract data at the document level for each quarter. Once all relevant data has been extracted from the ERP system, the relevant documents must be assigned to the individual transaction groups. In the case of complex companies, this assignment represents a challenge that should not be underestimated as, in some cases, there is no unique identifier for a transaction group that is necessary from a TP perspective. The 'mapping' of the ERP data to the corresponding transaction groups can initially be done by evaluating attributes, such as companies, country, account, time period, cost centre. In most cases, however, a residual amount of data remains. In most cases, however, a residual value remains which is then manually assigned to the transaction groups.[33]

Not many technologies exist to help companies in the case of audits, however, the technology-based solutions implemented in the other field of the TP life cycle can help to prevent future TP litigation.

4 LIMITATIONS OF TECHNOLOGIES

Technology solutions cannot only improve the quality of the information but also can ameliorate the efficiency of the key business processes and can therefore help companies to manage the practical challenges of the TP process. While more and more articles are analysing the benefits of the usage of technologies in TP, the limitation of such solutions need to be addressed and discussed as well.

The efficient technologies are commonly expensive and require significant investment in time and funds as well as multiple aspects for consideration necessary to implement technology in the operations of an organization successfully. The range of issues to be addressed can be overwhelming and, in addition, an IT project can often be delayed which can put further pressure on the organization.[34] Therefore, it is necessary to have the right project plan and preparation in advance.[35] Three key factors, i.e., quality data, suitable technology and skilled employees, should be in place to be able to efficiently implement and use a TP technology.[36]

The quality of data is crucial for the successful use of TP technology. While blockchain, AI, and other technologies can be powerful tools to document intra-group transactions to enhance end-to-end traceability, prevent information loss, and save time in reconciliation, human data entry errors and data with insufficient quality can

33. *Ibid.*
34. Emanuel Baptista et al., Tax Technology Applied to Supply Chain, OECD/International, October 2020.
35. For more details on what to consider before using a TP software *see* section 3.2 of this chapter.
36. M. Zackrisson, A. Bakker & J. Hagelin, AI and Tax Administrations: A Good Match, 74 Bull. Intl. Taxn., IBFD, 10 (2020).

poorly affect the efficiency of technologies.[37] During a TP process, dealing with large amounts of data is usual. When a technology-based solution is implemented, companies should ensure that the collected information not only be used efficiently but also protect the taxpayers' rights and privacy.[38] Security concerns related to preserving data integrity, breaches of personal data and privacy, rights of taxpayers, as well as ethical issues should be constantly considered. Data protection may not contribute to improving efficiency in a short term perspective, at least not until routines and workflows are in place, but it serves the long-term effectiveness.[39]

Technology will not prevent audits from happening and cannot completely replace tax advisors. However, in order to pursue a career in tax in the future, professionals need to understand the use of technologies. Implementing a new software can cause concerns among employees that can affect the work attitude; therefore, companies have to clearly explain the advantages of using technologies.[40] The organizational culture should support new ideas and be ready for change. Most importantly, focus should be on teaching and learning the skills needed to effectively use the implemented technology.

The chapter mentioned several technology solutions. Different technologies have diverse limitations. The DLT has great potential but might not be the best solution when the TP policy is different in the group entities and the HQ does not want to share complete transparency among all of the group participants. Notwithstanding, transparency is one of the key factors in TP and, with the Action 13 master file requirements to disclose important details involving TP policy, hiding information from group entities is becoming extremely difficult.[41] Blockchain has its critics besides its advantages as well. Namely, a blockchain network is decentralized across many computers, therefore, shutting down one computer on a blockchain does not disrupt the system. An attack against the blockchain can be a huge problem. Furthermore, transparency, a key element of blockchain, could allow hackers to exploit flaws in the system.[42] Defining the place of performance is essential for allocating the taxing rights, therefore, one of the main issues concerning the AI functions is whether it is attributed to the place it developed or to the place it operates. AI functions are lacking any physical substance and hence should be attributed to the jurisdictions of their performance. The current TP regulations focus on significant personal functions to distribute profits;

37. IBM Research Whitepaper, Blockchain/DLT: A Game-Changer in Managing MNCs Intercompany Transactions, June 2017.
38. S. Rao, The Potential Use of AI, Blockchain & Data Analytics in Transfer Pricing, 2 Digitax (2020).
39. M. Zackrisson, A. Bakker & J. Hagelin, AI and Tax Administrations: A Good Match, 74 Bull. Intl. Taxn., IBFD, 10 (2020).
40. S. Rao, The Potential Use of AI, Blockchain & Data Analytics in Transfer Pricing, 2 Digitax (2020).
41. S. Wagh, Potential Application of Blockchain in Multinational Transfer Pricing, March 2017, available at, https://www.linkedin.com/pulse/potential-application-blockchain-multinational-transfer-sagar-wagh/ (last accessed 29 March 2022).
42. B. Kuijper, T. Cameron & Z. Szatmari, Technology-Enabled Tax Compliance, 74 Bull. Intl. Taxn. 10 (2020), Journal Articles & Papers.

however, the rapid development of AI technologies reduces the primary importance of significant people functions at least in terms of routine business functions.[43]

Technology push challenges the whole organization; accounting and tax departments; as well as software engineers. Finding suitable technology and adapting it to overcome new challenges is especially difficult. In order to use technologies properly, MNEs must consider how these concepts and techniques structurally and culturally fit into their wider organization. The possibility to access technologies does not automatically provide benefits in the short term unless the organization has the readiness of data, the skills, and the staff needed.[44]

5 OUTLOOK

In the best of times, TP technology makes TPD more accurate, more efficient, and less subjective. However, for a year like 2020, technology is more of a necessity than a luxury as companies are forced to control internal costs while continuously managing external risks. Pre-COVID-19, businesses were operating with lean tax departments and even smaller in 2020; these departments are being tasked with the impossible. The only way to do more with less is by utilizing technology. TP-specific software can update professionals about international TP requirements, interpret the impacts of tax policy and reform, evaluate changes in the TP framework, and prepare accurate documentation thereby streamlining the whole TP compliance process. Further, with the advent of blockchain, machine learning, and AI, consumption and analysis of data are much quicker and more meaningful. As a consequence, it results in real-time actionable steps that can help MNEs mitigate risk, optimize opportunity, and maximize control.[45]

Technology-based solutions not only can help multinationals in hard financial times but can also support less-developed regions. Developing countries all over the world are searching for effective support to overcome their drawbacks against the more developed countries. It is important to mention that developed countries have the advantage in implementing blockchain and AI as these nations do not have any legacy issues of an old IT infrastructure.[46] With this huge advantage, future technologies can possibly further help developing countries for their catching up.

Although developed countries are trying to support small corporations in order to promote the usage of technologies, large digital MNEs are still at the forefront of utilizing technology-based solutions. They almost completely rely on AI technologies to perform their business functions at different locations around the world without any

43. S. Sim et al., Blockchain, Transfer Pricing, Customs Valuations, and Indirect Taxes: Transforming the Global Tax Environment, 26(4) Bloomberg BNA (June 2017).
44. M. Zackrisson, A. Bakker & J. Hagelin, AI and Tax Administrations: A Good Match, 74 Bull. Intl. Taxn., IBFD, 10 (2020).
45. M. Song, Tax Scrutiny and Transfer Pricing: What You Can Expect in 2021, Bloomberg Tax (December 2020).
46. Siddhesh Rao, The Potential Use of AI, Blockchain & Data Analytics in Transfer Pricing, 2020. Workshop paper based on the event 'The Potential Use of AI, Blockchain & Data Analytics in Transfer Pricing', jointly organised by the Global Tax Policy Center and the WU Transfer Pricing Center at the Institute for Austrian and International Tax Law, WU (Vienna University of Economics and Business).

physical or human presence. Companies like Google, Facebook, Amazon, Twitter, and other large MNEs that are responsible for creating significant challenges for the tax authorities and international tax order are the largest and most powerful AI companies in the world right now. As AI is developed to perform significant business functions in the first instance in a source country, the analysis of these functions would be a basis for determining what value is generated in the country and, consequently, what profits should be allocated there.[47] Taxation of technologies, taxpayers' rights, and compliance issues will arise together with these developments.

The future of international taxation and TP itself is constantly evolving. It is not easy but rather complicated to define what the future holds for multinational companies. However, they will definitely need to face the challenges of the globalized world. Therefore, digitalization and technology-based solutions will obviously raise increasing interest in the years to come.

6 CONCLUSION

The growing complexity of the intra-group transactions among different entities poses various challenges to international organizations. This chapter details the use of technology-based solutions and their role in simplifying the TP processes as part of their utilization. The chapter aims at providing detailed guidance for obtaining the most suitable and effective technologies for the different TP processes to overcome the evolving challenges that companies are facing with their TP operations. This chapter is targeted at showing the available technologies that can support multinationals in obtaining efficient results in TP and avoiding a manual, time-consuming workload. An additional goal of the chapter is to point out the benefits and the limitations of the technologies. Companies need to understand their processes in detail in order to effectively implement a technology-based solution. A well-established implementation plan that properly considers the possible limitations together with the expected benefits for the group can support multinationals in various ways. Finally, the chapter also demonstrates the outlook for TP technologies and shows the possible issues and developments for the areas. While TP technologies have not yet been well researched, it is certain that the utilization of such technologies will continue to evolve and will continue to be refined over time.

47. *Ibid.*

CHAPTER 28

Use of New Technologies in Transfer Pricing by Tax Authorities

Gabriela Capristano Cardoso & Sing Yuan Yong*

1 INTRODUCTION

Tax authorities, like any others, have experienced digital transformation as technology advanced through the years. The progression of new technologies such as machine learning (a subpart of AI), blockchain, and other technologies[1] enable tax authorities to work more efficiently. This is particularly important for those that typically lack resources such as the ones in developing countries and emerging economies. However, even for well-resourced tax authorities, the complexity of TP rules and the volume of related-party transactions make it virtually impossible to provide good quality service to taxpayers and undertake a sound risk assessment and TP audits without the use of new technologies.

The need for digitalization for tax authorities is enhanced by the ever-increasing digitalization of taxpayers, a trend accelerated by the COVID-19 pandemic as many of

* This chapter was finalized before the author joined the OECD and the opinions expressed in it are the author's and do not reflect those of the Organization, or its Member countries.

1. For further details on the use of new technologies by taxpayers, *see* Chapter 27 in this book.

them alike were forced to 'go digital' as quickly as possible in order to adapt to the restrictions on physical contact. While the COVID-19 pandemic will hopefully pass, the new trends in accelerated digitalization will remain.[2]

Tax Authorities 1.0,[3] a term used to identify tax authorities in the earlier stages of digitalization, if any, were characterized by the use of paper-based processes and many manuals and solid processes. However, this is no longer efficient considering the current stages of digitalization by taxpayers and the entire economy. Tax authorities need to consider opportunities arising from digitalization, including data analytical tools and blockchain. In particular, in TP control, the analysis of data is crucial for efficient tax authority practice.

In contrast, Tax Authorities 2.0, also known as 'e-administration', already provide services for taxpayers digitally and are able to optimize such services by, for example, using data analytics. Proceeding to Tax Authorities 3.0, the digital transformation of tax authorities goes one step further aiming to build-in compliance in many tax areas, including TP. With better access to data in real-time, tax authorities can better monitor the tax event and increase the focus on their auditing efforts. This is a significant opportunity for TP as it has the potential to reduce the compliance burden typically associated with TPD.

In the context of TP compliance, tax authorities generally operate on a risk assessment basis and select cases for further review. With improved technology, there is enhanced detection of possible non-compliance through better risk assessment modelling using increasingly substantial amounts of digital data and advanced analytical techniques.[4] As can be observed, TP compliance by tax authorities is mostly accomplished after the submission of the tax return and the relevant TPD. A real-time audit of controls, unlike what can be done for corporate tax and indirect tax, is more uncommon for TP at this juncture. This could be due to the method of implementing TP policies. While transfer prices may be established at the beginning of a period, depending on the system adopted by the MNE, monitoring and adjustments may occur on a monthly, quarterly, mid-yearly, or annual basis. However, it is still possible to obtain upfront certainty for TP. This can be done in terms of an APA in which TP arrangements are given certainty assuming critical assumptions are not effectuated. Accordingly, the use of technology by tax authorities has also further improved the APA processes.

Compared to the past, tax authorities collect more detailed information. In the TP context, BEPS Action 13[5] implemented the minimum standard for large MNEs to prepare a CbCR with aggregate data on the global allocation of income, profit, taxes paid, and economic activity among the tax jurisdictions in which it operates. The exchange of CbCRs among tax jurisdictions using the common transmission system

2. J. Owens & G. Capristano Cardoso, The Future of International Tax, Tax Notes International, vol. 103, p. 731.
3. OECD, *Tax Authorities 3.0: The Digital Transformation of Tax Authorities* (Paris: OECD, 2020).
4. *Ibid.*
5. OECD, *Transfer Pricing Documentation and Country-by-Country Reporting, Action 13: 2015 Final Report*, OECD/G20 Base Erosion and Profit Shifting Project (Paris: OECD Publishing, 2015).

provides jurisdictions where the MNE has a taxable presence with more information about the entire MNE.

There is also a trend for greater collaboration and cooperation between different tax authorities and between tax authorities and MNEs. This has given rise to multilateral programs such as the ICAP. Many of these efforts are complemented by the technology advancements that are discussed in subsequent parts of this chapter.

In this chapter, the authors explore relevant new technologies that can be used by tax authorities to facilitate TP analyses, taking into account the impact of the COVID-19 pandemic on the digitalization of tax authorities, and provide some considerations on implementation. As such, section 2 discusses the use of relevant new technology by tax authorities, and section 3 examines key aspects of implementation before concluding the chapter in section 4.

2 RELEVANT USE OF NEW TECHNOLOGY

Tax authorities around the world are in different steps of the digitalization process. Even within the same jurisdiction, various staff members have distinct levels of comfort in using new technologies. In this regard, tax authorities typically make use of both old and new technologies in order to provide better services for taxpayers, promote voluntary compliance, reduce errors, and perform risk assessment analyses and tax audits. These are of extreme relevance for TP analyses that tend to involve large amounts of data that need to be correctly processed by tax authorities – a time-consuming, resource-intensive, and prone-to-errors task. In this section, the authors discuss the advancement in e-services and the use of data analytics, including AI and blockchain in TP control by tax authorities.

2.1 e-Services

In order to meet the demands of taxpayers and more effectively manage taxpayer data and customer relationships, tax authorities have invested in the provision of e-services. These types of systems can also help tax authorities to improve resource management and promote voluntary compliance from taxpayers as they are typically more convenient and user-friendly than in-person interactions.

The provision of e-services typically constitutes the first phase of the digitalization of tax authorities. The range of such services can vary from providing guidance or making information available to taxpayers to prefiling of tax returns, tax payments, or reporting potential tax fraud. Moreover, many tax authorities have developed or are developing mobile applications to facilitate the use of e-services by taxpayers.[6]

E-services, such as prefiling of tax returns, can help to decrease the number of errors in filing tax returns and therefore reduce the tax gap thereby protecting countries' tax

6. Australia, Brazil, Chile, Mexico, Portugal, and Thailand are among the countries that have developed mobile applications available to taxpayers.

bases.[7] In a TP context in which large amounts of data are aggregated and voluntary compliance is desired, e-services can help facilitate the communication between taxpayers and tax authorities, provide a multitude of products or services for taxpayers to access relevant guidance and tax authorities' positions about relevant and recurrent issues, and help keep all information about the taxpayer organized and easy to access.

An increasing number of tax authorities have been investing in self-service offers for taxpayers. These can be supported by virtual assistants,[8] chatbots as well as tools and calculators on the tax authorities' website to assist taxpayers in predicting how much tax they owe.

However, e-services alone are not sufficient for facilitating a TP analysis. Tax authorities must properly analyse the data collected through the e-services that are provided. Tax authorities would also need to rely on other sources of information to complete their analysis. This could include, for example, information received from other parts of government and having access to other relevant cross-border information that can be obtained from external sources, taxpayers, or exchange of information with other tax authorities.

2.2 Data Analytics and AI

TP controls involve the analysis of substantial amounts of data. This exercise can be very time consuming and resource-intensive as well as prone to errors. Tax authorities can benefit from data analytics tools including advanced data analytics such as AI to help more rapidly and consistently assess the data received; improve the efficiency of administrative procedures; predict bad debts, fraud, or tax evasion attempts as well as aggressive tax planning or tax avoidance; and prioritize enforced collection.

Data analytics comprise a wide range of tools that can vary in complexity, on the amount of data that can be processed, and from a simple data collection to a more comprehensive analysis including those that are predictive and probabilistic. Predictive analyses aim at anticipating likely problems – for instance, with the accuracy of a tax return or the timing of a payment – so that tax authorities can consider which actions should be taken and when. Probabilistic analyses can help tax authorities understand future scenarios, for example, how taxpayers would likely react to a policy change in TP.

7. Among others, the tax authorities from Australia, Canada, Singapore, and the United States utilize an auto-fill mechanism of tax returns that prefile information already available to them, making filing easier and more convenient to taxpayers and reducing the likelihood of errors.
8. As an example, the Australian tax authorities use a virtual assistant, Alex, to support taxpayers on a twenty-four-hour basis.

Figure 28.1 Data Analytics

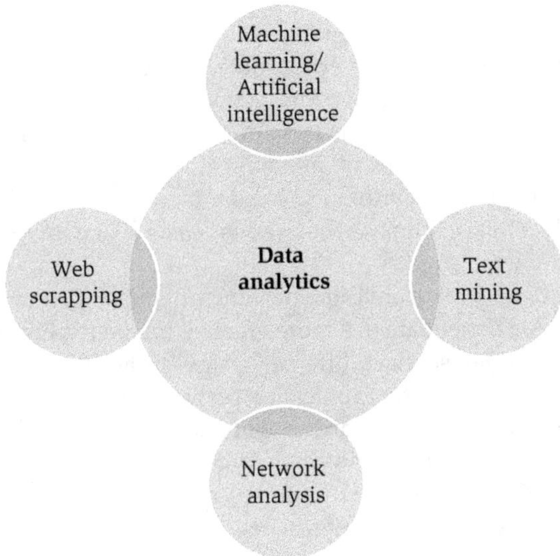

Tax authorities have been using data analytics for more than twenty-five years. In earlier years, much of the use was focused narrowly on case selection. With the emergence of advanced analytics, it is now possible to examine data or content using more sophisticated approaches such as pattern recognition, outlier detection, cluster analysis, experimental design, network analysis, and text mining. There are now new opportunities for the use of intelligence across all aspects of tax authorities' tasks (*see* Figure 28.1).[9]

In the case of TP, a predictive analysis coupled with increased information would have helped tax authorities perform a more adequate risk assessment and improve case selection. This would also aid tax authorities in focusing their efforts on appropriate areas.

Using the CbCR as one of the recent examples, data analytics can help achieve the main purpose of the use of the CbCR data that is employed for effective tax risk assessment. It is important to note that tax authorities who receive the CbCRs can only use them for risk assessment purposes and not for the purpose of making TP adjustments.[10] The information received is also used on an anonymized and aggregated basis for purposes of measuring BEPS under Action 11.[11] If a relevant risk is identified in the CbCR, tax authorities can request further information from taxpayers.

9. OECD, *Advanced Analytics for Better Tax Administration: Putting Data to Work* (Paris: OECD Publishing, 2016).
10. For further details on transfer pricing documentation, *see* Michael Lang, Raffaele Petruzzi, Giammarco Cottani, Alfred Storck (2018) Fundamentals of Transfer Pricing: A Practical Guide, Kluwer Law International, Chapter VII.
11. OECD, *Measuring and Monitoring BEPS, Action 11: 2015 Final Report*, OECD/G20 BEPS (Paris: OECD Publishing, 2015).

The process of the TP analysis has been made more efficient and effective with the use of technology. This has been the case for both MNEs and tax authorities. Processes that were previously manual such as the identification of functions, assets, and risks, accurate delineation of related-party transactions leading to a characterization of entities based on their functional and risk profile, and qualitative analysis for benchmarking could be optimized or replaced by automated processes such as AI, robotic process automation, or even excel macros. In most instances, the final step of the process remains as a manual review for either legal reasons when decisions on certain processes require human intervention or for assurance. It is likely that new technologies will not totally replace humans but rather ensure that human work is more efficient and less prone to errors.

Data analytics does not create anything new but attempts to allow tax authorities to do the same work using better data in a more efficient manner.[12] Finally, data analytics can also improve taxpayer services offered by tax authorities which can facilitate compliance and promote better communication between taxpayers and tax authorities.

In the case of TP control, tax authorities will use data analytics primarily for case selection and risk assessment. These allow for more focused tax audits and for productive use of tax authorities' (often limited) resources. However, there are other possibilities for the use of data analytics in TP, in particular when considering advanced data analytics.

Different uses of data analytics can expedite various steps of the TP analysis (*see* Figure 28.2). In Step 1, the accurate delineation of the actual transaction can likely benefit from it by identifying the relevant functions, assets, and risks and by providing an analysis of all comparability factors. Step 2, the recognition of the accurately delineated transaction, can be facilitated by using data analytics to determine whether the related-party transaction has commercial rationale and if it can be priced at arm's length. Step 3, the selection of the most appropriate TP method, can be achieved more efficiently by using data analytics to consider the facts and circumstances of the case in relation to the available TP methods. Finally, for Step 4, the application of the selected TP method can benefit from using data analytics for a more consistent and more rapid qualitative analysis of benchmarking studies and for identifying where comparability adjustments may be needed. In practice, data analytics is more commonly used in applying Step 4 of the TP analysis.

12. *Supra* n. 9.

Figure 28.2 Data Analytics Applied to the Different Steps of the TP Analysis

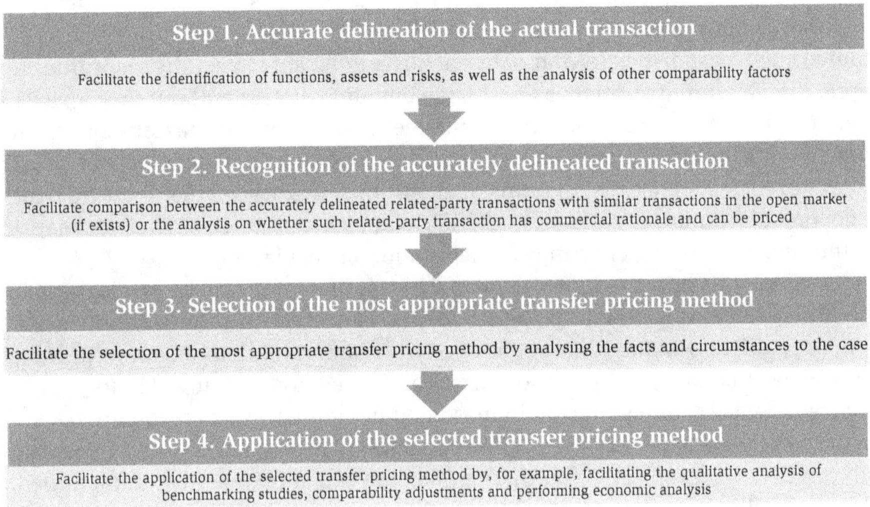

Data analytics can also simplify and enhance the effectiveness of the analysis of TPD which is often lengthy and complex. Tax authorities receive such documentation from multiple taxpayers, and a consequential significant number of resources are required for its analysis. It is not possible for tax authorities to meticulously analyse each item of documentation that is received. Data analytics can scan through the information searching for inconsistencies or particular risk areas and signal tax authorities to conduct a manual review.

Data analytics can also aid in avoiding and resolving TP disputes, for example, by facilitating a common interpretation of the facts of the case by recognizing patterns and assisting in the selection and application of the TP method. It can also improve consistency in a TP assessment or in the negotiation of TP disputes by analysing the case at hand against similar past cases and providing inputs on how such cases were resolved previously by the same tax authority. Should an international database of TP cases be created, this could further promote consistency worldwide on similar cases for jurisdictions following the OECD TPG. Besides greater consistency in the resolution of TP cases and, therefore, improved tax certainty for both taxpayers and tax authorities, the use of data analytics for TP dispute avoidance and resolution could greatly strengthen the application of the OECD TPG.

Using data analytics in the area of TP dispute avoidance and resolution also has its limitations. For example, it is important to have a good quality set of data which may be difficult to obtain considering the confidentiality of the MAPs and the unwillingness of some competent authorities using them to have more transparency in the way that cases are resolved as this could potentially reduce their negotiation power with other competent authorities. Moreover, it would be difficult to use data analytics to decide TP cases from both legal protection and competent authority procedure perspectives. After all, competent authority procedures, such as MAPs, are essentially a human procedure involving negotiation between competent authorities of different jurisdictions.

A potential issue with introducing complex data analytics to tax authorities' practices is that it may require training of the existing workforce and hiring specialized personnel such as statisticians and data scientists to be able to set the algorithms and interpret the data. In the same way that large amounts of data without the capacity to actually utilize the data in a meaningful manner is not useful for tax authorities, it is equally not efficient for setting bad algorithms or not having personnel to interpret the outcomes of the data analysis. In terms of algorithms, it is crucial that they are neutral and do not discriminate or favour specific taxpayers. It is also vital to keep the algorithm updated to reflect changes in legislation or regulations.

The necessary technology to use data analytics is in existence. The key is the ability of the tax authorities to build up the AI needed to instruct the software on what to search for in the information that is gathered. It is important that tax authorities build TP processes that are easily standardized and used for training AI. In terms of technology, optical character recognition, sometimes known as text recognition, can be used to identify certain characters and recognize patterns and classify information which can then be interpreted by AI. The outcome can subsequently be forwarded to the tax authorities.

In addition, the quality of the data imputed is the cornerstone of a well-working data analytics tool. Tax authorities need to ensure that both legislation and administrative practices are sufficiently clear to facilitate accurate data collection from taxpayers. If what is being asked from them is not transparent from a taxpayer perspective or if there is too much of a margin for interpretation, it is likely that the data that is collected may not be useful for data analytics. Moreover, the format of the data collection should be standardized as much as possible to facilitate the use of technology.

There are legal barriers to and practical issues in implementing data analytics such as availability of resources and particularly for advanced data analytics such as AI. It is unlikely that tax authorities will be able to use AI for making decisions on, for example, TP adjustments, as it is not always possible to have full transparency on how the decision was made by it. The algorithm can continue to evolve and 'learn' with its use and the data imputed in the system. Therefore, it would be difficult to defend the tax authorities' position to taxpayers and in dispute resolution procedures. Care should be taken that the use of data analytics does not infringe taxpayers' rights and that taxpayer data (often sensitive data shared in TP cases) are secured.

Finally, it is important to remember that TP is not an exact science and involves a significant amount of subjectivity from taxpayers and tax authorities alike. While technology such as data analytics can help to reduce subjectivity and enhance tax certainty, it may not be possible to completely eliminate human interpretation of the facts and circumstances and thus of the TP analysis. That is, as businesses evolve and legislations and administrative practices change, human intervention will be needed to ensure a fair and equal outcome of the analysis.

2.3 Blockchain

As a TP analysis requires the interpretation of reliable data on related-party transactions and the volume and complexity of such transactions continue to expand worldwide, a blockchain can provide a solution to transactional data collection and storage. It is crucial that tax authorities have access to this data to commence the TP analysis. However, the current high levels of TP data collected through TPD are not always reliable or easy to read. A blockchain can provide a solution to this important issue.

A blockchain is defined as a decentralized system based on a series of distributed ledgers (like a chain) for which no particular single party controls the data. As a decentralized system, all participants in the blockchain can provide inputs to the data with all changes being entirely visible to all participants in the blockchain. This also provides extra security to ensure that the data will not very likely become lost as it would be virtually impossible that all computers in the blockchain, typically dispersed regionally or worldwide, would become inoperable. It also makes it more difficult to hack the information as hackers would need to decode multiple nodes (a single part of the distributed ledger) in the blockchain (*see* Figure 28.3).[13]

Figure 28.3 Basic Blockchain Concept

The information imputed in a node is traceable and immutable, meaning that, in TP terms, once a related-party transaction is ledged in the blockchain, its information will be completely traceable, and all changes to this transaction will be visible in the blockchain. This would provide the tax authorities with the security that taxpayers could not manipulate the related-party transaction once it is on the ledger in the system and could provide better visibility of all aspects related to this transaction. What is even better is that the related-party transaction could also be linked to a smart contract, which is also possible with blockchains.

Smart contracts are standard contracts created and executed through the blockchain. Such contracts are low cost (as it does not require the assistance of legal professionals) and could potentially allow automated payments and self-execution. Translated to TP, smart contracts can provide a solution for the sometimes absence of related-party agreements in a TP analysis or the lack of trust that such agreements are at arm's

13. S. Sim et al., Blockchain, Transfer Pricing, Customs Valuations, and Indirect Taxes: Transforming the Global Tax Environment, Bloomberg BNA Insights, 6 June 2017.

length. Tax authorities could be afforded the opportunity to directly compare the related-party agreements with those with unrelated parties benefitting from more standardization of the contracts. Moreover, any changes to the agreement will be recorded in the blockchain and be visible to tax authorities, creating more transparency of the data and facilitating the detection of potential fraud, tax avoidance, or tax evasion attempts. For the latter purpose, blockchain could be combined with data analytics tools.

Tax authorities could potentially be on the same platform as taxpayers or have access to a taxpayer's private blockchain, helping them have real-time access to transactional data that could significantly facilitate assessments and reduce audits (or at least have better-targeted audits). For example, if the supplier enters a transaction on the ledger on the blockchain, and the tax authorities can access it, therefore, the taxpayer receiving the good may have more incentive to be compliant as he would be unable to conceal the information from the tax authorities.[14]

Considering the traceability of transactions, blockchain can be used to optimize the TP analysis. It can provide the tax authorities with a comprehensive history of the related-party transaction under analysis which could facilitate various stages of the TP analysis. Step 1 of the TP analysis, the accurate delineation of the transaction, could be facilitated by a blockchain as tax authorities would have a better overview of the transaction and would be able to trace a transaction and any changes to it. Step 2 of the TP analysis, the recognition of the accurate delineated transaction, could be expedited because a blockchain can provide tax authorities with a wider data set of potential comparables. It could therefore easily enable tax authorities to quickly identify whether the related-party transaction under analysis has commercial rationale and whether a price could be established under arm's length conditions. Step 3 of the TP analysis, the selection of the most appropriate TP method, could be facilitated by a blockchain as the better data set and visibility of the history of the related-party transaction can assist tax authorities in understanding which TP method could be suitable to price the transaction in a reliable manner. Finally, step 4 of the TP analysis, the application of selected TP method, could benefit from the larger data set and potentially better comparables provided by a blockchain (*see* Figure 28.4).

14. For example, the Shenzhen tax authorities implemented a pilot blockchain project in 2018 linking peer-to-peer payments for goods and services (e.g., through WeChat) to their system, having full visibility of such transactions. *See* S. Rao, The Potential Use of AI, Blockchain & Data Analytics in Transfer Pricing, beck.digitax, vol. 2, 2020.

Figure 28.4 Blockchain Applied to the Different Steps of the TP Analysis

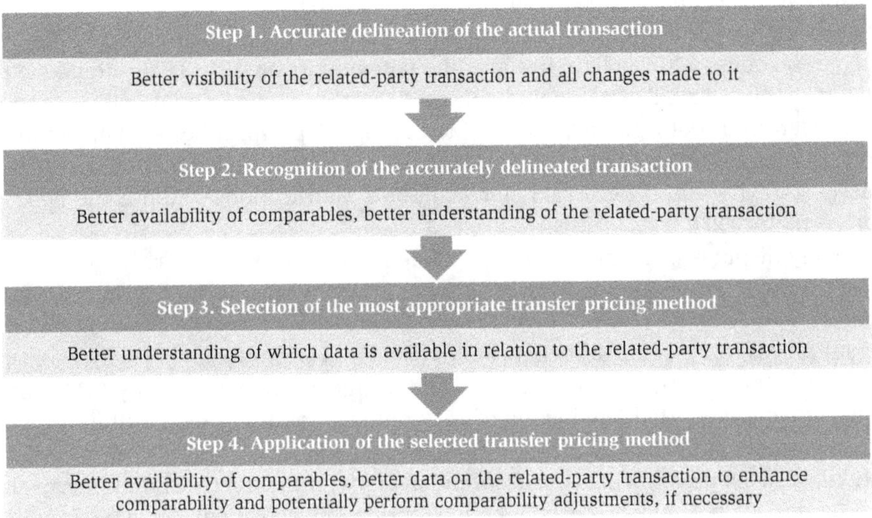

In particular, the potential availability of more comparables as blockchain transactions tends to be more standardized would help developing countries, as they typically suffer from a lack of comparables and resources to access commercial databases used by taxpayers. Proceeding forward, the greater availability of transaction-based data can promote the use of TP methods on a transactional basis instead of on an aggregated basis as often is the case currently due to the lack of information.

Traceability of related-party transactions is not only relevant for the TP analysis but could also be crucial in the area of deductibility of expenses, in particular in relation to intra-group services. According to Chapter VII of the OECD TPG, intra-group services can only be charged if they are actually rendered, provided a benefit for the receiving party, and an unrelated party would be willing to pay for such services or perform the services in-house. Moreover, the intra-group service should not be duplicated or considered a shareholder activity.[15] These discussions continue to be a significant source of disputes between taxpayers and tax authorities which could be reduced with the use of a blockchain or, if disputes still occur, negotiations could be facilitated by the information traceable in it.

Another significant area of TP dispute concerns intangibles. It is not always straightforward for taxpayers and tax authorities to agree on where the important functions related to the intangibles (specifically, the DEMPE functions) are performed. Therefore, the appropriate remuneration of the related parties involved in any of the DEMPE functions and where the residual profits related to the intangibles should be

15. For further details on intra-group services, *see* Michael Lang, Raffaele Petruzzi, Giammarco Cottani, Alfred Storck (2018) Fundamentals of Transfer Pricing: A Practical Guide, Kluwer Law International, Chapter IX.

allocated is sometimes not able to be discerned. A blockchain can facilitate those discussions by distinctly showing the steps from the development or acquisition of the intangible to its exploitation (as well as other functions).

By providing tax authorities with access to taxpayer data that is traceable and contemporaneous, a blockchain has also the potential to simplify TPD (often lengthy and overly complicated). This would substantially reduce the administrative compliance burden from both the taxpayer and tax authority perspectives as data could be more easily accessed on a real-time basis by tax authorities. They could make specific requests to taxpayers, if necessary, for additional clarifications without the need to submit lengthy TPD.

As many disputes in TP are heavily dependent on the facts of the case, blockchain can help to avoid or resolve disputes by providing tax authorities (and in international disputes, as often is the case in TP, all tax authorities involved in the dispute) with the relevant access to the same data that cannot be altered without leaving evidence. One example of a private blockchain used to avoid disputes is that created by IBM Global Financing which reported a reduction of 75% of the amount of time spent in disputes with its partners after the introduction of the blockchain.[16]

Multilateral cooperation in tax matters and intergovernmental collaboration can also benefit from a blockchain as exchange of information with taxpayer data could be achieved using this technology. Moreover, the immutable and real-time nature of the data could help prevent fraud, tax evasion, and tax avoidance.

As noted, a blockchain can provide tax authorities with better access to reliable data. Moreover, it can enhance the trust between taxpayers and tax authorities as it would provide security to tax authorities that the related-party transaction has not been altered. It will also provide the complete history of any potential changes made to the transaction. However, blockchain does not fully resolve the trust issue between taxpayers and tax authorities as it remains the responsibility of the taxpayer to enter the related-party transactions on the blockchain ledger. Thus, this initial data can either be omitted (i.e., never introduced in the blockchain) or manipulated prior to its introduction in the blockchain.

Historically, there has been information asymmetry between taxpayers and tax authorities with the former typically being the party with better access to their own groups' and peers' information. Blockchain has the potential to change this balance of information to provide tax authorities with the same access to information as taxpayers. What is also relevant for breaching this information gap is the timing when the information on related-party transactions is made available to tax authorities. The way that tax systems work inherently generates a timing issue between when the related-party transaction occurs when it is documented, and when it is potentially audited. A blockchain can give tax authorities access to real-time data on the related-party transaction and, in the event of a later assessment, the traceability of the transaction will significantly facilitate the discussions between taxpayers and tax authorities and provide effective input for the assessment.

16. *Supra* n. 13.

There are public and private blockchains. While the latter type may be more secure, tax authorities may be concerned that a private blockchain could be difficult or expensive to implement (and when providing training for personnel to use the blockchain). One possible solution to this concern is to have regional blockchains or to partner, whenever possible, with the private sector to create a shared platform.

While a blockchain is considered a secured platform, and only authorized personnel with the appropriate key can unlock its information, there are concerns that public blockchains (a potentially less expensive solution) may create confidentiality issues if non-authorized people somehow obtain access to taxpayers' sensitive data. In such a scenario, it would be difficult to determine who would be liable for the data leak as, once the information is entered into the blockchain ledger, it is beyond the control of one single party.

Countries' legislations and regulations would need to adapt to the use of a blockchain in order to regulate which types of information would be required to be imputed, who could have access, and who is liable in the unlikely event of a data leak, among other issues. Moreover, especially to be useful for TP, it would be necessary for jurisdictions to agree on an international standard for the use of blockchains.

Finally, tax authorities need to consider any legacy issues in the transition from old systems to blockchains. It may be burdensome to transfer the existing data to the blockchain, and it may ultimately not be the best technology in all cases. Each tax authority should consider if and to what extent a blockchain may be the most effective tool for its digital transformation.

3 IMPLEMENTATION

According to the OECD Innovation Index 2017, the majority of tax authorities have a below 50% innovation score with the median established at 40%.[17] In order to better navigate the new digital environment boosted by the COVID-19 pandemic and the rapid development of new business models, tax authorities must advance the use of new technologies. This must be accomplished with a clear vision and guidance[18] for going digital to avoid encountering undesirable implementation circumstances, such as taking legacy issues forward from old systems.

There are many possible technologies that tax authorities can leverage for purposes of TP control. However, the quality of data that is fed into these systems is very important. The best systems can deliver the most advantageous outcomes only if they are provided with accurate data. As mentioned in previous parts of this chapter, tax authorities are receiving more data than ever before. It is important that they ensure the accuracy of it before entering them into systems. Data may not be accurate if, for example, the design of the form that captures the data affords different interpretations by taxpayers. Those who are aware of such issues would have to either address these

17. OECD, *Tax Authorities 2019: Comparative Information on OECD and Other Advanced and Emerging Economies* (Paris: OECD Publishing, 2019), p. 37.
18. OECD, *Measuring the Digital Transformation: A Roadmap for the Future* (Paris: OECD Publishing, 2019).

inaccuracies or 'clean the data' prior to using it. In the event that the tax authorities are aware that such inaccuracies are minor and the resulting error is within a tolerable margin, they may still decide to consider using the data.

It is important that tax authorities recognize that technology, while being an enabler, would not mend the problems in the tax system. In terms of TP compliance, if the underlying factor that results in low compliance is due to, e.g., a lack of a transparent penalty regime, having good technology that greatly improves risk assessment and case selection would not address this problem. Another example could be when there are inaccuracies in the TP legislation, and it is unclear to the taxpayer which data is being requested. In such cases, even compliant taxpayers may be misled to submit inaccurate or irrelevant data; this cannot be resolved by having a digital system in place. Additionally, it is also important to consider the effects of technology and its potential interactions with the entire tax system and with other domestic and international regulations. For example, the protection of taxpayers' data must be observed.

It is important to ensure high levels of security when retaining and using taxpayer data as data leaks may occur. In TP, taxpayers need to submit substantial amounts of data to tax authorities that are, at times, commercially sensitive, and it is the tax authorities' responsibility to ensure that it is secured.

Once the tax authorities can ensure that the data is reasonably secured, data analytics tools need to be established to be able to use the data in an optimal manner. Merely having a data dump would not be of use to tax authorities. In fact, more data does not always mean better data and a better set of data does not always mean better use of it. Therefore, the quality of the data received and the ability to use the data effectively, e.g., by using a data analytics tool, is crucial to a successful implementation of a digital transformation by tax authorities.

For the reasons above, tax authorities need to also consider the resources that they have at their disposal to implement a digitalization project. New technologies can be very expensive and both software and hardware may need to be purchased to gain access to them. Human capital will also represent an important factor and is an expense to consider. Tax authorities will not only need to provide training for their current personnel to use the new technologies available to them but also recruit new personnel specialized in the use of new technologies. It is a trend that more modern and technologically advanced tax authorities have been employing data scientists, statisticians, and other personnel in the information communication and technology sector. Figure 28.5 represents some of the steps that tax authorities will need to take when implementing a digitalization project.

Figure 28.5 Implementation Steps

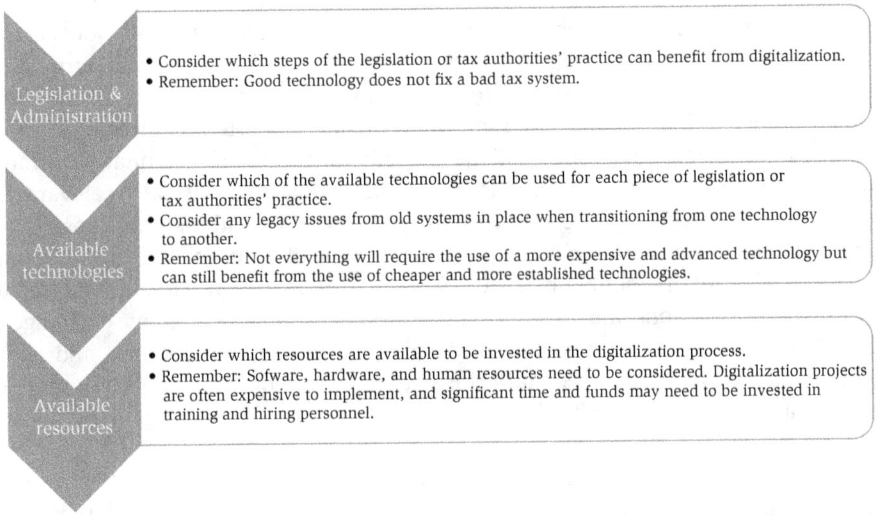

While tax authorities are in different stages of digitalization, the legislations and tax authorities' practices that are more likely to benefit from digitalization are those that establish clear and tested processes. Complex legislation or tasks performed by the tax authorities that require a high involvement of human resources or are very subjective may be more difficult to digitalize. Moreover, some legislation and administrative processes that were established prior to digitalization may no longer be needed in the future. For example, those for the service of notices to taxpayers in person or by mail may become obsolete if all taxpayers are converted to the digital mode with all correspondences and exchanges with the tax authorities occurring solely through the digital platforms.

Benefits from digitalization can range from a simplification of the application of legislation or administrative process to promoting more accuracy, certainty, transparency and, ultimately, trust in the tax system. While there are many factors to consider when going digital from a tax authority perspective, the benefits should typically outweigh the costs.

Available technologies must be considered in light of the resources available and how comfortable tax authorities' personnel are with the use of technologies. Sometimes, it is not efficient to implement very expensive technology for less complicated processes. It is also important to consider any legacy issues that tax authorities with existing digital processes may have when transitioning from one old technology to one that is more modern. The quality of the data and the management of data during the transitional period are key. The decision on which technology is ultimately better will depend on each tax authority and on which process is being digitalized as well as the short- and long-term effects of the digital transformation.

Implementation and running costs of digital systems should be considered, including the costs related to training and hiring of personnel, the decision for off-the-shelf modules, or creating their own systems. However, it is important to note that the resource investment in the implementation phase may be, at least partially, offset once the digital system is operating. Resources may be saved in the long term as a well-implemented digital system can free personnel from performing repetitive and time-consuming tasks, reduce common errors, ensure consistency, increase compliance, reduce the tax gap, and facilitate the identification of potential tax fraud, avoidance, and evasion schemes. These considerations are especially relevant for developing and emerging economies with limited resources and high tax gaps.

Technology can also assist in combating illicit financial flows related to TP not only by helping to identify potential tax fraud, avoidance, and evasion schemes and tracing related-party transactions and assets. It can also establish a more effective exchange of information between the tax authorities and other governmental and non-governmental entities. The tax authorities' digital system could be connected or communicate, for example, with the systems used by financial investigative units and banks.

Moreover, in many jurisdictions, there is a lack of communication between TP specialists, customs, and indirect taxes specialists. It is common that these departments do not communicate well which affords opportunities for tax arbitrage, double taxation, or double burden (i.e., formally not double taxation but nevertheless an economic burden on taxpayers if, e.g., a tax and a fee are charged on the same income). Having a digital system that can facilitate the interaction between direct taxes, in particular TP, indirect taxes, and customs can be very beneficial for jurisdictions. Tax authorities of developing countries that typically rely on substantial customs revenue can benefit from a consistent approach between the different departments within the government. Moreover, indirect taxes systems are typically at a more advanced stage of digitalization than TP systems. The latter can take examples and best practices from the former for building its own system and should ensure that the TP department communicates with the indirect taxes department.

Apart from facilitating tax authorities' processes and other benefits described in this chapter, technology may also help to develop efficient tax policies or test ideas for different tax policies prior to implementation.[19] The possibilities vary; however, perhaps the most significant impact in TP could be achieved with the simplification of TPD for both taxpayers (in preparing) and for tax authorities (in analysing). This could also occur by conducting an effective risk assessment to select TP cases for audit and for the facilitation of retrieval of documents and evidence for the audit discussion.

However, there are a number of other issues to consider when going digital. The various structures of tax authorities reflect different levels of approvals needed for certain processes.[20] There are distinct levels of comfort of tax authorities' personnel in using the new technologies and processes that are implemented. There will be related

19. *Supra* n. 2.
20. OECD, *Tax Authorities 2021: Comparative Information on OECD and Other Advanced and Emerging Economies* (Paris: OECD, 2021).

training that is necessary to develop capacity, and difficulties may arise in using new technologies. This could include a potentially negative impact on human interaction in bilateral or multilateral negotiations and cooperation in MAPs or APAs, cooperative compliance programmes (such as the ICAP), and joint or simultaneous audits. Connectivity issues should also be considered when implementing digital processes, in particular in developing countries where internet access may not be widespread or stable.

Taxpayers have also increasingly digitalized their systems, and this particularly accelerated due to the COVID-19 pandemic. They may have digital systems in place to, among others, monitor the increasing complexity and number of related-party transactions and their pricing, collect and store information to be used in TPD and tax audits, and monitor changes in legislation and regulations in multiple jurisdictions where they operate.[21]

It is crucial to establish a dialogue between taxpayers and tax authorities to ensure that both of their systems are able to communicate well as well as collect and process the same relevant data (*see* Figure 28.6). As taxpayers are typically ahead of tax authorities in digital transformation, tax authorities should seek inputs from the former when designing and implementing their own digital systems. This could be accomplished in the form of surveys, informal consultations with taxpayers, or by seeking a partnership with the private sector when this is possible. This would help tax authorities to build their digital systems by sharing both knowledge and resources and ensuring that they avoid illicitly favouring one taxpayer over another.

Figure 28.6 Interconnected Systems

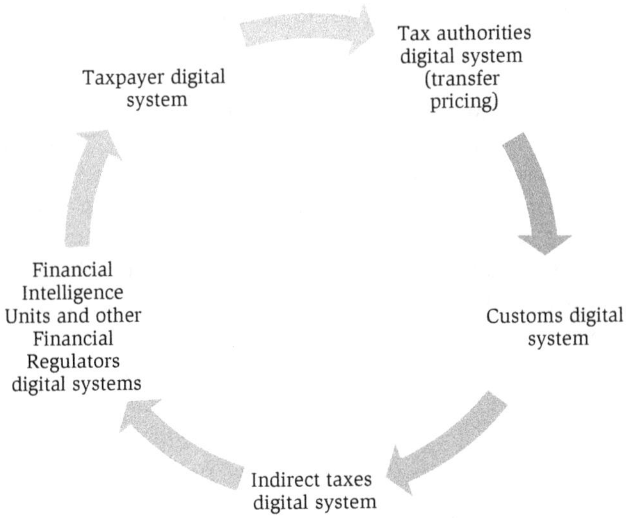

21. For further details on the use of new technologies by taxpayers, *see* Chapter 27 in this book.

Different tax authorities are in varying stages of digital transformation which could typically range from basic, consolidation, and optimization.[22] Figure 28.7 illustrates these different stages.

Figure 28.7 Different Stages of Digital Transformation for Tax Authorities

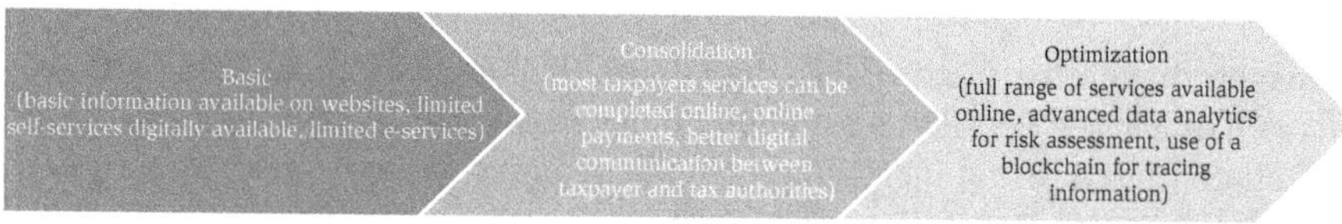

At what level a tax authority is currently at in its digital transformation and how far it can go depends on the readiness of the tax authority (including the resources available), quality of legislation and administrative processes, the interaction between the technology and other legislation (e.g., data privacy), and public support. Particularly intrusive processes established with technologies that may infringe a taxpayer's right to privacy or machine learning-based solutions that could ultimately make decisions on a taxpayer's assessment beyond the mere risk assessment phase may be problematic from the public's perspective.

TP audits typically involve enormous amounts of money and significant subjectivity in the interpretation of the specific facts and circumstances of the taxpayer. It is important to have sufficient transparency built into the systems that would allow taxpayers to understand why a certain decision was made and provide them with the necessary information to defend themselves in the event of an audit, court case, or MAPs. It is also relevant to guarantee that the degree of interference that occurs in the taxpayers' rights and guarantees are proportional to the decisions that are derived from programs that use AI.

As important as the quality of legislation and administrative processes are, the quality and neutrality of algorithms used in tax authorities' digital systems (typically for risk assessment or decision making) are of utmost relevance. Having people from a variety of backgrounds and considering different situations when setting the algorithm and ensuring that it is periodically updated would reduce the risk of the system being discriminatory or unfavourable to certain groups of taxpayers.

Technology can also greatly facilitate multilateral cooperation in tax matters which is a very relevant aspect of TP considering that TP legislation typically applies to cross-border transactions. The cross-border exchange of CbCR (following the implementation of BEPS Action 13)[23] using the common transmission system[24] platform developed by the OECD is perhaps the most relevant example of how technology can contribute to exchange of information and multilateral cooperation in a TP context. The common transmission system is also already used for exchange of information

22. WU Global Tax Policy Center, World Bank Group and EY, Digital Platforms: New Opportunities and Challenges for Tax authorities, Virtual Seminar, 31 March 2021 (unpublished).
23. *Supra* n. 5.
24. OECD, *Generic Status Message XML Schema: User Guide for Tax Authorities* (Paris: OECD, 2020).

pertaining to MAPs and is currently being considered for the exchange of information that will be required for the administration of Amount A and the tax certainty procedure of Pillar 1 of the OECD/G20/Inclusive Framework Digitalization of the Economy project.[25]

In relation to CbCR, the OECD Forum on Tax Administration has developed the TREAT, a tool designed to help tax authorities better identify certain tax risks using the information in the CbCR.[26] The TREAT builds on the guidance contained in the Handbook for Effective Tax Risk Assessment[27] and is a very welcomed tool for tax authorities receiving CbCRs.

In the EU context, unilateral tax rulings and APAs are also automatically exchanged electronically among the EU Member States based on Directive 2015/2376.[28] This is aimed to promote cooperation and transparency within the Union and aid in the fight against tax avoidance and aggressive tax planning. Likewise, under BEPS Action 5, unilateral tax rulings and APAs are also spontaneously exchanged electronically using the common transmission system among members of the Inclusive Framework.

Finally, once the new technology is implemented, it is critical to keep the system updated to reflect the rapidly changing regulatory framework. Changes in the legislation or administrative practices need to be quickly implemented into the new system to maintain its relevancy.

4 CONCLUSION

Digitalization of the economy and society will continue at an increasingly rapid pace that will likely have fundamental implications for tax policy and administration at both international and national levels. In particular with the impact of the COVID-19 pandemic, the digital transformation has been accelerated and tax authorities, like taxpayers, needed to establish digital processes in order to continue their operations.

The use of new technologies can, among others, enhance trust between taxpayers and tax administrations and promote tax compliance, reduce administrative burdens, and promote tax certainty. This chapter has shown how different technologies, such as data analytics (including advanced data analytics such as AI) and a blockchain, can help tax authorities in exercising their TP control in a more efficient manner. It has also briefly examined a number of limitations of the use of new technologies either from the

25. Statement on a Two-Pillar Solution to Address the Tax Challenges Arising from the Digitalisation of the Economy, https://www.oecd.org/tax/beps/statement-on-a-two-pillar-solution-to-address-the-tax-challenges-arising-from-the-digitalisation-of-the-economy-october-2021.pdf (last accessed 30 January 2022).
26. OECD, *OECD/G20 Inclusive Framework on BEPS Shows Progress in Implementing Tax Transparency Through Action 13 Country-by-Country Reporting* (Paris: 24 September 2020), https://www.oecd.org/tax/beps/oecd-g20-inclusive-framework-on-beps-shows-progress-in-implementing-tax-transparency-through-action-13-country-by-country-reporting.htm (last accessed 24 September 2021).
27. OECD, *Country-by-Country Reporting: Handbook on Effective Tax Risk Assessment* (Paris: OECD, 2017).
28. Council Directive (EU) 2015/2376 of 8 December 2015 amending Directive 2011/16/EU as regards mandatory automatic exchange of information in the field of taxation.

perspective of the technology itself or from a legal or practical perspective related to using such technology for TP control.

As noted in this chapter, there are varying levels of digitalization of tax authorities and different technologies that can be explored. Each provides distinct benefits and limitations and is better suited for different processes and the readiness of tax authorities. It is at the discretion of each tax authority to analyse the best approach for them according to their available resources and the level of digitalization of their taxpayers. It is important that tax authorities' digital systems communicate well with those of taxpayers and other government and non-government entities at both national and international levels. The digital system should be easy to use and be able to extract meaningful information to be utilized in TP control.

As analysed in section 2, all steps of the TP analysis can likely benefit from the use of new technologies. Moreover, different areas of the TP analysis can be facilitated such as the comparability analysis, functional analysis, TPD, and TP dispute avoidance and resolution.

Section 3 demonstrated that implementation is key. The quality of data should be observed in accordance with the garbage-in-garbage-out principle as even great technologies cannot work with a bad set of data. Further, the quality of the legislation and administrative processes should be taken into consideration, and tax authorities should bear in mind that technology cannot fix an inadequately functioning tax system. Finally, the design of algorithms must be neutral and transparent and not favour or discriminate against specific taxpayers. The digital transformation should always consider taxpayers' rights and ensure the security of their data.

Tax authorities should also adapt the capabilities of their workforce to this changing environment. Tedious repetitive tasks can be taken over by digitalization, freeing employees to work on more complex and valuable work. This is especially important in the TP context for which analysing enormous amounts of data can be time-consuming, and better use of the tax authorities' time may be to focus on the many complex issues typically present in TP cases.

While taxpayers are generally at the forefront of digital transformation when compared to tax authorities, the impact of technology on TP for both is converging. On the one hand, taxpayers are using technology to ensure, among others, centralization and consistency in the implementation of their TP policies as well as to better administer their data and TPD. On the other hand, tax authorities tend to approach TP traditionally from a jurisdictional perspective, i.e., protection of their own tax base, which can sometimes conflict with taxpayers' global systems. However, with advanced technologies, more cross-border exchanges of information, and the increase in multilateral cooperation in tax matters, tax authorities would likely also be driven to look more at the consistency in implementation of TP policies within an MNE at a global level.

Other Topics

CHAPTER 29

Transfer Pricing and Antitrust Rules

Marco D'Ostuni & Jacopo Figus Diaz[*]

1 INTRODUCTION

An interplay could exist between antitrust law and tax law.

In recent years, the interaction between EU competition law and tax law has focused on state aid cases, notably those concerning *FIAT*, *Amazon*, and *Apple*.[1] After all, Title VII of the TFEU reads 'Common rules on competition, taxation and approximation of laws'.

The aim of this contribution is to analyse and discuss a less debated area, i.e., how antitrust laws and TP may interact, including any potential points of contact or

* This chapter is based on a lecture, '*How to set Market Prices under Competition and Transfer Pricing Rules*', given by Marco D'Ostuni at the Vienna University of Economics and Business – Institute for Austrian and International Tax Law – Transfer Pricing Workshop, on 21 May 2019.

1. A list of state aid cases concerning Member States' tax rulings is available at, https://ec.europa.eu/competition/state_aid/tax_rulings/index_en.html (last accessed 30 January 2022).

discrepancies. Indeed, both antitrust law and tax law rely on certain economic concepts, notably prices and costs, and require a comparison between different transactions to assess the lawfulness of certain practices. Prices and costs are key issues in business economics and lie at the crossroads between microeconomic theory and marketing strategies.

Through the analysis of the antitrust and TP framework as well as by using a number of real cases, what the two branches of law may learn from each other and where material similarities or differences lie will be assessed.

2 FUNDAMENTALS OF ANTITRUST RELEVANT FOR TP

This section will provide an overview of certain basic principles and concepts of antitrust that may be relevant in the assessment of TP, specifically: the concepts of 'market price', 'relevant market', and 'undertaking'; and the use of prices, costs, or transaction comparisons.[2]

2.1 Absence of a Statutory Market Price Concept

Although antitrust rules have a primary objective to ensure free competition and the proper functioning of the markets (and although these terms are widely used in public and private enforcement), there is no statutory definition of the concepts of 'free competition' and 'market price' under EU competition law.

In a perfect competition scenario, the market price is set at the intersection between the market demand and the market supply curves. In such a situation, a firm's price for its product is equal to its marginal cost which is the amount paid for producing an extra unit of product; companies are price takers and cannot deviate from the market price (*see* Figure 29.1).

2. Various excellent handbooks on EU competition law are available. *See*, e.g., Bellamy & Child, European Union Law of Competition (in David Bailey and Laura Elizabeth Jones eds, 8th ed., Oxford, 2018); Alison Jones, Brenda Sufrin and Niamh Dunne, *Jones & Sufrin's EU Competition Law Text, Cases, and Materials* (7th ed., Oxford, 2019); Richard Whish and David Bailey, *Competition Law* (9th ed., Oxford, 2018); Jonathan Faull and Ali Nikpay, *The EU Law of Competition* (3rd ed., Oxford, 2014).

Figure 29.1 Equilibrium in a Perfect Competition Scenario

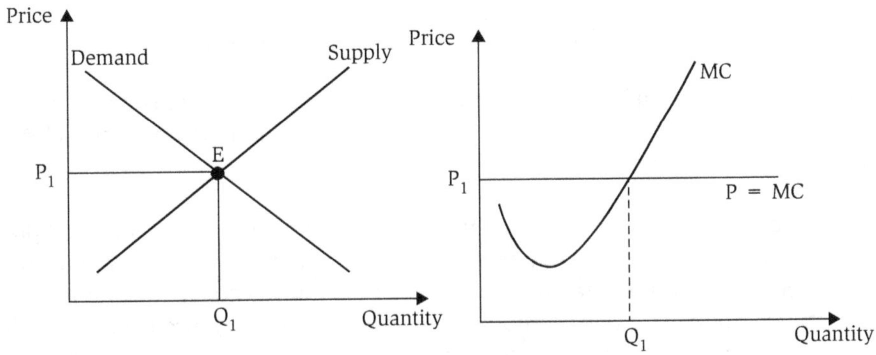

However, perfect competition is a theoretical market structure that rarely exists. It requires several factors, among which include: (i) a large number of buyers and sellers who have perfect information; (ii) homogeneity of the product in question; and (iii) absence of barriers to entry or exit from the market.

In the real economy, the degree of competition in a market varies depending on the market structure. At one end of the spectrum, there are markets in which fierce competition exists that are similar to perfectly competitive markets. In sharp contrast are markets where there is only one producer (i.e., the monopolist). Somewhat in the middle, markets that are, to varying degrees, concentrated where only a few leading firms are active (i.e., an oligopoly). In a competitive market (although not a perfectly competitive one), the market price will be relatively competitive approximate to that in a perfect competition scenario. By contrast, in an oligopolistic or a monopolist market, the market price will typically be set well above the competitive price (it will be the oligopolistic or monopoly price, respectively).[3]

However, market prices may not only depend on the relevant market structure; they may be altered by antitrust infringements, notably cartels, that typically result in higher prices that are applied by the cartel participants and therefore lead to artificially inflated market prices.

Besides the concept of 'market price', antitrust often relies on 'prices' and 'costs'. For antitrust purposes, these may refer to:

- a specific company's price and costs that may be above or below the market price or the prices and costs of other companies; or
- prices and costs that would have been applied or incurred in the absence of a specific transaction or infringement of competition law.

3. Richard Whish and David Bailey, *Competition Law*, 7-8 and 571 (9th ed., Oxford, 2018); Jonathan Faull and Ali Nikpay, *The EU Law of Competition*, §§ 1.65-1.71 and 1.78-1.82, 21-26 (3rd ed., Oxford, 2014); Frank Livesey, Oligopoly and Monopoly, 66-81 (in Brian Atkinson, Frank Livesey and Bob Milward eds, *Applied Economics*, Macmillan Publishers Limited 1998).

The latter type of 'price' is what adheres closer to and is often referred to as 'market price' in a perfect competition scenario.

2.2 The Concept of 'Undertaking' and 'Relevant Market'

In addition to prices and costs, two further key concepts of antitrust should be introduced for the purpose of this analysis: the notions of 'undertaking' and 'relevant market':

(1) Undertaking: EU competition law applies to agreements and unilateral practices put in place by undertakings which are defined based on a functional approach. An undertaking encompasses the entire economic entity or company group including all subsidiaries solely or jointly controlled by the same parent company provided that it engages in commercial or economic activities whether or not such activities are carried out for profit.[4] Antitrust rules therefore apply to transactions with or practices vis-à-vis unrelated parties that are performed by an entity engaged in economic activities.

As a result, antitrust does not apply to intra-group transactions, intra-group restructuring operations, or behaviour from entities that do not engage in economic activity (e.g., the EU Member States in the exercise of public powers). However, as will be discussed further in this contribution, intra-group transactions may be used as comparables relevant for antitrust purposes.

(2) Relevant product and geographic market: Practices that are relevant under antitrust rules (i.e., agreements, unilateral practices, and mergers and acquisitions) are assessed in the relevant product and geographic market. The concept of 'relevant market' under antitrust laws is defined by both product and geographic characteristics and is typically different from the definitions of market used in other contexts (e.g., companies often use the term 'market' generally to refer to the area where they sell products or to refer to the industry or sector more broadly). For antitrust purposes:
   - A relevant product market includes all products that are regarded as interchangeable or substitutable by the consumer by reason of the products' characteristics, their prices, and their intended use.[5]

4. There is no statutory definition of an undertaking in the TFEU. However, the CJEU (formerly known as ECJ) has interpreted this concept broadly. It has held that 'in competition law, the term "undertaking" must be understood as designating an economic unit for the purpose of the subject-matter of the agreement in question even if in law that economic unit consists of several persons, natural or legal' (*Hydrotherm Gerätebau GmbH v. Compact del Dott. Ing. Mario Andreoli & C. Sas. ECR 2999,* Case 170/83 (ECJ 1984) § 11). The CJEU has also clarified that 'in the context of competition law [...] the concept of an undertaking encompasses every entity engaged in an economic activity, regardless of the legal status of the entity and the way in which it is financed' (*Klaus Höfner and Fritz Elser v. Macrotron GmbH*, ECR I-01979, Case C-41/90 (ECJ 1991), § 21).
5. Cfr. Commission Notice on the definition of relevant market for the purposes of Community competition law, OJ C 372 (9 December 1997).

- A relevant geographic market comprises the area in which the conditions of competition are sufficiently homogeneous and can be distinguished from neighbouring areas because the conditions of competition are appreciably different in those areas.[6]

As a result, 'prices' and 'costs' in the antitrust world relate to products for which there is a relevant product and geographic market. An input that is not actually or potentially sold on the market is still relevant for TP purposes, however, it would rarely be relevant for antitrust purposes.

3 THE USE OF COMPARISONS IN ANTITRUST

As illustrated in more detail in other chapters, the assessment of TP often requires a comparison between different transactions.

Commercial or financial transactions between related parties are not necessarily driven by market forces. The arm's length principle seeks to adjust profits arising from such transactions by reference to the conditions that would be made between unrelated parties in comparable transactions under comparable circumstances.

The starting point of a TP analysis is therefore a comparability assessment aimed at establishing that no material differences between the transactions being compared affect the comparison or that reasonably accurate adjustments can be made to achieve comparability.

As mentioned in the OECD TPG,[7] comparability factors that might be relevant to the assessment include: (i) the characteristic of the property or services transferred; (ii) the functions performed (taking into account assets used and risks assumed); (iii) the contractual terms; (iv) the economic circumstances; and (v) the business strategies pursued by the parties.

The selection of the most appropriate TP method would follow. Traditional transactional methods are the most direct approaches for determining whether a tested transaction is at arm's length. Nonetheless, there are situations (e.g., when parties make valuable and unique contributions to the transaction or engage in highly integrated activities) when transactional profits methods may be more appropriate.

In antitrust, there are also instances when the assessment of a practice is based on a comparative analysis. The comparison may relate to prices or to costs.

3.1 Price Comparison: Antitrust Damages Action

A price comparison analysis and related tools are relevant in antitrust, particularly in the field of actions for damages caused by cartels or abuses of dominant position (referred to as 'private enforcement' of antitrust rules).

6. Cfr. Commission Notice on the definition of relevant market for the purposes of Community competition law, OJ C 372 (9 December 1997).
7. Paragraph 1.36 OECD TPG.

Under EU law, victims of cartels have a right to full compensation[8] which means that the person who has suffered harm should be placed 'in the position in which that person would have been had the infringement of competition law not been committed. It shall therefore cover the right to compensation for actual loss and for loss of profit, plus the payment of interest',[9] but it should not lead to 'compensation of harm exceeding that caused by the infringement of competition law to the claimant'.[10] Moreover, it is presumed that cartel infringements cause harm.[11]

In such actions, plaintiffs typically claim that the higher prices imposed by the cartel or paid as a result of a dominant company's abusive behaviour caused damage for which they request compensation. Simply stated, the damages quantification in private enforcement actions is often based on a comparison of (i) the price that the plaintiff paid for a product under the cartel against (ii) the price that the plaintiff would have paid for the same product absent the cartel. The delta between the two prices is generally referred to as the cartel 'overcharge'.[12]

The overcharge is often calculated pursuant to 'comparison-based methods': the price applied in the infringement scenario is compared with the price that would have been applied in a non-infringement situation and is calculated on the basis of price data observed on either:

- the same product and geographic market at a time before and/or after the infringement;
- the same product market but on a different, albeit similar, geographic market;
- a different product market with similar market characteristics; or
- the basis of a combination of the above scenarios.[13]

8. As early as in the 1970s, the CJEU held that the EU antitrust rules 'create direct rights in respect of the individuals concerned which the national courts must safeguard' (*BRT v. SABAM*, Reports of Cases 313, Case C-127/73 (ECJ 1974), § 17). In later rulings, the CJEU laid the foundation for the right of any natural or legal person to claim full compensation for the harm caused to them by an infringement of EU antitrust rules (*see*, e.g., *Courage and Crehan*, ECR I-06297, Case C-453/99 (ECJ 2001), §§ 25-26; *Manfredi*, ECR I-06619, Cases C 295/04-C 298/04 (ECJ 2006), §§ 89-91). These principles were subsequently reflected in the Directive 2014/104/EU of the European Parliament and of the council of 26 November 2014 on certain rules governing actions for damages under national law for infringements of the competition law provisions of the Member States and of the EU Text with EEA relevance OJ L 349 (5 December 2014) (Actions for Damages Directive).
9. Article 3 of the Actions for Damages Directive.
10. Article 12 of the Actions for Damages Directive.
11. Article 17 of the Actions for Damages Directive.
12. The European Commission has provided general guidance on the quantification of harm in antitrust damages actions, cfr. Communication from the Commission on quantifying harm in actions for damages based on breaches of Article 101 or 102 of the Treaty on the Functioning of the European Union Text with EEA relevance, OJ C 167 (13 June 2013) and commission staff working document, practical guide, quantifying harm in actions for damages based on breaches of Article 101 or 102 of the treaty on the functioning of the EU accompanying the communication from the commission on quantifying harm in actions for damages based on breaches of Article 101 or 102 of the Treaty on the Functioning of the European Union, https://ec.europa.eu/competition/antitrust/actionsdamages/quantification_en.html (last accessed 30 January 2022) ('Practical Guide On Quantifying Harm').
13. Cfr. Practical Guide On Quantifying Harm, pp. 16-21.

The strength of comparison-based methods lies in the fact that they use real-life data that are observed in the same or similar markets. Whether the level of similarity between infringement and comparable markets is sufficient for such a comparison to be used in quantifying harm depends on national legal systems.

That stated, other methods for calculating the overcharge exist that are not based on a comparative exercise. Among those, the most relevant are:[14]

- simulation models that simulate market outcomes on the basis of economic models; or
- cost-based and finance-based methods that, respectively, estimate market prices on the basis of costs of production and a reasonable profit margin for the undertakings or estimate whether the claimant has suffered harm and the amount of that harm on the basis of the financial performance of the claimant or the defendant.

3.2 Cost-Price or Cost-Price Plus Price-Price Comparison: Predatory Pricing and Excessive Pricing

A comparative analysis may also be relevant in the antitrust assessment of certain pricing conducts. Under EU law, antitrust authorities rely on cost-price or a cost-price plus a price-price comparison to establish whether certain behaviour may constitute unlawful predatory pricing or excessive pricing practices. Importantly, the cost-price analysis is an internal comparison, i.e., the comparison is between a company's own prices and costs.

Predatory pricing: Predatory practices may be generally defined as behaviour by a dominant company that applies low prices deliberately incurring losses or foregoing profits in the short term, so as to foreclose or be likely to foreclose its competitors and to strengthen or maintain its market power.[15]

Cost benchmarks that antitrust authorities are likely to use in the predatory pricing assessment may include:

- ATC.
- LRAIC (i.e., the average of all of the variable and fixed costs that a company incurs to produce a particular product).
- AAC (i.e., the average of the costs that could have been avoided if the company had not produced a discrete amount of extra output).
- AVC.

Under EU competition law, a dominant company's predatory practice is unlawful when the price that it applies is below its AVCs or its AACs depending on the specific case. If the price is above the company's AVCs or AACs but below the company's ATCs

14. Cfr. Practical Guide On Quantifying Harm, pp. 33-39.
15. Cfr. Communication from the Commission – Guidance on the Commission's enforcement priorities in applying Article 82 of the EC Treaty to abusive exclusionary conduct by dominant undertakings, OJ C 45 (24 February 2009) ('Guidance Paper') § 63.

or long-run average incremental cost, depending on the specific circumstances, a predatory practice is unlawful only if it is shown that the dominant company acted with predatory intent or pursuant to a predatory strategy. If the price is above the company's ATCs or long-run average incremental cost (again depending on the specific circumstances), the practice is not predatory.[16]

Excessive pricing: The imposition of high prices may also be subject to antitrust scrutiny as it may directly harm buyers and consumers. Under EU competition law, excessive pricing by a dominant company requires a two-step analysis: a cost-price comparison and a price-price comparison. Excessive pricing is unlawful when two cumulative conditions are satisfied:

(1) the difference between the dominant undertaking's costs and prices is excessive; and
(2) the price is unfair in itself or when compared with competitive benchmarks.[17]

Interestingly, there is no single method for identifying the competitive benchmark. Depending on the circumstances, the dominant company's price could be compared with the price of competing products, prices applied by the dominant company for the same product in other countries, or in other time periods (e.g., in the event of abrupt increases).[18]

3.3 Identification of the Relevant Transaction and Comparable

The identification of the appropriate (1) transaction to be compared and (2) term of comparison (i.e., the comparable circumstances) is a key issue in antitrust comparative analyses which may have substantial effects on the outcome of the comparative exercise.

16. *AKZO v. Commission*, ECR I-03359, Case 62/86 (ECJ 1991). *See also* Guidance Paper, §§ 64-66.
17. *United Brands Company and United Brands Continentaal BV v. Commission*, ECR 207, Case 27/76 (ECJ 1978), §§ 248-252. *See also* e.g., Bellamy & Child, European Union Law of Competition, § 10.123, 935 (in David Bailey and Laura Elizabeth Jones eds, 8th ed., Oxford, 2018); Alison Jones, Brenda Sufrin and Niamh Dunne, *Jones & Sufrin's EU Competition Law Text, Cases, and Materials*, 559-566 (7th ed., Oxford, 2019); Richard Whish and David Bailey, *Competition Law*, 735-743 (9th ed., Oxford, 2018).
18. Recently, European Commission Press release, *Antitrust: Commission accepts commitments by Aspen to reduce prices for six off-patent cancer medicines by 73% addressing excessive pricing concerns*, https://ec.europa.eu/commission/presscorner/detail/en/ip_21_524 (last accessed 30 January 2022). *See also* Italian Competition Authority case A480 – Price increase of Aspen's drugs, decision 26185 of 14 October 2016, available in an English translation at, https://en.agcm.it/dotcmsDOC/pressrelease/A480_eng.pdf (last accessed 30 January 2022). For comparisons with prices applied by competing undertakings, *see Corinne Bodson v. SA Pompes funèbres des régions libérées*, ECR 2479, Case 30/87 (ECJ 1988), § 31. For comparison with prices applied by the same undertaking *see* CJEU, 11 November 1986, *British Leyland Public Limited Company v. Commission of the European Communities*, ECR 3263, Case 226/84 (ECJ 1986), §§ 25-30.

The main variables to be considered include:

- the object of the transaction; and
- the relevant geographic and temporal perimeter.

Example

Company A, located in Country X and Company B, located in Country Y are part of the ABC Group. Company A decides to sell a product in Country X at CU 10 per unit for a limited period of time (e.g., six months). After the initial period of time, Company A increases the price to CU 20. The product AVC is CU 15 per unit.

A number of questions would typically arise in the cost-price comparison to assess if Company A's behaviour is an unlawful predatory pricing practice. By way of example:

- Should the price-cost comparison be limited to the initial 6-month offer period or should it take into account the post-offer period? (*relevant temporal period*).
- If the product AVC in areas closer to Company A's production plant was CU 9 due to lower transport costs, would the practice be considered predatory in those areas? (*relevant geographic perimeter*).
- Suppose that, instead of one offer, Company A launches two parallel offers: the same product is sold at a price of CU 10 to some customers whereas it is sold at a price of CU 15 to other customers. Should the prices of the two offers be combined for the purposes of the cost-price comparison? If so, should they be combined into a mere average (i.e., CU 10 + CU 15/2 = CU 12.5) or into a weighted average that takes into account other variables, e.g., the volumes sold at each price, the length of each promotional offer, etc.? (*object of the transaction*).

Further, both the relevant transactions and comparables may be affected and inflated by competition law infringements. For example, a cartel can increase the margin in seemingly comparable transactions above the competitive level. Suppose that:

- Company A manufactures the product in question in Country X.
- The cost of the product is CU 5.
- Company A sells the product to Company B in Country Y at CU 10.
- Company A sells the same product on the market in Country X and Country Z.

In Country X, Company A sells the product at a price of CU 12. In Country Z, where the price of the product is inflated by an unlawful cartel, Company A sells the same product at CU 15.

It follows that, as a result of a competition law infringement that alters prices, the price (CU 15) and mark-up (CU 10) applied by Company A in Country Z would not be suitable comparable transactions to assess Company B's TP.

4 ANTITRUST CONSIDERATIONS ON TP METHODS

From the antitrust experience, a number of considerations that may be relevant for the purposes of establishing the TP may be drawn.

First, like in the TP methods (especially in traditional transactional methods), the quantification of the antitrust damages is often based on a comparison of transactions which makes it necessary to identify the appropriate transaction as well as the geographic and temporal perimeter of the comparable. A regression analysis is a beneficial tool that is often used in antitrust litigation to identify alternative causes for the differences between the compared data sets and eliminate those from the comparison.

Suppose a cartel in the market for flour:

(1) The prices paid by bakeries to the milling companies during the cartel are compared with the same prices paid by bakeries in the pre-infringement period. The comparison shows a price increase of 20% during the infringement period.

(2) Suppose also that there are indications that the increase may not exclusively be due to the cartel as the cost of an important input (e.g., cereals) increased significantly during the cartel period.

(3) It will therefore be unclear how much of the increase in the price of flour is due to the cartel and how much is due to the increased input cost (i.e., the rise in the cereals' price).

A regression analysis may show the statistical relationship between input costs and flour price by observing data relating to the input costs (i.e., the cereals' prices) and the corresponding price of flour during a non-infringement period. In the case represented in Figure 29.2, data observation shows that past increases in the input costs were fully passed on to the flour price (e.g., when the cereal price increased CU 10 (from CU 50 to CU 60), the flour price also increased of CU 10 (from CU 120 to CU 130)).[19]

19. The example and Figure 29.2 are taken from the EU Commission, Practical Guide on Quantifying Harm, p. 27.

Figure 29.2 Communication on Quantifying Harm in Antitrust Damages Actions

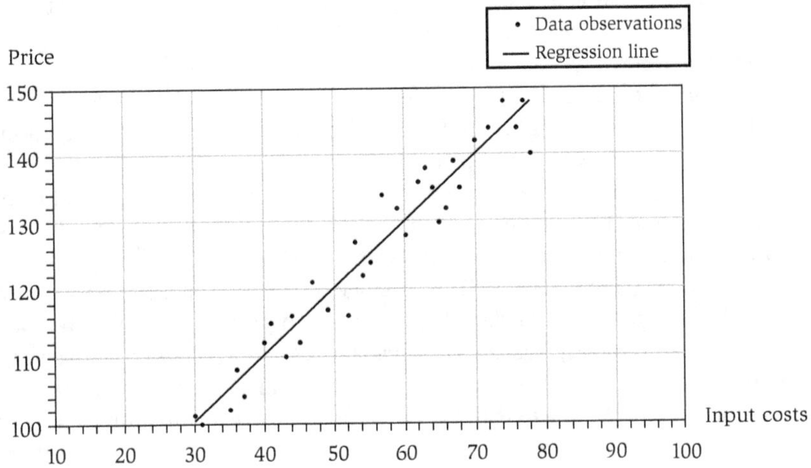

Second, with respect to the choice between traditional transaction methods and transactional profit methods for the TP quantification, it is worth noting that, also in an antitrust, empirical data are preferable to costs models. This is because economic models may lead to significantly different results depending on how the models are built.

Third, the identification of an appropriate margin in the resale price method may have antitrust implications. In margin squeeze practices, a dominant company charges a price for a product on the upstream market that, compared to the price it charges on the downstream market, does not allow an equally efficient competitor to trade profitably in the downstream market on a lasting basis.[20] The calculation of the appropriate margin for TP purposes may show that the actual margins that the dominant company applies downstream are too low; therefore, it may help to demonstrate that the practice constitutes an unlawful margin squeeze.

5 DIRECT RELEVANCE OF TP IN ANTITRUST CASES

Leaving aside the well-known state aid tax cases, it appears that the direct relevance of the TP in antitrust cases has thus far been limited.

20. Guidance Paper § 80.

Court Case

In *Glaxo France*,[21] the FCA exceptionally relied on the TP instead of costs to assess predatory pricing practices.[22] Based on the FCA's findings, the case can be summarized as follows:

(1) GlaxoSmithKline France (Glaxo France) previously purchased its drug, Zinnat®, an antibiotic that is commonly used in hospitals before operations, from its sister company, Adechsa GmbH.
(2) The FCA compared Glaxo France's sale price of Zinnat® to the TP that Glaxo France paid to its sister company; it concluded that the prices at which Glaxo France sold Zinnat® in France in 1999 and 2000 were predatory.
(3) Glaxo France challenged the FCA's reliance on the TP instead of on the costs for competition law purposes (as explained in section 3.2, the predatory pricing test is typically based on a price-cost comparison, e.g., between the price and ATC or AVC). In particular, Glaxo France argued that the TP is called upon to exclusively fulfil a monetary and fiscal function and is not equivalent to the remuneration of a supplier or a subcontractor that adheres to a logic of positive margin.[23]
(4) The FCA took into account the following elements to conclude that the TP could, in that case, be used as a reliable proxy for AVC:
    - Glaxo France did not provide its AVC or alternative measures of costs.[24]
    - The TP reflected a genuine transaction; it was not an artificial financial calculation.[25]
    - The TP was at an arm's length price as it was subject to audit by the tax authorities who found no issues.[26]
    - Glaxo France had a commercial autonomy within the group to fix its prices and operate on the market. According to the OECD's guidelines relied upon by Glaxo France, in these cases, the TP should correspond to a price of free competition.[27]

In Italy, Article 19 of the ARERA's administrative and accounting unbundling rules for companies operating in the electricity and gas sectors provides that:[28]

21. French competition authority, 14 March 2007, GlaxoSmithKline France (Glaxo France).
22. French competition authority decision 07-D-09 of 14 March 2007 concerning practices put in place by GlaxoSmithKline France (Glaxo France).
23. Glaxo France, §195.
24. Glaxo France, § 213.
25. Glaxo France, §196.
26. Glaxo France, § 210.
27. Glaxo France, §§ 197-206.
28. Working English translation of Article 19 of ARERA's integrated text of the provisions regarding the administrative and accounting separation (unbundling) for companies operating in the electricity and gas sectors and related publication and communication obligations, annex to ARERA's resolution of 18 January 2007, No. 11/07, approving the integrated text of the provisions regarding the obligations of administrative and accounting separation (unbundling) for companies operating in electricity and gas sectors and related publication and communication obligations as well as subsequent amendments.

> Regardless of the price actually paid, the value of the sales of goods and provision of services within a corporate group must be based on the principle of price of free competition or normal value, that is the price principle that would have been agreed upon between independent companies for identical or similar operations under similar or identical conditions in the free market.

In an ongoing investigation, the ARERA preliminarily ascertained that the intracompany agreements between a public utility company and its distribution arm were based on cost-plus and other calculation methods whereas the price of free competition should have been used. ARERA's proceedings are still pending.

6 CONCLUSION

In principle, antitrust and TP provisions are based on underlying different conceptual premises.

On the one hand, EU competition law relies on the concepts of 'undertaking', 'relevant product', 'geographic market', and various price and costs parameters.

On the other hand, the TP provisions rely on the notion of 'related parties', the arm's length principle, and the TP identification methodologies.

However, a comparative examination can help to identify material similarities or differences and improve on existing methodologies on both sides.

CHAPTER 30

Transfer Pricing and Customs Valuation

Karol Dziwiński[*]

* This work was reviewed by the WCO.

1 INTRODUCTION

A significant proportion of world trade is conducted by MNEs, and a substantial amount consists of the transfer of goods, intangibles, and services within MNEs. This makes international taxation, and in particular TP, a top priority for tax authorities as well as MNEs. As it is inherent in the activities of MNEs that they operate internationally, in the case of transactions involving goods, not only taxation but also the application of customs duties will be of concern for them. The coexistence of two sets of rules governing the imposition of charges in international trade will, of course, not be seamless taking into account various goals of the authorities responsible for the imposition of these charges, different rules binding in different jurisdictions, and usually no harmonization between tax and customs.

As the TP rules apply in transactions between related parties, the information used to settle such dealings at arm's length is also often employed by the MNEs for the analysis of the correct determination of the customs value of goods sold in cross-border transactions. However, if the use of the same data sets for both purposes might be attractive to MNEs, the tax and customs authorities often remain cautious. Nonetheless, it is an interesting concept and was also given attention in the international arena.[1] Another point of interest that can fall under scrutiny is the interplay between the TP adjustments and customs value. Finally, the administrative cooperation between tax and customs authorities also arises as an interesting point for developments, comprising areas such as exchange of information, advance rulings, and dispute resolution.

Taking into account that various common grounds exist between the TP and customs, this chapter will comprehensively examine the relationship between these two areas. The considerations will begin with the general introduction of the main principles governing customs valuation in order to then indicate the areas of interplay between the TP and customs and the reasons for this. In particular, the chapter will deal with the use of TP information for customs purposes, the influence of TP adjustments on customs valuation, and the administrative approaches towards the facilitation of the coexistence of the TP and customs.

1. This concept has been featured prominently in the work of the TCCV. It was established to ensure the uniformity in interpretation and application of the WTO Agreement (the Agreement) at the technical level. It is responsible for examining specific technical questions arising in the regular administration of the Customs valuation system of Members. It is also responsible for furnishing information and advice on any matters concerning the valuation of imported goods for customs purposes as may be requested by any members of the TCCV in the form of advisory opinion, commentaries or explanatory notes. It also facilitates, as requested, technical assistance to members to further the international acceptance of the Agreement.

2 THE PRINCIPLES OF CUSTOMS VALUATION

2.1 General Remarks

The discussion that is the primary point of this chapter shall begin with defining the main principles of customs valuation that are the background of the interplay between the TP and customs. Customs duties are intrinsically those that are imposed upon the importation of goods. It is important to emphasize that, contrary to the rules governing the TP, customs duties do not apply to services. The key issue in the imposition of customs duties is the determination of the appropriate customs value of imported goods and the choice of the appropriate tariff rate. This raises the issue of the correct determination of the customs value of imported goods that is primarily utilized as the basis for determining customs duty liability for imported goods when an ad valorem duty applies.[2] On one hand, the customs value is crucial for governments in securing consistent contributions to revenue and, on the other hand, is also important for issues such as accurate trade statistics, monitoring quantitative restrictions, applying tariff preferences, and collecting national taxes.[3]

2.2 Main Rules of Customs Valuation and Customs Valuation Method

Customs valuation is based, in principle, on the rules expressed in the WTO Agreement concluded during the 8th Round of Multilateral Trade Negotiations known as the Uruguay Round. Article 1 of the WTO Agreement stipulates the general rules that shall be respected when determining the proper customs value by indicating that it should be based on the transaction value, i.e., the price actually paid or payable for the goods when sold for export to the country of importation.[4] The WTO Agreement thus constitutes a basis for the determination of the customs value of goods. As all WTO Members are obligated to apply the provisions of the WTO Agreement,[5] it can be considered as a powerful tool composed of a solid foundation of the general rules governing customs valuation.

The customs valuation methodology that is established in the WTO Agreement contains a sequence of valuation methods with the transaction value method as the primary approach.[6] It has been reported by the WTO members that the transaction value method as envisaged in Article 1 of the WTO Agreement is employed for over

---

2. The Glossary of International Customs Terms defines ad valorem duties and taxes as 'duties and taxes which are collected on the basis of value'.
3. Cremer, I., Kitaura, M., *Customs Value*, in: Bakker, A., Obuoforibo, B. (eds), *TP and Customs Valuation: Two Worlds to Tax as One*, IBFD, 2009, p. 61.
4. The Preamble to the WTO Agreement states: '*[r]ecognizing that the basis for valuation of goods for Customs purposes should, to the greatest extent possible, be the transaction value of the goods being valued*'.
5. Cremer, Kitaura, *supra* n. 3, p. 64.
6. There are a series of methods that are explicated in the WTO Agreement. These are commonly referred to as the transaction value method, transaction of identical goods method, transaction value of similar goods method, deductive value method, computed value method, and the fall back option. These approaches are to be applied in a sequential order.

90% of all importations.[7] However, for the remaining cases, other methods exist. In general, the valuation methodology as envisaged in the WTO Agreement consists of the following valuation methods:

- transaction value method (Article 1);
- transaction value of identical goods (Article 2);
- transaction value of similar goods (Article 3);
- deductive value method (Article 5);
- computed value method (Article 6); and
- fall-back method (Article 7).

The transaction value method is the default 'go-to' method in customs valuation. However, if it proves inapplicable for assessing the value of the goods in a specific transaction, the WTO Agreement also envisages alternative valuation methods. These methods can be applied when the transaction value is rejected under certain circumstances. The first is not satisfying one or more of the conditions of Article 1 of the WTO Agreement. Another is when customs authorities have uncertainties regarding the truth or accuracy of the declared value that was conveyed to the importer, and these doubts were not clarified after the due consultation process was followed. Lastly, these methods are applicable if no actual sale of the goods has occurred. What is crucial to note in this context is that customs valuation adheres to a strong hierarchy of the valuation methods. Thus, the two primary rules can be described as follows:

(1) The transaction value method is the default method for every customs valuation.
(2) One method of valuation can only be applied if the preceding methods cannot be.

For example, the transaction value of the similar goods method can be considered only after it is established that the transaction value method and transaction value of identical goods method are not applicable. Thus, the importers are not allowed to freely decide which method is the most advantageous but must adhere to the hierarchy envisaged in the WTO Agreement. The rationale behind this approach is the simple fact that the transaction value method, as a rule, should be the approach that provides the most approximate estimation of the customs value of the goods as it is based on the price actually remitted for the goods. The other methods are less direct and hence do not deliver such reliable results. The following subparagraphs of this chapter will briefly deal with the general characteristics of each customs valuation method.

7. http://www.wcoomd.org/en/topics/valuation/overview/what-is-customs-valuation.aspx (last accessed 30 January 2022).

2.2.1 *Transaction Value Method*

According to the WTO Agreement, the transaction value of goods is the price actually paid or payable for the goods that are sold for export to the country of importation. As a rule, this price is based on the invoice price. Another element that can be used in the determination of the transaction value of goods is a series of cost elements that are not included in the invoice price (known as adjustments) that are to be added to the price to be established under Article 1. These adjustments are described under Article 8 which also provides for the inclusion in the transaction value of certain considerations that may pass from the buyer to the seller in the form of specified goods or services rather than in the form of money.[8]

Article 1 of the WTO Agreement first determines whether the concerned goods have been sold for export. This indicates that there is a transaction involving an actual international physical transfer of goods as the direct result of a sale between a seller and a buyer. The term 'sale' was not defined in the WTO Valuation Agreement, however, as a means of clarification, Advisory Opinion 1.1 indicated that the term 'sale' should be interpreted as widely as possible.[9] In addition, it also provides a list of situations that, as a rule, do not constitute a sale (e.g., free consignments, goods imported on consignment, goods imported by branches that are not separate legal entities, etc.). Article 1 also specifies certain situations and restrictions that may influence whether the declared price paid or payable will be accepted, for example, when the buyer and seller of the goods in question are related.[10]

When it has been established that the buyer and seller are related, the WTO Agreement stipulates that this does not constitute grounds in itself for regarding that the transaction price is unacceptable. The transaction value can still be accepted if there are no reasons to doubt that the relationship did not influence the price paid or payable. For this goal, customs authorities should examine the circumstances regarding the sale. In this respect, they should be prepared to examine the relevant aspects of the transaction, including the way in which the buyer and seller organize their commercial relationship and the method that is used to arrive at the price in question in order to determine whether the relationship has influenced the price. This examination can be performed, for example, by asking the following questions:[11]

(1) Has the price been settled in a manner that is consistent with the normal pricing practices of the industry in question?
(2) Has the price been settled in a manner that is consistent with the way the seller determines prices for sales to buyers who are not related to the seller?

8. Paragraph 1 of the General Introductory Commentary to the WTO Agreement, https://www.wto.org/english/docs_e/legal_e/20-val_01_e.htm (last accessed 30 January 2022).
9. The full text of this case can be found in the WCO Valuation Compendium, https://www.wcoomdpublications.org/en/products/valuation/customs-valuation-compendium (last accessed 29 March 2022).
10. The definition of related parties is contained in Article 15.4 of the WTO Agreement.
11. *See* World Customs Organization, *WCO Guide to Customs Valuation and Transfer Pricing*, 2018, p. 10.

(3) Can it be demonstrated that the price is adequate to ensure the recovery of all costs plus a profit that is representative of the firm's overall profit realized over a representative period of time (e.g., on an annual basis) in sales of goods of the same class or kind?

Finally, it must be emphasized that, in accordance with the provisions of the WTO Agreement, the customs authorities shall accept the customs value whenever the importer demonstrates that the value of goods as declared in the transaction between related parties closely approximates the value of a similar transaction between unrelated parties. It is important to note, however, that the use of such test values by the importer is only voluntary, and the initiative to use them belongs to the importer.[12] Nevertheless, manufactured goods often contain technology or intellectual property that is unique to the MNE and sold only between the related parties, therefore, such comparison prices are typically not available. Therefore, the test value option is used only minimally in practice.

Example

Company A, located in Country X is the parent company of ABC Group, and Company B, located in Country Y is a subsidiary of the same group. Company A sells its product to Company B. Country Y is hence the country of importation. The product is also sold by Company A to an unrelated buyer at the same commercial level and used for the same purposes as Company B at a higher price. It was established that the costs incurred by Company A who is the exporter in these transactions are the same for the transaction with Company B and with the unrelated buyer.

Both Company A and Company B are unable to explain the different prices when challenged by the customs authorities. Therefore, there are insufficient grounds to contend that the price differential is not significant. The transaction value in this case would therefore not be applicable. The transaction value of identical or similar goods imported by unrelated buyers may form the basis of the determination of customs value.

Example (continues from the previous example)

Company A sells the product only to Company B. In the examination of the sale's circumstances by the customs authorities, it was established that the price is adequate to ensure recovery of all costs plus a profit representative of Company A's (exporter) overall profit on goods of the same class or type over a representative period of time. Therefore, the transaction value in this case may be accepted.[13]

12. For further details on the procedures to be followed by customs and the importer, *see* Article 1.2 of the WTO Agreement.
13. *See* para. 3 of the Interpretative Note to Article 1 of the WTO Agreement.

The WTO Agreement lists the elements that should constitute the transaction value in addition to the price paid or payable.[14] In addition to the elements prescribed in Article 8.1 of the WTO Agreement, each customs administration has the option to decide whether they will include or exclude the elements in Article 8.2 of the WTO Agreement when determining the customs value. The majority of WTO members have decided, for example, to include the costs of transport; insurance and loading; and unloading and handling charges in the customs value, which is referred to as the CIF basis.[15] When the members do not choose to do so, the valuation is performed on what is referred to as the FOB basis.[16]

The determination of whether specific elements should be included in the customs value might be complicated, and customs authorities may possibly want to consult the importer to gather all necessary facts relative to the audited transaction. This is also important taking into account the fact that specific elements might be perceived as services or intangibles, and hence their customs' treatment might be different from the entire 'physical' good.

The discussed provision of the WTO Agreement opens up, in a certain way, the area of interplay between customs valuation and the TP. It indicates that, in order to accept the price actually paid or payable for the goods when sold for export as their value upon importation, the buyer and seller should not be related. In the event that they are, the transaction value should be accepted as not being influenced by this relation. Thus, the application of the transaction value method relies on a mechanism similar to the ALP which is the governing rule of the TP. At the same time, it has to be indicated that the characteristics of the transaction value method make it very similar to the CUP which is considered to be the basic TP method.

2.2.2 *Transaction Value of Identical Goods*

The transaction value of identical goods is the first alternative method to be used when the default transaction value method cannot be applied.[17] As the name indicates, it relies on the transaction value of identical goods sold for export to the same country of importation and exported at or approximately the same time as the goods being valued. In general, it should consider goods sold at the same commercial level and in substantially the same quantity as the goods being valued, however, in the case of certain differences, reasonable and appropriate adjustments can be made in order to apply this method. In the case that a number of transactions with identical goods is ascertained, the lowest customs value should be taken into account.

14. Article 8.1 of the WTO Agreement.
15. The CIF terms mean that the seller also contracts and pays the costs and freight that are necessary to transport the goods to the country of import. The seller also contracts for insurance against the buyer's risk of loss or damage to the goods during the carriage.
16. The FOB term means that the buyer would have to procure and pay the costs and freight that are necessary to bring the goods to the country of import. The buyer must also contract for insurance against risk or damage to the goods during carriage.
17. Article 2 of the WTO Agreement.

As the transaction value of identical goods examines transactions performed between unrelated parties, it can be compared to the use of the external comparables in the CUP method for TP purposes.

2.2.3 *Transaction Value of Similar Goods*

The third applicable method in the customs valuation hierarchy relies on the value of similar goods sold for export to the same country of importation and exported at or about the same time as the goods being valued. The WTO Agreement provides a comprehensive definition in Article 15 of similar goods indicating that such goods are not alike in all aspects but have similar characteristics and component material enabling them to perform the same functions and be commercially interchangeable.

From the above descriptions of the transaction value of identical goods and the transaction value of similar goods methods applicable in customs valuation, it certainly seems clear that both can be compared with the CUP method in the TP. They tend to rely on external comparisons; however, their primary focus lies on the characteristics of the goods which is similar to the CUP method.

2.2.4 *Deductive Value Method*

The deductive value method uses the price at which the imported identical or similar goods are sold by the importer in the country of importation to unrelated parties at a similar point in time to the importation being assessed. The customs value is arrived at by performing a series of deductions that include elements such as:

- a commission or the other elements of the price that are supposed to constitute the profit and cover the expenses connected with the sales of goods in the import country;
- the usual costs of transport and insurance and associated costs incurred within the country of importation; and
- potential exclusions from the customs value as envisaged by the domestic legislation as well as the customs duties and other national taxes payable in the country of importation by reason of the importation or sale of the goods.

The characteristics of the deductive value method clearly resemble the resale price method as known from the OECD TPG. However, this does not mean these two methods are identical. The first significant discrepancy concerns the time at which the value of goods shall be determined. While the arm's length transfer price is determined on the basis of actual transactions performed by the related party, i.e., the resale of goods, without considering when the goods are actually resold, the deductive value methods require declaring the value at the moment of importation, i.e., before the goods are resold. Further, the customs valuation in accordance with this method excludes certain costs incurred by the importer in the country of importation, for example, transportation costs.[18]

2.2.5 *Computed Value Method*

The computed value method is envisaged in Article 6 of the WTO Agreement. The computed value shall include elements such as the cost or value of materials and the manufacture of the imported goods, the amount that allows the exporter to cover general expenses and earn a certain profit as well as the costs of the items or services mentioned in Article 8, paragraph 2 of the WTO Agreement. What should be mentioned is that the computed value method might be used before the deductive value method at the request of the importer as envisaged by Article 4 of the WTO Agreement. Thus, Article 4 constitutes an exception to the general hierarchy of application of customs valuation methods.

Clearly, the computed value method bears resemblance to the TP CPM. Both of these methods rely on the computation of the costs necessary to manufacture goods and a benchmarking reference to the profit that a manufacturer is expected to make on the sale of the ready product. However, just as in the case of the relationship between the deductive value method and resale price method, the computed value method and CPM are also not identical. While the CPM deals with profits and general expenses separately, in the case of the computed value method, the profit mark-up and the general expenses are summed up together and considered as one value.[19] Further, a location to which the valuation pertains is also important as, in the case of customs valuation, the monetary worth of imported goods is always determined, meaning that the manufacturer of these goods is located in the other country. At the same time, in the case of the CPM, the arm's length price is determined in the country where the manufacturer is located.[20]

2.2.6 *Fall-Back Method*

The fall-back method is the last of the customs valuation methods, and it can be used when all previously-mentioned methods fail to determine the accurate value of the imported goods. In the case of this method, the customs value shall be determined using reasonable means consistent with the principles and general provisions of the WTO Agreement and Article VII of the General Agreement on Tariffs and Trade (GATT) 1994 on the basis of the data available in the country of importation.[21] As indicated by the WTO Agreement, the methods of valuation employed under the fallback method

18. Jablonska, U. *Linkage Between Valuations for TP, Customs and VAT on Cross-Border Transactions*, in: Petruzzi, R., Spies, K. (eds), *Tax Policy Challenges in the 21st Century*, Linde, 2014, p. 356.
19. Article 6(1)(b) of the WTO Agreement.
20. Maisto, G., *Cross-Border Valuation for Income Tax, Customs Duties and VAT*, Bulletin for International Taxation, Vol. 55, No. 3, IBFD, 2001, p. 111.
21. Cremer, Kitaura, *supra* n. 3, p. 83.

shall be the regular methods with the allowed reasonable degree of flexibility in the areas concerning identical goods, similar goods, deductive method, and computed method.

It must be emphasized that, even though a number of alternative valuation methods exist in customs, only the transaction value method has specific tests for related party transactions and is therefore of most relevance to TP issues.[22]

2.3 Administrative Issues in Customs

In order to make the image of the customs requirements in trade more complete, it is also necessary to briefly refer to the administrative issues connected with the importation of goods.

Firstly, in customs, specific documentation requirements exist. Mainly, the importer is required to submit a customs declaration that depicts the details of specific transactions and requires the importer to report a customs value of the imported goods. Depending on the jurisdiction, supplementary documentation might also be required to make a customs entry complete.[23]

Further, the adjustments of customs value and post-clearance checks of submitted customs documentation are possible. As the submission of a customs declaration is usually required directly upon the importation, there are no fixed annual deadlines as in the case of typical tax returns. Rather, there are time limits for the collection of any outstanding customs duties debts and for the repayment of overpaid duties.[24] In this context, it is also important to note that, even if doubts exist as to the customs value that cannot be explained directly at the border, the WTO Valuation Agreement foresees a possibility for the importer of the goods to withdraw them from customs. This can be done if the importer provides a sufficient guarantee in the form of a surety, a deposit or some other appropriate instrument, covering the ultimate payment of customs duties for which the goods may be liable.[25]

Finally, a recurring issue of granting advance rulings in customs shall be briefly discussed. While, in many countries, procedures exist for granting rulings with regard to the tariff classification or origin (with the EU's Binding Tariff Information and Binding Origin Information serving as prime examples),[26] an advance ruling for customs valuation is something rather unknown primarily because of the difficulty in establishing one specific value for a number of deliveries happening over time that might vary, even if slightly, between specific quantities. The WTO Trade Facilitation Agreement encourages members to issue advance rulings for other areas such as customs valuation. Therefore, in the current circumstances, the advance rulings as

22. Further information on all aspects of customs valuation can be found via the WCO website here, http://www.wcoomd.org/en/topics/valuation/overview.aspx (last accessed 30 January 2022).
23. Cremer, Kitaura, *supra* n. 3, p. 85.
24. Cremer, Kitaura, *supra* n. 3, p. 86.
25. Article 13 of the WTO Agreement.
26. BTI, https://ec.europa.eu/taxation_customs/business/calculation-customs-duties/what-is-common-customs-tariff/binding-tariff-information-bti_en; BOI, https://ec.europa.eu/taxation_customs/business/calculation-customs-duties/rules-origin_en (last accessed 21 April 2020).

known from tax law will not and, in fact, cannot be applied for customs valuation purposes.

3 INTERPLAY BETWEEN TP AND CUSTOMS VALUATION

With the theoretical background on the main principles of customs valuation, the areas of the interplay between customs valuation and the TP can now be analysed along with the consequences that this interplay brings for practice.

3.1 Diverging Goals of Tax and Customs Authorities

It can be observed that the goal of both customs valuation and TP methodologies is very similar. While customs authorities are establishing whether a price has been influenced by the relationship between the parties, the tax authorities' objective is to seek an arm's length price. Each is designed to ensure that the price is established as if the parties were not related and had been negotiated under normal business circumstances. It has also been noted that there are a number of similarities between the WTO and the OECD methodologies for customs valuation and the TP, respectively.[27]

However, these initial similarities do not mean that customs and the TP can be treated as comparable concepts and that the consequences of their coexistence are foreseeable and easily manageable. Fundamental differences exist in the goals behind the actions taken by both customs and tax authorities. The customs authorities' objective is to ensure all appropriate elements are included in the customs value and is not understated whereas the tax authorities' objective is to ensure that the transfer price does not include inappropriate elements and is not overstated. What does it mean? While customs authorities will be concerned with the price of the goods sold, the tax authorities examining TP issues will take into account the income arising from the terms and conditions of the transaction. This will subsequently lead to contradictory goals of both authorities. Customs authorities might be tempted to maximize the customs value of the imported goods in order to receive a higher customs duty while tax authorities will want to prevent overstating the amount of the transaction and claiming the excessive deductions. In addition, specific issues will be handled differently for customs and TP purposes which might, in turn, lead to difficulties in reconciling these two areas.

There are also a number of other differences in the approaches and their fundamentals between customs and tax authorities that are highlighted in Table 30.1[28] and explored further in the following sections of this chapter.

27. For a discussion on TP methods, *See* Michael Lang, Raffaele Petruzzi, Giammarco Cottani, Alfred Storck (2018) Fundamentals of Transfer Pricing: A Practical Guide, Kluwer Law International, Chapters III and IV.
28. Based on Fabio, M., *Customs Value and TP: WCO and ICC Solutions to Be Adopted by Customs Authorities*, Global Trade and Customs Journal, Vol. 15, No. 6, Kluwer Law International, 2020, p. 277.

Table 30.1 Differences Between TP and Customs Valuation

	TP	*Customs Valuation*
Main guidance	OECD TPG	WTO Agreement
Main principle	ALP	Price actually paid or payable
Determination of the value	Using comparables	Valuation methods
Assessment basis	Net profit/losses	Cost and profit (no net possible)
Assessment method	Aggregation	Transaction-by-transaction
Application of the valuation methods	Most appropriate method	Hierarchy
Documentation	Annual return	Customs declaration upon importation
Main focus of the authorities of the import country	High transfer price increases tax deduction	Low customs value decreases chargeable customs duty

3.2 ALP in View of Customs Valuation

As has already been mentioned, the main principle of the TP and customs valuation might seem similar. On one hand, the ALP indicates that the price of the transaction between related parties should be equal to that which would have been agreed on had the transaction been performed between unrelated parties. On the other hand, the price actually paid, taken into account in the case of customs, considers whether the price was not influenced by the relationship between the entities. Clearly then, the objective of both sets of rules is for the price to not be affected by the potential relationship between the seller and the buyer.

However, considering the dissimilarities in the areas of application of the discussed rules as well as different sources of supporting guidance (i.e., OECD TPG and WTO Agreement), the ALP as a TP concept should not be applied directly in the customs realm due to a number of reasons. These include various methods of arriving at the correct price which also includes elements to be taken into account in the calculation, possible differences in the interpretation of the term related parties and, finally, diverging goals of the respective authorities.

3.3 Data Range Used for the Assessment of the Transaction

The difference between TP and customs valuation also pertains to the scope of data used by the authorities to assess the audited transaction. An important source of discrepancy might be, for example, distinct periods being audited by tax and customs authorities. While the general rules will be stipulated in the local laws,[29] it can be expected that customs authorities will less frequently audit earlier periods as opposed to the tax authorities. Thus, when performing an audit, customs authorities should ensure that they use relevant TP data stemming from the same period as the audited customs data and to determine whether the used TP data has previously been audited or whether they might be still subject to further amendments.

When it comes to the profit to be examined by the customs authorities, they have the discretion to select between 'gross' or 'operating' profit depending on which is more beneficial for the examination purposes. Normally, operating profit is a better indicator of real profitability as it shows what is earned after all of the expenses have been paid. It is also the measure for which information concerning unrelated parties will most often be available. Operating profit is also the most common profit level indicator used when the net-CPM/TNMM is utilized for TP purposes. It is also important to note that, when referring to profits in deciding about whether the price is adequate to ensure recovery of all costs plus a profit, customs authorities will refer to the seller's (i.e., exporter's) profit. The TP data, however, will relate only to the profit made by the importer (i.e., buyer) and not the exporter. In this case, it is a question of whether the information is still relevant to customs authorities. It can be stated that, as the import value is the beginning point for the importer's profit calculation, information derived from the importer's profit can potentially assure customs authorities that the exporter/seller's profit is acceptable. This may subsequently confirm that the price of the imported goods is adequate for ensuring the recovery of all of the costs plus a profit and is therefore not influenced by the relationship.

Another issue that should be taken into account when analysing the transaction from customs and the TP perspectives is the determination of the tested party. Customs authorities focus on the importer and perform their analysis on a transaction-by-transaction basis. From the point of view of the TP, when applying profit-based TP methods such as the TNMM, it has to be taken into account that the tested party should be the less functionally complex entity in the transaction, which is often the importer. This places the focus on the MNE's profit in the country of importation (i.e., sales made by the taxable person). This can be tested against comparable transactions for deciding if the price in question is in accordance with the ALP.

Example

Company A located in Country X is the parent company of ABC Group, and Company B located in Country Y is a subsidiary of the same group. Company A is a manufacturer and sells its product to Company B who is a distributor. Company A sells this type of product exclusively to Company B, and Company B imports and purchases the product exclusively from Company A.

29. For example, in the EU, this period amounts to three years.

In 2020, Company B imported the goods manufactured by Company A using the transaction value that was based on the price stated on the commercial invoice. This invoice was then submitted to the customs authorities in Country Y. There was no indication that special circumstances between both companies existed that would prevent the use of the transaction value even though the companies were related.

After importation, customs authorities in country Y decided to review the circumstances surrounding the sale of goods between Company A and Company B as they were uncertain about the acceptability of the price.
Company B did not provide test values as a means of demonstrating that the relationship did not influence the price (as envisaged by Article 1.2(b) and (c) of the WTO Agreement). However, at the request of the customs authorities for additional information, Company B presented a TP study for the period 2019 prepared by an unrelated firm on behalf of Company B.

The data below illustrate relevant data for the importer, Company B:

Sales	100.0
COGS, i.e., price paid/payable to Company A in this case	75.0
Gross Profit	25.0
Operating expenses	20.5
Net operating profit	4.5
Net operating profit margin (benchmarked)	**4.5% of sales**

As Company A does not sell its products to unrelated buyers, Company B was unable to demonstrate that the price was settled in the same manner as in sales to unrelated parties, therefore, the TP study was needed. During the review of the circumstances surrounding the sale, customs authorities examined information discussed in the TP study with regard to the determination of whether the price had been settled in a manner consistent with the normal industry pricing practices. The conclusion drawn from the TP study are the following: the sales figure can be considered as being reliable since Company B is only selling to unrelated parties (and it is assumed that Company B is rationally seeking to maximize its profits in its dealings with arm's length parties):

(1) The amount of operating expenses can be accepted as being reliable since it is determined that these expenses are paid by Company B to only unrelated parties with Company B seeking to minimize its costs, and there is no evidence that any of these expenses have been paid at the request of the seller.

(2) The TP study confirms that Company B's operating profit margin of 4.5% is within the arm's length range (i.e., based on a benchmarking study of unrelated importers).
(3) The COGS of Company B reflects that the price paid or payable to Company B represents the transaction between Company B and its related party, Company A. This is the transfer price in question.

The arm's length COGS amount can be deduced by working backwards from the arm's length net margin of 4.5%. Therefore, if the derived COGS is equal to the relevant declared transaction value, it could be inferred that the price has not been influenced by the relationship between Company B and Company A. This demonstrates that information relating to the transactions between a related buyer and unrelated party distributors can be helpful and relevant to customs authorities when examining the circumstances surrounding sales between related parties.

The above example, however, is just an illustration of a possible method to use the data derived from TPD. Customs authorities may consider other approaches for examining the circumstances surrounding the sale, request additional information, and take into account the totality of all of the evidence that is available and relevant to the sales that are under consideration.

3.4 Scope of Information in TP and Customs Valuation

It has to be noted that the different scope of interest between the TP (aggregation) and customs (individual transactions) is also pertinent to the relevance of information from one area to the other. Therefore, customs authorities should carefully consider which information available to them from the TPD can actually be used in order to reliably determine or confirm the customs value.

The level of difficulty in the above case will be different depending on the characteristics of the business of the taxpayer. If it only trades a single or limited range of products, it most likely will be rather easy to choose the relevant data. A more complicated set-up with diverse products (or entire ranges) will definitely be more challenging for the customs authorities. This is not to state, however, that the TP data deriving from such a business will be of no benefit for the purposes of customs valuation.

In case the goods concerned are branded electrical kettles, and the range of goods incorporated in the TP study covers various branded electrical appliances (including microwaves, blenders, toasters, and kettles). The TP study confirms an acceptable arm's length range for those products taken as a group. The customs authorities may take into account the criteria provided in the third example in Interpretative Note to Article 1.2 of the WTO Agreement regarding the examination of the circumstances surrounding the sale, specifically, all of the costs plus a profit realized 'in sales of goods of the same class or kind'. In accordance with Article 15.3 of the WTO Agreement, 'goods of the same class or kind' should mean goods that fall within a group or range of goods produced by a particular industry or industry sector and include identical or similar goods.

The TP study and additional research (if necessary) may assure customs authorities that, in this case, the kettles and other electrical appliances may be considered as goods of the same class or type. Therefore, the details of costs and profits for the range of products may be relevant to each individual product within the group, including the kettle.

4 TP ADJUSTMENTS AND THEIR INFLUENCE ON CUSTOMS

4.1 General Information

As has already been indicated in the previous chapters of this book, TP adjustments are an important element of the reality of both MNEs and tax authorities. As it might happen that the TP adjustments will also pertain to transactions in which customs authorities are involved, it is important to understand the interplay between TP adjustments and customs value and consider potential remedies.

When discussing TP adjustments, it must be indicated that they might result in various consequences from the customs perspective, for example, the adjusted price for TP purposes might be more in accordance with the price actually paid or payable for customs valuation purposes. In the case of primary and corresponding adjustments, the adjusted price mentioned in the accounting will differ from the price actually paid between related parties. Hence, the customs authorities might be unable to determine if the relation between the entities influenced the price until the actual adjustment has been made.

Commentary 4.1 of the TCCV comprises an important principle with regard to any possible adjustments of the price, i.e., the price review clause. It should be included in the terms of the contract for the sale of goods and is applicable in situations in which the price of the goods is only provisionally determined upon importation. The final determination of the price should then be based on specific factors envisaged in the aforementioned contract. The application of such a tool allows for a certain extent of flexibility and also for the application of year-end adjustment in the TP which might influence the price of the imported goods. It is important to note, however, that the application of the price review clause should not preclude customs valuation under the transaction value method.

4.2 Possible Customs Treatment of TP Adjustments

4.2.1 Types of TP Adjustments and Potential Influence on Customs Valuation

As mentioned previously, there are a number of reasons why a TP adjustment may occur and different ways that it can be initiated.

In the case of adjustments initiated by the tax authorities, in many cases, they will not affect the price actually paid or payable as they will only influence the tax books. This will be the case for primary and corresponding adjustments. In the event of adjustments initiated by the taxpayer, they will usually involve the transfer of an actual amount of money or the issue of a debit or a credit note (in the case of corresponding/year-end adjustments) – hence, they could in fact influence the price actually paid for the purposes of customs valuation. Secondary adjustments in the TP, such as those that the tax authorities might insist on, and performed by the taxpayer will also involve an actual monetary transfer, and hence these adjustments could also influence the customs valuation.

It is important to note that the issue of TP adjustments influencing customs value has been a practical problem for many years and in various jurisdictions. An example of the approach taken towards attempting to effectively address potentially arising problems was provided in the *Hamamatsu* case decided by the CJEU.

Court Case[30]

In *Hamamatsu*,[31] the CJEU opined that transfer prices that are subjected to retroactive adjustments cannot be used for customs valuation purposes under the application of the transaction value method.

In the judgment, the CJEU held that the customs value must reflect the genuine economic value of imported goods at the time of the actual transaction and take into account all of the elements that have economic value such as selling commissions, transport costs, royalty and license fees, in pricing the good, etc. In cases when the transaction value method is the preferred method, however, is inadequate, alternative methods could be employed for determining customs value. Apart from situations that warrant adjustments to the actual price paid or payable, such as damages, quality defects. etc., the actual transacting price cannot be altered with subsequent adjustments. The judgment states that EU legislation does: ' ... *not permit an agreed transaction value, composed of an amount initially invoiced and declared and a flat-rate adjustment made after the end of the accounting period, to form the basis for the customs value, without it being possible to know at the end of the accounting period whether that adjustment would be made up or down*'. This ruling has led to different interpretations of its relevance and meaning by a number of commentators.

In the context of the point in time in which an adjustment is performed, it is important to differentiate between two situations, i.e., the adjustments performed before and after the importation. In the first case, the customs authorities should

30. The views and opinions expressed in this case do not necessarily reflect those of the TCCV or of the governments of WTO Members.
31. CJEU of 20 December 2017, C-529/16, *Hamamatsu Photonics Deutschland GmbH v. Hauptzollamt München*, For details, *see* Petruzzi, R., Prasanna, S., *Restricting the Interplay of TP and Customs Valuation*, Transfer Pricing International, Vol. 1, Linde, 2018, pp. 44-46.

consider the adjusted price of goods as the price for the purposes of customs valuation. In the second case, the adjustment is usually recorded in the accounts of the taxpayer, and the debit or credit note is issued after customs authorities clear the goods. Here, the approaches can vary. As demonstrated by *Hamamatsu*, the customs authorities might not take such an adjustment into account. On the other hand, this is not to state that this would be the case at all times as it might happen that the customs authorities will determine the value on the basis of the price adjusted in this manner. Such an approach would adhere to the already discussed price review clause. With this in mind, taxpayers should notify the customs authorities about the post-importation adjustment in order to afford these authorities an opportunity to assess the potential impact of a TP adjustment on customs valuation.

4.2.2 Final Determination of the Customs Value Following TP Adjustments

With reference to the point raised in the previous section about considering the already adjusted price as the customs value, the possible procedure that the customs authorities should implement in order to address this issue should also be considered.

In this context, it is important to indicate that Article 13 of the WTO Valuation Agreement envisages the possibility of delaying the final determination of the customs value. The application of this option requires customs authorities to offer a facility that allows importers to clear the goods on the provision of a security in cases when it becomes necessary to delay the final determination of the customs value at the time of customs clearance. In this case, it might be questioned if it is necessary to require importers to file a 'provisional' customs declaration with the indication of the value that is covered by a security for the potential duty that might become due. In the event that a substantial number of customs declarations are involved, such a requirement might constitute a significant resource constraint for both importers and the authorities, in particular as far as accounting and reconciliation procedures are concerned.

In order to facilitate potential issues connected with the TP adjustments, taxpayers could consider implementing a specific policy determining the criteria for the determination of the final transfer price (which will then also influence the customs value) which could be used in situations when the value of the goods will not be considered final upon importation. In order to make this policy beneficial, customs authorities should be notified of the existence of such a policy, or they might even require the concerned entity to submit it. Importantly, this policy could also be implemented as part of an APA concluded with the local authorities. After the final price has been determined, it will typically be required to report the final price to the customs authorities along with the information detailing the adjustment performed.

It is also important to note the provisions of Article 8 of the WTO Agreement which lists the elements that should be included in the customs value. In the case of a post-information TP adjustment, customs authorities should comprehensively examine the adjusted amount and consider its character in accordance with Article 8 in order to determine whether it should affect the customs value.

4.2.3 Practical Challenges

One of the most serious challenges when discussing the TP adjustments and their influence on the customs valuation is the determination of the mechanism and calculation method when it is decided that a retrospective adjustment of the customs valuation should be performed. In this context, the different transactional focus between the TP (aggregation) and customs (individual transactions) should be taken into account in order to derive a method that will allow identifying a link between the adjustment and specific consignment and calculate an appropriate adjustment.

Another possible issue is the situation in which customs authorities decide to perform an audit knowing that the taxpayer has the intention of performing a TP adjustment, but this adjustment has not yet been made. In such a case, the authorities will most likely take a unilateral decision on how to proceed – in the most optimistic case, they will consult the taxpayer to find a solution satisfying both parties.

The issue described above creates another and perhaps the most significant dilemma. Even though the basis for customs valuation and the TP are almost universally recognized around the world, there is still no unified global approach towards the customs treatment of the TP adjustments or vice versa. Therefore, there must be a recourse to the approach of the local customs authorities. As this problem embraces a wide variety of smaller issues (such as procedural matters), it is advisable for companies to discuss their cases with the authorities of respective countries.

5 USE OF TPD AND APAS FOR THE PURPOSES OF CUSTOMS VALUATION

5.1 Practical Use of the TPD

Even though no one-size-fits-all model exists for the use of the TPD for customs purposes, a solution proposed by the WCO is compliance-based audits which should be initiated taking into account risk criteria. This solution is deemed to be the most effective means for verifying the duty liability of MNEs. Such audits involve a structured examination of companies' financial systems, accounts, payment records, and any other relevant information.[32]

The use of the TPD might be beneficial for customs authorities also due to the fact that the related parties of the audited company will not always be inclined to share its profit information with the latter. Therefore, a practical recommendation for the customs authorities is to take into account information that is already available, i.e., in the TPD, to evaluate the circumstances surrounding the sale.

As MNEs prepare TP studies and reports to provide information for the purpose of tax audits (both internal and external), a question that has been accompanying discussions about the interplay between the TP and customs valuation was whether

32. World Customs Organization, *WCO Guide to Customs Valuation and Transfer Pricing*, 2018, p. 59.

such studies could be used when determining the customs value of imported goods. This would potentially reduce the compliance burden as readily-available information would not have to be produced twice. However, thus far, no uniform solution has been created in this respect. An interesting proposal regarding the use of TPD for customs purposes was proposed by the International Chamber of Commerce in its policy statement.[33] Proposal 6 includes a requirement to include additional information in the TPD that could be useful from the customs' perspective. Such a solution would require cooperation between tax and customs authorities in order to enact appropriate legislation, however, it could prove beneficial for both authorities and taxpayers by allowing saving time and providing a wider overview of the MNE's activity.

5.2 Advance Pricing Agreements

APAs[34] afford tax authorities and businesses the opportunity to confirm and agree in advance on the TP treatment of a specific transaction or group of transactions and, therefore, demonstrate the arm's length price. Customs administrations in certain countries identified that APAs can provide useful information for customs authorities when examining related-party transactions.[35] Conversely, also the requirements stemming from the rules of customs valuation might have to be considered during the work on an APA so that businesses do not need to prepare a specialized study based only on customs authorities' requirements.

Article 3 of the WTO Trade Facilitation Agreement[36] which requires customs administrations to make advance rulings available for classification and origin purposes also encourages customs to provide advance rulings (broadly similar to the concept of APAs in the context of the TP) for customs valuation. An advance ruling can provide business operators with certainty regarding how customs authorities will treat a related party transaction (or group of transactions) before the importation of the goods concerned. For an application for an advance ruling, customs authorities will examine the relevant information that is provided (which could be derived from a TP study or an APA) and make a decision that will be applicable in a specific set of circumstances. The decision in question might refer to the possible influence that the relationship between the buyer and seller might have on the price and if the transaction

33. International Chamber of Commerce, *ICC Policy Statement – Transfer Pricing and Customs Valuation*, 2015, p. 6.
34. For further information on APAs, *See* Michael Lang, Raffaele Petruzzi, Giammarco Cottani, Alfred Storck (2018) Fundamentals of Transfer Pricing: A Practical Guide, Kluwer Law International, Chapter V 5.
35. For example, in a private ruling issued on 30 August 2000, the US Customs Services indicated that the information included in an APA can be useful in the determination of the transaction value for the purposes of assessing a related party transaction under customs law. One of the examples might be an APA that envisages year-end adjustments. Such information might be used by the customs authorities as a means of challenging the originally declared customs value if the taxpayer took into account the possibility of adjusting income after the end of the year; *see* van Herksen, M, *Introduction*, in: Bekker, A., Obuoforibo, B. (eds), *Transfer Pricing and Customs Valuation: Two World to Tax as One*, IBFD, 2009, pp. 10, 232.
36. Available at, https://www.wto.org/english/tratop_e/tradfa_e/tradfa_e.htm (last accessed 30 January 2022).

value can be accepted. If it cannot be accepted, the decision can indicate what alternative method can be used as the valuation method.[37]

It is normal that an advance customs decision will not be issued based purely on an APA. Rather, the customs authorities will check whether the requirements of the WTO Agreement and the local law are fulfilled.[38] It is to be noted, however, that few customs administrations currently provide advance rulings for customs valuation purposes.

6 CONCLUSIONS

This chapter has illustrated the interplay between the TP and customs valuation in various areas with the most prominent being the influence of the TP adjustments on the results of the customs valuation. Subchapter 2 familiarized the readers with the general rules of customs valuation in order to build the background for further considerations. Subchapter 3 indicated the areas of interplay between the TP and customs valuation while the following subchapter 4 dealt with the issue of TP adjustments and their reconciliation with customs valuation. Finally, subchapter 5 provided an overview of how TPD can be used for the purposes of customs valuation.

37. WCO, *WCO Guide to Customs Valuation and Transfer Pricing*, 2018, pp. 67-68.
38. Cremer, Kitaura, *supra* n. 3, p. 87.

CHAPTER 31

Transfer Pricing and VAT

Pietro Bricchetto & Karol Dziwiński

1 GENERAL INTRODUCTION TO THE INTERPLAY BETWEEN TP AND VAT

1.1 Relevance of VAT

TP and VAT are areas of both domestic and international tax law that have gained significant importance over the years. The arm's length principle-based standards for the TP have been implemented by a number of countries, reaching 124 in 2019.[1] At the same time, the VAT is even more widespread with 168 countries having adopted a VAT/GST system until 2018. Arguably, the VAT is the most significant representative of the family of indirect taxes and, concerning its relevance as a source of revenues, it is a strong contender to direct taxes. For example, in the EU, the VAT is the second-largest source of budget revenue, even more so than corporate income tax (by a significant margin), and being approximate to the revenues generated by personal income tax.[2] A similar pattern can be also observed in various countries around the world that have implemented the VAT into their tax laws.[3]

1. For further details on the adoption of the TP around the world, *see* Michael Lang, Raffaele Petruzzi, Giammarco Cottani, Alfred Storck (2018) Fundamentals of Transfer Pricing: A Practical Guide, Kluwer Law International, Chapter 1.
2. Szymańska, A., *Dochody podatkowe w krajach Unii Europejskiej*, Wiadomości Statystyczne. The Polish Statistician, nr 5/2017 (672), Główny Urząd Statystyczny, pp. 79-99; Eurostat, *Tax Revenue Statistics*, https://ec.europa.eu/eurostat/statistics-explained/index.php/Tax_revenue_statistics#Direct_taxes_increased_in_2016.2C_while_indirect_taxes_remained_stable_and_social_contributions_decreased (last accessed 30 January 2022).
3. Lejeune, I., Daou-Azzi, J., Powell, M., *The Balance Has Shifted to Consumption Taxes: Lessons Learned and Best Practices for VAT*, in: Lang/Melz/Kristofferson (eds), *Value Added Tax and Direct Taxation: Similarities and Differences*, IBFD, 2009, pp. 61-62.

1.2 Increasing Importance of the Interplay Between TP and VAT

Taking into account the significance of both the TP and the VAT in countries around the world, a relevant question to ask seems to be whether these two, seemingly non-related, areas can overlap and what consequences this could cause.

In fact, as the VAT is also applicable to the transactions between related parties, a grey area exists that is not actually covered by a significant amount of local legislation or supranational guidance, which leads to doubts in practice. The issue at hand is the TP adjustments and the potential ramifications they might create for the VAT. Even though the problem has already been recognized and discussed for years by various stakeholders,[4] there has been no universal conclusion as to a possible solution.

The WCO and the OECD mentioned the issue briefly during the Second Joint WCO/OECD Conference on Transfer Pricing and Customs Valuation, which took place in 2007. The summary remarks mentioned postulates at the very general level such as encouraging dialogue between customs administration, tax authorities, and the business community; and the need for a comprehensive government approach or exploring the possibility of performing joint audits.[5] However, in spite of the initial works, the interaction between the TP and the VAT has never been the subject of specific guidance. Similarly, no binding conclusions were drawn during the International Fiscal Association congress held in Japan in 2007.[6]

The discussed topic remained overlooked on the international stage for years. However, as its relevance increased along with the number of countries implementing the TP and VAT provisions, the interest in solving arising issues or at least facilitating the coexistence of both areas of tax law also rose steadily. At the international forum, the EU, recognizing the problematic nature and relevance of the problem, issued two papers prepared by the VAT Committee[7] and the VAT Expert Group.[8] These two papers, even though not answering all of the questions in the discussed matter, significantly facilitated the approach towards TP and VAT adjustments for the EU Member States. The details of the guidelines will be discussed in section 3.4 of this chapter.

In view of the above considerations, the main goal of this chapter will be to examine the differences between the TP and the VAT and determine the ways in which these two areas interact with the specific focus on the TP adjustments and their influence on VAT settlements.

---

4. Ping, L., Silberztein, C., *Transfer Pricing, Customs Duties and VAT Rules: Can We Bridge the Gap?*, World Commerce Review, Volume 1, Issue 1, 2007, pp. 36-38.
5. Second Joint WCO/OECD Conference on Transfer Pricing and Customs Valuation Brussels (Belgium), 22-23 May 2007, https://www.oecd.org/ctp/transfer-pricing/38698312.pdf (last accessed 30 January 2022).
6. Desax, M., *An IFA Congress in Japan: At Last!*, p. 369, and *Subjects and Seminars of the 2007 Congress*, p. 371, both in: Bulletin for International Taxation, Volume 61, Issue 9, IBFD, 2007.
7. Value Added Tax Committee, Working Paper No. 923, 28 February 2017, taxud.c.1(2016) 1280928.
8. VAT Expert Group Paper, VEG No. 071 REV2, 18 April 2018, taxud.c.1(2018)2326098.

2 THE BASICS OF VAT

Before delving into the details of the relationship between the TP and the VAT, a few words must be stated about the main principles of the latter that will help to better understand the further considerations included in this chapter.

2.1 General Principles Regarding VAT

As indicated by the OECD, the overarching purpose of a VAT is to impose a broad-based tax on consumption that is understood to mean final consumption by private consumers.[9] In certain cases, it is also borne by entities involved in non-business activities. Thus, as such, the VAT should be neutral to businesses acting as professional operators.[10]

The functioning of the VAT relies on the collection of tax in a staged process through each business in the supply chain that remits the proportion of tax based on its margin.[11] Taking into account this specific model and the principle of neutrality of a VAT for businesses, a special mechanism should accompany the implementation of each VAT system which would relieve businesses from the burden of a VAT upon purchase of goods, services or intangibles. Such a system usually relies on the deduction of the amount of the VAT from the invoice received from the seller. Another important principle of it is the destination principle which envisages that, as a rule, supplies of goods, services, and intangibles are generally taxed in the jurisdiction where consumption occurs.[12]

As a rule that is usually accepted in the countries that implemented a VAT into their tax law, the taxable amount is everything that constitutes the consideration for the provision of goods, services, or intangibles. In addition, contrary to the TP, in a VAT, there is no overarching principle similar to the arm's length principle, meaning that the discussed taxable amount is of a subjective character and can be determined by the related parties in any way that matches their interests. In the context of the discussion in the following parts of this chapter, it is important to remember that the VAT can also be adjusted. However, in this case, the adjustments are aimed at correcting the amount of VAT due whenever the consideration originally agreed by the parties for a taxable supply of goods or services is subsequently increased or reduced. This can occur either because of agreements between the parties or because of other reasons (such as cancellation, refusal, or total or partial non-payment by the customer), but not due to determining the corporate income tax results in conformity with the arm's length principle.

All transactions subject to a VAT are usually also subject to reporting obligations. The process begins with invoices that have to be issued in order to confirm every taxable supply on tax returns that have to be submitted in intervals determined by the

9. Paragraph 1.2 of the OECD International VAT/GST Guidelines, OECD, Paris, 2017.
10. *Ibid.*, para. 1.4.
11. *Ibid.*, para. 1.5.
12. *Ibid.*, para. 1.12.

local law (usually monthly or quarterly). The taxpayers then have a number of required documentation obligations for which they have to register all of their transactions subject to a VAT.

In order to present how a VAT system can work, the following subchapter will refer to the example of a harmonized VAT within the EU indicating its main mechanisms and concepts.

2.2 Relevant EU VAT Rules

The EU VAT system has been widely harmonized among the Member States through the introduction of EU-wide legislation that is supposed to provide the basis for the relevant domestic provisions. The VAT Directive, in force since 2006, is the most important act in this respect.

2.2.1 'Subjective Value' and Consideration Actually Received by the Supplier (Article 73 of the VAT Directive)

When a taxable person[13] performs a taxed supply of goods or services[14] for which he is liable to pay a VAT, he must determine how much of it must be charged to the customer and/or reported on the VAT return. In order to do so, the taxpayer needs to establish the amount to which the VAT rate is to be applied, which is commonly referred to as the 'taxable amount'.

Title VII of the VAT Directive[15] deals with the determination of the taxable amount that is normally the price charged by the supplier for the supplied goods or services (provided that, in any case, a direct link can be established between the supply and the consideration received).[16] The VAT Directive also provides for specific rules determining which elements must be included[17] and which must be excluded[18] from the taxable amount as well as other provisions governing, *inter alia*, price adjustments, cancellations, returns, and discounts.[19] Title VII of the VAT Directive also contains (optional) anti-avoidance rules that allow Member States to levy a VAT on a transaction based on

13. Article 9(1) of the VAT Directive defines a 'taxable person' as '*any person who, independently, carries out in any place any economic activity, whatever the purpose or result of that activity. Any activity of producers, traders or persons supplying services, including mining and agricultural activities and activities of the professions, shall be regarded as "economic activity". The exploitation of tangible or IP for the purposes of obtaining income therefrom on a continuing basis shall in particular be regarded as an economic activity*'.
14. *See* Article 2 of the VAT Directive.
15. Articles 72-92 of the VAT Directive.
16. *See* Article 1(2) of the VAT Directive, stating that '*VAT entails the application to goods and services of a general tax on consumption exactly proportional to the price of the goods and services.*'
17. Article 78 of the VAT Directive.
18. Articles 79 and 87 of the VAT Directive.
19. Articles 87, 90 and 92 of the VAT Directive.

its 'open market value' rather than the consideration actually received, provided that certain conditions are satisfied.[20]

Under Article 73 of the VAT Directive, the taxable amount for a supply of goods or services carried out within the territory of each Member State shall include everything that constitutes consideration (either in money or in kind) obtained or to be obtained by the supplier in return for the supply. This is relevant regardless of whether the consideration is paid by the customer (as typically occurs) or by unrelated parties even in the form of price subsidies.

Pursuant to Article 83 of the VAT Directive, the same criteria apply in the case of intra-community acquisitions of goods.[21]

Under the main rule laid down by Article 73, the key elements of the VAT 'taxable amount' of goods and services are thus as follows:

(1) The taxable amount shall include everything that constitutes consideration regardless of its actual form (a consideration can be paid either in money or in kind, or it might even consist of an amount paid in money and partially of a payment in kind) provided it is capable of being expressed in money.
(2) The consideration must be obtained or is to be obtained by the supplier, meaning that not only the amounts received by the supplier but also those he should receive form part of the taxable amount.
(3) The consideration shall be paid 'in return' for the supply, meaning that there must be a 'direct link' between the goods/services supplied and the consideration received.[22]
(4) The consideration must be obtained from the customer or by an unrelated party, the identity of the person making the payment being of no relevance as long as a direct link can be established between the supply and the consideration.
(5) The consideration includes subsidies directly linked to the price of the supply, i.e., subsidies that constitute the entire or part of the consideration for the supply of goods or services and are paid by an unrelated party to the seller or supplier.[23]

20. Articles 72 and 80 of the VAT Directive.
21. Article 83 of the VAT Directive states that '*In respect of the intra-Community acquisition of goods, the taxable amount shall be established on the basis of the same factors as are used in accordance with Chapter 2 to determine the taxable amount for the supply of the same goods within the territory of the Member State concerned. (...).*'
22. Such a direct link is established if there is '*a legal relationship between the provider of the service and the recipient pursuant to which there is reciprocal performance, the remuneration received by the provider of the service constituting the value actually given in return for the service supplied to the recipient*' (*see*, amongst others, CJEU of 11 March 2020, C-94/19, *San Domenico Vetraria*, para. 21; of 3 July 2019, C-242/18, *UniCredit Leasing*, para. 69; of 22 November 2018, C-295/17, *MEO – Serviços de Comunicações e Multimédia*, para. 39; of 22 June 2016, C-11/15, *Český rozhlas*, paras 21 and 22 and the case law cited).
23. CJEU of 9 October 2019, Joined Cases C-573/18 and C-574/18, *C GmbH & Co. KG and C-eG*, para. 34; of 15 July 2004, C-144/02, *Commission v. Germany*, para. 31; of 22 November 2001, C-184/00, *Office des produits wallons*, para. 18.

The above rule has been constantly interpreted by the CJEU to mean that the general valuation principle within the VAT Directive is a subjective valuation and not an objective one.

The 'consideration' is indeed the value actually received (or to be received) in each specific case and not a value estimated according to objective criteria.[24]

As a consequence thereof, even if the price is too low or too high, if compared to the objective market value or even to the cost price of the goods or services concerned,[25] the taxable amount for VAT purpose should still be the actual sale price that reflects the actual consumption taking place and the legal character of the VAT as an indirect tax on this consumption.

A corollary of the subjective character of the taxable amount is that it should not, in principle,[26] exceed the sum finally received by the supplier and that the tax authorities may not, in any circumstances, require an amount of the VAT exceeding the tax that the taxable person received.[27] Examining it from this perspective, TP rules may be construed as deviating from the subjective value laid down as the tax base for the purposes of the VAT.

2.2.2 *Objective Valuation in VAT: The Open Market Value (Articles 80 and 72 of the VAT Directive)*

A notable exception to the main principle established by Article 73 of the VAT Directive – according to which the taxable amount comprises all sums that make up the consideration that has been or is to be obtained by the supplier from its customer – is laid down by Article 80 of VAT Directive. It establishes the conditions under which the Member States are allowed to revalue certain transactions, to (exceptionally) disregard the consideration freely agreed by connected parties, and take the 'open market value' as the taxable amount.

---

24. *See*, for example, the opinion of Advocate General Fennelly of 27 June 1996, C-288/94, *Argos*, para. 21.
25. The CJEU has often dealt with cases in which the consideration is lower than the cost price of the goods or services supplied. In Gåsabäck where the VAT treatment of food supplied by a hotel to its personnel for a consideration below cost price was examined, the CJEU stated that '*the fact that the price paid for an economic transaction is higher or lower than the cost price is irrelevant to the question whether a transaction is to be regarded as a "transaction effected for consideration". The latter concept requires only that there be a direct link between the supply of goods or the provision of services and the consideration actually received by the taxable person ...*' (CJEU of 20 January 2005, C-412/03, *Gåsabäck*, paras 22 and 36). In Campsa Estaciones de Servicio, the CJEU confirmed that '*the possibility of classifying a transaction as "a transaction for consideration" requires only that there be a direct link between the supply of goods or the provision of services and the consideration actually received by the taxable person. Thus, the fact that the price paid for an economic transaction is higher or lower than the cost price (...) is irrelevant as regards that classification*' (CJEU of 9 June 2011, C-285/11, *Campsa Estaciones de Servicio*, para. 25).
26. But *see* Article 80 of the VAT Directive.
27. *See* CJEU of 11 June 2020, C-146/19, *SCT*, para. 21; of 8 May 2019, C-127/18, *A-PACK CZ*, para. 17; of 6 December 2018, C-672/17, *Tratave*, para. 29; of 20 December 2017, C-462/16, *Boehringer Ingelheim Pharma*, para. 32; of 15 May 2014, C-337/13, *Almos*, para. 22; of 26 January 2012, C-588/10, *Kraft Foods Polska*, paras 26 and 27.

The *ratio legis* of this optional provision – which most of the Member States have implemented[28] – is to prevent tax evasion or avoidance in cases when the Member States would suffer a loss of tax revenues through the use by taxable persons of connected parties to derive tax benefits.[29]

With this aim, Article 80 of the VAT Directive contains an exhaustive list of circumstances in which the 'open market value' can be applied, and the fundamental principle of VAT neutrality laid down by Article 73 is derogated. As stated in this article, VAT must be exactly proportional to the prices, and tax authorities are therefore prevented from collecting VAT amounts exceeding those received by the taxable person. As an exception to the general rule, Article 80 of the VAT Directive must be interpreted strictly.[30] In this latter respect, it is worth noting that it clearly indicates that the open market value can be applied '*in any of the following cases*' but not in others.[31]

The scope of the 'open market value' rule laid down by Article 80 is therefore limited and only applies when:[32]

- the parties to the transaction are 'connected', and that connection has resulted in a value other than the usual market value being placed on the supply; the concept of connection is broadly defined by Article 80 since it encompasses '*family or other personal ties, management, ownership, membership, financial or legal ties as defined by Member States*'; and
- the person concerned by the transaction does not enjoy a full right of deduction. This is because the purpose of Article 80 of the VAT Directive is to prevent tax evasion or avoidance when applying artificially high or low prices to a supply which can only occur in cases when one of the parties involved does not have a full right of deduction.

28. The situation as of 1 November 2021 is summarized under the following link, https://ec.europa.eu/taxation_customs/system/files/2021-10/Notifications.pdf (last accessed 30 March 2022).
29. *See* Article 80(1) of the VAT Directive and Recital 26 of the Preamble to the same directive: '*To prevent loss of tax revenues through the use of connected parties to derive tax benefits, it should, in specific limited circumstances, be possible for Member States to intervene as regards the taxable amount of supplies of goods or services and intra-Community acquisitions of goods.*'
30. *See* CJEU of 26 April 2012, Joined Cases C-621/10 and C-129/11, *Balkan and Sea Properties ADSITs* (C-621/10) and *Provadinvest OOD* (C-129/11), para. 45; of 21 June 2007, C-453/05, *Ludwig*, para. 21; of 3 March 2011, C-41/09, *Commission v. Netherlands*, para. 58 and the case law cited.
31. *See* CJEU of 26 April 2012, Joined Cases C-621/10 and C-129/11, *Balkan and Sea Properties ADSITs* (C-621/10) and *Provadinvest OOD* (C-129/11), para. 50 and the opinion of Advocate General Sharpston delivered on 26 January 2012 in the same cases, para. 31. *See also* the explanatory memorandum to the proposal for a council directive amending Directive 77/388/EEC regarding certain measures to simplify the procedure for charging VAT, to assist in countering tax evasion and avoidance, and repealing certain decisions granting derogations; document COM(2005)89 final of 16 March 2005, in which the commission held that '*the scope of the re-valuation measure* [now Article 80 of the VAT Directive] *is limited. It is envisaged it will not be used in relation to normal everyday transactions, but apply only to a very small number of transactions made within specific categories and in specific circumstances*'.
32. According to the CJEU, if a supply is made between two connected taxable persons who have a full right of deduction using an artificially low or high price for their mutual supplies, that inherently cannot lead to tax evasion or avoidance or to any tax benefits (*see* CJEU of 26 April 2012, Joined Cases C-621/10 and C-129/11, *Balkan and Sea Properties ADSITs* (C-621/10) and *Provadinvest OOD* (C-129/11), para. 47: '… *where goods or services are supplied at an artificially*

More precisely, there are only three circumstances in which the 'open market value' might be imposed as the taxable amount of supplies between connected parties:

(1) when the consideration is lower than the open market value (undervaluation), the transaction is subject to VAT, and the recipient of the supply is not entitled to a full right of deduction of it;[33]
(2) when the consideration is lower than the open market value (undervaluation), the transaction is VAT exempt with no right to deduction, and the supplier is a partly exempt person (not having a full right of VAT deduction); by artificially undervaluing VAT exempt supplies, partly exempt businesses may indeed reduce the value of their VAT exempt turnover relative to the value of their taxable supplies and thus increase their recovery rate; and
(3) when the consideration is higher than the open market value (overvaluation), the transaction is subject to VAT, and the supplier is a partly exempt person not entitled to a full right of deduction of VAT; such a rule is aimed at businesses that do not have a full right to deduction and who inflate their taxable supplies to a fully taxable business connected to them (with full right of input VAT recovery); by increasing the value of its taxable supplies, the supplier manages to shift the balance between the value of the taxable and non-taxable supplies it is making in order to engineer an increase in the proportion of deductible VAT.

The three events and circumstances listed above represent a closed list that is explicitly restricted for expansion. As a consequence thereof, Member State's national legislation implementing said provision cannot provide that the taxable amount is to be the open market value of the transaction in cases other than those referenced in Article 80 (i.e., for example, in cases when the taxable persons involved are not connected and/or have a full right to VAT deduction).[34]

low or high price between parties who both enjoy a full right of deduction of VAT, there cannot be any evasion or avoidance of tax at that stage. It is only at the stage of the final consumer, or of a mixed taxable person enjoying only a proportional right of deduction, that an artificially low or high price can lead to a loss of tax revenue'.).

33. As pointed out by the commission in the explanatory memorandum to the proposal: '*This measure aims to combat avoidance where a taxable supply is made at a low value to a purchaser who is not able to deduct all his VAT and thus the lower amount of tax represents a real and lasting loss to tax revenues. The consideration is only set at that level because links exist between the supplier and purchaser. In order to apply the rule, Member States will need to define the relevant connections between the parties. This definition must be within the categories set out in the Directive*' (explanatory memorandum to the proposal for a Council directive amending Directive 77/388/EEC concerning certain measures to simplify the procedure for charging VAT, to assist in countering tax evasion and avoidance, and repealing certain decisions granting derogations; document COM(2005)89 final of 16 March 2005).
34. *See* CJEU of 26 April 2012, Joined Cases C-621/10 and C-129/11, *Balkan and Sea Properties ADSITs* (C-621/10) and *Provadinvest OOD* (C-129/11), para. 52. Since Article 80 of the VAT Directive unequivocally and exhaustively establishes the conditions to be satisfied for a Member State to be able to provide in its legislation for the possibility to derogate to the main rule laid down by Article 73, the court has established it has direct effect. This means that a taxable person who has objections against the application of the open market value to transactions other

The definition of what should be understood as the 'open market value' is contained in Article 72 of the VAT Directive. It is the full amount that, in order to obtain the goods or services in question at that time, a customer at the same marketing stage at which the supply of goods or services takes place would have to pay, under conditions of fair competition, to a supplier at arm's length within the territory of the Member State in which the supply is subject to tax. In the event of a supply of goods, the open market value is an amount that is not less than the purchase price of goods or of similar goods or, in the absence of a purchase price, the cost price determined at the time of supply if no comparable supply of goods can be ascertained. With respect to services, an amount that is not less than the full cost to the taxable person of providing the services is the open market value if no comparable supply of services can be determined.

The application of the 'open market value' rule is not very straightforward, and controversy has arisen with respect to its practical implementation since its introduction in European VAT legislation. As the guidance is rather limited (the VAT Directive does not provide any guidance on how the open market value should be calculated), debates revolve around the question of whether and to what extent it is possible to recur to the OECD TPG and local TP guidance for determining the open market value.[35]

According to some authors, there should be no opportunity for interactions between TP methods and the open market value assessment. This latter, by definition, restricts the application of potential methods to those that are price-related as profit-related considerations are not relevant for VAT TP purposes. Consequently, the application of OECD TP methods would be restricted to the CUP as the sole method complying with open market value requirements.[36]

In addition, Article 72 of the VAT Directive provides alternative methods if no comparables can be found, making reference to the purchase or cost price. The application of these criteria that could be justified by the nature and final aim of the VAT seems to be in contrast with the arm's length principle.

In light of the above, some authors reiterate that specific guidelines should therefore be provided within the VAT context by also taking into account the different structures, principles, and aims of the tax. Such a conclusion is somehow confirmed by the CJEU that has already had the occasion to limit the potential correlation between a direct tax rule (such as TP rules) and the rules established by the VAT Directive. In FCE Bank, the

---

than those listed in Article 80(1) of the VAT Directive can directly rely on the content of said provision to oppose the application of provisions of national law that are incompatible with it. In that case, should it prove impossible to interpret the relevant provisions of the national VAT legislation in conformity with Article 80(1) of the VAT Directive, the national court would have to desist from applying those provisions. In such a situation, Article 73 of the VAT Directive must be applied (since that provision also has direct effect), and the taxable amount should therefore be set at the level of the consideration actually received by the supplier.

35. *See* Santoro, E., *Transfer Pricing and Value Added Tax in the European Community: Is There Room for Interaction and, If So, Where?*, International Transfer Pricing Journal, Volume 14, Issue 3, 2007, pp. 155-156; Martins, A., *VAT Transfer Pricing Rules: A Portuguese Perspective*, Intertax, Volume 37, Issue 5, Kluwer Law International, 2009, p. 330; Derer, C., *Transfer Pricing Implications for VAT/GST*, in: Pfeiffer/Ursprung-Steindl (eds), *Global Trends in VAT/GST and Direct Taxes*, Linde, 2015, pp. 292-296; Matesanz, F., *Transfer Pricing Adjustments and VAT*, International VAT Monitor, Volume 26, Issue 5, 2015, pp. 297-298.

36. *See* Santoro, *supra* n. 35, pp. 154-155.

CJEU stressed that 'the OECD Convention is irrelevant since it concerns direct taxation whereas VAT is an indirect tax'.[37]

In spite of the above, other authors highlight that there is a strong case for aligning the arm's length principle and the VAT concept of open market value since both systems have the common goal of requiring a transaction value that is not influenced by the relationship of the parties to the transaction. In addition, the alignment of the two sets of (direct tax and indirect tax) rules would have the advantage of reducing the administrative burden imposed on businesses which is even increased by the margin of freedom granted to the Member States with respect to the local implementation.[38]

The lack of guidance at the EU or supranational level, on the one hand, and the need for clarity and legal certainty, on the other, has led certain Member States to solve the issue at the national level by prescribing an alignment with the income tax legislation. This is the case of Spain[39] and outside Europe, e.g., Japan,[40] that have introduced an express cross-reference into their national VAT legislation to the TP methods contained in the corporate income tax legislation.[41]

2.2.3 *Price Adjustments*

Article 90 of the VAT Directive requires the Members States to reduce the taxable amount (and, consequently, the amount of VAT payable by the taxable person) whenever part or all the consideration has not been received by the taxable person after a transaction has been concluded.[42]

Such a provision embodies one of the fundamental principles of the VAT system, according to which the taxable amount is the consideration actually received and the corollary of which is that the tax authorities may not charge an amount of VAT exceeding the tax paid by the taxable person.

37. CJEU of 23 March 2006, C-210/04, *FCE Bank*, para. 39.
38. Derer, *supra* n. 35, pp. 295-296. *See also* Idsinga, F., Kalshoven, B., van Herksen, M., *Let's Tango! The Dance Between VAT, Customs and Transfer Pricing*, International Transfer Pricing Journal, Volume 12, Issue 5, IBFD, 2005, pp. 199-209 and Matesanz, *supra* n. 35, pp. 297-298.
39. Matesanz, *supra* n. 35, p. 297. *See also* Article 79 of the Spanish VAT Law (Ley 37/1992), making a cross-reference to Legislative Royal Decree 4/2004, on the recast text of the Corporate Income Tax Act.
40. Ainsworth, R., *Transfer Pricing in VAT/GST vs Direct Taxation: A Paper on the Topic of Relations Between Associated Companies*, Working Paper 09-02, Working Paper Series, Law and Economics, p. 18.
41. A different approach has been adopted by other non-EU countries, such as Australia and New Zealand, that have developed a specific valuation system for GST purposes (*see* Ainsworth, *supra* n. 40, p. 28).
42. *See* Article 90 of the VAT Directive, in particular para. 1 that lists cases in which the taxable amount shall be reduced. In particular, said provision states that the taxable amount shall be reduced in case of: (i) cancellation, (ii) refusal, (iii) total or partial non-payment, or (iv) when the price is reduced after the supply takes place. In some language versions (among which the Italian is included), Article 90(1) of the VAT Directive provides for a fifth circumstance under which the taxable amount shall be reduced: termination of a contract for non-performance because it has become impossible to perform or because the terms are excessively onerous. *See* the opinion of Advocate General La Pergola of 27 February 1997, C-330/95, *Goldsmiths (Jewellers) Ltd v. Commissioners of Customs & Excise*, footnote 5.

3 INTERPLAY BETWEEN TP AND VAT

3.1 Differences Between TP and VAT

When discussing the interaction between the TP and the VAT, it seems necessary to realize the differences between both areas in terms of their main rules and concepts. Table 31.1 provides a condensed summary of these primary differences which will then be discussed in more detail in the following sections of this chapter.

Table 31.1 Direct Comparison Between TP and VAT

Area of Comparison	*TP*	*VAT*
Source of regulations	OECD Guidelines/domestic law	Domestic law/OECD International VAT/GST Guidelines/VAT Directive (in the EU)
Concept	OECD Arm's length concept	Everything which constitutes consideration for the supply
Assessment basis	Aggregated income	Consideration for specific transaction
Assessment period	Specific period	Moment of transaction
Valuation methods	TP methods	Consideration on an invoice/open market value

3.1.1 *Sources of Rules and the Main Concepts*

The issue of rules applicable in the TP and the VAT is the first area of significant differences. While the TP rules are based on the OECD TPG in the majority of the countries in the world, there is no such overarching guidance for the VAT. Even though the OECD VAT/GST Guidance also exists, its role is not as significant for worldwide VAT as that of the OECD TPG for the TP. Therefore, in the case of the VAT, special attention should be paid to the domestic rules in order to determine the correct VAT treatment of the analysed transactions. This is also relevant in the case of the TP, however, the TP rules around the world are more streamlined due to the position and importance of Article 9 of the OECD MTC and the OECD TPG that envisage the arm's length principle as an overarching principle for the TP and, for example, relevant TP methods.

When considering the differences between the main concepts behind the TP and the VAT, the objectivity criterion is perhaps the most important differentiating factor. For the TP, which is based on the arm's length principle, the most important aspect is the determination of the prices in transactions between related parties at the same level at which the transaction would be priced between unrelated prices. This approach requires the performance of the comparability analysis and prevents, in principle, a free determination of the price to be paid for delivered goods or provided services. At the same time, the value taken for the determination of the taxable basis for VAT purposes is usually described as subjective as the transacting parties are free to determine the actual consideration to be paid for the delivery of goods or provision of services.[43] In this context, they are usually not bound by any reference to the value taken in a similar transaction between unrelated parties. This situation of course leads to abuse in the form of artificially overpriced or under-priced deliveries in order to obtain specific VAT benefits. In this context, certain jurisdictions introduced specific exceptions to the main rule that are supposed to prevent this type of abuse (e.g., Articles 72 and 80 of the VAT Directive within the EU that were already discussed in the earlier parts of this chapter).[44]

3.1.2 *Assessment of Transactions*

When discussing the issue of assessment of transactions, two separate points shall be analysed, specifically, the assessment basis and the assessment period.

In the case of the assessment basis, it should be noted that, in the TP, there is a clear tendency to aggregate the transactions to arrive at an arm's length outcome. This is directly due to the fact that the TP is mainly concerned with the profitability of the entities and thus the aggregation approach facilitates the determination of the profitability. In addition, it is also useful, for example, in the case of closely linked or continuous transactions where the separation would not really be in accordance with the essence of the transaction. Similarly, bundling transactions as a component of a so-called portfolio approach aimed to achieve a better return is another example of when the aggregation of transactions is the most effective for MNEs.[45] This is also due to the fact that, very often in the TP realm, it is almost impossible to determine arm's length conditions of a separate transaction, for example, due to a scarcity of comparables that could provide a reliable point of reference.

At the same time, the VAT assessments rely almost exclusively on a transaction-by-transaction basis. The aggregation happens, but it is an exception to the rule – for example, in situations when the deliveries or provisions of services are so closely correlated that it would not make any sense to consider them separately for VAT purposes as their goal was to offer the purchaser the full package and, most likely, the purchaser would not be interested in obtaining only one of the elements separately. Nevertheless, this type of approach is an exception to the rule in the VAT realm, and

43. Lucas Mas, M.O., *Value Added Tax*, in: A. Baker, B. Obuforibo (eds), *Transfer Pricing and Customs Valuation: Two Worlds to Tax as One*, IBFD, 2009, p. 193.
44. van den Brekel, R., van Doesum, A., van Kesteren, H., *VAT Effects of Year-End Transfer Pricing Adjustments*, EC Tax Review, Volume 4, Kluwer, 2017, p. 184.
45. Paragraph A.3.1 of the OECD TPG.

the regular approach is to account for every transaction separately.[46] Undoubtedly, there are two reasons for this state of things. First, the fact that the VAT is a neutral tax from the perspective of the taxpayers and its burden lays on the customers makes it necessary to monitor every delivery or the provision of services to the final customer. Second, as a consequence of this character of the VAT, every transaction must also be documented separately with an invoice and reported to the tax authorities (in certain countries, also at a supranational level, for example, in the EU in the event of intra-community supplies).

Proceeding to the assessment period, specific and significant differences can also be identified between the TP and the VAT. The regular practice among MNEs is to determine financial indicators such as projected margins at the beginning of the fiscal year. These indicators are somewhat of a guidance to be taken into account over the course of the year. However, in the case of financial results that diverge from those projected at the beginning of the financial year, it is usual practice to perform appropriate year-end adjustments that bring the actual results in accordance with the financial projections. It is important to indicate that TP settlements will usually be performed once per year and disclosed on the corporate income tax return,[47] which automatically also limits the number of adjustments performed by an MNE.

Contrary to the TP settlements, the VAT usually focuses on the specific moment when the transaction has been performed and the VAT became chargeable[48] even if certain exceptions might exist to this general rule.[49] This fact is confirmed by the issue of an appropriate document, usually a VAT invoice.[50] In addition, it should be indicated that the settlement periods in the VAT are usually more frequent than in the TP (predominantly one month or one quarter). In addition, they are connected with disclosing all relevant information about the taxable transactions to the tax authorities (either by means of a VAT return or an automatized system based on, for example, the SAF-T technology).[51]

3.1.3 Valuation Methods

The TP and the VAT are also significantly different regarding the methods that are used to arrive at the final value of the analysed transaction. In general, the rules applicable for TP purposes seem to be fairly more complex than those applicable in the VAT realm.

46. In the EU, confirmed by the case law of the CJEU, e.g., CJEU of 14 June 2007, Joined Cases C-434/05 and C-445/05 Horizon College and Haderer; of 8 December 2016, C-208/15, Stock'94; of 18 October 2018, C-153/17, Volkswagen Financial Services (UK); *see also* Mas, *supra* n. 43, p. 197.
47. Mas, *supra* n. 43, p. 196.
48. Article 63 of the VAT Directive.
49. *See* e.g., Articles 64-67 of the VAT Directive.
50. For further conditions regarding VAT invoices, *see* Article 220 of the VAT Directive.
51. For further details, *see* Forum on Tax Administration, *Guidance Note: Guidance for the Standard Audit File: Tax Version 2.0,* OECD, April 2010; Majdańska, A., Dziwiński, K., *The Potential of a Standard Audit File: Tax in the European Union – A Chance for Coordinated VAT Administration?,* Bulletin for International Taxation, Volume 72, Issue 10, IBFD, 2018, pp. 582-594.

As already discussed in the earlier chapters of this book, TP rules envisage that the transactions between related parties shall adhere to the arm's length principle.[52] The process of arriving at this result entails, according to the OECD TPG, a small number of steps such as the identification of the commercial or financial relations, recognition of the accurately delineated transaction, selection of the most appropriate TP methods best reflecting the characteristics of the transaction (with the number of available methods making this step more complex) and, finally, the application of the selected method.

In this view, the valuation of transactions for VAT purposes seems comparatively easier. In a vast majority of the cases, the taxable amount is the amount paid or payable for the delivery of goods or provision of services. Hence, VAT, in principle, does not follow any overarching rule like the arm's length principle but rather taxes what the customer is willing to pay for the good or service. Depending on the jurisdiction, the rules might vary and impose specific modes of determining the taxable amount.[53]

Arguably, the difference in the valuation of transactions between the TP and the VAT is significant, and they make the coexistence of these two sets of rules complicated, in particular in the situation when they directly interact, such as adjustments in both ways. The determined values of the transactions for TP and VAT purposes might differ significantly which, as a result, can also influence their further reconciliation.

3.2 Missing Harmonization

When discussing the interaction between the TP and the VAT, it must be noted that one fundamental difference makes it challenging to reconcile the respective goals in these two areas. It consists of the fact that the TP can be classified as a part of the direct tax system concerning transactions between related parties while the VAT is the most significant example of an indirect tax that remains neutral to taxpayers. This dissimilarity will influence the coexistence of both discussed areas in almost any jurisdiction beginning with the fact that, usually, within the apparatus of tax authorities in a specific country, different teams are responsible for the TP and the VAT. Perhaps the most significant example of their difficult coexistence can be the EU where direct taxes are not the EU organs' area of competence while indirect taxes including the VAT are which was expressed by the publication of a binding law, i.e., the VAT Directive.[54] This act, obligatory for the Member States to implement, provides some solid grounds for the uniform understanding and application of the discussed tax across a number of countries. At the same time, in spite of certain efforts of the EU to at least coordinate the taxation among the Member States, designing tax policy and specific rules, such as those for the TP, remains within the sphere of competencies of the Member States with

52. For further details, *see* Michael Lang, Raffaele Petruzzi, Giammarco Cottani, Alfred Storck (2018) Fundamentals of Transfer Pricing: A Practical Guide, Kluwer Law International, Chapter I 'Introduction to Transfer Pricing' and Chapter II 'Accurate Delineation and Recognition of Actual Transactions'.
53. For example, the already discussed open market value in the EU.
54. *See* http://www.europarl.europa.eu/factsheets/en/sheet/81/indirect-taxation (last accessed 30 January 2022).

not much coordination between the respective regulations and practices that also pertain to the interaction of the TP and the VAT.[55]

The example of the EU is a significant one to demonstrate their difficult coexistence; however, it is also the reality of all countries where these two areas are regulated. An important remark in this aspect is to mention that in the majority of the cases, the TP rules are based on the arm's length principle as envisaged in Article 9 of the OECD MTC which grants a certain degree of comparability between various rules. At the same time, the VAT/GST systems around the world are based on the same principles that should also facilitate the understanding of potential ramifications that the TP adjustments might have on the VAT settlements. Nevertheless, a lack of harmonization between these two areas and no global guidance makes it necessary to always conduct a careful analysis that will depend on the facts of the case and on the specific local regulations.

3.3 TP Adjustments and Their Influence on VAT

The recurring issue in the interplay between the TP and the VAT is the consequences that adjustments in one area might have on the other. Therefore, the aim of the following subchapters will be to provide more details on the practical approach towards the analysed issue.

3.3.1 Categories of TP Adjustments

In order to determine the influence of the TP adjustments on the VAT, a brief recap of the main characteristics of such adjustments is needed. While this book has already provided an in-depth view of this issue, this chapter will reiterate them for the purposes of further analysis.[56]

Primary adjustments are those that tax authorities in a first jurisdiction make to a company's taxable profits as a result of applying the arm's length principle to transactions involving a related party in a second tax jurisdiction.[57] Thus, a certain part of the profit resulting from the entire transaction is moved from one entity to another (and thus also jurisdiction). It should be noted, however, that no actual money transfer is involved in this adjustment, but there is only a change in the tax accounts.

A corresponding adjustment can be treated as an 'answer' to the primary adjustment. It modifies the tax liability of the related party in a second tax jurisdiction and is performed by the tax authorities there. It corresponds to a primary adjustment made by the tax authorities in a first tax jurisdiction so that the allocation of profits by the two

55. *See* http://www.europarl.europa.eu/factsheets/en/sheet/80/direct-taxation-personal-and-company-taxation (last accessed 30 January 2022).
56. For further details on the TP adjustments, *see* Michael Lang, Raffaele Petruzzi, Giammarco Cottani, Alfred Storck (2018) Fundamentals of Transfer Pricing: A Practical Guide, Kluwer Law International, Chapter I, pp. 27-28.
57. Glossary, OECD TPG, p. 28.

jurisdictions is consistent.[58] This logical coherence among them will be ensured if the interpretation and implementation of the arm's length principle are the same or devoid of any crucial divergences among both respective tax authorities. Similar to the primary adjustment, the corresponding adjustment also does not involve an actual money transfer between the related parties.

In accordance with the definition provided by the OECD, the secondary adjustment arises from imposing tax on a secondary transaction.[59] Briefly, it means that this adjustment involves an actual monetary transfer by creating a secondary transaction in order to reflect the changes in the tax accounts effectuated by the previous adjustments. Usually, this adjustment is performed in the form of a constructive dividend, equity contribution, or constructive loan.[60]

Finally, the last type of TP adjustment, which is perhaps the most interesting when considering its influence on the VAT, is the compensating adjustment. According to the definition, it is an adjustment in which the taxpayer reports a transfer price for tax purposes that is, in the taxpayer's opinion, an arm's length price for a tested transaction, even though this price differs from the amount actually charged between the related parties. This adjustment would be made before the tax return is filed,[61] which is why it is usually also referred to as a 'year-end adjustment'. The compensating adjustments, due to their nature, involve a monetary transfer (usually from a mother company to a subsidiary) and are primarily performed by the taxpayers in order to ensure that their year-end settlements adhere to the profit allocation projected at the beginning of the year.[62]

3.3.2 *TP Adjustments Influencing VAT*

Whenever an adjustment to a company's taxable profit is made, the key issue for VAT is to determine whether such an adjustment:

- should be taken into account as more or less consideration of a pre-existing supply of goods or services already made, i.e., as an adjustment to a price already paid, leading to a modification of the taxable amount of that transaction for VAT purposes; or
- should be regarded as the consideration of an autonomous and independent taxable transaction for VAT purposes (i.e., as the consideration for a separate supply of goods or services made for consideration); or
- is of no relevance for VAT purposes.

Since TP regulations do not create new categories of transactions subject to the VAT (and the VAT Directive does not provide for specific rules concerning the VAT ramifications of TP adjustments), reference must be made to ordinary VAT rules.

58. *Ibid.*, p. 25.
59. *Ibid.*, p. 30.
60. Santoro, *supra* n. 35, p. 158.
61. *Supra* n. 27, p. 25.
62. Santoro, *supra* n. 35, p. 162.

Therefore, in order for a TP adjustment to assume relevance for VAT purposes, it shall be regarded as the 'consideration'[63] (either in cash or in kind) of a taxable transaction.[64]

In the lack of consideration, there is no taxable transaction, and the TP adjustment is clearly beyond the scope of the VAT.

In light of the above, non-voluntary adjustments such as primary, secondary, and corresponding adjustments[65] that do not qualify as 'consideration' do not usually lead to a taxable transaction and are therefore considered as being outside the scope of VAT.[66] In particular:

(1) Primary adjustments have little or no VAT effects[67] since they are made at the initiative of the tax authorities, and they only affect the calculation of profits for direct tax purposes. In addition, these adjustments are merely reflected in the tax accounts without any actual balancing payment or monetary transfer changing the financial situations of the parties. It cannot be stated, therefore, that the said adjustments represent a modification of the initial taxable amount since they do not alter the consideration agreed by the parties. Nonetheless, primary adjustments might indicate that the envisaged transaction is under- or overvalued also for VAT purposes. In such a case, if one of the parties is not entitled to a full right of deduction (and the country concerned has implemented anti-avoidance VAT rules such as those established by Article 80 of the VAT Directive), primary VAT adjustments might

---

63. According to settled case law of the CJEU, a transaction is made for consideration within the meaning of Article 2, para. 1 of the VAT Directive and hence is taxable only if there is a direct link between the service supplied and the consideration received.

Such a direct link is established if there is a legal relationship between the provider of the service and the recipient pursuant to which there is reciprocal performance, the remuneration received by the provider of the service constituting the actual consideration given in return for the service supplied to the recipient.

64. In this latter respect, a supply of goods or services is subject to the VAT when made for consideration by a taxable person acting as such pursuant to Article 2(1) of the VAT Directive. In order to become relevant for VAT, a transaction thus has to fulfil three cumulative conditions:

- the transaction shall be attributable to a taxable person (i.e., pursuant to Article 9 of the VAT Directive, any person carrying out an economic activity whatever the purpose or results of that activity; *subjective* condition);
- the transaction shall fall into one of the existing categories of taxable transactions for VAT purposes (specifically: supply of goods, supply of services, intra-community acquisition of goods; *objective* condition); and
- the transaction shall be deemed to be performed within the territory of the Member State concerned pursuant to the territoriality or place-of-supply rules laid down by the VAT Directive for each taxable transaction (*territorial* condition).

65. For further details, *see* VEG No. 65, *Possible Implication of Transfer Pricing*, para. 2.1.5, *Transfer pricing adjustments*, taxud.c.1(2017)1513583, 29 March 2017, pp. 6-10.
66. For further details, *see* VEG No. 71 REV2, *Paper on topic for discussion. Possible VAT implications of Transfer Pricing*, para. 2.2.1.1, *Non-voluntary Transfer Pricing Adjustments*, taxud.x.1(2018)2326098–EN, 18 April 2018, p. 6.
67. van den Brekel, van Doesum, van Kesteren, *supra* n. 44, p. 185; Matesanz, *supra* n. 35, pp. 35, 295-299.

also lead to adjustments of the VAT taxable amount irrespective of the lack of balancing payments between the parties.[68]

(2) Corresponding adjustments should, in principle, not trigger any VAT consequence. Since they are mere reflections of primary adjustments (even if performed by other tax authorities with the aim of avoiding double taxation in the second tax jurisdiction), the considerations under (1) above remain valid here. In addition, this type of adjustment is usually performed as a change in the capital accounts of the parties, and hence it does not represent the consideration of any supply and consequently falls outside the scope of the VAT.[69]

(3) Secondary adjustments are also made at the sole initiative of the tax authorities of certain countries with a view to make the actual allocation of profits consistent with primary adjustments. They might take the form of constructive dividends, constructive equity contributions, or constructive loans; all of them represent mere financial flows that are, in principle, not to be regarded as the consideration of taxable supplies for the purposes of VAT.[70]

Regarding year-end adjustments made at the initiative of the taxpayer, the definition of compensating adjustments provided by the OECD TPG[71] seems to indicate that such adjustments also only have a direct tax effect. Such a conclusion is certainly valid for compensating adjustments that are only made at the level of the direct tax accounts of the parties without a balancing payment.

However, some VAT issues may arise from compensating adjustments with balancing payments, i.e., when consideration arises from a compensation adjustment in order to balance the cash position of the companies involved in the transaction. In so far as the adjustments are voluntarily made and may be attributed to a transaction or, at least, to a series of specific transactions, they can be considered as either (i) a modification

68. *See* for instance Martins, *supra* n. 35, pp. 328-329; Santoro, *supra* n. 35, p. 147; such an approach is also shared by the UK tax authorities *see* HMRC International Manual, section INTM486010, Interaction with VAT: '*Transfer pricing adjustments or compensating adjustments made under TIOPA10/Part 4 have no direct VAT consequences. However, where a business undertakes a transaction with an associated business other than on an arm's length basis, then there may be a question about whether the value of the underlying supply for VAT purposes is less than the open market value. If so, then, depending on whether the conditions specified in VATA94/SCH6 are met, there may be scope for making a direction that the open market value is used for VAT purposes. This is most likely to be an issue if the two parties to the transaction are not in the same VAT group, or if a member of the VAT group is involved in making supplies that are exempt for VAT purposes (as then the value of supplies to other members of the VAT group may affect the amount of input tax that can be recovered).*'

69. Idsinga, Kalshoven, van Herksen, *supra* n. 38, p. 207. *See also* CJEU of 29 April 2004, C-77/01, *EDM*; of 26 June 2003, C-442/01, *KapHag*.

70. For other arguments on this topic, *see* Dziwiński, K., *Transfer Pricing and VAT: An Analysis of Two Overlapping Disciplines*, TPI Transfer Pricing International, Volume 1, Linde, 2020, p. 30.

71. Compensating adjustments are defined as 'An adjustment in which the taxpayer reports a transfer price for tax purpose that is, in the taxpayer's opinion, an arm's length price for a tested transaction, even though this price differs from the amount actually charged between the related parties. This adjustment would be made before the tax return is filed.'

of the consideration already paid for the goods or services in question or even as (ii) the entire consideration for one or more separate and independent taxable transactions.

In order to be seen as *the consideration for a supply already provided*, the compensating adjustment balancing payment and the previous taxable supply must be closely connected (i.e., a direct link must exist between the balancing payment and those supplies). Business agreements and TPD – as well as debit or credit notes and/or any other VAT document eventually issued by the parties – may contain useful indications as to whether a direct link actually exists between the year-end adjustment and the previously made supplies (in this regard, *see also* section 3.3.4.1 of this chapter).

When, for instance, the parties agree on an annual adjustment of their transfer prices with an intent to considering changes in both the market conditions and in the functions performed by the parties in the course of the year, there undoubtedly exists a direct link between the year-end balancing payment and the supplies made in the same period.

The circumstance that the compensating adjustment and the balancing payment are made to comply with the arm's length principle is of no relevance: If the parties agree on a price adjustment and it is reflected in their financial accounts, it becomes part of the consideration obtained or to be obtained pursuant to Article 73 of the VAT Directive (*see* section 2.2.1 above).

Compensating adjustments with balancing payments may also be seen as the *consideration of a separate and independent taxable supply for VAT purposes*. This is the (not uncommon) case of year-end adjustments characterized by the parties as service fees (such as 'marketing fees', 'advertising fees', etc.). One of the reasons for MNEs to explore the possibility to treat year-end adjustments as a remuneration for a separate service rather than as retroactive price adjustments of their supplies is to reduce the administrative burden of year-end adjustments.

The qualification of the adjustments as consideration for a taxable supply of services is sometimes certainly acceptable. This is the case if, for instance, a parent company makes a compensating adjustment in favour of a subsidiary providing shared services within the group. However, it must be to the extent the services are actually made available to the parent company[72] and performed on the basis of specific service agreements between the parties.[73] Under these circumstances, indeed, a direct link can be established between the compensating adjustment balancing payment and the service made available to the paying company.

In light of the above, the following conditions have to be satisfied for a year-end voluntary TP adjustment to display VAT effects:

72. It is worth pointing out that the CJEU has repeatedly held that, even if a service is not actually used, the fact that it is made available is a service in itself (*see* CJEU of 21 March 2002, C-174/00, *Kennemer Golf & Country Club*, para. 40 and of 23 December 2015, Joined Cases C-250/14 (*Air France-KLM*) and C-289/14 (*Hop!-Brit Air SAS*)).

73. *See* CJEU of 18 June 2020, C-276/18, *KrakVet*, para. 66; of 20 June 2013, C-653/11, *Paul Newey*, para. 43: '*Given that the contractual position normally reflects the economic and commercial reality of the transactions and in order to satisfy the requirements of legal certainty, the relevant contractual terms constitute a factor to be taken into consideration* ...' in categorizing a taxable transaction.

(1) they must entail balancing payments (i.e., an actual financial element reflected in the accounts of the parties);
(2) the TP adjustment and the balancing payment related thereto must be directly linked to one or more specific VAT taxable supplies.

Example

Company A, located in Country X and Company B located in Country Y are part of the ABC Group. Company A operates as a local LRD in Country X: it purchases finished products from one single counterpart, e.g., the affiliated Company B. As a limited risk distributor of the products within Country X, under the TP policy of the group, Company A is only responsible for the promotion of the products within its local market.

For direct tax purposes, the transfer prices applied by Company B to Company A for the finished products are set by applying a TNMM return on sales basis, ensuring Company B receives an arm's length remuneration for the functions performed in the local market in accordance with the OECD Guidelines.

The TP policy of the group provides that:
(1) At the beginning of each fiscal year, the price of the finished goods sold by Company B to Company A for subsequent distribution in Country X are approved by Company B; the parties agree that such a price does not change during the fiscal year.
(2) Considering the limited risk profile of Company A, this latter recharges (through the issuance of separate invoices) to Company B the costs of advertising and promotion exceeding a certain 'threshold' that is budgeted and verified on an annual basis.
(3) Moreover, by the end of each year, a compensating payment may also be paid by Company B to Company A if, also considering the extra-costs recharge under let. b., Company A's profit is lower than expected.
As far as the VAT implications of the adjustments, the following shall be considered:
(4) The recharge to Company B of the costs for advertising and promotional activities exceeding the pre-established 'threshold' qualify as a separate taxable transaction for VAT purposes, i.e., as a supply of (advertising and promotional) services rendered by Company A and to be separately invoiced by the latter to Company B. Such a supply is generally taxable in the place where the customer has established his business (i.e., in Country Y) for which the latter shall apply local VAT through the reverse charge mechanism.
(5) The (additional, if any) 'compensating adjustment' aimed at reaching Company's A agreed profit margin is not a taxable transaction for VAT purposes because:

(a) it does not constitute consideration given in exchange for the previous supply of goods sold by Company B to Company A (i.e., it is not an adjustment to the price already paid by Company A to Company B which, as required by the contract, does not change); and
(b) there is no direct link with the supply of finished goods sold by Company B to Company A.

In such a scenario, the compensating adjustment is to be considered outside the scope of the VAT.

A different situation would have arisen if a transfer price revision had been contractually envisaged since the beginning. If, for example, the TP policy had provided for retroactive pricing adjustments of the finished products, Company B should have issued debit or credit notes to Company A. They must have been cross-referenced to the original invoices and have had the same VAT treatment as the initial transactions.

3.3.3 *Upward and Downward Adjustments*

In the event of year-end TP adjustments with balancing payments that can be directly attributed to already made VAT taxable transactions, only two possibilities may materialize:

(1) the prices that have been used for the supplies (of goods and services for consideration) carried out in the course of the year are too low from a TP perspective so that the compensating adjustment will amount to an upward adjustment for the supplier; or
(2) the prices used during the year were too high so the compensating adjustment will amount to a downward adjustment.

This chapter focuses on the VAT implications of upward and downward year-end compensating adjustments relating to previous supplies of goods and services for consideration only. If the adjustment clearly relates to previous taxable supplies, credit notes, or additional invoices shall normally be issued which are cross-referenced to the original invoices.

As far as EU VAT is concerned, the following situations may materialize in connection with adjustments that clearly relate to taxable supplies of goods already carried out as:

(1) *Supplies of goods within one Member State.* According to the relevant provisions of the VAT Directive, the local supplier has initially charged its (affiliated) customer with local VAT[74] that was, in principle, recovered by the

74. *See* Articles 2(1)(a), 32 and 33 of the VAT Directive.

latter. If prices are to be adjusted upwards,[75] the supplier should pay additional VAT – because of the increase in the consideration actually received – and, provided this VAT is charged onwards in a valid VAT invoice to its customer, the latter may, in principle, recover it.

From the supplier's perspective, a debated issue is one concerning the tax period in which the year-end adjustment should be processed for VAT purposes, i.e., whether the supplier has to adjust the initially filed VAT return or rather include the additional VAT on the return in which the year-end adjustment is finally made. According to some authors, year-end adjustments that can be directly linked to supplies already made should, in principle, be settled through the VAT returns of the periods in which the taxable supplies were deemed to take place for VAT purposes and were consequently initially registered.[76] On the contrary, the VEG's opinion is that '*the chargeable event for Transfer Pricing Adjustment should ... be the moment when the decision is made to voluntarily adjust the taxable amount for VAT purposes. At the same time, a debit/credit note is issued*'.[77]

For the recipient of the original supply, an upward adjustment means that he will be confronted with an additional charge of the VAT. As long as he does not suffer from a limitation to his right to a VAT deduction (meaning he does not have a special VAT status that disallows input VAT recovery and exclusively carries out transactions for which a right of VAT deduction exists), the additional amount of the VAT should be fully recoverable and should not result in an extra cost for him.

The VAT Directive prescribes that the right of a VAT deduction arises at the time the tax becomes chargeable and must, in principle, be exercised during the same period.[78] However, the same directive provides that the

75. From a VAT viewpoint, supplies of goods for consideration are deemed to be carried out (and shall be taxed) in the location where the goods are placed at the time the supply takes place regardless of the place of establishment/tax residence of the parties (*see* Articles 32 and 33 of the VAT Directive). This means that, although it is not a particularly frequent case (since most of the supplies of goods carried out by a member of an MNE to another are either VAT exempt intra-community supplies of goods or VAT exempt export sales, entailing the physical dispatch of the products outside the MS of departure), it may happen that related parties established in different countries make domestic supplies of goods that are not dispatched or transported and are therefore subject to the VAT in the country where the goods are located at the time when the supply takes place (an example could be that of a German manufacturing company selling finished products to a US based affiliated company without the goods being transported outside the German territory. The supplies of the goods made by the German company for consideration would, in this case, be subject to German VAT regardless of the fact that the US affiliated company is not established nor does it have a permanent establishment/fixed establishment in Germany). This shows that even domestic supplies of goods for consideration (i.e., supplies of goods made within one Member State) may be subject to transfer pricing rules and adjustments as far as they are concluded between related parties established in different tax jurisdictions.
76. van den Brekel, van Doesum, van Kesteren, *supra* n. 44, p. 188. The author's position is grounded on the wording of Article 63 of the VAT Directive pursuant to which the chargeable event shall occur, and the VAT shall become chargeable when the goods or services are supplied.
77. *See* VEG No. 71 REV2 of 18 April 2018, p. 5.
78. Articles 167, 179, 180 and 182 of the VAT Directive.

exercise of the right of an input VAT deduction is subject to the condition of holding an invoice that meets the invoicing requirements.[79] The correction of deductible VAT through the issuance of an adjusted invoice should therefore not result in a retroactive adjustment of the deductible VAT.[80] The right to deduct the additional VAT shall hence be fully granted as long as – further to the upwards adjustments with balancing payments – the supplier issues a debit note/correcting invoice so that the substantive and formal conditions triggering the right of deduction are truly satisfied.

If prices should be adjusted downwards, the opposite occurs:

- the supplier should reduce the taxable base of the supplies already made[81] and recover the excess (output) VAT that he has initially paid; while;
- the customer should recompense the tax authorities the (input) VAT it has deducted or recovered. In this latter respect, the VAT Directive provides for a legal basis[82] to adjust the VAT deduction when it is lower than that to which the taxable person was entitled. In this latter respect, the CJEU has recently[83] confirmed that, when a business is confronted with retroactive price adjustments relating to one or more specific transactions, the VAT that has initially been deducted by the taxpayer in relation to those purchases must be adjusted. Additionally, it must be done regardless of the issuance of a proper credit note (or other VAT relevant document) by the business granting the retroactive discount. The CJEU ruling had retrospective price adjustments deriving from volume discounts relating to multiple transactions previously carried out as its objective. However, it could equally apply to other retroactive price adjustments that can be linked to one or more specific transactions such as certain voluntary year-end compensating adjustments with balancing payments.

From a practical perspective, downward year-end adjustments directly linked to already made supplies are normally settled with the issuance of VAT credit notes. The judgment of the CJEU shows that an input VAT deduction shall be adjusted regardless of the issuance of a credit note by the person granting the discount and/or making the TP adjustment balancing payment clearly relating to previous supplies.

(2) *Cross-border supplies of goods from one Member State to another.*

From a VAT viewpoint, intra-community B2B transactions imply two different taxable events inextricably bound to each other: (i) an intra-community supply by the supplier of the goods that is deemed to be made in

79. Article 178 of the VAT Directive.
80. *See* CJEU of 21 March 2018, C-533/16, *Volkswagen AG* and the Opinion of Advocate General of 26 October 2017, C-533/16, *Volkswagen AG*, para. 91.
81. *See* Article 90 of the VAT Directive which, in the case of price adjustments, requires a reduction of the taxable base of the supplies already made.
82. Articles 184-186 of the VAT Directive.
83. *See* CJEU of 28 May 2020, C-684/18, *World Comm Trading*.

the EU country of departure of the goods[84] where it shall be exempted from local VAT with right of deduction[85] and (ii) an intra-community acquisition of the same goods[86] that is considered to occur in the EU country of arrival of the goods[87] where the transaction value of the goods shall be subject to the local VAT rate by the (affiliated) customer.[88] The buyer is indeed the person liable to pay the VAT on the intra-community acquisition[89] so he must report it in his VAT return and (in principle) pay the VAT due on it. If the buyer has a right to fully recover input VAT, he can deduct the VAT on the acquisition in the same VAT return with no actual VAT payment to the tax authorities.

There are several administrative obligations and requirements to be fulfilled by both the supplier and the customer in connection with an intra-community supply and intra-community acquisition of goods, respectively. The supplier must report the intra-community supply of goods in its periodical VAT return and must also periodically submit declarations of his intra-community supplies to the tax and customs administration (referred to as 'recapitulative statement' or 'EC Sales Listing').[90] In addition to EC Sales Listings, suppliers carrying out intra-community supplies must also periodically file Intrastat reports for statistical purposes (listing the value of these supplies exceeds certain thresholds).[91]

84. Article 32 of the VAT Directive.
85. Article 138 of the VAT Directive. As pointed out by the CJEU on 27 September 2007, C-409/04, *Teleos plc and others*, from this provision, it can be derived that a VAT exempt intra-community supply of goods occurs if all of the following conditions are met:

    (1) The supplier shall be a taxable person, and the customer shall also be a taxable person or a non-taxable legal person.
    (2) The right to dispose of the good as the owner shall be transferred to the purchaser.
    (3) The goods shall be dispatched or transported to another Member State.
    (4) The goods shall physically leave the territory of the Member State of supply.

86. Article 20 of the VAT Directive.
87. *See* Article 40 of the VAT Directive laying down the main rule according to which the place of an intra-community acquisition of goods shall be deemed to be the place where dispatch or transport of the goods to the person acquiring them ends.
88. Following Article 83 of the VAT Directive, the taxable amount of intra-community acquisitions of goods shall be established on the same factors that are used to determine the taxable amount for the supply of the same goods within the territory of the Member State concerned. Therefore, the taxable amount of an intra-community acquisition of goods is, in principle, the consideration obtained or to be obtained by the supplier.
89. Article 200 of the VAT Directive.
90. *See* Article 262 of the VAT Directive. The information provided to the tax authorities through the EC Sales Listings is exchanged between the Member States via what is referred to as the 'VAT Information Exchange System' (VIES) that enables the tax authorities of the Member State where the goods arrive (i.e., the Member State where the taxable intra-community acquisition is deemed to occur) to compare the intra-community acquisitions recorded by the purchaser in his local VAT return with the intra-community supplies recorded by the supplier in the EC Sales List.
91. The rules on Intrastat reporting are laid down in Regulation (EC) 638/2004 of the European Parliament and of the Council of 31 March 2004 on Community Statistics relating to the trading of goods between Member States and repealing Council Regulation (EEC) 3330/91.

When compensating adjustments on the value of the intra-community supply (and, consequently, of the corresponding intra-community acquisition) have to be made for TP purposes, a balancing payment is also exchanged by the parties. This latter is clearly attributable to the previous intra-community transactions, all the above filings must be amended accordingly.

Example

Company A located in Country X, Company B located in Country Y, Company C located in Country Z, and Company D located in Country V are part of the ABC Group. Company A manufactures its products in Country X, and they are subsequently sold and dispatched to its affiliates B, C, and D. The supplies of finished products from Company A to Companies B, C, and D qualify under EU law as intra-community supplies of goods since they are transported or dispatched from one Member State to another in the course of the supply (i.e., from Country X to either Country Y, Z, or V), meaning that Company A performs an intra-community supply of goods in Country X, the goods leave this Member State of dispatch VAT-free, and the distributing companies (either Company B, C or D) buying the goods effect a taxable intra-community acquisition of the goods in the Member State of arrival. This occurs through the reverse charge mechanism (i.e., with no actual payment of VAT to the extent that the buyer is entitled to fully deduct input VAT).

In the event of a year-end compensating adjustment with a balancing payment clearly relating to the intra-community supplies of the products carried out in the course of the year:

(1) Debit or credit notes shall be issued by Company A to the affiliated Companies B, C, and D which must be cross-referenced to the original invoices and have the same VAT treatment (i.e., the VAT exemption regime applicable to intra-community supplies) as the initial transactions.
(2) The buyers (i.e., Companies B, C, and D) will instead be confronted with an additional reverse charge of VAT (in the case of upward adjustments) or with the need to adjust input and output VAT originally applied on the intra-community acquisitions (in case of downward adjustments).

In both cases (upward or downward adjustments), no material VAT consequences would arise (provided that the buyers – Companies B, C, and D – are entitled to fully deduct input VAT). However, mainly administrative obligations would have to be accomplished such as the correction of Intrastat declarations and EC Sales Lists by both the supplier (Company A) and the customers (Companies B, C, and D). Since some Member States require the adjustments to be reported in the month in which the initial supply has taken place, Companies A, B, C, and D must determine whether this is the case in the Member States where they are established and whether they have to retroactively adjust their VAT and Intrastat returns as well as their EC Sales Listings.

(3) *Cross-border supplies of goods from a Member State to a non-EU Country.* Coherently with the nature of the VAT as a tax on consumption, supplies of goods exported out of the EU are exempt from it.[92] Compensating adjustments with balancing payments directly linked to previous VAT exempt export sales should therefore not lead to major VAT issues for the supplier. However, certain customs and VAT implications may arise for the importer of the goods in the non-EU Country. The actual implications may widely vary depending on the country of the importer and should be further investigated on a country-by-country basis.

As far as cross-border supplies of services are concerned, different territoriality rules apply depending on the type of services. Since 1 January 2010, the EU legislation has provided for two main place-of-supply rules (each of which has its own set of exceptions) that depend on the VAT status of the customer:[93]

- in the case of B2B supplies (i.e., services rendered to taxable persons or customers regarded as such for the purpose of applying the place-of-supply rules), the services are subject to a VAT where the customer has established its business[94] and, if supplied cross-border, the recipient of the service shall self-assess local VAT (which, in principle, is recoverable at the same moment) while;[95]
- in the case of B2C supplies (i.e., services rendered to non-taxable persons), the services are subject to a VAT where the supplier has established his business,[96] and it is generally due by the latter.[97]

92. Article 146 of the VAT Directive.
93. *See* Council Directive 2008/8/EC of 20 February 2008, amending Directive 2006/112/EC as regards the place of supply of services.
94. *See* Article 44 of the VAT Directive. In the case of customers established in multiple jurisdictions, the services are subject to a VAT where the customer has established the fixed establishment to which the service is provided (*see* Articles 20-22 of Council Implementing Regulation (EU) No. 282/2011).

    Exceptions to the general place-of-supply rule apply for the following B2B services: (i) services connected with immovable properties; (ii) passenger transport services; (iii) cultural, educational, and similar services; (iv) restaurant and catering services; (v) restaurant and catering services on board ships, trains, or aircraft; (vi) short-term hiring of means of transport.
95. Article 196 of the VAT Directive.
96. Article 45 of the VAT Directive.

    Exceptions to the general place-of-supply rule apply for the following B2C services: (i) intermediary services; (ii) services connected with immovable properties; (iii) passenger transport services; (iv) cultural, educational, and such like services; (v) valuations and work on movable tangible property; (vi) restaurant and catering services; (vii) restaurant and catering

Since TP rules and adjustments only apply to cross-border transactions (to the extent they are carried out between related parties), upwards adjustments with balancing payments clearly related to B2B cross-border supplies of services already made would result in additional VAT to be applied by the customer through the reverse charge mechanism. On the contrary, downward adjustments would lead to a downward adjustment of the VAT that the customer had originally both self-assessed and, in principle, deducted. In addition, invoicing and reporting obligations (the latter even in both countries depending on the place of establishment of the parties) would also have to be fulfilled.[98]

Example

Company A located in Country X and Company B located in Country Y are part of the ABC Group. Company A functions as a toll manufacturer for the parent Company B. Under this structure, Company B is the owner of the raw materials and the finished goods, and it pays Company A a manufacturing fee for the manufacturing services. The toll fee is a fixed amount to be paid quarterly which is determined on the basis of the cost-plus method with a mark-up being a percentage of the manufacturing costs and not the value of the end product.
From a VAT perspective, the toll fees qualify as the consideration for the supply of manufacturing services rendered by Company A to Company B that is subject to the general place-of-supply rules for services (according to which a VAT is due in the country where the customer has established its business).[99] It is therefore subject to a VAT in Country Y where it shall be applied by Company B through the reverse charge mechanism.[100] Certain invoicing and reporting obligations have to be accomplished by Company A in Country X and, depending on the country concerned, Company B might also be required to file recapitulative statements in Country Y for the tolling services it had received by Company A (and for which it is liable to account for a VAT under the reverse charge mechanism).[101]

services on board ships, trains, or aircraft; (viii) hiring of means of transport; (ix) electronically supplied services, telecommunication, as well as radio and television broadcasting services.

97. Article 193 of the VAT Directive.
98. *See* Article 220(1)(1) of the VAT Directive (according to which every taxable person shall ensure that an invoice is issued in respect of supplies of services he has made to another taxable person) and Article 262, para. 1, let. c) of the VAT Directive (which provides for the obligation to file recapitulative statements also in respect with cross-border services subject to the B2B default place-of-supply rule). Please note that, although the VAT Directive does not authorize them to that effect, several Member States require taxable persons to file recapitulative statements in respect of the services they have received from abroad and for which they are liable to account for a VAT under the reverse charge mechanism.
99. Article 44 of the VAT Directive.
100. Article 196 of the VAT Directive.
101. *Supra* nn. 94 and 95.

In the case of a year-end compensating adjustment with balancing payments clearly relating to the manufacturing services previously supplied by Company A to Company B on the basis of the toll manufacturing agreement:

(1) Debit or credit notes shall be issued by Company A to Company B that must be cross-referenced to the original invoices and have the same VAT treatment (i.e., subject to a VAT in Country Y where Company B is established) as the initial transactions; in addition, Company A shall also amend the recapitulative statement originally filed in Country X where it had listed the toll manufacturing services rendered to Company B.

(2) Company B will instead be confronted with an additional reverse charge of VAT (in the case of upward adjustments) or will need to adjust input and output VAT originally applied on the intra-community acquisitions (in the case of downward adjustments) in Country Y.

The VAT returns and recapitulative statements mentioned above might need to be amended retroactively depending on the Member States concerned.

An upwards year-end compensating adjustment with balancing payments clearly related to B2C supplies of services already made has adverse consequences for the recipient of the services that would, in this case, bear the cost of additional unrecoverable VAT to be applied by the supplier in the Member State where he is established. In the case of downward adjustments, the supplier would instead be entitled to recover excess (output) VAT initially applied on the supply which must also be repaid to the customer in order to avoid unjust enrichment of the supplier.

If the adjustment is considered as a separate taxable supply (and not as more or less consideration for taxable supplies of goods or services already made), it will generally be qualified as the consideration for a supply of services. However, it is important that such a classification is contractually justified and that a direct link between the service actually provided and the compensating adjustment balancing payment can be established in order to be accepted by the tax authorities.[102]

3.3.4 *Other Elements Influencing the Interplay*

3.3.4.1 *Legal Relationship Between the Entities*

As mentioned in section 3.3.2, the possibility of qualifying a TP adjustment as more or less consideration of a taxable supply of goods or services already made depends on the existence of a direct link between that consideration (i.e., the balancing payment reflecting the compensating adjustment) and the previous supply. In the latter respect, the link between a supply and a consideration must be regarded as 'direct' if there is a legal relationship between the supplier and the recipient of the supply pursuant to which there is reciprocal performance. Additionally, the remuneration received by the

102. Derer, *supra* n. 35, pp. 295-296.

provider of the supplier constitutes the value actually given in return for the goods or services supplied to the recipient.[103]

The condition of 'legal relationship' requires that there is an underlying legal relationship between the supplier and the customer on the basis of which the goods or services have been supplied; a consideration was stipulated and the prices were consequently paid; and the adjustments to the prices can be justified. Such a legal relationship may be evidenced by either business agreements or TPD as well as by the general correspondence, purchase orders, debit or credit notes, and/or any other VAT document eventually issued by the parties.[104]

3.3.4.2 Type of Entities

The type of entities conducting the transactions may also play a role in determining the VAT implications of TP adjustments with balancing payments.

While TP rules apply in a uniform way to all cross-border transactions performed by the members of MNEs (e.g., local subsidiaries),[105] VAT taxable supplies (i.e., supplies of goods and services 'for consideration') may only materialize when a 'legal relationship' can be established between two separate legal entities. This is one of the aspects under which the VAT and corporate income tax TP principles depart significantly.

Supplies of goods and services by the same taxable person are generally not subject to a VAT since a taxable person is prevented from engaging in a 'legal relationship' with itself and, with the absence of a legal relationship, there can be no supply 'for consideration' nor a taxable event for a VAT.[106] On this basis, in *FCE Bank,*[107] the CJEU has established the principle that a branch and its head office that are the same legal entity for civil law purposes must be treated as a single taxable person for VAT purposes. This results in the supply of services between the two entities not falling within the scope of the VAT.[108]

103. *See* CJEU of 3 March 1994, C-16/93, *Tolsma*, para. 14.
104. *See also* van den Brekel, van Doesum, van Kesteren, *supra* n. 44, p. 186, according to whom the terms 'legal relationship' shall not be interpreted too strictly.
105. In this context, the term 'subsidiary' refers to the company (i.e., the autonomous legal entity) for which shares have been acquired by the parent company/holding company. The term 'branch' is commonly referred to as the permanent establishment or the fixed establishment of a business. In terms of the VAT, the CJEU has provided guidance on the meaning of 'fixed establishment' for the purpose of determining the place of supply, clarifying that '*an establishment must possess a sufficient degree of permanence and a structure adequate, in terms of human and technical resources, to supply the services in question on an independent basis*' (CJEU, of 17 July 1997, C-190/95, ARO Lease, para. 16). This test has been codified in Article 11 of Council Implementing Regulation (EU) No. 282/2011 of 15 March 2011 laying down implementing measures for Directive 2006/112/EC on the common system of VAT.
106. *See* section 3.3.4.1 of this Chapter as well as CJEU of 3 March 1994, C-16/93, *Tolsma*, para. 14.
107. CJEU of 23 March 2006, C-210/04, *FCE Bank*.
108. The European Commission appears to be of the same opinion, stating that '*where a single legal entity has more than a fixed establishment, services rendered between the establishments shall not be treated as supplies*' (*see* COM (2003)822 final, 2003/0329 CNS).

    It is worth noting that, unlike services, the cross-border transfer of goods would instead normally be taxable even when carried out between two establishments of the same company

When, however, the branch belongs to a VAT group thereby forming part of a new taxable person,[109] the head office and its branch should not be considered to be the same taxable person for VAT purposes even though they are legally bound to one other.

In this latter respect, the CJEU confirmed in *Skandia America*[110] that, even if businesses constitute the same legal entity, they may become separate taxable persons for VAT purposes when one of them belongs to a VAT group. Thus, VAT grouping provisions are given precedence over the legal ties between the entities. This should not be considered to be in contradiction with the conclusions in *FCE Bank* (where the relationship between the head office and its branch was not influenced by the presence of any VAT group).

In light of the above, compensating adjustments aimed at again establishing the arm's length conditions of supplies between a branch and its head office, or *vice versa*, should therefore not display VAT effects. This is valid regardless of the fact that balance payments are made and may be directly ascribed to the transaction that had previously occurred between the two entities unless one of them participates in a VAT group.

If, indeed, one of the entities (either the branch or the head office)[111] of the same legal person joins a VAT group pursuant to Article 11 of the VAT Directive, such an entity dissolves itself from the simultaneously existing legal form and becomes part of a new separate taxable person for VAT purposes (specifically, the VAT group). Any supplies of goods or services exchanged between the two entities – as well as

---

irrespective of whether the entities are considered to be the same or different taxable persons. In particular:

- in the case of importation, it is the mere physical entry of the goods into the EU territory that effectuates the application of the VAT on a taxable amount equal to their customs value regardless of the identity of the parties involved (*see* Articles 2, para. 1, let. d), 30, and 85 of the VAT Directive); while
- the transfer by a taxable person of goods forming part of his business assets to another Member State will normally be treated as a supply of goods for consideration. Therefore, a deemed intra-community acquisition materializes in the country of arrival of the goods where VAT shall apply on a taxable amount equal to the purchase price of the goods or of similar goods or, in the absence of a purchase price, the cost price determined at the time of the supply (*see* Articles 17, 20, and 83 of the VAT Directive).

109. Article 11 of the VAT Directive.
110. CJEU of 17 September 2014, C-7/13, *Skandia America Corporation USA, filial Svergie v. Skatteverket*.
111. On 30 October 2019, the Swedish Supreme Court asked the CJEU for a preliminary ruling (reference to the Case is C-812/19, *Danske Bank*) on whether services provided by a Danish head office – that is a member of a local VAT group – to a fixed establishment in Sweden should be subject to Swedish VAT. To a certain extent, the case mirrors the *Skandia America* case, and it refers to the situation known as 'reverse Skandia' (where the head office is part of a VAT group, but the branch is not).

     While the EU VAT Committee has already adopted non legally binding guidelines (by a large majority) for which they recognize the application of Skandia and reverse Skandia (*see* the guidelines resulting from the 105th meeting of 26 October 2015, DOCUMENT A – taxud.c.1(2016)7465801 – 886), the actual application differs from one country to another, especially regarding the reverse-Skandia situation.

compensating adjustments directly attributable to such supplies – would, in this case, display VAT effects as if they were incurred between separate and unrelated parties.

3.3.4.3 *Direct Link Between the Adjustment and the Transaction and Remuneration and the Transaction*

The existence of a legal relationship between the parties is not inherently sufficient to qualify the compensating adjustment (and the corresponding balancing payment) as an adjustment of the consideration that was originally received by the supplier in return for the supplies of goods and services previously made in the course of the year.

In order for year-end adjustments to display effects on the VAT taxable amount, they must therefore be capable of being split and directly linked to specific supplies of goods and services that were carried out during the year.

The sources that can be used to examine whether a link exists between the year-end adjustment and the previously made supplies are exactly the same as the basis on which the existence of a legal relationship is also verified, i.e., agreements and TPD, as well as debit or credit notes and/or any other VAT document eventually issued by the parties.

The TP method adopted by the group can also be relevant for the purpose of establishing whether a direct link between the adjustment and the transaction is present. From a VAT perspective, it appears that, if one of the 'traditional transactional methods'[112] is applied, a direct link will be more evident since it would be easier to assign the adjustment to a certain specific transaction, or at least to a series of transactions, than if a 'transactional profit method'[113] was used.[114]

In addition, the circumstance that the year-end adjustment is related to homogeneous supplies (i.e., supplies of the same goods or services) carried out throughout the year would facilitate establishing a link. If, on the contrary, the adjustment was to be made for a wide variety of goods and services supplied throughout the year (heterogeneous supplies), it may prove to be difficult to establish a direct link with such supplies on an individual basis.[115]

According to the VEG:[116]

(1) If there is no direct link with the initial supplies and no contractual obligation to make a balancing payment, it may be assumed that the balancing payment (if any) is aimed at reaching an agreed profit margin. In such a case, the adjusting payment is not a consideration for a taxed supply already made but

112. That is comparable uncontrolled price method (CUP method), resale price method, and cost-plus method.
113. That is TNMM or transactional profit split method.
114. van den Brekel, van Doesum, van Kesteren, *supra* n. 44, p. 187 and Matesanz, *supra* n. 35, p. 298, FN 18.
115. van den Brekel, van Doesum, van Kesteren, *supra* n. 44, p. 187.
116. *See* VEG No. 71 REV2, Paper on topic for discussion. Possible VAT implications of Transfer Pricing, 18 April 2018, taxud.x.1(2018)2326098 -EN, pp. 7-8.

a mere payment of money falling beyond the scope of the VAT with no VAT consequences.[117]

(2) Moreover, when business agreements or contracts refer to the treatment of TP adjustments, the contractually agreed treatment should be adhered to by the parties, and the following options are available:

Definition TP Adjustment as per the Contract	*VAT Treatment*
Contract defines adjustments to reach guaranteed profit margin	Adjustment relates to a 'profit adjustment' – this is not a taxable transaction – no debit or credit note or any other document to be issued
Contract defines adjustment for previous supplies – reference is made to a period during which transactions happened, list of invoices numbers attached, breakdown of the adjustment to each supply	Taxable transaction – supply of goods (or services) – debit or credit note to be issued – same VAT treatment as initial transaction
Contract defines the adjustment as billing of variances between actual and budgeted cost of marketing or administrative expenses	Taxable amount is adjusted, i.e., further (less) consideration for a 'supply of services' – debit or credit note to be issued
Contract defines the adjustment as a profit split (e.g., in case of a joint venture)	Adjustment relates to a 'profit adjustment' – this is not a taxable transaction – no credit or debit note to be issued

3.3.5 *Customs, VAT, and TP*

An interesting issue that should be mentioned in the discussed context is the imposition of VAT upon the importation of goods. The basis for the determination of the amount of tax in this aspect is the customs value of the goods determined in accordance with the rules of customs valuation.[118]

A question that arises in the above context is what happens to the amount of import VAT in the case of a customs adjustment performed due to an earlier TP adjustment. It seems that the only correct answer in this case will be that the import VAT, as a rule, should follow the customs adjustments. Therefore, whenever a TP adjustment influences the customs value of the imported goods and, hence, an adjustment to the

117. In these circumstances, it would be helpful to both tax authorities and businesses that any document issued to evidence payments that are made between the parties but are outside the scope of VAT are not described as 'invoices' (since tax authorities might otherwise assume that a VAT must be due) and had an agreed description such as 'Transfer Pricing Payment Request'.

118. For further details on customs valuation and its interplay with TP, *see* Chapter 30 of this book.

customs valuation will be performed, the amount of the import VAT will also have to be adjusted to properly reflect the change in the customs value. It will definitely depend on the local circumstances whether tax authorities will be equally keen to accept such changes in the case of both upward and downward adjustments.

3.4 EU Approach

As previously mentioned, the dissonance and lack of harmonization between the TP and the VAT has been an increasing issue over the last few years. In this context, the EU recently created guidance on a common understanding of the issue among its Member States. The VAT Committee issued the first related paper in February 2017[119] while the VAT Expert Group followed with the release of the second one in April 2018.[120] It must be noted that these papers are not a binding source of EU law and, due to their character, are inherently limited in application to the Member States of the EU. It is nonetheless interesting to more comprehensively examine the approaches taken by the EU VAT experts and the solutions they proposed to solve the issue at hand.

When assessing the potential influence of TP adjustments on VAT settlements, the VAT Committee focused on the three elements which are necessary to consider in order to determine whether a transaction falls within the scope of the VAT at all. These elements are:

- existence of consideration (i.e., an actual financial element reflected in the accounts of the parties);
- existence of supply (consideration must be paid in return for a particular supply); and
- existence of a direct link between supply and consideration (a direct link between payment and supply which, according to the case law of the CJEU, can be established if a legal relationship exists between the supplier and the recipient that entails a reciprocal performance).

Importantly, in the above context, the VAT Committee stated that open market value is an exception to the main principle governing the valuation of transactions for VAT purposes. Therefore, the adjustment to the VAT settlement on the basis of an earlier TP adjustment will also, in general, be an exception to the rule. Otherwise, the open market value reflecting the TP's arm's length principle would become the new norm for the VAT.[121]

In the following paper released by the VAT Expert Group in 2018, the neutrality of the VAT was emphasized as the overarching principle that should not be influenced by the TP adjustments and thus none of the stakeholders should bear the consequences of

119. Supra n. 8.
120. Supra n. 9.
121. This might happen in Luxembourg after the state issued circular No. 790 issued on 18 January 2019 dealing with the taxable base for transactions between related parties; for further details *see* http://www.aed.public.lu/actualites/2019/01/18_Circulaire790/20190118_Circulaires_790.pdf (last accessed 22 September 2020).

a TP-based VAT adjustment. Interestingly, the VAT Expert Group indicated a simplification practice under which the right to recover VAT would be the basic criterion in order to determine whether a TP adjustment should also cause the need to adjust the VAT settlements. In view of the experts, if only one of the parties to the transaction has the full right of recovery, an adjustment for VAT purposes might be required if the three criteria for taxation with VAT mentioned in the committee paper are fulfilled. Further, the view that the TP adjustments that were performed at the initiative of the tax authorities should not cause the necessity to perform a VAT adjustment was also confirmed by the committee. This approach should definitely be accepted as the TP adjustments performed at the initiative of the tax authorities usually do not bear any actual financial adjustments, i.e., these are only adjustments in the accounts that do not involve any monetary flow. In addition, the VAT Expert Group recommended that no negative VAT consequences should arise for taxpayers from TP adjustments, not even when the VAT taxable base should be amended. In particular, even if adjustments were required for VAT purposes, these should not lead to the application of penalties, late payment interest, and/or retroactive adjustments of deductible VAT.

With regard to the above guidance provided by the two entities, it should be noted that it constitutes valuable assistance towards creating a common understanding of the discussed issue in the EU. However, it has two significant disadvantages. First, it is not exhaustive and does not solve all issues connected with the interplay between the TP and the VAT. Second, it is not a legal act, meaning that it can only have an explanatory character, and the Member States are free to apply it or not to do so. The fact that it is an EU document makes it certainly relevant but only to the EU Member States; in other countries, it might only have a character of a general source of reference. Nevertheless, the guidance seems to find a good compromise at the general level to the complicated issue of the interplay between the TP and the VAT, and it also accords with the approach already discussed in the earlier parts of this chapter.

3.5 Country Practice

The interplay between the TP and the VAT is still a rather unexplored issue that is also visible when analysing country practices around the world. Thus far, very few countries have decided to introduce any respective guidance and, in the others, the issue was dealt with by the local courts. The following part of this chapter presents the approaches taken in Austria and Italy.[122]

122. Other countries that dealt with the issue of interplay between the TP and the VAT include, for example, Luxembourg (*supra* n. 121) and Turkey where the guidance mainly focuses on deductions of a VAT paid during importation regarding disguised profit distribution via transfer pricing. (*see* Maarten Schreuder, VAT Implications of Transfer Pricing Adjustments in Europe, Deloitte, 19 December 2017, https://www.taxathand.com/article/8928/European-Union/2017/VAT-implications-of-transfer-pricing-adjustments-in-Europe), (last accessed 30 January 2022).

3.5.1 *Austria*

Austria was possibly the first country that introduced any type of guidance regarding the interplay between TP and VAT adjustments. The country's national TP guidelines were issued in 2010 and included a subchapter dealing with the discussed issue. In 2021, the Austrian TP guidelines were updated and the approach towards the influence of TP adjustments on VAT was modified.[123]

The Austrian VAT Act envisages in certain cases the application of a so-called 'normal value' as a taxable amount instead of the actually invoiced amount.[124] In general, the normal value is the equivalent of the open market value envisaged by the VAT Directive. In the case of intra-group services, it must be examined for VAT purposes whether the conditions for the application of the normal value are fulfilled or not. If so, the normal value corresponds to the transfer price for corporate tax purposes. Thus, if the transfer prices for intra-group services are adjusted and the conditions for the application of the normal value are met, the normal value forms the basis of assessment for VAT purposes.[125] In these cases, the relevant provision of the Austrian VAT Act forms the legal basis for the subsequent claim for VAT as a result of a transfer price correction. A possible secondary adjustment through the recognition of transfer pricing-related credit and liabilities therefore does not lead to a change in the taxable amount according to the Austrian VAT Act.

If the conditions for the application of normal value are not met, a transfer price adjustment by recognizing transfer pricing-related credit and liabilities leads to an adjustment of the taxable amount under the Austrian VAT Act.[126] The adjustment may be waived if it has no effect on tax revenue and if it does not disrupt the VIES.[127]

If supplies or other services are provided between group companies free of charge, the normal value does not apply.[128] If in such a case a transfer price adjustment is made for income tax purposes by means of a hidden distribution or hidden contribution (no recognition of transfer pricing-related credit and liabilities by the group companies), there is also no change in the taxable amount. Whenever there are predominantly non-deductible costs (expenses) due to the hidden distribution, there will be no input tax for VAT purposes. Subsequent resale, withdrawal or provision free of charge of such items is not subject to VAT.[129] If, on the other hand, input tax is not excluded because at least half of the costs (expenses) are deductible, this may result in a withdrawal or another service pursuant to specific provisions of the Austrian Tax Act. The basis of assessment is then determined according to the purchase price of a good (with related costs) or the costs necessary to provide the service.

123. VPR 2021, Verrechnungspreisrichtlinien 2021, https://findok.bmf.gv.at/findok?execution=e100000s1&dokumentId=ace379c9-6082-4d25-b31a-456515264bee (last accessed 30 March 2022).
124. §4 para. 9 of the Austrian VAT Act (Umsatzsteuergesetz 1994).
125. Paragraph 4.1.4.1. of the Austrian TP Guidelines.
126. §16 of the Austrian VAT Act (Umsatzsteuergesetz 1994).
127. Paragraph 4.1.4.2. of the Austrian TP Guidelines.
128. Paragraph 4.1.4.3. of the Austrian TP Guidelines.
129. Austrian Supreme Administrative Court (Verwaltungsgerichtshof, VwGH) of 27 June 2018, Ra 2017/15/0019.

3.5.2 *Italy*

In Italy, the interplay between the TP adjustments and the VAT was explained by the tax authorities in three tax rulings having at their object the effects of TP year-end adjustments on the VAT settlements in transactions between related parties.[130]

We will focus on the first one since the three rulings are consistent with each other and with the observations expressed by both the VAT Committee and the VAT Expert Group.

Tax Ruling No. 60 of 2 November 2018

In the case at hand, the Italian authorities analysed transactions between company Alfa located in Italy and its related party, company Beta, located outside of the EU. *Beta* was the legal and economic owner of a brand X and the related ingenuity. It operated as a principal in the process of production and distribution of branded goods with brand X and made the brand and imaginative contrivance available at no cost to all related parties involved in the production of branded goods. Alfa, under a contract with Beta, was a contract assembler and made its equipment available to another related party – Italian Gamma, operating as a contract manufacturer – in order to manufacture branded products. Alfa was also coordinating the sales and the manufacturing of goods through the distribution network of the group as well as managing logistics and controlling the quality of the products in the interest of Beta. The finished products manufactured by Gamma were thus sold to Alfa that subsequently sold them either to Beta (for subsequent distribution in the North American and world markets) or to Delta (for subsequent distribution in the EMEA market).

All transfer prices of the finished X-branded goods adhered to the TP policy in order to target the arm's length remuneration of each of the affiliated companies. The contract between Alfa and Beta envisaged, in accordance with the general TP policy of the group, that an appropriate TP adjustment will be performed in order to align the results so that they reflect the arm's length principle in the event that Alfa's profit margin in a fiscal year falls outside the interquartile range. Thus, whenever Alfa incurred operational losses associated with the manufacture and distribution of branded products, Beta paid Alfa an upward contribution. The issue in question was whether these contributions were relevant from the VAT perspective and thus created a necessity to perform a VAT adjustment.

130. Ruling No. 60 of 2 November 2018 (https://www.agenziaentrate.gov.it/portale/documents/20143/307292/Interpello+60+2018_Risposta+n.+60+del+2018.pdf/aae4bb1a-5404-b61d-330a-bbe77ab3c6d7 (last accessed 30 March 2022)), Ruling No. 529 of 6 August 2021, (https://www.agenziaentrate.gov.it/portale/documents/20143/3744575/Risposta+529+del+2021.pdf/43e6524f-5d5b-b840-49c6-d7010a442518 (last accessed 30 March 2022)) and Ruling No. 884 of 30 December 2021 (https://www.agenziaentrate.gov.it/portale/documents/20143/4002792/Risposta+n.+884_2021.pdf/fe0dc4d1-7f27-b9f6-5de5-b23427a1aa18 (last accessed 30 March 2022)).

The Italian authorities referred extensively to the main principles of VAT indicating that a TP adjustment will influence the taxable base for VAT purposes if:

- a consideration was agreed upon among parties;
- the transactions for the provision of goods or services were duly identified; and
- there was a direct link between the transactions and the consideration.

In particular, the importance of a direct link between the transaction and the consideration was stressed by the authorities as, in their view, it was not possible to identify such a link in the analysed transaction. Due to the fact that all three above criteria have to be fulfilled for a TP adjustment to have an influence on VAT, the Italian Revenue Agency decided that no adjustment was needed in the case at hand.

In particular, the Italian authorities considered that the payment (if any) to be made by Beta to Alfa: (i) *does not represent the consideration for a separate service supplied by Alfa* since the latter has no obligations other than those provided by the contract with Beta (i.e., production of X-branded goods in accordance with technical specifications and volumes given by Beta) already remunerated by the transfer prices agreed for the sale of said goods between the same companies; and (ii) *does not represent an adjustment of the consideration for the X-branded goods* since '*by reading the agreement in force between Alfa and Beta, a direct link between said cash contribution/adjustment and the single supplies of X-branded goods carried out between the parties seems missing. As a consequence, said amounts should in principle qualify as cash contributions, out of the scope of VAT*'.[131]

131. By their Ruling No. 529 of 6 August 2021 the same Italian Tax Authorities came to the opposite conclusion, confirming that TP adjustments voluntarily made by the taxpayer may in principle affect the VAT taxable base of supplies between related parties. In that specific case, however, the related parties had agreed from the beginning that: (i) at the time of each supply, a provisional price would have been applied (so-called Target supply price); and (ii) subsequently, on a quarterly basis, the parties would have made a final adjustment to the price provisionally applied, through a so-called Profit true up. This latter was determined 'analytically for each type of product sold', thus actually 'redefining the initial sale price' (i.e., the true consideration) of each supply. In light of these specific circumstances, a 'direct link' was deemed to exist between the quarterly adjustments and each single supply to which they were allocated.

The VAT treatment of TP year-end adjustments was then once again addressed by the Italian Tax Authorities in their Ruling No. 884 of 30 December 2021, whereby the adjustments made by an Italian company belonging to a multinational group operating in the fashion industry were deemed to fall outside the scope of Italian VAT, since: (i) the sole purpose of the adjustments was to bring the foreign subsidiaries' operating margin within the interquartile range, and it was not possible to attribute such adjustments the nature of consideration for an autonomous and independent supply of goods and/or services; and (ii) although involving the recognition of an extra costs for the foreign subsidiaries, aimed at lowering their operating margin, the adjustments were not directly related to the original supplies of finished products made by the Italian company.

Taking into account the earlier considerations included in this chapter, the conclusion of the Italian tax authorities should be accepted as correct. Therefore, the adjustment performed in the form described in the case at hand could not be treated as causing any VAT consequences due to not fulfilling all of the discussed criteria. An important point to note in the context of this case is the difference between the TP and the VAT – where the first is primarily concerned with establishing the conditions of a transaction so that they are in line with the arm's length principle, the latter usually considers the price paid between the entities and only sporadically takes into account the actual market value. Therefore, the adjustments in these two areas also have different characters. Those performed for TP purposes aiming to reach the market level and those for the VAT mainly happening in order to reflect changes in the consideration for supplies of goods or services eventually agreed by the parties and actually reflected in their financial accounts.

3.6 Potential Remedies

The differences between the TP and the VAT described in the previous paragraphs might create issues, especially regarding tax adjustments. While an adjustment for TP purposes might be carried out in order to reflect arm's length market conditions, a VAT adjustment might not be necessary due to the fact that the VAT does not rely on the arm's length principle. The latter adjustment would rather be required if specific circumstances occurred that could influence the price of the goods or services provided. This might include, for example, issuing a correction invoice at a later point in time that was due to, for instance, a wrong price calculation on the original invoice or because of a supervening agreement aimed at redetermining the price originally agreed and paid or to be paid by the parties.[132] One conclusion that can be drawn in this context is that the reasons for performing an adjustment for TP and VAT purposes might be entirely different, therefore, an adjustment in one area will not necessarily cause a respective adjustment in the other area in every situation. In addition, taking into account all of the differences between the TP and the VAT, when a need to perform an adjustment occurs, it might not always be possible to align the outcomes, and mismatches might remain.

At the same time, it seems that there is not and will not be a unified solution that could answer all of the above issues. The far-reaching differences between the TP and the VAT prevent applying consistent treatment to all cases of TP and VAT adjustments.

The interpretative solution given by the Italian Tax Authorities in the three cases analysed so far (Rulings No. 60 of 2 November 2018, No. 529 of 6 August 2021 and No. 884 of 30 December 2021) are consistent with each other and with the observations expressed by both the VAT Committee (Value Added Tax Committee, Working Paper No. 923, 28 February 2017, taxud.c.1(2016)1280928) and the VAT Expert Group (VEG No. 71 REV2, Paper on topic for discussion. Possible VAT implications of Transfer Pricing, 18 April 2018, taxud.x.1(2018) 2326098 –EN).

132. Every country individually determines the rules of correcting its VAT, e.g., https://www.gov.uk/guidance/how-to-correct-vat-errors-and-make-adjustments-or-claims-vat-notice-70045#VAT-errors-submitted (last accessed 29 September 2020).

Therefore, it seems that the best solution that would facilitate the coexistence of both areas of tax law is a better exchange of information between the tax authorities dealing with the TP and the VAT which would help determine whether an audit is required. On the taxpayer's side, the only imaginable solution is possibly the fulfilment of the documentation requirements that could help identify the interdependencies between TP and VAT adjustments.[133] In addition, tax authorities could provide specific guidance akin to that proposed by the EU in order to clarify in which situations TP adjustments will influence VAT settlements and how to analyse a potentially disputable transaction.

4 CONCLUSIONS

This chapter aimed to explain the issue of the interplay between the TP and the VAT. Subchapter 1 provided a general overview of the increasing importance of VAT and its overlaps with the TP. Subchapter 2 dealt with the specific features of the VAT, including binding rules within the EU. Finally, subchapter 3 extensively addressed the issue of the interplay between the TP and the VAT, discussing the differences between the areas and their ramifications, the influence of TP adjustments on the VAT and regional approaches, including guidance provided by the EU and practice in two countries. Finally, it also provided ideas for potential remedies for alleviating the consequences of the differences between the TP and the VAT.

133. *See* section 3.3.4.3 of this Chapter and VEG No. 71 REV2, *Paper on topic for discussion. Possible VAT implications of Transfer Pricing*, 18 April 2018, taxud.x.1(2018)2326098 -EN, pp. 7-8.

Table of Cases

Index

O

P

R

S

T

U

V

W

www.ingramcontent.com/pod-product-compliance
Lightning Source LLC
LaVergne TN
LVHW020003031026
849161LV00023B/864

* 9 7 8 9 4 0 3 5 3 5 1 5 9 *